An Expanding World
Volume 20

Theories of Empire,
1450–1800

AN EXPANDING WORLD
The European Impact on World History, 1450–1800

General Editor: A.J.R. Russell-Wood

Please note titles may change prior to publication

An Expanding World
The European Impact on World History 1450–1800

Volume 20

Theories of Empire,
1450–1800

edited by
David Armitage

Ashgate

VARIORUM

Aldershot • Brookfield USA • Singapore • Sydney

This edition copyright © 1998 by Ashgate Publishing Limited, and Introduction by David Armitage. For copyright of individual articles refer to the Acknowledgements.

Published in the **Variorum Expanding World Series** by

Ashgate Publishing Limited
Gower House, Croft Road
Aldershot, Hampshire GU11 3HR
Great Britain

Ashgate Publishing Company
Old Post Road
Brookfield, Vermont 05036–9704
USA

ISBN 0–86078–516–5

British Library CIP data
>Theories of Empire, 1450–1800.
>(An Expanding World: The European Impact on World History, 1450–1800: Vol. 20).
>1. Imperialism–History.
>I. Armitage, David.
>325. 3' 2' 09

US Library of Congress CIP data
>Theories of Empire, 1450–1800/edited by David Armitage.
>p. cm. – (An Expanding World: The European Impact on World History, 1450–1800: Vol. 20).
>Includes one essay in Spanish. Collection of 15 essays originally published 1949–1995. Includes bibliographical references.
>1. Europe–Territorial expansion. 2. Imperialism–History.
>3. Europe–Colonies. 4. Europe–Foreign relations.
>I. Armitage, David, 1965–   . II. Series.
>D210. T45   1998   97–43882
>327 . 4–dc21   CIP

Printed in Great Britain by Galliard (Printers) Ltd, Great Yarmouth

AN EXPANDING WORLD 20

Contents

Acknowledgements

The chapters in this volume are taken from the sources listed below, for which the editor and publishers wish to thank their authors, original publishers or other copyright holders for permission to use their material as follows:

Chapter 1: J.S. Richardson, '*Imperium Romanum*: Empire and the Language of Power', *Journal of Roman Studies* LXXXI (London, 1991), pp. 1–9. Copyright © 1991 by The Society for the Promotion of Roman Studies, London.

Chapter 2: John Robertson, 'Empire and Union: Two Concepts of the Early Modern European Political Order', in ed. John Robertson, *A Union for Empire: Political Thought and the British Union of 1707* (Cambridge, 1995), pp. 3–36. Copyright © 1995 by Cambridge University Press.

Chapter 3: John M. Headley, 'The Habsburg World Empire and the Revival of Ghibellinism', *Medieval and Renaissance Studies* VII (Chapel Hill, NC, 1978), pp. 93–127. Copyright © 1978 by The University of North Carolina Press. Used by permission of the publisher.

Chapter 4: Franz Bosbach, 'The European Debate on Universal Monarchy', first publication. Copyright © 1998 by Franz Bosbach.

Chapter 5: Victor Frankl, 'Imperio Particular e Imperio Universal en las Cartas de Relación de Hernán Cortés', *Cuadernos Hispanoamericanos* CLXV (Madrid, 1963), pp. 443–482. Copyright © 1963 by the Instituto de Cultura Hispánica, Madrid.

Chapter 6: John H. Elliott, 'The Seizure of Overseas Territories by the European Powers', in ed. Hans Pohl, *The European Discovery of the World and its Economic Effects on Pre-Industrial Society, 1500–1800* (Stuttgart, 1990), pp. 43–61. Copyright © 1990 by John H. Elliott.

Chapter 7: Anthony Pagden, 'Dispossessing the Barbarian: The Language of Spanish Thomism and the Debate over the Property Rights of the American Indians', in ed. Anthony Pagden, *The Languages of Political Theory in Early Modern Europe* (Cambridge, 1986), pp. 79–98. Copyright © 1986 by Cambridge University Press.

Chapter 8: Nicholas P. Canny, 'The Ideology of English Colonization: From Ireland to America', *William and Mary Quarterly* (3rd series) XXX, no. 4 (Williamsburg, VA, 1973), pp. 575–598. Copyright © 1973 by The Omohundro Institute of Early American History and Culture. Reprinted by permission of the author and The Omohundro Institute of Early American History and Culture.

Chapter 9: W.J. Eccles, 'Sovereignty-Association, 1500–1783', *Canadian Historical Review* LXV, no. 4 (North York, Ontario, 1984), pp. 475–510. Copyright © 1984 by The University of Toronto Press Incorporated. Reprinted by permission of The University of Toronto Press Incorporated.

Chapter 10: C.H. Alexandrowicz, 'Freitas Versus Grotius', *British Yearbook of International Law* XXXV (Oxford, 1960), pp. 162–182. Published 1960 by Oxford University Press.

Chapter 11: G.D. Winius, 'Millenarianism and Empire: Portuguese Asian Decline and the "Crise de Conscience" of the Missionaries', *Itinerario* XI (Leiden, 1987), pp. 37–51. Copyright © 1987 by *Itinerario*, c/o Rijks Universiteit Leiden.

Chapter 12: Jacob Viner, 'Power Versus Plenty as Objectives of Foreign Policy in the Seventeenth and Eighteenth Centuries', *World Politics* I (Baltimore, MD, 1949), pp. 1–29. Copyright © 1949 by The Johns Hopkins University Press.

Chapter 13: Norbert Kilian, 'New Wine in Old Skins? American Definitions of Empire and the Emergence of a New Concept', in ed. Erich Angermann, Marie-Luise Frings and Hermann Wellenreuther, *New Wine in Old Skins: A Comparative View of Socio-Political Structures and Values Affecting the American Revolution* (Stuttgart, 1976), pp. 135–152. Published by Ernst Klett Verlag, Stuttgart. Copyright © 1976 by Norbert Kilian.

Chapter 14: Timothy E. Anna, 'Spain and the Breakdown of the Imperial Ethos: The Problem of Equality', *Hispanic American Historical Review* LXII, no. 2 (Durham, NC, 1982), pp. 254–272. Copyright © 1982 by Duke University Press. Reprinted with permission.

Chapter 15: James Tully, 'Aboriginal Property and Western Theory: Recovering a Middle Ground', *Social Philosophy and Policy* XI (Cambridge, 1994), pp. 153–180. Copyright © 1994 by Cambridge University Press.

Every effort has been made to trace all the copyright holders, but if any have been inadvertently overlooked the publishers will be pleased to make the necessary arrangement at the first opportunity.

***

David Armitage thanks those who have contributed essays to this volume, as well as Joyce Chaplin, Thomas Cohen, Constantin Fasolt, Chad Ludington, Joan-Pau Rubiés and John Russell-Wood, for their help and comments.

General Editor's Preface

A.J.R. Russell-Wood

An Expanding World: The European Impact on World History, 1450–1800 is designed to meet two objectives: first, each volume covers a specific aspect of the European initiative and reaction across time and space; second, the series represents a superb overview and compendium of knowledge and is an invaluable reference source on the European presence beyond Europe in the early modern period, interaction with non-Europeans, and experiences of peoples of other continents, religions, and races in relation to Europe and Europeans. The series reflects revisionist interpretations and new approaches to what has been called 'the expansion of Europe' and whose historiography traditionally bore the hallmarks of a narrowly Eurocentric perspective, focus on the achievements of individual nations, and characterization of the European presence as one of dominance, conquest, and control. Fragmentation characterized much of this literature: fragmentation by national groups, by geography, and by chronology.

The volumes of *An Expanding World* seek to transcend nationalist histories and to examine on the global stage rather than in discrete regions important selected facets of the European presence overseas. One result has been to bring to the fore the multicontinental, multi-oceanic and multinational dimension of the European activities. A further outcome is compensatory in the emphasis placed on the cross-cultural context of European activities and on how collaboration and cooperation between peoples transcended real or perceived boundaries of religion, nationality, race, and language and were no less important aspects of the European experience in Africa, Asia, the Americas, and Australia than the highly publicized confrontational, bellicose, and exploitative dimensions. Recent scholarship has not only led to greater understanding of peoples, cultures, and institutions of Africa, Asia, the Americas, and Australasia with whom Europeans interacted and the complexity of such interactions and transactions, but also of relations between Europeans of different nationalities and religious persuasions.

The initial five volumes reflect the changing historiography and set the stage for volumes encompassing the broad themes of technology and science, trade and commerce, exploitation as reflected in agriculture and the extractive industries and through systems of forced and coerced labour, government of empire, and society and culture in European colonies and settlements overseas. Final volumes examine the image of Europe and Europeans as 'the other' and the impact of the wider world on European *mentalités* and mores.

An international team of editors was selected to reflect a diversity of educational backgrounds, nationalities, and scholars at different stages of their professional careers. Few would claim to be 'world historians', but each is a recognized authority in his or her field and has the demonstrated capacity to ask the significant questions and provide a conceptual framework for the selection of articles which combine analysis with interpretation. Editors were exhorted to place their specific subjects within a global context and over the *longue durée*. I have been delighted by the enthusiasm with which they took up this intellectual challenge, their courage in venturing beyond their immediate research fields to look over the fences into the gardens of their academic neighbours, and the collegiality which has led to a generous informal exchange of information. Editors were posed the daunting task of surveying a rich historical literature and selecting those essays which they regarded as significant contributions to an understanding of the specific field or representative of the historiography. They were asked to give priority to articles in scholarly journals; essays from conference volumes and *Festschriften* were acceptable; excluded (with some few exceptions) were excerpts from recent monographs or paperback volumes. After much discussion and agonizing, the decision was taken to incorporate essays only in English, French, and Spanish. This has led to the exclusion of the extensive scholarly literature in Danish, Dutch, German and Portuguese. The ramifications of these decisions and how these have had an impact on the representative quality of selections of articles have varied, depending on the theme, and have been addressed by editors in their introductions.

The introduction to each volume enables readers to assess the importance of the topic *per se* and place this in the broader context of European activities overseas. It acquaints readers with broad trends in the historiography and alerts them to controversies and conflicting interpretations. Editors clarify the conceptual framework for each volume and explain the rationale for the selection of articles and how they relate to each other. Introductions permit volume editors to assess the impact on their treatments of discrete topics of constraints of language, format, and chronology, assess the completeness of the journal literature, and address *lacunae*. A further charge to editors was to describe and evaluate the importance of change over time, explain differences attributable to differing geographical, cultural, institutional, and economic circumstances and suggest the potential for cross-cultural, comparative, and interdisciplinary approaches. The addition of notes and bibliographies enhances the scholarly value of the introductions and suggests avenues for further enquiry.

I should like to express my thanks to the volume editors for their willing participation, enthusiasm, sage counsel, invaluable suggestions, and good judgment. Evidence of the timeliness and importance of the series was illustrated by the decision, based on extensive consultation with the scholarly community, to expand a series, which had originally been projected not to exceed eight volumes, to more than thirty volumes. It was John Smedley's initiative which gave rise to discussions as to the viability and need for such a series and he has overseen the publishing, publicity, and marketing of *An Expanding World*. As

General Editor, my task was greatly facilitated by the assistance of Dr Mark Steele who was initially responsible for the 'operations' component of the series as it got under way; latterly this assistance has been provided by staff at Variorum.

The Department of History,
The Johns Hopkins University

Introduction

David Armitage

The expansion of Europe has an intellectual history, just as intellectual history carries the traces of European expansion. The early-modern overseas empires of Spain, Portugal, France, Britain and Holland had to be justified, not only to their competitors but also to themselves, and their effects on the metropolitan nations as well as the native and later colonial populations had to be accounted for, understood and explained. The territorial and economic expansion of the early-modern monarchies and republics accordingly generated an extensive corpus of argument and reflection, cast within familiar discourses of human nature, political organisation, salvation history, economic order and international relations.[1] Though much of the resulting material was intentionally tactical some of it attained the abstraction of theory, and had novel applications beyond its contingent purposes; at the same time, philosophers shouldered the ideological task of justifying overseas enterprise, and political theory in particular would thereafter bear the marks of early-modern Europe's expanding world.

From early-modern theories of empire, all roads led to Rome, and from Rome to Troy.[2] All of the European empires – including those east of the Urals, and in the successor states of European colonies in the Americas – looked back to classical Rome as an inspiration and an aspiration. The Roman Empire had grown from a settlement supposedly founded by Trojan fugitives into a regional power in northern Italy and from thence to mistress of, if not the known world (since parts of Asia, Africa, Britain and Ireland remained beyond its control, though not its ken), then of the whole world worth knowing. At its greatest extent, the Roman Empire encompassed the Mediterranean *oikoumene* defined by Greek geographers as the extent of the terrestrial universe and was in that sense the first universal empire. Yet, as J. S. Richardson shows (see chapter 1 below), it was only in the time of Julius Caesar and Augustus that the term *imperium* came to carry a territorial dimension.[3] *Imperium* was originally the authority given to

---

[1] The best starting-point for understanding this body of argument is now Anthony Pagden, *Lords of All the World: Ideologies of Empire in Spain, Britain and France c. 1500 – c. 1800* (New Haven, 1995), which supersedes the earlier classic study by Richard Koebner, *Empire* (Cambridge, 1961).

[2] On Troy see Marie Tanner, *The Last Descendant of Æneas: The Hapsburgs and the Mythic Image of the Emperor* (New Haven, 1993), together with the important review by R. J. W. Evans, 'The Sun Also Sets', *The New York Review of Books*, 17 February 1994, pp. 25–27.

[3] On Roman conceptions of *imperium* see also Andrew Lintott, 'What Was the "Imperium Romanum"?', *Greece and Rome*, XXVIII (1981), pp. 53–67, *idem, Imperium Romanum: Politics and Administration* (London, 1993); and P.A. Brunt, '*Laus Imperii*', in his *Roman Imperial Themes* (Oxford, 1990), pp. 288–323.

a magistrate to act on behalf of Rome and its citizens in peace and war, whether at home (*domi*) or abroad (*militiæ*). As Rome grew, it came to mean authority in the abstract, detached from any particular holder; the formerly hard-and-fast boundary between *imperium domi* and *imperium militiæ* gradually dissolved; and Rome and its dependencies were considered to form a single unit, the *Imperium Romanum*. The belatedness of this territorial application should constrain any easy assimilation of the Roman Empire to the later European empires, not least because the vernacular cognates of *imperium* retained its connotations of political authority long after the term had again been extended spatially across the oceans of an expanded world.

Despite the barbarian invasions, the sack of Rome in 410 CE, and the end of the Western Empire in 476 CE, the idea of the Roman Empire did not die, and the Imperial title passed from the Carolingians through the Ottonian and Salian Franks and the Hohenstaufens on to the Spanish Habsburgs and thence to the Austrian Habsburgs.[4] However, the Emperor's claim to the Empire, and the implied universal authority it brought with it, did not go unchallenged.[5] The Byzantine Emperors claimed that the Eastern Empire was the true successor to Rome as at various times did the '*Papacy*,... no other, than the Ghost of the deceased *Romane Empire*, sitting crowned upon the grave thereof', in Thomas Hobbes' contemptuous words.[6] The division of the Empire into its Eastern and Western parts, and the disputes between the Papacy and the Emperor, made it increasingly obvious that if competing powers could claim the Roman mantle of universalism with equal right, then universalism had been overcome by particularism. The collision between particular claims to authority and universalist aspirations to hegemony would remain at the heart of theories of empire until the late eighteenth century, and would not be fully resolved until the development of federalist theories in the Early American Republic.

Particularist claims to supreme authority and a confederal conception of the Empire added two further dimensions of the Roman inheritance – *imperium* as sovereignty, and *imperium* as rule over multiple dominions. The transformation of imperial provinces into barbarian kingdoms in the latter days of the Western Empire had shown that the unitary Roman Empire, which extended citizenship

---

[4] Robert Folz, *The Concept of Empire in Western Europe from the Fifth to the Fourteenth Century*, trans. Sheila Ann Ogilvie (London, 1969); Marc Bloch, 'The Empire and the Idea of Empire under the Hohenstaufen', in his *Land and Work in Medieval Europe*, trans. J.E. Anderson (London, 1967), pp. 1–43.

[5] On later theories of the Empire and their transformation see Hanns Gross, *Empire and Sovereignty: A History of the Public Law Literature in the Holy Roman Empire, 1599–1804* (Chicago, 1973), Karl Otmar Freiherr von Aretin, *Das Alte Reich, 1648–1806* (Stuttgart, 1993) and Constantin Fasolt, *The Shadow of the Emperor: A Study and Translation of Hermann Conring's "Discursus Novus de Imperatore Romano-Germanico"* (forthcoming).

[6] Thomas Hobbes, *Leviathan* (1651), ed. Richard Tuck (Cambridge, 1991), p. 480.

to all of its conquered peoples, had become an imperial federation, a 'Roman Empire, of which other kingdoms are dependencies', as Isidore of Seville had defined it in the seventh century.[7] The twelfth-century recovery of Roman law strengthened both these legacies, as some jurists stressed the fact that the *Digest* (XIV. 2. 9) identified the Emperor (and, by extension, his successors, whether Imperial or Papal) as the lord of all the world (*dominus mundi*), while others accepted the diversity of polities within Europe and argued that each ruler had the authority of an emperor within his own kingdom (*rex in regno suo est imperator*).[8]

The Empire was by then but one among many *imperia*, and the traditions of Rome could be appropriated to defend particular sovereignty as readily as to claim universal authority, within Europe and in its overseas dependencies. The European overseas empires depended upon the constitutional structures of their parent states for their own definition, and imperial disputes often reproduced metropolitan contests. The realisation that early-modern Europe was a 'Europe of composite monarchies' has clarified the nature of the connection between early-modern state-building and contemporary overseas expansion.[9] The classic nineteenth-century model of the nation-state as the necessary unit of political history obscured the fact that 'Europe, the initiator of one of the world's major processes of conquest, colonization and cultural transformation, was also the product of one' after the fall of the Roman Empire,[10] and that the European monarchies were created from diverse territories and peoples, brought together by dynastic inheritance, conquest or political union. Early-modern Europe encompassed a variety of political forms, with a multiplicity of political theories to explain them. The period between Charles V's accession to the Holy Roman Empire and the Union between England and Scotland (1519–1707) was pivotal in European political theory, as John Robertson argues (see chapter 2 below).[11] In the context of constitutional innovation within Europe and external expansion beyond Europe, theorists like Hugo Grotius, Juan de Solórzano, Thomas Hobbes and James Harrington formulated novel theories of conquest, intervention,

---

[7] Isidore of Seville, *Etymologiæ* (c. 622–33), IX. 3. 2, cit. Folz, *Concept of Empire*, p. 7.

[8] Walter Ullmann, 'The Development of the Medieval Idea of Sovereignty', *English Historical Review* LXIV (1949), pp. 1–33; Quentin Skinner, *The Foundations of Modern Political Thought*, 2 vols. (Cambridge, 1978), I, 'The Renaissance'.

[9] J. H. Elliott, 'A Europe of Composite Monarchies', *Past & Present* CXXXVII (1992), pp. 48–71; Mark Greengrass, ed., *Conquest and Coalescence: The Shaping of the State in Early Modern Europe* (London, 1991).

[10] Robert Bartlett, *The Making of Europe: Conquest, Colonization and Cultural Change, 950–1350* (London, 1993), p. 314.

[11] See also John Robertson, 'Union, State and Empire: The Britain of 1707 in its European Setting', in Lawrence Stone, ed., *An Imperial State at War: Britain from 1689 to 1815* (London, 1994), pp. 224–57.

sovereignty and international relations with their eyes upon activity overseas as well as on domestic political developments.[12]

The union of diverse territories was the norm within Europe, and the theoretical issues raised by composite monarchy and confederation provided precedents for dealing with overseas dominions. Empire could be the equivalent of union, at least in Solórzano's conception of the Spanish Monarchy's relationship with its provinces abroad. It could also be a form of union, as in James VI and I's vision of Britain as a united monarchy of England and Scotland in which neither kingdom would be subordinate to the other as a unitary empire without dependent provinces.[13] However, union could also be the alternative to empire, as when the United Provinces confederated defensively against the Spanish Monarchy,[14] or the Swiss Cantons founded their alliance to counter the Holy Roman Empire. Solórzano was a belated apologist for imperial unity as the Spanish Monarchy settled into irretrievable decline; few of James VI and I's subjects shared his dream of a British empire of equals; and the Dutch ruthlessly insisted on Grotius' arguments in favour of their empire of the seas to make the United Provinces master of new, non-territorial species of empire. The diversity of these political forms, and of the political theories which underlay them, is a reminder that there was no single European theory of empire and hence no common ideological project of 'imperialism' in post-Reformation Europe.

The headship of the Holy Roman Empire remained the most prestigious attribute of secular kingship in early sixteenth-century Europe.[15] When the Imperial dignity descended upon Charles V in 1519, it was united *de facto* to Europe's most extensive body of overseas possessions to create the most far-flung empire the world had ever known, greater even than the Roman Empire, which had never burst the bounds of the Pillars of Hercules to extend westward into the Atlantic.[16] Charles's two realms nevertheless remained legally distinct. The

---

[12] On whom see also Hedley Bull, Benedict Kingsbury and Adam Roberts, eds., *Hugo Grotius and International Relations* (Oxford, 1990); James Muldoon, *The Americas in the Spanish World Order: The Justification for Conquest in the Seventeenth Century* (Philadelphia, 1994) (on Solórzano); Noel Malcolm, 'Hobbes, Sandys, and the Virginia Company', *The Historical Journal* XXIV (1981), pp. 297–321; David Armitage, 'The Cromwellian Protectorate and the Languages of Empire', *The Historical Journal* XXXV (1992), pp. 531–55 (on Harrington).

[13] Compare David Armitage, 'Making the Empire British: Scotland in the Atlantic World, 1542–1707', *Past & Present* CLV (May 1997) pp. 34–63; *idem*, 'The Scottish Vision of Empire: Intellectual Origins of the Darien Venture', in John Robertson, ed., *A Union for Empire: Political Thought and the British Union of 1707* (Cambridge, 1995), pp. 97–118.

[14] Compare Martin van Gelderen, *The Political Thought of the Dutch Revolt, 1555–1590* (Cambridge, 1992); Benjamin Schmidt, 'Innocence Abroad: The Dutch Imagination and the Representation of the New World, c. 1570–1670' (Ph. D. dissertation, Harvard University, 1994).

[15] Compare Gaston Zeller, 'Les Rois de France Candidats à l'Empire: Essai sur l'Idéologie Imperiale en France', *Revue Historique* CLXXIII (1934), pp. 273–311, 497–543.

[16] Ramón Menendez Pidal, *El Idea Imperial de Carlos V* (Buenos Aires, 1941); Frances A.

existence of the Holy Roman Empire debarred the Spanish Monarchy from becoming the Spanish Empire and, despite the messianic expectations aroused by the discovery of America, even those who hailed Charles's universal monarchy did not necessarily take it to include his lands in the New World. Chief among the Habsburg imperial panegyrists was Charles's own Chancellor, Mercurino Gattinara, who expected his master to revive Dante's vision in the *Monarchia* of a pan-European (and by that definition, universal) empire centred upon Italy, 'the garden of the Empire'.[17] As John Headley argues (see chapter 3 below), Gattinara's neo-Ghibelline, apocalyptic and Erasmian vision of empire 'remain[ed] firmly focused on Europe, and appears quite unaffected by the American experience and Castile's presence in the New World'.[18] Gattinara's contemporary, the Navarrese jurist Michael de Ulcurrunus, shared this indifference to the New World and concentrated, like Gattinara, on the threats to Christendom, from Lutheranism and the Turk, rather than on Spain's new opportunities in the Americas.[19] Similarly, the messianic hopes pinned on the return from the dead of the Portuguese King Sebastian imagined an empire in the Iberian peninsula and North Africa and deliberately overlooked Portugal's dominions in South America and Asia in favour of reviving the heroic greatness lost at the battle of El-Ksar-el-Kebir in 1578.[20] Even the first generations of Protestant theorists – including Luther and Calvin – remained indifferent to the native peoples of the New World as they worked out their novel theories of salvation history and church government.[21]

The union of the Spanish Monarchy and the Holy Roman Empire in the person of Charles V nevertheless raised the spectre of a Habsburg universal monarchy in Europe, fuelled by the bullion of the Indies and the trade of Seville.

Yates, 'Charles V and the Idea of the Empire', in her *Astræa: The Imperial Theme in the Sixteenth Century* (London, 1975), pp. 1–28; Earl Rosenthal, '*Plus Ultra, Non Plus Ultra*, and the Columnar Device of the Emperor Charles V', *Journal of the Warburg and Courtauld Institutes* XXXIV (1971), pp. 204–28.

[17] Dante, *Monarchia* (c. 1320), ed. Prue Shaw (Cambridge, 1995); Charles T. Davis, *Dante and the Idea of Rome* (Oxford, 1957).

[18] See also John M. Headley, 'Gattinara, Erasmus and the Imperial Configurations of Humanism', *Archiv für Reformationsgeschichte* LXXI (1980), pp. 64–98; *idem*, 'Rhetoric and Reality: Messianic, Humanist, and Civilian Themes in the Imperial Ethos of Gattinara', in Marjorie Reeves, ed., *Prophetic Rome in the High Renaissance Period* (Oxford, 1992), pp. 241–70.

[19] Diana Perry, '"*Catholicum Opus Imperiale Regiminis Mundi*": An Early Sixteenth-Century Restatement of Empire', *History of Political Thought* II (1981), pp. 227–52.

[20] Lucette Valensi, *Fables de la Mémoire: La Glorieuse Bataille des Trois Rois* (Paris, 1992); compare Luís Filipe F.R. Thomaz, 'L'Idée Imperiale Manueline', in Jean Aubin, ed., *Le Découverte, Le Portugal et L'Europe: Actes du Colloque Paris, les 26, 27 et 28 Mai 1988* (Paris, 1990), pp. 35–103.

[21] George Huntston Williams, 'Erasmus and the Reformers on Non-Christian Religions and *Salus Extra Ecclesiam*', in Theodore K. Rabb and Jerrold E. Seigel, eds., *Action and Conviction in Early Modern Europe: Essays in Memory of E. H. Harbison* (Princeton, 1969), pp. 319–70.

The language of universal monarchy provided its opponents with a counter-theory of the Empire, not as the apocalyptic vehicle of Christianity, joining the whole world under 'one shepherd with one flock' in a reign of perpetual peace, but rather as European hegemony for the Habsburgs. Franz Bosbach shows that this conception of universal monarchy drew upon earlier theories of the succession to the Roman Empire, the universal *imperium* of the Emperor, and the evangelical destiny of the Empire (see chapter 4 below). However, after the elevation of Charles V it became a means of understanding international politics as the competition between Habsburg and Bourbon aspirations to political hegemony through to the age of Louis XIV (and indeed beyond);[22] it would also later provide a language to criticise the putative monopolies threatened by France, Holland or England over international trade.[23] Apprehensions that one European power was aiming at universal monarchy could be used to inspire others to ally against the potential aggressor, so that what began as an analytical theory of empire ultimately became a justification for defensive aggression within Europe.[24] This transformation of the language of universal monarchy indicates a major stage in the passage from a providentialist theory of empire, whose roots lay in the Christianisation of the Roman Empire under Constantine[25] to the economic interpretation of hegemony that underpins modern theories of imperialism. However, though universal monarchy proved to be a useful tool for understanding European politics, its horizons barely encompassed the Americas or Asia, except insofar as the profits of the Indies were held to have strengthened the European states in their contests for hegemony.

The major exception to the Eurocentricity of universal monarchist discourse was the imperial vision of Hernán Cortés, as eccentric as it was original. Cortés promised Charles V that he could 'ser monarca del mundo' and recreate the Empire as a truly universal monarchy, spanning the European continent, traversing the Atlantic, and stretching from New Spain over the Pacific decades before Philip

---

[22] See also Franz Bosbach, *Monarchia Universalis: Ein politischer Leitbegriff der frühen Neuzeit* (Göttingen, 1986); Rodolfo De Mattei, 'Il Mito della Monarchia Universale nel Pensiero Politico Italiano del Seicento', *Rivista di Studi Politici Internazionali* XXXII (1965), pp. 531–50; John Robertson, 'Universal Monarchy and the Liberties of Europe: David Hume's Critique of an English Whig Doctrine', in Nicholas Phillipson and Quentin Skinner, eds., *Political Discourse in Early Modern Britain* (Cambridge, 1993), pp. 349–73.

[23] On the economic redefinition of universal monarchy in the age of mercantilism, see Steven C. A. Pincus, *Protestantism and Patriotism: Ideologies and the Making of English Foreign Policy, 1650–1688* (Cambridge, 1996); *idem*, 'The English Debate over Universal Monarchy', in Robertson, ed., *A Union for Empire*, pp. 37–62.

[24] Compare E.V. Gulick, *Europe's Classical Balance of Power* (New York, 1955); Michael Sheehan, *The Balance of Power: History and Theory* (London, 1996).

[25] On which see for example Averil Cameron, *Christianity and the Rhetoric of Empire: The Development of Christian Discourse* (Berkeley, 1991) and Garth Fowden, *Empire to Commonwealth: Consequences of Monotheism in Late Antiquity* (Princeton, 1993).

II would acquire a Hispano-Portuguese empire on which the sun never set.[26] Cortés achieved his premature and novel theory of empire by drawing on the particularist conception enshrined in the *Siete Partidas*, the thirteenth-century legal code of Alfonso X, which he applied to the dominions of the Mexica 'emperor' Moctezuma, as Victor Frankl shows (see chapter 5 below).[27] In his *Second Relation* from Mexico (1519), Cortés promised Charles V that he 'might call [him]self emperor of this kingdom with no less glory than that of Germany which, by the Grace of God, Your Majesty already possesses'.[28] This implied the existence of multiple empires for Charles's glory, one acquired by election from the German princes, the other by donation from his new vassal, Moctezuma, or by his faithful servant Cortés's conquest. Conquest implied the defeat of a worthy enemy; donation implied a secular juridical basis for Charles's dominions in New Spain, distinct from the papal grant of new territories in the Antilles and Tierra Firme to the Castilian crown in 1493. Like Gattinara back in Europe, Cortés imagined a neo-Ghibelline empire for Charles V, though his vision was predicated on a new empire in the Americas, beyond the authority of the Papacy, while Gattinara's remained bounded by the Mediterranean.

All of the European powers faced Cortés's dilemma of legitimating a novel position with intellectual resources that were necessarily traditional. Almost all of them adopted some form of Cortés's solution, and claimed that their unparalleled assertions of dominion were, in fact, precedented. Despite the continuity of the Western Empire and the longevity of classical and medieval languages of empire, 'the large-scale European seizure of overseas territories from the sixteenth century onwards constituted a new and distinctive phase in the continent's relationship with the outside world', as J. H. Elliott's essay emphasises (see chapter 6 below). There were theoretical precedents for Christian relations with infidels, dating back to the Mongol threat to Europe in the thirteenth century, and these were kept current in the canonistic tradition underlying the papal bulls of donation of 1493.[29] The settlements on Madeira and the Azores, and the conquest of the Canaries in the fifteenth century, offered some practical

---

[26] See also John M. Headley, 'Spain's Asian Presence, 1565–1590: Structures and Aspirations', *Hispanic American Historical Review* LXXV (1995), pp. 623–46.

[27] Compare J.H. Elliott, 'The Mental World of Hernán Cortés', *Transactions of the Royal Historical Society* XVII (1967), pp. 41–58, and Anthony Pagden, '"Con título y con no menos mérito que el de Alemania, que Vuestra Sacra Majestad posee": Rethinking the Conquest of Mexico', in his *The Uncertainties of Empire: Essays in Iberian and Ibero-American Intellectual History* (Aldershot, 1994), ch. XIII.

[28] Hernán Cortés, *Letters from Mexico*, ed. and trans. Anthony Pagden (rev. edn., New Haven, 1986), p. 48.

[29] James Muldoon, *Popes, Lawyers, and Infidels: The Church and the Non-Christian World, 1250–1550* (Philadelphia, 1979).

precedents,[30] though these did not combine territorial conquest with economic enterprise in the manner that would be characteristic of later European seizure of overseas territories. Competition for land and trade among the European powers, and the shattering of Christendom by the Reformation, necessitated a more demanding justification for conquest than the supposedly universal authority of the Church by which the world had been carved into Spanish and Portuguese spheres of influence in the 1490s. Accordingly, the right of exclusive possession came to override the earlier claims of first discovery, so that states needed both to settle, 'plant' or colonise overseas territory and, crucially, to provide ideological justifications for their settlements against the claims both of the native peoples and those of their European competitors.[31]

The papal attribution of sovereignty (*imperium*) in the Americas did not carry with it a right of property (*dominium*), and therein lay a challenge for the Catholic powers, as Anthony Pagden shows (see chapter 7 below). The newly-discovered lands could not be appropriated on the grounds that they were unoccupied, since they patently had a resident population; arguments for the next three hundred years therefore turned as much upon justifications for dispossessing the native peoples as they did upon asserting positive rights of ownership against other European states.[32] The Spanish Dominicans were the first to construct such arguments, though in the process of justifying the Castilian crown's particular dominion in the Americas, they undermined the claims of both the Papacy and the Empire to universal jurisdiction. Instead, as Francisco de Vitoria argued, the Spanish could legitimately claim the rights of travel, commerce and preaching the gospel to the 'barbarians', with only the last enforceable by arms if denied.[33] Even this left the Castilian crown with no right of *dominium* in the New World, a right that could only be restored to the Spanish by a theorist like Juan Gines

---

[30] Felipe Fernández-Armesto, *The Canary Islands After the Conquest* (Oxford, 1982); Peter Russell, 'Influencia del Descubrimiento de Canarias sobre el Debate Medieval Acerca de los Derechos del Hombre Pagano y de los Estados Paganos: La Documentación Portuguesa', *Revista de Historia Canaria* XXXVI (1978), pp. 9–32.

[31] L.C. Green and Olive P. Dickason, *The Law of Nations and the New World* (Edmonton, 1989); Patricia Seed, *Ceremonies of Possession in Europe's Conquest of the New World, 1492–1650* (Cambridge, 1995); John T. Juricek, 'English Claims in North America: A Study in Legal and Constitutional Thought' (Ph. D. dissertation, University of Chicago, 1970); *idem* 'English Territorial Claims in North America under Elizabeth and the Early Stuarts', *Terrae Incognitæ* VII (1975), pp. 7–22; Kent McNeil, *Common Law Aboriginal Title* (Oxford, 1989).

[32] Generally, see J.H. Parry, *The Spanish Theory of Empire in the Sixteenth Century* (Cambridge, 1940); Silvio Zavala, *The Political Philosophy of the Conquest of America* (Mexico City, 1953); Lewis Hanke, *The Spanish Struggle for Justice in the Conquest of America* (Boston, 1965).

[33] Francisco de Vitoria, 'On the American Indians' (1539), in Anthony Pagden and Jeremy Lawrance, eds., *Vitoria: Political Writings* (Cambridge, 1991), pp. 231–92.

de Sepúlveda, who argued that civil peoples should exercise *dominium* as well as *imperium* over the barbarians.

The Spanish debate over 'dispossessing the barbarian' had the signal effect of diverting the argument over property to natural law, and hence to the objectively identifiable characteristics of native peoples.[34] If the criteria for the ability to exercise *dominium* were such traits as type of social organisation, marriage customs, religious observance and, at base, rationality, ethnographic observation became the necessary foundation for political claims. This ethnographic turn was not unique to the Spanish. Nicholas Canny argues that the English began their anthropological engagement with the Gaelic inhabitants of Ireland in the 1560s, just as the Spanish debate was dying down after the death of Bartolomé de las Casas, the man who had done most to keep it alive (see chapter 8 below).[35] The English in Ireland followed a theoretical path similar to that traversed by the Spanish between 1493 and 1551, except that their trajectory had begun with the Anglo-Norman invasions of the twelfth century. The papal bull *Laudabiliter* (1155) had empowered Henry II to invade Ireland,[36] which was thereafter held by right of conquest, as Edmund Spenser remarked in 1596: 'all is the conqueror's, as Tully to Brutus saith'.[37] After the English Reformation had made any claim from papal donation inoperable, Henry VIII was proclaimed 'King of Ireland' by the Irish Parliament, thereby adding a second crown to the imperial crown of England. When the English under Elizabeth I wanted to reassert control over the increasingly independent Irish lordships, they executed a move similar in consequence, if not in substance, to that made by the Spanish Dominicans a generation earlier. Many of these 'New English' came to Ireland already possessed of an image of the barbarian derived from reading Spanish ethnographers such as José de Acosta, and as a result brutalised a native population they recognised as uncivilised because pagan. These traits marked the Irish as barbarians and the English as the bearers of a civilising mission to them. That categorisation could justify dispossession in Ireland as readily as it could in New Spain, though the Spanish cultural mission would encompass such expedients as intermarriage between conquerors and

---

[34] Anthony Pagden, *The Fall of Natural Man: The American Indian and the Origins of Comparative Ethnology* (2nd edn., Cambridge, 1986).

[35] Compare D.B. Quinn, 'Ireland and Sixteenth Century European Expansion', in T. Desmond Williams, ed., *Historical Studies* I (London, 1958), pp. 21–32; Nicholas P. Canny, *The Elizabethan Conquest of Ireland: A Pattern Established, 1565–1576* (Hassocks, 1976).

[36] James Muldoon, 'Spiritual Conquests Compared: *Laudabiliter* and the Conquest of the Americas', in Steven B. Bowman and Blanche E. Cody, eds., *In Iure Veritas: Studies in Canon Law in Memory of Schafer Williams* (Cincinnati, 1991), pp. 174–86.

[37] Edmund Spenser, *A View of the Present State of Ireland* (1596), ed. R.L. Renwick (Oxford, 1970), p. 9.

conquered that would rarely be countenanced in subsequent British colonial enterprises.[38] Later, the English in Ireland would rely increasingly on legal rather than cultural arguments for *dominium*.[39]

The New English settlers in Ireland were concerned to prove that native rights of sovereignty had passed to the English Crown by right of conquest or by an act of the Irish Parliament. There was therefore no question that the Gaelic Irish had once held *dominium*; the argument in the late sixteenth century was who held it then, and where *imperium* lay. By contrast, the Spanish had taken for granted that the Mexica and the Inka had possessed *imperium*; their argument was instead over rights of *dominium*. Similarly, the French and the Dutch generally recognised the sovereignty of native peoples as, on occasion, would the English in North America.[40] Such recognitions of sovereignty are not only of theoretical importance, as W. J. Eccles shows (see chapter 9 below), because the transfer of sovereignty from first nations to Euro-American settlers made between the sixteenth and the eighteenth centuries underlies the sovereign claims of current successor states such as Canada.[41]

The French in the 1520s were the first European nation to challenge the papal division of the world between the Portuguese and the Spanish, as Francis I had demanded to see the provision in Adam's will that had bequeathed half the world to Spain.[42] The lack of papal donation apart, the French initially proceeded in their claims to sovereignty along lines laid down by the Spaniards, by making land-grants which carried with them a duty to evangelise the Indians. However, since French activities in North America tended to concentrate less on colonial settlement than on concentrated missions and dispersed economic activities such as fur-trapping, they became more dependent on co-operative relations with native peoples, and increasingly respectful of their sovereign claims. The French were more keen to enter into treaty-relations with the First Nations than most other European powers, and they found more willing partners in the diplomatically-sophisticated Iroquois confederation. Dominion over Indian lands which had been negotiated by the French passed to the British under the terms of the Treaty of Paris (1763)

---

[38] J.H. Elliott, *Britain and Spain in America: Colonists and Colonized* (Reading, 1994).

[39] Hans Pawlisch, *Sir John Davies and the Conquest of Ireland: A Study in Legal Imperialism* (Cambridge, 1985).

[40] Dorothy V. Jones, *License for Empire: Colonialism by Treaty in Early America* (Chicago, 1990).

[41] Compare Robert A. Williams, Jr., *The American Indian in Western Legal Thought: The Discourses of Conquest* (New York, 1990).

[42] On the French experience see also Sigmund Diamond, 'An Experiment in Feudalism: French Canada in the Seventeenth Century,' *William and Mary Quarterly* 3rd ser., XVIII (1961), pp. 3–34; Brian Slattery, 'French Claims in North America, 1500–59', *Canadian Historical Review* XLIV (1978), pp. 139–69; Olive P. Dickason, *The Myth of the Savage and the Beginnings of French Colonialism in the Americas* (Edmonton, 1984).

and thence was transmitted to their successor governments in the Canadian federation. This has meant that First Nations' claims to property in their lands and sovereignty over them against the Canadian government must be adjudicated according to both fact and law. Early-modern theories of both *dominium* and *imperium* are therefore still at issue in contemporary tribunals in Canada, as they remain in the United States, Australia and New Zealand.

By and large, there was one procedure for America, another for India (*alia enim India, alia Americana ratio est*), as the Dutch jurist Hugo Grotius observed in 1609.[43] The legal position in the East Indies was radically different from that in the West Indies since India had been known to (and had traded with) the Romans and had been partly conquered by Alexander, so that no claims of first discovery could be made. The peoples of the subcontinent and Indonesia had legal traditions as ancient in many cases as those of the European nations, and were treated as equal and sovereign partners in treaty-making under international law.[44] (The process by which these peoples were excluded from the family of nations in the late eighteenth century is beyond the scope of this volume, though their earlier inclusion should caution against any assumption that European dealings with Asian peoples were conducted, at all times, within a homogeneous discourse of 'Orientalism'.) Grotius denied Portuguese sovereignty over any part of the East Indies by according the local rulers full sovereign rights, and argued for freedom of the seas (*mare liberum*) on the Vitorian grounds that the rights to travel and trade were admissible according to natural law. In making this last claim, Grotius was also probably drawing on his knowledge that freedom of navigation was a principle of Indian law and a practice throughout the East Indies, as Alexandrowicz plausibly suggests (see chapter 10 below). Grotius's arguments for the sovereignty of the East Indian princes and for the freedom of the seas provoked the most wide-ranging dispute over theories of empire since the Spanish debates of over half a century earlier, a dispute that drew responses to *Mare Liberum* from jurists in Scotland (William Welwod, *An Abridgement of All Sea-Laws* [1613]), England (John Selden, *Mare Clausum* [c. 1618]), Portugal (Justo Seraphim de Freitas, *De Justo Imperio Lusitanorum Asiatico* [1625]) and Spain (Juan de Solórzano, *De Indiarum Jure* [1629]).[45] The origins and aftermath of

---

[43] C.H. Alexandrowicz, 'Grotius and India', *The Indian Year Book of International Affairs* III (1954), pp. 357–67.

[44] See more generally C.H. Alexandrowicz, *An Introduction to the History of the Law of Nations in the East Indies (16th, 17th and 18th Centuries)* (Oxford, 1967).

[45] For other treatments of this dispute see Samuel Muller, *Mare Clausum: Bijdrage tot de Geschiedenis der Rivaliteit van Engeland en Nederland in de Zeventiende Eeuw* (Amsterdam, 1872); Thomas Wemyss Fulton, *The Sovereignty of the Sea* (Edinburgh, 1911), ch. 9; W.S.M. Knight, 'Seraphin de Freitas: Critic of *Mare Liberum*', *Transactions of the Grotius Society* XI (1926), pp. 1–9; Richard Tuck, *Philosophy and Government, 1572–1651* (Cambridge, 1993), pp. 169–79, 212–14.

the debate between Grotius and his critics suggest the need to follow two relatively undeveloped avenues for research: into other Dutch imperial ideologies[46] and into non-European contributions to western theories of empire.[47]

Claims to dominion over land and sea provided the ideological foundations for the early-modern European overseas empires, though on that basis were erected competing millenarian and mercantilist theories of imperial destiny and purpose. The Spanish, Portuguese, French and English had all grounded their claims to expansion on the duty to evangelise, through the papal bulls and royal charters, so that each of the sixteenth-century empires could claim to have a religious mission. It was not inevitable that such evangelical purpose should be translated into a millenarian conception of imperial destiny, though the biblical typology of the Four Empires prophesied in the Book of Daniel certainly gave sanction to the identification of any one of these empires as the vehicle for the millennium.[48] The history of specifically Protestant theories of empire – in England, Scotland, the United Provinces, France and Sweden – remains largely unwritten, though scattered treatments exist that would allow a comparative study to be undertaken.[49]

Both Protestant and Catholic Reformations cast the territorial and economic rivalry between Catholic and Protestant powers in terms of the apocalyptic battles

---

[46] See C.R. Boxer, *The Dutch Seaborne Empire 1600–1800* (London, 1965), chs. 4, 8; P.J. Drooglever, 'The Netherlands Colonial Empire: Historical Outline and Some Legal Aspects', in H.F. van Panhuys, ed., *International Law in the Netherlands* I (1978), pp. 103–65.

[47] For one striking example of the latter see Richard H. Grove, *Green Imperialism: Colonial Expansion, Tropical Island Edens and the Origins of Environmentalism, 1600–1860* (Cambridge, 1995); on a more controversial case see Donald A. Grinde, Jr., and Bruce E. Johansen, *Exemplar of Liberty: Native America and the Evolution of Democracy* (Los Angeles, 1991) and 'Forum: The "Iroquois Influence" Thesis – Con and Pro', *William and Mary Quarterly*, 3rd ser., LIII (1996), pp. 587–636.

[48] Werner Goez, *Translatio Imperii* (Tübingen, 1958); Adriano Prosperi, 'New Heaven and New Earth: Prophecy and Propaganda at the Time of the Discovery and Conquest of the Americas', in Reeves, ed., *Prophetic Rome in the High Renaissance Period*, pp. 279–303; John Leddy Phelan, *The Millennial Kingdom of the Franciscans in the New World* (2nd edn., Berkeley, 1970); J.A. De Jong, *As the Waters Cover the Sea: Millennial Expectations in the Rise of Anglo-American Missions 1640–1810* (Kampen, 1970).

[49] For example, David S. Lovejoy, *Religious Enthusiasm in the New World* (Cambridge, Mass., 1985), ch. 1; Avihu Zakai, *Exile and Kingdom: History and Apocalypse in the Puritan Migration to America* (Cambridge, 1992); Roger A. Mason, 'The Scottish Reformation and the Origins of Anglo-British Imperialism', in Mason, ed., *Scots and Britons: Scottish Political Thought and the Union of 1603* (Cambridge, 1994), pp. 161–86; Arthur Williamson, 'Scots, Indians and Empire: The Scottish Politics of Civilization, 1519–1609', *Past and Present* CL (Feb. 1996), pp. 46–83; Simon Schama, *The Embarrassment of Riches: An Interpretation of Dutch Culture in the Golden Age* (London, 1987), ch. 2; Frank Lestringant, *Le Huguenot et le Sauvage: L'Amérique et la Controverse Coloniale, en France, au Temps des Guerres de Religion (1555–1589)* (Paris, 1990); Michael Roberts, *The Swedish Imperial Experience 1560–1718* (Cambridge, 1979); Susanna Åkerman, *Rose-Cross Over the Baltic* (forthcoming).

of salvation history. The Iberian empires carried with them the memory of the reconquest of the peninsula as an enterprise which had combined the imperative of advancing the true religion, the necessity of treating alien peoples as vassals, slaves or converts, and the economic benefits of plunder. Behind that particular historical experience also lay the Catholic European legacy of the crusades and the Papacy's long-term support for conquest legitimated by spiritual necessity. Apocalyptic history could explain failure as readily as success, and though millenarian theories of empire, especially in Spain and Portugal, celebrated expansion in the sixteenth century, in the seventeenth century they seem to have been more indebted to the perception of decline.[50] George Winius' essay illustrates the way in which geo-political and economic competition could be cast in millenarian terms, in this case as missionaries in the Portuguese *Padroado* of the East Indies struggled to understand the successful incursions into their territories by the heretical Dutch (see chapter 11 below).[51] The reactions of Ardizone Spinola and Fernão de Queyroz offer a teasing example of the ways in which one form of European activity – the struggle for domination of the East Indian spice-trade – could be theorised in terms of another – the battle for conversion of the infidel before the Last Days. The episode of Portuguese-Dutch competition in the East Indies also indicates the need for more histories of the mutual perceptions among the European empires, because they encountered each other in the expanding world almost as often as they met the colonial 'Other'.

If millenarianism provided one major theory by which contemporaries understood European expansion as a common, and competitive, enterprise, then mercantilism provided another. 'Mercantilism' as a body of supposedly identifiable and coherent doctrine is the invention of modern historians, and the first systematic exposition of the 'mercantile system' came from Adam Smith, who sought to undermine its principles in Book IV of *The Wealth of Nations* (1776).[52]

---

[50] See especially Alain Milhou, *Colón y su Mentalidad Mesiánica en el Ambiente Franciscanista Español* (Valladolid, 1983); Pauline Moffit Watts, 'Prophecy and Discovery: On the Spiritual Origins of Columbus's "Enterprise of the Indies",' *American Historical Review* XC (1985), pp. 73–102.

[51] Compare 'Messianism and Millenarianism in the Luso-Brazilian World', special issue, *Luso-Brazilian Review* XXVIII, no. 1 (1991); C.R. Boxer, 'Faith and Empire: The Cross and the Crown in Portuguese Expansion, Fifteenth-Eighteenth Centuries', *Terrae Incognitae* VIII (1976), pp. 73–89; *idem, The Church Militant and Iberian Expansion, 1440–1770* (Baltimore, 1978).

[52] From a vast historiography see especially Eli F. Hecksher, *Mercantilism* (2 vols., London, 1955); Donald Winch, *Classical Political Economy and Colonies* (London, 1965); D.C. Coleman, ed., *Revisions in Mercantilism* (London, 1969); Lars Magnusson, *Mercantilism: The Shaping of an Economic Language* (London, 1994) and, more generally, Albert O. Hirschman, *The Passions and the Interests: Political Arguments for Capitalism before its Triumph* (Princeton, 1977); Terence Hutchinson, *Before Adam Smith: The Emergence of Political Economy, 1662–1776* (Oxford, 1988); John Dunn, ed., *The Economic Limits to Modern Politics* (Cambridge, 1990).

Smith's target was the British Atlantic empire,[53] though the term later found as much currency as a description of the theory and practice of non-imperial European states, such as cameralist Prussia, and hence had no necessary connection with European overseas expansion. However, the emphasis on the division of world trade which is central to most definitions of mercantilism has made it a peculiarly useful tool for understanding the economic competition between the early-modern empires, not least because it was in the context of that competition that the foundations of mercantilism as a doctrine were laid. As Viner's classic discussion showed, mercantilism linked what might be called the interior and the exterior of state policy, and combined a theory of state power with recommendations about how it was to be achieved: primarily by cornering a larger share of the supposedly inflexible sum of international commerce, thereby making plenty the parent of power (see chapter 12 below). Mercantilist theory was therefore a peculiarly appropriate descriptive theory of imperial antagonism, though whether it provided the theoretical impetus behind such antagonism is more debatable. Henceforward, European expansion would be understood primarily in economic terms, as theories of *imperium* gave way to recognisably modern doctrines of imperialism.[54]

The colonial independence movements in the Americas in the late eighteenth and early nineteenth centuries made possible those modern theories of imperialism by bringing to an end the classic early-modern empires of Britain and Spain. The first decolonisation movements in the western hemisphere helped to redefine empire not solely negatively, by allowing commerce rather than conquest to become the dominating principle in the remaining European empires, but also positively, as new political forms arose on the ruins of old imperial structures.[55] As Norbert Kilian shows (see chapter 13 below), in the two decades after 1776, institutional innovation in the new American republic generated new federalist, republican, providential and progressive theories to stabilise and analyse what Alexander Hamilton proudly called 'an empire in many respects the most

---

[53] E.A. Benians, 'Adam Smith's Project of Empire', *Cambridge Historical Journal* I (1925), pp. 249–83; C.R. Fay, 'Adam Smith, America, and the Doctrinal Defeat of the Mercantilist System', *Quarterly Journal of Economics* XLVIII (1933–34), pp. 304–16; Andrew S. Skinner, 'Mercantilist Policy: The American Colonies', in his *A System of Social Science: Papers Relating to Adam Smith* (Oxford, 1979), pp. 184–207.

[54] Again from a huge literature see, for example, Wolfgang J. Mommsen, *Theories of Imperialism*, trans. P.S. Falla (Chicago, 1980) and Bernard Semmel, *The Liberal Ideal and the Demons of Empire: Theories of Imperialism from Adam Smith to Lenin* (Baltimore, 1993).

[55] On the British Empire see David Armitage, *The Ideological Origins of the British Empire* (Cambridge, 1999); Eliga H. Gould, *The Persistence of Empire: British Political Culture and National Identity, 1714–1783* (Chapel Hill, forthcoming); Thomas R. Metcalf, *Ideologies of the Raj* (*The New Cambridge History of India III: 4*) (Cambridge, 1994).

interesting in the world'.[56] It would be interesting because doubly remarkable: first, as an 'Empire for Liberty', combining two values – freedom and extent – which the republican tradition had held to be incompatible, and second as a polity which combined 'these United States' into a single federal structure after 1787.[57] Though American historians have, like the Founding Fathers, wished rather to emphasise the rupture rather than the continuity between the American Republic and the First British Empire, that empire had been federal in practice, if not in theory, and thereby provided the structure for the newly united states.[58]

The collision between metropolitan and colonial theories of empire precipitated rebellion in British America.[59] As Timothy E. Anna suggests, the Latin American independence movements arose from similar disagreements about the purposes of the Spanish empire, and led in their turn to the redefinition of theories of empire, monarchy and republicanism (see chapter 14 below). Spanish-American *criollos* defined their identity through history, reaching back to the Spanish conquests for their legitimacy and the native nobility for their identity. The Spanish kingdoms became separate states rather than members of a federation because they had been ruled as distinct viceroyalties integrated into the Spanish Monarchy, not colonies of Spain. They had conspicuously not been treated as equals by the metropolitan government, and the declaration by the Cortes of the 'indisputable concept that the Spanish dominions of both hemispheres form a single monarchy, a single nation, and a single family' came too late to restrain the rebellions of *criollos* already possessed, unlike the colonists of British America, of their own independent identities before they revolted.[60] Both the

---

[56] James Madison, Alexander Hamilton and John Jay, *The Federalist Papers* (1788), ed. Isaac Kramnick (Harmondsworth, 1987), p. 87.

[57] See also Gerald Stourzh, *Alexander Hamilton and the Idea of Republican Government* (Stanford, 1970); J.G.A. Pocock, *The Politics of Extent and the Problems of Freedom* (Colorado Springs, 1988); Judith Shklar, 'Montesquieu and the New Republicanism', in Gisela Bock, Quentin Skinner and Maurizio Viroli, eds., *Machiavelli and Republicanism* (Cambridge, 1991), pp. 265–79; Peter S. Onuf and Nicholas Onuf, *Federal Union, Modern World: The Law of Nations in an Age of Revolutions, 1776–1814* (Madison, 1993).

[58] Jack P. Greene, *Peripheries and Center: Constitutional Development in the Extended Polities of the British Empire and the United States, 1607–1788* (Athens, Ga., 1986); *idem*, 'The Imperial Roots of American Federalism', *This Constitution* VI (1985), pp. 4–11.

[59] Bernard Bailyn, *The Ideological Origins of the American Revolution* (rev. edn., Cambridge, Mass., 1992) and J.C.D. Clark, *The Language of Liberty, 1660–1832: Political Discourse and Social Dynamics in the Anglo-American World* (Cambridge, 1993) offer sharply different accounts of that collision and its nature.

[60] See also Anthony Pagden, *Spanish Imperialism and the Political Imagination: Studies in European and Spanish-American Social and Political Theory, 1513–1830* (New Haven, 1990), chs. 4–6; David Brading, *The First America: The Spanish Monarchy, Creole Patriots and the Liberal State, 1492–1867* (Cambridge, 1991); Benedict Anderson, *Imagined Communities: Reflections on the Origin and Spread of Nationalism* (rev. edn., London, 1991), ch. 4, 'Creole Pioneers'.

British King-in-Parliament and the Spanish Monarchy had hoped that declarations of equality, the ties that bound colonists to metropolitans, and the economic benefits of mercantilism would be sufficient to hold their Atlantic empires together. However, each foundered on what Anna calls 'the inherent ideological contradiction of empire', that the modern empires did not distribute the benefits of citizenship equally as Rome had, and that proclamations of good will from the metropolis rang hollow in the Americas, when North American colonies were treated like viceroyalties and Spanish-American viceroyalties were treated like colonies.[61]

The imperial roots of the American federation and the viceregal infrastructure of the Latin American republics are reminders that the theoretical legacy of the early-modern empires still shapes contemporary political concerns. Yet, as Richard Tuck and James Tully (among others) have stressed, political theory also carries freight from the period of European expansion of which contemporary theorists need to be aware.[62] Almost all of the major early-modern political theorists had some stake in the ideological justification of European rights to property, dominion or freedom of trade in the wider world: for example, Grotius argued on behalf of the Dutch East India Company; Hobbes held shares in the Virginia Company; and Locke co-wrote the Fundamental Constitutions for his patron, Shaftesbury's Carolina plantation, owned shares in the Royal African Company, and elaborated an agriculturalist theory of property that would be used to justify European dispossession of native lands well into the eighteenth century.[63] Tully argues that, since a central problem for western political theory between Grotius and Kant was precisely the ideological justification of European property, the underlying assumptions of European traditions of political thought – whether liberal, communitarian or nationalist – can hardly provide impartial adjudication in contemporary land-disputes between First Nations and the governments of the European empires' successor-states (see chapter 15 below). The imperial origins of contemporary theories of property, rights, liberty and sovereignty must be

---

[61] Compare J.H. Elliot, 'Empire and State in British and Spanish America', in Serge Gruzinsi and Nathan Wachtel, eds., *Le Nouveau Monde-Mondes Nouveaux: L'Expérience Américaine* (Paris, 1996), pp. 365–82.

[62] Richard Tuck, *Sorry Comforters: Political Theory and the International Order from Grotius to Kant* (Oxford, forthcoming); *idem*, 'Rights and Pluralism', in James Tully, ed., *Philosophy in an Age of Pluralism: The Philosophy of Charles Taylor in Question* (Cambridge, 1994), pp. 159–70; James Tully, *Strange Multiplicity: Constitutionalism in an Age of Diversity* (Cambridge, 1995).

[63] On Locke see especially James Tully, 'Rediscovering America: The *Two Treatises* and Aboriginal Land Rights', in his *An Approach to Political Philosophy: Locke in Contexts* (Cambridge, 1993), pp. 137–76, and Barbara Arneil, *John Locke and America: The Defence of English Colonialism* (Oxford, 1996); compare Thomas Flanagan, 'The Agricultural Argument and Original Appropriation: Indian Lands and Political Philosophy', *Canadian Journal of Political Science* XXII (1989), pp. 589–602.

discovered before the inequities of European expansion be successfully overcome, while the history of that expansion cannot justly be written without discriminating the particularity of each nation's imperial ideology while also acknowledging the non-European contribution to the formation of western political theory. This volume attempts to map some of the ways in which the expanding world affected the political imaginations of European theorists. However, it also shows that there is much work still to be done to provide a fully comparative history of theories of empire from *imperium* to imperialism, and thereby to reveal the imperial features on the face of modern political theory.

Bibliography

Alexandrowicz, C. H., *An Introduction to the History of the Law of Nations in the East Indies (16th, 17th and 18th Centuries)* (Oxford, 1967).

Armitage, David, *The Ideological Origins of the British Empire* (Cambridge, 1999).

Arneil, Barbara, *John Locke and America: The Defence of English Colonialism* (Oxford, 1996).

Bosbach, Franz, *Monarchia Universalis: Ein politischer Leitbegriff der frühen Neuzeit* (Göttingen, 1986).

Boxer, C. R., *The Dutch Seaborne Empire, 1600–1800* (London, 1965).

—, *The Portuguese Seaborne Empire, 1415–1825* (London, 1969).

Brading, David, *The First America: The Spanish Monarchy, Creole Patriots and the Liberal State, 1492–1867* (Cambridge, 1991).

Brunt, P. A., *Roman Imperial Themes* (Oxford, 1990).

Bull, Hedley, Benedict Kingsbury and Adam Roberts, eds., *Hugo Grotius and International Relations* (Oxford, 1990).

Dickason, Olive P., *The Myth of the Savage and the Beginnings of French Colonialism in the Americas* (Edmonton, 1984).

Doyle, Michael W., *Empires* (Ithaca, 1986).

Elordny, Eleuterio, *La Idea del imperio en el pensamiento español y de otros pueblos* (Madrid, 1944).

Finley, M. I., 'Colonies – An Attempt at a Typology,' *Transactions of the Royal Historical Society* XXVI (1976), 167–88.

Folz, Robert, *The Concept of Empire in Western Europe from the Fifth to the Fourteenth Century*, trans. Sheila Ann Ogilvie (London, 1969).

Gliozzi, Giuliano, *Adamo e il Nuovo Mundo: La nascita dell'antropologia come ideologia coloniale: dalle genealogie bibliche alle teorie razziali* (Florence, 1976).

Goez, Werner, *Translatio Imperii* (Tübingen, 1958).

Green L. C. and Olive P. Dickason, *The Law of Nations and the New World* (Edmonton, 1989)

Hanke, Lewis, *The Spanish Struggle for Justice in the Conquest of America* (Boston, 1965).

Headley, John M., *Church, Empire and World: The Quest for Universal Order, 1520–1640* (Aldershot, 1997).

Kennedy, Dane, 'Imperial History and Post-Colonial Theory', *Journal of Imperial and Commonwealth History* XXIV (1996), pp. 345–63.

Knorr, Klaus E., *British Colonial Theories 1570–1850* (Toronto, 1944).

Koebner, Richard, *Empire* (Cambridge, 1961).

Kupperman, Karen Ordahl, ed., *America in European Consciousness, 1493–1750* (Chapel Hill, 1995).

Lestringant, Frank, *Le Huguenot et le Sauvage: L'Amérique et la controverse coloniale, en France, au temps des Guerres de Religion (1555–1589)* (Paris, 1990).

Magnusson, Lars, *Mercantilism: The Shaping of an Economic Language* (London, 1994).

Pidal, Ramón Menendez, *El Idea Imperial de Carlos V* (Buenos Aires, 1941),

Muldoon, James, *Popes, Lawyers, and Infidels: The Church and the Non-Christian World, 1250–1550* (Philadelphia, 1979).

—, *The Americas in the Spanish World Order: The Justification for Conquest in the Seventeenth Century* (Philadelphia, 1994).

Pagden, Anthony, *The Fall of Natural Man: The American Indian and the Origins of Comparative Ethnology* (2nd edn., Cambridge, 1986).

—, *Spanish Imperialism and the Political Imagination* (New Haven, 1991).

—, *The Uncertainties of Empire: Essays in Iberian and Ibero-American Intellectual History* (Aldershot, 1994).

—, *Lords of All the World: Ideologies of Empire in Spain, Britain and France c. 1500 – c. 1800* (New Haven, 1995).

Parry, J. H., *The Spanish Theory of Empire in the Sixteenth Century* (Cambridge, 1940).

Pocock, J.G.A., *The Machiavellian Moment: Florentine Political Thought and the Atlantic Republican Tradition* (Princeton, 1975).

Seed, Patricia, *Ceremonies of Possession in Europe's Conquest of the New World, 1492–1650* (Cambridge, 1995).

Skinner, Quentin, *The Foundations of Modern Political Thought* (2 vols.; Cambridge, 1978).

Tanner, Marie, *The Last Descendant of Æneas: The Hapsburgs and the Mythic Image of the Emperor* (New Haven, 1993)

Tuck, Richard, *Sorry Comforters: Political Theory and the International Order from Grotius to Kant* (Oxford, forthcoming).

Tully, James, *Strange Multiplicity: Constitutionalism in an Age of Diversity* (Cambridge, 1995).

Williams, Jr., Robert A., *The American Indian in Western Legal Thought: The Discourses of Conquest* (New York, 1990).

de Witte, Charles-Martial, *Les Bulles pontificales et l'expansion Portugaise au XVe siècle* (Louvain, 1958).

Yates, Frances A., *Astræa: The Imperial Theme in the Sixteenth Century* (London, 1975)

Zavala, Silvio, *The Political Philosophy of the Conquest of America* (Mexico City, 1953).

1

Imperium Romanum: Empire and the Language of Power

J.S. Richardson

The vocabulary of empire, as it has developed in European contexts since the period of the Roman empire, reveals clearly enough the significance of the inheritance of Rome for the regimes which have followed it. From Charlemagne to the Tsars, from British imperialism to Italian Fascism, the language and symbols of the Roman republic and the Roman emperors have been essential elements in the self-expression of imperial powers. Such communality of language, by creating a sense of familiarity in the mind of a modern observer of the Roman empire, may hinder a proper understanding of antiquity, because the importance of the after-life of these words and symbols tends to obscure the nature of the contexts from which they originated. An obvious parallel instance can be seen in the case of the word 'democracy', where the adoption of the Athenian term to describe a series of political developments in the modern world which claim some connection with the Greek notion of *demokratia* has tended to make more difficult the modern understanding of what happened at Athens in the fifth and fourth centuries B.C.[1]

To establish and illustrate this point, the best term to examine is the crucial one, from which indeed the basic vocabulary of empire and imperialism has been developed, the word *imperium*. During the period of the growth and establishment of the Roman empire, from the third century B.C. to the early decades of the first century A.D., the meaning of the word seems to have undergone a shift, or more precisely an extension, of meaning. The earlier significance, the right of command within the Roman state, vested in the magistrates and pro-magistrates who were responsible for the official activity of the Roman people, was never lost, but in addition the meaning 'empire', in an increasingly concrete, territorial sense came to be a normal usage, so that, at least from the second half of the first century A.D., *imperium Romanum* is used as we would use 'Roman empire'.[2] Given the concurrent use of these two significances of the word, and assuming at least a continuum of meaning (which is probable if the second, as will be suggested below,[3] develops chronologically after the first is firmly established), it should be possible to discover more about each concept by examining ways in which the two relate to one another. It would be interesting to attempt to account for the change, even if it were no more than a movement in linguistic usage; but the importance of the concept of *imperium* in its original significance for the understanding of the political ideas of the Romans and the importance of the process which produced the *imperium Romanum* in its extended sense suggest that a fresh look at *imperium* may help to clarify the nature of Roman imperialism.

I

The secular activity of the Roman state (as a modern constitutional analyst might describe it) in the period of the republic may be summarized in two words: war and law. In the ancient world, of course, the distinction between sacred and secular did not divide the activity of the state in this fashion: the relations of a community with the gods was, as Aristotle observed in the case of the Greek *polis*, the prerequisite for all the others.[4] It is also true, of course, that Romans of all classes were interested in matters other than the military and the legal: all were involved in some fashion or other with activity which we would call economic, and a few were interested in matters of literature and art; but these were not areas which concerned the

* Earlier versions of this paper were read to meetings of the Classical Association of Scotland and the Leicester/Nottingham Seminar on War and Society. I take this opportunity to thank those who discussed this topic with me then, and also many other colleagues who have done so since, especially Michael Crawford, John North, and Andrew Wallace-Hadrill.

[1] For the use of Roman imperial imagery in late antiquity and the early middle ages, see M. McCormick, *Eternal Victory* (1986); for the Renaissance period, F. A. Yates, *Astraea* (1975); and in modern times, D. Mack Smith, *Mussolini's Roman Empire* (1976). On ancient and modern democracy, see for instance M. I. Finley, *Democracy, Ancient and Modern* (1973), esp. ch. 1.

[2] Thus, for instance, Pliny, *NH* VI.26.120: 'durant, ut fuere, Thebata et, ductu Pompei Magni terminus Romani imperi, Oruros, a Zeugmate L.CC.'; Tac., *Germ.* 29.1: '(Batavi) Chattorum quondam populus et seditione domestica in eas sedes transgressus in quibus pars Romani imperii fierent.'

[3] See below, III.

[4] Aristotle, *Politics* 1382b 11–13.

J. S. RICHARDSON

Roman state as such. To put the point in terms which might have meant something to Romans of the period of the republic, these were not in the public domain, not part of the *res publica*, the business of the *populus Romanus*.[5] The work of the officials of the city of Rome and of its senate and popular assemblies was taken up with legislation and jurisdiction (that is to say, with *leges* or their equivalent, and with *iura*); or with the declaration, prosecution and ending of wars, and the various processes which led up to war or its avoidance, in other words, what we now call foreign policy.

Central to all this activity was, of course, the *imperium* of the magistrates and pro-magistrates. Only magistrates proposed *leges* and were responsible for jurisdiction;[6] only magistrates and pro-magistrates were able, through their *imperium*, to command. The very word implies such command: *imperium* is to *imperare* as *desiderium* is to *desiderare*.[7] The nature of *imperium* is controversial and mysterious, and it may well be that any attempt to import exactitude into a discussion of its origins and development before the third century B.C. is fruitless and wrong-headed;[8] but the reports which later authors give of those origins are certainly an important indicator of the attitudes of the time at which they wrote. Even in the period of the late republic and early empire, with which this article is concerned, at least a certain element of the mysterious is to be expected: in part *imperium* belongs not to the precise complexities of constitutional law but to the proper obscurities of religion.[9] Although closely associated with the elected magistrates, it was not election by the *comitia centuriata* which gave the consul or the praetor his *imperium*. Election had to be followed by the curious formality of the *lex curiata*, passed in the late republic by a vestigial assembly consisting of thirty lictors, as a result of which the magistrate was given the right to take the auspices.[10] Once he had been voted the *lex curiata*, the magistrate elect proceeded to take the auspices to confirm the acceptance by Jupiter of his holding of the *imperium*.[11] It was not only the people who decided, but also the god. This is particularly clear in the case of the dictator, who was not of course elected, but who, having been nominated by the consul, was appointed by the rite of the auspices — 'is ave sinistra dictus populi magister esto', as Cicero describes the process in his ideal constitution in the *de legibus*.[12] For the tenure of the *imperium*, election could be avoided, but the acquisition of the *auspicia* and the *lex curiata* could not.

By the late republic, the precise significance of the detail of the *auspicia* had to a considerable degree been lost, and both Cicero and Dionysius of Halicarnassus lament the tendency to ignore the proper ritual connected with the *imperium* and the magistracies.[13] The basis of the earlier understanding had, however, left its mark on the practice of the state. According to Dionysius, the magistrates down to his own time went through the ceremony early in the morning of the day of their entry to office, and a favourable omen was announced, even if none was seen.[14] Although Ap. Claudius Pulcher as consul in 54 argued that he did not need a *lex curiata* to hold *imperium* in his *provincia* of Cilicia, nonetheless he attempted to provide himself with one, even though this involved bribing the augurs.[15] Similarly the importance of Jupiter and the particular relationship of the god to the holder of *imperium* remained a fundamental aspect of the celebration of the triumph by a successful *imperator* on his return to Rome.

[5] On the meaning of *res publica* as *res populi*, see Cic., *de rep.* 1.25.39, 27.43, 32.48; P. A. Brunt, *The Fall of the Roman Republic* (1988), 2 and 299.

[6] Though, as Kunkel has pointed out, others who were not magistrates were also involved in jurisdiction (W. Kunkel, 'Magistratische Gewalt und Senatsherrschaft', *ANRW* 1.2 (1972), 3–23, at 12–13).

[7] U. Coli, 'Sur la notion d'imperium en droit public romain', *RIDA* 7 (1960), 361–87, at 361.

[8] On problems of interpretation of *imperium*, see the comments of H. S. Versnel, *Triumphus* (1970), 313–19; and most recently, A. Drummond, *CAH* VII.22 (1989), 188–9.

[9] *contra* A. Heuss, 'Gedanken und Vermutungen zur frühen römischen Regierungsgewalt', *Nachr. Akad. Wiss. Gottingen. Phil.-Hist. Kl.* (1982), 377–454, at 433, who argues, correctly, that this notion is at the root of Mommsen's understanding of *imperium*, though not explicitly stated; A. Giovannini, 'Magistratur und Volk: ein Beitrag zur Entstehungsgeschichte des Staatsrechts', in W. Eder (ed.), *Staat und Staatlichkeit in der frühen*

römischen Republik (1990), 406–36, at 428f. See the commentary on the latter by E. Badian, *ibid.* 462–75, esp. 468–9.

[10] Cic., *de leg. agr.* II.10.27, II.12.31.

[11] Dion. Hal. II.5–6; cf. Mommsen, *StR* I³.81 and 609, A. Magdelain, *Recherches sur l'imperium* (1968), 36–40. Versnel, op. cit. (n. 8), 313–55 gives a useful account of various views on the *lex curiata* as well as his own, but he had not read Magdelain. For the importance of Jupiter in connection with *imperium* and *auspicia*, see J. R. Fears, 'Jupiter and Roman imperial ideology', *ANRW* 2.17.1 (1981), 3–141, at 9–55.

[12] *de leg.* III.3.9; cf. Magdelain, op. cit. (n. 11), 28–9.

[13] Cic., *ND* II.3.9, *de div.* II.36.76; Dion. Hal. II.6; cf. Magdelain, op. cit. (n. 11), 16.

[14] Dion. Hal. II.6. J. Linderski, 'The augural law', *ANRW* 2.16.3 (1986), 2146–312, at 2293–4, suggests that assistance may have been given to the god by the use of caged birds.

[15] Cic., *ad Att.* IV.18.4; *ad fam.* 1.9.25; *ad Q.f.* III.2.3.

This multi-strandedness of the power of the Roman magistrate, by which the magistracy itself and the *imperium/auspicium* complex are seen as, at least in principle, separable, provided great strength and flexibility when it became necessary to adapt the institution to meet new needs. The obvious case, of course, is that of non-magistrates (i.e. private citizens[16]) with the *imperium* of magistrates *pro consule* or *pro praetore*, created either by prorogation of an already existing command; or (as in the case of the men sent to Spain in the last years of the third and first years of the second century B.C.) by vote of one or other of the popular assemblies; or, and perhaps most remarkably, by means of the creation of *imperium* holders by the *praetor urbanus* on the order of the senate.[17] None of these held a magistracy, but each held the *imperium* and used it outside the city, that is to say held *imperium militiae* as opposed to *domi*. This distinction between the two areas in which *imperium* could be exercised, *domi* and *militiae*, also seems to have originated in the localization of the auspices,[18] and thus to have become linked to the different activities, military and judicial, which took place both inside and outside the city. If this is correct, it suggests that the growth of the notion of a multiplicity of *imperium* holders, operating outside the city, and not restricted numerically by the number of magistracies, developed from an understanding of the power and position of the *imperium* holder in which the *auspicia* were of significance.

The distinction between *domi* and *militiae* continues to be found in the late republic, particularly in contexts in which the operation of *imperium* is linked to the possession of the *auspicia*.[19] It was not true by the late republic that Romans lived only within the *pomerium* (the original definition of *domi*) nor even within one mile of the walls of Rome (the definition which replaced it for many purposes during the republic);[20] and by the time of Cicero, of course, a proconsul, who had *ex hypothesi* no possibility of exercising his *imperium* in Rome, was able to hear cases under the *ius civile*.[21] The mere fact that the *domi/militiae* distinction continues to be found widely in descriptions of *imperium* shows the continuing importance of the link with *auspicia*.[22]

This understanding of what *imperium* was helps to clarify the attitudes of the ruling élite to the growth of empire, and the relationship between individual careers and the activity of the *res publica*. First, given that the passages in which the *domi/militiae* distinction is used appear to include all uses of *imperium* under this double description, all the activity of a holder of *imperium* outside the category of actions *domi* belongs to the category of actions *militiae*: that is to say, whatever is not part of the 'domestic' activity of the holders of consular and praetorian *imperium* in Rome is part of their military activity.

Second, as already mentioned, the whole activity of the Roman state was divisible into the two categories of war and law, which find their parallel in the two fields of exercise of the *imperium*. This suggests that the activity of Rome *qua* state was carried out by these men. It should be noted further that the power that they exercised in order to carry out this role was given to each of them as individuals following (normally) their election, but by means of the *lex curiata* and the auspices. The people might choose which individual was to hold the *imperium*, but it was the individual who, through the use of the auspices, received it from, or at least with the active connivance of, the god. However much one might wish to play down Mommsen's belief that the *imperium* of the magistrates was in principle absolute,[23] and emphasize instead the power of the oligarchy (after the manner of Syme or Kunkel[24]) or even of the people (following Fergus Millar, and, in modified fashion, John North[25]), it remains the case that the executive of the Roman state was a group of magistrates, susceptible to influence and to advice which, when it came from the senate, could rarely be ignored, and who were in power for only brief periods; but nonetheless not capable of being stopped within their own sphere of action except by the intervention of another magistrate (an event which occurred

[16] On the status of pro-magistrates during the republic as *privati*, see Livy XXXVIII.42.10; Mommsen, *StR* 1³.642.

[17] Livy XXIII.34, XXVIII.46, XXXV.23, XLII.35; cf. Mommsen, *StR* 1³.681 n. 6.

[18] E. Meyer, *Römischer Staat und Staatsgedanke*² (1961), 119–21; Magdelain, op. cit. (n. 11), 72–3; *contra* A. Giovannini, *Consulare imperium* (1983), 9–15. The most telling evidence for this is the significance of the auspices which the *imperium* holder takes before leaving the *pomerium* (Magdelain, op. cit. (n. 11), 40–5).

[19] Cic., *de leg.* II.12.3; *de div.* I.2.3.

[20] Mommsen, *StR* 1³.61–70.

[21] Mommsen, *StR* 2³.102–3.

[22] Thus esp. Cic., *de div.* I.2.3; Sallust, *Cat.* 29.2–3, 53.2; Livy I.36.6.

[23] So Heuss (n. 9).

[24] Kunkel, op. cit. (n. 6), 3–22.

[25] Fergus Millar, 'The political character of the classical Roman republic', *JRS* 74 (1984), 1–19; John North, 'Democratic politics in Republican Rome', *Past & Present* 126 (February 1990), 3–21.

with great rarity).[26] The magistrates were indeed members of the senatorial élite and were elected to their magistracies by the people, but the *imperium* which gave them power was a gift from Jupiter. Each individual member of the élite class depends directly on the people to gain election to the magistracies of the city, and thus to the *imperium* which provides him with the power to act on behalf of the city and thus to advance his own standing.

The position is beautifully presented in a quotation preserved from a speech of Scipio Aemilianus: 'ex innocentia nascitur dignitas, ex dignitate honor, ex honore imperium, ex imperio libertas.'[27] Here personal virtue (*innocentia*), once recognized (*dignitas*), leads, by way of the magistracy voted to the individual by the people (*honor*), to the acquisition of power in the state by the individual (*imperium*); and thus to the culmination of the list with the freedom which guarantees not only the position of the state with regard to other states, but also the position of the individual within it. The crucial link in the ascending sequence is that between the individual and the state, and that is represented by *honor* and *imperium*, magistracy and power. For the purposes of the present investigation, it is important to note that the two are not identical, for, as we have seen, *imperium* is separable from the magistracies (as the very designation *pro consule* indicates), and hence occupy two steps on the ascending ladder of Scipio's sentence;[28] and that whereas the magistracy was essentially collegial, and, as deriving from the people, was part of the corporate nature of the *res publica*, the *imperium*, at least as the Romans of the late republic and early principate saw it, was handed on directly from the kings, and always contained within itself the possibility of tyrannical power.[29]

II

What then of the promised link between Roman notions of power and the nature of the Roman empire? In the context of this article, it should be noticed that, in contrast to many more recent empires, the Roman empire was from the beginning organized by the political executive of the city of Rome. In this respect Rome, like all other empires before the early modern period, did not develop mercantile structures which undertook the process of imperialist expansion, as did, for example, the British and the Dutch in the sixteenth and seventeenth centuries.[30] This observation has recently been confirmed by analyses, inspired by the work of Immanuel Wallerstein, of the structures of 'world-systems', both political and economic.[31] Even in terms of the primarily economic analysis adopted by such approaches, it is clear that in empires such as that of Rome, economic interests, though always significant, were secondary to political and military interests. Under such circumstances, the way in which the military and political executive of such a state regarded itself is likely to have important consequences for the empire which emerged from their activities. In many cases the empires of the pre-early modern period reflect directly the aspirations of the emperors who created them.

In the Roman case, there does not appear to have been an economic drive, of the sort which was to lead to the British and Dutch territorial empires. This is not to say that the Romans were not keen to profit from the growth of Roman power and influence throughout the Mediterranean, nor even (a far more debatable proposition) that such desires may not have contributed to the development of imperialism; but certainly the agencies which were used to produce the empire, as we see it in the late first century B.C. and early first century A.D., were not commercial. Under these circumstances it is highly significant that military power, *imperium*, was entrusted to individual members of the Roman élite in the way it was. The *imperium* of the Roman magistrate and pro-magistrate was not a distributed portion of the

[26] Mommsen, *StR* 3.1088, n. 3 records only three cases: M. Furius Crassipes, *praet.* 187 in Gaul (Livy XXXIX.3.1–3); M. Aemilius Lepidus, *procos.* 136 in Nearer Spain (App., *Ib.* 83.358); and L. Hortensius, *praet.* 170 during the war against Perseus (Livy XLIII.4.8).
[27] Isid., *etym.* 11.21.4 = *ORF* I².21 fr. 32.
[28] Isidore in fact cites this sentence as an instance of a *climax*.
[29] Cic., *de rep.* 11.32.56; Livy 11.1.7. See Brunt, op. cit. (n. 5), 15–17 and 331.

[30] See C. R. Boxer, *The Dutch Seaborne Empire* (1965); B. Gardner, *The East India Company* (1971); Jean Sutton, *Lords of the East: the East India Company and its Ships* (1981); for a comparison of the two, see C. D. Cowan, *New Cambridge Modern History* 5 (1961), 417–29, esp. 419–20.
[31] cf. G. Woolf, 'World-systems analysis and the Roman empire', *JRA* 3 (1990), 44–58.

total power of the Roman state, issued from a finite pool (so to speak), but could be multiplied through the issuing, with the co-operation of the god, of identical *imperia* to a potentially infinite number of persons. On occasion, indeed, those who had already held such power could be recommissioned *en bloc* to fulfil the needs of the state. In 211, when Hannibal was camped outside the city and there was fear of disruption within, the senate decreed that all those who had been dictators, consuls or censors in the past should be *cum imperio* until such time as the enemy departed from the walls.[32] Even in less abnormal times, it was possible to create additional individuals with the *imperium* required. Moreover, because what they were given was *imperium*, they were in principle capable of undertaking any of the tasks for which *imperium* was necessary. It is remarkable, for instance, that, when in the third century B.C. additional commanders were needed, firstly in the context of the First Punic War, and then in 227 to command in Sicily and Sardinia, the men to be sent were not designated as consuls, but as praetors, a magistracy apparently devised (or perhaps revived) in 366 for judicial not military purposes (that is for service *domi* not *militiae*). The ancient sources make no comment on this surprising change of direction in the magistracy. This is surely because what mattered about these people was not that they had been elected by the people to a particular magistracy, but that they had been given their allocation of that strange but essential substance, *imperium*.

III

If the *imperium* by which the members of the senatorial élite in Rome waged war on behalf of the state was a power, almost a substance, affirmed by the gods to particular individuals, the question remains as to how this affected the way in which warfare itself was seen, and also that ultimate outcome of warfare, the Roman control of the world, the *imperium Romanum*. In part, as suggested above,[33] this is a question of linguistic usage: why did the expression *imperium Romanum* come to be used to express 'empire' rather than the power of a magistrate or pro-magistrate? It is worth noticing at this point that this second meaning is different in two important respects from what has been discussed hitherto: it is about only one of the two spheres of application of the *imperium* of a magistrate, *militiae* but not *domi*; and it is not individual but corporate, relating to the power/empire of the *populus Romanus* rather than of any particular Roman. It was, of course, always true that in some sense the power of the magistrate was that of the *populus Romanus*, in that wherever the *imperium* holder was, there the power of the *populus Romanus* was to be found. In the case of the *imperium Romanum*, in the sense of 'empire', however, the identification with the *res publica* is much stronger and the central importance of the *imperium* holder seems to have disappeared almost entirely.

This second point can be seen clearly even in those rare passages in the literature of the late republic and early empire in which *imperium populi Romani*, used in a wider sense than simply 'power of the magistrate', includes the notion of *domi* as well as that of *militiae*. For instance, Livy can make the tribune C. Canuleius ask, when contending with patrician opponents about his bill on *conubium*, 'denique utrum tandem populi Romani an vestrum summum imperium est? regibus exactis utrum vobis dominatio an omnibus aequa libertas parta est?'[34] In this context, the form of *imperium*, in so far as it is relevant to the argument Livy is presenting, is both *domi* and *militiae*, since Canuleius suggests the consul will call up the army to threaten the *plebs* and their tribune. Yet even in this deliberately heightened and paradoxical passage (Mommsen described it as 'politische Speculation, nicht technische Rede'[35]), the question at issue is precisely who it was that held the *imperium*, whether it was to the magistrates or to the people that the army owed its allegiance.

When we come to examine the use of the word used in this larger sense and in a *militiae* context, it is immediately apparent that there is a whole gamut of meanings from the most abstract (that is 'power' with little or no territorial implication) to the most concrete ('empire'

[32] Livy XXVI.10.9.
[33] Above p. 1.
[34] Livy IV.5.1; 'And finally, is the highest *imperium* yours or the Roman people's? What was gained by the expulsion of the kings — domination by you or equal liberty for all?'.
[35] Mommsen, StR 1³.22 n. 2.

in the sense of a sharply delimited area). When the author of *ad Herennium* uses the phrase 'imperium orbis terrae',[36] his context suggests he is describing something abstract rather than concrete: he states that this *imperium* is something to which 'omnes gentes, reges, nationes, partim vi partim voluntate consensuerunt'. Similarly, when subject peoples even under the republic are described in official documents as being *sub imperio* (as in the *foedus Callatinum*[37]), it is probable that here the meaning is abstract rather than concrete. When Horace talks of 'adiectis Britannis imperio',[38] or Augustus asserts 'Aegyptum imperio populi Romani adieci',[39] the *imperium* in question could be taken as either 'power' or 'empire'. At the other end of the scale, St Augustine, in reviewing the disasters which afflicted the world before the coming of Christ, delimits the area with which he proposes to deal in the following words: 'quod ad Romam pertinet Romanumque imperium tantum loquar, id est, ad ipsam proprie civitatem, et quaecumque illi terrarum, vel societate coniunctae, vel condicione subiectae sunt, quae sint perpessae ante adventum Christi, cum iam ad eius quasi corpus rei publicae pertinerent.'[40] This is clearly an *imperium* which comprises a territorial area (and, incidentally, does not include the whole of the *orbis terrae*). It is apparent that we are not dealing with two alternative and incompatible meanings, but with the co-existence of a pair of meanings, of which in any particular case one is likely to be more dominant than the other.

A systematic investigation of the word *imperium* confirms that, of course, its use to refer to something more wide-ranging than the power of the Roman magistrate does not begin with the late republic or early empire.[41] A fragment of the tragedian Accius, from the mid-second century B.C., refers to the 'Argivum imperium', meaning the kingdom of Argos;[42] and Cicero frequently associates *imperium* with *urbs*, *civitas*, and *res publica* in contexts which suggest that it is almost a synonym for these words;[43] while Varro describes the socio-political arrangements of the bees as being like those in human *civitates*, having a *rex*, *imperium*, and *societates*.[44] For Cicero *imperium* in this sense can also have abstract qualities, such as *dignitas*, *gloria*, and *nomen*,[45] but can also be treated almost as an abstract, listed along with *dignitas* and the others as an attribute of the state.[46] It also has a temporal extension (though admittedly the time-span is usually external),[47] and a spatial extension (often, though not invariably, world-wide).[48]

Thus far it might appear that there is good reason to assume that there was already in the last century of the republic a use of the word *imperium* which coincides with the English 'empire'. A comparison with the usage of the early imperial period, however, suggests that, although the territorial connotations of *imperium* were undoubtedly present at an early stage, the full development had not taken place. First, and most obviously, the use of the phrase *imperium Romanum* does not occur until after Cicero's death. The first occurrence is in Sallust, who, in a retrospective passage in the *Catiline*, describes Carthage as having been 'aemula imperi Romani'.[49] This new usage coincides with a more territorial notion of the *imperium Romanum*. Although Livy refers to boundaries of *imperium*, he is describing situations in the past, in which even Cicero was prepared to allow that there had been limits;[50]

[36] *ad Her.* IV.13.

[37] *ILLRP* 516, line 12; though not, interestingly, in the *lex repetundarum, FIRA* I².7, line 1. The usage *sub imperio* continues in the texts of the jurists (cf. Paulus D.XXXVI.1.27; Gaius 1.53).

[38] Hor., *carm.* III.5.4.

[39] *RG* 27.1.

[40] Augustine, *de civ. Dei* 3.1.

[41] For this purpose, a data-base was constructed containing the passages listed in the *Thesaurus Linguae Latinae*, VII.1, 578–81 *s.v.* 'imperium' IIIA ('metonymice, ad quod potestas pertinet'); supplemented by a search of the *PHI* disk, using the Ibycus system.

[42] Accius, 231–2 (Ribbeck).

[43] Cic., *Rosc. Am.* 18.50; *div. in Caec.* 69, 2 *Verr.* II.34.85, *Rab. perd.* 12.33, *Cat.* 1.13.33, II.9.19, III.8.19–20, *Arch.* 10.28, *Sest.* 8.19, 9.20, 24.53, *Vatin.* 6.14, *Balb.* 8.22, *de orat.* 1.46.201; cf. Caes., *BG* 1.33.2.

[44] Varro, *RR* III.16.6.

[45] Cic., 2 *Verr.* IV.11.25, *Manil.* 4.11.

[46] Cic., *Phil.* III.5.13, *de orat.* 1.44.196.

[47] Cic., *Rab. perd.* 12.33.

[48] World-wide: Cic., *Cat.* III.11.26, *Sest.* 31.67; slightly less so: Cic., *Balb.* 17.39, and, of an earlier period, *prov. cons.*, 12.31. On the more modest side, cf. Caes., *BG* IV.16.4. On conceptions of empire in the Ciceronian period, see P. A. Brunt, 'Laus imperii', in P. D. A. Garnsey and C. R. Whittaker (eds), *Imperialism in the Ancient World* (1978), 159–91 = *Roman Imperial Themes* (1990), 288–323 (with further discussion at ibid. 433–80).

[49] Sall., *Cat.* 10.1. The only other possible case of such a use before this is a quotation by Valerius Maximus of Scipio Nasica Serapio, complaining in 133 B.C. about the consul of that year, P. Mucius Scaevola, that 'dum iuris ordinem sequitur, id agit ut cum omnibus legibus imperium Romanum corruat' (Val. Max. III.2.17 = *ORF* I².38 fr.4). Given Valerius Maximus' tendency not to quote accurately (there is, after all, no reason why he should) and the interval of ninety years before the next occurrence, it is probably safe to assume that this was not precisely what Serapio said.

[50] Livy XXI.2.7, XXVII.8.17, XXXVII.35.5, XXXVII.54.23; cf. Cic., *prov. cons.* 12.31.

and Vergil could still describe Caesar's *imperium* as bounded only by Oceanus.[51] It is more significant that the new *imperium* has not only extension but parts, so that Velleius can write of events 'in hac parte imperii',[52] and Tacitus of Agricola's desire to make Ireland 'valentissimam imperii partem'.[53] Cicero's only use of such an expression was to express his disgust when Verres yielded the control of his naval squadron to the Syracusan Cleomenes.[54] Here Cicero surely means 'a part of our power', not 'a section of our empire'. Another instance of the same phenomenon, and an explanation of it, has recently been given by Dietmar Kienast,[55] who observes that when Cicero stated that after Sulla a change had come about in the nature of Roman control of the world, so that what had previously been virtually a *patrocinium orbis terrae* was now in reality *imperium*, he was referring to mastery of the world rather than an empire;[56] and that the notion of the empire as a coherent unit, expressed by the phrase *corpus imperii*, first appears in Ovid, and thereafter becomes an imperial cliché.

The sense of 'empire' as a territorial entity which these changes suggest indicates that when Cicero, his contemporaries, and predecessors used *imperium* to describe a national or political structure, they had in mind something less well-defined. A similar usage might be found in the English word 'power', which since the eighteenth century has also had the meaning, 'a state or nation from the point of view of its having international authority or influence'.[57] It is not, of course, possible to be precise about the exact significance of so wide-ranging and elusive a word, but the pattern of usage to which I have drawn attention supports the view of Lewis and Short that the transferred, concrete meaning 'dominion', 'realm', 'empire' becomes especially frequent during and after the Augustan period.[58] If this is correct, the reasons for the shift are not hard to surmise. The already existing senses of *imperium* meaning a 'power' as well as the power of the magistrate, combined with the concentration of *imperium* in the hands of a single individual, will have made the use of *imperium* to describe the corporate power of the Roman state increasingly natural. It was, after all, in this period that those areas of the world which were defined as under the *imperium* of the emperor were seen to coincide in effect with the extent of the influence of Rome as a world 'power'. The shift thereafter to such expressions as those of Tacitus, who describes the Egyptian towns of Elephantine and Syene as 'claustra olim Romani imperii', or the empire as a whole as 'immensum imperii corpus' then becomes almost inevitable.[59]

IV

This brief examination of the nature and the semantics of the Roman *imperium* suggests a number of conclusions. First, there does appear to be a shift in the usages of the word *imperium* in its wider sense of the empire of the Roman people, from a concept which, in the period after Sulla, already included some notion of concrete shape and size, to one referring to a more precisely determined physical entity. This extension of meaning coincides with the first appearances of the term *imperium Romanum*, and with the emergence of those supremely powerful holders of *imperium*, Julius Caesar and then Augustus.

Second, the area of activity covered by the description *militiae*, which if it does not exactly mean 'war' certainly relates to matters military rather than civilian, was far larger than the practice of warfare as such. In the earlier stages of the growth of Roman power in the Mediterranean region, it will have applied to all the activity of a holder of *imperium* outside the boundaries of the city itself, and thus all that work which we normally call 'provincial

[51] Verg., *Aen.* 1.286–7.
[52] Vell. Pat. 11.97.1.
[53] Tac., *Agr.* 24.
[54] Cic., 2 *Verr.* v.32.85: 'iis tu nostri imperii partem dedidisti'.
[55] D. Kienast, 'Corpus imperii', in G. Wirth *et al.* (eds), *Romanitas-Christianitas (Festschr. J. Straub)* (1982), 1–17.
[56] Cic., *de off.* 11.8.27; Kienast, op. cit. (n. 55), 3.
[57] *The Shorter Oxford English Dictionary* (revised ed., 1973), s.v. power II(b).

[58] Lewis and Short s.v. *imperium* IIB(1)b; cf. also Rosenberg, *RE* IX.2 (1916), 1210–11. The word *provincia* shows a similar development through the first centuries B.C. and A.D., during which period the dominant meaning shifts from 'task assigned to an *imperium*-holder' to 'area under Roman administration'. See A. W. Lintott, 'What was the *imperium Romanum*', *Greece & Rome* 28 (1981), 53–67; J. S. Richardson, *Hispaniae* (1986), 1–10; contra J.-M. Bertrand, 'A propos du mot *provincia*', *Journal des Savants* (1989), 191–215.
[59] Tac., *Ann.* 11.61; *Hist.* 1.16.

administration'. War, that is to say, was the context not only of the acquisition but also of the establishment of what became the Roman territorial empire.

Third, the *imperium* itself, the power through which the Roman state waged war, and from which the empire came, was distributed in a way which shows that, both in the theory and practice of the middle and late republic, it was separable from the magistracies and the responsibility of particular individuals, normally chosen by the people, hence making possible the multiplication of the number of *imperium* holders. Indeed I would suggest that it was the nature of that power — the *libertas* which depended on *imperium* in the formulation of Scipio Aemilianus — which gave room for the motivation of the long series of military commanders, culminating in the *principes* of the late republic, and which led to the emergence of the territorial empire.

It might at first sight seem odd that it was on *imperium* that this individual liberty of action depended. After all, Cicero believed, as he expounds at length in the second book of the *de republica*, that the *imperium* originated with the kings, and attributed to Numa the first use of the *lex curiata de imperio*.[60] He was probably wrong,[61] but that is not the point. The oddity lies in the link between *libertas* and *imperium*, when the latter was believed to originate in a period when, inasmuch as they were ruled by a king, the Roman people did not possess the former.[62] The problem is, of course, unreal, for it is not primarily the *libertas* of the people of which Scipio Aemilianus was speaking.[63] Under a monarchy the one person who has *libertas* is the king, who is the only person (so Cicero and his contemporaries believed) to possess *imperium*. It is then no wonder that the holder of *imperium* under the republic was in a position to conduct himself with an almost regal independence.

Augustus in turn was well-placed to take every advantage of the inheritance provided for him by the republican understanding of *imperium* as a power fit for a king. He is said to have considered taking the name Romulus, which might have been appropriate for someone who, as a new founder of Rome, could be said, like his predecessor, to have been marked out for his task by Jupiter, but in the end to have preferred a name which was less reminiscent of kingship.[64] There were, however, other ways to express predominance. Among them was inevitably the question of the *imperium* of the *princeps*. Although much remains debatable about this important topic, two matters which concern this paper may be noted. First, Augustus' *imperium*, as formulated after his illness in 23 B.C., was superior to that of the other magistrates and pro-magistrates, and was primarily seen as *militiae* rather than *domi*. This emerges from Dio Cassius' account of the new proposals of 23, in which he not only specifically states the superiority of Augustus' power, but also mentions that a special ruling was given that this power, unlike all other cases of *imperium militiae*, would not lapse when the holder crossed the *pomerium* and entered the city.[65] Second, though this is less clear, he seems to have concentrated into his own hands the *auspicia militiae*. This seems the most obvious explanation for the means he used to ensure that M. Licinius Crassus was prevented from claiming the right to deposit in the temple of Jupiter Feretrius the *spolia opima* as a result of killing in battle Deldo, the chieftain of the Bastarnae, while proconsul in Macedonia in 29.[66] The same explanation probably applies to the cessation of triumphs celebrated by those who were not members of the imperial family after 19 B.C. Although Crassus was allowed, by whatever means, to celebrate a triumph in July 27,[67] which would have required recognition in some sense of the validity of his *auspicia*, it may be that for Crassus, as for members of the emperor's family later, the holder of the *auspicia* was able to allow a delegation of his authority.[68]

[60] Cic., *de rep.* II.13.25.

[61] So Magdelain, op. cit. (n. 11), 30–2, *contra* Mommsen, *StR* 1³.609 n. 3.

[62] cf. Cic., *de rep.* 1.32.48; Ch. Wirszubski, *Libertas as a Political Idea at Rome during the Late Republic and Early Principate* (1950), 7–30. On the concept of *libertas*, see now P. A. Brunt, 'Libertas in the Republic', in *The Fall of the Roman Republic* (1988), ch. 6.

[63] See the comment of Brunt on Scipio's aphorism: 'In other words a man was most free when he had the fullest right to enforce his own will' (op. cit. (n. 62), 312).

[64] Suet., *Aug.* 7.2; Dio Cassius LIII.16.7. On Julius Caesar's use of the Romulus motif, see St. Weinstock, *Divus Julius* (1971), 175–99.

[65] Dio Cassius LIII.32.5.

[66] Dio Cassius LI.24.4 says this was because Crassus

was not αὐτοκράτωρ, which has usually been taken to mean that he did not have full *imperium* (e.g. R. Syme, 'Livy and Augustus', *HSCP* 64 (1959), 27–87, at 43–6 = *Roman Papers* 1 (1979), 400–54, at 417–21). However Livy's note about the *spolia opima* of A. Cornelius Cossus, which was, on Livy's account, a matter of interest to the emperor, makes the question of whose *auspicium* was involved central to the argument (*contra* R. Combès, *Imperator* (1966), 162–5).

[67] *Inscr. It.* 13. 87 and 571.

[68] cf. P. Catalano, *Contributi allo studio del diritto augurale* 1 (1960), 442–3; compare also the case of Q. Valerius Falto in 241 (Val. Max. II.8.2; J. S. Richardson, 'The triumph, the praetor and the senate in the early second century B.C.', *JRS* 65 (1975), 50–63, at 51–2).

The particular effect of Augustus' settlement of 23 upon the empire was to put into formal terms what had already been his position before that date, and indeed that of Julius Caesar before him. Although in strict legal terms there were of course other holders of *imperium* besides the *princeps*, in practice he had concentrated the power into his own hands. The *imperium* was effectively unified in a way that it had not been, as Cicero's contemporaries would have seen it, since the age of the kings. It is not surprising, then, that at this same time the notion of the empire, the *imperium Romanum*, as a unified *corpus* also emerged.[69]

The message was present clearly enough in the decoration of the Forum of Augustus. There stood, on the left of the temple of Mars Ultor, which formed the focal point of the end of the forum, the statues of Aeneas, his son Iulus and the members of the Julian *gens*, arranged in the niches of the portico which made up the left-hand side of the forum; and, on the other side, the statue of Romulus and the most important men of the republic, those who, in Suetonius' words, had made 'imperium populi Romani ex minimo maximum', wearing triumphal dress.[70] The *gens Iulia* and the *triumphatores* of the republic formed a continuum, which had its origins in the founder of the Julii and in the king, son of the god Mars, who had first held *imperium* and (according to the Augustan *Fasti Triumphales*) first celebrated a triumph on the first day of the first year of the foundation of the city.[71] In the midst of the forum stood a triumphal chariot, honouring Augustus himself, voted, as he tells us in the final section of the *Res Gestae*, by the senate, and below which was placed the tablet recording the award to him of the title Pater Patriae.[72] This was to be the setting in which the senate would consider the award of triumphs, from here those who went with *imperium* to the provinces would set forth, and it was here that, if they were successful, they would come to be rewarded with *ornamenta triumphalia*.[73] In such a context the commanders of the forces of the Roman people could not fail to realize that it was *imperium militiae*, passed down from the kings through the great individuals of the republic, that had made the *imperium Romanum*; nor indeed amid such surroundings did it need to be stated explicitly that it was from the exercise of *imperium* throughout the known world that monarchy had made its return to Rome.

---

[69] Compare the conclusions of C. Nicolet, *L'Inventaire du monde* (1988) that the Augustan period saw the appearance of a new spatial understanding of the Roman world, though N. Purcell (*JRS* 80 (1990), 178–82) believes that this development had begun during the last century B.C. Purcell's suggestion that Roman conceptual geography was linear rather than spatial coincides with the view presented here of *imperium* being essentially seen as the power held by particular magistrates and pro-magistrates, since in geographical terms this would appear as a network of lines of movement of *imperium*-holders, spreading out from Rome. If, as I suspect, Nicolet is right to see a more spatial view developing in the Augustan

period,.this would in turn coincide with the shift in the dominant meaning of the word *imperium* towards a delimited area.

[70] Suet., *Aug.* 31.5; Ovid, *Fasti* v.563–6; Vell. II.89.4; Pliny, *NH* XXII.6.13; Gellius, *NA* IX.11.10; F. Coarelli, *Guida archeologica di Roma* (1974), 107–11; P. Zanker, *Augustus und die Macht der Bilder* (1987), 213–17 (= *The Power of Images in the Age of Augustus* (1988), 210–15).

[71] *Inscr. It.* 13.1.64–5 and 534: 'Romulus Martis f. rex ann. [I] / de Caeninensibus k. Mar[t.]'.

[72] *RG* 35.1.

[73] Suet., *Aug.* 29.2; Dio Cassius LV.10.3–5.

2
Empire and Union:
Two Concepts of the Early
Modern European Political Order
John Robertson

I

FROM a purely British vantage point, the relation between union and empire is likely to seem quite straightforward. The formation of the United Kingdom of Great Britain in 1707 was so quickly followed by the expansion of British commerce and the acquisition of territory overseas, in North America and India, that a close, even a causal, connection between the Union and the British Empire could be taken for granted. Few might go as far as to claim that the achievement of Anglo-Scottish Union was a sufficient explanation for the acquisition of empire: both English and Scottish historians would wish to trace the roots of overseas imperial enterprise in the two countries back into the seventeenth and even the sixteenth centuries. But the disproportionate numbers in which Scots merchants, soldiers and administrators contributed to – and benefited from – imperial activity in the eighteenth century were to ensure that the Empire acquired its 'British' identity earlier and with fewer reservations than many of the domestic institutions of the newly united state.

The assumption of a straightforward correlation between union and empire has been strengthened by the conviction that the union was a one-off occurence, a singular British solution to the anomaly of two neighbour kingdoms sharing the same monarch. The anomaly had threatened the sovereign statehood which independent kingdoms were

Versions of this chapter were given as papers to the Early Modern Europe Seminar at Oxford and the Seminars in European and British History 1500–1800 at the Institute of Historical Research, London, and as lectures in the Universities of Bonn and Bayreuth: I am grateful to participants on these occasions for their helpful comments. I am more particularly indebted to Franz Bosbach, J.H. Burns, J.H. Elliott, George Garnett and H.G. Koenigsberger for specific observations. Responsibility for the judgements made, however, is entirely mine.

JOHN ROBERTSON

supposed to enjoy; but by forming a new, unitary state, the Union of 1707 enabled the British to gain the advantage over their continental rivals, the French above all, whose aspirations to such statehood were still compromised by the archaic political structures of *ancien régime* monarchy. Viewed in this light, the Union was not only the foundation of the Empire; it was itself an exceptional achievement, confirming and enlarging the gulf between British and continental patterns of political development.[1]

Indispensable as it may have become to a British historical consciousness, this is an understanding of the relation between union and empire whose historical supports are fast dissolving. The predicament in which England and Scotland found themselves in the seventeenth century, sharing the same monarch, was by no means as anomalous as the conventional account would suppose. On the contrary, historians now suggest, 'composite' monarchy was the European norm: almost every ruling dynasty of consequence – Habsburg, Bourbon and Vasa as well as Stuart – had acquired multiple titles, and exercised authority over a number of territories, which might not even be contiguous.[2] The potential advantages of closer unity between their territories were, moreover, well known to these rulers: over the sixteenth and seventeenth centuries there were many examples of the imposition or negotiation of more formal unions.[3] The belief that the British problem was exceptional, and that its solution, a negotiated union, was unique, can no longer be sustained. The Union of 1707 belongs within a European setting, and should be thought of as the British variant of a wider pattern.[4]

While the structural characteristics of composite monarchy have been re- assessed by modern historians, however, much less attention has been devoted to the terms in which contemporaries themselves understood and discussed the European political order, and forms of union in particular. Without a knowledge of these, it is impossible to gauge the extent to which union was discussed in the same terms in England and Scotland as elsewhere in Europe. As J.H. Elliott has commented,

[1] An assumption still to be found in the otherwise valuable work of Brian P. Levack, *The Formation of the British State. England, Scotland, and the Union 1603–1707* (Oxford, 1987), p. vi.
[2] The most prominent and persuasive exponents of this new understanding of early modern Europe have been H.G. Koenigsberger and J.H. Elliott. See H.G. Koenigsberger, '*Dominium regale* or *Dominium politicum et regale*', in his *Politicians and Virtuosi. Essays in Early Modern History* (London, 1986): also his 'Composite states, representative institutions and the American Revolution', *Historical Research*, 62, 148 (1989); and J.H. Elliott, 'A Europe of composite monarchies', *Past and Present*, 137 (1992).
[3] Elliott, 'A Europe of composite monarchies', pp. 62–8. Also, Mark Greengrass (ed.), *Conquest and Coalescence: The Shaping of the State in Early Modern Europe* (London, 1991).
[4] I have previously attempted to develop such an approach in: John Robertson, 'Union, state and empire: the Britain of 1707 in its European setting', in Lawrence Stone (ed.), *An Imperial State at War: Britain from 1689 to 1815* (London, 1994).

4

EMPIRE AND UNION

historians of political thought have hitherto offered little help, their pre-occupation with the concept of sovereignty leading them to neglect investigation of concepts more appropriate to the phenomenon of composite monarchy.[5] It is to such an investigation that this introductory chapter is intended to contribute.

At the centre of my inquiry will be the ways in which contemporaries understood the two concepts of 'empire' and 'union'. Not only was there more than one understanding of each; the concepts themselves were closely associated with others in current usage. The development of the concept of empire in particular was complicated by the existence of the – Holy Roman – Empire, an association which encouraged the elaboration of a synonym, 'universal monarchy', to convey the more general idea of rule over extensive territory.[6] Meanwhile 'empire' itself continued to be used in another, apparently contrary sense, to indicate the autonomy of individual kingdoms. I shall argue none the less that the two ideas shared a common emphasis on the territorial extent of a monarch's authority, and further that they were associated with a specific idea of union as 'incorporation' under one ruling head. This association of ideas crystallised during the first half of the sixteenth century, under the monarchies of Charles V and Henry VIII, and provided the conceptual framework for the Anglo-Scottish Union debate initiated by James VI and I in the opening decade of the seventeenth century.

From the 1620s, however, this pattern of ideas was to be shaken by new developments in political thinking, developments which altered and enlarged contemporaries' understanding of the concepts of empire and union. There emerged a new doctrine of pre-emptive defence and legitimate conquest, yielding an approach to union considerably more aggressive than that hitherto associated with the idea of universal monarchy. On the other hand, there also emerged a second, rival concept of union, understood as a confederation of more or less equal states. By contrast with the idea of incorporating union, confederal union was represented as antagonistic to extensive territorial empire.[7] As the case of

---

[5] Elliot, 'A Europe of composite monarchies', pp. 48–50, 52–4.
[6] Study of the idea of universal monarchy has until now been almost exclusively the preserve of German scholars (who should be exempted from Elliott's strictures): most recently: Franz Bosbach, *Monarchia Universalis. Ein politischer Leitbegriff der frühen Neuzeit* (Göttingen, 1988).
[7] This too has long been a subject of interest to German scholars. Perhaps the best-known German student of federalism is Otto Gierke (1841–1921): in English are *Natural Law and the Theory of Society 1500–1800*, trans. Ernest Barker, 2 vols. (Cambridge, 1934), and *Community in Historical Perspective*, trans. Mary Fischer, ed. Antony Black (Cambridge, 1990). But see now also: Reinhart Koselleck, 'Bund, Bündnis, Föderalismus, Bundesstaat', in Otto Brunner, Werner Conze and Reinhart Koselleck (eds.), *Geschichtliche Grundbegriffe. Historisches Lexicon zur politisch-sozialen Sprache in Deutschland*, vol. I: A–D (Stuttgart, 1972).

JOHN ROBERTSON

the United Provinces demonstrated, however, confederal union was not thereby incompatible with another, novel, concept of the empire, that of the empire of the seas, pursuit of which might be distinguished from the territorial ambition of universal monarchy. Thus by the time that the Scots and the English returned to the issue of the union, in the last decade of the seventeenth century and the first of the eighteenth, the interrelation of ideas of empire and union had been both reinforced and opened to new and divergent interpretations. The debate which preceded the Union of 1707 will be understood only if it is recognised as an outcome of an already long and complex discussion of the place of empire and union in the European political order.

II

The Monarchy of Charles V recast the mould of European politics. Modern historians may wish to emphasise the limits upon the effective exercise of his authority, but Charles himself, his advisers, alarmed contemporaries and later, more impartial observers (up to Montesquieu and Hume in the mid eighteenth century) had no doubt that the sheer extent of his inheritance made possible monarchy on a scale not seen since the Roman Empire. What Charles could not do was entitle the Monarchy as a whole an 'Empire'. Election as Holy Roman Emperor in 1519 rounded off his inheritance, but his other kingdoms, Castile at their head, insisted that the Imperial title would not have precedence in their territories. Limits on his use of the title, however, did not prevent Charles and his supporters from exploiting the universal associations of the Roman idea of empire.[8]

The image of Charles as a Roman emperor was variously portrayed. The biographical *Istoria Imperial y Cesarea* (1547) by the Spanish historian Pedro Mexia (subsequently translated as *The Imperiall History: or Lives of the Emperors, from Julius Caesar, the First Founder of the Roman Monarchy* (1623)) cast Charles V as the direct successor of the Roman Emperors.[9] Titian's great equestrian portrait of Charles after Muhlberg in the same year made the identical point, with rather more style. Well before then, as John Headley has argued, the Imperial Chancellor Gattinara had been making sophisticated political use of the Roman imperial model. Forced to abandon his early belief that Roman

[8] Frances Yates, *Astraea. The Imperial Theme in the Sixteenth Century* (London, 1975, pbk repr. of 1985), part I: 'Charles V and the idea of empire'.
[9] Pedro Mexia, *Istoria Imperial y Cesarea* (1547), trans. as *The Imperiall History: Or Lives of the Emperors, from Julius Caesar, the First Founder of the Roman Monarchy*, translation by W.T., corrected by Edward Grimeston (London, 1623).

6

EMPIRE AND UNION

Law would provide a single, universal basis for Charles' authority, Gattinara had adapted the Roman idea of 'client kingdoms' to accommodate individual states within an imperial framework.[10] Most evocative of all, however, was Charles's choice of emblem, the ship sailing beyond the Columns of Hercules, with the motto *'plus ultra'*: testimony to an ambition even more universal than the Roman.

Charles V was also the beneficiary of the recent revival of another imperial tradition, that forged in the great conflict between the Holy Roman Emperor and the Papacy. This might be a conflict in which few Emperors had gained the advantage; simply by joining the conflict, however, they had continued to associate their title with the pretension to universal authority, eliciting such powerful intellectual supports as Dante's *Monarchia*. In the fifteenth century, moreover, Empire and Papacy had temporarily made common cause against the 'national' monarchies and the Conciliar Movement. From this convergence had come a 'dualist' case for the universal authority of Emperor and Pope, as in the *Monarchia* (c.1430–43) of Antonio Roselli, who borrowed many of Dante's arguments, and in the still more enthusiastic imperialism of Roselli's pupil, Aeneas Sylvius Piccolomini, later Pope Pius II.[11] By the early sixteenth century Papal publicists such as Cajetan once again had the confidence to proclaim their master's supreme authority.[12] But the dualist argument continued to enjoy support, being restated in Spain in 1525, in the *Catholicum Opus Imperiale Regiminis Mundi* of Michael of Ulcurrunus.[13] More aggressively, Gattinara encouraged renewed interest in Dante's *Monarchia*, and there were publicists at Charles V's court who would justify even the Sack of Rome in 1527.[14] Prophecy offered a further

[10] John M. Headley, 'The Habsburg world empire and the revival of Ghibellinism', *Mediaeval and Renaissance Studies* (Chapel Hill, 1978), pp. 93–127.
  For accounts of the Romans' own understanding of their *'imperium'*: Richard Koebner, *Empire* (Cambridge, 1961), pp. 1–17; and Andrew Lintott, 'What was the *'Imperium Romanorum'*?', *Greece and Rome*, 28, 1, (1981), 53–67. Koebner's pioneering account of the history of the concept of 'empire' was, unfortunately, thinnest in relation to the period covered by this chapter.
[11] J.H. Burns, *Lordship, Kingship and Empire. The Idea of Monarchy 1400–1525* (Oxford, 1992), ch. 5, 'Monarchy: Papacy and empire'. Roselli's *Monarchia* was first printed in 1487, and republished in Germany in 1611, in a collection of texts which served as sources for the seventeenth-century debate over the Imperial constitution. Piccolomini's *De ortu et authoritate Romani Imperii* is dated to 1446.
[12] Burns, *Lordship, Kingship, and Empire*, pp. 138–45; Paolo Prodi, *The Papal Prince. One Body and Two Souls: The Papal Monarchy in Early Modern Europe*, trans. Susan Haskins (Cambridge, 1987), p. 24.
[13] Diana Perry, ' "*Catholicum Opus Imperiale Regiminis Mundi*". An early sixteenth-century restatement of Empire', *History of Political Thought*, 2, 2, (1981).
[14] Headley, 'Habsburg world empire', pp. 104–7; J.A. Fernandez-Santamaria, *The State, War and Peace. Spanish Political Thought in the Renaissance 1516–1559* (Cambridge, 1977), pp. 38–49; Marcel Bataillon, *Erasme et L'Espagne* (Paris, 1937), ch. 5.

JOHN ROBERTSON

justification for universal pretensions. Gattinara set the idea of a crusade against the Turk in this perspective in the 1530s;[15] but it was most fully developed in the work of the Lutheran Johann Sleidan, whose *Quattuor summis imperiis* (1556) cast the Empire as the harbinger of the Fifth Monarchy foretold in *Daniel*.[16] The willingness of even the Lutherans to accept the Empire's universal mission offers powerful testimony to its continued appeal. By exploiting anew the universal associations of the imperial idea, in both its Roman and its Christian forms, Charles V and his publicists re-established its identification with the exercise of authority over extended territory: if the concept of empire, *imperium*, was itself no longer used exclusively in this sense, that of 'universal monarchy' became its recognised synonym.[17]

Significant as this reaffirmation of the idea of empire would be, it may be thought to have been offset by the simultaneous consolidation of another usage of the concept, that embodied in the phrase '*rex in regno suo est imperator in regno suo*'. Of twelfth-century origin, and often coupled with another, '*rex qui superiorem non recognoscit*', the phrase had been deployed since the thirteenth century by the Kings of France and Naples in particular at the expense of the Emperor's authority. By the late fifteenth century many of Europe's monarchies, including the Scottish, had claimed for themselves the status of an imperial crown. But the most resonant statement of the claim was still to come, in 1533. In the words of the preamble to the Act in Restraint of Appeals:

> Where by dyvers sundrie old autentike histories and cronicles it is manifestly declared and expressed that this Realme of Englond is an Impire, and so hath ben accepted in the worlde, governed by oon supreme heede and King having the dignitie and roiall estate of the Imperiall Crowne of the same, unto whom a Body politike, compacte of all sortes and degrees of people . . . ben bounden and owen to bere next to God a naturall and humble obedience.[18]

That these few words were sufficient to give the idea of empire a lasting place in English political thinking is not in doubt; less clear, perhaps, is what that idea signified. The common view is that this was a straightforward declaration of national sovereignty, and further, by virtue of its inclusion in a statute, of parliamentary participation in that sovereignty. Recent

---

[15] Headley, 'Habsburg world empire', pp. 114–15.

[16] J. Sleidan, *Quattuor summis imperiis* (1556).

[17] On the promotion of Charles V as a universal monarch: Bosbach, *Monarchia Universalis*, ch. 3: 'Die Universalmonarchie Karls V'.

[18] *An Acte that the Appeles in suche cases as have ben used to be pursued to the See of Rome shall not be from hensforth had ne used but wythin this Realme* (1533: 24 Henry VIII, c. 12), in *The Statutes of the Realm*, vol. III (1817), p. 427.

EMPIRE AND UNION

studies of the Act's intellectual genesis suggest, however, that the matter was considerably more complicated.

A number of strands of contemporary 'imperial' thinking can be identified in the preamble. One, elucidated by Walter Ullmann, was the Roman Law argument that since the *ecclesia* had been constituted by authority of the Emperor, his *imperium* rightly extended to all ecclesiastical matters.[19] When this claim seemed insufficient, Henry VIII's advisers turned to a second, native source of imperial inspiration: the historic pretension of the English Monarchy to exercise rule by lordship or conquest over others, and in particular over Scotland and Ireland. Coupled with the supposition of England's historic independence from papal jurisdication, Graham Nicholson has suggested, it was these territorial claims which informed the anglicising of the formula '*Rex est imperator in regno suo*'.[20] Thus while the claim of empire was designed to exclude the jurisdiction of the Pope, and, by extension, of the Emperor, it did not entail a repudiation of the 'universal' associations of imperial authority.[21] To the contrary, the preamble implied a reassertion of the English Crown's ambition to extend its territorial authority at the expense of its neighbours.

A further dimension to the language of the Act of Appeals underlines the territorial aspect of empire. The realm of England was also characterised as a 'body politic'. This concept too had strong mediaeval roots. It was a term which evoked both the religious imagery of the *corpus mysticum* (an imagery exploited by jurists no less than by theologians) and the more strictly juridical attributes of the corporation.[22] In the fifteenth century, J.H. Burns has argued, it had become central to discussions of monarchy. It underlay Sir John Fortescue's distinction between *dominium regale* and *dominium politicum et regale*, permitting him to accommodate parliament as an organ of the body politic of which the king was the head. But the concept had other implications besides, as both Fortescue and contemporary French theorists appreciated. The image of the body naturally placed a

[19] Walter Ullmann, 'This Realm of England is an Empire', *Journal of Ecclesiastical History*, 30, 2 (1979), 175–203.
[20] Graham Nicholson, 'The Act of Appeals and the English Reformation', in C. Cross, D. Loades and J.J. Scarisbrick (eds.), *Law and Government under the Tudors* (Cambridge, 1988); also John Guy, 'Thomas Cromwell and the intellectual origins of the Henrician Revolution', in A. Fox and J. Guy, *Reassessing the Henrician Age* (Oxford, 1986).
[21] See J.P. Canning, 'Law, sovereignty and corporation theory, 1300–1450', in J.H. Burns (ed.), *The Cambridge History of Medieval Political Thought* c.350–c.1450 (Cambridge, 1988), pp. 464–73, on the possibility of distinguishing the claim to be an emperor in one's kingdom from the claim not to acknowledge a superior.
[22] Ernst Kantorowicz, *The King's Two Bodies. A Study in Medieval Political Theology* (Princeton, 1957); J.P. Canning, 'Law, sovereignty and corporation theory', in *Cambridge History of Medieval Political Thought*, pp. 473–6.

JOHN ROBERTSON

premium on the unity of the realm: a monarchy ought to be 'incorporating'.[23] If therefore the realm was an empire as well as a body politic, as the Act of Appeals proclaimed in the case of England, it would seem to follow that such a realm should incorporate the territories over which it exercised imperial authority. Through the concept of the body politic, in short, empire was drawn into association with union by incorporation.

In the event neither the Scots nor the Irish had to wait long to feel the consequences of such thinking. To the Irish, Henry and his advisers carefully spelt out their understanding of the logic of his imperial status. By the Act of the Irish Parliament which in 1541 elevated Henry from Lord to King, the crown of Ireland was itself declared to be imperial, but one none the less 'united and knit to the imperiall crown of England'.[24] A year later the Scots were treated more bluntly, their (rather older) claim to possess an imperial crown being swept aside by a renewed declaration of the English King's claim to superiority – and hence, implicitly, to a superior 'empire'. Explicit, aggressive use of imperial rhetoric was then made by Somerset, in pursuit of a dynastic union between Edward VI and Mary Stuart. The idea had some enthusiastic Scottish supporters, but to many more it seemed a cover for the traditional English pretension to superiority.[25] Elizabeth eschewed imperial designs upon Scotland (having to be cajoled into limited intervention by Cecil) – but endorsed them in Ireland, where settlement schemes were likened to Roman colonisations.[26] More generally, as Frances Yates demonstrated in her classic study, the Queen and her image-makers proved themselves to be imaginative exponents of the imperial theme. Elizabeth might herself prefer to be cast as Astraea, the virgin goddess whose return to the world heralded the fifth and final age of empire, an age of union and peace. But the original theme of independence from the Papacy was renewed by Protestant apologists, while others made free use of the columnar device of Charles V to assert a pretension to independent maritime empire.[27]

[23] J.H. Burns, 'Fortescue and the political theory of *Dominium*', *Historical Journal*, 28 (1985); *Lordship, Kingship and Empire*, ch. 3: 'Lordship and Kingship: France and England' – a discussion to which this paper is greatly indebted.

[24] M. Perceval-Maxwell, 'Ireland and the monarchy in the early Stuart multiple Kingdom', *Historical Journal*, 34, 2 (1991), p. 280.

[25] For the claim against the Scots: *A Declaration, conteynyng the iust causes and consyderations, of this present warre with the Scottis, wherein also appereth the trewe and right title, that the Kinges most royall majesty hath to the soverayntie of Scotlande* (1542), repr. in J.A.H. Murray (ed.), *The Complaynt of Scotland* (London, for the Early English Text Society, 1882), pp. 191–206, and set in context by Roger A. Mason, 'The Scottish Reformation and the origins of Anglo-British imperialism', in Roger A. Mason (ed.), *Scots and Britons: Scottish Political Thought and the Union of 1603* (Cambridge, 1994), pp. 168–70.

[26] Mason, 'The Scottish Reformation and the origins of Anglo-British imperialism' p. 181; Nicholas Canny, *Kingdom and Colony. Ireland in the Atlantic World 1560–1800* (Baltimore and London, 1988), chs. 1–2.

[27] Yates, *Astraea*, part II: 'The Tudor Imperial Reform'.

EMPIRE AND UNION

A similar exploitation of the imperial idea, Yates also observed, was occurring in late sixteenth-century France. Represented between columns as the Gallic Hercules in the age of Astraea, Henri IV posed as the reconciler of Europe; and his minister Sully prepared his 'Grand Dessein' by which the French Monarchy would guarantee this peaceful new order. Behind these professions of pacific intent, however, might be thought to lie more familiar universal pretensions. With the title *Rex Christianissimus,* and a descent from Charlemagne, King of the Franks before he had had himself crowned Emperor, the King of France had an older and better claim to universal monarchy than any so far mustered by a King or Queen of England. His assassination may have left Henri IV's own intentions unclear; but his Bourbon heirs left no doubt which of the two French imperial traditions was to be taken more seriously.[28]

It is none the less a mistake to suppose – as Yates appears to have done – that the mantle of empire had simply been passed from Charles V to the national monarchies of England and France. There was no doubt among contemporary observers, in these countries and throughout Europe, that the leading imperial power of the age, the current aspirant to universal monarchy, was one of the two monarchies between which Charles V had divided the Habsburg inheritance: specifically, the Spanish Monarchy of Philip II. Even if the Spanish Habsburgs scrupulously avoided any pretension to the title of Emperor, out of respect for their Austrian cousins, their publicists readily exploited the universal associations of the imperial idea.

One of these was Giovanni Botero, the Piedmontese ex-Jesuit whose *Della Ragion di Stato* (1589) gave its name to a genre of political writing that in the early seventeenth century became particularly asssociated with Catholic monarchies.[29] Deliberately reversing Machiavelli's order of preference, Botero put the preservation of states, '*il conservare*', before conquest, '*l'aggrandire*' – a choice clearly more suited to the circumstances of the Spanish Monarchy in the later sixteenth century.[30] Botero also suggested that 'disunited' states were not necessarily at a disadvantage compared to those whose territories were joined together. Unity might

[28] Yates, *Astraea,* part III: 'The French Monarchy'; Maximilian de Bethune, Duc de Sully, *Memoires ou Oeconomies Royales d'Estat Domestiques, Politiques et Militaires de Henry le Grand* (Paris, 1644), IV, pp. 57–89, esp. pp. 77–89; 'Discours sur les Magnifiques Desseins du Roy Henry le Grand'. Sully characterised his new European order as 'cette Republique Monarchie Tres-Chrestienne' (p. 79).

[29] Robert Bireley, *The Counter-Reformation Prince. Anti-Machiavellianism or Catholic Statecraft in early modern Europe* (Chapel Hill and London, 1990).

[30] Giovanni Botero, *Della Ragion di Stato* (1589), Bk I, ch. 5, edn of Luigi Firpo (Turin, 1948), pp. 58–60, trans. by P.J. and D.P. Waley as *The Reason of State* (London, 1956), pp. 5–7. On the appropriateness of the theme: J.H. Elliott, 'Foreign policy and domestic crisis: Spain 1598–1659', in his *Spain and its World 1500–1700* (New Haven and London, 1989), p. 114.

JOHN ROBERTSON

give strength to an empire (*imperio*), but it also rendered it more vulnerable to corruption. By contrast if the parts of an '*imperio disunito*' could stand separately, and assist each other, the empire might be as strong as if it were united. As an example, Botero pointed to '*Il Dominio di Spagna*', whose separate states formed an empire joined by the sea.[31]

A separate *Relationi del Mare* (1598) clarified the importance which Botero attached to the sea. Distinguishing between 'oceans' and 'Mediterraneans' (the latter being defined as great lakes joined to oceans by a Straits of Gibraltar), Botero pointed to the situation of the Mediterranean between Africa, Asia and Europe, and to its concentration of cities and traffic, as the explanation for Europe's leadership of the rest of the world in commerce.[32] This suggests a view of the Spanish Monarchy as founding its empire primarily upon a Mediterranean base – a view in line with the priority which Botero attached to unifying Europe to meet the threat from the infidel Turk.[33]

Botero's preference for '*il conservare*' did not mean that he ignored conquest. Recognising that it occurred, he recommended means to consolidate authority over territories so acquired, and particularly recommended a policy of assimilation, such as the Romans had offered the Albans and the Sabines. An instance from modern times was provided by the Poles, whose '*imperio*' had been enlarged by their having incorporated ('*incorporato*') the territories of their foreign-born monarchs into the Crown of Poland.[34] The physical unity of a monarchy's parts might not be essential to its preservation; but in a case of conquest it was none the less desirable that the territories be juridically 'incorporated' within the monarchy's empire.

The case for the Spanish Monarchy was put still more aggressively by the Neapolitan Tommaso Campanella. Mixing reason of state with astrology and imperial prophecy, his *Monarchia di Spagna* (composed 1600 – 1) was the least inhibited of proposals for a universal monarchy in Europe.[35] Perhaps because it was too aggressive, however, Campanella's

[31] Botero, *Della Ragion di Stato*, Bk I, chs 7, 8, pp. 63–8; *Reason of State*, pp. 9–13.
[32] Giovanni Botero, *Relationi del Mare*, in *Aggiunte di Gio. Botero benese alla sua Ragion di Stato* (Pavia, 1598), pp. 81–95. Other examples of 'Mediterraneans' were the Baltic, Red, Caspian and Persian Seas.
[33] Richard Tuck, *Philosophy and Government 1572–1651* (Cambridge, 1993), pp. 65–7.
[34] Botero, *Della Ragion di Stato*, Bk V, chs 1, 7; Bk VIII, chs 6, 7, 18, pp. 175–9, 190–5, 255–8, 268; *Reason of State*, pp. 95–8, 107–8, 157–8, 167.
[35] Tommaso Campanella, 'Della Monarchia di Spagna' (1600–1), published in German in 1620 (see below, note 47), in Latin as *De Monarchia Hispanica* (Amsterdam, 1640), and in English as *A Discourse touching the Spanish Monarchy*, [trans. Edmund Chilmead] (London, 1654; repr. 1660 with a Preface by William Prynne); on the composition and publication of the work, L. Firpo, *Bibliografia degli scritti di Tommaso Campanella* (Turin, 1940), pp. 56–67, is indispensable. Recent studies are: Anthony Pagden, 'Campanella and the universal monarchy of Spain', in his *Spanish Imperialism and the*

EMPIRE AND UNION

work did not find official favour, and remained unpublished for twenty years; in its own kingdoms, that of Naples not least, the acceptability of the Monarchy continued to lie in its willingness to respect local privileges. The point, as Elliott has observed, was rendered with particular clarity by the Castilian jurist Juan de Solórzano Pereira, when he described the European kingdoms of the Monarchy as forming a union of equals, *aeque principaliter*.[36] But the jurist made this concession the better to insist upon the primacy of Castilian authority in the Indies. In the *De Indiarum Iure* (1629), and again in the *Politica Indiana* (1647), Solórzano Pereira expressly characterised the Indies as 'provinces', 'united and incorporated' by accession to the Crown of Castile. If it had to be acknowledged that the Indies had originally been granted to Castile by Papal donation, this did not mean that they were held on the same terms of vassalage as the Kingdom of Naples.[37] Solórzano Pereira used the term *imperium* only occasionally in relation to the Monarchy, but 'province' had obvious imperial associations, and was now explicitly connected to the idea of union by incorporation. Out in the Indies, at least, ideas of empire and incorporating union could be regarded as correlative. As we shall now see, the point was not lost on contemporary European observers, despite the Spanish Monarchy's continued profession of very different principles as the basis of its rule within Europe.

III

The association of the ideas of empire and union by incorporation was a prominent feature of the first Anglo-Scottish Union debate, initiated by James VI of Scotland on his accession to the thrones of England and Ireland in 1603. James entered his long-awaited inheritance with a strong sense that a mere dynastic union must be consolidated if it was to last, and with clear views of his own as to how to achieve this. As he lost no time in telling his first English Parliament, in March 1604, only an incorporating union made sense. Joined as they were by nature, religion, language and manners, the two Kingdoms of Scotland and England – Ireland had no part in his proposal – ought to regard themselves as one wife to James as their husband, one body to the King their head – for surely no reasonable man would wish James to be a polygamist, or to have a divided and monstrous body. Where the Saxon Kingdoms had been united by

Political Imagination (New Haven and London, 1990), and Tuck, *Philosophy and Government*, pp. 69–72.

[36] Juan de Solórzano y Pereira, *Politica Indiana* (1647, Madrid, 1972), Bk IV, ch. xix, s. 37. Elliott, 'Composite monarchies', pp. 52–3.

[37] Johannes de Solórzano Pereira, *Disputationem de Indiarum Jure* (Madrid, 1629), Bk III, ss. 46, 47, 67; *Politica Indiana*, Bk V, ch. xvi, s. 12.

JOHN ROBERTSON

Bellona, he added, this would be a peaceful union, fastened by the ring of Astraea.[38] When he returned to the matter in 1607, James again argued in corporeal terms, for one body under his headship. But having in the meantime encountered English opposition, James now emphasised that such a union would be tantamount to a peaceful conquest of Scotland by England, since the latter would always be the seat of the Court and government. Only the English should not treat Scotland 'like a naked province': 'I hope you meane not I should set Garrisons over them, as the Spaniards doe over Sicily and Naples, or governe them by Commissioners . . .'. Avoid this, and the union would 'advance the greatnesse of your Empire seated here in England', providing security against both 'intestine Rebellion' and enemies abroad.[39] Among those enemies was of course the Papacy; but although James would show himself as defiantly imperial towards papal pretensions as any Tudor, he clearly wished to distinguish the ecclesiological from the territorial connotations of the term. It should be possible to join two imperial crowns without subordinating one kingdom to the other. As James presented it, union by incorporation would be the basis of a British empire, but the empire he had in mind was an empire of peace, an empire without a province.

The responses to James's proposal ranged from the enthusiastic to the obstructive, and indicate a wider spectrum of conceptions of union's relation to empire. Prominent among the enthusiastic were Francis Bacon and Sir Thomas Craig, both of whom viewed the union as an opportunity for empire in a more expansive sense. In an early contribution to the debate, Bacon drew a distinction between unions *'compositio'* and *'mistio'*. Composite unions, in which the political bodies remained separate under one sovereignty, were the more usual; but the late revolt of Aragon in defence of its liberties had demonstrated their vulnerability. Much happier, therefore, were mixed unions, by which political bodies were joined under a new form. To Bacon there had been no better exponents of such unions than the Romans, who had freely naturalised all with whom they had incorporated. Just as in nature the greater draws the lesser, so had the Romans united with the Sabines, and so should England unite with Scotland.[40] Anglo-Scottish union would in turn be the prelude to the plantation of Ireland, and hence the union of all three of James's

---

[38] James I, 'A Speach . . . delivered . . . on Monday the xix day of March 1604, being the First Day of the First Parliament', in C.H. McIlwain (ed.), *The Political Works of James I* (Harvard, 1918, repr. New York, 1965), pp. 269–80.

[39] 'A Speach to both the Houses of Parliament, the last day of March 1607', in McIlwain (ed.), *Political Works of James I*, pp. 290–305.

[40] Francis Bacon, *A Brief Discourse of the Happy Union Betwixt the two Kingdoms of Scotland and England* (1702), in *The Works of Francis Bacon*, ed. J. Spedding, R.L. Ellis and D.N. Heath (London, 1857–74), X: *The Letters and the Life*, III, pp. 90–9.

EMPIRE AND UNION

kingdoms, 'such a trefoil as no prince except yourself (who are worthiest) weareth in his crown . . .'.[41] Later Bacon was to elaborate the implications of this conception of union in still more expansive terms in the essay 'Of the true Greatnesse of Kingdomes and Estates', endorsing Machiavelli's idea of empire as increase, and expressing particular admiration for the imperial prowess of the Spaniard.[42]

Still more was made of the Spanish example by Thomas Craig in his *De Unione Regnorum Britanniae Tractatus* (1605). *Hispaniae Regnum* was explicitly characterised as an *Imperium*, the most powerful in existence. As such, it was the model to be followed by Britain. By fusing the two *regna* of Scotland and England, each with its *jura majestatis*, into *unius Regis imperium*, Craig argued, the British would achieve a union truly *incorporationis*. This would be the case even if, as in the Spanish Monarchy, or in the Polish – Lithuanian Union, there was no union of the two kingdoms' laws: while Craig believed that their common basis in feudal law ought to facilitate their assimilation, it was not a necessary condition of an incorporating, imperial union. Likewise, Craig saw no reason why the creation of *unum Regnum et Imperium* should be incompatible with the retention of the two kingdoms' separate offices. Like James, Craig urged the English to recognise that they would gain much more by such a union than if they conquered Scotland; but he was convinced that it would be equally to Scotland's advantage to be part of an imperial British Monarchy. United, Britain had the potential to be at least as formidable as *Hispanicum Imperium* itself.[43]

Not all responses to James's proposal were as sanguine as this. Many Scots feared that the Union would reduce their kingdom to 'ane pendicle' of England, endangering the liberties on which its own 'impyir' depended.[44] Two ways of avoiding that fate were canvassed. One was to

[41] Francis Bacon, *Certain Considerations touching the Plantation in Ireland* (1606/9), in *Works*, XI: *Letters and Life*, IV, pp. 114–26, quotation on p. 114. Bacon crowned this flattery by adding 'for indeed unions and plantations are the very nativities or birthdays of kingdoms' (p. 116).

[42] Francis Bacon, 'Of the true Greatnesse of Kingdomes and Estates', *Works*, VI, pp. 444–52; Recent studies of Bacon's treatment of empire are J.H. Martin, *Francis Bacon, the State and the Reform of Natural Philosophy* (Cambridge, 1992) esp. pp. 129–40; and Markku Peltonen, 'Politics and science: Francis Bacon and the greatness of states', *Historical Journal*, 35, 2 (1992).

[43] Sir Thomas Craig, *De Unione Regnorum Britanniae Tractatus* (1605), ed. and trans. C. Sanford Terry, *Scottish History Society*, vol. LX (Edinburgh, 1909): pp. 40–2 (Latin), 261–2 (English), 57–9 (Latin), 283–5 (English), 73 (Latin), 303 (English), 139–55 esp. 153 (Latin), 390–411 esp. 408 (English), pp. 170–93 (Latin), pp. 431–60 (English).

[44] John Russell, 'A Treatise of the Happie and Blissed Union' (1604), in *The Jacobean Union. Six Tracts of 1604*, edited B.R. Galloway and B.P. Levack for the *Scottish History Society*, Fourth Series, vol. XXI (Edinburgh, 1985), pp. 89–91, 97. A similar sentiment was expressed by the Scottish Estates, when in August 1607 it responded to reports of

JOHN ROBERTSON

ensure that political union was accompanied by complete religious and ecclesiastical union, on Scottish terms. Later the object of the Solemn League and Covenant, this was advocated at the time by millenarian mathematician Robert Pont.[45] The other was to settle for what an anonymous commentator termed an 'imperfect incorporation', such as the Romans had agreed with the Tuscans, and the Poles with the Lithuanians. While stopping short of what was imposed upon the vanquished Sabines, this ought to be sufficient to secure a common naturalisation, and hence access to each other's commerce, without sacrificing the two kingdoms' separate laws and customs.[46]

Justification for these Scottish apprehensions was provided by the response of most English commentators. English obstruction of James's proposals, it should be emphasised, was not all gratuitous. As the well-informed Sir Henry Savile pointed out, a dynastic union was unlikely to be perpetual: successful unions required a stronger basis, such as could only be provided by conquest, or by the authority of a parliament. 'For . . . I am of opinion', he wrote, 'that by the authority of the parliament with us, or an assembly of estates elsewhere, a state inferiour may be inseparably united to his superiour.'[47] More directly, this was to say that England already possessed the authority to impose union upon Scotland; and until union was accepted on English terms, there was no reason to compromise existing English liberties. Implicitly aligning the Henrician claim of empire with parliament as much as with the crown, Savile and the English parliamentarians held out for a union that would simply incorporate Scotland into an English empire.[48]

James's speech to the English parliament by advising him that:

> . . . we nevir meant . . . to except aganis onie confounding as it wer of these two befoir separated kingdomes in one glorious monarchie and impyre of the whole Yle, but onlie that this your Majesteis antient and native Kingdome sould not be so disordourit and made confusit by turneing of it, in place of a trew and freindlie Unioun, into a conquered and slavish province to be governed by a Viceroy or Deputye, lyke suche of the King of Spaynes provinceis as your Majestie in your Heynes said speech maid mentioun of.

> in *The Register of the Privy Council of Scotland: Vol VII 1604–1607* (Edinburgh, 1885), pp. 535–6.

[45] Robert Pont, 'Of the Union of Britayne' (1604), in *The Jacobean Union*, pp. 1–38; on Pont see Arthur H. Williamson, 'Number and national consciousness: the Edinburgh Mathematicians and Scottish political culture at the union of the crowns', in Mason (ed.), *Scots and Britons* pp. 193–7.

[46] 'A Treatise about the Union of England and Scotland, to King James the 1st' (1604), in *The Jacobean Union*, pp. 39–74, esp. 56–61.

[47] Sir Henry Savile, 'Historicall Collections left to be considerd of, for the better perfecting of this intended union between England and Scotland' (1604), in *The Jacobean Union*, p. 193.

[48] As Conrad Russell points out, 'The Anglo-Scottish Union 1603–1643: a success?' in A. Fletcher and P. Roberts (eds.), *Religion, Culture and Society in Early Modern Britain: Essays in Honour of Patrick Collinson* (Cambridge, 1994), the clear implication of this position was that there had been no union at all in 1603. See also: Jenny Wormald,

EMPIRE AND UNION

IV

The political and intellectual horizons of the Jacobean Union debate were those of the era of Spanish hegemony. That era came to an abrupt end after 1618, in the protracted conflicts which resulted from the challenge to Habsburg authority in Bohemia, and the lapsing of the Twelve Years' Truce between the Spanish Crown and the rebel United Provinces. At first, in the 1620s, the Habsburgs held their ground, intellectually as well as militarily. Campanella's *Monarchia di Spagna* was finally translated and published in Germany, probably by Besold, even as Imperial and Spanish armies were driving James's son-in-law Frederick Palatine from his Kingdom and his Electorate.[49] From 1630, however, both the course of the war and the discussion of empire were summarily transformed by the intervention of a new and unanticipated belligerent, the Vasa Monarchy of Sweden.

Veiled behind almost two centuries of modern Swedish neutrality, the devastating impact and predatory opportunism of the Vasa Monarchy are still too easily missed. Hugh Trevor-Roper has drawn attention to the ruthless taste with which the Swedish armies plundered the artistic wealth of Habsburg Europe, culminating in the gratuitous looting of Prague in 1648.[50] But there has been no comparable study of the intellectual world of Vasa aggression, even though the dynasty was as determined in its head-hunting of philosophers as it was in its plundering of the arts. What can be identified are two very different lines of justification for Swedish aggression; their inconsistency may be regarded as characteristic of Vasa opportunism.

One source of inspiration on which the Vasas were always happy to draw was the national identity myth, which cast the Swedes as descendents of the Goths, who in turn stemmed from the earliest people of the Bible.[51] Among the most ambitious exponents of this idea, it seems, was Gustav Adolf's tutor Johann Bure, or Bureus. His writings set runic and linguistic scholarship to work to render the Gothic origin myth compatible

'The creation of Britain: multiple kingdoms or core and colonies?', *Transactions of the Royal Historical Society*, Sixth Series, II (1992); Bruce Galloway, *The Union of England and Scotland 1603–1608* (Edinburgh, 1986), esp. pp. 30–57, 93–136; and Levack, *The Formation of the British State*, esp. pp. 31–48, 51–8.

[49] Thomas Campanella, *Von der spanischen Monarchy* (Frankfurt, 1620 and 1623); on these German editions: Firpo, *Ricerche Campanelliane*, pp. 56–67.

[50] Hugh Trevor-Roper, *The Plunder of the Arts in the Seventeenth Century* (London, 1970), pp. 40–51, reprinted in his *From Counter-Reformation to Glorious Revolution* (London, 1992), pp. 125–7.

[51] Michael Roberts, *The Swedish Imperial Experience 1560–1720* (Cambridge, 1979), pp. 70–5; and B. Ankarloo, 'Europe and the glory of Sweden: the emergence of a Swedish self-image in the early seventeenth century', in Goran Rystad (ed.), *Europe and Scandinavia. Aspects of the Process of Integration in the Seventeenth Century* (Lund, 1983), pp. 237–44.

JOHN ROBERTSON

with the prophetic framework of Daniel's Four Monarchies, and to present the Vasas as the heirs to the *translatio imperium* by which the Goths had succeeded the Romans.[52]

When the exigencies of policy-making while on campaign demanded arguments more likely to make an immediate impression on German foes and allies, however, Gustav Adolf could turn for justification to a quite different, and on the face of it improbable, authority: Hugo Grotius' *De Jure Belli ac Pacis* (1625). The received picture of Grotius is of course that of the peace-maker; and it is true that he ended this work with an admonition to preserve peace.[53] It is also true that Grotius rejected as grounds for just war the very arguments which Bureus found so compelling: the pursuit of universal empire, and the call to fulfil biblical prophecies.[54] But elsewhere in Grotius's discussion of what constitutes a just war, and of what is permissible in such a war, Gustav Adolf had no difficulty finding other grounds to justify his actions. For in identifying war between sovereigns with the conflict of individuals in the state of nature, Grotius had made two critical concessions. He construed the right of self-defence as extending to pre-emptive action, and he admitted a right to exact punishment.[55] Once a just war had been initiated, moreover, Grotius allowed that it might be pursued until the enemy had been conquered, his property taken, and the conquered people absorbed by the victors.[56] Grotius did urge clemency towards the conquered: the example to be followed was that of the Romans, who had admitted their former enemies the Albans, the Sabines and the Latins to membership of the *civitas*.[57] In the case of the Sabines in particular Grotius believed that there had been a *de jure* union, with a full communication of rights between the two peoples.[58] But it remained clear that that union was the result of conquest: in context, the mutual communication of rights appears as no more than a wise concession by the victors to the

[52] Johannes Bureus (1568–1652) is mentioned by Roberts, *Swedish Imperial Experiences*, pp. 72–3, and is discussed at various points in Susanna Åkerman, *Queen Christina of Sweden and her Circle. The Transformation of a Seventeenth-Century Philosophical Libertine* (Leiden, 1991), pp. 92–3, 114, 198.

[53] Hugo Grotius, *De Jure Belli ac Pacis Libri Tres* (1625), Bk III, ch. xxv. In the series *Classics of International Law*, *Carnegie Endowment for International Peace*, 2 vols. (Oxford, 1925): vol. I: the 1646 edition; vol. II: trans. F.W. Kelsey.

[54] *De Jure Belli*, II, xxii, 13–15.

[55] *De Jure Belli*, II, i, 2, 16; the implications of these concessions have been pointed up by Richard Tuck, *Sorry Comforters. Political Thought and the International Order from Grotius to Kant* (Oxford, forthcoming).

[56] *De Jure Belli*, III, iv–viii. It was these arguments that Gustav Adolf found particularly helpful when negotiating under pressure on campaign in Germany: Michael Roberts, 'The political objectives of Gustavus Adolphus in Germany 1630–32', in his *Essays in Swedish History* (London, 1967), p. 95.

[57] *De Jure Belli*, III, xv, 3.

[58] *De Jure Belli*, II, ix, 9.

EMPIRE AND UNION

vanquished. Not since Machiavelli had conquest been justified so aggressively: Grotius had certainly earned his reward of appointment in 1635 as Swedish ambassador to the Court of France.[59] Disdaining almost all the existing arguments for empire, whether from prophecy, reason of state or scholastic jurisprudence, the *De Jure Belli* offered instead a straightforward argument for union by right of conquest.

Following the Peace of 1648, the focus of the debate shifted away from Sweden. The young Queen Christina appears to have repudiated her father's aggression, converting to Rome and abdicating in search of an alternative, eirenic cenception of universal monarchy, for which the thrones of Naples or of Poland appeared more suitable than the Swedish.[60] Conquest theory was nevertheless made welcome by others, nowhere more so than in England. In 1651 Hobbes's *Leviathan* offered a justification of power based on conquest even starker than that conceded by Grotius. Not only did Hobbes argue that contracts of obedience to a conqueror were as valid as any other; redeploying the language of the body politic to insist upon the unitary character of a commonwealth, he determined that all separated territories of a commonwealth must be regarded as 'provinces', being but subordinate 'systems' of the sovereign body.[61] Over the 1650s a number of English political writers, notably Marchmont Nedham and James Harrington, were to revive the older, Machiavellian idea of empire by 'increase' or conquest: Rome, they reminded readers, was most aggressively imperial as a republic.[62] But it was Hobbes who was at the leading edge of conquest theory, reinforcing

---

[59] On his conduct in the post, which was hardly what Öxenstierna desired: Hugh Trevor-Roper, 'Hugo Grotius and England', in *From Counter-Reformation to Glorious Revolution*, pp. 65–77.

[60] Åkerman, *Queen Christina of Sweden and her Circle*, esp. part IV.

[61] Hobbes, *Leviathan* (1651), ed. Richard Tuck, (Cambridge, 1991), chs xx, xxii, and 'A Review, and Conclusion', pp. 138–9, 155–60, 485–6. Hobbes wrote

> This word Province signifies a charge, or care of businesse, which he whose businesse it is, committeth to another man, to be administered for, and under him; and therefore when in one Common-wealth there be divers Countries, that have their Lawes distinct one from another, or are farre distant in place, the Administration of the Government being committed to divers persons, those Countries where the Sovereign is not resident, but governs by Commission, are called Provinces. (pp. 158–9)

[62] James Harrington, *Oceana* (1656), in *The Political Works of James Harrington*, ed. J.G.A. Pocock (Cambridge, 1977), pp. 320–33. David Armitage has sought to qualify Harrington's enthusiasm for empire, in 'The Cromwellian Protectorate and the languages of Empire', *Historical Journal*, 35, 3 (1992). But the distinction which Harrington draws between the 'patronage' and the 'empire' of the world (*Oceana*, p. 323) seems to me to be no more than the republican obverse of the distinction between a beneficent and a harmful universal monarchy; a little later Harrington simply refers to 'the empire of the world' as appertaining to 'a well-ordered commonwealth' such as he is proposing (*ibid.*, p. 329). For a comment on the imperialism of English republicans: A.B. Worden, 'English Republicanism', in J.H. Burns with Mark Goldie (ed.) *The Cambridge History of Political Thought 1450–1700*, (Cambridge, 1991), pp. 466–7.

JOHN ROBERTSON

Grotius's challenge to the traditional Habsburg idea of a dynastic territorial *imperium*.

The awakening of English interest in conquest theories had a specific context. In 1650–51, even as Hobbes was writing *Leviathan*, the armies of the Commonwealth succeeded where so many kings had failed, and summarily conquered both Ireland and Scotland. The experience of defeat, followed by enforced union, changed for ever the relationship of each country to England. In Ireland a lasting wedge was driven between Protestant settlers and the indigenous and 'Old English' Catholics. In Scotland it would be widely if grudgingly acknowledged that the union offered some benefits; but never again could the Scots deceive themselves that the English lacked the will or the means to conquer them. The conquest of the 1650s would hang heavily over all the subsequent Scottish discussion of union, up to 1707.

The advent of Grotian conquest theory did not, however, mark the end of the idea of universal monarchy. On the contrary, it too was to be restated, after 1660, in terms more aggressive than ever before. Set on campaigns of territorial acquisition in the Low Countries and the Rhineland, Louis XIV seems to have been the first ruler since Charles V to sanction the explicit presentation of himself as an aspirant to universal monarchy. His case was made by Antoine d'Aubery, in his *Justes Pretentions du Roi sur l'Empire*, a work which so appalled the Imperial Librarian that he promptly re-issued it for the edification of Europe in a Latin abridgement as *Axiomata politica Gallicana* (1667).[63] This was a quite unrestrained statement of the dynastic priority of the French Monarchy, whose claims to an *imperium* without limit between the heavens and the oceans were traced back to Charlemagne. As King of the Franks, Charlemagne had been the heir to the Empire of Rome, ruler of Germany as well as of France, and *Dominus* of the city of Rome and the Papacy within it. In his case, therefore, the papal conferral of the title of Emperor had been but an acceptance of his rightful overlordship. When later the German kings had received the title, however, it had been an acknowledgement of their inferior status, and the closed imperial crown had been a mark of their subordination to the Pope and to the King of France. On these grounds, Aubery maintained, most of Germany was justly subject to Louis already: and when the happy dynastic union of Louis to his Spanish Queen bore fruit, the Dauphin would inherit 'the

---

[63] For the relationship between the *Justes Pretentions* and the *Axiomata politica Gallicana*: Franz Bosbach, 'Eine französische Universalmonarchie? Deutsche Reaktionen auf die europäische Politik Ludwigs XIV', in Jochen Schlobach (ed.), *Vermittlungen. Aspekte der deutsch-französosischen Beziehungen vom 17. Jahrhundert bis zur Gegenwart* (Berne, 1992), pp. 56–7.

EMPIRE AND UNION

Empire of the entire sea and the entire earth, and consequently a Universal Monarchy'.[64]

It was to similarly brazen statements of Bourbon dynastic ambition that Franz von Lisola responded in his *Bouclier d'Estat et de Justice, contre le dessein manifestement découvert de la Monarchie Universelle, sous le vain pretexte des pretentions de la Reyne de France* (1667). The aim of the French King, Lisola demonstrated, was far more than the conquest of a few provinces. It should be likened to a Vesuvian eruption, which would give him 'l'empire absolue' within Europe, and make him 'maitresse absolue de commerce'. To maintain the liberty of Europe against such a danger, Lisola invoked the Duc de Rohan's principle of a balance between the powers of France and the House of Austria. Claiming that the Habsburgs had historically been Europe's bulwark against universal monarchy, he urged the members of the Empire to unite behind them to resist the French.[65]

Lisola's tract was only the first and most famous of a flood of denunciations of Louis XIV as a universal monarch, from every corner of Europe. As an argument on behalf of the Habsburgs, however, its significance lay rather in marking the close of the tradition which had supported their pretension to imperial monarchy. Shattered politically by Vasa and Bourbon aggression, bypassed intellectually by a new strain of conquest theory, a monarchy which had aspired to be Roman while putting dynastic right before conquest was now being presented, however improbably, as the guardian of Europe's liberty. Nor, despite the best efforts of Lisola and, later, Leibniz, could even that role be credibly sustained. For Habsburg authority within the Empire itself rested, after 1648, on a new basis, while the ambitions of Louis XIV would only be frustrated if an alliance could be made with the United Provinces and the Stuart Monarchy in Britain. And in this new political context the discussion of empire had finally to come to terms with the existence of an alternative idea of union, by leagues or confederations. There had emerged in early modern Europe, we now need to recognise,

---

[64] Antoine D'Aubery, *Axiomata politica Gallicana* (1667), Lib. I, cap. i; II, i–iii; III, i, 10–11, ii, iii, esp. 35: 'Delphino Franciae, ex matrimonio Regis, Ludovici XIV & Reginae, Maria Theresiae, nato, promittunt omnes rerum circumstantiae infallibitur futurum Imperium totius maris & totius terrae, & consequenter Monarchiam Universalem.'

[65] [Franz von Lisola], *Bouclier d'Estat et de Justice. Contre le dessein manifestement découvert de la Monarchie Universelle, sous le vain pretexte des pretentions de la Reyne de France*, (1667), Articles I, VI; for a fuller analysis of the arguments of Aubery and Lisola, Bosbach, 'Eine französische Universalmonarchie?', pp. 54–68, and *Monarchia Universalis*, ch. 6: 'Die Universalmonarchie Ludwigs XIV'; and for the range of other devices by which Louis' aggrandisement was portrayed: Peter Burke, *The Fabrication of Louis XIV* (New Haven and London, 1992), pp. 71–83, 179–80.

JOHN ROBERTSON

another form of union besides incorporation into a territorial *imperium*, and another form of empire besides the territorial.

V

Leagues of cities or nobles were widespread in mediaeval Europe, where they offset the hierarchic but fractious structures of vassalage; the concept itself existed in a range of synonyms, in Latin and in the vernaculars.[66] Leagues were particularly prevalent, however, in the German territories of the Empire. The most successful had been the Hanseatic League, in the north, and the Swiss Confederation, or Eidgenossenschaft, in the South. The member cities of the Hanse were renowned for their devotion to commerce rather than territorial aggrandisement; but even at its strongest, in the fourteenth century, the co-ordinating powers of their Diet, the *Hansetag*, had been limited. By contrast the Swiss Confederation, a composite league of Alpine communities and riverine cities, had grown steadily in extent and cohesion since the thirteenth century; early in the sixteenth century its independence was recognised by its nominal overlords, the Habsburgs, (although it remained formally within the Empire until 1648). Despite briefly threatening to dominate northern Italy, the Confederation, like the Hanseatic League, was averse to territorial expansion. Adjoining the Confederation in south-western Germany was the more recently formed Swabian League (1488–1534), whose willingness to accept Maximilian and then Charles V as its head indicated that leagues might also be used to strengthen Imperial authority. The experiment, however, was cut short by the Reformation, and the ensuing confessionalisation of leagues. The activities of the Lutheran Schmalkaldic League (1530–47), and later of the Huguenot and Catholic Leagues in France, left monarchs and their jurists no reason to suppose that leagues were other than undesirable agents of religious division and political subversion.[67] Nevertheless, the confederal idea survived. The successive leagues formed from the 1560s by the aggrieved provinces of the Netherlands might be subversive of the Habsburgs' authority; but the Dutch resisted confessionalisation, despite the prominence of calvinists in the revolt, and in the Union of Utrecht (1579) they committed themselves to both provincial autonomy and religious freedom. Although it required another three decades to determine exactly which

[66] Koselleck, 'Bund, Bündnis, Föderalismus, Bundesstaat', *Geschichtliche Grundbegriffe*, I, pp. 582–600.
[67] H.G. Koenigsberger, 'Liga, Ligadisziplin und Treue zum Fursten im Westeuropa der frühen Neuzeit', in Paolo Prodi (ed.), *Glaube und Eid. Treueformeln, Glaubensbekenntnisse und Sozialdisziplinierung zwischen Mittelalter und Neuzeit* (Munich, 1993), pp. 173–8.

EMPIRE AND UNION

provinces would belong to the Union, the growing likelihood of its success, culminating in the Spanish concession of a Twelve Years' Truce in 1609, did much to restore the credibility of confederal leagues as alternatives to imperial and incorporating monarchy.

The potential of these leagues was noted with particular enthusiasm by the Venetian political writer, Trajano Boccalini, whose *Ragguagli di Parnasso* (1612–13) repeatedly attacked the Spanish pretension to universal monarchy, along with the arguments of supporters such as Botero. Suggesting that the monarchies of Europe had every reason to regard such leagues as a greater threat than individual republics, Boccalini pointed to the strict equality maintained between their members, and to the attraction they exerted over their neighbours precisely because they showed no inclination to make slaves of others.[68]

For a short time at the outset of the seventeenth century it did indeed seem that the age of the confederation might be at hand. While the Spanish Habsburgs remained unable to overcome the Union of the Netherlands, the Austrian Habsburgs found themselves facing a grand Confederation of their Bohemian, Moravian, Austrian and Hungarian Estates. Modelling itself on the constitution of the Polish–Lithuanian Commonwealth, the Confederation declared its intention in 1619 to make the Bohemian Crown, and hence the Empire itself, genuinely rather than formally elective, and to uphold the principle of religious liberty.[69] In the event the Confederation quickly went down to defeat in 1620, but its inspiration, the Polish–Lithuanian Commonwealth, survived. Despite the repeated assaults of Gustav Adolf, the Commonwealth continued to offer a working example of a large-scale territorial union. Here, if anywhere, was an indication of what the alternative to territorial monarchic *imperium* might look like. The Commonwealth was based upon a formal union, negotiated with unusual care; its structure was egalitarian and radically decentralised, most powers lying in the regional Dietines (Sejmiki), which chose and mandated the delegates to the common Diet (Sejm), whose decisions in turn required unanimity; and it was committed to religious toleration.

It is by no means clear, however, that the Commonwealth was actually

[68] Trajano Boccalini, *I Ragguagli di Parnasso* (1612–13), in the translation by Henry [Carey] Earl of Monmouth, *Advertisements from Parnassus: in Two Centuries, with the Politick Touchstone* (London, 1674), pp. 138–46. On Boccalini, Tuck, *Philosophy and Government*, pp. 101–3.

[69] See the important articles by Gottfried Schramm, 'Armed conflict in east-central Europe: Protestant noble opposition and Catholic royalist factions 1604–20', and especially Inge Auerbach, 'The Bohemian Opposition, Poland-Lithuania, and the outbreak of the Thirty Years War', both in R.J.W. Evans and T.V. Thomas (eds.), *Crown, Church and Estates. Central European Politics in the Sixteenth and Seventeenth Centuries* (London, 1991).

JOHN ROBERTSON

understood as an alternative form of union, either by its members or by external observers. The terms of the Union of Lublin, agreed in 1569 after the Diets of the Kingdom of Poland and the Grand Duchy of Lithuania had accepted separate Acts of Union, were themselves indicative. While the title, laws and offices of the Grand Duchy were retained, the union was none the less declared incorporating: Kingdom and Duchy were to become 'one inseparable and indistinguishable body . . . one united Commonwealth', with one Diet and one elected ruler.[70] This would ensure the naturalisation of the two nobilities as equal citizens of one Commonwealth. Contempory observers, such as Botero, evidently had no difficulty in accepting this account of the Union. A further obstacle to understanding the Commonwealth as a new kind of union was the persistence of Aristotelian categories of political interpretation. In these terms it was obvious to Bodin, as later to the German Hermann Conring, that the Polish constitution was aristocratic. To the Poles, by contrast, it was a matter of honour that the Commonwealth was counted as a monarchy. That the crown was strictly elective (with no allowance for pre-election), that the nobility possessed rights of resistance unknown anywhere else, made no difference: Poland remained a monarchy. (The extent to which there was a separate Lithuanian view of these matters is unclear.) In this Aristotelian framework the application of the concept of confederation was limited to the legitimation of resistance, and did not refer to the more general structure of the union; in so far as Polish commentators referred to the union with Lithuania at all, it was to the original dynastic union under the Jagiellons in 1385.[71]

The possibility that the Polish – Lithuanian Commonwealth might come to be regarded as an alternative model of union was in any case destroyed by the calamities which befell it in the 1640s and 1650s. Following the revolt in the Ukraine in 1647 and the subsequent political crisis, the reputation of the Polish nobility and their 'liberties' was irretrievably damaged. Far from offering a model of union, the Commonwealth had by 1700 become a byword for feudal anarchy.

Yet just as one apparent opportunity was lost, the middle years of the

[70] H.E. Dembkowski, *The Union of Lublin. Polish Federalism in the Golden Age* (Boulder and New York, 1982), quotation from the Act of Union, p. 175.

[71] Jean Bodin, *Six Livres de la Republique* (1576), in the trans. by Richard Knolles, corrected by K.D. McRae, *The Six Bookes of a Commonweale* (Cambridge, MA, 1962), Bks I, ch. x, and IV, ch. iii, pp. 166, 472. The persistence of the Polish commitment to monarchy is illustrated by Francisco Marinio [Johann Sachs], *De Scopo Reipublicae Poloniae adversus Hermannum Conringium* (Warsaw, 1665), and Christoph Hartknoch, *De Republica Polonica Libri Duo* (Frankfurt and Leipzig, 1678). For comment, Robert Frost, '"Liberty without License?" The failure of Polish democratic thought in the seventeenth century', in M.B. Biskupski and James S. Pula (eds.), *Polish Democratic Thought from the Renaissance to the Great Emigration* (New York, 1990), pp. 29–54.

EMPIRE AND UNION

century saw the idea of equal union gain new strength elsewhere – ironically in the very monarchy which the Polish model had been used to challenge in 1619, the Empire itself. The Peace of Westphalia in 1648 not only ended the Thirty Years' War, it wrought a fundamental change in the status of the Empire. In political terms, the main beneficiaries of the Peace were of course the Princes, whose powers were enhanced at the expense of the Emperor. But the Peace also reaffirmed the unity of the Empire under the Emperor, and gave it a formal juridical status which it had hitherto lacked. Signed by the various members of the Empire as independent states, the Peace constituted a treaty *jure gentium*; as such, German jurists proceeded to argue, it should be regarded as a Fundamental Law for the Empire, the basis of a specifically Imperial Public Law or ReichsRecht. The ascription of a specific juridical status to the Empire was reinforced by Conring's assault on the historical thesis that there had been a *translatio imperii* from the Roman to the German Emperors. There was an increasing tendency for jurists and publicists to abandon the prefix 'Holy Roman', with its universal pretensions, and to identify the Empire exclusively with the German territory.[72] So understood, the Peace of Westphalia effectively marked the end of the Empire (though not of course of the larger, Central European Habsburg Monarchy) as a monarchic *'imperium'*, and its reconstitution on a basis much more akin to a juridical union of equals, whose relations with each other and with the Emperor were governed by a common Public Law.

In the Empire as in Poland, however, discussion of the constitution as a form of union was still impeded by adherence to Aristotelian political categories. Again Bodin was the *bête noir*, his insistence that the Empire too was an aristocracy provoking fierce controversy among German thinkers, controversy happily fanned by interested outsiders like the Swedes.[73] What transformed this debate was the appearance in 1667, the same year as the exchange between Aubery and Lisola, of Samuel Pufendorf's *De Statu Imperii Germanici*. Written in the guise of reflections by a travelling Italian, Severino da Monzambano, the book was a deliberately provocative assault on the shibboleths of Imperial

---

[72] On Westphalia: Hanns Gross, *Empire and Sovereignty. A History of the Public Law Literature in the Holy Roman Empire 1599–1804* (Chicago and London, 1973, repr. 1975), pp. 293–310; on the supposed *translatio imperii*: K.O. Freiherr von Aretin, 'Il problema della *Renovatio Imperii Romanorum*. Pretese universali e realtà costituzionale del sacro romano impero dal xvi al xviii secolo', in *La Nozione di Romano tra cittadinanza e universalità*, Da Roma alla Terza Roma, Documenti e Studi, Studi II (Naples, 1984), pp. 73–87.

[73] Julian H. Franklin, 'Sovereignty and the mixed constitution: Bodin and his critics', in *The Cambridge History of Political Thought 1450–1700*, pp. 298–328, though with an anachronistic tendency to arraign the Germans for failing to understand the modern theory of sovereignty; Tuck, *Philosophy and Government*, pp. 124–7.

25

JOHN ROBERTSON

constitutionalism. After an historical introduction in which he virtually admitted the justice of the French claim that Charlemagne had held Germany as part of the Kingdom of France, Pufendorf proceeded systematically to expose the inadequacy of the traditional Aristotelian categories of analysis. In those terms, Pufendorf argued, the Empire could only ever be regarded as an 'irregular' form, a constitutional 'monster'.[74] The scandal caused by this one simile made the book's reputation – but was soon regretted by its author, since it distracted attention from his attempt to construct an alternative account of the Empire as a particular form of union.

Pufendorf deferred to monarchy to the extent of admitting that the most perfect union *(perfectissima unio)* would be achieved in a well-ordered kingdom. But Germany could not now be reformed into a monarchy without enormous upheaval. The direction in which it tended was, rather, towards a system of confederates or allies *(systema foederatorum* or *sociorum)*, united in an unequal league.[75] The *De Statu Imperii* closed with an impassioned argument that the 'state interest' of the German Empire lay in the continuation of this process, until it formed a true 'system of states' *(systema civitatum)*. In an Empire so constituted, the Princes would treat each other as equals, while the Emperor would be bounded by the law and by a perpetual council. Liberty of religion would be secure, and the defence of Germany provided for.[76]

In later works of general jurisprudence Pufendorf further clarified the principles behind the idea of 'systems of states', and openly acknowledged its derivation from Hobbes. A system of states existed when several states were joined by a league so as to appear to constitute one body, but each none the less retained sovereign power.[77] On the last point Pufendorf was particularly insistent: a state which lost its sovereignty would be reduced to a 'province'. Those which had come closest to forming a 'system of

---

[74] Severino da Monzambano, [i.e. Samuel Pufendorf], *De Statu Imperii Germanici* (1667, in the revised edition of 1684), chs. I, sects. viii, xii–xv, and VI, sect. ix; translated as *The Present State of Germany, or an Account of the Extent, Rise, Form, Wealth, Strength, Weaknesses and Interests of that Empire*, by Edmund Bohun, (London, 1690, 1696), pp. 11–13, 18–24, 152–4.

[75] *De Statu Imperii Germanici*, VI.ix, VII.vii, pp. 237–40, 265–8; *Present State of Germany*, pp. 153–4, 175–7.

[76] *De Statu Imperii Germanici*, VIII.iv–x, esp. pp. 289–94; *Present State of Germany*, pp. 192–6; Gross, *Empire and Sovereignty*, pp. 311–23. See also James Moore and Michael Silverthorne, 'Protestant theologies, limited sovereignties: natural law and conditions of union in the German Empire, the Netherlands and Great Britain', below, pp. 178–84.

[77] 'Systemata civitatum nobis appellantur plures una civitates, vinculo aliquo ita inter se connexae, ut unum corpus videantur constituere; quarum singulae tamen summum in sese imperium retinent.' Samuel Pufendorf, *De Systematibus Civitatum*, in *Dissertationes Academicae Selectiores* (Uppsala, 1677), and in *Politica Inculpata* (Lund, 1679), p. 228 of the latter edition.

EMPIRE AND UNION

states' in Pufendorf's terms were the Achaian League in the ancient world, and the Union of the Netherlands in the modern.[78]

Once the scandal of the monster simile wore off, Pufendof's ideas exerted considerable influence upon jurists attracted by the idea of a Reichssystem.[79] But there were also critics, notably Leibniz. In his *Caesarinus Fürstenerius* (1677) (itself but one chapter in an epic challenge to every aspect of Pufendorf's philosophy), Leibniz attacked Pufendorf's simple Hobbesian insistence on the indivisibility of sovereign power, in order to argue that the 'territorial superiority' of the German Princes remained compatible with the continued ascription of a universal authority to the Empire. In the course of this argument, Leibniz expressly distinguished a confederation (*confoederatio*) from a union (*unione*): a confederation might be likened to a *societas*, but only a union formed a body (*corporis*), and hence a new *persona civilis* or *respublica*. Any comparison of the Dutch confederation with the German Empire was accordingly invalid.[80] Perhaps what is most revealing about this exchange, however, is the move that neither participant was able to make. Neither Pufendorf, with his clear-cut alternatives of monarchy and a system of states, nor Leibniz, with his refusal to admit that a confederation was a union, was in a position to draw the modern distinction between a 'confederal' and a 'federal' union. This conceptual incapacity may be thought at odds with German reality, since the Emperor still possessed important powers; nevertheless, the distinction would not begin to be drawn for another hundred years. In the meantime, despite Leibniz's criticism, it was Pufendorf's straightforward definition of union as either confederal or monarchic that won general acceptance.

The conviction that only a strict confederation offered a coherent alternative to monarchy was powerfully reinforced by the seventeenth-century achievements of the United Provinces or States of the Netherlands – and by the terms in which it was defined as a union by contemporaries. The Union of Utrecht in 1579, to which the United Provinces traced its foundation, had itself been little more than a defensive league, a step towards the formation of a General Union of all the Netherlands. It did not repudiate the Habsburgs' sovereignty, and fell short of a comprehensive

---

[78] *De Systematibus Civitatum*, in *Politica Inculpata*, pp. 226–83; more concisely in Samuel Pufendorf, *De Jure Naturae et Gentium* (1672, in the edition of Amsterdam, 1698), Bk VII, cap. v, ss. xvi–xxi, pp. 714–21, and in the translation *Of the Law of Nature and Nations*, (London, 1703), pp. 184–89.

[79] Bernd Roeck, *Reichssystem und Reichsherkommen. Die Diskussion uber die Staatlichkeit des Reiches in der politischen Publizistik des 17. und 18. Jahrhunderts* (Stuttgart, 1984).

[80] G.W. Leibniz, *Caesarini Fürstenerini Tractatus de Jure Suprematus ac Legationum Principum Germaniae* (1677), in *Gothofredi Guillelmi Leibnitii . . . Opera omnia* (Geneva, 1768), vol. III, part iii, caps x–xi, pp. 357–61; trans. in *The Political Writings of Leibniz*, trans. and ed. Patrick Riley, (Cambridge, 1972), pp. 114–20.

JOHN ROBERTSON

constitution. It did, however, enunciate two clear principles, guaranteeing the traditional privileges and freedoms of each province and town, and securing individual religious freedom.[81] As the Revolt took hold in the seven northern provinces, and these won the breathing space of the Twelve Years' Truce in 1609, institutional consolidation gradually followed. Each province had its own Estates and Stadtholder, and sent delegates to the Estates General, which proceeded by unanimity. The formal equality of the Union was of course complicated by the real pre-eminence of Holland; but while Holland's leaders might sometimes treat the other six provinces as their inferior allies, they were always careful to exert their influence from within the institutions of the Union. A potentially greater complication was the independent role of the House of Orange, whose head was by tradition Captain-General of the Union's armies and navy, and whose exact constitutional relation to the Estates General was never strictly defined.[82]

To begin with, the political theory of the Dutch Revolt was that of resistance against tyranny, political and religious; and when the rebellious provinces sought a collective identity, they found it in the myth of the ancient Batavians, who had heroically defied Roman imperial despotism.[83] From the 1580s, however, a debate developed on the implications of the Union of Utrecht's reservation of provincial liberties; and a number of writers began to articulate the principle that sovereignty lay in the individual states.[84] There are signs that Grotius contemplated the qualification of this principle, either through the emergence of superiors within a league, or through the strengthening of the central institutions of the Union (but not the House of Orange).[85] But the principle of States'

---

[81] A translated version of the Treaty of Utrecht is given in E.H. Kossman and A.F. Mellink (eds.), *Texts concerning the Revolt of the Netherlands* (Cambridge, 1974), pp. 165–73; J.C. Boogman, 'The Union of Utrecht: its genesis and consequences', in J.C. Boogman and G.N. van der Plaat (eds.), *Federalism. History and Current Significance of a Form of Government* (The Hague, 1980), pp. 5–35.

[82] H. Wansink, 'Holland and six allies: the Republic of the seven United Provinces', in J.S. Bromley and E.H. Kossman (eds.), *Britain and the Netherlands, Vol. IV Metropolis, Dominion and Province* (London, 1971).

[83] Martin van Gelderen, *The Political Theory of the Dutch Revolt* (Cambridge, 1992). E.H.N. Mout, 'Ni Prince ni Etat', in André Stegman (ed.), *Pouvoir et Institutions en Europe au XVIième Sièle* (Paris, 1987), pp. 117–30; and 'Ideales Muster oder erfundene Eigenart. Republikanische Theorien während des niederländischen Aufstands', in H.G. Koenigsberger (ed.), *Republiken und Republikanismus im Europa der Frühen Neuzeit* (Munich, 1988).

[84] *Texts concerning the Revolt of the Netherlands*, pp. 255–9: 'About the present condition of government in the Netherlands, 1583', and pp. 274–81: 'A short exposition of the rights . . . of Holland and West Friesland . . . 16 October 1587', by Francis Vranck.

[85] Grotius, *De Jure Belli*, I.iii.21; and other writings discussed by Tuck, *Philosophy and Government*, pp. 162–4, (though cf. pp. 192–3 for later arguments apparently upholding the principle of States' sovereignty).

EMPIRE AND UNION

sovereignty became widely accepted, and later in the century was powerfully endorsed by the Friesland jurist Ulrik Huber, possibly under the influence of Pufendorf. Given this principle, Huber was clear that the Union must be regarded as a *foedus aequale*: in effect, as a confederation.[86] There was also general agreement that such a union was defensive only, on the model of the Achaian League in ancient Greece, with no interest in territorial acquisition.[87]

Foreign observers who overcame their anti-republican prejudices sufficiently to examine the Dutch constitution sometimes showed the beginnings of a subtler understanding. Both Cardinal Bentivoglio, in the first half of the century, and, later, Sir William Temple appreciated that sovereign power was in practice divided between the Provinces and the Estates General. Even so, Temple still believed it impossible to range the United Provinces (like the state of Poland) 'under any particular names of goverment that have yet been invented'.[88] In the absence of a coherent account of the division of powers within the Union, it was the jurists' understanding which seems to have prevailed.[89] As in the case of the Empire, this understanding may have done less than justice to the complex reality of Dutch politics; but the impression that the only form of union coherent enough to withstand imperial monarchy was a confederation of equal, sovereign states had gained still more ground. Well before 1700, it seems, it had been accepted that confederation was the (sole) alternative to incorporation.

If the Dutch was, within Europe, a purely defensive union – a union against territorial empire – its relation to empire overseas was another

[86] Ulrik Huber, *De Jure Civitatis libri tres* (Franeker, 1684, 3rd edn 1698), Bk I. ch. xvii, paras. 8–14. In 1698 Huber added a discussion of the German constitution, suggesting that the Empire too should be regarded as a *foedus aequale*: Bk I, sect. iii, ch. 3, paras. 17–19. Cf. Moore and Silverthrone, 'Protestant theologies, limited sovereignties', below, pp. 184–9.

[87] Huber, *De Jure Civitatis*, I.xvii.10; for the identification of the Dutch with the Achaians, cf. Boccalini, *Ragguagli di Parnasso*, (in the 1674 translation), pp. 175, 197–8, 201–2, and Henry Stubbe, *The History of the United Provinces of Achaia* (London, 1673), 'To the Reader'. What was known about the Achaian League derived from Polybius: see W. Den Boer, 'The Dutch Republic and Antiquity', in Boogman and van der Plaat, *Federalism*, pp. 47–64.

[88] Guido Bentivoglio, *Historicall Relations of the United Provinces of Flanders*, trans. Henry [Cary], Earl of Monmouth, (London, 1652), Bks I, chs iv, v, and III, vii, pp. 4, 7, 45–8. Sir William Temple, *Observations upon the United Provinces of the Netherlands* (1673), ed. Sir George Clark (Oxford, 1971), pp. 52 (ch. ii), 127–8 (ch. vii), 133–5 (ch. viii); and *An Essay upon the Original and Nature of Government* (1672), in *The Works of Sir William Temple*, 2 vols. (London, 1720), I, p. 96.

[89] The caution of this judgement reflects my inability to read the vernacular literature. The *Bibliography of Dutch Seventeenth-Century Political Thought. An Annotated Inventory, 1581–1710*, comp. G.O. van de Klashorst, H.W. Blom and E.O.G. Haitsma Mulier (Amsterdam and Maarssen, 1986), indicates the existence of a limited amount of further material.

JOHN ROBERTSON

matter. There, as Richard Tuck has pointed out, the Dutch were ruthless in deploying the arguments of Grotius to proclaim their freedom to sail and trade there they would, to use pre-emptive force whenever necessary, and to assume the rights of conquest over the goods of those they overpowered.[90] In their own eyes, the Dutch sought no more than – in Grotius's phrase – the 'freedom of the seas', and that on behalf not of the state but of private bodies, the East and the West India Companies. But by treating goods at sea equally with those on land as open to pre-emptive conquest, Grotius's doctrine went far further than previous accounts of the sea as a basis for empire. It eliminated Botero's distinction between 'mediterraneans' and 'oceans', with its implication (also evident in Charles V's columnar emblem) that empire overseas depended upon, and was an offshoot of, empire within Europe. Equally, it dispensed with Solórzano Pereira's assumption that territories acquired overseas must be 'provinces' of a specific European monarchy, held by an 'incorporating' union. Goods and territory could legitimately be acquired anywhere in their own right, without having to be regarded as an extension of a prior European *imperium*. Within Europe itself, the aggressive edge of Grotius's theories might be masked by the United Provinces' deliberate repudiation of territorial acquisition on their own account; overseas, the Dutch had no such inhibitions.

Not surprisingly, the point was appreciated most clearly by the main rivals to the Dutch for maritime supremacy, the English. Long remembering that they had been the victims of an early instance of Dutch ruthlessness, the Amboyna massacre of 1623, the English regarded it as obvious that what the Dutch sought was the 'empire of the seas'. Hostility to the Dutch on this account reached a peak in the anti-republican climate of the 1660s, when a spate of pamphlets accused them of attempting to establish no less than a universal monarchy by sea.[91] But this was name-calling, since the English by no means rejected the pursuit of maritime empire on their own account. In John Evelyn's words, 'a spirit of commerce, and strength at sea to project it, are the most certain marks of greatness of empire'.[92] Just as the English had shown none of the restraint of the Dutch in acting on the implications of Grotian-Hobbesian conquest theory at the expense of their neighbours, so they showed a similar impatience with the doctrine of the freedom of the seas, countering it with a succession of Navigation Acts, and a frank avowal of

[90] Tuck, 'Grotius and Selden', in *The Cambridge History of Political Thought 1450–1700*, pp. 503–4; more fully in *Sorry Comforters*, ch. 2.
[91] S.C.A. Pincus, 'Popery, trade and universal monarchy: the ideological context of the outbreak of the second Anglo-Dutch War', *English Historical Review*, 422 (1992), pp. 1–29.
[92] J. Evelyn, *Navigation and Commerce, Their Original and Progress* (London, 1674), p. 15.

EMPIRE AND UNION

their own maritime imperial ambitions. By 1700 it was common ground in English political and economic debate that the sea was England's natural empire, and that the interest of state must be identified with that of commerce.[93] Between them, the Dutch and the English thus added a new dimension to the concept of empire, making it possible to detach it from its previous identification with the territorial ideal of universal monarchy.

VI

1672 was the decisive year for the empires and unions of early modern Europe. By gratuitously invading and almost over-running the entire Netherlands, Louis XIV had come within an ace of accomplishing both his own univeral monarchy and the ruin of the United Provinces and its commerce. Even in failure, he transformed the alignment of forces in Europe, and the relation between the United Provinces and England in particular.

Somehow the Province of Holland held out, but the republican regime of de Witt was brought down, and with it the policy of preserving diplomatic independence. In its place the newly restored Stadtholder William of Orange set about 'constructing the alliances which would secure both his own country and Europe from the French King's dreadful ambition. Above all he looked to England, and when his Stuart cousins denied him, he took the extraordinary risk of invading England to secure the crown. The risk was offset, however, by the knowledge that English public opinion now regarded France, not the United Provinces, as the pre-eminent enemy. After 1672, as Steven Pincus will show in the following chapter, relentless pamphleteering stirred the British into an obsession with the threat of a French universal monarchy, an obsession which contributed strongly to the acceptance of the invasion and revolution of 1688, and which continued unabated into the 1690s.[94] Exploiting this climate of Francophobia, William proceeded to devote himself to harnessing the resources of all three of his kingdoms for the ultimate struggle over the Spanish Succession, which was expected to follow the now imminent death of Charles II, the last Spanish Habsburg.

---

[93] For some (chronologically rather scattered) expressions of this idea: Koebner, *Empire*, pp. 68–77; for a much more systematic account of the key economic arguments: Istvan Hont, 'Free trade and the economic limits to national politics: neo-Machiavellian political economy reconsidered', in John Dunn (ed.), *The Economic Limits to Modern Politics* (Cambridge, 1990).

[94] Steven Pincus, 'The English debate over universal monarchy', below pp. 37–62: until Pincus uncovered the evidence, the scale of pamphleteering on this subject had passed virtually unnoticed.

JOHN ROBERTSON

At stake in the conflict, it was anticipated, would be no less than the preservation of the 'Liberties of Europe' from a Bourbon universal monarchy, and, closely related to those liberties, England's own freedom to pursue its natural empire of the sea.

It was in this European setting that the question of union returned to Britain after 1688. Over the course of this volume, contributors will explore in greater detail a number of specific ways in which this setting was understood, alongside the concerns, cultural, religious and legal as well as political, which informed the Scottish response to it. In the remainder of this introductory chapter, I shall confine myself to outlining the extent to which the Anglo-Scottish Union debate of 1698–1707 exploited the conceptual resources made available by two centuries of European discussion of empire and union.

Perplexed by the erratic, mercenary behaviour of Scottish politicians, William had by his death reached the conclusion that further union of the two kingdoms was desirable, and he and his ministers expected it to take the form of an incorporating union of parliaments. Additional urgency was lent by the realisation that his successor, Anne, would have no heirs, creating an opportunity for a return of the exiled heirs of James II. Even so, it appears to have been assumed that the Scots would simply accept the English Parliament's choice of the Hanoverian succession, and that they would be content with the minimum of economic concessions.

The Scots, however, believed that there was room for manoeuvre. Resentful of the ever-mounting pressure on the historic sovereignty of their kingdom, the Scottish elite was persuaded to support, in quick succession, two initiatives designed to restore its economic and political autonomy. The first was the Darien Scheme of 1698–1700, an attempt to establish a commercial *entrepôt* on the isthmus of Panama. As David Armitage demonstrates, the venture embodied a distinct and original conception of commercial empire, in which trade would not be concentrated in the hands of metropolitan merchant monopolies.[95] The flaw in the scheme was the Scots' inability to give military support to the Darien colonists: an intensely irritated William and an enraged London merchant community simply left the colonists to their fate at the hands of the Spanish. Nevertheless, the Scots' commitment to the scheme was a strong indication that closer union of the British kingdoms would be hard to reconcile with an exclusively English empire of the sea.

Frustrated in this attempt to develop an independent maritime empire, the Scottish elite was the more easily persuaded to take advantage of the political opportunity provided by the prospect of an open succession.

[95] David Armitage, 'The Scottish vision of empire: intellectual origins of the Darien venture', below, pp. 97–118.

EMPIRE AND UNION

Deferring to the intelligence of Andrew Fletcher, the Scottish Parliament signalled that it would only accept the Hanoverian successsion if the crown's powers were curtailed. Parliament should become the guarantor of Scotland's sovereignty. This was not a declaration of independence as such: what Fletcher and his allies sought was a re–negotiation of the terms of the union between the two kingdoms, reconstituting it as, in effect, an equal or confederal union. Informing their argument, it is clear, was the now well–established conviction that confederal union was the one coherent alternative to incorporation: what was envisaged was a sort of United Provinces of Great Britain.[96]

Fletcher's initiative ensured that the Scots were presented with a choice: there was, in principle, a geniune alternative to the offer of incorporation emanating from London. Unfortunately, the confederal idea faced a crucial difficulty: the requirement of equality. Within a union of the three Kingdoms as they stood England would inevitably continue to predominate; but to create equal units would require the break–up of all three Kingdoms, with (as Fletcher tacitly admitted) the consequent sacrifice of the historic sovereignties which confederal union was supposed to preserve. Here, perhaps, Pufendorf's pre-emption of a distinction between 'confederal' ·and 'federal' union proved critical. When they had the opportunity, in 1703–4, the Scottish advocates of confederation were reluctant to qualify their insistence on equality as a condition of such a union with any admission that there might also be central or 'federal' institutions with distinct powers. There was a definite sense in which the adherents of confederal union allowed themselves to be hoist by the rigidity of their conceptual inheritance.[97]

Increasingly aware of the dangers of keeping the succession open when there was no credible Protestant alternative to the Hanoverians, Scottish political opinion had by late 1705 swung back to those making the case for an incorporating union of parliaments. The strength of this case lay in its promise to exchange political weakness for civil, and especially economic, benefits. Relentlessly the advocates of incorporation criticised the existing Scottish Parliament as little better than a Polish Diet, whose survival was too high a price to pay for a notional independent 'sovereignty'. (So far had Poland now fallen from offering a model of a successful union.) Once they shared a common legislature with the English, however, the Scots would gain the same security for their liberty

[96] John Robertson, 'Andrew Fletcher's vision of Union', in R.A. Mason (ed.), *Scotland and England 1286–1815* (Edinburgh, 1987); and 'An elusive sovereignty: the course of the Union debate in Scotland 1698–1707', below, pp. 205–7.

[97] As two of Fletcher's early associates, James Hodges and George Ridpath, were later to acknowledge, by moving away from the idea of confederation: see Robertson, 'An elusive sovereignty', below, pp. 208–10, 213–15.

33

JOHN ROBERTSON

and property as the English, and the same economic opportunities. Specifically, England's maritime empire would be open to their participation. Although this was not the form of empire which the Darien projectors had had in mind, the belated concession by English negotiators of free trade with England and its overseas colonies could be presented as generous compensation for the sabotage of the Darien Scheme.[98] Empire was, finally, being offered to the Scots in return for incorporating union.

Nevertheless, the term chosen to characterise this 'exchange' of incorporating union for maritime empire contained a critical ambiguity. For the preferred reference of the incorporating unionists was to Grotius's definition of union as a 'communication' of rights, such as the Romans had offered the Sabines. This was repeatedly cited as authoritative re-assurance that an incorporating union entailed no surrender of sovereignty, but its transfer into a new body politic.[99] As Fletcher early pointed out, however, the reference was flawed: Grotius himself had presented Rome as conquering the Sabines before incorporating them into its empire.[100] Behind the reassuring concept of 'communication' there lay the dark shadow of Grotian conquest theory. In the event, the threat of conquest was played down during the debate. Protestant opponents of the Union feared to provoke an English invasion, since it would only give the Jacobites their chance; the English, meanwhile, had no wish to be diverted from the war on the continent. But the threat was none the less present – and drawn to the Scots' attention at strategic moments by English minsters:[101] after Cromwell's success in the 1650s, it was an unavoidable, intrinsic dimension of Anglo-Scottish relations. In Grotian (and *a fortiori* in Hobbesian) terms, the English possessed both the power and the right to have enforced the process of Anglo-Scottish 'communication' by a simple pre-emptive strike. There was more justice than even King James had supposed in his remark, 100 years earlier, that an incorporating union was tantamount to the peaceful conquest of Scotland by England.

The implication is reinforced when the Union of 1707 is viewed from the perspective of the English parliament. For the Parliament which accepted the Treaty of Union was the direct descendant of the Parliament

[98] Laurence Dickey, 'Power, commerce and natural law in Daniel Defoe's political writings 1698–1707', below, p. 95; Armitage, 'Scottish Vision of Empire', below, pp. 116–18.
[99] See above for the Grotian doctrine, pp. 18–19; and for the use of it in the Union Debate, Robertson, 'An elusive sovereignty', below, p. 221 and n 78.
[100] Andrew Fletcher, *An Account of a Conversation concerning a Right Regulation of Governments for the Common Good of Mankind* (Edinburgh, 1704), in *The Political Works of Andrew Fletcher* (London, 1732), pp. 408–9; also Robertson, 'Andrew Fletcher's vision of Union', pp. 213–14.
[101] For examples, Robertson, 'An elusive sovereignty', below pp. 204, 211n.40.

EMPIRE AND UNION

which had proclaimed the imperial status of the realm of England in 1533, and to which in 1604 Sir Henry Savile had confidently ascribed the power of uniting an inferior state to its superior. If it now accepted an Act of Union which formally ended its independent existence, it did so knowing that in every respect bar its style and a limited addition to its membership the new Parliament of Great Britain would be as its English predecessor. In this perspective, incorporating union was, as James's critics had insisted it must be, a straightforward enlargement of England's 'empire'. The Scots may have accepted union in return for the prospect of empire overseas; but the English Parliament was at least equally interested in the empire to which it had laid claim since 1533, an empire of territory within Britain, now afforced by the threat of conquest. From this point of view the limited concession of a new style, unacceptable a century earlier, was now worthwhile, since English interests would remain predominant in a British parliament, while the resources of Scotland would be added to the struggle against French universal monarchy in Europe, and to the defence and enlargement of empire overseas.

The debate preceeding the Union of Scotland and England in 1707 was thus one outcome of two centuries of European discussion of the ideas of empire and union, ideas constitutive of the early modern European political order. Far from being *sui generis*, the formation of Britain, its Union and its Empire in the eighteenth century can only be appreciated in the European context. A union which it was suggested might be confederal, but was in the event incorporating, though on a parliamentary rather than a dynastic basis; a union intended to facilitate the pursuit of maritime, commercial empire, but which was also, in historical effect, an extension of the territorial empire of one party over the other: this was a union framed in terms reaching far back into history of European political thought. In its principles as well as in its circumstances, British union was a thoroughly European event.

The union agreed in 1707 was of course only one of several eighteenth-century outcomes of the early modern debate over empire and union. Among others whose accompanying debates are equally in need of investigation, two which stand out are the Spanish Monarchy's *Nueva Planta* of 1707–16, uniting Aragon with Castile, and, at the other end of the century, Joseph II's remarkable attempt to remodel the Austrian Habsburg Monarchy. Of more direct concern to this volume, however, are the outcomes of the British Union itself, outcomes explored in the final three chapters. One was in Ireland. At the turn of the seventeenth century incoporating union was the ideal of the Protestant Anglo-Irish; but the English Parliament saw no advantage, and some economic disadvantage, in absorbing its Irish counterpart. Anticipating this rebuff,

JOHN ROBERTSON

Molyneux encouraged his fellow Protestants to reassert their parliament's autonomy on the basis of a distinctively Anglo-Irish version of Grotian conquest theory.[102] But the question of Ireland's relation to the British Empire remained: and when the Anglo-Irish Ascendancy as well as the Empire were threatened at the end of the eighteenth century, incorporating union would offer both Dublin and Westminster an all too ready-made outcome to the crisis.

By contrast, incorporating union did not offer a solution to the crisis in relations between Britain and its North American colonies. While Scottish settlers and administrators in the colonies strove to interpret the imperial union in terms similiar to those of mutual 'communication', at Westminster the Parliament of Great Britain remained adamant in its refusal to compromise its imperial sovereignty.[103] Faced with such rigidity, the colonists were reluctantly obliged to form themselves into a union. At first this took the conventional form for a union against empire, a confederation. But when the constraints of confederation quickly became apparent, a new distinction began to be drawn. A union of states, it was suggested, might be 'federal' as well as 'confederal' – and might then aspire to an 'empire' of it own. In the words with which Alexander Hamilton addressed his fellow Americans in 1787, as they prepared to draw up the constitution of this new union:

> . . . you are invited to deliberate a new Constitution for the United States of America. The subject speaks its own importance; comprehending in its consequences, nothing less than the existence of the Union – the safety and welfare of the parts of which it is composed – the fate of an empire, in many respects, the most interesting in the world.[104]

The creation of the United States of America would simply give the age-old association of union and empire a new lease of life.

[102] Jacqueline R. Hill, 'Ireland without Union: Molyneux and his legacy', below, pp. 277–84.
[103] Ned Landsman, 'The legacy of the British Union for the North American Colonies: provincial elites and the problem of Imperial Union', below, pp. 304–11; J.G.A. Pocock, 'Empire, state and confederation: the War of American Independence as a crisis in multiple monarchy', below pp. 346–7.
[104] Alexander Hamilton, *The Federalist*, no. 1, 27 October 1787.

3
The Habsburg World Empire and the Revival of Ghibellinism

John M. Headley

On 8 September 1517 Charles of Burgundy set sail from Flushing, Zeeland, in order to claim his Spanish kingdoms, recently left rulerless by the death of his grandfather, Ferdinand of Aragon.[1] As the fleet that bore the youthful king to Castile stood out toward the English Channel, there could be descried, painted on the sails of the royal flagship, the emblem devised by the court physician Marlianus: the two columns of Hercules and the intertwined inscription *Plus Oultre*—"still further." To the knights of the Order of the Golden Fleece who had gathered in the choir of Saint Gudule the previous year to hear Marlianus's oration, there could have been little doubt as to the emblem's preeminent meaning. For at that time the orator had set forth a worldwide empire and called Charles a new Hercules or Atlas superbly qualified to bear its responsibilities. Nor for that matter could there have been much doubt in the minds of the awed populace of Brussels, as it watched in March of the same year the funeral cortege of Ferdinand of Aragon wind its way through the narrow streets of the city. There stood in the last car, for all to behold, a soldier in full armor with sword upraised surrounded by Amerindians and at the back of the car a golden globe with the motto *Ulterius nisi morte*, suggestive of universal expansion. And in the young king himself there could be

*I wish to express my gratitude to the John Simon Guggenheim Memorial Foundation for a grant that allowed me to accomplish some of the research for this paper. I also want to take this opportunity to thank the staff of the Biblioteca Reale di Torino, the Bibliothèque municipale de Besançon, the Bibliothèque Royale Albert Ier, the Münchner Universitätsbibliothek, the Haus-Hof und Staatsarchiv, the Biblioteca Marciana, the Humanities Room, Wilson Library, University of North Carolina, and Dr. Carlo Revelli of the Biblioteche Civiche di Torino.

John M. Headley

no uncertainty, for had not his grandfather in a final letter before dying instructed Charles to conquer Islam and to evangelize the antipodes? To a Europe that had seen in the past two decades the materialization of a new world beyond the seas conjoined with the results of Habsburg nuptial diplomacy that piled crowns and soon hereafter the imperial title upon Charles of Burgundy in such a way as to stagger the contemporary imagination, the new ruler awakened grave anxieties as well as boundless hopes. But to the courtiers and humanists who pressed around Charles, the device of Marlianus betokened the drive to universal Christian empire. It was at once a pledge and an aspiration.[2]

To appreciate the excitement and the foreboding that the young Habsburg prince awakened, we need to remind ourselves of the current mental outlook that allowed men to experience themselves as participants in a prophetic scheme of history. It is well known that medieval religious and political prophecy had received its ultimate stamp under the influence imparted by the twelfth-century Calabrian abbot, Joachim of Flora. Here was to be found the idea of that progressive trinitarian elaboration of world history, culminating in the Age of the Spirit with its profound sense of *renovatio*, renewal. The Joachimite pattern juxtaposed the greatest earthly beatitude and the greatest tribulation, and in its development looked to an outstanding ruler, a monarch of the whole world, a second Charlemagne, repeatedly identified either with a current French Rex Christianissimus or with a German Rex Romanorum who would renew the church, chastise its ministers, conquer the Turk, and—like David—gather all sheep into one fold. Some expositors of the Joachimite tradition believed that an angelic pope, a *pastor angelicus*, shunning temporal goods and collaborating with the Savior-Emperor, would rule the Holy See. The astrologer-prophet Johann Lichtenberger represented one of the most recent and well-known expressions of this cast of thinking. In his *Prognosticatio* of 1488 he awaited the appearance of a Burgundian world emperor who would arise as a Second Charlemagne, the prince and monarch of all Europe, in order to reform the churches and the clergy. Throughout this vast literature that captured the historical imagination of successive generations and that associated grave foreboding with great hope, there moved as a continual refrain a

Habsburg World Empire and Ghibellinism

single text in which profound anxiety gave way to joyous release, the text of John 10:16: "et fiet unum ovile et unus pastor."[3]

On that September day in 1517, he who embodied Habsburg destiny and represented for many the Savior-Emperor, had left behind in the Charterhouse of Scheut outside Brussels, forgotten and apparently removed from further political assignments, the man who would soon orchestrate the various themes of imperial *renovatio*, reform, and world order adumbrated by poets and humanists into a vast scheme of Ghibelline realization. But the events of the autumn of 1517—whether the departure of Charles for Spain or the posting of theses by a Saxon monk—seem to have left Mercurino Arborio de Gattinara irrevocably behind on the sidelines of the developing imperial drama. Scion of local nobility in Piedmont, product of a stiff juristic training and of almost a decade as a successful, even renowned, lawyer in Turin, champion of a most exalted appreciation of the law, Gattinara had distinguished himself by his zeal in the service of the Habsburg dynasty[4]. As chief architect of the notorious League of Cambrai against Venice, as a negotiator for the Archduchess Margaret and the Emperor Maximilian in a number of capacities, and as president of Burgundy since 1508, Gattinara had sacrificed every waking moment to the advancement of the dynasty. His rigorous application of Roman law in the province of Franche-Comté against a fractious nobility and his inflexible manner had produced such turmoil there that the Habsburg praetorian prefect of Burgundy, as he was inclined to envisage himself, had witnessed in these past months the erosion of both his personal finances and his political support. His relentless and brilliant services to the Habsburgs had prevented his fulfilling a vow, taken in 1513 and commuted by the pope, which had now brought him to the Charterhouse of Scheut in August of 1517 where he was to remain for the next seven months.[5] To his enemies in Franche-Comté as well as to those in the archduchess's government at Malines—and probably to himself—Gattinara's career as diplomat, administrator, and principal magistrate for the Habsburgs was over.

In his autobiography Gattinara later mentions how in the first month of his withdrawal to the monastery of Scheut he composed a small book, dedicated to Charles and designed to be presented to him before his departure. In this treatise Gattinara hailed the future

John M. Headley

monarchy of the world and the triumph of the Christians in the person of Divus Carolus, and he predicated supreme monarchy for Charles. Of this treatise only a fragment, a highly apocalyptic fragment, has survived. We can only surmise its contents.[6] But there can be no doubt as to its spirit and intent. The fallen magistrate was swept up in the current mood of apocalyptic expectation and imperial aspiration. In the charged atmosphere of the moment his sources were ready at hand. Nevertheless, it may be noted that Gattinara was a friend and reader of Jean Lemaire de Belges, the former court chronicler of Margaret.[7] In his treatise on the schisms and councils of the church Lemaire had warned that in the twenty-fourth and last schism secular princes would be constrained to undertake the reform of the clergy as proved by several prophets, sibyls, astrologers, holy persons, and mathematicians. He proceeded to quote them and, while mentioning Abbott Joachim, he drew most heavily upon Johann Lichtenberger.[8]

Having already suffered deposition from office, Gattinara emerged from his meditation and penance at Scheut in May 1518.[9] On his way homeward he apparently entertained notions of entering the service of his original master, Duke Charles of Savoy. But he was never to reach his destination. For in Spain Charles's grand chancellor, Jean Le Sauvage, had died in June; this second most important office at court and the one that was at the bureaucratic center of government needed a skilled jurist and experienced administrator. The gravity of the problem did not end here. In Germany, the aging emperor and in the Netherlands his gifted daughter Margaret, who embodied the imperial aspirations of the dynasty, must both now attend to the future election of a Habsburg to the Holy Roman Empire.[10] The narrow Flemish nationalism of Chièvres, who as grand chamberlain was the most prominent person in the entourage of Charles, could not provide the necessary vision of and justification for a world empire.[11] The archduchess and the emperor knew their man. Despite his recent fall from office, the ex-president of Burgundy's preeminent legal knowledge, his awesome capacity for work, and his absolute devotion to the dynasty were never in doubt and made him the only logical candidate.[12] On 15 October 1518 Mercurino de Gattinara took the oath of office between the hands of Charles in Saragossa.

Habsburg World Empire and Ghibellinism

In the ensuing twelve years up to his death the new "Grand Chancellor of all the realms and Kingdoms of the King"[13] would count for more than any other single person in the entourage of Charles. The relationship between the aged, experienced dynastic servant and the young emperor, which needs to be defined and elaborated beyond the picture so splendidly drawn by Karl Brandi, cannot concern us here. Neither can the reorganization of the Spanish central administration, nor the immense diplomatic activity of these years deflect us from our course. We seek the possibly less ambitious and more ambiguous task of defining and assessing the contours of a mind and a policy that can best be referred to as Ghibellinism. In a splendid article on Charles V and the idea of empire Frances Yates has noted among a number of sixteenth-century litterateurs the main features of Ghibelline aspiration: namely, the renewal of the empire, the emergence of an ideal master of the world, and the reign of justice and peace in a new golden age.[14] But what proves fruitful in the case of poets and philosophers will not suffice in the case of a statesman whose advice and policies were to be of paramount significance for European politics in this period. Thus without forsaking entirely the categories of Dr. Yates, we propose to study Gattinara's Ghibellinism under three broad topics: the educing of the idealized emperor; the reduction of the pope to his properly pastoral office; and the place of Italy in the emerging world *monarchia*. None is exclusive and all are so interrelated as to make it difficult to consider one without the other two.

Among the innumerable tasks confronting Gattinara on his arrival in the Iberian peninsula, the most subtle and absorbing was the portrayal of an emperor who would draw not only the youthful Habsburg but also his Spanish subjects to the vocation of empire. The first formal opportunity occurred with the need to respond publicly to the ambassadors of the German electors who brought the news of Charles's election as Holy Roman Emperor. On 30 November 1519, St. Andrew's Day, the patron saint of Burgundy, the grand chancellor delivered the speech of acceptance at Molina del Rey. The divinely inspired election of Charles, we are told, signified the restoration and renewal of the empire hitherto diminished and almost effaced. With the renewal of *sacrum imperium* the

John M. Headley

Christian Commonwealth may receive necessary care, the Christian religion be increased, the Apostolic See stabilized, and the enemies of Christians exterminated so that the promise of the Savior that there will be one sheepfold and one shepherd may be fulfilled. God has indeed shown his favor that the empire divided under Charles the Great to the extent that most of it was overrun by enemies of the Christian religion is now able to be reestablished under Charles the Greatest and be led back to the obedience of the true and living pastor himself. Justice and peace embrace.[15]

In the first of those many *consultas* or memoranda whereby Gattinara sought to educate his master for the great opportunity that spread out before him and to advise him on all political matters, the grand chancellor reacted to the news, hardly a week old, that Charles had been elected Holy Roman Emperor:

Sire: God the creator has given you this grace of raising you in dignity above all Christian kings and princes by constituting you the greatest emperor and king who has been since the division of the empire, which was realized in the person of Charlemagne your predecessor, and by drawing you to the right path of monarchy in order to lead back the entire world to a single shepherd. Thus it is very reasonable that your imperial and Caesaric Majesty, in order to avoid the vice of ingratitude, should recognize his Creator as true distributor of all goods rendering to him appropriate thanks and attributing to him due praise by eschewing all ambition and vainglory . . . as well as those temptations and vices which might distract and repel [your] exercise of virtues and good works.[16]

Gattinara evidently felt responsible for the moral upbringing of the prince, a presumption that would not make any easier his relationship to Charles, and although he never had the time nor probably the desire to compose a *Speculum principis*, the equivalent can be deduced from successive *consultas*.

In pursuing his task Gattinara warns Charles that the exalting of the Christian faith, the growth of the Christian Commonwealth and the preservation of the Holy See, all for the attainment of universal peace, will be impossible without monarchy.[17] After correlating peace and monarchy, he then raises the theme that would be the continuing preoccupation of a lifetime of dynastic service—justice.

Habsburg World Empire and Ghibellinism

For the administration of that justice which is the queen of all virtues by which emperors, kings and princes rule and dominate, as God has given you the title of emperor and legislator and as it belongs alone to you to declare, interpret, correct, emend, and renew the imperial laws by which to order the entire world, it is most reasonable that in following up the suggestions (*vestiges*) of the good emperor Justinian, your Caesaric Majesty should early select the most outstanding jurists that one may find to undertake the reformation of the imperial laws and to advise on all possible means for the abbreviation of trials and for presenting such clear laws that the entire world may be inclined to make use of them and that one may say in effect that there is but a single emperor and a single universal law.[18]

Placing Justinian as a model before the emperor, Gattinara cites the contemporary jurist Celsus to the effect that the emperor is the vicar of God in his empire in order to accomplish justice in the temporal sphere.[19] He is the prince of justice.[20] The Dantesque vision of a jurist-emperor, who is the guardian and expositor of Roman law and who as *dominus mundi* champions justice and the law by a sort of preeminent moral and juridical authority but does not impose them by force, had received further support during the fourteenth century in the teaching of Bartolus.[21] This vision is now resurrected. Together with peace, justice completes the two great correlates of Augustine—*justitia et pax*—vital to Gattinara's view of universal monarchy.[22]

The response of Castilians to Charles's acceptance of the imperial office was almost totally negative. Whatever exhilaration and pride some *letrados* and humanists might have felt at the awareness of their king's being emperor was inevitably stifled by the profound anxiety that it produced among Charles's new subjects. And although Gattinara could not have been alone in urging the acceptance,[23] even if the royal council as early as 5 September 1519 had moved to proclaim that the title and office of emperor would not be exercised to the prejudice of Charles's Spanish kingdoms,[24] the question of Castile's new role in a world empire coupled with the abrupt departure of their king for Germany led directly to the revolt of the *comunidades*. In the Crown of Aragon, however, matters were different. Indeed, the town counselors of Barcelona, on hearing the news of their king's coronation at Aachen in 1520,

John M. Headley

enthusiastically responded in a remarkable Catalan proclamation wherein they hailed Charles as another Charlemagne, who, in using their city as the staging base for those expeditions that would recover Jerusalem, would subjugate the Turk, unite the two empires, the eastern and western, achieve the unification of the churches, Catholic and Orthodox, and realize a golden age wherein the lion would lie down with the lamb—ideas long nursed by readers of Ramón Lull.[25]

National opinion in both Castile and Aragon would ultimately be able to tolerate Charles's addition of the imperial dignity to his many crowns and dominions by claiming the emperor to be richer in Spain than in Germany and by respecting the providential mission of Charles as protector of Christendom.[26] Although this careful cultivation of the feeling of the Hispanic peoples is most evident in the imperial addresses to successive *cortes* after Charles's return in 1522, his departure from Spain in 1520 required the attention of both royal council and chancellery.[27] Among the papers constituting part of the personal file of Gattinara at the Biblioteca Reale in Turin is one, written in a fine humanist hand, that shows signs of having been circulated within the chancellery or possibly the royal council for revisions and additions before it appeared in its published form under the title *The Address of Charles, King of the Romans, in the Spanish Cortes, immediately before his Departure*. The tract constitutes a Latin reworking of the heart of the famous speech by Pedro Ruiz de la Mota, bishop of Badajoz, to the *cortes* of Santiago de Compostela on the early afternoon of 31 March 1520. The Latin tract is more compressed than the Castilian speech; the address has been shifted from the third to the first person with the king directly speaking; and while the development of the argument in the tract generally follows that of Mota's speech, the classical examples and emphases are different. Apparently directed toward that literate Spain beyond the immediate *procuradores* gathered at Santiago and designed to mollify the rising passions of Charles's Castilian subjects, the work could hardly have appeared in print without Gattinara's approval and, indeed, his direct participation. The existence of the manuscript together with the final Latin printed version and even a later German version demands a reconsidera-

Habsburg World Empire and Ghibellinism

tion of Mota's famous speech as a collective enterprise on the part of the royal council.[28]

As for the content of the Turin manuscript, empire, we are told, is not attained by whim or ambition but is bestowed by God alone. Charles here claims that the empire of Spain with its far-flung European possessions and with another, a gold-bearing world attached, would have sufficed, but the pressure of the Turk and the needs of religion as well as the welfare and dignity of his Spanish realms demand that he add Spain to Germany, the name of Caesar to that of Spanish king. Rome would have never had her empire if she had not sent forth men equal to the task. He promises to return to Spain, the citadel, staging base, and support of his kingdoms. The manuscript ends on the heroic note that while other peoples serve pleasure and utility, Spain alone is born to honor—to live and die for honor.[29]

In Gattinara's representation of the emperor to that monarch himself and to his Spanish subjects the messianic note is tempered by a moral concern feeding on classical models and examples that show the influence of humanism. Just as Dante in those letters that hailed the advent of the Emperor Henry VII in Italy applied to the ostensible Savior Emperor scriptural texts properly pertaining to the Messiah, likewise Gattinara since his early years in Habsburg service had exercised the same practice. In 1514 he had identified the Emperor Maximilian and the protection he must afford his daughter and grandson with the eagle of Deuteronomy 32:11 tending her young and John 10:30: "I and the Father are one." Repeatedly in the autobiography he clothes the emperor and his providential mission in these hues.[30] In accordance with earlier Ghibelline practice reminiscent of the Hohenstaufen chancellery, the sacralization of the imperial office perilously approaches the blasphemous. Yet in the *consultas*, where he directly addresses the emperor, the moral strain is uppermost. Gattinara never tires of drilling into the still impressionable mind of Charles the importance of an emperor's exercising justice, clemency, magnanimity, fortitude, liberality, and temperance, or of presenting models of Greek and Roman emperors.[31] In a remarkable series of articles that Gattinara circulated among the members of the Council of State early in the winter of

John M. Headley

1523–24 for their criticism and reactions, under the rubric *amour des subjects*, the grand chancellor set forth one of his most used and favorite texts drawn from Seneca's *De clementia*: that for a ruler his subjects' love constitutes an impregnable fortress. In enjoining his master how he must present himself, be seen and known by his subjects, Gattinara encourages Charles to go into the churches, pass through the towns, and even go into the fields, entering into honest conversation with his people.[32] Although the aged chancellor's moral instruction and exhortation would in the long run wear on Charles so that the monarch would always breathe more freely during Gattinara's absences, nevertheless they left their impress upon the victor of Pavia, the conqueror of Tunis, so that his modesty and *gravitas* raised Charles head and shoulders above the deportment of his royal contemporaries. For our purposes here it should be noted that Gattinara conceived the moral stature and *providentia*[33] of the emperor as vital to the pacification of Spain, following his return in 1522, and vital also to providing the links between the emperor and other lands within the far-flung *monarchia*. In his idealized understanding of the Holy Roman Empire and the presently envisaged monarchy of the world Gattinara conceives of it less as a legal and administrative construct and more as something depending upon moral stature.

Sire, your grandeur and the security of your affairs do not consist in holding Milan nor other states which hereafter you would be able to conquer and master, but it consists in winning the hearts of men and causing through them that kings, dukes, princes and potentates come to your devotion and obedience and recognize you as overlord. This is the way by which the Romans and others had the monarchy of the world, the remnants of which you ought to follow in order to attain thereto.[34]

A second aspect of Gattinara's Ghibellinism is his attitude toward the pope. The pope is considered chiefly a political and administrative figure—the ruler of the Papal States, the grantor of *cruzadas* and taxes upon the clergy so valuable to late medieval secular authorities. As with many notables in pre-Tridentine Europe before Luther began to draw attention to the papacy, Gattinara participated in a broad current of belief that saw the pope preeminently in political terms and sought to reduce him to his originally pastoral office. Nevertheless it would be a major misconstruing of

Habsburg World Empire and Ghibellinism

Gattinara's personality and career as chancellor to view him as religiously indifferent or as making religious issues the mere instruments of political ends. He was the first of Charles's counselors to assert the need for a council. The papal nuncio at Worms, Aleander, himself the epitome of a politicised ecclesiastic, saw Gattinara and Chièvres as using the issue of Luther to gain political ends. Yet while Chièvres thought that the whole Luther disturbance could be handled, Gattinara was impressed by its popular dimensions and saw the necessity of a council.[35] His frequent recourse to monastic retreats, his enthusiastic support of Erasmus as the preeminent teacher of the orthodox faith and as a middle way, his continuing desire to see the life of the clergy reformed—all argue for a seriously experienced catholicism that was neither Roman nor papal.[36]

Gattinara was ready enough to withstand any effort on the part of the pope to intervene in secular matters while advancing the claims of his imperial master to intrude upon the realm of the spiritual. In 1522 he continued to support Juan Manuel, the imperial ambassador at Rome, despite the determined campaign of Pope Adrian to get rid of him. Reading over the diplomatic correspondence, Gattinara grumbles, "The pope will content himself with what is reasonable and leave it to us to ask advice of whom we like."[37] When he drew up the instructions for Miguel de Herrera as special envoy to Italy and to the pope in November 1525 his tone becomes more menacing: "[Tell] His Holiness that if he does not want to use his office of common pastor for the tranquility of Italy and of Christendom, then we will be forced to use our office as emperor, and His Holiness ought to take note that we still have in our hands the King of France and that he is in our power to leave when we wish it."[38]

The imperial victory at Pavia in February 1525 encouraged Gattinara to urge the emperor, shortly after the receipt of the news, to make the pope call a council to extirpate the errors of the Lutheran sect, reform the affairs of Christendom, and mobilize effective action against the Turk. If the pope should excuse himself, then the emperor as *advocat et protecteur* of the church should undertake the convoking of a council.[39] As the diplomatic situation darkened and the conniving of Pope Clement with France and sundry Italian

John M. Headley

states threatened to remove the imperial grip upon the peninsula, Gattinara's insistence that Charles seize the initiative became more strident. In July 1526 he composed one of his longest *consultas*. Therein he urged the emperor to realize the goal of one sheepfold and one shepherd by going to Italy and by convoking a council for the reform of the church and the extirpation of heresies. He would subject the Lutherans to the truth of evangelical doctrine in which he believed, the sect to be for the most part grounded, win them over as much as possible by amnesty, clemency, and pardons, and thus turn with renewed strength against the Turk.[40]

Amidst the deepening diplomatic crisis the grand chancellor found an outstanding spokesman for his ideas in the person of Alfonso de Valdés, who had been a permanent scribe in the imperial chancellery since 1521 and became one of its Latin secretaries in 1526.[41] Under the direction and guidance of the Council of State and the grand chancellor, Valdés had been entrusted with the task of composing the official government report on Pavia. Therein Valdés identified the Spaniards as the elect people of God and presented the imperial victory as releasing Charles to attack the Turks and the Moors, recover the empire of Constantinople, and retake the Holy Sepulchre in Jerusalem, thus fulfilling the words of the Redeemer, "Fiet unum ovile et unus pastor."[42] Now with the slipping of Pope Clement VII back into the French orbit and the materialization of the League of Cognac, Gattinara was able to look to Valdés's stalwart assistance in leading the diplomatic offensive against Pope Clement during the summer and fall of 1526.

In the remarkable replies that were delivered over to the papal nuncio Baldassare Castiglione at Granada, 17 and 18 September 1526, if the hand proclaimed the work of Valdés, the voice was clearly that of Gattinara.[43] In a conscious effort to obtain the understanding and approval of secular and ecclesiastical princes, magistrates and citizens throughout the Habsburg empire, the grand chancellor arranged to have the correspondence between pope and emperor together with related materials published at Alcalá, Antwerp, Cologne, and Mainz.[44] The first imperial reply to Clement and the letter to the Sacred College of Cardinals interest us here. The former letter, while raking up all past wrongs inflicted by Rome upon Charles, repeatedly finds the pope neglectful of his

Habsburg World Empire and Ghibellinism

pastoral duties, which is another way of saying that he is deeply involved in preparations for war directed against the very one who is the most obedient prince in all Europe and seeks only the good of Italy.[45] Rather than a shepherd and a mediator, the pope has become a wolf, a partisan, a begetter of war. The letter reaffirms those *duo luminaria* both instituted by God that should rule cooperatively, bring peace to Christendom and war against the Turk. It concludes on the menacing note that if the pope refuses to exercise his responsibilities as a father and pastor, the emperor must have recourse to a general council, which he now begs the pope to convoke for healing the wounds of Christendom.[46] Pressing the point still further, the imperial chancellery on 6 October dispatched a letter to the College of Cardinals, asking it to call a council if the pope demurred.[47] The consternation that these letters created in Rome was dulled only by the sack of the city itself.[48] And as the imperial propaganda campaign reached its crescendo, Gattinara for good measure tried to enlist the efforts of the prince of humanists to publish a definitive edition of Dante's *De monarchia*.[49] But Erasmus's view of Christian polity was not that of Gattinara, and the *editio princeps* of Dante's work would have to wait three more decades before another spectacular clash between emperor and pope promoted its publication.[50]

More important than the refusal of Erasmus was the caution and reluctance of the emperor concerning the conciliar policy of his minister. Although a council for Gattinara was an obvious means of realizing necessary ecclesiastical reform, as well as a political lever to embarrass a vacillating pope, Charles was probably more realistic in recognizing the highly sensitive nature of the conciliar issue; either wisely or out of native Habsburg dilatoriness he refused to be rushed along. In actual fact, his own interest in a council did not permit resort to such extremes, and it is quite possible that the conciliar issue contributed to the rupture between the emperor and his chancellor that occurred in March 1527.[51]

The reasons for Gattinara's withdrawal from government and trip to Italy were complex and a long time in maturing. Although these reasons cannot concern us here, one is relevant to the present issue. There is some evidence that his belief in the imminence of the *pastor angelicus* drew him to Italy at this time.[52] When he arrived

John M. Headley

in Monaco, the chancellor was greeted with the news of Rome's sack by the imperial army. Unable to refrain from his customary task, so recently relinquished, of counseling the emperor, Gattinara promptly sat down to communicate his advice in this instance. In his autobiography he tells us that he presented the emperor with two alternatives: either Charles could approve the deed, the pope being not the pastor but the robber, disturber, and waster of Christendom, having assumed arms for himself and turned a deaf ear to the imploring requests for a council; or, if he could not accept the rigor of this advice nor condone the actions of his soldiers, Charles could proclaim his horror of the event and manifest his desire for a peace and the submission of his case to a general council. In actual fact, what Gattinara wrote to the emperor on this occasion, included amidst a series of recommendations and directions, was that His Majesty must purge himself of blame before all Christian princes; that Valdés must write good Latin letters and in them ask for the convocation of a council to heal divisions and extirpate heresies. While awaiting a response, the emperor should make his own preparations for a council. Gattinara concluded that with a victorious army in Italy the emperor would be on *le droit chemin de la monarchie*.[53]

Gattinara's suggestion to the emperor may have served as the initial impetus that led to Valdés's composition of his notorious dialogue on the sack of Rome. With his customary enthusiasm the chancellery's Latin secretary, entering into the spirit of things, asserted at the end of the *Lactancio* dialogue that Christ founded the church and the emperor restored it.[54] If the passionate Valdés proved to be more Erasmian than Erasmus, it could also be said that his Ghibelline zeal sometimes exceeded that of his master, Gattinara.[55] Although it is doubtful that the chancellor himself would have gone so far as to equate the emperor with Christ regarding their services to the church, he was ultimately responsible for the entertainment of such an idea within the imperial chancellery. Likewise, it is also doubtful that he would have gone so far as his cousin, Giovanni Bartolomeo di Gattinara, the emperor's leading negotiator at Rome, who in writing back to Charles casually inquired what sort of Apostolic See, if any, ought to remain in Rome and how it ought to be maintained other than entirely under

Habsburg World Empire and Ghibellinism

the control of the prince.[56] Gattinara participated in that world of thought and policy that had not yet experienced the impact of Luther's reformation upon the papacy.[57] At the same time he belonged to more than a century of political experience that recognized that ultimately more could be gained in cooperation with the pope than in opposition and more specifically that pope and emperor, papacy and empire, needed each other. Thus it is not surprising that Gattinara should write during this same period that if the pope should come to Spain to negotiate, he, Gattinara, would eagerly return to do business.[58] Although the pope himself did not go to Barcelona in 1529 to negotiate, his legate did, and the resulting treaty of Barcelona brought to an end Gattinara's express anti-Romanism and conciliarism and, in effect, thereby undercut his own Ghibellinism.

Italy and its role within the *monarchia* constitute the final aspect of our inquiry into Gattinara's Ghibellinism. To Dante Italy was the garden of the empire, to Petrarch a land most holy destined to be the mistress of all the world, and to Paolo Giovio, the contemporary historian of Charles V's reign, she was that infallible ladder of true monarchy. Nor did one have to be a Ghibelline to admire Italy's centrality within Christendom. A century after Giovio, Richelieu would allow in his *Political Testament* that Italy was deemed the heart of the world and the preeminent part of the Spanish empire.[59] By the beginning of the sixteenth century Italy had become the decisive arena for the clashing ambitions and rival claims of Valois and Habsburg. On first coming to the office of chancellor and continuing throughout the succeeding decade Gattinara in all his *consultas* drummed into his master's ear that Italy was the principal foundation of his empire, and lacking it, his honor was void and the growth of his empire jeopardized. He who would counsel ignoring Italy, counseled the emperor's shame and ruin.[60] Repeatedly over the years Gattinara urged Charles V to come to Italy, secure his justice and order there, and complete the pacification of the land. When Gattinara speaks of Italy, he can mean the entire peninsula well known to the Roman jurist that he was, but he can also suggest the traditional notion of the *regnum Italicum*, which included only the north and central portions of the peninsula. For he frequently distinguishes Italy from Naples and Sicily and con-

[107]

John M. Headley

tinually reverts to the problems of the comity of independent states north of the Neapolitan kingdom.[61]

Another distinctive feature of his attitude toward Italy is that this Burgundo-Piedmontese statesman has no feeling for Rome and its *Mystik*, which he seems to transfer to Italy as a whole. Rather than Rome, the cities of Milan and Genoa occupy his constant attention, and he never tires of insisting that they are together the gateway to Italy: the two duchies are the keys and bastions for keeping and dominating all Italy reduced to the emperor's subjection and as the seat and scepter for dominating the world.[62] Here he defined a strategic truth that made the Genoa-Milan axis the veritable hinge of the entire Habsburg position in Europe, an axiom that would be affirmed long after the chancellor had passed from the scene.[63]

How did Gattinara approach the problem of Italy's liberty, namely the independence of her city-states, which for his contemporary, Francesco Guicciardini, provided the social and political bases for Renaissance culture? The solution to the Italian riddle lay through Milan. He who controlled that city would be master of Italy. Gattinara steadfastly opposed the generals—Lannoy, De Leyva, Moncada, Pescara—who would seize Milan outright, impose a military solution upon the Italian problem, and reach an accord with France at the expense of Italy.[64] For this reason he brooked the emperor's wrath and refused to apply the seals of office to the treaty of Madrid on 14 January 1526. Instead he urged that the present duke, Francesco Sforza, be invested with the imperial fief of Milan and that the imperial army be reduced to a small effective force whose maintenance would not ruin the Milanese. By preserving this state in his devotion the emperor would accomplish more than by having a lieutenant hold it outright, for according to the chancellor, subjects are more inclined to employ their lives and property for the defense of their estate and their immediate lord when they know him to be on good relations with the emperor. Gattinara's reasons for propping up the existing regime in Milan stemmed from a more precise appreciation of the emperor's position with respect to the pope and Venice. To seize Milan would transgress treaties and understandings with both.[65] Gattinara's reliance upon a league and upon

Habsburg World Empire and Ghibellinism

awakening native elements within Italy points to a looser and more general imperial hegemony.

Since the end of 1523 and with increasing urgency during and after the negotiations for the treaty of Madrid Gattinara advocated a union with the Italian states. Italy was in his mind always the center and basis of the Habsburg empire. "Italy is to be preserved for him more by love than by force and with their love he will be able to dominate all the world and without it His Majesty will thrust his kingdoms and affairs into peril and never will he be able to recover himself without necessity and work."[66] Once the emperor united with Italy, the pacification of his land might be extended to a general pacification within Christendom, which would bring the kings of England and France into an alliance against Turk and heretic.[67] In adjusting these two essentially opposing conditions—the independence of the Italian states and Italy's imperial role—Gattinara invoked the relationship between ancient Rome and her client states within the Holy Roman Empire.[68] He could warn that by using force rather than love and humanity, Rome had taken longer to master the rest of Italy than to conquer the world.[69]

Gattinara's appeal to the Roman Empire seems to have been fundamental to his solution to the Italian problem. Gasparo Contarini, after five years as Venetian ambassador to the imperial court, emphasized this feature in his *relazione* to the Senate. He distinguished the two rival parties within the imperial council, one led by Gattinara, the other by the Viceroy Lannoy. In characterizing the former, he says that the Romans, Cyrus, and others who have produced something like universal monarchies have nevertheless not ruled all directly but have had other kings and other friendly republics that have favored them, enjoying their fraternity. This was the way that the chancellor guided His Imperial Majesty.[70] The contemporary sources for the basis of his appeal to the Roman Empire lie beyond the scope of our present inquiry, but it can be observed that as a jurist trained in the Roman law Gattinara was doubtlessly aware of the *jus Italicum* that, developing out of the Republic and constituting a basic feature of the pre-Diocletian empire, extended the legal status of Italian cities to non-Italian provincial cities and communities; it comprised various

John M. Headley

rights of a public and private character such as self-government and exemption from supervision by the governor of the province.[71] Thus particularly for Italy and to some extent elsewhere *monarchia* connoted ideally not a uniformly organized empire but a looser Habsburg hegemony that would give room to local privileges, provincial customs, native institutions.[72]

It would be a mistake, however, to believe that Gattinara intended to apply in equal measure to all other lands and kingdoms in the *monarchia* the policy of clemency and relaxed guidance that distinguished his treatment of Italy. Although love, clemency, justice are the preeminent characteristics in the chancellor's conception of a world order, when dealing with a pronounced enemy and any allies of that enemy Gattinara reveals a more aggressive and oppressive drive in his thinking.

France represented the one discordant note in the existing political scene that prevented the rapid realization of Gattinara's Ghibelline dream. France blocked any mobilization of the Christian world on the part of the emperor for war against the Turk. More immediately, she had her own claims to Naples and to Milan. Gattinara nursed an invincible distrust of France, and the first step in his contribution to the emperor's diplomacy was to bring the papacy and England into the lists against France. By the treaty of Windsor, immediately preceding the court's departure for Spain in 1522, the allies agreed on a dismemberment of France. The idea of a virtual *Vernichtungskrieg* in the early sixteenth century may seem to cast a curious light on chivalric-dynastic politics.[73] Nevertheless, since the prevailing image of European polity at this time still was supremacy and empire rather than competitive balance, our shock is diminished and the high stakes for which Valois and Habsburg struggled become evident.[74] After the imperial victory at Pavia, Gattinara sought to realize that reduction of France whereby the emperor might regain his rightful possession of Burgundy, obtain a corridor through southern France, and remove forever the French grip from northern Italy. The chancellor recommended the Habsburg possession of Languedoc and Provence—an idea that was receiving some ventilation in the chambers of imperial government at the time. To obtain the legal arguments for affording the emperor this ready access to Italy, Gattinara undertook the ransacking of

Habsburg World Empire and Ghibellinism

the archives at Barcelona.[75] Three years later, after his return to court and power, Gattinara in the midst of a bitter struggle with France and England composed a *consulta* predicated on a false report concerning the death of the king of France. Gattinara called for the restoration of the empire to its original vigor with the reacquisition of Dauphiné, the Arelate kingdom, "y otras tales." Through the Dauphin, at the time his prisoner, the emperor would establish a sort of protectorate over France without destroying the kingdom. And under the guise of avenging Queen Catherine of England and her daughter, the emperor could take the island realm. In the midst of considering a Scottish alliance in order to implement such a design, Gattinara breaks off, interrupted by other work,—or by the truth that his great enemy still lived.[76] Despite its interest and its value for defining the aggressive element, at its most inflated, in Gattinara's conception of the *monarchia*, not much weight should be given the document. Probably written early in the winter of 1527–28, it belongs to what Fernand Braudel calls the time of bulging files, the winter plans, when the servants of government could concoct the most grandiose schemes, when, before the blazing hearth in the cozy chamber, no plan seemed too difficult, no policy too bizarre—all only to disintegrate before the harsh realities of the spring.[77]

In the construction of Charles's monarchy the special care that Gattinara directed toward Italy and her imperial role supports his claim that he was an Italian, seeking the liberty of Italy.[78] *Libertà d' Italia*—the words appear repeatedly on the lips and quills of the leading Italian political thinkers and actors during those very years that saw the death agony of that independence usually signified by the phrase and that had made the Italian Renaissance possible. Both Gattinara's Florentine contemporaries Machiavelli and Guicciardini could agree with him in perceiving a vital connection between the destiny of Milan and the liberty of Italy. Yet both could now strenuously oppose the Habsburg *monarchia d' Italia* as they had earlier opposed French domination.[79] However marginal an Italian Gattinara might be and whatever his tangled motives, he appeared to some Italians as one trying to moderate the impact of foreign domination upon the peninsula. The papal nuncio to Castile, Baldassare Castiglione, writing to the archbishop of Capua,

John M. Headley

could observe that no one in Spain had such a good mind for Italian affairs as Gattinara.[80] Contarini, who often had some caustic comments to make about Gattinara, could remark that he was a second Joseph in that both had the opportunity to benefit their people—Joseph, the Hebrews and Gattinara, the Italians.[81] He did not disguise his relief when in July 1525 Gattinara's resignation was refused, and he considered the chancellor's return to the Council of State a reason for all Italians to rejoice.[82] For his own part Gattinara could afford to represent himself to Contarini as ready to dare all for the liberty and welfare of Italy.[83] Prematurely in 1522 he could claim the merit of having freed his country from the barbarians.[84] And ever on the prowl for funds to support the insatiable war machine, reducing its numbers and its pillaging to effective control, Gattinara could approach Contarini as a fellow Italian and in his efforts to obtain a contribution from Venice, express his deep desire to remove the ruinous Spanish soldiery from the country.[85]

In the supreme crisis of the Italian Renaissance that culminated in the sack of Rome *libertà d' Italia* had a variety of meanings according to the minds of the leading protagonists. Insofar as he could realize and maintain it during the few years remaining to him, Gattinara's accommodation was certainly the most realistic, the most practical; apart from Italy's role in his Dantesque theory of empire, Gattinara squarely confronted the problem of adjusting his land to the facts of Spanish might and the French menace. In this respect Castiglione was more perceptive of current political realities than were his two Florentine contemporaries.[86] The solutions of Machiavelli and Guicciardini either failed to materialize or were shattered by events. Gattinara, the child of both Dante and Bartolus, strove to construct a broad enough conception of monarchy to allow for those two poles around which Italy's life continued to move—universalism and particularism.[87] By the treaty of Barcelona, 29 January 1529, the emperor capitalized on the recent destruction of the French army before Naples and his alliance with Genoa and the fleet of Andrea Doria—an alliance for which Gattinara had provided the groundwork and impetus.[88] The treaty, described by contemporaries as Gattinara's masterpiece, provided for the decisive accommodation between emperor and pope. And while it sounded the death knell of the Florentine republic, it led to

Habsburg World Empire and Ghibellinism

the General League of Italian States realized at Bologna at the end of the year. Gattinara, by then a dying man, accompanied his master to Italy, received his long-desired cardinal's hat; months later Charles received the imperial crown from Pope Clement at Bologna. As the emperor and his suite moved northward toward Germany, the mood that settled upon Italy, according to Benedetto Varchi, eyewitness and historian of these events, was one of incredulous relief:

> For [the emperor] had succeeded not as barbarously as people had imagined, [judging from] the cruelty done by his ministers and soldiers, but most consummately and very benignly and even beyond the believing of many had returned the State of Milan to the duke. It was thought by some . . . who had observed his manners and actions that it had not been by chance and without art that he had so pleasingly caressed all and had sought with such industry and benevolence to oblige all who were able to aid or impede his enterprises.[89]

The pacification of Italy was the last and greatest service that Gattinara rendered his master. Not without its uncertainties and ambiguities, this Spanish domination of the peninsula would be secured by the treaty of Cateau-Cambrésis thirty years later and would endure for a century and a half.

The treaty of Barcelona destroyed the recrudescence of Ghibellinism that we have tried to define here. But Gattinara's Ghibellinism, which attempted to integrate notions of the ideal emperor, antipapalism, and the central role of Italy into an overall conception of world empire, evaporated not because it was unrealistic or irrelevant or even successfully contested but because much of it could be attained through other means—by cooperation with the pope. To our own age the illusion of empire seems the grandest of all at the beginning of what is traditionally considered the modern period. In his pursuit of explaining the present out of the past, the historian of this period all too often becomes mesmerized by the apparently triumphant march of the "national state" to the neglect of those other polities, the city-state and the conception of empire as a broad hegemony, both of which are treated as so much political debris. And yet in their time it was this that Valois and Habsburg struggled to obtain, the supreme magistracy of Europe—this the reality, this the goal. Neither a phantom nor a mirage, empire

John M. Headley

conceived as a leadership of Europe, a broad hegemony steadied by the presence of the Ottoman threat, was later to receive sufficient realization in Spanish diplomacy, bureaucracy, and armed might to hypnotize a century of French statesmen.

In conclusion, any assessment of Gattinara's conception of empire would need to note that it was not so doctrinaire as to be incapable of change during the twelve years of his chancellorship. In this respect the revolt of the *comunidades* seems to have had a salutary effect not only upon Gattinara but also upon other members of the imperial government in making them realize the limits of the possible in the politics of their age. Gattinara's early vision of a uniform law and uniform justice came to be tempered by an enforced respect for native institutions and customs and the value of the *cortes*.[90] On the other hand, the orientation of his view of empire remains firmly focused on Europe and appears quite unaffected by the American experience and Castile's presence in the New World. That the chancellor shared this basic blindness with his contemporaries becomes astonishing only when we reflect that here was a man who knew and had dealt directly with Hernán Cortes; who was a friend and correspondent of Peter Martyr of Anghiera, the first historian of America; and finally who had worked intimately with and given decisive support to Las Casas in his efforts to reform the government of the Indies.[91] Third, Gattinara's idea of empire is essentially moral, legal, and fully capable of admitting national differences; there is no distinction between the concept of universal monarchy and Christian empire.[92] Finally, in his preoccupation with empire, as it applied to an essentially Romanic world, the juristic elements, composing his view of universal monarchy, seem to recede behind eschatological and prophetic ones. In the last months of effective work, Gattinara's mind strained beyond the immediate negotiations with the pope to that final mobilization of Christendom under the emperor's leadership in a crusade against the Turk.[93]

The contemporary prophetic-eschatological understanding of history caused Europeans to experience themselves as participants in a cosmic drama, not as observers in an impersonal process. And 1529–30 can be designated the most apocalyptic year of the sixteenth century. During the autumn of 1529 Suleiman's hordes ad-

Habsburg World Empire and Ghibellinism

vanced upon and besieged Vienna. The Ottoman cataclysm, which could be understood only in universalist terms, sent tremors throughout Europe and convulsed the humanist community. Erasmus, quite expectably, composed the least apocalyptic and the most reluctantly bellicose tract among those that flooded from the press. His *Consolation concerning the Turkish War together with an Exposition of Psalm 28* was the last work ever to be read by Gattinara.[94] More vehement and disturbed was Juan Luis Vives, outstanding proponent of peace and concord among Christian princes, who now rejected any accommodation and urged common action against the Turk.[95] From a cardinal of the church came a remarkably Ghibelline response to the mounting crisis of the age. In his vast historical enterprise, the *Scechina*, completed in 1530 and addressed to the emperor, Giles of Viterbo saw Charles V as the new Cyrus who would cleanse the church; the true king of Jerusalem, who would shepherd the flock into one fold; the church's advocate and even messiah in the struggle against Islam.[96] In a similar vein, the Spanish humanist and Aristotelian, Juan Gines Sepúlveda, product of Bologna and resident at Rome, had greeted Charles's appearance in Italy with an *Exhortation—to War against the Turks* in which he summoned the emperor to that most holy and sacred war, to that task most befitting the office of *imperator*, whereby Jerusalem and "all the remaining lands of the earth might be added to the power and most holy religion of Christians."[97]

During these same months came from the presses of Wittenberg in Saxony a number of tracts bearing upon war and the Turk, culminating in a *Military Sermon* of a very different nature indeed from that of Sepúlveda's *Exhortation*. Martin Luther fully experienced the apocalyptic nature of the moment; at no time in his life was he so certain of the imminence of the world's end as in late 1529 and early 1530.[98] Nevertheless, in calling upon Germans and Europeans to accept the leadership of the emperor in war against the Turk, Luther drove home a distinction that would prove a fatal blow to empire itself. In accordance with his profound belief that Christians were not so many that they could get together in mobs (say nothing of armies), Luther insisted that the subject obey his ruler in war against the Turk but that this duty was not to be understood as part of a crusade, not a holy enterprise, and the

[115]

John M. Headley

emperor should undertake its leadership simply as a secular ruler and not as some sort of universal head or vicar of Christendom.[99] Implicit here is that unraveling of the essential bonds of empire, similar to that already occurring in the ecclesiastical sphere. For despite the trivial witticism of Voltaire, the traditional empire was holy—its sacral character evident in Roman law, in an anointed ruler, and in that ruler's special role as champion of the church. To deny this role, to reject holy war and make crusade into just another secular struggle, had the effect of decisively advancing the disintegration of the Holy Roman Empire. Luther and Sepúlveda—two worlds in irreconcilable conflict!

But when the two Habsburg brothers, Charles and Ferdinand, met in the Tyrol and conferred at length far into the spring, while the diet summoned to Augsburg anxiously awaited their attendance, none could have surmised that process of disintegration soon to be released within the *Reich*: the formation of an independent political league, the consolidation of the territorial church, confessional strife, foreign intervention, and at the end that bitter moment before Metz where the imperial motto *Plus Oultre* had to withdraw before the besieged, who flaunted in conscious defiance the counterdevice of an imperial eagle chained to the Herculean columns with the inscription *Non Ultra Metas*—"not beyond these limits," not beyond Metz.[100] It was May 1530, the high noon of the Habsburg empire in Europe. As the cardinal lay dying at Innsbruck, the true dimensions of the crisis of empire lurked obscurely in the immediate future. When on 5 June Charles's great minister closed his eyes upon the world, who could have said with certainty that an accommodation might not yet be made with the Lutheran specter and that Europe might not be drawn closer to the realization of one sheepfold, one shepherd?

NOTES

1. The following abbreviations are used throughout the notes to this paper: Bibl. Marc.—Biblioteca Marciana; BMB—Bibliothèque municipale de Besançon; BR—Biblioteca Reale di Torino; BRA—Bibliothèque Royale Albert Ier; HHSA—Haus-, Hof- und Staatsarchiv.

2. On Marlianus and the columnar device of Charles V see the excellent article of Earl E. Rosenthal, "The Invention of the Columnar Device of Emperor Charles V at the Court of Burgundy in Flanders in 1516," *Journal of the Warburg and Courtauld Institutes* 36 (1973): 198–230.

3. What follows in this paragraph is indebted to the magisterial study of Marjorie Reeves, *The Influence of Prophecy in the Later Middle Ages: A Study in Joachimism* (Oxford, 1969), esp. pp. 350, 365, 386–87, 431, 447, 507, and passim.

4. The first study of Gattinara appears to have been a Kiel University dissertation of the eighteenth century, written by Philip Frederick Hane, which constitutes a part of his *Historia sacrorum* (Kiel, 1728) that was intended to serve as a highly schematized *Handbuch* for the systematic representation and study of Protestant church history. In accordance with the Melanchthonian tradition Gattinara was here presented as a would-be Protestant. I am indebted to Dr. Birgitte Hvidt of Det Kgl. Bibliotek, Copenhagen, for a reproduction of its copy, that of Kiel University Library having been destroyed in the last war. The Munich University Library has a Leipzig, 1729 copy, 4° H. eccl. 1969 (2). In March and May 1753, M. de Courbezon read two papers to the Academy of Besançon on Gattinara (BMB, MS 1102, vol. 2, fols. 402–31; and Fonds de l'Academie, MS 5, fols. 131v–42). There followed Carlo Tenivelli's "Vita di Mercurino da Gattinara," an unpublished manuscript composed in 1781 and read in the Accademia di Torino on 12 December 1782 (BR, Misc. 114.6). The first real biography of Gattinara was that of Carlo Denina, *Elogio storico di Mercurino di Gattinara Gran Cancelliere dell' imperadore Carlo V e cardinale di S. Chiesa*, Piemontesi Illustri, Vol. 3 (Torino, 1783), which still has merit. Only in the nineteenth century did a number of limited studies of Gattinara begin to appear: M. Huart, *Le Cardinal Arborio de Gattinara Président du Parlement de Dole et chancellier de Charles-Quint* (Besançon, 1876); M. Le Glay, "Études biographiques sur Mercurino Arborio di Gattinara," *Société royale des sciences . . . de Lille. Memoires* 31 (1847): 183–260; Gaudenzio Claretta, "Notizie per servire alla vita del Gran Cancelliere di Carlo V., Mercurino di Gattinara," *Memorie della reale accademia della scienze di Torino* 47 (1897): 67–147 and Gaudenzio Claretta, "Notice pour servir à la vie de Mercurin de Gattinara, Grand Chancelier de Charles-Quint d'àpres des documents originaux," *Société savoisienne d'histoire et d'archéologie* 37 (1898): 245–344. Both Le Glay and Claretta are important for the documents published therein. The event that raised the history of Gattinara's career above the local and obscure and placed it in the main current of historical scholarship was the publication of his autobiography and related documents at the beginning of the twentieth century by Carlo Bornate. See Carlo Bornate, ed., "Historia vite et gestorum per dominum magnum cancellarium . . . con note, aggiunte e documenti," *Miscellanea di storia Italiana* 48 (1915): 233–568. (Hereafter this work will be cited in the following fashion: the autobiography itself, Bornate, "Vita;" the annotations, Bornate, "Noti;" the completion of the autobiography which itself extends only until August 1529, Bornate, "Aggiunte;" several important memoranda and some correspondence, Bornate, "Documenti.") Since Bornate's publication a number of outstanding historical works have given a significant, even crucial role, to Gattinara: Karl Brandi, *The Emperor Charles V*, trans. C. V. Wedgwood (London, 1954); Marcel Bataillon, *Érasme et l'Espagne* (Paris, 1937); Manuel Giménez Fernandez, *Bartolomé de Las Casas*, 2 (Seville, 1960); and Fritz Walser, *Die spanischen Zentralbehörden und der Staatsrat Karls V* (Göttingen, 1959). Although quite incom-

John M. Headley

plete, the best bibliography for Gattinara can be found in Karl Brandi, *Kaiser Karl V.* 2 vols. Vol. 2, *Quellen und Erörterungen* (Darmstadt, 1967), p. 43.

5. P. De Wael, "Collectanea rerum gestorum et eventuum Cartusiae Bruxellensis," 1625, (BRA call number 7043), vol. 1, fol. 157v; Joan. Bapt. de Vaddere, "Historia monasterii nostrae dominae de gratia," Anderlac 1691, (BRA call number 11616), fols. 145–49. Concerning the pressure applied on Margaret to dismiss Gattinara from his office as president of Burgundy, see her letter of May 1518 to the Duke of Savoy, published in Max Bruchet, *Marguerite d'Autriche, Duchesse de Savoie* (Lille, 1927), pp. 407–8. Gattinara's presidency was made further untenable by a complicated lawsuit in which he was himself the defendant. The case provides a splendid example of the operations of justice in the early sixteenth century and has been recognized as such and examined with care only by Andreas Walther, *Die burgundischen Zentralbehörden unter Maximilian I und Karl V* (Leipzig, 1909), pp. 30–38. Walther's assessment, however, relied upon the archives of the Grand Council at Malines without reference to or knowledge of Gattinara's own account in the autobiography and papers in the Gattinara family archives at Vercelli. Cf. Bornate, "Vita" and Bornate, "Noti," pp. 256–66. Although the case very much involved the purchase and forced resale of the Chevigny estate by Gattinara, there is ample evidence that the trial had its political reverberations in Franche-Comté and in the Netherlands government at Malines.

6. Bornate, "Vita" and Bornate, "Noti," pp. 266–67.

7. The correspondence between Gattinara and Margaret of Austria published in L. M. G. Kooperberg, *Margaretha van Oosterrijk, Landvoogdes der Nederlanden, tot den vrede van Kamerijk* (Amsterdam, 1908), pp. 357–58, cf. p. 343, reveals Gattinara's interest in the reception of one of Lemaire's latest works. In the prologue to his *La concorde du gendre humain* (Brussels, 1508), written to honor the conclusion of the peace of Cambrai by Margaret, Jean Lemaire writes: "A noble et magnifique personne Messire Mercurin des seigneurs de Gattinaire docteur en tous droitz. Conseillier de Lempereur, de Larchiduc et de madame leur fille et tante. Et leur president de la conte de Bourgoigne et du pays de Bresse Jehan Lemaire." M. E. Kronenberg, *Nederlandsche Bibliographie van 1500 tot 1540*, 2 ('S-Gravenhage, 1940), no. 3375.

8. Jean Lemaire de Belges, *Oeuvres*, edited by J. Stecher (Geneva, 1969), 3:351–55.

9. On the dating of Gattinara's stay at Scheut I am here following De Wael and HHSA (Belgien), PC 72, fols. 9–10, which is a copy of the act of destitution dated 22 February 1517 (1518). Margaret's letter to the duke of Savoy, May 1518 (see n. 5 above), speaks of the event as having occurred in the recent past. But cf. Le Glay, "Études," pp. 208–10, which dates Gattinara's leaving Scheut as May 1517. At Malines and Dole the new year began at Easter.

10. On the leading role played by Margaret in the imperial election and the background to Gattinara's appointment as grand chancellor see the important work of Walser, *Die spanischen Zentralbehörden*, pp. 141–42. Published posthumously, this work has been reorganized, supplemented, and completed by Rainer Wohlfeil, who in places is as much the author as Walser.

11. On this point see Andreas Walther, *Die Anfänge Karls V* (Leipzig, 1911), pp. 186–87 and the chapter on Chièvres.

12. Walser, *Die spanischen Zentralbehörden*, pp. 161–63; see also the letter of Margaret to Maximilian of 1513 in M. Le Glay, ed., *Correspondance de l'empereur Maximilian Ier et de Marguerite d'Autriche . . . 1507–1519*, 2 vols. (Paris, 1839), 2:243–44.

13. Brandi, *Emperor Charles V*, p. 90.

14. Frances A. Yates, "Charles Quint et l'idee d'empire," *Fêtes et Cérémonies au temps de Charles Quint*, IIe Congrès de l'Association internationale des Historiens de la Renaissance (Paris, 1960), p. 64.

15. Both the copy of the *Responsiva oratio* in the Bibliothèque Nationale and that

Habsburg World Empire and Ghibellinism

in Luxembourg Bibliothèque Nationale being unavailable, that printed in Hane, *Historia sacrorum*, pp. 58–60 was used here:

ut divino satisfiat obsequio, Reipublicae consulatur, sacrum Imperium restauretur, Christianae religioni incrementum accedat, Apostolica sedes stabiliatur, ipsa Petri navicula diu fluctuans, in salutis portum de[d]ucatur: perfidorum quoque Christiani nominis hostium exterminatio sequatur, hincque Salvatoris sententia impleatur, ut fiat unum ovile, & unus pastor . . . Quid praeterea laudabilius iis adscribi posset, quam quod ex ipsa praeteritarum, praesentium & futurarum rerum animadversione eum Imperatorem futurum decernerent, qui diminutum ac fere exhaustum Imperium restaurare posset, qui implumem Aquilam refoveret, renovaret, ac ad propriam naturam deduceret . . . Faxit itaque Deus optimus maximus, ut hujusmodi Imperium sub Carolo magno divisum, & ut plurimum a Christianae religionis hostibus occupatum, sub Carolo Maximo valeat instaurari, ad ipsiusque vivi & veri pastoris obedientiam reduci.

Cf. Kronenberg, *Nederlandsche Bibliographie*, 2, no. 3369.

16. Bornate, "Documenti," pp. 405–6. On the date upon which Charles received the news of his election see his letter to the viceroy of Cerdeña in Manuel Fernandez Alvarez, ed., *Corpus Documental de Carlos V.* (Salamanca, 1973), 1:81.

17. Bornate, "Documenti," p. 406.

18. Ibid., p. 408.

19. Walser, *Die spanischen Zentralbehörden*, p. 174.

20. Bornate, "Documenti," p. 507.

21. Cf. Dante *De mon.* 1.11–14. Except for one parallel not treated by Brandi, the present author has intentionally avoided considering specific influences of Dante on Gattinara, which can be found in the excellent article by Karl Brandi, "Dantes Monarchia und die Italienpolitik Mercurino Gattinaras," *Deutsches Dante-Jahrbuch* 24 (1942): 1–19. On Bartolus's appreciation of the emperor's power rather than as expositor of particularistic sovereignty see Jan Baszkiewicz, "Quelques remarques sur la conception de Dominum mundi dans l'oeuvre de Bartolus," (Bartolo da Sassoferrato. Il Studi e documenti per il VI Centenario) *Convegno commemorativo del VI centenario di Bartolo* (Perugia, 1959), pp. 9–25.

22. Cf. Aug. *De civ. dei* 19. 12–28. In his remonstrance to the Emperor Maximilian of September 1514, entitled "Remonstrances de Messire Mercurin de Gatinare [*sic*], President de Bourgongne faictes à Maximilian I Empereur sur les traverses causées à sa personne et au Parlement par le Marschal de Bourgongne" (BMB, Collection Chifflet, t. 187, fols. 116–34). Gattinara twice quotes the famous *Remota iustitia . . .* (*De civ. dei* 4. 4) and draws a fairly extensive passage from Augustine's treatment of Psalm 84(85): 11, cf. Aug. *Enarr. in Ps.* 84, Corpus Christianorum 39. 1172. ll. 14–20. I am here dependent upon a late sixteenth- or early seventeenth-century copy of the "Remonstrance," fols. 127v, 133, and 120. I wish also to take the opportunity to thank Mme. O. Paris and the staff of the Bibliothèque municipale de Besançon for making this material available to me; the manuscript is important with respect to Roman law and humanism and is being prepared for publication.

23. According to Mota's speech (see below) the election was accepted, "mas con el parescer de todos los grandes y perlados, caballeros y personas del su Consejo que en su corte se hallaron, que no solo lo aconsejaron pero firmaronlo de sus nonbres." *Cortes de los antiguos reinos de León y de Castilla*, La Real Academia de la Historia, 5 vols. (Madrid, 1882), 4:294. Walser, *Die spanischen Zentralbehörden*, p. 142, would support the belief that behind the hard-won unanimity, ultimately presented by the royal council, was more than just the sole initial vote of Gattinara for the acceptance, as the chancellor would have us believe from his autobiography. Cf. Bornate, "Vita," pp. 272–73.

24. Alonso de Santa Cruz, *Crónica del emperador Carlos V*, edited by Ricardo Beltrán y Rózpide and Antonio Blázquez y Delgado-Aguilera, 5 vols. (Madrid,

John M. Headley

1920–25), 1:204; Juan Beneyto Perez, *España y el problema de Europa: Contribución a la historia de la idea de imperio* (Madrid, 1942), pp. 253–54.

25. Quoted in Joan Reglà Campistol, *Introduccio a la Historia de la Corona d'Aragó. Dels origens a la Nova Planta* (Palma de Mallorca, 1969), pp. 102–4.

26. Ricardo del Arco y Garay, *La idea de imperio en la política y la literatura españolas* (Madrid, 1944), pp. 135–36. Cf. Beneyto Perez, *España*, pp. 216, 231.

27. Brandi, *Quellen*, pp. 153–54; Walser, *Die spanischen Zentralbehörden*, p. 178; and the important collective *consulta* composed by Gattinara to the emperor at the end of 1523 printed in the appendix, Ernest Gossart, *Espagnols et Flamands au XVIe siècle: Charles Quint roi d'Espagne*, (Brussels, 1910), pp. 245–46.

28. Here is not the place for an exhaustive analysis and conclusive identification of BR, St. d'Ital. 75 (Miscellanea politica del secolo XVI), but the following general points may be made to suggest that it preeminently constitutes a fragment of Gattinara's chancellery files: forty-three separate items (39.9 percent of the total material) can be immediately identified as by, to, or read by Gattinara, according to the address, marginal comments, or endorsement; forty-eight separate items (32.1 percent) can be associated with him as ambassadorial instructions, relevant political affairs, communications of his cousin Giovanni Bartolomeo Gattinara to the emperor, copies of treaties that would be likely for reference, along with the splendid exposition of the office of grand chancellor composed apparently at Gattinara's request and for his benefit by the Audiencier Philippe Hanneton (fols. 683–86v; cf. Claretta, *Notice*, p. 312); twenty-seven separate items (25.5 percent) appear more removed but still belong to the period and might well have constituted part of Gattinara's system of reference; nine separate items (2.5 percent) derive from the decades immediately after Gattinara's death and must have been bound into the *mazzo* at a later date, perhaps in the nineteenth century. (Cf. also below, nn. 38 and 75). BR, St. d'Ital. 75, fols. 569–70 is written in a fine humanist, roman hand that would suggest the work of the Latin secretaries, Gaspar Argillense or Sanchez de Orihuela. (Cf. Luis Nuñez Contreras, *Un registro de cancelleria de Carlos V. El MS 917 de la biblioteca nacional de Madrid* [Madrid, 1965], p. xxix). The changes in the draft appear to be stylistic; what seems to be another hand has written "pene alio orbe," then crossed out "orbe" and completed the rendering of "con otro nuevo mundo de oro fecho para él" (*Cortes*, 4:294–95) from the original with "aurifero orbe," (fol. 569v). The published Latin version reveals a considerable number of stylistic changes beyond the draft, and although it includes those changes and additions made in the draft it has a concluding section the manuscript for which is lacking. This manuscript may well have become separated and lost from the present *mazzo*, BR, St. d'Ital. 75. I have used here the Münchner Universitäts bibliothek copy, 4 Hist. 2580, entitled *Caroli Ro [manorum] Regis Recessuri adlocutio in conventu Hispaniarum*. Only two known copies exist in the United States: one at Harvard designated as "Rome, J. Mazochius, 1519" and the second at the New York Public Library designated as "Augsburg? 1520?" I have not yet been able to consult the New York copy, but the Munich version constitutes a separate edition quite distinct from that identified by Harvard as Mazochius's. The catalog of the Bibliothèque nationale (26:1049) not only indicates the presence of a copy of the Latin publication but also a German one (cat. no. Mp. 1570). Upon inspection the latter would appear to derive from the press of Michael Hillen in Antwerp if the banderole on the title page bearing the letters MHAV can be so credited. The "aurifero orbe" passage is here rendered "unnd eyner andern/also tzu reden guldene welt" sig. [Av]. Antonio Palau y Dulcet, *Manual de librero hispanoamericano* (Oxford-Madrid-Barcelona, 1950), 3:172, tentatively suggests Augsburg as the place of publication for the Latin version but gives the impossible date 1518. Late 1520 or early 1521 would be more likely. But more important to know is the place of publication of the Munich copy, which must wait upon an analysis of watermarks and other bibliographical evidence. Another level

Habsburg World Empire and Ghibellinism

of analysis that needs to be pursued before we can gain greater insight into the authorship of the speech attributed to Mota and into the public image that the royal-imperial council sought to project is a close examination of the literary sources and overall content of the speech. Menéndez Pidal has pointed out the use of Claudian (XXX [XXIX] *Laus Serenae*, ll. 64, 66) [*Hispania*] *contulit Augustos. . . . haec generat qui cuncta regant* for the idea that while other lands may be rich in material resources, Spain produces world rulers. Ramon Menéndez Pidal, ed., *Historia de España* (Madrid, 1966), 18:xxviii. With the recrudescence of the imperial theme during these years the late Roman imperial poet enjoyed renewed attention. Although it cannot be argued that any one person exercises a monopoly over the citing of an earlier author, particularly at a time of revived interest in that author, it is worth noting that in his Remonstrance of 1514 (see above, n. 22) Gattinara had drawn two passages from Claudian's *Panegyricus de quarto consulatu Honorii Augusti* (ll. 276–77, 267–68; cf. BMB (Coll. Chif.), t. 187, fol. 131v) for quotation. Of Mota's classical interests, on the other hand, we know nothing except that he was adept at several languages. But to keep this largely circumstantial evidence in proper perspective, Peter Giles in his panegyric celebrating the entry of Charles into Antwerp in 1520 will quote the same passages from Claudian in the same reverse order (*Hypotheses sive argumenta spectaculorum*; [Antwerp, 1520], sig. [bii]; cf. sig. ci). As it is most improbable that Giles had ever seen Gattinara's manuscript, it would seem that both secretary and chancellor drew from a common secondary source. In the same line of argument, one may note in the ostensible speech of Mota the following statement: "ya sabeis que asy como no es menos virtud conservar lo ganado que adquerirlo de nuevo, asi no es menor vituperio no seguir la victoria, que ser vencido" (*Cortes*, 4:295), which seems to have its root in the very common Latin proverb *Non minor est virtus quam querere, parta tueri* (Hans Walther, ed., *Lateinische Sprichwörter und Sentenzen des Mittelalters* [Göttingen, 1963–67], no. 18042; cf. no. 5200) that Gattinara develops at some length again in his "Remonstrance" (fol. 125v). Furthermore, it may be observed that the particular designation of America as a "new gold-bearing world" seems to have had some currency in the circles of the imperial chancellery, for in August 1521 as leading member of Charles V's delegation to the Calais conference, Gattinara composed a public denunciation of Francis I's politics, wherein he stated that by equipping his fleets, the emperor propagated the dominion of Christ *in novo aurifero orbe*. Pierre de Vaissiere, ed., *Journal de Jean Barrillon*, 2 vols. (Paris, 1899), 2:227. Finally, to sum up, we are merely arguing here that the authorship of the speech attributed to Mota may be collective and in its several redactions a product of the royal council. At least the question needs to be considered in the light of this possibility. For even the best Spanish historians Mota's speech has tended to become one of the great vested interests of Spanish historiography: Jose Antonio Maravall, *Carlos V y el pensamiento politico del renacimiento* (Madrid, 1960), p. 112, while accepting Mota's speech at face value, can argue without any apparent reason that Gattinara's speech to the cortes of Valladolid in 1523 represents a collective enterprise. We merely suggest here that on better grounds the reverse may be argued.

29. BR, St. d'Ital. 75, fol. 570: "meminerit caeteras gentes voluptati et utilitati servire solam hispaniam ad honorem natam pro honore et vivere posse et mori." In the Latin printed edition this passage appears at sig. Aiiv. Here as in all other cases throughout this article the manuscript and typographical abbreviations will be silently expanded.

30. See the remarks of A. P. d'Entrèves, *Dante as a Political Thinker* (Oxford, 1952), pp. 37 and 51, on Dante *Ep.* 5 and *Ep.* 7. 2 (Toynbee ed.) On Gattinara, BMB, (Coll. Chif.) 186, fol. 128v and Bornate, "Vita," pp. 323, 325, 356, 363.

31. Bornate, "Documenti," pp. 408–9.

John M. Headley

32. Gossart, *Espagnols et Flamands*, pp. 245–46. Cf. Seneca *De clem.* 1. 19. 6: "Unum est inexpugnabile munimentum amor civium."

33. On *providentia* as exercised by Roman emperors see M. P. Charlesworth, "The Virtues of a Roman Emperor," *Proceedings of the British Academy* 23 (1973): 105–33, esp. 118 ff. Gattinara does not use the term itself, but the notion is present. On the religious and particularly chivalric background to the formation of Charles V's moral character and the previous influence of such persons as Chièvres, Margaret, Glapion, Adrian of Utrecht, see the suggestive remarks by Carlos Clavería, *Le Chevalier Délibéré de Oliver de la Marche y sus versiones españolas del siglo XVI* (Zaragoza, n.d.), pp. 48–50, 68–69.

34. Gossart, *Espagnols et Flamands*, pp. 250–57.

35. Paul Kalkoff, *Die Depeschen des Nuntius Aleander vom Wormser Reichstage 1521* (Halle a. S., 1897), pp. 102, 112; A. Wrede, ed., *Deutsche Reichstagsakten unter Kaiser Karl V*, Jüngere Reihe (Gotha, 1896), 2:521, 827.

36. Bornate, "Vita," pp. 263–66, 343, 354. Cf. P. S. Allen et al., eds., *Opus epistolarum Des. Erasmi Roterodami*, 12 vols. (Oxford, 1906–58), 4:479. Cf. also Vaddere, "Historia Monasterii," on his exemplary conduct at Scheut.

37. See G. A. Bergenroth, ed., *Calendar of Letters, Despatches and State Papers relating to the Negotiations between England and Spain* (London, 1866), 2:375 (hereafter cited as *SP Span.*).

38. BR, St. d'Ital. 75, fol. 39v: "el dicho duque [Sessa] y vos como devos mismos sin mostrar de tener comission de nos sobrello, de dezir a su santidad que no queriendo su santidad de usar de officio de comun pastor por la quietud de ytalia y de la cristiandad que ental caso seriamos forcado usar de nuestro officio como emperador y que su santidad debria pensar que tenemos ahun en nuestras manos el Rey de francia y que es en nuestro poder de saltar lo quando querremos y usando con el de liberidad y dexando nos delo que le havemos pedido fazer lo nuestro amigo." The editors of *SP Span.* apparently ignored Herrera's Instructions (fols. 37–40v), together with other relevant materials to be found in this *mazzo*.

39. Karl Brandi, "Nach Pavia: Pescara und die italienischen Staaten, Sommer und Herbst 1525," Berichte und Studien zur Geschichte Karls V., 17, *Nachrichten von der Gesellschaft der Wissenschaften zu Göttingen*, Philologisch-Historische Klasse (1939), pp. 202–3; cf. Bornate, "Vita," p. 348. See also Hubert Jedin, *A History of the Council of Trent* (London, 1957), 1:227–28, 240–41 for Gattinara's use of a council.

40. Bornate, "Documenti," 502–3: "se assossegaran en alguna forma los dichos tumultos de allemagna: y los culpados de haver sostenido y favorecido los dichos errores de luthero . . . se podran assegurar y mas facilmente retirarse de los dichos errores; especialmente dandoles camino con que rectamente se pueda determinar la verdad de la doctrina evangelica en la qual principalmente se funda la dicha secta."

41. Andreas Walther, "Kanzleiordnungen Maximilians I, Karls V, und Ferdinands I," *Archiv für Urkundenforschung* 2 (1909): 388; Marcel Bataillon, *Erasmo y España* (Mexico, 1966), p. 231.

42. Sigs. Aviiv–Aviiiv. The collective authorship of the report on the battle of Pavia and of similar public statements of the imperial government stemming from the chancellery is evident from the title of the Pavia tract: *Relacion delas nuevas de Italia sacadas delas cartas que los capitanes y comisario del Emperador y Rey nuestro señor han escripto a su magestad: assi dela victoria contra el rey de Francia come de otras cosas alla acaecidas: vista y corregida por el señor gran Chanciller y consejo de su magestad.*

43. Ibid., pp. 335–37. But cf. Bornate, "Vita," pp. 332–33. The detailed legal and diplomatic knowledge evident particularly in the first reply to Clement VII points to Gattinara as both presiding over and participating in the production of that double compilation entitled *Pro Divo Carolo eius nominis quinto Romanorum Imperatore Invictissimo, pio, felice, semper Augusto, Patrepatriae, in satisfactionem quidem sine talione eorum quae in illum scripta, ac pleraque etiam in vulgum aedita fuere, Apologetici libri duo*

Habsburg World Empire and Ghibellinism

nuper ex Hispanis allati cum alijs nonnullis, quorum catalogos ante cuiusque exordium reperies (Mainz: Joannis Schoeffer, 1527). (This is the definitive edition.)

44. *Pro Divo*, p. 1. The imperial propaganda campaign of 1526–27 deserves separate, extensive treatment. The main features can only be mentioned here. According to the colophon the first to appear was the Cologne edition (March 1527) *Epistolae duae altera Clementis VII . . . altera Karoli*, which included only the first of Clement's two letters and Charles's reply (Bibl. Marc. Miscell. 2451.5). The Miguel de Eguía edition (Alcalá, April 1527) included all materials bearing on the controversy between emperor and pope except the very brief second letter from Clement. I have consulted copies both in BMB (Coll. Granvelle) and HHSA (Belgien), PA 94, fols. 1–40v. The Antwerp editions are numerous: a Latin edition by Joannes Graphaeus including both the French and the papal controversies (19 August); the same in Dutch (12 September); a Latin edition of the French controversy by Michael Hiller (August); a Latin edition of the French controversy by Marten de Keyser (1527); a French edition of the same by Willem Vorstermann; then two Latin editions of 1527 that include both controversies: *Pro Carolo V apologetici II* jointly by Gottfried Dumaeus and Marten de Keyser and another by Joannes Graphaeus identical with his first. See Kronenberg, *Nederlandsche Bibliographie*, 1–3, nos. 1263, 1266, 1264, 1265, 1269, 3297, and 0721, respectively. As privileged printer to the chancellery of the empire at Mainz, Joannes Schoeffer was the obvious agent for the purveying of these materials within the *Reich*. Cf. F. W. E. Roth, "Die Mainzer Buchdruckerfamilie Schoeffer," *Beihefte zum Centralblatt für Bibliothekswesen* 9 (Leipzig, 1892): 3–11. Parts of the two controversies would enjoy reprintings in the course of the century and the several parts constituting the Mainz edition can be found distributed through Melchior Goldast's *Politica imperialia* and *Collectio constitutionum imperialium*. On the financing of the Eguía edition see Bataillon, *Erasmo y España*, p. 230.

45. *Pro Divo*, pp. 32, 76.

46. Ibid., pp. 77–80, 84.

47. Ibid., pp. 98–99.

48. The papal reaction to the materials in *Pro Divo* can be followed in Bergenroth, *SP Span.*, 3/1:1039, 1045–47, 1056–58, 3/2:8–9, 37–42, 76–77.

49. Allen et al., *Opus epistolarum*, 6:470–71.

50. For the political and literary background to the publication of the *De monarchia* and its German translation, see the valuable study of Andreas Burckhardt, *Johannes Basilius Herold. Kaiser und Reich im protestantischen Schrifttum des Basler Buchdrucks um die Mitte des 16. Jahrhunderts* (Basel and Stuttgart, 1967), pp. 194–212. Burckhardt disputes the suggestion made by Peter Bietenholz that the manuscript of the *De monarchia*, presumably sent by Gattinara to Erasmus, served as the basis for printer's copy.

51. On the different positions taken by Gattinara and the emperor concerning a council see Gerhard Müller, "Zur Vorgeschichte des Tridentinums: Karl V und das Konzil aährend des Pontifikates Clemens' VII," *Zeitschrift für Kirchengeschichte* 74 (1963): 87, 91–94. Although in the opinion of the present writer Müller is correct in distinguishing between the two developing positions, he errs in attributing to Gattinara purely political motives.

52. J. S. Brewer, James Gairdner, and R. H. Brodie, eds., *Letters and Papers, Foreign and Domestic, on the Reign of Henry VIII* (London, 1862–1932), 4/2, no. 4977.

53. Bornate, "Vita," p. 348; HHSA (Belgien), PA 94, fols. 451–52v; cf. Brandi, *Quellen*, p. 185.

54. Alfonso de Valdés, *Diálogo de las cosas ocurridas en Roma*, ed. José F. Montesinos (Madrid, 1969), p. 155.

55. For a presentation of Valdés that emphasizes the influence of Gattinara rather than of Erasmus, cf. Sosio Pezzella, "Alfonso de Valdés e la politica religiosa di Carlo V," *Studi e Materiali di storia della religioni* 36 (1965): 211–68, esp. pp. 223, 265–68.

John M. Headley

56. Brandi, *Quellen*, p. 182.

57. Cf. Bergenroth, *SP Span.*, 4:195–201, 209–10, 235–38.

58. HHSA (Belgien), PA 94, fol. 446: "Et qui si avant mon embarquement survenoit nouvelle certaine de la venue du pape en barcelonne je me detiendroye illeques pour non faillir au service de votre maieste en telle coniuncture."

59. *Par.* 6. 105; T. Neri, G. Martellotti, E. Bianche, N. Sapegno, eds., *Francesco Petrarca. Rime, Trionfi e Poesie Latine* (Milan/Naples, [1951]), p. 804, "Ad Italiam"; Paolo Giovio, *Epistolae*, ed. Giuseppe Guido Ferrero (Rome, 1956), 2:10; on Richelieu see Hermann Weber, "Richelieu und das Reich," in *Frankreich und das Reich im 16. und 17. Jahrhundert* (Göttingen, n.d.), p. 39.

60. Bornate, "Documenti," p. 429.

61. Cf. Claretta, *Notice*, p. 323: Remonstrance of 1523 to Charles; Gossart, *Espagnols et Flamands*, p. 250; *Cortes*, 4:348: to the *cortes* of 1523 Gattinara says that the fall of Rhodes allows the Turk to threaten "sobre Napoles e Italia." Cf. also F. de Laiglesia, *Estudios históricos 1515–1555*, 3 vols. (Madrid, 1918), 1:367 for the continuation of this cortes in 1524: where Gattinara speaks of the kingdoms of Naples and Sicily and "todos los potentados de Italia." On the medieval understanding of Italy in connection with the notion of the *regnum Italicum* see B. H. Sumner, "Dante and the *Regnum Italicum*," *Medium Aevum* 1 (1932): 22–23.

62. Gossart, *Espagnols et Flamands*, pp. 250 ff.; cf. the original HHSA (Belgien), PC 68, fol. 22–22v, which indicates general agreement within the royal council.

63. See Alva's advice in Federico Chabod, "¿ Milan o los Países Bajos? Las discusiones en España sobre la 'alternitiva' de 1544," *Carlos V (1500–1558). Homenaje de la Universidad de Granada* (Granada, 1958), pp. 345–64, 369–70; also idem, *Storia di Milano nell' epoca di Carlo V*, Fondazione Trecanni degli Alfieri ([Torino, 1971]), pp. 55–56, 101–7 and passim where the emphasis falls upon the centrality of Milan.

64. Federico Chabod, *Lo stato di Milano nella prima metà del secolo XVI* (Roma, 1955), p. 26; Eugenio Albèri, ed., *Relazioni degli ambasciatore venete al senato*, 2 vols. (Firenze, 1840), 2:57; Brandi, "Nach Pavia," p. 219.

65. Gossart, *Espagnols et Flamands*, pp. 250–57.

66. Bornate, "Documenti," pp. 463–69: *consulta* Sept. 1525.

67. Ibid., p. 462: *consulta* Sept. 1525.

68. Gossart, *Espagnols et Flamands*, p. 257.

69. Bornate, "Vita," p. 307.

70. Albèri, *Relazioni*, p. 59.

71. Adolf Berger, "Encyclopedic Dictionary of Roman Law," *Transactions of the American Philosophical Society*, n.s. 43/2 (1953): 530.

72. Brandi, "Nach Pavia," p. 151. Cf. also Bergenroth, *SP Span.*, 2:517, for Gattinara's favorable reaction to the pope's support of Siena's independence, while urging it in December 1522 to pay annually a certain sum to the emperor in recognition of his suzerainty.

73. Cf. John Lynch, *Spain and the Habsburgs: Empire and Absolutism*, 2 vols. (New York, 1964), 1:80.

74. Cf. Michel François, "L'idée d'empire en France sous Charles-Quint," *Charles-Quint et son temps*, Colloques internationaux du Centre National de la Recherche Scientifique 30 September–3 October 1958 (Paris, 1958), p. 30, who quotes the Venetian ambassador Marion Cavelli in his *relazione* of 1546, concerning the differences that oppose France to Charles, that the bone of contention was not some particular state "ma ad un certo modo della superiorità ed arbitrio della Christianità." See also Giovio, *Epistolae*, 1:282 and Maravall, *Carlos V*, pp. 98–99.

75. Brandi, "Nach Pavia," p. 206. On the ransacking of the archives at Barcelona to equip Gattinara with legal arguments for the occupation of Languedoc and Provence there are scattered among the papers in BR, St. d'Ital. 75, which has been identified here as preeminently being part of Gattinara's personal working file, fols.

Habsburg World Empire and Ghibellinism

28–30v, 190–221v, materials under the title *Acta & documenta in authentica forma extracta ex regis archivis Barchinonae Comitatuum Civitatum, Terrarum, Castellorum, ac Jurium in Gallia per comites Barchinonae & deinde per Reges Aragoniae acquisitorum & post per plures annos possessorum ac consequentes ad Caesarem nunc gloriose Imperantem & Regna[n]tem spetantium [sic] et pertinentium.* Gattinara will draw upon these materials for his memorandum, written during the negotiations leading up to the treaty of Madrid, the French version of which appears in BR, St. d'Ital. 75, fols. 642–74v under the title *Informacion des droicts et querrelles de la maison de Bourgoinge [sic] contre France Sur les demandes faictes depuis La prinse du Roy de France pour parvenir a bonne paix.* The Latin version of this memorandum was published by Bornate, *Memoire de Chancelier de Gattinara sur les droits de Charles-Quint au duché de Bourgogne* (Brussels, 1907), which finds among its biblical citations John 10:16 and Psalm 84(85):11. Cf. Bergenroth, *SP Span.*, 3/1:93–94. See also HHSA (Belgien), PA 92, fol. 11 on the search through the Barcelona archives for legal claims to Languedoc.

76. HHSA (Belgien), PA 95, fols. 324–27, esp. 326v–27: "Si a este effecto queriendo su magestad apoderarse y assegurar del dicho reyno de Inglaterra: se hauria de hazer con color del desaffyo y por el drecho que su magestad puede iustamente pretender al dicho reyno: mejor que el rey que agora lo possee: por muchos cabos: o si sera mejor mostrar de hazerlo: por vengar la injuria de la reyna y para que la princessa su hija no quede bastarda: ny privada de la succession paterna: sin mostrar que su magestad quiera occupar el dicho reyno por si."

77. Fernand Braudel, *The Mediterranean and the Mediterranean World in the Age of Philip II*, 2 vols. (New York, 1973), 1:254. But cf. Bergenroth, *SP Span.*, 3/2:577–79, 878, 887 for the reality of this issue and the diplomatic mission of Cornelius Scepperus, Gattinara's subordinate and humanist friend, to Scotland.

78. Rawdon Brown, ed., *Calendar of State Papers and Manuscripts existing in the Archives and Collections of Venice 1520–1526* (London, 1869), 3, no. 401 (hereafter cited as *SP Venice*).

79. Chabod, *Lo stato*, pp. 8–16.

80. Carlo Bornate, "L'apogeo della casa di Absburgo e l'opera politica di un Gran Cancelliere di Carlo V," *Nuova Rivista Storica*, 3 (1919): 417.

81. Brown, *SP Venice*, 3, no. 956.

82. Ibid., no. 1064.

83. Ibid., nos. 401, 438; Ernest Gossart, "L'apprentissage politique de l'empereur," in *Espagnols et Flamands*, p. 196.

84. Brown, *SP Venice*, 3, no. 461.

85. Ibid., no. 1069.

86. Vittorio Cian, *Un illustre nunzio pontificio del Rinascimento Baldassar Castiglione*, Studi e testi, 156 (Città del Vaticano, 1951), pp. 126–28.

87. See the well-balanced and insightful article of Giovanni Barbero, "Idealismo e realismo nella politica del Gattinara, Gran Cancelliere di Carlo V," *Bollettino storico per la Provincia di Novara* 58 (1967): 3–18.

88. On Gattinara's continuing concern for Genoa and her role in the *monarchia* see Brown, *SP Venice*, 3, no. 746; Brandi, "Nach Pavia," p. 208; HHSA (Belgien), PA 91/3, fols. 258, 333v; PA 92, fol. 13; PA 94, fol. 470v; PA 95, fol. 326.

89. Benedetto Varchi, *Storia fiorentina* (Cologne, 1721), p. 355. "Lasciò l'Imperadore tutta l'Italia piena di grandissimo sospetto, perciocchè, sebbene egli era riuscito non mica barbaro, ed efferato, come se l'erano immaginato le genti, per le crudeltà fatte da Ministri, e soldati suoi, ma costumatissimo, e benigno molto, e sebbene aveva, oltre il credere di molti, renduto lo Stato di Milano al Duca, si conosceva però da chi vi badava che . . . i quali avevano osservato i modi, e l'azioni sue, che non fosse stato fatto a caso, e senz'arte l'aver elgi così piacevolmente accarezzato ognuno, e cercato con ogni industria, e amorevolezza di farsi benevoli, e obbligati tutti coloro, i quali potevano, o aiutare l'imprese sue, o impedirle." On the appar-

John M. Headley

ently conscious effort made by Spaniards at this time to ingratiate themselves with Italians and reduce the shock of Spain's dominance in the peninsula cf. Bergenroth, *SP Span.*, 4/1: 484–85, 568–69, 585.

90. See, for example, Gattinara's mid-October 1521 letter to the emperor, HHSA (Belgien), PC 4, fols. 181–181v, on Diego de Mendoza's coming as viceroy to Catalonia from Valencia, where he had gained a bad reputation. Gattinara manifests alarm that Mendoza, who needs to be bridled, is against the form of the constitution of the country and the privileges of the city of Barcelona, which he scandalizes. Published in Karl Lanz, ed., *Aktenstücke und Briefe zur Geschichte Kaiser Karls V* (Wien, 1853), Monumenta Habsburgica, Zweite Abteilung, 1:386–87. Cf. also Walser, *Die spanischen Zentralbehörden*, pp. 178–83.

91. On Europe's "mental shutters" coming down before the immense novelty of America see J. H. Elliott, *The Old World and the New 1492–1650* (Cambridge, 1970), chap. 1; on Cortes's relation to Gattinara see Antonio de Solis, *Istoria della conquista del Messico* (Venice, 1715), pp. 490–505; on Pietro Martyro Anghiera see his *Opus epistolarum Petri Martyris Mediolanensis* (Alcala, 1530), passim; on Las Casas see his *Historia de las Indias*, ed. Agustin Millares Carlo and Lewis Hanke (Mexico-Buenos Aires, 1951), 3:278–363 and Manuel Giménez Fernández, *Bartolome de las Casas* (Seville, 1960), 2: passim.

92. But cf. the well-known article by Ramon Menéndez Pidal, "La idea imperial de Carlos V," which first appeared in the *Revista Cubana* 10 (1937) and attained its definitive form as the preface to volume 18 of *Historia de España*, edited by the same author. For a good criticism, other than those of Brandi and Rassow, of Menéndez Pidal's distinction between *monarquía universal* and *universitas christiana* see Chabod, *Storia*, p. 132. See also the articles by Menéndez Pidal and J. Vicens Vives in *Charles-Quint et son temps*, Colloques internationaux du Centre National de la Recherche Scientifique 30 September–3 October 1958 (Paris, 1958), pp. 1–21 and the discussion therein. On Gattinara's recognition of national differences, see Walser, *Die spanischen Zentralbehörden*, pp. 171–74.

93. Bergenroth, *SP Span.*, 4/1:620. By *cruzada* Gattinara intends here the special indulgence tax authorized by the papacy, not "crusade" itself; but the diplomatic activity of these months with respect to obtaining support from England and France can be traced in Bergenroth, *SP Span.*, 4/1:279–80, 297–98, 307, 338–45, 397–98, 411–14.

94. J. Clericus, ed., *Desiderii Erasmi Roterodami opera omnia* (Leiden, 1704), 5:345–68, esp. pp. 367–68; see Allen et al., *Opus epistolarum*, 8:463, the important letter of Scepperus to Erasmus, 28 June 1530.

95. Carlos B. Noreña, *Juan Luis Vives* (The Hague, 1970), p. 225.

96. John W. O'Malley, *Giles of Viterbo on Church and Reform* (Leiden, 1968), pp. 116, 130, 176–77.

97. J. G. Sepulveda, "Ad Carolum V. Imperatorem invictissimum ut facta cum omnibus Christianis pace bellum suscipiat in Turcas, Cohortatio," *Opera, cum edita, tum inedita* (Madrid, 1780), 4:373–74: "Age igitur, Imperator felicissime, et omnes cunctandi moras abrumpe, omissisque his bellis, quae, si verum quaerimus, parum habent et emolumenti et dignitatis, optatissimaque pace Christianis reddita, ad haec propera, in haec toto animo et cunctis opibus incumbe, ad quae officium te Imperatoris vocat, pietas hortatur tum in patriam, tum in Deum et religionem, quae cum libertate et salute reipublicae Christianae . . . in summum discrimen adducitur . . . ut miseram Graeciam et finitimas Christianorum regiones cum Byzantio regia jam pridem Romanorum Imperatorum in libertatem asseras, et minoris Asiae opulentissimae regionis, et finitimarum gentium usque Mesopotamiam et Aegyptum imperio potitus, in sancta urbe Hierusalem teste nostrae redemtionis oculata . . . ut te Imperatore et bellum administrante, reliquus terrarum orbis ditioni Christianorum et sanctissimae religioni adjiciatur."

[126]

Habsburg World Empire and Ghibellinism

98. John M. Headley, *Luther's View of Church History* (New Haven and London, 1967), pp. 245–46.

99. *D. Martin Luthers Werke* (Weimar, 1909), 30/2:173–74, 189; cf. also 114, 130–31, esp. 130, ll. 27–28, which clash with Gattinara's statement to the cortes of Valladolid of 1523—"de que Dios nuestro Sennor merritisimamente le hizo Rey e sennor, e sobre los quales le elegió e constituyó su bicario y generalmente de toda la cristiandad, cuya universal cabeça es su Alteza," *Cortes*, 4:335.

100. On this point see Earl Rosenthal, "Plus Ultra, Non Plus Ultra, and the Columnar Device of Emperor Charles V," *Journal of the Warburg and Courtauld Institutes* 34 (1971): 216.

4

The European Debate on Universal Monarchy

Franz Bosbach

1. Introduction

In early modern Europe the idea of Universal Monarchy was the subject of a debate established by contemporaries in order to form a judgement on the question of how international
politics should take shape. The special question under discussion was not in what way
different states or nations could be united within one dominion, but rather how the union of
different dominions could be avoided. Therefore it ought to be said that Universal Monarchy
appears to have had a rather bad image, at least at first sight, though there were some exceptions which have to be dealt with in the course of this essay.

There were some aspects in the debate over Universal Monarchy which had a general
characteristic significance. The theme of Universal Monarchy only qualifiedthe foreign
policy of a certain number of states, and in this respect two things were
remarkable:

1. Universal Monarchy applied only to European great powers and the concept was only
    used in such situations, where one of them was suspected of illegal power politics against
    the rest of Europe.
2. Universal Monarchy appeared mostly in debates over conflicts and events that stood in
    connection to the rivalries between the house of Habsburg and the French king. The
    conflict between the Habsburgs and France formed one of the determinants of interna-
    tional politics in early modern Europe from the sixteenth to the eighteenth century, and
    Universal Monarchy accompanied, so to speak, the struggle of these two powers down
    the ages. Normally it was a Habsburg or a French ruler who became the universal
    monarch, as either the emperor of the Holy Roman Empire, the king of Spain or the king
    of France. And it was from this context that the debate over Universal Monarchy derived
    its decisive impulse.

To give an answer to the question, what the significance of Universal Monarchy was in the
context of European international politics, and how the debate developed, it is necessary to
evaluate the political literature of the contemporary publicists concerned with foreign affairs,
for this is the source material where political events are observed and commented on most
closely. Most often the subject of the discussions was not a theoretical
problem of politics or of international relations, but rather an argument used in a propagandistic manner for or against certain political practices. The study of these discussions offers
an insight into the so to say 'normal' and popular level of political thought of most of the
people of the time. Of course only a few of them took part in that discussion by writing
personally, but those who made contributions did so in front of the general public and in front
of people who were interested and could read and buy the publications, in particular the
pamphlets. Since it was the intention of these publicists to arouse public interest, they had to
be at least understandable if not convincing. That means that the language and the arguments
had to correspond with the political standards and ideas known and accepted

by the general public of the time. There are two distinctive groups of source material.

1. The first group consists of the propagandistic pamphlets. In early modern Europe pamphlet literature was an obvious and essential part of any politics and therefore of international politics as well. This kind of literature was directed to a public audience and ideas of Universal Monarchy were employed for the purpose of propaganda in order either to criticize or to defend the politics of the government.
2. The second group of writings is formed by official or semi-official statements and declarations of governments participating in a political or military conflict. It includes the manifestos published by every belligerent power as a legitimation of its wars; moreover it includes the texts of treaties, instructions for ambassadors and similar things.

In the following the question to be answered is, how the debate over Universal Monarchy developed. For this purpose a special procedure is needed. Considering the wide range of variations and the multiplicity of arguments it is most helpful to speak only of the decisive elements of the debate, that is, not to ask for the specific and individual character of a single pamphlet but to ask what is common, what can be found in all the contributions which contributed to the discussion. Indeed there are some arguments and subjects of crucial importance for the debate as a whole, what these are will become clear by dealing with the contents of propagandistic arguments. Once the structure of the debate has been elaborated in this way, the changes which the concept of Universal Monarchy underwent in different periods will become clear.

As I mentioned in the beginning, I will touch first on the medieval elements and traditions linked to the idea of Universal Monarchy. In a second part I will describe the main characteristics of the debate over Universal Monarchy in early modern Europe by tracing the discussions which took place in a period of decisive influence over the thinking on universal empire, the time of the Emperor Charles V, in the first half of the sixteenth century. In a third part I will outline shortly the essential aspects of the development after Charles V up to the middle of the seventeenth century, and then I will speak in detail fully of Universal Monarchy during the time of Louis XIV.

2. The Medieval Foundation

The first question refers to the medieval traditions which are reflected in the debate over universal monarchy. This question is helpful since at the beginning of early modern times both the expression and the idea denoted by the term had been largely defined already and certain meanings fixed. The ideas expressed by the term of Universal Monarchy resulted from a long period of reflection upon the problems of government and sovereignty and supreme universal power. When the unity of church and world, of *sacerdotium* and *imperium*, broke apart in the eleventh century, laymen and clergymen started debating how the relationship of ecclesiastical and secular order should be and how secular politics could be organised independently. In this context Universal Monarchy stood for the government of the universal powers, the papacy and the empire. At that time people did not say Universal Monarchy but only *Monarchy*. The pope governed in the *Monarchia Ecclesiae*, the emperor in the *Monarchia Imperii*.

Monarchia was a Greek loanword, already introduced with its universal meaning into the Latin world by Isidore of Seville in the seventh century.[1] Isidore defined the universal monarchy as a *singularis principatus*, as a single princely government such as that of Alexander among the Greeks and that of Caesar among the Romans. According to its singularity this government was called *monarchia*.

What *Monarchia* meant in the concrete sense, as defined by legal terms, was the common way in which questions of government used to be described. The crucial mark of universal power was seen in the *iurisdictio*, the supreme legislative and judicial power. This power included the right to universal legislation as well as the exemption of the political actions of the universal ruler from any restrictions of the positive law.

During the middle ages the debate over Universal Monarchy was concerned with the question whether the universal government of the emperor was independent from the pope or whether the emperor could exercise his universal jurisdiction only by order of the pope. There were different opinions, divided between two major concepts: one called the hierocratic concept, the other the dualistic concept. According to the hierocratic concept the pope was superior to the emperor in all matters even in the *temporalia*, the secular affairs. The symbol of their relationship was the representation of the pope as the possessor of the two swords, and later on it was the identification of pope and emperor with the sun and the moon. According to the dualistic concept there were two totally independent fields of action for pope and emperor. The most striking argument of this concept was based on the interpretation of the medieval empire as part of the ancient *Imperium Romanum*. The idea of the continuance of the Roman Empire referred to the doctrine of the four world empires of which the prophecy of Daniel spoke in the Bible. The idea was that the medieval emperor succeeded the Roman emperors and was a ruler of the continuing Roman Empire, which was regarded as the last universal empire and the last of the famous four monarchies. In conformity with this interpretation the ancient Roman law was adopted and used as an imperial law by the emperor. This Roman law described the emperor as *dominus mundi* so that the claim to world domination could also be based on this legal tradition.

The medieval ideas of Universal Monarchy, of which the essential aspects have been outlined here, had been elaborated in a steady debate by theorists since the eleventh century. At any time there were advocates of the theocratic theory as well as the dualistic conception. Here is not the place to mention individual contributions, but what is important is the fact that already in medieval times a theory of government had been elaborated for the emperor of Christendom, which claimed universal authority for him in secular politics. So the only question was, if there ever would be an emperor who could actually transfer these theories into actual power politics.

3. The Structure of the Debate on Universal Monarchy in Early Modern Europe

The debate on Universal Monarchy of the early modern period differs remarkably from that of the Middle Ages. Its character was changed from a mainly theoretical discussion to a

---

[1] Isidore de Sevilla, *Etymologiae* 9.3.23: 'Monarchae sunt, qui singularem possident principatum, qualis fuit Alexander apud Graecos et Julius apud Romanos. Hinc et monarchia dicitur'.

political one by its connection with international politics in Europe. This was not by accident. Since Charles V had been elected Emperor of the Holy Roman Empire in 1519 he was the first ruler in European history who appeared to be able to obtain political supremacy among the European nations because of the enormous dimensions of his territories and of his resources. Since his time every kind of foreign policy suspected of domineering over other European states could be interpreted in terms of Universal Monarchy. There were three different main periods of debate:

1. The time of Charles V, in the first half of the sixteenth century.
2. The time of the Spanish preponderance from Philip II to the end of the Thirty Years' War in 1648.
3. The French preponderance in the time of Louis XIV during the second half of the seventeenth century and during the war of the Spanish succession.

The enumeration shows clearly that the idea of Universal Monarchy was fixed in European international politics. It was used for discussing the policy of any state that at the time tended to be in a position of preponderance.

4. The Time of Charles V

During the reign of Charles V in the first half of the sixteenth century there were two different views in the debate: one in favour of Charles V and his politics and arguing in a positive sense, the other fighting against him and arguing in a negative sense. In the following the central arguments of both sides will be described systematically and set against each other in order to make a comparison. In detail it will be asked what expressions were used to designate Universal Monarchy, what kind of territory was attributed to it, how it was legitimized, and what its main distinctive marks were. Finally it must be considered what propagandistic purpose the idea of Universal Monarchy served.

4.1. Propaganda for Charles V

First it must be mentioned that the propaganda which argued in favour of Charles V used the idea of Universal Monarchy especially after 1519, the year of his imperial election, until 1530. This coincides exactly with the period when Mercurino Gattinara held the chancellorship.

On this side of the debate Universal Monarchy was founded mostly on the medieval traditions of universal imperial rulership, though Empire and Monarchy were not congruent. People knew very well that the emperor of the Holy Roman Empire did not have any real universal authority or at best very little. Nevertheless, both the vocabulary and the ideas developed for the Universal Monarch during the Middle Ages served to explain and to defend the policy of Charles V.

4.1.1. Terminology and Territory
The medieval traditions already become clear by regarding the expressions *Monarchia* and *Monarcha*. Both were employed for the emperor and in doing so the universal character of his rulership was taken for granted. The quotations

illustrate the usage of these terms by a German and a Spanish example.[2] Universality meant two different things at the same time. First it referred to the superiority of the emperor over all the other rulers and second it designated the area of imperial authority, which was regarded as universal and not circumscribed by any political borders.[3]

The definition of the territory as universal was based on two traditions. One of them derived from the usage of ancient Roman law, where the world in general was described as the field of imperial government.[4] But such expressions were not meant to be used in a literal sense. Most often they did not refer to the whole world but only to Europe. The same author, Sauromanus, from whom the last quotation was taken, defines in succeeding passages only Europe including Greece as the field of action for the emperor.

Even more vague was the second mode of expression which derived from the Christian and theological thought of the middle ages. It defined the emperor first of all as the secular arm of the church and therefore it conceded the Christian society as a whole to the imperial rulership.[5]

4.1.2. Legitimation There were five arguments propagated in favour of Charles V to answer the question why a universal government was needed on earth. All of them laid particular emphasis on the divine and religious character of universal emperorship.

1. First argument, The divine right: God himself founded the Universal Monarchy.[6]
2. The second argument was based on the idea of the *translatio imperii* and was most popular in the German part of the Empire. It meant that the ancient Roman Empire constituted the last of the four world empires foreseen in Daniel's vision and that it was still alive in form of the empire of Charles V after having been transferred from Rome to the north by the pope at the time of Charlemagne.

---

[2](1520) Georgius Sauromanus, *Hispaniae Consolatio* (n.p. 1520), fol.C2': 'Quis enim rex, quis princeps qui praeter sanguinis cognationem atque necessitudinem non multis nominibus si genus, si potentiam, si legitimam electionem et deorum et hominum consensum spectemus, et amicum et imperatorem regemque suum salutet. Itaque cum is [Carolus] iure sit monarcha, velint et eundem esse, agnoscere nec usquam quod sine gravi piaculo fieri ncn potest, a dei iudicio alio provocare'; (1524) Alvaro Guitierres de Torres, *El sumario de las maravillosas y espantables cosas que en el mundo han acontescido* (Toledo, 1524), 89: 'Quando alegremente fue elegido para el regimiento de la altissima e mayor prefectura del mundo que es la monarchia del imperio romano'.

[3](1520) Sauromanus (cf.n.2) fol.D3': 'Propterea sic apud animum vestrum viri Hispanici statuite imperatorem, regem inquam regum, non unius regni aut provinciae concludi par esse, sed plane mundanum oportere esse, totum tcti ubique corpori permistum et nullam stabilem et fixam sedem, nullum certum domicilium habentem'; (1520) Cornelius Graphaeus, *Divi Caroli Caesaris Opt. Max. desyderatissimus ex Hispania in Germaniam reditus* (Antwerpen, 1520), fol.A3: 'Maximus ille hominum, regum rex maximus ille/Carolus, orbis amor, dominator maximus orbis/Imperii inmensi visurus regna...'.

[4](1520) Sauromanus (cf.n.2), fol.B2: '[Carolus] profiscitur, ut delati et suscepti imperii munus expleat, hoc est ut tandem orbem terrarum concordia, uno imperio, uno sceptro coniungat'.

[5](1547) Cesare Delfini, *De summmo Romani pontificis principatu et de ipsius temporali ditione demonstratio* (Venice, 1547), fol.B3: 'Nam veluti in civili...pollitia primus gradus imperatori uni debetur, ita etiam primus gradus in politia ecclesiastica solummodo papam concernit, sicut enim status hominum saeculares pro commodo et honore cuiuslibet eorum certa pace mansiva de iure per imperatorem disponuntur, gubernantur et corriguntur, pari ratione status ecclesiasticorum...per papam...disponi...debent'.

[6](1520) Sauromanus (cf.n.2), fol.C3: 'Cum Deus ipse optaret tale in rebus humanis quandoque regnum prospicere, quale in coelo est, illud simulacrum mortalibus condidisse rerumque omnium summam saepe uni detulisse'.

6   FRANZ BOSBACH

3. Third argument: The Universal Monarchy had been foreseen and announced by prophecies.[7]
4. Fourth argument: God himself had disposed the election of the emperor and he still supported the politics of Charles V.[8]
5. Fifth argument: The virtues of Charles V by which he seemed better qualified than any other ruler for the universal government.[9]

All the arguments for legitimation of a universal imperial government were strongly influenced by the medieval concept of Universal Monarchy. The most striking arguments were the divine right of Universal Monarchy and the personal qualification of Charles V for a universal government.

4.1.3. The Practice of Universal Government   The description of the practice of Universal Monarchy was based also on the medieval mood and structure of describing universal powers and it was specifically influenced by juridic and theological thought. That becomes clear by regarding the functioning and the results of universal government.

1. Charles V as Universal Monarch exercised universal jurisdiction and all other rulers were bound to his law.[10] Two conclusions can be drawn from such a juridical position. On the one hand all the other rulers had to obey the emperor and to promote his politics.[11] The second conclusion is that it was up to the emperor to settle the conflicts among Christian rulers and to eliminate any political grievances.[12]
2. The results of a well organized universal rulership were calculated in a universal dimension too and were described as a service for the universal church as well as for human society. The ideal at which universal government had to aim consisted in uniting mankind into one herd of sheep under only one shepherd. This image symbolised the universal order of the world under Christian faith and imperial government.[13] These were the theoretical limits within which the concrete tasks of the universal monarch were placed.

---

[7] (1520) Graphaeus (cf.n.3), fol.B3-B3': 'unus erit tum pastor et unum erit omnium ovile/ talia saecla olim cecinere Sybillae/talia multicipli praedicunt omine vates'.

[8] (1528) Gonzalo Arredondo y Alvarado, *Castillo inexpugnable defensorio d'la fee y concionatorio admirable para vencer a todos enemigos espirituales y corporales* (Burgos, 1528), 8: 'Seyendo yo [Carlos] por Dios constituydo emperador'; (1536) *Pasquillus Romanus ad rectores civesque Galliae* (s.l., 1536), fol.3': 'Occurrite igitur [Carolo] a superis nobis misso. Veniet enim fortis et potens rebellibus omnium deorum atque hominum auxilio munitus'.

[9] (1520) Sauromanus (cf.n.2), fol.C2': 'Si genus, si potentiam, si legitimam electionem [Caroli] et deorum et hominum consensum spectemus'.

[10] (1528) Arredondo (cf.n.8), fol.6': 'Y pues que...las leyes os [i.e. Carlos] llaman y dizen ser señor del mundo y esto por razon como dizen los doctores de protecion, defendimiento y iurisdicion'; fol.17: 'a quien pertenece conder leyes quitar y corregir'.

[11] (1520) Sauromanus (cf.n.2), fol.d2: 'Siquando simultates et controversiae...inter caeteros reges...inciderint, ille potentior, veluti arbiter et disceptator protinus intercedat, res dubias componat, surgentia bella reprimat'.

[12] (1520) Sauromanus (cf.n.2), fol.d2: 'nunc caeteri reges huic [i.e. uni totius mundi rectori] ut fabri et ministri architecto in omnium pulcherrimo opere haud gravate obsequantur'.

[13] (1520) Sauromanus (cf.n.2), fol.d2: 'Qui...monarchiae imaginem...restitueret...quae nobis aurea illa Saturni et Augusti saecula reduceret, quibus regnantibus non alia de causa mortales beatos fuisse quam quod fere omnes unum regem et unum populorum pastorem summa concordia agnoscerent'.

It was his task to guarantee the welfare of mankind in all secular and spiritual matters, which especially meant the maintenance of universal peace by taking care of universal justice and by preventing conflicts among the other rulers.[14]

The task of peace-keeping did not only refer to the political community of Christianity but also included the defence of the Christian states against aggressors from outside, especially the Ottoman Turks. The war against the Turk was regarded as the special task of the universal ruler. By defending Christianity against Turkish aggression Charles had to guarantee the freedom of Christendom from slavery and at the same time accomplish his task as a defender of the church and propagator of Christian faith.[15]

4.1.4. The Propagandistic Use of Universal Monarchy The propaganda in favour of Charles V used the argument of Universal Monarchy in two different ways for its purposes.

1. First of all, Universal Monarchy was the argument for the right of the emperor to aggressive political behaviour and especially for using military power. Imperial politics were defined as aiming at enlarging the territory of the empire as well as at waging war against the Turk. Both objectives depended on each other, because by going to war against the Turk not only was Christianity was rescued from a imminent danger but at the same time the emperor gained an overwhelming fullness of power.[16]

Following this interpretation the emperor, after the successful defeat of the Turks, would augment his empire on a large scale; and this would be the decisive step to transform his empire into a Universal Monarchy.[17]

2. Pointing out the aggressive imperial power politics which aimed at defending Christendom and at enlarging the empire was only one way of discussing the monarchical theme. The second argument linked the concept of Universal Monarchy directly to the concrete political behaviour of the emperor in the international context of Europe itself. The objective was to legitimate Charles' political actions and to discredit those of his enemies.

---

[14](1528) Arredondo (cf.n.8), 8: 'Seyendo yo [Carlos] por Dios constituydo emperador y electo para a todos aprovechar et a ninguno dañar y deviendo ser defensor de la fee y religion christiana et universal yglesia et congregacion de los fieles xristianos et su capitan...unir y no segregar devo y tengo a la universal xristiandad, al los buenos induziendo a mas bien e a los malos atrayendo a vien, porque no obren mal...y no permitir que por passiones de inquietos principes y reyes y otras señorias dominio siquier temporales siquier ecclesiasticos injustamente haziendo y biviendo subceda derramamiento de sangre humana...'.

[15](1529) Baptista Pizacharus, *Ad Carolum V.Caesarem augustissimum pro Francisco Sfortia insubrum duce oratio* (Rome, ca. 1529), fol.C1: 'Converte, quaeso Caesar, converte contra veros tui imperii inimicos iram et arma, contra foedissimum et inpurissimum Turcarum regem, Christi et religionis nostrae hostem. En vides illum fines tui imperii invadere, depraedari, Turcas ipsos hominum genus barbarum...patieris Christiano nomini tam diu insultare, Christianorum fines in dies infestare, imperium et ditionem late propagare'.

[16](1529) Pizacharus (cf.n.15), fol.C1: 'Res eo adducta est, Caesar, ut vel tibi totius orbis imperium contingat vel Turcarum regi, neque enim cum eo ullae honestae conditiones de pace sperandae sunt'.

[17](1520) Graphaeus (cf.n.3), fol.B3': 'Te Libyes, te Asiae populi, te extrema per orbem / regna petunt optantque.../comprendes palmo totum cum gentibus orbem/ et solus magni dominus vocitabere mundi'.

For that purpose the usual way of arguing was by interpreting the political actions of Charles V as making an effort to accomplish his task of waging war against the Turk, whereas the politics of his adversaries were delineated as trying to put obstacles into his way. The most striking argument in that context claimed that the essential condition for going to war against the Turk was to make peace in Christendom. So first of all the emperor had to strive after peace among the Christian rulers. It was claimed that the emperor was justified in using force against those who resisted his efforts, who made trouble or war, because they became an obstacle to the imperial duty of defending Christianity.[18]

No wonder that in the imperial propaganda the king of France, Francis I, turned out to be the first and most important disturber of peace. He competed with Charles V for supremacy in Europe and was his almost constant foe in armed struggles. Especially in 1528 and 1536 imperial propaganda made use of just this argument.

4.1.5. Summary   Summing up, it may be said that the propaganda arguing in favour of the policy of Charles V works out a picture of Universal Monarchy, which mainly consists of elements of Roman law and of Christian theological thought of the middle ages. Following that image Universal Monarchy designates a worldwide rulership of a single person over all other rulers. The function of the universal monarch is to preserve peace and welfare in Christendom, to augment and defend the faith, and to eliminate the menace of the Turk. It is argued that for fulfilling these tasks the emperor Charles V, as the Universal Monarch, must be superior to all other Christian kings and princes both in authority and in political power.

4.2. Propaganda against Charles V

The important role attributed to Universal Monarchy in the political thought of early modern Europe is illustrated by the fact that even the opponents of Charles V made use of it, though there was a remarkable difference in their deployment of it. Unlike the argumentation of the partisans of Charles V who put a positive value on Universal Monarchy, the political enemies of the emperor argued against any kind of universal empire. On this side the concept of Universal Monarchy appeared to be of an ominous nature and it was that negative image which could be used in the propagandistic battle against the policy of Charles V.

According to the method of the previous section, the following seeks the essential elements forming the picture of Universal Monarchy in order to compare the mood and structure of the argumentation of both sides.

4.2.1. Terminology and Territory   The participants in the propagandistic debate do not show any difference in their usage of terms describing Universal Monarchy and its territory. The Monarchy of the Emperor was regarded as universal, and universal meant either the whole world or Christendom. So in this regard the same terms and ideas can be found on both sides.

---

[18] (1528) Arredondo (cf.n.8), fol.8': 'Cesen...las rebuluciones, ligas, patos, defensiones, comociones, debatimientos, et parcialidades de la Christiandad, que yo [Carlos] prometo ser el primero que vaya et passe et emplee mi persona, et todo lo que Dios me dio en su servicio y defensa de su sancta yglesia, et catholica, et sincera et sancta fee en detrumiento de los infieles espurcissimos Turcos, Agarenos, Sarracenos, et Esmaelitas'.

UNIVERSAL MONARCHY   9

4.2.2. Legitimation   Although both sides accepted the idea of an universal empire, they differed from each other in their assessment of this kind of government. The publicists in opposition to Charles V denied that such an empire could claim any kind of legitimacy, because it appeared to be nothing but an unjust rule. The motive from which a monarch aspired after Universal Monarchy seemed to them not to be caused by his care for religion and universal welfare, but by his thirst for glory and honour, in Latin called *libido dominandi*. In this way he offended against the traditional rules of good government, and his politics were considered mere robbery.[19]

4.2.3. The Practice of Universal Government   The practice was described so as to correspond perfectly to the motives. Universal Monarchy turned out to be a mere tyranny, because the subjects were kept in unchristian slavery and treated as the personal property of the universal ruler.[20]

4.2.4. The Propagandistic Use of Universal Monarchy   Considering such attributes ascribed to Universal Monarchy, it is clear that its function in the anti-imperial propaganda could only be to discredit the policy of Charles V. His political actions were supposed to form single steps towards his real aim, which was the abominable Universal Monarchy. Upon the pretext of defending his policy as efforts made for the benefit of religion and the welfare of Christendom Charles V appeared to be trying to realise his real scheme.[21]

The second kind of argument against the emperor in that context worked by denouncing the tactics of Charles V which helped him to reach his long-term objective. This procedure was marked by gradual aggression. First, only one state was conquered, then followed the next one. In this way every armed action of the emperor could be interpreted as an aggression against all the European states, even if only one of them were actually attacked. The conclusion was drawn, that all of them were justified in combining their armed forces to wage all together a just war against the potential universal tyrant.[22]

---

[19](1527) *Legitimation of Thomas More for his negotiations with France*, in Jean Du Mont, *Corps Universel* 4/1 (Amsterdam, 1726), 495: 'Inexplebilis dominandi cupido ea retrosaeculis exempla orbi protulit, ut in quocumque pullulaverit, merito bonis omnibus debeat esse suspecta, ne sine omni rerum discrimine sacra simul et prophana confundens, undecumque dabitur, commoditatem semper et auxilium sit captatura et simulato religionis fideive praetextu omnia sub eo velamine factura, quae suam causam promoveant et libidini utcumque explendae quoquomodo inservitura videantur'.

[20](1535) Guillaume De Bellay to the Princes of the league of Schmalkalden, in *Corpus Reformatorum* 2 (Halle, 1835), 1012: 'Nisi enim brevius dicendum ipsi esset, eorum amentiam esse ostensurum, qui in Germania regnum constituere et servitutem inducere molirentur. Esse enim vere servitutem eo propellere, ut cogaris repudiare, quos velis conciliatos'; (1552) Manifesto of the German Princes against Charles V, in Friedrich Hortleder, *Handlungen und Außschreiben deß Teutschen Kriegs Kaiser Carls des Fünfften* 1 (Gotha, ²1645), 1297: 'Als den führnehmsten und höchsten puncten dieses offenen außschreibens...haben wir...angesehen...was massen man...uns allesampt zugleich entlich zu einem solchen unerträglichen viehischen erblichen servitut, joch und dienstbarkeit, wie in andern nationen vor augen ist, zu bringen vorhat'.

[21](1552) Manifesto against Charles V (cf.n.20), 1295: 'Da doch klärlich vor augen lieget daß es [dem Kaiser]... umb die religion nicht je so hoch, sondem je so viel wo nicht mehr darumb zu thun gewesen, daß er unter dem schein der gespalteten religion sein eigen domination, nutz und gewalt durchdringen und erlangen möchte.'

[22](1552) *Adversus impudentissima Caesarianorum mendacia pro Henrico secundo rege Francorum christianissimo iusta defensio* (n.p., 1552), fol.A4': 'Re diu multumque concertata stetit ad extremum illa vetus sententia: subiugandam esse prius Germaniam, nullo negotio postea Galliam opprimi posse'.

4.3. Summary

The answer to the question what Universal Monarchy in the first half of the sixteenth century meant, can be formulated in four points:

1. The partisans of Charles V as well as his opponents regarded Universal Monarchy as a theoretical concept of empire, which was set over all the Christian rulers and played the dominant role in interpreting events in the field of international relations.
2. The propaganda which argued in favour of Charles V's Universal Monarchy signified the superelevated and perfect emperorship. It was especially marked by being authorized to give instructions to all the other rulers in Christendom as well as by having such a strong position that it could bring his authority to effect by power politics. The authority of the universal monarch was based on his tasks of defending the faith and securing peace within Christianity as well as outside against a menacing Turk.
3. In the anti-imperial propaganda, Universal Monarchy was likewise regarded as a con-siderable augmentation of the dominion of Charles V towards a supremacy over all other rulers, but this augmentation was interpreted as a corrupted rulership which disqualified itself as tyranny according to the traditional theories of government. Because of its corrupted and tyrannical character Universal Monarchy turned out to be unjust rule, and offended the standards of morals and ethics.
4. On both sides of the debate the theme of Universal Monarchy was used to legitimate political actions: it justified the policies of Charles V just as it gave his enemies their right to resistance.

5. The Period of Spanish Preponderance

5.1. The Essential Aspects of the Development

It may be said that the period of Charles V had fundamental significance for the debate on Universal Monarchy in early modern Europe. It was here that the medieval ideas of a universal empire were transferred to the questions of European international politics. Both the terminology and the essential elements of the picture were determined in a decisive manner. It is especially typical of this epoch that the idea of supranational government remained a serious alternative, at least in theory, to the actual emergence of independent early modern states. The function of such a universal power was linked to the field of international politics. It should be entitled to direct the common affairs of all European states, especially the questions of peace and war. Certainly there were some change afterwards in the form of accommodations to new developments and circumstances in European politics. In this respect three points are especially important.

1. The association of the imperial dignity of the Holy Roman Empire with Universal Monarchy came to an end. The emperor and the Roman–German empire ceased to play a major part in European power politics. First the Spanish members of the House of Austria and the Spanish kingdoms moved up to their place, followed later on by Louis XIV who became the decisive figure during the second half of the seventeenth century.

Accordingly, the debate on Universal Monarchy was focused on them.

2.   The second point refers to the propaganda itself. When Charles V was emperor a positive interpretation was used by his publicists in order to defend and to legitimize his European politics. This kind of argument disappeared almost entirely from the debate in the centuries that followed. Universal Monarchy could be used by political propaganda only for the negative evaluation of foreign politics.

3.   In spite of the negative image of Universal Monarchy the concept of a universal authority superior to the individual rulers and the endeavour of maintaining order and peace in European international relations continued to exist. And the predominant powers made use of that thought for their own propaganda.

5.2. The Universal Monarchy of the Spanish Kings

There were two favourable factors for diverting the debate on Universal Monarchy from the emperor Charles V to his successor in the Spanish kingdoms. The Spanish kings remained members of the house of Habsburg and so they were still in some contact with the imperial title, which remained with the other branch of the family in Vienna. The second factor was that Spain took over the task of defending the Catholic Church, which was until then a specific imperial duty. By adopting this responsibility Spain claimed a position among the European rulers that was similar to that of the emperor.

The debate on the Spanish Universal Monarchy was brought to its culmination during the Thirty Years' War from 1618 to 1648 when the enemies of Spain regarded the aspiration of the house of Habsburg to Universal Monarchy as the main cause of the war. In anti-spanish propaganda the impending Universal Monarchy lost to some extent its universal character and looked more and more like the predominance of one European state due to its political and military strength. The questions of the legitimation and the practice of universal government continued to be discussed in the traditional way with the help of criteria taken from morals, ethics, law and religion which together contributed to the condemnation of Universal Monarchy as unjust tyranny. Also similar to the methods of arguing during the time of Charles V was the use made of Universal Monarchy for propagandistic purposes. The enemies of Spain utilized it for demonstrating the justice of their war against Spain. Every military or even political action of the Spanish government against one of its adversaries was linked with the threat of the gradually progressing designs of the Spanish kings toward Universal Monarchy. Spanish politics could be interpreted in that way as a menace to all European states which had got a reason for uniting their arms and for waging a just war against the Spanish foe.

On the other hand Spanish propaganda made use of the traditional ideas of Universal Monarchy in order to defend Spanish politics. The strength of Spanish dominion was justified in religious terms as divinely granted. It was said that the Habsburgs had got their mighty power because they had been elected defenders of the Catholic Church in Europe. Therefore the political task of Spain was to defend the church against heretics and in addition to that to defend Europe against the Turk as well as to keep the peace among the Christian rulers. All these arguments show that the concept of a universal empire as an institution needed for the common welfare was still very much alive.

It may be summarized that even in the time when the emperor had less political influence in European power politics the idea of Universal Monarchy continued to the employed by being modified slightly and by being transferred to other powers which were suspected of aiming at hegemony.

6. Louis XIV

The epoch of Louis XIV marks the keypoint in the European debate on Universal Monarchy. Because of his offensive and almost always aggressive foreign policy the French monarch superseded Spain and the house of Habsburg in becoming the ruler to whom the opponents attributed the title of Universal Monarch.

But in some respects the concept changed remarkably. Traditional arguments were set aside, and variances were introduced at a large scale. This can be demonstrated by asking again about the structural elements which are linked with the idea of Universal Monarchy in the propagandistic debate. They were the same as in the previous periods, and therefore it must be asked what expressions were used to designate Universal Monarchy, what kind of territory was attributed to it, how was it legitimized, and how its practice took shape.

6.1. Terminology and Territory

The conceptual starting point of the debate was the same as in the previous epochs. Even now the terms *Universal Monarchy* or simply *Monarchy* were natural and substantial components of the discussion over French politics.[23]

There were some variances or synonyms, which reflected clearly their provenance from the medieval dispute over papal and imperial universal government. So the terminology of Roman law was used if the *Imperium* or the *Dominatus* were mentioned, and the term *Christianity* conveyed the language of Christian theology.[24]

While the traditional context is still to be seen in these expressions, other terms qualified the French design more in accordance to the political circumstances of the time so that here the French Universal Monarchy appeared to become not a universal empire but rather a powerful kingdom.[25]

---

[23] (1667) Title of Jean Paul François Lisola, *Bouclier d'Estat et de justice contre le dessein manifestement découvert de la monarchie universelle sous le vain prétexte des prétentions de la reyne de France* (n.p., 1667).

[24] (1681) Gottfried Wilhelm Leibniz, *Aufforderung zum Widerstand gegen Frankreich*, in *Politische Schriften* 2 (Berlin, 1963), 443: 'Nosti quae sequuntur, quae non tam de regibus indiscriminatim, quam de magnis terrarum praedonibus, qui Heroes videri volunt, et vulgo Conquaestores appellantur, intelligenda censeo. Horum plerosque in flore aetatis violento exitu periisse historiae loquuntur. Quis est qui sciat, quem huic destinarit Deus: nam cum providentiae liberalitate abutatur, et generalem quendam Dominatum sive Monarchiam Universalem affectet, sentiet haud dubie aliquando sibi a superiore manu metas figi, quas nulla unquam vi superabit'; (1702) Dutch Declaration of War against France, in Jean Du Mont, *Corps Universel* 8/1 (Amsterdam, 1731), 114: 'Requerant tous rois, princes, républiques et états, qui ont à coeur et aiment leur propre salut, leur liberté, et celle de toute l'Europe, de recevoir notre déclaration, comme y aiant été contrains et forcés pour la défense et protection de nous et de nos sujets et de toute l'Europe, et de s'opposer avec nous aux pernicieux desseins des rois de France et d'Espagne et à leur trop grand pouvoir, dont ils veulent se servir pour se rendre maistres de toute la Christienté'.

[25] (1689) *Fecialis Gallus* (Frankfurt, 1689), 7: '[Galli] non ante his consiliis cedendum putant quam regnum Europae expugnaverint'.

But altogether there was no restriction on a special line of tradition; on the contrary, traditional and new terms are used indistinguishably on the same occasion. So the example mentioned in the last quotation offers four variances.[26]

It becomes clear that the traditional way of speaking of Universal Monarchy had become variable according to the fact that the presumed Universal Monarch was not yet the emperor but instead still a European king.

6.2. The Universal Monarch

The twofold aspect of Universal Monarchy, namely traditional and at the same time actualized, is still more evident in the description of the qualifications attributed to the universal ruler. Here the tradition was still vigorous so that the French Universal Monarchy could be described as a new empire. At the same time the French policy toward Germany could be suspected of trying to adopt the dignity of the emperor for the French king in order to achieve the suitable basis for a French Universal Monarchy.[27]

But it was also possible that the argumentation worked without the imperial element. In that case the French king was expected to achieve the Universal Monarchy only as a result of his political and military strength.[28]

Universal ruling was seen as to be based on universal jurisdiction and legislation. In this regard the terminology abided by the traditional wording.[29]

The multiplicity of variances to be found in definitions of the term Universal Monarchy at the time of Louis XIV is exemplified in a dissertation that appeared in 1681 at the university of Leipzig. The author defines Universal Monarchy in two ways: Either it designates a large dominion built up by conquering and incorporating other states; or it can be organized by a structure that follows the example of the Holy Roman Empire as it had been described in 1667 by Samuel Pufendorf. He interepreted the Empire as a special constitutional system where several states have been bound together so that they seemed to form a unique body

---

[26] (1689) Fecialis Gallus (cf.n.25), 6: 'per orbem impium dominatum stabiliri'; 7: 'regnum Europae'; 13: 'dominatio orbis'; 60: 'quintam monarchiam emoliri'.

[27] (1690) *Los verdaderos intereses de los principes de Europa en la estado presente de las cosas* (n.p., n.d., ca. 1690), 12: 'Francia esta oy verdaderamente en la positura en que otras vezes se malició estava la casa de Austria. Ella es actualmente el terror de sus vezinos. Amenaza poner grillos a toda Europa, y aspira infaliblemente à la dominacion universal. No es imaginacion vana, ni supuesto falso. No ay cosa mas cierta, y palpable, que haverse Francia querido apoderar del Imperio Germanico'.

[28] (1673) *Le colloque des royaumes sur le projet fait en France, qu'il ne faloit qu'un roy, une loy et une foy* (s.l., s.d., ca. 1673): 'Le roi de France parle:.../ Que'étant Dieu seul, et puis qu'il n'a qu'un soleil/il ne faudra qu'un roi, qui n'ait point son pareil:/ vous regnant sur les cieux, et moy dessus la terre./ Les princes Allemans, ces petits potirons,/ et tous ces roitelets du froid Septentrion,/ l'Espagne et l'Empereur mes seront tributaires'.

[29] (1685) Gatien de Courtils de Sandras, *Nouveaux intérests des princes de l'Europe où l'on traite des maximes qu'ils doivent observer pour se maintenir dans leurs états et pour empêcher qu'il ne se forme une monarchie universelle* (Cologne, 1685), 22of.: 'Dans le temps que la politique s'acordait avec ses entreprses, il a trouvé le secret de vaincre les saisons, de surmonter la rapidité des plus grands fleuves, et en un mot de faire la loi à toute l'Europe, et pour ainsi dire à toute la nature'.

14   FRANZ BOSBACH

under one head. The author of the dissertation accepted this definition as suitable for a Universal Monarchy.[30]

6.3. The Attributes of Universal Monarchy

Unlike the definition cited above, the description of the attributes of Universal Monarchy remained far more traditional. The individual elements did not differ from those used in the previous periods. That means that the legitimation, the formation and the practice of a French monarchy were criticized exactly in the same way as they had been at the time of Charles V or of the Spanish kings.

In regard to the legitimation, all legal grounds that could be given at that time for proving the legitimacy of domination were refused because they were either non-existent or deceptive.

1. There was found no legal title to such a universal empire. If the French maintained such a title as they did, for example, in the case of the Reunions, then they simply deceived.[31]
2. There were no prophecies which predicted a French universal rulership.[32]
3. Neither was there any divine providence for the French design.[33]
4. The French claim of a special duty to defend the universal church appeared to be nothing but presumption and pretext.[34]

---

[30] (1681) Gottlob Christian von Doelau, *De monarchia universali quae Europae imminere dicitur* (Leipzig, 1681), fol.A3: 'Sensus quaestionis duplici adhuc modo potest intelligi: Uno, quo monarchia universalis est magnum imperium, quod incrementum sumsit absorptis aliis, iisque pluribus civitatibus, et in unum secum corpus redactis quod evenire solet, vel quando victor devictarum civitatum cives in suas quoque sedes transfert aut iure prioribus civibus exaequat, vel quando devictae civitates antiquis in sedibus relinquuntur et extincto quod penes se antea habebant imperio, victrici civitati mere fiunt subditae. Altero, quo monarchia universalis idem est, ac systema plurium civitatum, quae vinculo aliquo peculiari ita inter se connexae sunt, ut unum corpus sub uno capite constituere videantur confer nobiliss[imi] Pufendorfi dissertationem de systemat[ibus] civitat[um]. Utrovis modo hic accipias monarchiam, nobis perinde fuerit; tummodo civilem intelligas, non ecclesiasticam, qualem Pontifex per orbem christianum satis artificiose extruxit'.

[31] (1684) *Prédiction sur la destinée de plusieurs princes et états du monde* (Antwerpen, 1684), 1of.: 'J'ai entendu parler qu'il y a un prince dans le monde, qui veut prendre tout l'univers et prétend que toute la terre est de son domaine et que ce qu'il ne peut conquérir par l'épée, il le fait devorer par une meschante beste, qu'il nourrit dans une de ses villes, nommée Mets, et qu'il appelle "Dependance"'.

[32] (1684) *Das regiersüchtige Franckreich, worinnen der europäischen Welt sonderlich aber Franckreichs regiersucht ... vorgestellet werden* (s.l., 1684), 63: 'Was die sogenandte fünffte oder universalem monarchiam anbelanget, ist davon schon vor vielen zeiten her geschrieben und anschläge gemachet worden, ob und wie solche aufzurichten sey oder nicht: diejenigen, welche sonder regiersüchtige und partheyische affecten der sache genauer nachdencken, halten dieses werck fast gantz für ohnmöglich, wenn man es durch menschliche anschläge zu vollführen gedächte; denn kein weiser wird in abrede seyn: Quod res sit humanis consiliis altior'.

[33] (1678) Armin Brunner, *Der erfährte Hahn* (Freystadt, 1678), 18f.: 'Es bilden sich zwar die Frantzosen ein, daß ihr König von Gott insonderheit zur allgemeinen regierung der gantzen welt außerwehlet und zu dem end mit ohngewohnlichen gemüts und leibesgaben außgerüstet worden sey; deßwegen auch die überschrifft, nec pluribus impar, bey obgedachten königlichen sinnbild gelesen wird. Welches so viel sagen soll, daß wie eine sonne viel länder bescheinen kan, also seye auch ihr könig tüchtig vieler länder regierung zu verwalten. Daß aber dieses mehr eine schmeicheley als ein warhaffter wahn sey, haben wir schon oben mit mehrerem außgeführet'.

[34] (1685) Courtilz de Sandras (cf.n.29), 231f.: 'Et de fait tout le but que le roi de France peut avoir en cela, c'est de se faire chef de Catholiques Romains, afin que sous prétexte de religion il puisse se fraier le chemin à des

5. The examples show that following the anti-French propaganda there was nothing that could legitimate a French Universal Monarchy. This included also the personality of the monarch and his qualifications for rulership. The French king appeared to be disqualified by moral and ethical criteria and the description of his character did not differ from those of his universal predecessors.[35]

6. The true character of French Universal Monarchy was so negative that it could only be put on a level with the dominion of the Turk, the common foe of all Christian states.[36]

6.4. The Practice

Because of the absence of legitimation and the bad conduct of the monarch a French Universal Monarchy could be nothing but a clearly unjust rule. The same impression results from the description of how French universal government was practised. The opponents of the French mentioned three aspects especially.

1. There was no legal title for interfering in international politics. The French monarch tried to obtain the domination of European politics either by resorting to ruse and deception or by appealing to arguments with which universal politics could be justified, that is, defending religion, securing common welfare, waging war against the Turk. But all these reasons were interpreted as pretexts and therefore could be refuted.
    Advocating the church and religion seemed only to be a cloak under which the French monarch served his self-interest.[37]
    The legitimation of French international politics as taking care of peace, liberty and the welfare of Christianity served only to strengthen French universal hegemony.[38]

---

grandeurs, où tout puissant qu'il est, il voioit encore beaucoup de dificulté à ariver...Enfin est-ce là le moien de se fraier le chemin à l'Empire'.

[35] (1667) *Respuesta de España al tratado de Francia sobre las pretensiones dela reyna christianissima* (s.l., 1667), 135: 'No passa de aqui por aora el discurso sobre la declaracion Francesa de su designio de monarquia universal en la cabeza de su Rey...y tambien para la advertencia y consideracion de las potencias y politicos d'Europa, que han visto en esta era, y estàn viendo tantos escritos de la Francia fatigados en buscar, sin hallar, titulos a su Rey para la pertenencia, y conquistas de todos los dominios de los principes de la Christiandad, y han visto juntamente y ven sus empressas usurpadoras de provincias, y estados agenos, sin mas titulo ni motivo, que el condenado por el historiador Romano, que es tener por causa para la guerra el deseo de dominar, y por la mayor gloria el mayor Imperio'.

[36] (1686) *La cour de France turbanisée et les trahisons démasquées en trois parties* (Cologne, 1686), 215: 'Nous avons deux ennemis irreconciliables, les Turcs d'un côté et la France de l'autre; l'un est le boureau et l'autre la torture, le premier est universel à toute la Chrêtienté, l'autre insatiable, et d'une ambition démesurée'.

[37] (1672) *Ein sendschreiben, weiches Sincerus Germanus an Ludovicum Seldenum abgehen lassen* (s.l., 1672), fol.B2': 'Es ist nunmehr nichts neues, daß man die religion zum deckmantel der regiersucht und den namen Gottes durch eine schändliche entheiligunge, zum kunstgriffe die herschafft zu erweitern, mißbrauchet'.

[38] (1673) *Von der allgemeinen Monarchie uber die gantze Welt, von der allerchristlichsten königlichen Majestät in Franckreich zu beherrschen* (s.l., 1673), fol.A2': 'Dann die experientz es sattsam außweiset, was in Welsch- und Teutschland und andern ländern vor gross confusion und unruhe entstanden, da selbige dem allgemeinen Imperio nicht gehorchen, sondern sich selbst zu regieren unterwunden. Damit nun solche unruhe beruhiget und die christenheit nicht gäntzlich möge untergehen, ist von uns nach reiffer erwegung beschlossen worden, daß ein herr und monarch über die gantze welt regieren solte'.

The French king did not defend Christendom against the Turk but used instead the Turkish menace for enlarging his own empire.[39]

2. The second aspect touches the more detailed circumstances of universal rule. The argumentation reflected two different ways of arguing: one was still rooted in the traditional terminology, the other referred more to the actual political circumstances.

As in the periods before, the subjects of an Universal Monarch were considered to be slaves without any personal rights and obliged to do whatever their ruler demanded.[40]

The most important element of a universal rulership was still the universal jurisdiction.[41]

Apart from these traditional arguments there were other descriptions which stood in direct relation to the actual political events. They laid particular stress on the international importance that the function of *arbiter belli et pacis* implied and they presumed that the French king strove for that office. But as he was supposed to aim at the Universal Monarchy he appeared to act not only as arbitrator of international conflicts, as was commonly accepted by international law, but to go beyond that by trying to become superior to all the other states whose conflicts he was arbitrating and finally to claim to be the only one on whose decision peace and war in Europe depended.[42]

3. The description of the effects of French Universal Monarchy was also divided in tradition and actuality. The interpretation of French politics as disturbing the peaceful relations among the European states was traditional.[43]

---

[39] (1684) Gottfried Wilhelm Leibniz, *Mars Christianissimus, autore Germano-Gallo-Graeco, ou apologie du Roi très-chrestien contre les Chrestiens*, in *Politische Schriften* 2 (Berlin, 1984), 491: 'Allés donc vous sousmettre au joug que la France vous offre,...en mettant au plustost le Roy tres Chrestien en estat de combattre les Turcs et les heretiques. Si cela vous couste vostre liberté, vous vous consolerés en considérant, que c'est pour l'accroissement du Royaume de Jesus Christ, que vous souffrés une perte si grande'.

[40] (1677) *The present state of Christendom and the interest of England with regard to France in a letter to a friend* (1677), in *The Harleian Miscellany* 8 (London ³1810), 111: 'As it is without dispute, that the French aim at universal dominion (which is only a more plausible cover for that universal slavery which must create it) so is it accounted as indubitable a principle, that the conquest of Flanders must be the foundation of it'.

[41] (1684) Leibniz, *Mars christianissimus* (cf.n.39), 491: 'Car il est Vicaire General de Dieu pour exercer souverainement toute la jurisdiction et puissance temporelle...les loix ordinaires ne l'obligent point, et sa grandeur est la seule mesure de sa justice, puisque tout ce qui sert à l'augmenter, sert à la gloire de Dieu...'.

[42] (1670) Gottfried Wilhelm Leibniz, *Bedencken, welcher gestalt securitas publica interna et externa und status praesens im Reich iezigen umbständen nach auf festen fuß zu stellen* (1670), in *Politische Schriften* 1 (Berlin, ³1983), 181: 'Diese Monarchie kan ich nun nicht beßer nennen als Arbitrium rerum. Ein solches Arbitrium rerum hatten die Römer unter ihren bundsgenoßen...Durch welchen gelinden und freundlichen Namen die Römer ebensoviel erlangten, als wenn sie sie alle überwunden hätten...Sie genoßen ihre beyhülffe sowohl an Geld und Volck nach belieben, sie waren schieds-leute aller ihrer streitigkeiten, und dafern einer oder der andere sich sperrete, schleunige und einen schein des rechtens habende Executores'.

[43] (1667) *Respuesta de España* (cf.n.35), 135: 'Y en la constitucion presente de Europa, la razon y la experiencia haze demonstracion, que una monarquia universal no podria fundase sino es con la aniquilacion injusta de tantos Reynos, y dominios justos en que està dividido el orbe Christiano; y consiguientemente con la maldad, y la injusticia condenada en los Romanos, y que la union de las dos coronas assombraria con notorio riesgo y commocion la libertad, y la quietud de los demas reynos, y estados de la Christiandad, atribuyendose sin duda al cuerpo unido de dos potencias tan mayores, el designio de oprimir a las demas, y de arribar a la monarquia universal'.

Another argument was relatively new. The concept of peaceful and undisturbed relations among the European states was increasingly identified with the metaphor of the balance of power. This concept of political balance was propagated as the new ideal for European politics and thus the assumed French universal monarch became the negative equivalent to that idea.[44]

6.5. The Propagandistic Use

The principle of balance of power conflicted with Universal Monarchy and became more and more the regulative norm for international politics in Europe. This development provoked changes in the argumentation of publicistic texts. Universal Monarchy had almost always been a negative concept, which had to be attacked, but the political equilibrium represented a positive concept. Therefore from this time on the use of military force could be legitimized by the intention to keep or to restore balance of power. This happened for the first time in an official governmental statement when England entered into the war of Spanish succession in 1702.[45]

6.6. Summary

Universal Monarchy represented during the time of Louis XIV a political concept of order in the field of international relations which had been propagated in Europe for a long time past. It meant a form of government which was superior to the individual states but which included them. The way of evaluating its details and effects was a traditional one. Most often the elements of the running theory of government set the standard for criticizing its legitimation, its practice and its effects. In principle the concept of Universal Monarchy turned out to be a negative one because it was supposed to disturb international relations.

But the description of the debate would be incomplete without mentioning the pro-French propagandistic publications. Certainly they did not use the term Universal Monarchy, but nevertheless preeminence was claimed above all European princes for the king of France. As the European state system was seen at that time to be structured in a hierarchical order, ranking higher could also mean more authority and more privileges and influence among the rulers. The French side linked the claim to preeminence of the French king with his right to act as arbitrator and to determine international relations. They justified this claim in the same way as their opponents but contrary to them they did so by pointing out that this kind of universal rule met all the conditions of good government. For legitimation they appealed to divine providence, to prophecies and legal titles; moreover they put forward the personal qualifications of their monarch and his virtuous behaviours, and finally they proved

---

[44] (1701) *The present succession of Spain considered and a view of its consequences to the rest of Europe, particularly England and Holland* (London, 1701), 12:'For my part, I expect nothing but universal war in Europe, even in our days, to set up an universal monarchy; and it is plain, we all have reason to apprehend it, seeing the ballance of power now absolutely broke'.

[45] (1702) *English Declaration of War against France*, in Jean Du Mont, *Corps Universel* 8/1 (Amsterdam, 1731), 115: 'pour conserver la liberté et la balance de l'Europe et pour abatre le pouvoir exhorbitant de la France'.

that it would be for the best of all, for church and religion as well as for the secular welfare of the subjects.[46]

7. Conclusion

To draw a conclusion it may be asked, why, for such a long time, Universal Monarchy could be used for evaluating international relations. It seems to me that two reasons especially must be mentioned.

1. The first reason is that in the field of foreign policy in early modern Europe concepts and traditions survived which commonly are related to the middle ages. The concept of a world as a purposive unit of all men, hieratically structured and with a transcendental purpose of being, remained part of popular political thought at least in a rudimentary form until the eighteenth century.
2. There was no accepted institution that could prescribe standards of political behaviour for international politics and make them compulsory. The concept of sovereignty ruled out any kind of foreign control over the monarch. Therefore conventions of international law and ethical or moral principles depended to a certain degree on the willingness of politicians. Against this background the concept of Universal Monarchy was used for evaluating foreign policy. It contained a number of ideas by the help of which all kinds of international events could be linked and compared with the common elements of the theory of good government. During the time when some early modern states developed into independent political units and were differentiated from each other, nothing could be more dangerous for the existence of an independent ruler than aggression and military pressure from outside. It was this problem that the concept of Universal Monarchy aimed at by accusing aggression of unjustness, by appealing for international help and by supplying arguments for waging just war.

---

[46] Examples are Antoine Aubery, *Des justes prétentions du roi sur l'Empire* (Paris, 1667); Gabriel de Loberan de Montigny, *Les grandeurs de la maison de France* (Paris, 1667).

5

Imperio Particular e Imperio Universal en las Cartas de Relación de Hernán Cortés

Victor Frankl

En un sublime estudio de la evolución de la Idea imperial de Carlos V, Ramón Menéndez Pidal llamó la atención sobre un pasaje que se encuentra al principio de la llamada Segunda Carta de Relación, firmada por Hernán Cortés el día 30 de octubre de 1520 y despachada al Emperador —según la indicación al comienzo de la Tercera Carta de Relación— el 5 de marzo de 1521. El pasaje reza: «He deseado que V. A. supiese las cosas desta tierra; que son tantas y tales, que... se puede intitular de nuevo emperador della, y con título y no menos mérito que el de Alemaña, que por la gracia de Dios V. S. M. posee» (1). El ilustre historiador-filólogo interpreta el significado de estas memorables palabras diciendo que en ellas «por primera vez se da a las tierras del Nuevo Mundo una categoría política semejante a las de Europa, ensanchando el tradicional concepto del imperio; Cortés quiere que el César dedique al Nuevo Mundo todo el interés debido, como a un verdadero imperio».

Pero Menéndez Pidal llega a esta interpretación aislando el pasaje cortesiano citado, tanto en atención al contexto de la carta respectiva como en atención a la situación jurídica y vital de Cortés válida en el momento de escribirla y a las ideas jurídico-políticas que constituyeron el fundamento ideológico de la Conquista. Además, Menéndez Pidal no tiene en cuenta el problema jurídico-histórico y jurídico-filosófico que radica en el hecho de que Cortés sostiene, en la Segunda Carta de Relación, una determinada idea de imperio —la del imperio particular y limitado, que permite la yuxtaposición de varios imperios de análogo título jurídico— que corresponde, en efecto, hasta cierto punto a la realidad, pero no al contenido ideológico del Imperio romano-

---

(1) RAMÓN MENÉNDEZ PIDAL: *Idea imperial de Carlos V* (Col. Austral. Buenos Aires, 1941, p. 34). El ilustre historiador-filólogo hace escribir a Cortés las palabras citadas «en abril de 1522», «después de entrar en México... noticiándole (al emperador) estar pacificada toda aquella inmensa tierra de Moctezuma», o sea las localiza en la Tercera Carta-Relación de Cortés, de 15 de mayo de 1522, que describe el sitio y la toma de Tenochtitlan, encontrándose ellas en realidad en la Segunda Carta-Relación, de 30 de octubre de 1520, cuyo relato no conduce sino hasta la narración de los preparativos para el sitio de la capital.

germánico; a más de esto, no tiene en cuenta que Cortés mismo en sus Cartas de Relación Cuarta y Quinta sostendrá otra idea de imperio, opuesta a aquélla, de definido carácter universal. No existe, que yo sepa, ninguna investigación del significado, de la función en la obra cortesiana, y del material conceptual de construcción, ni de una ni de otra de las dos ideas antitéticas de imperio, ni tampoco del camino que va de una a otra en la mente de Cortés. Reconoceremos que el problema de las dos ideas opuestas de imperio que aparecen sucesivamente en las Cartas cortesianas constituye uno de los problemas clave del mundo intelectual del Conquistador, cuya solución nos franqueará el camino hacia la comprensión de los elementos constitutivos del mismo.

Examinemos, ante todo, la cuestión de dónde tomó Cortés el material conceptual y la actitud intelectual para interpretar el imperio como particular a secas, es decir, como efectivo Imperio «de Alemania» y posible Imperio «de Nueva España», incluso blindándolo contra toda competencia de la idea universal de imperio mediante una indirecta irónica (no comprendida por la ciencia histórica); pues Cortés, quien había preguntado a un indio si era vasallo de Moctezuma o si era de otra parcialidad alguna, le atribuyó una respuesta en forma de otra pregunta, a saber, «¿quién no era vasallo de Moctezuma?», interpretando el Conquistador esta contestación en el sentido de que el indio habría querido decir que Moctezuma «allí era señor del mundo», y poniendo en ridículo, de tal modo, la idea del imperio universal; oponiendo, además, a aquella idea huera, no el mito auténtico de la universalidad imperial, el romano, sino la concepción «hegemonial» de imperio, según el estilo del imperio leonés-castellano de la Edad Media, mediante la declaración hecha en presencia del indio, de «que otros muy muchos y muy mayores señores que no Muteczuma eran vasallos de V. A.... y que así lo había de ser Moctezuma y todos los naturales destas tierras» (2). (No requiere ninguna explicación el que esta pequeña escena magistralmente descrita no entraña ni un gramo de verdad objetiva, pues Cortés hubiese imposibilitado su plano de adueñarse del poderío azteca revelándolo en este momento de una marcha muy arriesgada aún hacia la capital, pero precisamente por esta ausencia indudable de verdad, esta escena manifiesta con tanta claridad lo que pensaba Cortés en esta época de la Segunda Carta-Relación a

---

(2) *Cartas y relaciones de Hernán Cortés al Emperador Carlos V* (Ed. Gayangos. París, 1866, pp. 58-59). Cf. JUAN BENEYTO PÉREZ: *España y el problema de Europa* (Madrid, 1942, p. 240). Beneyto Pérez no percibe la altanera ironía con que Cortés hace decir a aquel indio con respecto a Moctezuma: «Allí era señor del mundo.»

propósito de la estructura del Imperio y lo que suponía que Carlos V pensase al respecto.)

Cortés se encuentra, sosteniendo la concepción del imperio particular, dentro de una tradición específicamente española, la cual se forma paso a paso desde el siglo IX (incluso, como opina José A. Maravall, desde la temprana época gótica de España) (3). El contenido de la misma consiste en destacar la unidad de España y su independencia respecto a cualquier universalismo imperial, y aun en reclamar para España misma un «imperio» limitado a su territorio, imperio éste que adopta, desde el desarrollo pleno de la Reconquista, es decir, desde la formación de Estados independientes dentro de España, concebida sin cesar como unidad, un carácter «hegemonial», o sea, el de la supremacía especialmente de León-Castilla sobre los otros Estados españoles; en cuanto imperio «particular», empero, tuvo que entrañar la tendencia de comprender también el Imperio romano-germánico —teóricamente interpretado por sus partidarios desde la época de los Hohenstaufen como universal— como Imperio «de Alemaña» solamente, es decir, asimismo como imperio «particular», y aun de considerar como posibles a otros «imperios» igualmente limitados (4). Las «Siete Partidas» de Alfonso X —tan íntimamente conocidas por Hernán Cortés— atribuyen al imperio, y a pesar·de recalcar la altura incomparable de su dignidad, un territorio limitado (Part. II, Tit. I, Leyes III, VII, VIII); la «Primera Crónica General de España», de Alfonso X, asimismo arraigada profundamente en la conciencia española, destaca el carácter «hegemonial» del imperio de Julio César como «sennor que manda et sennorea sobre otros et sobre reys», y recuerda, además, que el rey don Alfonso VI ha sido llamado «emperador»; la crónica personal de Alfonso X, escrita por Sánchez de Valladolid, califica su elección imperial de elección para «emperador de Alemania», y aún se sabe, a raíz de una carta de Alfonso X, que éste consideró la posibilidad de adquirir un Imperio hispánico-norteafricano (5). Esta tradición del im-

---

(3) José Antonio Maravall: *El concepto de España en la Edad Media* (Instituto de Estudios Políticos. Madrid, 1954, p. 443).

(4) *Respecto a la persistencia de la idea de la unidad de España durante la Edad Media, alta y tardía.* Cf. Juan Maravall, *Op. cit.*, p. 429: *Sobre el concepto de monarquía en la Edad Media española* (Estudios dedicados a Menéndez Pidal, tomo V, C. S. I. C., Madrid, 1954), pp. 405 ss. *Con respecto a la idea del Imperio español, «particular»*. Cf. R. Menéndez Pidal: *El Imperio hispánico y los cinco Reinos* (Instituto de Estudios Políticos, Madrid, 1950); Percy Ernst Schramm: *Das kastilische König- und Kaisertum während der Reconquista* (Festschrift für Gerhard Ritter Tübingen, 1950); P. E. Schramm: *Das kastilische Königtum in der Zeit Alfons d. W.* (Festschrift für Edmund E. Stengel, Münster-Köln, 1952); Alfonso García Gallo: *El Imperio medieval español* (en: Historia de España, Estudios Publ. en la Revista «Arbor», Madrid, 1953, pp. 108 ss.). *Respecto al carácter «hegemonial» de la idea imperial de España*. Cf. Edmund E. Stengel: *Kaisertitel und Souveränitätside* (Weimar, 1939).

(5) *Respecto a la actitud intrínsecamente contradictoria de las Siete Partidas relativa al Imperio.* Cf. R. W. and A. J. Carlyle: *A History of Mediaeval Poli-*

perio «particular» no se extinguió como lo cree Hermann J. Hüffer
con Alfonso X, sino que sigue viviendo sin interrupción hasta la época
de Carlos V, trasmitiéndose desde el siglo XIII hasta el XVI por varios
canales perfectamente determinables (6): El Romancero —conservado
en la memoria de Cortés tan cabalmente como las «Siete Partidas»—
relata, en el «Cantar de Rodrigo», el ofrecimiento del Papa de coronar
«emperador de España» al rey don Fernando y la altanera contestación del Cid quien califica esta posición —en cuanto hegemonía sobre
los «cinco reynos de España»— de ya ganada y conceptúa como fin el
«conquerir el emperio de Alemania, que de derecho ha de heredar-
lo» (7). También la historiografía y la filosofía jurídica de la tardía
Edad Media española conservan aquella tradición: Rodrigo Sánchez
de Arévalo —según J. A. Maravall, «el más claro exponente de nuestro
siglo XV»— enseña en su «Historia Hispánica» que las partes disociadas
de la «monarquía de España» en otros tiempos se hallaron gobernadas
por una autoridad única que *aliquando imperator Hispaniarum appe-*
llabatur, y en su tratado *De origine ac differentia principatus impe-*
rialis et regalis, que los reyes de España y Francia ejercen una soberanía imperial en sus países respectivos, y que el imperio, por tanto, no
posee ningún dominio universal, sino solamente el señorío sobre sus
territorios específicos, asimismo en las sesiones de las Cortes de León-
Castilla aparece ocasionalmente (Briviesca, 1387) el concepto de «Emperadores de Alimania» (8). De tal modo, el esquema conceptual polí-

---

tical Theory in the West (Vol. V, 3d, imp. Edinbourgh-London, 1950, p. 148).
Los pasajes aludidos en el texto de la Primera Crónica General de España, publi-
cados por R. MENÉNDEZ PIDAL (Univ. de Madrid, Facultad de Filosofía y Letras.
Ed. Gredos. Madrid, 1955, tomo I, p. 90; tomo II, p. 643. *Crónica del rey don Al-*
fonso X (Bibl. de Aut. Esp., tomo 66. Madrid, 1933), p. 13. La carta de Alfonso X, mencionada en el texto, ha sido dirigida al Obispo de Cuenca en el año 1264.
Cf. ANTONIO BALLESTEROS Y BERETTA: *Alfonso X, emperador electo de Alema-*
nia (discurso de rec. en la Real Academia de Historia. Madrid, 1918), p. 72 (Cf
J. A. MARAVALL: *El concepto de España,* p. 488).
(6) La tesis —indudablemente falsa— de HERMANN J. HÜFFER, de que la idea
imperial española en la época de Alfonso X «se ha extinguido ya desde hace mucho tiempo». Cf. por último, en: H. J. HÜFFER: *Die mittelalterliche spanische*
Kaiseridee (estudios dedicados a Menéndez Pidal, tomo V. Madrid, 1954, páginas 361 ss.). Cf. Respecto a la persistencia de la idea imperial española del Medio
Evo hasta la época de Carlos V, J. A. MARAVALL: *El concepto de España...,* pp. 490;
Sobre el concepto de monarquía..., pp. 413 ss.
(7) Cf. *Reliquias de la poesía épica española,* pub. por R. MENÉNDEZ PIDAL (Madrid, 1951, pág. 288). También en otros romances relativos al Cid, «Entrada del rey
Fernando y de Rodrigo en Francia», «Ruy Díaz, a las puertas de París», figura el
concepto de «emperador alemano» (C. *Reliquias...,* pp. 279, ss. I.).
(8) En atención a Rodrigo Sánchez de Arévalo. Cf. J. A. MARAVALL: *El con-*
cepto de España, p. 432; *Sobre el concepto de monarquía,* pp. 413, 415; T. y J. CA-
RRERAS Y ARTAU: *Historia de la filosofía española,* Fil. cristiana de los siglos XIII
al XV (Madrid, 1943, pp. 540-41); JUAN BENEYTO: *Los orígenes de la ciencia polí-*
tica en España (Instituto de Estudios Políticos. Madrid, 1949, pp. 311-315); J. BE-
NEYTO: *España y el problema de Europa* (Madrid, 1942, pp. 143-144). Las Cortes
mencionan a los «Emperadores de Alimania» en Briviesca, 1387 (Ed. Cortes de
León y Castilla, II, 397) *(cit.* por J. BENEYTO PÉREZ: *España y el problema de*
Europa, pp. 145, 159).

tico usado por Cortés en su propuesta de un «Imperio de Nueva España» equiparado al «Imperio de Alemaña», así como el pensamiento
acompañante de una estructura «hegemonial» del dominio de Carlos V,
en cuanto dominio sobre «señores», aparecen arraigados en los elementos de la tradición española, cuyo conocimiento puede atribuirse a Cortés con seguridad o alta probabilidad, en especial, en las obras del
Rey Sabio y el Romancero (9).

Examinemos ahora el fondo de intereses que pudo producir la in-
clinación de Cortés a adoptar aquella idea de imperio. Consideremos,
ante todo, que la equiparación entre el «Imperio de Alemañia» y el
de Nueva España, sugerido por Cortés al principio de su Segunda
Carta-Relación, entraña un juicio jurídico-político relativo al fundamento del dominio español sobre México, que hace contrastar este
fundamento con el fundamento jurídico del dominio español sobre
las partes anteriormente descubiertas y ocupadas de las Indias, o sea,
las islas y costas del mar Caribe. Mientras que este último fundamento
consiste en la llamada «donación papal» de las Indias a los Reyes de
Castilla, tal cual ella ha sido formulada para los fines de la Conquista
en el «Requerimiento» (10), el dominio de Carlos V sobre la Nueva
España tiene que poseer, para podérselo equiparar con su dominio
sobre Alemaña, un título jurídico meramente secular, análogo a la
votación de los príncipes electores y a la eficacia práctica del principio
de herencia en la sucesión de los habsburgos en el imperio. Y, efecti-
vamente, desarrolla la Segunda Carta-Relación —sin habérselo notado hasta la ciencia histórica— tal título jurídico especial de Carlos V
relativo al dominio sobre la Nueva España: se encuentra en la protohistoria de los aztecas, ideada, como veremos, por Cortés y expuesta
en tres escalones cuidadosamente calculados, resultando de este esta-
blecimiento de un fundamento especial, independiente de la donación
papal, del dominio mexicano de Carlos V un desprendimiento ideológico del territorio de la Nueva España respecto al círculo jurídico-
político del mar Caribe. Comprenderemos en seguida qué interés pudo
Cortés ver en esto.

---

(9) Respecto al conocimiento de Cortés relativo a las Siete Partida de Alfonso X, Cf. mi detenida investigación titulada: *Hernán Cortés y la tradición de
las Siete Partidas* (Revista de Historia de América, México; desde 1960 aceptada
para la publicación). En atención al conocimiento de Cortés relativo al Romancero,
Cf. abajo, las notas 17-20.

(10) En materia del «Requerimiento», concebido por JUAN LÓPEZ DE PALACIOS
RUBIOS (texto en: B. DE LAS CASAS: *Historia de las Indias*, Lib. III, c. 57; más
exactamente: MANUEL SERRANO Y SANZ: *Orígenes de la dominación española en
América*, tomo I, Madrid. 1918, pp. 292-294), y del fundamento jurídico del mismo,
la «donación papal», Cf. E. STAEDLER, en: *Archiv für kathol. Kirchenrecht*, tomos 117 (1937) y 118 (1938); JOSEPH HÖFFNER: *Christentum und Menschenwür-
de* (Trier, 1947, pp. 160 ss.; LEWIS HANKE: *La lucha por la justicia en la conquista de América* (B. Aires, Ed. Sudamericana, 1949, pp. 47 ss.).

Reproduzcamos, ante todo, las tres formulaciones de la protohistoria azteca, ponderando su significado jurídico en orden a las pretensiones cortesianas. La primera formulación se la atribuye a Moctezuma como declaración hecha inmediatamente después de la recepción ceremoniosa de los españoles en Tenochtitlan. El texto respectivo de la «Segunda Relación» reza:

> «Muchos días há que por nuestras escrituras tenemos de nuestros antepasados noticia que yo ni todos los que en esta tierra habitamos no somos naturales della, sino extranjeros y venidos á alla de partes muy extrañas; é tenemos asimismo que á estas partes trajo nuestra generación un señor, cuyos vasallos todos eran, el cual se volvió á su naturaleza, y después tornó á venir dende en mucho tiempo, y tanto, que ya estaban casados los que habían quedado con las mujeres naturales de la tierra, y tenían mucha generación y fechos pueblos donde vivían; é queriéndolos llevar consigo, no quisieron ir, ni menos recibirle por señor; y así se volvió. E siempre hemos tenido que de los que dél descendiesen habían de venir á sojuzgar esta tierra y á nosotros, como á sus vasallos. E según de la parte que vos decís que venis, que es á do sale el sol, y las cosas que decís dese grand señor ó rey que acá os envió, creemos y tenemos por cierto él ser nuestro señor natural; en especial que nos decís que él há muchos días que tiene noticia de nosotros. E por tanto vos sed cierto que os obedeceremos y ternemos por señor en lugar de ese gran señor que decís...; é bien podeis en toda la tierra, digo en la que yo en mi señorio poseo, mandar á vuestra voluntad, porque será obedecido y fecho, y todo lo que nosotros tenemos es para lo que vos dello quisiéredes disponer. E pues estais en vuestra naturaleza y en vuestra casa, holgad y descansad del trabajo del camino y guerras que habeis tenido» (11).

En esta exposición, Carlos V aparece como descendiente del conductor primordial de los aztecas y, por tanto, como señor natural de los mismos, representado legítimamente por Cortés, y México, como «naturaleza» de los españoles, hermanos carnales de los aztecas quienes habrían salido, en tiempos inmemorables, de la misma tierra de origen de aquéllos; los aztecas desempeñan, de tal modo, en este presunto discurso de Moctezuma, el papel de colonizadores españoles de antaño, quienes reconocen emocionados su dependencia perpetua de la Madre Patria. (Parece sorprendente que los historiadores modernos, seducidos por una confianza mal aplicada en la veracidad de hecho del relato cortesiano, no hayan comprendido más el sentido palmario de este discurso ficticio, a pesar de que un historiador de la propia época de Cortés, Gonzalo Fernández de Oviedo —como todavía veremos— lo interpreta con íntima comprensión; es verdad, por otra parte,

---

(11) GAYANGOS, pp. 86-87. La fórmula «estáis en vuestra naturaleza» tiene que entenderse, sin duda, en sentido estrictamente jurídico, según Part. IV, Tít. XXIV, Ley I y ss., como declaración de la consanguinidad hispánico-azteca.

que Cortés omite en este discurso —caracterizado por una ausencia total en el tenor de todo acento místico-religioso, acaso en el sentido del «mito de Quetzalcoatl», y por el uso exclusivo de conceptos jurídico-políticos racionales de procedencia feudal toda precisión en la indicación de hechos, fechas y lugares, sin duda, para no provocar por una demasía de claridad la desconfianza del lector, conservando Cortés, con la maestría del gran escritor nato en el tono del relato protohistórico, el murmullo misterioso, peculiar de tales evocaciones de un pasado mítico, como lo escuchamos retumbando aún en fuentes semi-indígenas de época poscortesiana, por ejemplo, en la *Relación del origen de los indios*, del Códice Ramírez, o en la *Historia general de las cosas de Nueva España*, de fray Bernardino de Sahagún) (12).

La segunda exposición de la protohistoria azteca se realiza, estando Moctezuma ya prisionero de los españoles, y en presencia de la aristocracia azteca, la cual, de tal modo, encuentra la oportunidad de confirmarla y de manifestarse reconociendo a Carlos V como señor; esta exposición repite primero la historia ya conocida del conductor originario y de la desobediencia de su pueblo, llegando empero a una intensificación dramática del gesto de despedida de aquél, para conseguir una base apropiada para una apelación no menos dramática de Moctezuma a la nobleza azteca y para la declaración de fidelidad de la última hacia el emperador:

---

(12) Es sorprendente que ANGEL DE ALTOLAGUIRRE Y DUVALE: *Descubrimiento y conquista de México* (Historia de América, ed. A. Ballesteros y Beretta, tomo VII, Barcelona, 1954, pp. 175-176), se fíe del carácter histórico de la presunta reproducción verídica de la protohistoria azteca por Cortés y del supuesto fundamento de esta última, el «mito de Quetzalcoatl», hasta el extremo de resumir simplemente la protohistoria azteca según el relato cortesiano, insertando en ella el concepto «Quetzalcoatl», como si el Moctezuma cortesiano lo hubiese usado: «El Emperador (scil. Moctezuma) ...pasó a hacerle (scil. a Cortés) una visita, en que expuso que por las profecías de su religión sabía cómo habían de venir hombres de Oriente, súbditos de Quetzalcoatl, y que él, cumpliendo la voluntad de los dioses, se sometía al Rey de España»; un proceder absolutamente inadmisible desde el punto de vista del método histórico, pues produce en el lector la impresión de ser Cortés mismo un testigo explícito del mito de Quetzalcoatl y de su función fundamental en el logro de la conquista. SALVADOR DE MADARIAGA: *Hernán Cortés* (B. Aires. Ed. Sudamericana, 1951) basa toda la biografía del Conquistador en la exposición introductoria del mito de Quetzalcoatl, dando con ello a su libro un neto carácter novelístico. EULALIA DE GUZMÁN, en cambio, la investigadora mexicana de los hechos de Cortés, declara en su comentario a la Segunda Carta Relación del mismo *(Relaciones de Hernán Cortés a Carlos V sobre la invasión de Anahuac*, tomo I, Libros Anahuac, 1958, pp. 223, 227) «que Quetzalcoatl no figura en ninguna tradición ni escritura, como dios o como hombre, guiando a nahuatlacas vasallos suyos, de extrañas tierras, al Anahuac». Con respecto al mito de Quetzalcoatl, posterior a la obra de Cortés, Cf. Fr. BERNARDINO DE SAHAGÚN: *Historia general de las cosas de Nueva España*, Lib. VIII, prol. y cap. VII (ed. Biblioteca Porrua, por ANGEL M. GARIBAY, tomo II, 1956, pp. 281-282; 293); Don FERNANDO DE ALVA IXTLILXOCHITL: *Historia de la nación Chichimeca*, cap. I (obras históricas de D. F. de A. I., publ. por A. Chavero, tomo II, México, Ed. Nac., 1952, pp. 21 ss.).

«... por manera que no quisieron volverse con él, ni menos lo quisieron recebir por señor de la tierra; y se volvió, y dejó dicho que tor-
naria ó enviaria con tal poder, que los pudiese costreñir y atraer a su
servicio. E bien sabeis que siempre le hemos esperado, y segun las
cosas que el capitan nos ha dicho de aquel rey y señor que le envió
acá, y segun la parte de do él dice que viene, tengo por cierto, y así
lo debeis vosotros tener, que aqueste es el señor que esperábamos, en
especial que nos dice que allá tenia noticia de nosotros. E pues nuestros
predecesores no hicieron lo que á su señor eran obligados, hagámoslo
nosotros, y demos gracias a nuestros dioses porque en nuestros tiempos
vino lo que tanto aquellos esperaban... de aquí adelante tengais y obe-
dezcais á este gran rey, pues él es vuestro natural señor, y en su lugar
tengais á este su capitan; y todos los tributos y servicios que fasta aquí
á mí me haciades, los haced y dad á él... (Los nobles aztecas) respon-
dieron que ellos le tenian por su señor, y habian prometido de hacer
todo lo que les mandase... é que desde entonces para siempre se daban
ellos por vasallos de V. A. y desde allí todos juntos y cada uno por sí
prometían, y prometieron, de hacer y cumplir todo aquello que con el
real nombre de V. M. les fuese mandado, como buenos y leales vasallos lo deben hacer, y de acudir con todos los tributos y servicios que
antes al dicho Muteczuma hacian y eran obligados... Lo cual todo pasó
ante un escribano público, y lo asentó por auto en forma» (13).

Si esta última afirmación pierde todo su valor probatorio por haber
informado Cortés al emperador al principio de la Segunda Carta-
Relación que «en cierto infortunio agora nuevamente acaecido... se
me perdieron todas las escrituras y autos que con los naturales destas
tierras yo he hecho», la presunta oración de Moctezuma pierde toda
probabilidad interna —prescindiendo de la imposibilidad de una afirmación de un origen español de los aztecas— por figurar en aquélla
una alusión indudable a los versículos San Matheo XIII/16-17 (San
Lucas X/23-24): «Mas bienaventurados vuestros ojos porque ven,
y vuestras orejas porque oyen. Porque en verdad os digo que muchos
profetas y justos codiciaron ver lo que veis, y no lo vieron: y oír lo
que oís, y no lo oyeron.»

Por cierto, este manifiesto anacronismo cambia de aspecto si lo
relacionamos con la tercera exposición de la protohistoria azteca,
insertada en la Segunda Carta-Relación: pues ella comprende nada
menos que la declaración de Moctezuma y de los nobles aztecas que
sus antepasados habrían procedido de un país cristiano, siendo cristianos, y precisamente del mismo de que había venido recientemente
Cortés, a saber, la España católica; de manera que la alusión a aquellos versículos bíblicos adquiere el buen sentido de basarse en una
evocación del pasado cristiano de la raza. El tercer pasaje —formulado

─────────────
(13) GAYANGOS, pp. 98-100.

en relación con la presunta purificación del adoratorio principal de los aztecas, que Cortés se atribuye, y con su «discurso de Areópago» pronunciado, según dice, en esta oportunidad— reza como sigue:

> «Y todos, en especial el dicho Muteczuma, me respondieron que ya me habían dicho que ellos no eran naturales desta tierra, y que había mucho tiempo que sus predecesores habían venido á ella, y que bien creían que podrían estar errados en algo de aquello que tenían, por haber tanto tiempo que salieron de su naturaleza, y que yo, como mas nuevamente venido, sabría mejor las cosas que debían tener y creer, que no ellos; que se las dijese y hiciese entender y que ellos harían lo que yo les dijese que era lo mejor» (14).

La pregunta de si Cortés aprovechó, para la elaboración de esta falsa protohistoria de los aztecas, algún material conceptual auténtico de los mismos, transformándolo quizá según sus finalidades políticas propias, tiene que ser contestada negativamente, con la más alta probabilidad. El llamado «mito de Quetzalcoatl», siempre de nuevo aducido como fuente de aquella protohistoria, no está documentado, que yo sepa, sino a base de exposiciones bastante posteriores a las Relaciones de Cortés, y es de suponer que ha sido sacado de estas mismas y de los acontecimientos trágicos y consecuencias próximas de la Conquista, en el sentido de un conato mitológico de explicación (15). De lado español, a lo sumo se podría remitir a la idea —comprobable en orden al año 1512— de la posibilidad de una conversión de los indios al cristianismo efectuada en la época apostólica, pero mediante un viaje de misión de un apóstol a las Indias y no a raíz de la venida de un grupo de indios procedente de un país cristiano (16). Todas las teorías afines a la protohistoria azteca de Cortés, que encontramos en autores españoles —es decir, en Fernández de Oviedo y en Las Casas—, son considerablemente posteriores a ella y suponen manifiestamente la tesis de Cortés; se las tratará más abajo. Tendremos que quedar, por de pronto, en que la protohistoria azteca de la Segunda Carta de Relación consiste en una ficción de Cortés con fines políticos, considerándola como tal su conocedor más inteligente, su coetáneo Fernández de Oviedo, si bien con cierta restricción, que se mencionará.

Ahora bien: ¿cuál es el sentido político de esta ficción de protohistoria y en qué conexión se encuentra ella con la idea particular

---

(14) GAYANGOS, p. 107.
(15) Cf. arriba, la nota 12, hacia el final.
(16) Cf. FRAY MATÍAS DE PAZ: *Del dominio de los Reyes de España sobre los indios* (ed. Silvio Zavala y A. Millares Carlo, en: JUAN LÓPEZ DE PALACIOS RUBIOS: *De las islas del mar Océano*, Bibl. Americana, Fondo de Cult. Económ., México, 1954, pp. 249-250). Respecto a la fecha del tratado, Cf. la introducción por S. ZAVALA, p. 30

de imperio aplicada a México, según su formulación al principio de la- Segunda Carta-Relación? La protohistoria azteca confiere al dominio de Carlos V sobre México un fundamento jurídico similar al fundamento de su poder sobre el Imperio alemán: una combinación entre una especie de derecho consuetudinario de herencia y el reconocimiento por los príncipes (la «elección»); un fundamento, por tanto, completamente independiente de la base jurídica de su poder sobre las Islas y Tierra-Firme del Mar Caribe, a saber, la «donación papal». Y si Cortés aquella posición mexicana de Carlos V, fundada en la protohistoria azteca, intitula «imperio» (utilizando el concepto «particular» del mismo, según la tradición de las Siete Partidas y del Romancero), lo hace, sin duda, para exhibir en forma sugestiva la perfecta independencia de la Nueva España, conquistada por él, respecto al ámbito de la jurisdicción más antigua de la dinastía de Cristóbal Colón y, por consiguiente, también de la jurisdicción del «Teniente de Almirante» Diego Velázquez, representante en la Isla Fernandina de la autoridad hereditaria de Diego Colón. El título sugerido por Cortés a Carlos V, de «Emperador de la Nueva España», debía impedir cualquier intento de incorporar· los nuevos territorios de su conquista en las Indias Occidentales concedidas a los «Reyes» de Castilla por «donación papal» y fundamentar, al mismo tiempo, la unidad indivisible de la Nueva España, amenazada siempre de nuevo por la intervención rapaz de otros conquistadores, con o sin la instigación de lado de Diego Velázquez; y es característico que Cortés intitule al conductor primitivo de los aztecas, ficticio antepasado de Carlos V, siempre «Señor» y nunca «Rey», para mantener estrictamente separados, hasta en los títulos de gobierno, los nuevos territorios cortesianos de los territorios de la jurisdicción de la dinastía del almirante-descubridor.

De este modo aparece, detrás de la idea del «Imperio mexicano» y de la protohistoria ficticia de los aztecas, destinada a cimentar aquélla, el amenazante problema cortesiano de la violación de la Ley, mediante la cual Cortés se había emancipado de la autoridad de su superior Diego Velázquez, ejecutando el acto de «población» de la Villa-Rica-de-la-Vera-Cruz y comenzando la expedición de conquista del interior, en contraposición abierta a la expresa «instrucción» de Velázquez, la cual había restringido su actividad a mera navegación costanera con fines de exploración y comercio de trueque («rescate») con los indígenas (17). Estará indicada una breve descripción de aquel acontecimiento que debía quedar suspendido sobre la futura vida

_____

(17) Cf. RICHARD KONETZKE: *Hernán Cortés como poblador de la Nueva España* (en: Estudios Cortesianos, IV. Centenario de H. Cortés, ed. Inst. G. Fernández de Oviedo, C. S. I. C., Madrid, 1948, pp. 341-381).

de Cortés como una nube oscura preñada de rayos, imprimiendo a todas las Cartas de Relación la conciencia perpetua de la presencia del espíritu vengador de Velázquez, y con esto el carácter agustino-dualista de una lucha continua de Cortés contra la *civitas terrena* o satánica encarnada en el gobernador de la Isla Fernandina.

Diego Velázquez —quien gestionaba en la época de la firma de la «Instrucción» cortesiana, el 23 de octubre de 1518, en la Corte española, para sí mismo, mediante un negociador, la autorización para la población y conquista de las regiones descubiertas bajo sus auspicios de Yucatán y del Golfo de Campeche (tratando de infringir el privilegio exclusivo de descubrimiento y conquista en las Indias Occidentales de Diego Colón, del mismo modo como después Cortés quebrantará el privilegio velazqueño, relativo a los territorios del sudeste de México)—; Diego Velázquez, digo, encomendó a Cortés las tareas fútiles fijadas en la «Instrucción», sin duda, con el solo objeto de sostener su propia reclamación de estos territorios contra posibles rivales hasta la llegada de la autorización esperada. Cortés, empero, estuvo decidido de antemano —como se comprobará en seguida— a aprovechar para sí mismo el momento histórico en que aquellos territorios recién descubiertos y calificados de ricos por sus descubridores fuesen, desde el punto de vista legal, en cierto sentido, «tierra de nadie»; el medio jurídico para librarse de las limitaciones de la instrucción velazqueña sería la apelación directa a la Corona, a título de los intereses superiores del rey y de la nación, comprendidos en la no observación de las mismas, y la utilización de los recursos de Derecho basados en el acto mismo de poblar. El hecho de que en esto mismo consistió el plan originario de Cortés resulta —de una manera que no deja lugar a dudas—, de una parte, de la grandiosidad, muy superior a las necesidades de un mero viaje a lo largo de la costa, del equipo de su acción naval y, de otra, del análisis de una conversación sostenida entre Cortés y su oficial Hernández Puertocarrero, mediante el intercambio lleno de alusiones de trozos de romances tradicionales, en el momento preciso de acercarse la flota cortesiana a San Juan de Ulúa, la última estación antes de la arribada decisiva al lugar de la posterior Villa-Rica-de-la-Vera-Cruz. En esta conversación —conservada por Bernal Díaz del Castillo y utilizada por la ciencia con la finalidad exclusiva de demostrar el íntimo conocimiento de los conquistadores relativo al Romancero (18)— cita Puertocarrero

(18) Cf. R. Menéndez Pidal: *Los romances de América y otros estudios* (Buenos Aires, Col. Austral, 1941, p. 9); Alfonso Reyes: *Letras de la Nueva España* (México, Col. Tierra Firme, Fondo de Cul. Económ., 1948, p. 9). Bernal Díaz del Castillo: *Historia verdadera de la conquista de la Nueva España*, tomo I (Ed. J. Ramírez Cabañas, México, 1950, cap. XXXVI, p. 155).

las palabras iniciales del romance «Montesinos se venga de Tomillas» («Cata Francia, Montesinos, Cata París la ciudad...»), añadiendo: «Yo digo que mire las tierras ricas, y sabeos bien gobernar», y, según Bernal Díaz, «Cortés bien entendió a qué fin fueron aquellas palabras dichas, y respondió: «Denos Dios ventura en armas, como al paladín Roldán, que en lo demás, teniendo a v. m. y a otros caballeros por señores, bien me sabré entender.» Ahora bien: en aquel romance de Montesinos solicita éste —informado por su padre del papel satánico desempeñado por Tomillas respecto al destierro de la familia del protagonista—, a la vista de París, que su padre

Le quisiese dar licencia,
Que en París quiere pasar,
Y tomar sueldo del Rey...
Por vengarse de Tomillas,
Su enemigo mortal;
Que si sueldo del Rey toma
Todo se puede vengar (19).

Estos dos últimos versos, empero, representan un símbolo inequívoco del gran plan de Cortés de destruir la autoridad de Velázquez mediante la apelación directa a la Corona y la entrada en la esfera de la autoridad directa del rey, vigente en todo acto de «población» como fundamento jurídico de la misma (20). No carece de interés que el mismo Bernal Díaz admite, en ocasión posterior, el sentido político de la alusión de Puertocarrero al romance de Montesinos, interpretándola mediante las palabras: «quiso decir que (Cortés) se quedase por capitán general» (21). Es indudable, por tanto, que Cortés ya emprendió su viaje, ordenado primero y prohibido después por Velázquez, con la intención de quebrantar las «Instrucciones» del mismo (22).

El plan se realiza de tal modo que —según la explicación de la llamada Primera Carta de Relación, destinada a defender la acción ante la Corona, reduciéndola a estrictos principios jurídicos— los partidarios de Cortés en el pequeño ejército expedicionario apelan a él solicitando que «pueble» conforme a Derecho español y nombre las autoridades municipales; la infracción de las restricciones comprendidas en las «Instrucciones» de Velázquez se la justifica —según mi propia demostración presentada en mi trabajo *Hernán Cortés y la tradición*

---

(19) «Montesinos se venga de Tomillas»: Romancero general, tomo I, número 383 (Bibl. Aut. Esp., 2.ª ed., Madrid, 1859), pp. 257-259.
(20) Todo acto de población supone la autorización de parte de la Corona, Cf. José M. Ots Capdequi: *Instituciones* (Historia de América, tomo XIV. Barcelona, 1959, p. 270).
(21) Bernal Díaz del Castillo: *Op. cit.*, cap. XLII, tomo I, p. 176.
(22) Cf. R. Konetzke: *Op. cit.*, p. 344.

de las Siete Partidas— remitiendo a dos de los principios jurídicos alfonsinos, a saber: el de la superioridad incondicional del «pro de todos los homes comunalmente» sobre «la pro de algunos» (Part. III, Tít. XXVIII, Ley VIII) y el de la legitimidad de la derogación de leyes vigentes en caso de que «hobiese en ellas alguna cosa contra la Ley de Dios, o contra derecho señorio, o contra grant pro comunal de toda la tierra, o contra bondat conoscida» (Part. I, Tít. I, Ley XVIII) (23). Cortés declara su conformidad, ejecuta la «población» y nombra a los funcionarios municipales, en nombre de los reyes Juana y Carlos y anticipando la necesaria autorización de parte de la Corona; acto seguido, el cabildo que acaba de ser nombrado de tal modo «examina» —conforme al antiguo privilegio de los ayuntamientos de Castilla— el poder de mando de Cortés, basado en la Instrucción de Velázquez, lo declara caduco y nombra ahora *motu proprio,* en nombre de los reyes, a Cortés alcalde mayor, justicia mayor y capitán general, invocando el principio del Derecho de Gentes de la necesidad de una autoridad que garantice a los miembros del ejército expedicionario el «poder vivir entre sí en concordia et en paz» (Part. I, Tít. I, Ley II) (24).

Se reconoce que este fino tejido compuesto de conceptos jurídicos de las Siete Partidas —que denota la mano del diestro jurisperito Cortés, quien había escrito, sin duda alguna, esta Primera Carta-Relación (firmada después por un grupo de sus partidarios) (25)— presenta un agujero: se encuentra en la declaración del nuevo Consejo municipal de que ha llegado —después de un examen cuidadoso de los poderes e instrucciones de Cortés— a la convicción de que éstos ya caducaron y que por eso Cortés no disponía ya de ninguna autoridad valedera sobre el ejército expedicionario; pues en atención a esta declaración, decisiva con respecto a todo el futuro del movimiento cortesiano, no se invoca ningún principio jurídico ni se alega ningún fundamento. No se puede encontrar tampoco tal fundamento sino en el parecer de que con el acto de poblar en el continente, y en una región totalmente desconocida a Colón (fundador y piedra angular del círculo jurídico de Santo Domingo, al cual perteneció también Diego Velázquez, el «Teniente de Almirante»), toda autoridad arraigada en el

(23) Cf. mi trabajo: *Hernán Cortés y la tradición de las Siete Partida,* aceptado en el año 1960 para la publicación en la «Revista de Historia de América», México.

(24) Cf. el detallado análisis de la estructura jurídica de la llamada «Primera Carta de Relación», de Cortés, que se encuentra en mi trabajo mencionado en la nota precedente.

(25) La demostración de la paternidad literaria de Cortés respecto a la «Primera Carta de Relación» —demostración que se basa en la perfecta analogía de la «Primera Carta» con las otras cortesianas de Relación tanto con respecto a la estructura ideológica como al estilo —véasela en mi trabajo citado en la nota 23.

sistema jurídico del mar Caribe *eo ipso* habría dejado de existir. Y se comprende cuánta importancia daba Cortés —quien durante la redacción de la Segunda Carta de Relación esperaba aún la aprobación imperial de su insubordinación relativa a Diego Velázquez y de su expedición de conquista, basada en ella— a la comprobación, al menos aparente, de la peculiaridad del círculo jurídico mexicano y de su independencia esencial de la esfera jurídica del Mar Caribe, fundada en la teoría de la «donación papal», mediante su ficción de la protohistoria azteca y su programa derivado de ésta de un «Imperio de Nueva España». Esto significa, empero, que la idea de tal imperio no ha sido concebida, como cree Menéndez Pidal, en atención a Europa y con la finalidad de una equiparación ideológico-política de los Mundos Viejo y Nuevo, sino en orden a la región de origen del movimiento conquistador mexicano, o sea Cuba y su fuente de derecho, Santo Domingo, y con la finalidad de la liberación ideológico-política de la nueva conquista, del cordón umbilical jurídico que la ató a aquélla.

Constituye una especie de comprobación retroactiva de la exactitud de esta interpretación, si nos damos cuenta del cambio que se operó en la ficticia protohistoria azteca de Cortés al entrar en el círculo cultural del mar Caribe, y precisamente en la obra de Gonzalo Fernández de Oviedo, a quien se puede bien calificarlo de conciencia histórica personificada de Santo Domingo (26). Oviedo habla —sin duda, por sugestión de Cortés, cuyas «Cartas de Relación» las transcribe directamente para su propio relato de la Conquista de México— del «Imperio occidental de las Indias, Islas y Tierra-Firme del Mar Océano» de Carlos V, pero este imperio, que figura en la «dedicatoria» y en el capítulo final de su *Sumario de la natural historia de las Indias*, de 1526, equivale a la totalidad de los territorios hispanoamericanos, sin admitir aquella línea divisoria entre el círculo jurídico de México y el del mar Caribe, trazada por Cortés mediante su concepto del «Imperio de Nueva España». Y en su *Historia General y Natural de las Indias, Islas y Tierra-Firme del Mar Océano* (primera parte, 1535) expone Oviedo una teoría —paralela a la protohistoria azteca de Cortés —de un dominio primordial de los reyes de España sobre las Indias Occidentales, según la cual «estas Indias» serían idénticas con las «Islas Hespérides», denominadas así de «Hespero», duodécimo rey de España, y precisamente, «según Beroso», en el año 1658 a. C., así que

---

(26) Cf. Pedro Henríquez Ureña: *La cultura y las letras coloniales en Santo Domingo* (en P. H. U.: Obra crítica, ed. Fondo de Cult. Económ., México, 1960, pp. 350, 408-409); Mariano Picón Salas: *De la conquista a la independencia* (Col. Tierra Firme, Fondo de Cult. Económ., México, 1944, pp. 54-56-57); Alberto M. Salas: *Tres cronistas de Indias, Pedro Mártir, Oviedo, Las Casas* (Fondo de Cult. Económ., México, 1959, pp. 74 ss.).

hasta el año 1535 d. C., el de la publicación de su obra y tesis, tres mil ciento noventa y tres años de legítimo dominio de España sobre «estas islas o Indias Hespérides» habrían pasado. Pero en contraposición a la tesis cortesiana, según la cual el objeto de la dominación primordial de España habría sido la tierra firme de México, ligada de tal modo en forma especialmente estrecha a la Madre Patria, considera Oviedo como tal objeto las islas agrupadas alrededor de Santo Domingo, constituyendo ellas, por tanto, la base permanente del Imperio colonial de España: esta tesis de Oviedo forma, en cierto sentido, el contra-golpe ideológico de Santo Domingo contra el México cortesiano, después de haber fracasado todas las tentativas prácticas de Diego Veláz-quez —teniente en la Isla Fernandina del almirante dominicano— de aniquilar a Cortés y de conservar de este modo la primacía del círculo insular. Y no carece de interés, a propósito de esto, que Oviedo, hacien-do relatar en la segunda parte de su obra a Moctezuma la protohistoria azteca, dentro del ambiente de la entrevista con Cortés y en segui-miento del texto de éste, añada que en aquella protohistoria o se había tratado de un «novelar ó traer á ssu propossito confabulaçiones de mañoso é sagaz é diestro capitan» o que «estas gentes tenian alguna noticia de lo que allí (scil. en la primera parte, libro II, cap. III, de la *Historia* de Oviedo) se tractó del rey XII de España, llamado Hespe-ro» (27): en este pasaje tan significativo aparece Cortés vencido ideo-lógicamente por el historiador dominicano, si se permite llamarlo así. Por lo demás, opone Oviedo a Cortés en la misma segunda parte de su obra una protohistoria de los aztecas de carácter plenamente realista, en que los hace proceder de Nicaragua (28).

Las Casas —quien igualmente acepta la tesis cortesiana del Imperio Occidental, sin aplicarla a un territorio determinado de las Indias o contraponerla en cierto modo a la tesis de la donación papal, como lo hace Cortés, sino que habla de un «soberano imperial y universal prin-cipado de las Indias», concedido a los reyes de Castilla por el Papa (29)— sostiene también una tesis protohistórica, afín hasta cierto punto a la

---

(27) Gonzalo Fernández de Oviedo: *Historia general y natural de las Indias, islas y Tierra Firme del Mar Océano* (ed. Real Ac. de Hist., por J. Amador de los Ríos, Madrid; Prim. Parte, 1851, pp. 14-18); seg. parte, tomo II, 1.853, pp. 285 ss., 297). Cf. José Miranda: *Introducción al sumario de la Natural Historia de las Indias,* de Oviedo (Fondo de Cult. Económ., México, 1950, pp. 62 ss.).

(28) Gonzalo Fernández de Oviedo: *Op. cit.,* seg. parte, tomo II, pp. 533-524.

(29) La teoría lascasiana del «soberano imperial y universal principado de las Indias», de los Reyes de Castilla (en *Treinta proposiciones muy jurídicas,* prop. XVI-XIX; *Tratado comprobatorio del imperio soberano, etc.,* Bibl. Aut. Esp. to-mo CX, pp. 253, 350 ss.). De la cual Las Casas saca la importante consecuencia de hacer persistir, bajo el «Imperio de los Reyes de Castilla, los dominios autóno-mos de los Reyes y señores indianos, según el modelo alegado por él del Imperio Romano —Germánico del Medio Evo— no se la puede comprender, en mi con-cepto, sino como consciente golpe en contra de la tesis cortesiana relativa al «Imperio» directo sobre México del «Emperador de Alemania».

protohistoria azteca de Cortés, pero no limitada como ella a México, sino aplicada a todos los pueblos de las Indias: declara imaginable que las costumbres de comer carne humana haya sido traído a los indios por intermedio de los escitas, quienes quizá habrían poblado, procedentes de Europa, ciertas partes de la Tierra Firme (30). Y a base del hecho de que la *Primera Crónica General de España,* de Alfonso X, narra que los godos habrían sido llamados también escitas por haber permanecido ellos en época temprana de su historia por mucho tiempo en Escitia (31), sería dable pensar que Las Casas se haya imaginado una colonización de las Indias procedente de la más antigua España gótica, acercándose bastante, a ser así, al concepto cortesiano de la colonización protohistórica de México desde la España cristiana. Desde el punto de vista de nuestro tema, el interés de estas concepciones lascasianas radica en el criterio de la unidad y totalidad indianas, expresadas por ellas, criterio éste que excluye la posibilidad de separar y aislar un determinado grupo étnico dentro de esta totalidad indiana, según la ficticia protohistoria azteca de Cortés.

Para concluir esta interpretación de la sugerencia cortesiana de un título imperial fundado en el dominio sobre Nueva España, quisiera añadir que este título parece revestir importancia también en orden a la organización político-social y económica de Nueva España: pues a base del mismo es probable que se resuelva el problema —no tenido en cuenta hasta ahora por la ciencia; pero, sin duda, muy importante— del porqué Cortés llame la adjudicación (notificada al emperador al final de la Tercera Relación) de un grupo de aztecas a cada uno de los conquistadores españoles, con el objeto de prestación personal y material de los mismos, «depósito», en vez de llamarla, según costumbre ya inveterada en el espacio del Caribe, «encomienda». El concepto «depósito» abarca, en sentido estrictamente jurídico (según Part. V, Tít. III, Leyes V, VIII, IX, XII), el riguroso deber de devolución del objeto depositado, siendo inalienable el derecho de propiedad del poseedor, en este caso, del Estado o de la Corona; en tanto que el concepto de «encomienda», con su carácter feudal y sus tonos concomitantes moral-religiosos del deber de cristianizar a los indios, etc., oscurece este derecho inalienable de disposición de la Corona sobre ellos. Ahora bien: la Partida II, Título I, Ley VIII, establece expresamente que, por cierto, el rey está autorizado para entregar a quien quiera una villa o fortaleza a título hereditario, pero no el emperador,

---

(30) Fr. Bartolomé de las Casas: *Apologética historia de las Indias* (Nueva Bibl. de Aut. Esp., tomo XIII; *Historiadores de las Indias,* tomo i, ed. Serrano y Sanz, Madrid, 1909, p. 540). Cf. Lewis Hanke: Bartolomé de las Csas, *An interpretation of His Life and Writing* (The Hague, 1951, p. 79).

(31) *Primera crónica general de España* (ed. R. Menéndez Pidal, tomo I; Universidad de Madrid, Fac. de Fil. y Letras, Madrid, Gredos, 1955, pp. 216-217).

que, como «siempre augusto» por esencia, carece de la facultad para aminorar los bienes del imperio por medio de donaciones. Por consiguiente, corresponde a este concepto de imperio, de las Partidas —es decir, al concepto del imperio localizado y particular, sostenido también por Cortés en sus tres primeras Cartas de Relación, seguramente el concepto «depósito», pero no el de «encomienda», que en conformidad con su estructura feudal entrañaba la tendencia a la sucesibilidad. Es probable, por tanto, que la elección por Cortés del concepto «depósito», nuevo en la historia de la institución de encomienda, esté ligada a la idea cortesiana del «Imperio de Nueva España», y que aquel concepto haya sido creado, del mismo modo como esta idea de imperio, en contraposición consciente al círculo jurídico del Mar Caribe (32).

El interés de Cortés por la ideología del «Imperio de Nueva España» y por el deslinde, fundado en ella, respecto al círculo jurídico del Caribe, se extinguió en el momento del reconocimiento oficial de la conquista cortesiana en forma del nombramiento de Cortés para gobernador, capitán general y justicia mayor de Nueva España, efectuado el 15 de octubre de 1522 (33); la exploración de la costa mexicana del Océano Pacífico, en cambio —que comienza inmediatamente después de la rendición de la capital azteca y se halla descrita ya en forma enfática en la misma Tercera Carta de Relación, en la cual Cortés informa al emperador sobre la toma de Tenochtitlan—, abre el camino para una nueva comprensión de la trascendencia general del dominio sobre México como puente hacia un verdadero gobierno mundial del emperador y, por tanto, para una nueva forma de la idea de imperio: la universal, según la tradición gibelina. En la Cuarta Relación, de 15 de octubre de 1524, declara Cortés, a continuación inmediata de la ponderación de la importancia incomparablemente grande atribuída por él a sus barcos, que están en construcción a la costa del Océano Pacífico, lo siguiente: «Tengo por muy cierto que con ellos (los navíos)... tengo que ser causa que V. Ces. M. sea en estas partes señor de más reinos y señoríos que los que hasta hoy en nuestra nación se tiene noticia..., creo que con hacer esto no le quedará á V. Excels. más que hacer para ser monarca del mundo» (34). Las acciones de descubrimiento conducentes a este fin —y, en

---

(32) En la bibliografía del ramo no se atribuye ninguna importancia a la diferencia entre «encomienda» y «depósito»: Cf. SILVIO ZAVALA: *La encomienda indiana* (Madrid, 1935, pp. 41 ss.); SILVIO ZAVALA: *Ensayos sobre la colonización española en América* (B. Aires, Emecé, 1944, pp. 140 ss.). Solamente SALVADOR DE MADARIANA: *Op. cit.*, p. 547, hace constar que el concepto «depósito» constituye un «vocabulario nuevo», sin tratar empero de aclarar su significación.

(33) Cf. ROGER BIGELOW MERRIMAN: *Carlos V, el emperador* (B. Aires, Espasa-Calpe, 1949, p. 296).

(34) GAYANGOS, p. 308.

especial, el descubrimiento, considerado por Cortés como probable, de un canal interoceánico a través del Continente americano— se las caracteriza, algunas páginas más abajo, mediante una imagen muy peculiar, que combina la idea antigua de la «Fortuna principis» con la idea místico-renacentista del «mago» (variedad del *spiritualis homo)*, a quien la naturaleza se revela espontáneamente, y con la idea de las Siete Partidas relativa al pueblo obligado a decir a su rey siempre la verdad: Cortés confía en el éxito de sus esfuerzos de descubrimiento precisamente «porque en la real ventura de V. M. ninguna cosa se puede encubrir» (35). Esta sorprendente combinación de ideas, empero, comprende la concepción de que la naturaleza universal misma es propensa a abrirse al príncipe, a revelarle la «verdad», a entregarse a su servicio. Reconoceremos en seguida la importancia de esta concepción —síntesis peculiar entre la idea estoico-renacentista de la correspondencia mágica entre el mundo humano y la naturaleza, y la idea aristotélico-tomista del universo como organización jerárquica de fines— para la conformación de la nueva idea cortesiana del emperador del mundo, interpretado como supremo fin del universo.

En un pasaje algo posterior de la misma Cuarta Relación observa Cortés con respecto al apresamiento por los franceses de las joyas enviadas por él al emperador —que en este hecho se encuentra también algo satisfactorio, porque «los franceses y los otros príncipes á quien aquellas cosas fueren notorias, conocerán por ellas la razón que tienen de se sujetar á la imperial corona de V. Ces. M. pues demás de los muchos y grandes reinos y señoríos que en esas partes V. A. tiene, destas tan divisas y apartadas, yo el menor de sus vasallos tantos y tales servicios le puedo hacer» (36). En esta frase se manifiesta, una vez más, el amplio saber jurídico de Cortés, quien estuvo informado sobre la posición de Francia dentro del sistema ideológico imperial-romano, no reconociendo ella *in temporalibus* «de facto» ninguna supremacía del emperador, estándole subordinada, empero «de jure» y «debiendo» reconocerlo como señor, según el criterio

---

(35) GAYANGOS, p. 315. Respecto al concepto de la «Fortuna Principis», Cf. W. WARDE FOWLER: *Caesar's Conception of Fortuna* («The Classical Review», volumen XVII, London, 1903, pp. 153 ss.); FRANZ KAMPERS: *Die Fortuna Caesarea Kaiser Friedrichs II* (Historisches Jahrbuch der Görresgesellschaft, año 1928, páginas 208 ss, esp. pp. 212-213, 226-227); HARRY ERICSSON: *Caesar und sein Glück* (Eranos, Acta Philologica Suecana, Göteborg, 1944, pp. 57 ss.); FRITZ TAEGER: *Charisma* (Stuttgart, tomo I, 1957, p. 181; tomo II, 1960, pp. 22 ss.). Respecto al tema del «Spiritualis homo», Cf. KONRAD BURDACH: *Rienzo und die geistige Wandlung seiner Zeit* (Vom Mittelalter zur Reformation, II/I, Berlin, 1913-1928, pp. 538 ss. 564 ss.). Respecto a la idea renacentista del «Magus», Cf. WILL-ERICH PEUKERT: *Pansophie* (1936); KARL JOËL: *Der Ursprung der Naturphilosophie aus dem Geiste der Mystik* (Jena, 1926, pp. 8 ss). El pasaje aludido en el texto de las *Siete Partidas* (Part. II, Tít. XIIII, Ley V), reza: «El pueblo..., debe siempre decir palabras verdaderas al rey, et guardarse de mentirle llanamente.»

(36) GAYANGOS, p. 317.

de la Glosa a la Decretal *Per venerabilem,* aceptado por Juan de Torquemada en su *Opusculum ad honorem Romani imperii et dominorum Romanorum* (1467-68), cuya importancia para la forma final de la idea imperial de Hernán Cortés llegaremos a conocer (37).

Pues en la Quinta Carta de Relación, de 3 de septiembre de 1526, aparece una variante de la idea universal de imperio, de suma originalidad creadora, cimentada por Cortés —sin habérselo notado la ciencia histórica— en un principio básico de la cosmología teleológica del aristotelismo cristiano: Cortés informa al emperador hacia el final de la Carta-Relación —después de haberle dado varias veces el tratamiento de monarca universal en forma cortesana y sin peculiaridad filosófico-teológica— que había comisionado un destacamento militar para subyugar a los bárbaros chichimecas del Noroeste, «porque no haya cosa supérflua en toda la tierra, ni que deje de servir ni reconocer á V. M.» (38). Pues bien, este concepto de que no debe haber nada «supérfluo» en este mundo se basa, según su significación y su texto, en la fórmula aristotélico-tomista: *Natura nihil facit frustra* (39). Cortés lo vincula a la idea imperial en el sentido de que todo en este mundo encuentra su finalidad en servir al emperador. Pero ¿es que Cortés mismo ha establecido esta asociación de ideas entre el principio teleológico universal y la idea de imperio universal, o la adoptó ya hecha de algún sostenedor de esta última, de orientación aristotélico-tomista? Con eso estamos ante la pregunta por una posible inspiración literaria de la idea universal de imperio de Cortés.

El tratado *De Monarchia,* de Dante —cuyo cimiento averroísta del imperio universal comprendido como garante de la continua transformación, en medio de una paz universal, del intelecto «potencial», común a toda la Humanidad, en intelecto «activo»; es decir, en cultura viva, carece, por lo demás, de toda comparabilidad con la concepción cortesiana— no entra en cuenta como modelo sugestivo de la misma por no haber sido impreso sino en 1559 (40); la propuesta de una publicación de un manuscrito de la *Monarchia,* de Dante,

(37) Cf. W. KIENAST: *Deutschland und Frankreich in der Kaiserzeit* (Leipzig, 1943, pp. 98 ss., p. 104; resp. a la glosa de Huguccio de Pisa al Decretum Gratiani); FRIEDRICH AUGUST FREIHERR VON DER HEYDTE: *Die Geburtsstunde des souveränen Staates* (Regensburg, 1952, pp. 36-37; resp. a la glosa a la Decretal «Per venerabilem»).

(38) GAYANGOS, p. 491.

(39) *Natura nihil facit frustra:* Aristóteles. Pol. I, 2 (1253 a 9); De Coelo, I, 4 (271 a 33). D. Thom. De Coelo, I, lect. 8, núm. 14; In II Sent., dist. 25, q. 1, a. 1; Summa c. Gentes, lib. II, cap. 55; lib. II, cap. 79. Cf. RAIMUNDO PANIKER: *El concepto de la naturaleza* (Inst. Luis Vives, de Fil. C. S. I. C., Madrid, 1951, páginas 399-400).

(40) Cf. KARLA ECKERMANN: *Studien zur Geschichte des monarchischen Gedankens im 15. Jahrhundert* (Abhandlungen Z. Mittleren und Neueren Geschichte, Heft 73, Berlin-Grunewald, 1933, p. 157).

de propiedad del canciller imperial Gatinara, hecha por éste a Erasmo
pocos meses después de la redacción de la Quinta Carta de Relación
por Cortés, no llegó a ejecutarse (41). La extensa obra de Antonio
de Roselli: *Monarchia, sive Tractatus de potestate Imperatoris et
Papae* —que había ido creciendo en la época del Concilio de Basilea
hasta su dedicación al emperador Federico III, y que ha sido impresa
varias veces en la segunda mitad del siglo xv y a principios del siglo xvi (42)— no puede ser considerada tampoco como fuente de inspiración de la Idea cortesiana de emperador universal, porque no cimienta su concepto del monarca universal de modo naturalista-racionalista
en el sentido de la cosmología aristotélico-tomista, como lo hace Cortés,
sino de modo espiritualista según la tradición del dualismo y pesi-
mismo moral de San Agustín: habiendo deducido, en el profundo
capítulo 37 de la Parte Primera, de la dualidad espiritual-corporal de
la naturaleza humana, la dualidad de las finalidades de la misma
y de los poderes destinados a dirigirla, declara con respecto a la naturaleza humana terrenal que ella *proclivis est ad malum ab adolescen-
tia sua... nam ad motum et actum peccati naturali movemur ins-
tinctu...*, por lo cual ella necesita al *Caesar qui per naturalia documenta et temporales potestates genus humanum ad temporalem feli-
citatem dirigit scilicet sedatis tempestatibus nostrae mortalitatis hu-
manae* (43). Tampoco la insistencia, correspondiente al agustinismo
de Roselli, en el aspecto histórico-filosófico de su mística de imperio
—la caída de Adán, primer emperador universal, no podía ser com-
pensada sino administrando justicia al Dios-Hombre, el sucesor de
aquél en el dominio universal, el emperador romano (44)— no encuentra ni la sombra de una analogía en las Cartas de Cortés. El pequeño
tratado, de orientación imperial-universal, de Eneas Silvio (más tarde
Papa Pío II): *de Ortu et Auctoritate Romani Imperii*, de 1446, por
otra parte, carece del amplio fondo de la Teleología y Cosmología
aristotélico-tomistas —el cual aparece reducido a un providencialismo
neo-estoico bastante trivial—, así que tampoco este tratado entra en
consideración como fuente posible de la concepción cortesiana (45).

Por cierto, la idea del emperador y del imperio universales no
fueron desconocidas en España. Hacia fines del siglo xiv Pedro López

---

(41) Cf. MARCEL BATAILLON: *Erasmo y España* (Fondo de Cult. Económ. México, 1950, tomo i, p. 270).

(42) Cf. KARLA ECKERMANN: *Op. cit.*, caps. II y V.

(43) En MELCHIOR GOLDAST: *Monarchia S. Romani Imperii*, tomo I (Hano-
viae, 1611, p. 721).

(44) En MELCHIOR GOLDATS: *Op. cit.*, Pars V, cap. XXII, p. 550; Cf. Pars I,
cap. XXXVI, p. 270.

(45) Aeneae Silvii Piccolominii Senensis, olim Pii II Pont. Max., de ortu et
authoritate S. Romani Imperrii, lib. I (Moguntiae, 1535), esp. caps. V y VII. Cf.
G. KALLEN: *Aeneas Silvius als Publizist* (Köln, 1939).

de Ayala la había aplicado, en su *Crónica del rey Don Pedro,* a Octaviano; al mismo tiempo, aproximadamente, Francesc Eiximenis, en su *El Crestià,* a Roma en general (46). También el pensamiento de un dominio universal del soberano de España surge repetidas veces: en Juan de Mena, con relación al rey Juan II; en el bachiller Palma y otros, en punto a los Reyes Católicos; en los «Capítulos del Reino» de los comuneros castellanos —al menos según el relato de Sandoval—, respecto a Carlos V y sus antecesores (47). Pero solamente *un* tratado había utilizado antes de la época de Carlos V aquella idea de la monarquía universal para la interpretación ideológica del Imperio romano-germánico: el sucinto *Opusculum ad honorem Romani imperii et dominorum Romanorum,* del gran teólogo español Juan de Torquemada, O. P., de 1467-68, que en su apología —dirigida contra el tratado de Rodrigo Sánchez de Arévalo *De origine ac differentia principatus imperialis et regaeis*— de la idea del imperio universal concibe, precisamente, aquel fundamento cosmológico aristotélico-tomista de la misma, que hemos encontrado, en forma aún más concentrada, en el pasaje en cuestión de la Quinta Carta de Relación de Hernán Cortés, quien, como jurisperito, pudo conocer el *Opusculum* con suma facilidad. Torquemada parte de la tesis de que el «Ser-de-Dios» del imperio (comprendido como universal) no se lo deba entender en el sentido de una cimentación divina directa del mismo, coincidente con la creación divina del mundo, sino en el sentido de una conformidad del imperio universal con la razón dada por Dios al hombre, y declara, apoyándose en el libro XII de la Metafísica de Aristóteles: *Entia nolunt male disponi; pluralitas principatuum non est bona; unus ergo princeps.* Y prosigue diciendo: *Quod est debitum et expediens esse in hominibus secundum rectam rationem, est debitum esse iure gentium... Illud secundum rectam rationem in moribus dicitur, quod habet conformitatem ad bonitatem, quae est in rebus naturalibus, quia ars imitatur naturam, quantum potest. Sed potestas principatus imperialis est huiusmodi, quia in naturalibus inferiora reguntur por superiora et multitudo per unum. Unde totum universum ad modum exercitus ordinatur sub uno principe, qui est Deus, ut dicitur XII° Metaphisice. Ergo quod unus post Deum super omnes homines visibili conversatione principetur, est conveniens iuri naturali* (48).

---

(46) Cf. J. A. MARAVALL: Sobre el concepto de la monarquía, *Op. cit.,* páginas 414-415.

(47) Cf. J. A. MARAVALL: Sobre el concepto de la monarquía, pp. 416-417; El concepto de España, *Op. cit.,* p. 499.

(48) El pequeño tratado de Torquemada ha sido publicado como apéndice del artículo de HUBERT JEDIN: *Juan de Torquemada und das Imperium Romanum* (en Archivum Fratrum Praedicatorum, vol. XII, 1942. Roma, Ist. Stor. Domenicano di S. Sabina, pp. 247-278). El texto citado por mí, Cf. pp. 272-273. Cf. CARRERAS Y ARTAU, *Op. cit.,* pp. 540-541.

En este pasaje está formulada, precisamente, la visión cosmológica unitaria del universo, que reúne en un sistema único, mediante conceptos de carácter aristotélico-finalista, los mundos de la naturaleza y de la sociedad humana, y que hemos encontrado como fundamento de la idea del emperador universal en la frase arriba comentada de la Quinta Carta-Relación de Hernán Cortés: según aquella visión expuesta por Torquemada del universo, éste forma una ingente conexión de fines, en la cual cada cosa aspira al «bien» y, por tanto, todas a la unidad, que consiste —en atención a las relaciones humanas terrenales— en el imperio; el estilista magistral Hernán Cortés tuvo que añadir solamente la fórmula contundente, suministrada, empero, también por Aristóteles-Tomás de Aquino, «¡Nada superfluo en toda la tierra!», para obtener la impresionante definición de su ideal imperial, al final de la Quinta Carta-Relación. Estamos autorizados, por tanto, a admitir la hipótesis de que la lectura del mencionado tratado de Torquemada haya contribuído a producir en Cortés el tránsito desde la idea particular de imperio a la idea universal del mismo.

Pero, naturalmente, supone esta transformación en la esfera de las ideas políticas cortesianas también una evolución correspondiente, favorable a la acogida de la idea del imperio universal por el alto destinatario de las Cartas-Relaciones en la Corte española. Y, en efecto, en aquellos años transcurridos entre las Cartas-Relaciones Segunda y Quinta —o sea considerándolo del lado de España, desde la ultimación del levantamiento de las Comunidades y la subsiguiente vuelta a España de Carlos V en verano de 1522, hasta la rápida ascensión de éste al apogeo exterior de su vida, la victoria de Pavía a fines de febrero de 1525— se habían operado importantes cambios en la esfera de la historia del espíritu, el centro de los cuales estuvo en la Corte del emperador, quien iba fundiéndose rápidamente en uno con la Nación española. En estos años se va originando el erasmismo español, caracterizado por la concentración unilateral en un aspecto único de la vasta obra de Erasmo, matizada de diversas maneras, a saber: el postulado de la Reforma de la Iglesia y por la vinculación de este postulado con la idea de la monarquía universal (no sostenida, en realidad, por Erasmo), considerándose esta monarquía como potencia impulsora y espacio de realización de la reforma universal. Los sostenedores principales de esta combinación de ideas son el secretario imperial Alfonso Valdés —quien, la manifiesta en el parte oficial de la victoria de Pavía, redactado por él, y después del mencionado lapso de tiempo, en sus libros *Diálogo de las cosas ocurridas en Roma* y *Diálogo de Mercurio y Carón*— y el canciller Gatinara, que la matiza de un modo especial a raíz de su predilección por la idea de Dante relativa al emperador universal. También el *Tractatus regiminis mundi*, del jurista imperial Miguel de Ulzurrun —publicado en el mismo año de 1525—, representa esta atmósfera ideológica. En mayo o junio de este año se publica la traducción española de la obra de más relieve dentro del programa erasmiano de la Reforma de la Iglesia, el *Enchiridion militis christiani*, que logra una difusión inaudita y llega rápidamente a constituir una verdadera revolución espiritual (49).

Ahora bien: encontramos reflejos indudables de este movimiento erasmista en las Cartas cortesianas de Relación: la Cuarta, de fecha 15 de octubre de 1524, abarca una diatriba verdaderamente «erasmiana» contra los abusos indignos de un cristiano, del clero superior en México, que, según Cortés, se encuentra, con respecto a su actitud moral, profundamente por debajo de los sacerdotes paganos de los indios, y la Quinta, de 3 de septiembre de 1526 (como ya antes una carta cortesiana dirigida al emperador, de fecha 15 de octubre de 1524), contiene una idea directriz del erasmismo reformador, a saber: la de «una nueva iglesia, donde más que en todas las (partes) del mundo Dios Nuestro Señor será servido y honrado», que se levantará, como Cortés espera, en Nueva España (50). Por tanto, no parece demasiado arriesgado suponer que también el acentuado destacar de la idea del emperador universal, en la Cuarta, y aún más, en la Quinta Carta de Relación, esté en relación con aquellas corrientes, de dirección a la vez erasmista e imperial-universalista, en la Corte de España, y que éstas hayan sido tomadas en consideración por Cortés al redactar sus Cartas de Relación, hallándose él perfectamente informado, según parece, hasta respecto a los acontecimientos y cambios más sutiles acaecidos en el ambiente cortesano o sabiéndolos extraer, al menos, de las comunicaciones recibidas por él desde España.

A propósito de esto surge la pregunta de si la idea cortesiana de imperio y de emperador universales se limita a una mera fórmula

---

(49) Cf. M. Bataillon: *Op. cit.*, tomo I, pp. 182 ss., 222 ss. y 263 ss.
(50) La diatriba cortesiana contra el clero secular: Cf. *Gayangos*, pp. 319-320; El concepto de la «Nueva Iglesia»: *Cayangos*, pp. 327, 488. Este concepto de la «Nueva Iglesia» se le conoce solamente como formulado por Vasco de Quiroga, quien en su *Información en Derecho* pronostica el advenimiento de una «Iglesia nueva y primitiva» en el Nuevo Mundo, suponiéndose que Vasco de Quiroga haya tomado este concepto directamente de Erasmo (Cf. M. Bataillon: *Op. cit.*, tomo II, p. 447), sin tener en cuenta que se encuentra en las Cartas cortesianas, de donde pudo sacarlo mucho más fácilmente que de Erasmo, cuanto más que Vasco de Quiroga como oidor de la Segunda Audiencia, destinada para aconsejar a Cortés, estuvo en contacto con éste. Cortés tiene el derecho paterno a esta idea grande y profunda de que el Nuevo Mundo estaba destinado para cuidar de una «Iglesia nueva», aunque solamente el apostólico Vasco de Quiroga inspire a ella el espíritu de Pentecostés.

de cortesía, inventada en atención a las corrientes imperialistas mencionadas, o si Cortés la abrazó con su fe y la convirtió de tal modo en una fuerza capaz de influir sobre la realidad. Con otras palabras: la indomable voluntad cortesiana de descubrimiento y conquista, que abarca todas las costas del Océano Pacífico, con inclusión de las lejanías de Asia envueltas en la vagorosa luz mágica de leyendas medievales, y que se manifiesta con tanta pasión en las Cartas Cuarta y Quinta de Relación, ¿está fundada en la idea de imperio universal, como voluntad de realización de las pretensiones comprendidas en ella, según Cortés lo quiere hacer creer (51), o se origina aquella voluntad universal de descubrimiento y conquista meramente de la nueva imagen universal de espacio y del nuevo tipo de hombre del Renacimiento, ávido de actividad abarcadora del mundo (52), que encuentran en la idea universal de imperio a lo sumo una analogía, un adorno ideológico? Claro está que esta pregunta no puede contestarse con exactitud científica, sino que queda entregada a la apreciación psicológica de acuerdo con la impresión general de la personalidad de Cortés, a la cual el investigador haya llegado. En todo caso es un hecho demostrable que en las cartas cortesianas, en general, no puede atribuirse la significación de una realidad auténtica, de una fuerza determinante del acaecer histórico, al factor ideológico, a los pensamientos filosóficos y teológicos oriundos de la tradición medieval, que no raras veces tienen que cumplir directamente la función de «ideologías de encubrimiento». La interpretación cortesiana, por ejemplo, de la contraposición Cortés-Velázquez en la Primera Carta de Relación —la cual se considerará aún en la exposición siguiente— mediante los conceptos del dualismo agustiniano, haciendo el primero el papel del *rex justus,* perteneciente al reino de Dios, y el segundo el papel del *tyrannus,* perteneciente al reino de Satanás, forma una ficción que sirve en parte para la finalidad literaria de dar realce mítico-teológico al simple acto de insubordinación, y en parte para la finalidad jurídica de poder aplicar a Velázquez ciertas advertencias y condenaciones de las Siete Partidas. Con claridad insuperable muestra el carácter meramente ficticio de la utilización de elementos de la tradición escolástica la alocución de Cortés, pronunciada en Tlaxcala con motivo del alarde al tiempo de partirse

(51) Cf. *Gayangos,* p. 308, citado arriba en nota 34; Cf. también *Gayangos,* p. 466, tratado más abajo en el texto correspondiente a la nota 79 (en que Cortés interpreta la urgencia de su actividad vuelta hacia el Universo mediante la imagen del apóstol, según San Marcos XVI/15, pero mandado por el Emperador).

(52) Cf. EGMONT ZECHLIN: *Das europaische Weltbild und die Entdeckung Amerikas* (Veröffentlichungen des Reichsinstituts für Seegeltungsforschung, Leipzig, 1944); GUSTAV ADOLF REIN: *Voraussetzungen und Beginn der grossen Entdeckung* (en «Historia Mundi», fundada por Fritz Kern, tomo VII, Basel, 1957).

para poner cerco a México, y que se refiere a las «justas causas y razones» para reanudar la guerra contra los aztecas. Esta alocución está conservada en dos formas: en resumen, al principio de la Tercera Carta de Relación; y por extenso, en las «Ordenanzas militares y civiles mandadas pregonar por don Hernando Cortés en Tlaxcala, al tiempo de partirse para poner cerco a México» (53). La exposición respectiva de la Tercera Carta parte de la afirmación —sin duda, contraria a la verdad— de que los aztecas «sin causa ninguna» se habían rebelado contra los españoles y los habían echado fuera de toda su tierra (siendo la causa con toda seguridad la terrible matanza de los nobles aztecas reunidos sin armas con motivo de una fiesta religiosa, matanza ésta ejecutada por orden de Alvarado o —como opina el fray Diego Durán— por orden de Cortés mismo) (54); la alocución extractada pasa después a los argumentos de la doctrina tradicional escolástica sobre la «guerra justa», en referencia casi textual a la reproducción de esta doctrina, incluída en las Siete Partidas (Part. II, Tít. XXIII, Prólogo) (55). Las «Ordenanzas» son más detalladas, parten del concepto agustiniano de «Ordo» en cuanto fundamento de las «Ordenanzas» militares y le hacen seguir como primer postulado la amonestación dirigida a los soldados de que su motivo principal en la guerra en vísperas tenga que ser «apartar y desarraigar de las dichas idolatrías á todos los naturales destas partes, y reducillos... al conocimiento de Dios y de su santa fe católica; porque si con otra intención se hiciese la dicha guerra, sería injusta, y todo lo que en ella se oviese obnoxio é obligado á restitución»: este pasaje procede de Santo Tomás, quien en la *Summa Theologica*, expone lo siguiente (II/II, 66, 8, ad 1): «Si los que saquean a los enemigos hacen guerra justa, lo que por violencia adquieren en la guerra, se hace suyo propio, y esto no tiene razón de rapiña y, por consiguiente, no están obligados a la restitución; aunque puedan en la toma del botín los que hacen una guerra justa pecar por codicia según la mala intención, esto es, si pelean no por la justicia, sino principalmente por el botín... Pero si los que lo toman hacen una guerra injusta, cometen rapiña y están obligados a la restitución.»

---

(53) El resumen de la alocución cortesiana: Cf. *Gayangos*, pp. 165-166; las *Ordenanzas militares y civiles*, en Col. de Documentos para la Hist. de México, ed. J. García Icazbalceta, tomo I (México, 1858, pp. 445 ss.).

(54) Respecto a la matanza de los nobles aztecas por orden de Alvarado o —tal vez— de Cortés mismo, Cf. EULALIA GUZMÁN: *Relaciones de Hernán Cortés a Carlos V sobre la invasión de Anáhuac* (Libros Anáhuac, México, 1958, páginas 397 ss.). También la exposición apologética de ANGEL DE ALTOLAGUIRRE Y DUVALE, Op. cit. en nota 12, pp. 219-228), defiende solamente los motivos, sin cambiar el estado de las cosas.

(55) Cf. SILVIO ZAVALA: *Ensayos sobre la colonización española en América* (B. Aires, 1944, pp. 83-84).

No requiere ninguna explicación que en este caso la utilización de conceptos tomistas no sirve sino para el engaño de otros quienes conocieren el texto de las «Ordenanzas», y acaso para que los soldados se engañen a sí mismos, careciendo aquellos conceptos de todo poder para influir sobre la realidad.

No carece de interés, a propósito de la referencia a esta ineficacia de los elementos de la tradición escolástica —que figuran como adornos conceptuales, destinados para demostrar la cultura intelectual de Cortés y para ofuscar la conciencia de los soldados mediante el «como si» de la presencia (meramente verbal) de estas argumentaciones esco-lásticas—, observar el orden de los argumentos presentados por Cortés en el exordio de las «Ordenanzas» para demostrar la necesidad de las mismas. Primero, se hace presente que «por muchas escrituras y corónicas auténticas nos es notorio e manifiesto cuanto los antiguos que siguieron el ejercicio de la guerra, procuraron é trabajaron de introducir tales y tan buenas costumbres y ordenaciones, con las cuales y con su propria virtud y fortaleza, pudiesen alcanzar y con-seguir victoria y próspero fin en las conquistas y guerras que hobiesen de hacer y seguir; é por el contrario vemos haber sucedido grandes infortunios, desastres é muertes á los que no siguieron la buena cos-tumbre y orden que en la guerra se debe tener...». Segundo, figura el argumento teológico-metafísico de que «la orden es tan loable, que no tan solamente en las cosas humanas, mas aun en las divinas se ama y sigue... como que ella sea un principio, medio y fin para el buen regimiento de todas las cosas». Tercero, Cortés recuerda que «los pasados (españoles) fallaron ser necesario hacer ordenanza é cos-tumbres por donde se rigiesen é gobernasen aquellos que hubiesen de seguir é ejercer el uso de la guerra», para llegar —cuarto— a hacer constar que «á los Españoles que en mi compañía agora están é estuvieren é á mí nos es mucho mas necesario é conveniente seguir é observar toda la mejor costumbre y órden que nos sea posible... por tener por enemigos y contrarios á la mas belicosa y astuta gente en la guerra... que no tiene número, é nosotros tan pocos y tan apar-tados y destituidos de todo humano socorro». Se reconoce que el argu-mento teológico-metafísico —que, como el más general, hubiese debido figurar, según principios de la lógica, en primer lugar— se halla puesto en segundo lugar, entre el argumento humanista-renacentista de la ejemplaridad de los antiguos en los asuntos de la guerra, y el argumento (expuesto en forma breve, como mero pensamiento de transición hacia el cuarto argumento práctico y concreto) de la ejem-plaridad de los antepasados españoles; y resulta a las claras de esta misma posición del argumento teológico-metafísico que Cortés lo consideró más bien como un adorno intelectual, no atribuyéndole una trascendencia suficiente, ni para él ni para sus soldados, como para ponerlo al principio de sus «ordenanzas», como punto de partida de su argumentación.

Con claridad insuperable muestra la específica estratificación existente en el alma de Cortés entre lo que consideró en esta época de su vida como realidad práctica y lo que consideró como mera ideología superpuesta teóricamente a ella, el pasaje que se encuentra hacia el final de la Segunda Carta de Relación, en que el conquistador expone los motivos de su decisión de no retirarse, después de la huída de los españoles de Tenochtitlan (la «Noche Triste») hasta la costa, sino de mantenerse firme en la sierra mexicana, organizando desde aquí la reconquista de la capital; el pasaje respectivo reza: «E yo, viendo que mostrar á los naturales poco ánimo, en especial á nuestros amigos, era causa de más aína dejarnos y ser contra nosotros, acordándome que siempre á los osados ayuda la fortuna, y que éramos cristianos, y confiando en la grandisima bondad y misericordia de Dios, que no permitiría que del todo pereciésemos, y se perdiese tanta y tan noble tierra como para V. M. estaba pacifica y en punto de se pacificar... me determiné de por ninguna manera bajar los puertos hácia la mar... porque en ello me parecia que, demás de ser vergonzoso á mi persona, y á todos muy peligroso, á V. M. haciamos muy gran traicion» (56). El punto de partida y la base de todo el razonamiento los forma la consideración práctico-realista de que una actitud de pusilanimidad de parte de los españoles en su situación de entonces significaría la ruina; sobre esta consideración se pone, como segundo estrato, el pensamiento perteneciente a la filosofía vulgar del Renacimiento, que Maquiavelo formula en *Il Principe* (cap. XXV) diciendo: «la fortuna è donna: ed è necessario, volendola tenere sotto, batterla e urtarla»; y sólo después, como tercer estrato, todavía más ligero y vaporoso, a decirlo así, aparece la argumentación cristiano-teológica, la referencia a la bondad de Dios, en estrecha asociación con la idea feudal del servicio imperial. Y como una especie de síntesis de la argumentación, después de haber sacado la conclusión de la misma, se presenta, primero, la referencia —reveladora de una orgullosa conciencia de sí mismo, muy de tipo renacentista— a la vergüenza que significaría para Cortés la retirada a la costa; segundo, la advertencia relativa al peligro para todos, entrañada en esta retirada, y tercero, el recuerdo del motivo feudal, a saber: la traición respecto al emperador, que significaría tal repliegue hasta Vera Cruz. Se diría que en los dos pasajes cortesianos analizados habla un típico

(56) *Gayangos*, pp. 142-143.

hombre de Renacimiento, de estructura maquiavélica, para quien en el primer plano de su conocimiento se encuentra su altanera conciencia de sí mismo y los razonados intereses políticos y militares prácticos; pero que —debido a la efectiva importancia de la herencia medieval en el Renacimiento español (57)— conserva también una plenitud de conceptos patrísticos y escolásticos en su mente, utilizándolos (no raras veces diluídos en la ligerísima ideología careciente de toda eficacia práctica) por razones de la impresión literaria o de su virtud jurídica.

Pero, a pesar de que conforme a eso la aparición de nuevos esquemas ideológicos en la mente de Cortés no se expresa casi nunca en un cambio de su actitud relativa a la realidad empírica, ni ofrece nuevos motivos de su acción, sino más bien nuevas imágenes de la exposición literaria, nuevos conceptos de la retórica apologética; esta circunstancia no disminuye la importancia de un problema no resuelto por la ciencia, incluso ni siquiera observado por ella, a saber: el problema de la descripción de la evolución intelectual, de la «historia del espíritu» de Hernán Cortés. Considerando que algunos rasgos básicos de esta evolución se han hecho patentes por medio de nuestro estudio de las fases de la transformación de la idea cortesiana de imperio, quiero tratar de esbozar, para dar remate al presente trabajo, las líneas principales de la «historia del espíritu» de Cortés desde el momento de la redacción por él de la Primera Carta de Relación, que constituye el primer documento cortesiano en que podemos hacernos cargo de lo peculiar de su mentalidad.

El debido punto de partida de tal investigación lo constituye el exacto conocimiento, por parte de Cortés, de las Siete Partidas, probado por la Primera Carta de Relación; tal conocimiento demuestra la cultura jurídica de Cortés y se halla conforme con la presencia a lo largo de todas las Cartas de Relación de numerosos conceptos latinos, concernientes especialmente a la jurisprudencia, y con los copiosos latinismos estilísticos que se encuentran ante todo en los exordios de las Cartas (58). Además, pertenece a este primer estado comprobable de la cultura personal de Cortés el dualismo agustiniano, algo difuso, que no presupone ningún conocimiento directo de San Agustín y que sirve a Cortés para dar mayor relieve a su disensión

---

(57) Cf. José Antonio Maravall: *Carlos V y el pensamiento político del Renacimiento* (Inst. Est. Polít., Madrid, 1960), Introducción: *El sentido del Renacimiento en España*. Cf. mi libro *El Antijovio*, de G. Jiménez de Quesada, y las concepciones de realidad y verdad en la época del Manierismo y de la Contrarreforma, en víspera de publicarse por el Instituto de Cultura Hispánica.

(58) Cf. arriba las notas 23 y 25.

con Diego Velázquez. El fondo popular de aquella cultura jurídica y de este agustinismo de Cortés lo constituye su saber amplio y vivaz relativo al Romancero; y de la combinación entre la tradición de las Siete Partidas y la tradición del Romancero se origina la idea particular de imperio de la Segunda Carta de Relación, que hemos investigado especialmente. La Segunda Carta abarca, empero, también una prueba indudable de la familiaridad de Cortés con la filosofía de Santo Tomás, familiaridad ésta que no puede interpretarse como una adquisición hecha en este mismo período de la vida de Cortés, absorbido por las graves tareas de la conquista de Tenochtitlan-México, sino que se tiene que comprender como una parte integrante de los fundamentos mismos de la cultura personal del conquistador.

Este conjunto de conceptos de alta cultura queda estacionario, según parece, hasta la época determinada por la Tercera Carta de Relación, o sea hasta la terminación completa de la conquista de México. En la Cuarta Carta —separada de la Tercera por más de dos años de trabajo constructivo de un hombre perspicaz de Estado— aparecen, al lado del fundamento ideológico de cuño tomista fielmente conservado, nuevos estímulos intelectuales: además de una transformación de la idea de imperio en el sentido universalista, y dentro del margen de una concepción cósmica, la cual hace suponer la lectura, ocurrida ya entonces, del tratado de Torquemada relativo al imperio universal romano, se manifiesta un elemento nominalista-relativista procedente de la tradición de Guillermo de Occam, proporcionado a Cortés probablemente por los franciscanos llegados a México pocos meses antes de la redacción de la Cuarta Carta. La Quinta Carta, escrita después de la dramática expedición cortesiana a las Hibueras, prueba que Cortés prosigue su nuevo camino indicado, según parece, por los franciscanos, surgiendo, al lado del universalismo imperial, que ha sido conceptuado a base de la filosofía aristotélico-tomista y por sugestión del *Opusculum* de Torquemada, una insinuación de la teoría escotista de conocimiento y el concepto agustiniano del tirano, que evidencia por primera vez la lectura directa de la obra principal de San Agustín. Y no es una mera coincidencia que sería San Agustín quien determinaría le evolución espiritual de Cortés durante los últimos años de su vida, que transcurrirán ya más allá del lapso de tiempo comprendido por las Cartas de Relación: sobre los fundamentos tomistas de la formación intelectual de Cortés —que le ofrecieron valiosos elementos de argumentación y exposición ideológicas, pero ninguna experiencia de una regeneración religiosa interior— se elevarán las ideas de San Agustín relativas a la omnipotencia de Dios y la impotencia del hombre como energías que provocarán la transformación en el fondo del alma de Cortés, haciendo de un hombre mundano del Renacimiento a un hombre de la Contrarreforma. Esta evolución espiritual de Cortés, caracterizada a grandes rasgos en las líneas precedentes, consideraremos aún en forma algo más detallada, por tratarse científicamente de una tierra virgen.

La Primera Carta de Relación —que comprende la apología, basada en las Siete Partidas, del acto de la población veracruzana y de la violación por ella de las instrucciones de Velázquez (y que ha sido redactada, sin duda alguna, por Cortés mismo, aun cuando no firmada por él, sino por un grupo de sus oficiales— utiliza también conceptos del dualismo agustiniano de la «Ciudad de Dios» y de la «Ciudad terrenal», o sea Ciudad de Satanás, para profundizar teológicamente el antagonismo entre Cortés y Velázquez; sustituyendo, empero, a ese respecto, el principio central de la *Ciudad de Satanás*, de San Agustín, la superbia, por el pecado por excelencia de la Edad Media tardía y del capitalismo temprano, la codicia, que figura también, de modo análogo, como pecado fundamental en las Siete Partidas (59); mientras que a Diego Velázquez se lo caracteriza como «movido más a codicia que a otro celo», poniéndoselo de tal manera —según Part. II, Tít. III, Ley IV y Part. II, Tít. V, Ley XIII— entre los culpables de pecados mortales y servidores de Satanás, indicados para que el rey auténtico los aleje de sí por traer ellos mucho daño (según Part. II, Tít. IX, Ley II), se presenta a Cortés por distinguido por «muy gran celo y deseo del servicio de Vuestras Majestades»; y al paso que Velázquez aparece revestido, en virtud de su actuación de gobernador de la Isla Fernandina, de los atributos del tirano clásico, según Aristóteles (Part. II, Tít. I, Ley X), se revela Cortés a sí mismo —en cuanto llamado para tener a sus compañeros de armas «en justicia y gobernación»— a la luz del *Rex justus*, de San Agustín (60). Se comprende

---

(59) J. HUIZINGA hizo observar, en su obra maestra *El otoño de la Edad Media*, que en esta época la «Superbia» —que había sido considerada por San Agustín como pecado fundamental— cede el puesto a la «Avaritia», refiriéndose al versículo «Radix omnium malorum est cupiditas» (I. Timot. 6/610) a la «Avaritia». (Huizinga, El otoño..., ed. «Rev. de Occidente», Argentina, B. Aires, 1947, pp. 38-39). El texto respectivo de las Siete Partidas (Part. II, Tít. II, Ley IV) reza: «Los santos y los sabios se acordaron en esto, que la cobdicia es muy mala cosa, así que dixieron por ella que es madre et raiz de todos los males... es grant pecado mortal quanto á Dios, et grant malestanza al mundo» (Cf. Part. II, Tít. V, Ley XIII). Part. II, Tít. IX, Ley II, añade la advertencia dirigida al rey de que no utilice los servicios de hombres pobres «porque probedat trae a los homes á grant cobdicia, que es raiz de todo mal»; por lo cual, la «Primera Carta de Relación» que tanto pone de relieve la «codicia» de Diego Velázquez, termina solicitando los firmantes de la Carta que el rey lo separe de sus cargos. (Para mayores detalles, véase mi trabajo citado en la nota 9).

(60) Los rasgos característicos de Velázquez en cuanto «tirano», según la «Política», de Aristóteles, y Part. I, Tít. I, Ley X, véaselos: *Gayangos*, p. 27. Los rasgos característicos de Cortés como «rex justus», según San Agustín: *Gayangos*, pp. 21, 28. Respecto al origen agustiniano del antagonismo entre «Tyrannus» y

que la presencia de estos elementos del dualismo agustiniano en la Primera Carta de Relación no implica necesariamente la suposición de un conocimiento directo de la obra *De Civitate Dei*, de San Agustín, pues no contando el hecho de que algunos de ellos figuran en las Siete Partidas —la pericia de las cuales era muy difundida entre los soldados de la conquista y puede quedar por supuesta en una persona activa en funciones de administración pública, como era Cortés durante su estadía en la Isla Fernandina (61)—, el dualismo agustiniano había penetrado en los espejos de príncipes y doctrinas políticas de la alta y tardía Edad Media y se había convertido en una parte integrante de la conciencia política general (62).

La Segunda Carta de Relación que presenta al principio el concepto realista particularista del Imperio, para cimentarlo después mediante una protohistoria azteca artificiosamente construida (la cual supone, probablemente, de su parte, el conocimiento de movimientos protohistóricos de amplios espacios, ejecutados a base de la autoridad de un «conductor», como los expone, por ejemplo, la *Primera Crónica General de España*, de Alfonso X, en su *Estoria de los Godos* (63), abarca al mismo tiempo ideas tomistas, íntimamente afines al principio aristotélico-tomista que fundamenta, en la Quinta Carta, la idea del imperio universal. Y es el concepto de la naturaleza, de Cortés, que, mirándolo bien, resulta ser tomista; aparece en el conjunto siguiente: «Salí una noche —cuenta Cortés— con cien peones y con los indios nuestros amigos y con los de caballo, y a una legua del real se me cayeron cinco de los caballos y yeguas que llevaba, que en ninguna manera los pude pasar adelante, y hícelos volver. E aunque todos los de mi compañía decían que me tornase, porque era mala señal, todavía seguí mi camino, considerando que Dios es sobre natura» (64). Cortés rechaza de tal manera la superstición del destacamento —la cual procede de la antigüedad clásica, pasando por el Medievo al Renacimiento, y consiste en la interpretación de ciertos acontecimientos naturales como indicios de mal agüero—, poniendo el conquistador el acontecimiento respectivo en su lugar en el nexo causal universal, elaborado por el aristotelismo cristiano de la alta

«Rex justus», Cf. ERNST BERNHEIM: *Mittelalteriliche Zeitanschauungen in ihrem Einfluss auf Politik und Geschichtsschreibung*, Teil I (Tübingen, 1918, pp. 46 ss.).
(61) Cf. SILVIO ZAVALA: *Ensayos sobre la colonización española en América* (B. Aires, 1944), p. 84. R. MENÉNDEZ PIDAL recalca la unión de las armas y las letras jurídicas, tradicional en España, en su libro *La España del Cid* (2.ª ed. Buenos Aires, 1943, pp. 448-451).
(62-a) Cf. R. W. and A. J. CARLYLE: *A History of Mediaeval Political Theory in the West*, v. VI, 2nd impr. (Edinburgh-London, 1950), passim: WILHELM BERGES: *Die Fürstenspiegel des hohen und späten Mittelalters* (Stutgart, 1952), passim.
(63) *Primera Crónica General de España* (publ. por R. Menéndez Pidal, Madrid, 1955, pp. 216-217).
(64) *Gayangos*, p. 64.

Edad Media, de la naturaleza creada por Dios y obediente a sólo Dios (65). La tesis de Cortés «Dios es sobre natura» forma una abreviación de la sentencia de Santo Tomás: «Naturalia soli Deo, qui est auctor naturae, subduntur» *(Summa Theol.* III, q. 13, a. 3, sed contra); ella expresa la idea tomista de la naturaleza como «instrumento de Dios» *(Summa Theol.* 1/II, q. 1, a. 2, resp.; q. 6, a. 1, ad 2), y entraña la interpretación de aquel incidente nocturno de «que —como dice Santo Tomás— los defectos que acontecen en las cosas naturales, aunque están fuera del orden de las causas particulares, no por esto se hallan fuera del orden de las causas universales, y principalmente de la causa primera, que es Dios, a cuya providencia nada puede escapar» *(Summa Theol.* I/II, q. 93, a. 5, ad 3).

Con los acontecimientos relatados en la Tercera carta, de 15 de mayo de 1522 —o sea del cerco y de la toma de la capital mediante una operación «anfibia» ingeniosamente concebida (66), y de la subsiguiente fundación del Estado hispánico-azteca nuevo—, termina el período de la situación de Cortés fuera de la ley (la cual constituye, como se ha demostrado más arriba, el punto de partida de la concepción de la idea particular de imperio, orientada en orden a México y a Alemania); y no por mera coincidencia aparece al final de esta Carta-Relación, como último efecto de esta idea de imperio, el uso del concepto «depósito» en vez del concepto «encomienda», creado en atención a las islas Antillas para caracterizar la situación de servicio de los indios respecto a los españoles. El 15 de octubre de 1522 firma el emperador en Valladolid el decreto que nombra a Cortés gobernador, capitán general y justicia mayor de Nueva España, legalizando de tal modo la posición del mismo y cancelando la penalidad de su acto de insubordinación relativo a Velázquez. La Cuarta Carta-Relación, firmada exactamente dos años después de este nombramiento, contiene ya —en lógica conformidad con la nueva situación— la nueva idea de imperio universal. Además abarca esta Carta testimonios del afluir de nuevos pensamientos: Cortés conoce ahora —probablemente a raíz de una lectura de Livio— el sentido más profundo y el *pathos* del concepto de la «necesidad», puesto por Maquiavelo en el centro de su doctrina. Escribe al emperador lo siguiente: «Por las diferencias que Diego Velázquez ha querido tener conmigo, y por la mala volun-

---

(65) Cf. respecto a la superstición de los soldados: ALFRED LEHMANN: *Aberglaube und Zauberei* (Stuttgart, 1925). Respecto al concepto de la naturaleza, presupuesto por Cortés, Cf. RAIMUNDO PANIKER: *El concepto de la naturaleza* (Inst. Luis Vives, C. S. I. C.; Madrid, 1951, p. 401); JOSÉ ANTONIO MARAVALL: *Sobre naturaleza e historia en el humanismo español* (en Historia de España, estudios publ. en la revista «Arbor», de Madrid, 1953; pp. 243-244); ETIENNE GILSON: *L'Esprit de la Philosophie Médiévale* (Etudes de Phil. Médiév., t. XXXIII, París, 1948, p. 351).
(66) Cf. C. HARVEY GARDINER: *Naval Power in the Conquest of México* (Austin, Univ. of Texas Press, 1956).

tad que a su causa y por su intercesión don Juan de Fonseca, obispo de Búrgos, me ha tenido..., no he sido proveído de artillería ni armas, cómo tenia necesidad..., y porque no hay cosa que mas los ingenios de los hombres avive que la necesidad, y cómo yo ésta tuviese tan extrema y sin esperanza de remedio, pues aquellos no daban lugar que V. S. M. la supiese, trabajé de buscar órden para que por ella no se perdiese lo que con tanto trabajo y peligro se habia ganado»; y Cortés consiguió hallar en el país mismo cobre y estaño y producir piezas de artillería (67). Con fuerte insistencia manifiesta el conquistador al final de la Cuarta Carta de Relación el relativismo de principio en orden al cambio necesario de los criterios de juicio, y aun el derecho a contradecirse a sí mismo, en vista de los aspectos continuamente cambiantes de la realidad y de la plenitud inmensa de los posibles casos y situaciones, diciendo: «Siempre tendré cuidado de añadir lo que mas me pareciere que conviene, porque cómo por la grandeza y diversidad de las tierras que cada dia se descubren, y por muchos secretos que cada dia de lo descubierto conocemos, hay necesidad que á nuevos acontecimientos haya nuevos pareceres y consejos, y si en algunos de los que he dicho ó de aquí adelante dijére á V. M. le pareciere que contradigo algunos de los pasados, crea V. E. que nuevo caso me hace dar nuevo parecer» (68). Se presenta en este pasaje, según parece, un caso de aplicación a la situación de continua modificación y dilatación del horizonte intelectual, producida por los progresos del descubrimiento y de la exploración de la tierra, de la doctrina de Averroes, transcrita por Guillermo de Occam en su *Dialogus,* que «secundum diversitatem qualitatem et necesitatem temporum expedit regimina et dominia mortalium variari» (que conviene que cambien las formas de gobierno de los hombres, en conformidad con la diversidad, la propiedad y la necesidad de las épocas) (69). Es de suponer que han sido los sabios franciscanos —llegados a México pocos meses antes de la terminación de la Cuarta Carta de Relación, el 13 de mayo de 1524— quienes transmitieron a Cortés este concepto del gran franciscano inglés. Puede ser que no carezca de cierta importancia respecto al aparecer de la idea de imperio universal en la misma Cuarta Carta el hecho de que aquella tesis relativista de Guillermo de Occam se encuentra en su tratado *De juribus romani imperii* —el último de la

---

(67) *Gayangos,* p. 311. Cf. MACHIAVELLI: *Discorsi sopra la prima deca di Tito Livio,* lib. III, cap. XII; FRIEDRICH MEINECKE: *Die Idee der Staatsräson in der neueren Geschichte* (2. Aufl. München-Berlin, 1925, p. 47).

(68) *Gayangos,* p. 323.

(69) GUILLERMO DE OCCAM: *Dialogus III/2/1,* cap. V (ed. M. Goldast en *Monarchia S. Romani Imperii,* vol. II, Hanau, 1613, p. 876. Cf. FRIEDRICH AUGUST FREIHERR VON DER HEYDTE: *Die Geburtsstunde des souveränen Staates* (Regensburg, 1952, pp. 112 ss.).

parte tercera de su *Dialogus*—, en que el franciscano inglés defiende la monarquía universal, aunque desde otro punto de vista que Cortés y su fuente inmediata, Torquemada, a saber, desde el punto de vista del interés general de la humanidad y de la soberanía inherente a ella (70) (en tanto que Torquemada y, siguiendo a éste, Cortés cimienta el imperio universal mediante consideraciones peculiares de la cosmología tomista, es decir, aristotélica).

Varios de los rasgos más característicos de la impresionante Quinta Carta de Relación están relacionados directamente con la probable infiltración de la influencia franciscana en el mundo intelectual de Hernán Cortés, originalmente orientado en sentido tomista. La Carta está encabezada por la no admisión del postulado ciceroniano *(De oratore*, II, lib. XV, 63) de que el historiador manifieste no sólo el hecho o dicho en cuanto tal, sino el «cómo», el «quo modo», del mismo, declarando Cortés: «Decirlas (cosas) como pasaron, ni yo las sabria significar, ni por lo que yo dijese allá se podrian comprender.» Y en el curso del relato de la Carta, Cortés vuelve sobre el mismo pensamiento, sobre lo indecible del acontecer en su verdadera realidad e individualidad y sobre su esencia, incomprensible para el lector ajeno a ellos, declarando: «Pues querer yo decir y significar á V. M. la aspereza y fragosidad deste puerto y sierras, ni quien mejor que yo lo supiese lo podría explicar, ni quien lo. oyese lo podría entender, si por vista de ojos, no lo viese é pasando por él no lo experimentase.» Este aserto corresponde a la manera de pensar tanto tomista como escotista-franciscana, según la cual solamente lo general puede ser el objeto del entendimiento racional, y, por tanto, de la definición, lo individual, empero, se presenta exclusivamente a la experiencia inmediata de los sentidos, sustrayéndose a toda demostración racional *(Individuum est ineffabile)* (72); pero Duns Escoto, el principal filósofo franciscano, había introducido en esta doctrina común del tomismo y de la escuela franciscana un acento especial por su distinción aguda entre *quidditas* (esencia general y definible) y *haecceitas* (singularidad, peculiaridad individual), y por su insistencia en que el individuo entraña más que la esencia genérica *(individuum exprimit plus quam quidditatem)*, presentándose este «plus» de lo meramente individual exclusivamente como existente, pero de ningún modo como comprensible *(haecceitas non sen-*

(70) Cf. ALOIS DEMPE: *Sacrum Imperium* (München-Berlín, 1929; pp. 521 ss.).
(71) *Gayangos*, pp. 395, 433.
(72) Cf. ARISTÓTELES: *Phys* I, 5.189 a 5; S. THOMAS: *Summa Theol.* I. q. LXXXVI, a. 1. Cf. G. M. MANSER, OP.: *La esencia del Tomismo* (2.ª ed., trad., por V. García Yebra, Inst. Luis Vives, de Fil., C. S. I. C., Madrid, 1953, p. 291; E. GILSON: *Le Thomisme* (Etudes de Phil. Médiév. t. 5, 5e, éd., Paris, 1948, pp. 304 ss.).

titur) (73). Resulta que aquellos asertos de Cortés relativos a lo indecible de la realidad del acaecer y a la necesidad de experimentarla para conocerla constituyen otras tantas pruebas de la influencia franciscana sobre la mente de Cortés en esta época tardía de su conquista.

Asimismo, el concepto —ya mencionado como indicio de la influencia erasmiana— de «una nueva iglesia, donde mas que en todas las (partes) del mundo Dios Nuestro Señor será servido y honrado» y que se levantará en Nueva España «si estorbo no hay de los que mal sienten destas cosas y su celo no es enderezado á este fin», asimismo este concepto, digo, tiene una vertiente hacia el franciscanismo. Pues esta consigna de la «novedad» aplicada a temas religiosos pertenece a la peculiar tradición de la Orden franciscana. En la primera biografía oficial de San Francisco, escrita por Tomás de Celano, se recalca que el Santo había llegado en la última época de la existencia del mundo como «evangelista nuevo», trayendo al universo una «santa novedad», infundiendo en los corazones de los elegidos un «espíritu nuevo» y aun transmitiéndoles un «nuevo rito y nuevos símbolos», de manera que por él «los antiguos milagros se habían renovado», después de haber «plantado él la vid fructífera según nuevo orden, pero antigua costumbre» (74). Se reconoce cómo estas imágenes específicamente franciscanas se reflejan en la visión de la «Nueva Iglesia» de Cortés, y cómo la veneración personal del conquistador ante los abnegados *Fratres Minores* (los recibió de rodillas cuando llegaron a la capital, se hizo acompañar por dos de ellos durante su fatal expedición a las Hibueras, y de vuelta de ésta, su primer camino fué al convento franciscano, donde se quedó durante seis días) se manifiesta simbólicamente en la Quinta Carta.

Pero el hecho más importante que se puede considerar como resultado de la influencia franciscana sobre Cortés es, sin duda, su contacto directo con la obra principal de San Agustín *La ciudad de Dios*, pues agustinismo y franciscanismo se encuentran desde siglos estrechamente ligados (75). Es cierto que la lectura de esta obra de Cortés no está comprobada por ningún testimonio directo; pero se la puede inferir,

---

(73) Cf. Etienne Gilson: *Jean Duns Scot* (Etudes de Phil. Médiév. tom. XLII, Paris, 1952, pp. 544-547). Un caso análogo de un claro conocimiento de la definitiva imposibilidad de comprender y describir los elementos histórico-individuales, fundada igualmente en la influencia de la epistemología del Escotismo, se encuentra en el importante epílogo de la *Crónica de don Alvaro de Luna*, escrita entre 1453 y 1460, tal vez por Gonzalo Chacón. En mi obra relativa al *Antijovio*, citada más arriba (núm. 56), analizo por primera vez este caso notable de una influencia de la doctrina epistemológica de Duns Escoto sobre la Historiología.

(74) Cf. Ernst Benz: *Ecclesia Spiritualis* (Stuttgart, Kohlhammer, 1934, páginas 64 ss.).

(75) Cf. Etienne Gilson: *La Philosophie au Moyen Age* (2e éd., Paris, 1952, pp. 587-588).

demostrarla indirectamente, como única fuente posible del específico concepto agustiniano de «tirano» que aparece en la Quinta Carta y que nos sirve de «fosil conductor». Mientras que en la Primera Carta de Relación la actividad de Diego Velázquez como gobernador de la Isla Fernandina está calificada de «tirania», según el concepto clásico de «tirano» formulado en la *Política*, de Aristóteles, como gobernación ejercida con injusticia, arbitrariedad y egoísmo y asegurada mediante la provocación refinada de temor y discordia entre los súbditos (aun cuando no usando expresamente la voz «tirano»), y al principio de la Segunda Carta se atribuye a Moctezuma «tiranía» en el mismo sentido aristotélico de un gobierno despótico sin justicia (76), aparece en la Quinta carta el concepto de «tirano» en un sentido totalmente diferente, específicamente agustiniano, a saber, en el sentido de una rebelión contra el orden legítimo y el señor legítimo. Así como San Agustín en *La ciudad de Dios* declara que el ángel satánico ha caído porque «en casi tiránica altivez prefirió gozar de súbditos al ser súbdito» y llama a los enemigos de los emperadores piadosos Constancio y Teodosio «tiranos» y hace morir al emperador Graciano «a hierro tiránico» (77), así Cortés hace constar en la Quinta Carta que ciertas personas lo acusan ante el emperador de «no tener esta tierra en su poderoso nombre, sino en tiránica e inefable forma, dando para ello algunas depravadas y diabólicas razones» (78). De la misma manera, Cortés llama en la Quinta Carta a los indignos lugartenientes encargados por él del Gobierno de México durante su ausencia en la expedición a las Hibueras «tiranos» que le habrían tenido «injuriado y destruído» (79). La procedencia agustiniana de este concepto insólito —es decir, no aristotélico— de «tirano» es tan clara como la atmósfera agustiniana de los conceptos acompañantes de las «depravadas y diabólicas razones» y de las «serpentinas lenguas» atribuídas a los autores de la calumnia, conceptos que entrañan la suposición de la continua presencia y actividad de las fuerzas satánicas en hombre y mundo, tal cual la había concebido San Agustín (de manera totalmente diferente de la doctrina optimista y racionalista de Santo Tomás) (80). Tenemos que admitir la hipótesis de que Cortés haya leído la obra *De Civitate Dei*, de San Agustín, en esta época del

---

(76) *Gayangos*, pp. 27-28; 53.
(77) Cf. Ernst Bernheim: *Op. cit.*, p. 47.
(78) *Gayangos*, p. 484.
(79) *Gayangos*, p. 481.
(80) *Gayangos*, p. 485. Cf. mi trabajo *El descubrimiento de la Nada por la Filosofía medieval y la Ontología existencialista de Santo Tomás* («Revista Bolívar» núm. 27, Bogotá, 1954, pp. 187 ss.); Adolf Harnack: *Lehrbuch der Dogmengeschichte*, III (4.Aufl. Tübingen, 1910, pp. 210 ss.); Joseph Mausbach: *Die Ethik des hl. Augustinus*. I (Bd. 2.Aufl. Freiburg, 1929, pp. 118, 131, 142-145); Etienne Gilson: *L'Esprit de la Philosophie Médiévale* (2e éd. Paris, 1948), chap. VI; E. Gilson: *Le Thomisme*, pp. 497 ss.

ocaso de su estrella, probablemente en las semanas entre su vuelta a México de la expedición a las Hibueras, el 19 de junio de 1526, y la terminación de su Quinta Carta-Relación, el 3 de septiembre del mismo año.

Para redondear la imagen ofrecida por la Quinta Carta, de un notable progreso en la intensificación y profundización de los contactos de Cortés con la tradición religiosa y con las raíces patrísticas y hasta bíblicas de la misma, quiero llamar la atención del lector sobre el pasaje en que el conquistador se representa a sí mismo como apóstol mandado por el Emperador para dar testimonio de Dios. Utilizando el versículo de San Marcos XVI/15: «Et dixit eis: Euntes in mundum universum praedicate Evangelium omni creaturae», Cortés informa a Carlos V que había dicho a ciertos indios que «traje mandado de V. M. —a quien todo el universo es subjecto— que viese y visitase toda la tierra, sin dejar cosa alguna, y hiciese en ella pueblos de cristianos..., así para la conservación de sus personas y haciendas como por la salvación de sus ánimas» (81). Si se compara con este pasaje las utilizaciones anteriores por Cortés de textos bíblicos, utilizaciones de indudable carácter blasfemo por tratarse siempre de manifestaciones de intentos meramente políticos del conquistador —en la Segunda Carta aplica a las disensiones entre los indios, tan favorables a Cortés para «más aína sojuzgarlos», «maneando con los unos y con los otros», el versículo de San Lucas XI/17: «Omne regnum in seipsum divisum desolabitur», y en la segunda exposición de la protohistoria azteca, que se encuentra en la misma Carta, Cortés introduce, como hemos visto, una alusión al versículo de San Mateo XIII/16-17—, se comprende que ahora, en la Quinta Carta-Relación, el aprovechamiento del Evangelio en las relaciones cortesianas está haciéndose mucho más compatible con el significado y con la dignidad de la Sagrada Escritura que antes.

Esta profundización que se produjo en el nombre de San Agustín de la conciencia religiosa de Cortés continuó, en parte, bajo el empuje más y más recrudescente de los golpes del destino, en parte —y esto durante sus últimos años de vida, pasados en España— bajo la influencia de la Contrarreforma, en pleno desarrollo en esta época. Indico, en pocas palabras, estos reveses de fortuna, posteriores a las «Cartas de Relación», e interpreto al final un último testimonio en forma de carta para aclarar la dirección de la evolución religiosa de Cortés, pero a la vez el resultado final de las transformaciones de su idea de imperio. A continuación de la vuelta de Cortés de las Hibueras sigue la «residencia» tomada a Cortés por el Gobierno español, es decir, la

(81) *Gayangos*, p. 466.

479

pesquisa de toda su gestión financiera y política (82); después, su regreso a España en el año 1528, con el fin de defender su causa ante el emperador; la restricción de su autoridad en México al mando militar, separándose de éste el gobierno civil y la administración suprema de la justicia, que se encargaron primero a una Audiencia y después a un virrey, Antonio de Mendoza, lo cual produjo el desposeimiento total de Cortés respecto al gobierno del país conquistado por él durante los años de su renovada permanencia en México, entre 1530 y 1540; también los amplios designios abrigados por él en esta época de una exploración y conquista de toda la costa del Océano Pacífico, con inclusión de los países del este de Asia, fracasaron, ante todo por razón de la resistencia, primero, de la Audiencia, y después, del virrey. Nuevamente de vuelta en España, en 1540, trató de restablecer su posición participando en la expedición de Argel de Carlos V; incluso esta tentativa malogró a causa de la desconfianza del emperador contra Cortés. Este siguió viviendo aún hasta el 2 de diciembre de 1547, y llegó a ver aún, de este modo, los primeros pasos de la Compañía de Jesús y la victoria de Esmalcalda, de Carlos V, y con ello, el primer despliegue impetuoso de la Contrarreforma. La última carta —profundamente amargada— de Cortés a Carlos V, enviada desde Valladolid el 3 de febrero de 1544, revela toda la esencialidad del cambio operado en el fondo del alma del conquistador. En esta carta escribe lo siguiente: «Pensé que el haber trabajado en la juventud me aprovechara para que en la vejez tuviera descanso, y así ha cuarenta años que me he ocupado en no dormir, mal comer y á las vezes ni bien ni mal, traer las armas á cuestas, poner la persona en peligros, gastar mi hacienda y edad, todo en servicio de Dios, trayendo ovejas en su corral muy remotas de nuestro hemisferio, é inoctas y no escritas en nuestras escrituras, y acrecentando y dilatando el nombre y patrimonio de mi rey, ganándole y trayéndole á su yugo y real cetro muchos y muy grandes reinos y señoríos de muchas bárbaras naciones y gentes, ganados por mi propia persona y expensas, sin ser ayudado de cosa alguna, antes muy estorbado por muchos émulos é invidiosos que como sanguijuelas han rebentado de hartos de mi sangre. De la parte que á Dios cupo de mis trabajos y vigilias asaz estoy pagado, porque seyendo la obra suya, quiso tomarme por medio, y que las gentes me atribuyesen alguna parte, aunque quien conociere de mí lo que yo, verá claro que no sin causa la divina Providencia quiso que una obra tan grande se acabase por el más flaco é inutil medio que se pudo hallar, porque á solo Dios fuese el atributo» (83). Ahora bien: este

---

(82) Cf. R. B. MERRIMAN: *Op. cit.*, pp. 209-210: A. DE ALTOLAGUIRRE Y DUVALE: *Op. cit.*, cap. XXII.
(83) *Gayangos*, pp. 567-568.

último pensamiento decisivo procede de San Agustín. «Potestas nostra ipse—scilicet Deus—est», se lee en la temprana obra *Soliloquia* (II, 1, 1), lo cual reaparece en su obra de vejez, de orientación antipelagiana, *De Gratia Christi* (Lib. I, cap. 25, n. 26), en forma más amplia, exponiendo el santo: «Non solum enim Deus posse nostrum donavit et adiuvat, sed etiam velle et operari operatur in nobis» (No solamente nuestro poder obrar nos dió Dios y coopera en él, sino también el querer y obrar El produce en nosotros). Ha sido San Agustín, por consiguiente, quien condujo a Cortés más allá de la utilización meramente teórico-ideológica de los elementos de la tradición tomista, colocándole en el gran movimiento del Contrarrenacimiento, que abarca tanto el luteranismo y calvinismo como la Contrarreforma católica, aunque la poderosa fórmula cortesiana «a solo Dios» —afín al «Sola-Fide», principio de Lutero— fuese impropia en la Contrarreforma, al menos después del Tridentinum.

Es verdad que en aquella frase cortesiana se une, con el fundamento agustiniano, un elemento procedente de San Pablo, formulado en la Epístola II a los corintios XII/9-10, de la manera siguiente: «Y me dijo (el Señor): Te basta mi gracia, porque la virtud se perfecciona en la enfermedad. Por tanto, de buena gana me gloriaré en mis enfermedades para que more en mí la virtud de Cristo. Por lo cual me complazco en mis enfermedades, en las afrentas, en las necesidades, en las angustias por Cristo: porque cuando estoy enfermo, entonces soy fuerte.» El esbozo que hemos encontrado en la Quinta Carta-Relación de un autorretrato de Cortés en actitud de apóstol (según San Marcos XVI/15), ha adquirido una tremenda realidad: en la carta de 3 de febrero de 1544, Cortés dirige la palabra al emperador, a pesar de toda la humildad acentuada, y aun por medio de ella, como sucesor de San Pablo, como verdadero apóstol de los indios, hablando de sí mismo de manera muy similar a como lo hizo el apóstol arquetípico de los gentiles (84). Y esto significa que Cortés —originalmente un político según el corazón de Maquiavelo, actuando al dictado del mero «interés» y de la mera «conveniencia» y manejando todos los recursos de la filosofía tomista, esco-

---

(84) Un caso análogo de una adopción de fórmulas simbólicas mediante las cuales San Pablo había caracterizado su posición de apóstol de Jesucristo, por una persona que pretendió igualar su actuación a la del apóstol arquetípico de los gentiles, presenta el Emperador Otón III, quien con motivo de su visita a Polonia, en los años 999-1000, de cierta aspiración misional, se hizo intitular «Servus Jesu Chriti et Romanorum imperator augustus secundum voluntatem Dei salvatorisque nostrique liberatoris». (PERCY ERNST SCHRAMM aclaró en su libro *Kaiser, Rom und Renovatio*, I, Teil, Studien der Bibliothek Warburg, Leipzig, 1929, pp. 141-146, el significado de una intentada igualación a San Pablo, de Otón III, ocultada en aquella fórmula. Cf. mi trabajo *La idea del imperio español y el problema jurídico-lógico de los Estados-misiones en el Paraguay*, en Estudios de Historia de América, ed. Instituto Panamericano de Geografía e Historia, Comisión de Historia, México, 1948, p. 49).

tista, occamista, agustiniana y de la jurisprudencia alfonsina para propiciar al emperador (85)— se ha convertido, para su propia conciencia, en un sucesor, no del todo indigno, del apóstol de los gentiles, con toda humildad aparente haciendo frente al emperador, de igual a igual, y aun, conforme al sentido oculto de su pretensión de apóstol, como titular de una dignidad más alta que la suya. Este es el último aspecto de la metamorfosis de la idea de imperio de Hernán Cortés.

---

(85) El concepto de la «conveniencia» tiene en las Cartas de Cortés ya el mismo sentido que tendrá en el siglo XVIII como «Droit de convenance», o sea, como derecho a la violación del derecho por razón de Estado (Cf. F. MEINECKE: *Op. cit.*, pp. 322 ss.). En este sentido escribe Cortés, por ejemplo, con respecto al arresto de Moctezuma: «Me pareció... que convenía al real servicio y a nuestra seguridad que aquel señor estuviese en mi poder» *(Gayangos, p. 88).*

6

The Seizure of Overseas Territories by the European Powers

John H. Elliott

PRECONDITIONS

'The establishment of the European colonies in America and the West Indies', wrote Adam Smith in a famous phrase, 'rose from no necessity'.[1] A vast literature has accumulated around the fifteenth-century European background to the overseas voyages of discovery — the motivations, the technology, the methods which made it possible for Europeans to break through the confines of their traditional space, and, in due course, to encompass the globe — but much of this literature has tended to ignore the distinction made by Smith between the 'project of commerce' which, as he saw it, took Europeans to the East Indies, and the 'project of conquest' which occasioned the establishment of the Spaniards, and in due course other European nationals, in the Americas.[2] Instead, the tendency has been to subsume into a single process, conceptualized as 'overseas expansion' or 'imperialism', a whole range of Early Modern European activities, running all the way from commerce to conquest, which were not always, or necessarily, mutually supportive or even mutually compatible.

There are solid reasons for this tendency to merge activities which Adam Smith found it convenient to separate. It is enough to look at the Cortés expedition of 1519 to the coast of Mexico, which was authorized as an expedition for *rescate* (trade and barter) and was transformed by its commander into an expedition of conquest, to appreciate the fineness of the line dividing one form of activity from another. Attempts at classification therefore tend to look artificial, and would have appeared largely meaningless to many of the sixteenth-century Europeans who ventured overseas in pursuit of profit. But in spite of this, it is not immediately apparent why so much European activity in the non-European world should have taken the particular form of the seizure and settlement of other peoples' territories. Adam Smith himself seems to have been rather puzzled: it 'arose from no necessity'.

As they developed the skills, the experience and the daring to make long-distance oceanic voyages, fifteenth and sixteenth-century Europeans were faced with a range of possibilities in their approach to the non-European civilizations with which

---

1   *The Wealth of Nations*, ed. Edwin Canham, 2 vols. (repr. London, 1961), II, p. 68.
2   *Ibid.*, p. 75.

44   John H. Elliott

they came into contact. These possibilities might be crudely summarized as trading, raiding, or conquest and settlement, or some combination of the three. Of these options, conquest and settlement beyond the confines of Europe itself was the one least pursued by medieval Europeans. The Crusader states, Iceland and Greenland — these represented the extent of medieval European overseas expansion before the fifteenth-century settlement of Madeira and the Azores, and the conquest of the Canaries. In this respect, the large-scale European seizure of overseas territories from the sixteenth-century onwards constituted a new and distinctive phase in the continent's relationship with the outside world.[3]

Medieval precedents for overseas conquest and settlement were therefore limited, although there were some important internal precedents within Europe itself — the colonization movement into central and eastern Europe, the activities of the Catalan Grand Company in fourteenth-century Greece, and, above all, the prolonged process, part conquest, part colonization, of the *reconquista* of the Iberian peninsula from Islam. But, while precedents existed, they hardly seem sufficient of themselves to have ensured that the conjunction of conquest with economic enterprise would become so dominant a feature of Europe's relations with non-Europeans. Nor is it clear, as the discussion of protection costs in European overseas commercial enterprise has indicated,[4] that this conjunction was the most economically beneficial method of operation for those who adopted it. The Portuguese empire in India was hardly a shining example of the advantages of the use of force over peaceful commercial competition.[5]

To what impulses, then, were Early Modern Europeans responding when, in the words of that sensitive sixteenth-century French observer, Henri de la Popelinière, they chose to hazard 'leur vie, leur bien, leur honneur, et conscience, à troubler l'aise de ceux qui comme frères domestiques en cette grande maison mondaine ne demandaient qu'à passer le reste de leurs jours en paix et contentement'?[6] For Adam Smith, comparing the first modern European colonies with those established by Greece and Rome, the former, unlike the latter, derived from no 'irresistible necessity, or clear and evident utility'.[7] 'Irresistible necessity' for him seems to have been defined by excess of population, and in this respect, although there may have been local situations — as in the lands of the Order of Santiago in fifteenth-century

3   For this point, see J. R. S. Phillips, *The Medieval Expansion of Europe* (Oxford, 1988), pp. 254–5.
4   See the essays by Frederic C. Lane, grouped together as part III of his *Venice and History* (Baltimore, 1966), and the comments of Niels Steensgaard, *The Asian Trade Revolution of the Seventeenth Century* (Chicago and London, 1973), pp. 16–21.
5   M. N. Pearson, *The Portuguese in India* (*The New Cambridge History of India*, I.1, Cambridge, 1987), pp. 74–5.
6   *Les Trois Mondes* (Paris, 1582), p. 38.
7   *Wealth of Nations*, II, p. 68.
8   Mario Góngora, 'Regimen señorial y rural en la Extremadura de la Orden de Santiago en el momento de la emigración a Indias', *Jahrbuch für Geschichte von Staat, Wirtschaft und Gesellschaft Lateinamerikas*, 2 (1965), pp. 1–29.

The Seizure of Overseas Territories by the European Powers   45

Extremadura[8] — where restricted opportunities at home encouraged dreams about seizing and settling new territories abroad, a Europe slowly recovering from the demographic catastrophe of the fourteenth century had no great compulsion to export its people. The position slowly changed as the demographic losses were made good, and Europe's population once again began to press hard on resources. Late sixteenth and early seventeenth-century England seems to have been the first society in which the promotion of overseas settlement was linked with assertions of overpopulation at home;[9] but only in the decades after 1760, when the whole scale of European migration to America is transformed,[10] does the occupation of overseas lands begin to look like an 'irresistible necessity' deriving from the vast upsurge of Europe's population.

It seems, therefore, that we should look elsewhere than to population pressure as an explanation for Early Modern Europe's move to seize overseas territories. Nor should we necessarily expect to find that 'clear and evident utility' for which Adam Smith looked in vain as a motive for the initial establishment of European colonies, although there may well have been more of this than he was prepared to allow. The occupation by the Portuguese of the Atlantic islands in the fifteenth century was in large part prompted by their desire to increase the area available to them for the growing of cereals and sugar-cane.[11] But in general the seizure of territories resulted from a complicated variety of motives, springing partly from aspirations and predispositions that had developed in Europe, and especially Mediterranean Europe, during the Middle Ages, and partly from local circumstances in the overseas territories themselves.

A glance at a map of the world in 1800 suggests that the largest share of overseas territories in European hands had fallen to what might be called the three 'conquest societies' of late medieval or sixteenth-century Europe: Portugal, Spain, and England. Portugal and Spain had forged many of their social aspirations and characteristics in their long holy war with Islam. This war had given them a traditional, hereditary enemy, the Moslem world, against which they measured themselves, and in response to which they had developed a militant, crusading tradition that was kept alive, even as the Moslem danger within the Iberian peninsula itself receded, by the proximity of the Moors of North Africa. The continuation of the *reconquista* across the Straits of Gibraltar in the fifteenth and early sixteenth centuries was therefore a natural prolongation of a well-proven process — a prolongation that seemed all the more necessary in view of the resurgence of the Moslem world as the Ottoman Turks

9   Cf. Richard Hakluyt, 'Discourse of Western Planting' (1584), in *The Original Writings and Correspondence of the Two Richard Hakluyts*, ed. E. G. R. Taylor (Hakluyt Society, Second Series, vol. 77), p. 234: 'wee are growen more populous than ever heretofore: So that nowe there are of every arte and science so many, that they can hardly lyve one by another, nay rather they are readie to eate upp one another.'
10   Bernard Bailyn, *Voyagers to the West* (New York, 1986), p. 24.
11   V. De Maghalães Godinho, *A economia dos descobrimentos henriquinos* (Lisbon, 1962), p. 81.

John H. Elliott

continued their inexorable advance. The extension of Europe's room for manoeuvre through the development of its navigational skills created for the first time, at the end of the fifteenth century, the possibility of waging the holy war on a global scale, and of outflanking Islam by way of the Indian Ocean and Asia.

The *reconquista* had also instilled in the Castilians and Portuguese certain assumptions about the character and proper treatment of wealth, land, and alien peoples. As might have been expected of societies engaged for centuries in warfare along a moving frontier, wealth was conceived in the essentially portable terms of gold and booty. Land was seen in terms of lordship, and alien peoples in terms of vassals, slaves, and converts.[12] These attitudes, which were not confined to nobles and *hidalgos*, coexisted with more calculating attitudes towards commerce, profits and improvement — attitudes to be found in the commercial and sea-faring centres of Portugal, Andalusia, and northern and Mediterranean Spain, and reinforced in the later Middle Ages by the influx into the Iberian peninsula of Italian, and more especially Genoese, merchants and capital.[13] At times, the tension between the two sets of attitudes reached breaking-point, as in the expostulation of a Venetian factor on Cabral's voyage: 'If you wish to trade, you do not rob competitors' ships'.[14] But the particular commercial aspirations of late fifteenth-century Europe — the pressing need for bullion, the hunger for spices, the desire to acquire new land for the development of sugar plantations — created at least a temporary union of interest which enabled the merchant and the military man to cooperate in their enterprises and talk the same aggressive language.

Conditions, however, first in North Africa and then in the lands bordering the Indian Ocean, did not prove conducive to large-scale territorial conquest. The Portuguese and the Spaniards in turn were to discover that the Moslem societies of North Africa were too rich, sophisticated and populous to lend themselves to easy conquest; all they could secure was a series of footholds, beginning with Ceuta in 1415 and gradually extending around the African coastline during the following decades — forts, factories and *presidios* that could be used for raiding and trading, and for tapping the traffic in gold and slaves of the African interior.[15] This pattern was to repeat itself when the Portuguese moved into Asia. Deflected eastwards by the new and glittering possibilities of the Indian and Asian trades, they could make use of their superior naval technology and gunnery to seize an initial advantage and string together an empire of scattered bases running from the west coast of Africa to the Moluccas. But they failed at critical points, as at Aden; and India was to prove as unfavourable as North Africa to inland penetration and large-scale conquest. La Popelinière, attempting in 1582 to analyse their failure, ascribed it not to lack of

12   See Pedro Corominas, *El sentimiento de la riqueza en Castilla* (Madrid, 1917).
13   See Charles Verlinden, *The Beginnings of Modern Colonization* (Ithaca and London, 1970).
14   Cited by Steensgaard, *The Asian Trade Revolution*, p. 84.
15   Andrew C. Hess, *The Forgotten Frontier* (Chicago, 1978), especially ch. 3; Fernand Braudel, 'Les espagnols en l'Afrique du nord de 1492 à 1577', *Revue Africaine*, 69 (1928), pp. 184–233 and 351–428; E. W. Bovill, *The Golden Trade of the Moors* (Oxford, 1958).

The Seizure of Overseas Territories by the European Powers　　　47

volonté but of *puissance*. The Portuguese found themselves confronting old-established and powerful states, and highly civilized societies which soon learnt to imitate their methods of warfare; and they came to conclude, in La Popelinière's words, that 'le jeu ne valait pas la chandelle'.[16] Modern analyses have added little to this sixteenth-century diagnosis.

The Spaniards, too, were deflected from North Africa, but by the very different world of America. Here, as reported by Columbus in his account of his first voyage, was the prospect of incalculable gold (*oro sin cuento*), rhubarb and cinnamon, spices and cotton, and slaves 'from among the idolators'.[17] It was a list of desiderata well calculated to appeal to mercantile and military elements alike in the Spain of the late *reconquista*. Columbus held out the prospect of wealth as booty, and of wealth through trade and development; and this, as it soon became apparent, in a world that, unlike the Moslem world, had apparently never heard of the Christian gospel, and was therefore ripe for evangelization. This itself was not only an important incentive to intervention by the Castilian crown and church, but also made it possible to secure the requisite papal authorization for the conquest (under certain specified conditions) of infidel societies which the medieval canon law tradition had come to recognize as viable entities with their own legitimate rights to dominion and property.[18] In the Christendom of the late fifteenth century there was no more essential precondition than this for the seizure of overseas territory.

By the time Cortés landed on the coast of Mexico in 1519, many of the characteristic features of Castilian *reconquista* society had reproduced themselves on the far side of the Atlantic: raiding, plunder, enslavement and exploitation under the sign of the cross, in a new, Caribbean, world with a moving frontier. But there was another element of the *reconquista* in Spain that was less in evidence in the Antilles: settlement and colonization. In spite of the efforts of the Spanish crown through its governor, Nicolás de Ovando, to stabilize the society of Hispaniola through the founding of cities and the *repartimiento* of the indigenous inhabitants to settlers in return for their instruction and conversion,[19] the catastrophic decline of the native population and the reports of gold and booty to be won further to the west left Antillean society in flux, as adventurers moved from island to island, and on to the mainland, in the pursuit of easy riches. This was less the seizure of territory than its laying waste by bands of marauders.

'Without settlement there is no good conquest, and if the land is not conquered, the people will not be converted. Therefore the maxim of the conqueror must be to settle.'[20] This maxim expressed the philosophy of Hernán Cortés, whose first-hand

---

16　*Les Trois Mondes*, pp. 51—53.
17　Cristobal Colón, *Textos y documentos completos*, ed. Consuelo Varela (2nd. ed., Madrid, 1984), 'Carta a Luis de Santangel' (15 Feb. 1493), p. 145.
18　Cf. James Muldoon, *Popes, Lawyers and Infidels* (Philadelphia, 1979).
19　Ursula Lamb, *Frey Nicolás de Ovando, gobernador de las Indias (1501–1509)* (Madrid, 1956).
20　Francisco López de Gómara, *Historia general de la Indias* (Madrid, 1852), p. 181.

John H. Elliott

knowledge of the destruction of the Antilles left him determined to avoid a repeat performance as Montezuma's Mexican empire fell into his hands. The dispersal of the *conquistadores* through the continent continued, especially as reports began to percolate back of the fabulous riches of Peru — already a myth in the 1520's before its conquest by Pizarro in the 1530's made them a reality.[21] But two features of Spain's expanding world in mainland America helped to ensure that the Spaniards would subject substantial parts of it to a 'good conquest', in Cortés' understanding of those words. The first of these was the presence, especially in the central Mexican plateau and the Andean highlands, of large, sedentary populations. The second was the appearance of substantial quantities of gold and silver artefacts, followed by the discovery in both regions, in the 1540's and 1550's, of exceptionally rich silver deposits.

To Castilians and Andalusians living in the world of the *reconquista*, infidel settled populations, capable of being subjugated, implied simultaneously souls for salvation, and bodies to provide tribute and labour; while gold and silver hinted at the presence of mines capable of yielding a steady flow of bullion for the Spanish crown, and unparalleled wealth for private individuals. Consequently, the seizure of the American mainland — the acquisition of an 'empire of the Indies' — came to be seen as justifying an investment of men, money and national energy on a scale that would have been unthinkable without the prospect not only of instant bonanzas, but also of continuing long-term yields. This investment, like the reconquest of southern Spain from the Moors, proved attractive for differing reasons to the various sectors of Castilian society — crown, church, *hidalgos*, merchants, peasants and artisans — and the seizure of central and southern America could therefore assume the form of a collective enterprise, conducted, as the *reconquista* had been conducted, under the supervisory regulation of a king to whom belonged the ultimate lordship (*señorío*) of the newly conquered lands.

The Spanish crown, however, was operating within the framework of a competitive European state-system, in which any accretion of wealth and power by one state had immediate repercussions on its rivals. For this reason, its new-found wealth of the Indies was bound to spark off a fresh round of competition, together with attempts at imitation. In promoting voyages of exploration Ferdinand and Isabella had themselves been responding in part to the overseas successes of their Portuguese fellow-monarch, the self-proclaimed 'Lord over conquests, navigation and trade with Ethiopia, Arabia, Persia and India.'[22] As Spain tightened its grasp on the Indies Portugal countered by moving in the 1530's to take possession of Brazil, where the indigenous population proved less amenable to subjugation and exploitation than that of Mexico and the Andes. Through the device of parcelling out the land into fourteen captaincies (in fifteen lots) held by twelve *donatários*, who were to settle and develop the land at their own expense under the system of obligatory cultivation (*sesmaria*)

21   Antonello Gerbi, *Il mito del Perù* (Milan, 1988), pp. 24–26.
22   Steensgaard, *The Asian Trade Revolution*, p. 84.

already employed in the Atlantic islands,[23] the crown hoped to save the actual or potential resources of Brazil from falling into the hands of Portugal's European rivals.

National and dynastic rivalries in Europe, therefore, were already operating by the middle decades of the sixteenth century to encourage the occupation of fresh chunks of overseas territory, either to provide additional protection for those areas already seized, or to serve as a form of reinsurance against the loss of future potential assets. Where Brazil was concerned, brazilwood might be the immediate attraction to other European predators, especially the French,[24] but there was always the hope that gold would be discovered; and although it was to be almost two hundred years before this particular dream was realized, the highly profitable development of large sugar plantations on the fertile Atlantic littoral of Brazil was to make it a particularly valuable prize by the early seventeenth century. From the first stages of their movement overseas, Portuguese and Spaniards had taken formal possession of foreign soil in the name of their respective monarchs.[25] Now, as European rivalries were carried over into the non-European world, and other European rulers, beginning with Francis I, refused to acknowledge the validity of the papal arbitration of new-found lands to the Iberian monarchs, the convention was gradually developed that right to exclusive possession was to be based on fixed and permanent establishment.[26] In this way, the seizure and occupation of territory became a *sine qua non* of the overseas activity of European societies, with their highly developed territorial consciousness.

For all the activity of the French in Brazil, and later, in the West Indies and Canada, they were to be late and — before the nineteenth century — not spectacularly successful players in the process of carving up and occupying large areas of the non-European world. While the religious divisions and civil upheavals of sixteenth-century France were no doubt an impediment to sustained and effective overseas enterprise in the important initial stages of the game, the English, although beginning later, were to prove themselves more adept. One important reason for this may be that, unlike the French, but like the Spaniards and Portuguese, they too were a 'conquest society' when they launched out on overseas enterprise. Their chosen land of conquest — unlike the southern half of the Iberian peninsula — was to be an adjoining island, rather than part of the mainland; and the people to be subjugated and converted were not Moors, but Gaelic Catholics. But there are indications that the sixteenth-century conquest of Ireland, like the medieval Iberian conquest of Islamic Spain, was

---

23   Verlinden, *Beginnings of Modern Colonization*, p. 220.
24   C. A. Julien, *Les débuts de l'expansion et de la colonisation françaises (XVe–XVIe siècles)* (Paris, 1947), chs. 2 and 4.
25   Cf. Cortés at Vera Cruz, who 'took possession of the country, and of all the land as yet unexplored, in the name of the Emperor Don Carlos, King of Spain' (Francisco López de Gómara, *Cortés, the Life of the Conqueror by his Secretary*, Engl. trans., ed. L. B. Simpson, Berkeley and Los Angeles, 1964, p. 66).
26   Julien, *Les débuts*, p. 114.

50   John H. Elliott

a useful prelude, and perhaps even an essential precondition, for the subsequent successful occupation of overseas territory.[27]

The English crown considered that it had established its title to most of Ireland as a consequence of the Norman offensive of the twelfth and thirteenth centuries. Although the native Irish had subsequently repossessed much of the land, it was therefore taken for granted in the sixteenth century, when schemes were put forward for the establishment of 'plantations' or 'colonies' of English and Scottish settlers, that they were occupying land that was already the rightful property of the crown. Justification for settlement in areas previously unconquered was found in the argument of land utility, since it seemed wrong that good Irish soil should go uncultivated.[28] Add to this the assumption that the native Irish were to all intents and purposes pagans, and that — in the words of Queen Elizabeth — it was necessary to 'bring in that rude and barbarous nation to civility',[29] and it is clear that a battery of arguments was already in place for subsequent justification of the seizure and settlement of land in North America. Nor is it a coincidence that several of the pioneers of the first projects for British settlement in America — Sir Humphrey Gilbert, Sir Walter Raleigh, Thomas White, Ralph Lane — were closely associated with schemes for Irish plantations. Ireland for the English, like Andalusia for the Spaniards, served as a useful laboratory for developing the ideas and techniques which would make possible the subsequent establishment of overseas empire.

Although the first successful British settlement in mainland America, that of Jamestown in 1607, was to be conducted under the auspices of a joint-stock company, it would be a mistake to read into this an exclusively commercial orientation to the new enterprise. As with the attempts directed by the Welsers to conquer and exploit Venezuela in the 1530's and 1540's,[30] the efforts of the Virginia Company were characterized by a mixture of motives and interests — a hunger for precious metals; desire for trade with the natives; hopes of plunder; vague schemes for colonization.[31] In both instances, the desire was for quick profits; and in both instances the companies failed. As in Ireland, there was a strong *conquistador* element in the Jamestown settlement. Like the *conquistadores*, many of the first Jamestown settlers were adventurers who dreamt of finding gold and silver, had no taste for routine work, and looked forward to living on the tribute and the labour of a servile Indian population. But the Indians of Virginia, unlike those of Central Mexico and the Andes, did not

27   The theme of the conquest and colonization of Ireland as a prelude to the colonization of America, which was argued by David Beers Quinn in *The Elizabethans and the Irish* (Ithaca, 1966), esp. ch. 9, has been developed by Nicholas Canny, notably in *The Elizabethan Conquest of Ireland. A Pattern Established, 1565–1576* (New York, 1976), and *Kingdom and Colony. Ireland in the Atlantic World, 1560–1800* (Baltimore and London, 1988).

28   Canny, *The Elizabethan Conquest*, pp. 118–19.

29   *Ibid.*, p. 121.

30   Juan Friede, *Los Welser en la conquista de América* (Caracas, 1961).

31   Wesley Frank Craven, *Dissolution of the Virginia Company. The Failure of a Colonial Experiment* (New York, 1932), p. 29.

prove to be usable Indians. The Virginia settlement was to be saved by the development of a crop, tobacco, which was to be cultivated not by the Indians but, in the first instance, by indentured servants from England, and subsequently by African slaves.

This transformation of the colony's prospects inevitably transformed also the settlers' attitude to the land and its indigenous inhabitants. Now that land had become desirable, its acquisition along the banks of the river James became a principal objective of the colonists. This meant, as in Ireland, the development of a 'pale', which by 1633 consisted of 300,000 acres of land cleared of Indian title.[32] In effect, an Indian frontier had been established; and in spite of sporadic attempts to maintain it, and to guarantee the rights of Indians to the lands beyond it, it was constantly being pushed back under the pressure of population growth in the settler community, and of insatiable hunger for more land for the planting and cultivation of tobacco.

The experience of Virginia suggests, and that of British settlements to the north, in New England, confirms that there were important distinctions between the British and Spanish approach to the seizure of territory in the Americas. The Spaniards, on arrival, would find a pretext for 'conquering' large areas of territory deep into the interior, and then would subsequently, and slowly, fill in the conquered areas by founding cities and settlements. The British, on the other hand, were more likely to establish a base, settle a relatively narrow coastal or riverine strip, and then, by degrees, push back the boundaries and, with the boundaries, the Indians. This process, as in New England and the Middle Colonies, might often be very slow. For generations, the settlers clung close to the Atlantic seaboard, held back partly by geography and fear of the Indians, and partly, at least in the Puritan colonies of New England, by a strict social discipline which for a surprisingly long time managed to contain the pressures generated both by immigration and by natural, and exceptionally vigorous, population growth.[33] It was only with the late eighteenth century and the coming of independence that the boundaries were finally breached, and tidal waves of migrants moved westwards across the Appalachian mountains to seize and settle the lands of the interior.

This difference between the British and the Spanish approach to the seizure of Indian territory may in part derive from differences, at least in emphasis, in their attitudes to the land. In spite of high-sounding claims, both countries displayed initial uncertainties about their titles to land in the Americas. Cortés engineered a 'voluntary' transfer of Montezuma's imperial title to the Emperor Charles V; and, in apparent imitation of the Spanish precedent, Captain Christopher Newport, on the instructions of the Virginia Company, 'crowned' a reluctant 'Emperor' Powhatan in 1608, as a

---

32   Wesley Frank Craven, 'Indian policy in Early Virginia', *William and Mary Quarterly*, 3rd series, 1 (1944), pp. 65–82.

33   See for example, Philip J. Greven, *Four Generations. Population, Land and Family in Colonial Andover, Massachusetts* (Ithaca and London, 1970).

vassal of James I.[34] But the Spaniards, setting aside legal niceties and papal authorization, soon came to regard the Indies as a 'conquest' of the Crown of Castile, entitling the crown, in theory at least, to free disposal of the land. For its part, the English crown, in blithe disregard for any prior Indian rights, gave the Massachusetts Bay Company the right to 'have and to hold, possess and enjoy all and singular the aforesaid continent, lands, territories, islands, hereditaments, and precincts, seas, waters, fishings. . .'[35]

Yet for both colonizing powers, a nagging question remained. This was well put by Robert Gray in his *A Good Speed to Virginia* (1609): 'The first objection is by what right or warrant we can enter into the land of these Savages, take away their rightfull inheritance from them, and plant ourselves in their places, being unwronged or unprovoked by them.'[36] The Spanish crown, although anxious to prevent the development of a feudal aristocracy in the Indies, had no compunction about exercising its rights as a conqueror to reward *conquistadores* for their services with grants of land; but it also recognized prior Indian titles. Influenced, however, by Roman Law conceptions of land-ownership, it drew a distinction between those lands actually used by Indian communities for production, and those that stood vacant, and it was these latter which it distributed to Spaniards.[37] Once the vacant land was distributed, however — and large quantities became available as the indigenous population shank and Indian communities were regrouped at the command of their European rulers — the distinction between ownership and use tended to be forgotten, in spite of viceregal efforts to ensure that land allocated to settlers should be forfeited if it were not promptly exploited.[38]

In British America, a similar distinction was drawn between land ownership and use, with consequences that — given the pattern of Indian life over large parts of North America — were even more detrimental to Indian rights than in Mexico and Peru. English settlers failed to realize that Indian concepts of property related not to the land, but to what was on the land at different seasons of the year. As a result, they occupied land which in their eyes, but not in Indian eyes, was being left shamefully unused; and when they purchased Indian land, as distinct from seizing it, the mutual misunderstanding as to what in fact was being bought and sold led to countless incidents.[39] The general tendency, however, was for the crown simply to grant large tracts of land to the colonists, on the basis both of its own presumed rights of sovereignty and the

---

34   For Cortés, see J. H. Elliott, 'Cortés, Velázquez and Charles V' in Hernán Cortés, *Letters from Mexico*, trans. and ed. Anthony Pagden (1971; revised reprint, New Haven and London, 1986), pp. xxvii–xxviii; for Newport, *The Complete Works of Captain John Smith*, ed. Philip L. Barbour (3 vols., Chapel Hill, 1986), I, p. 237.

35   Cited by William Cronon, *Changes in the Land. Indians, Colonists and the Ecology of New England* (New York, 1983), p. 71.

36   Cited by Craven, 'Indian Policy in Early Virginia', p. 65.

37   Woodrow Borah, *Justice by Insurance* (Berkeley and Los Angeles, 1983), pp. 38–9.

38   François Chevalier, *La Formation des grand domaines au Mexique* (Paris, 1952), p. 178.

39   Cronon, *Changes in the Land*, pp. 65–9.

assumption that land that was unfenced and uncultivated was not being properly used. The seizure of Indian land therefore came to be justified in terms of a doctrine of 'improvement' — a word that was to be widely used in British settlements in mainland America and the West Indies in the seventeenth and eighteenth centuries.[40] The contrast was with the 'wilderness' which the colonists had found on their arrival. They 'came to a wilderness', wrote William Penn, but 'it was not meet that [they] should continue it so.'[41]

In speaking the language of improvement, British settlers — whether they were New England farmers, Virginian tobacco-growers, or Caribbean sugar-planters — were in effect using as justification for their occupation of American Indian territory a term expressive of the accumulative and developmental approach to resources that was steadily gaining ground in pre-industrial England. The extent to which the Spaniards in America shared the same approach remains unclear. As Hernán Cortés showed with his Cuernavaca sugar plantation and his plans for Pacific trade, there was a strong entrepreneurial element among some at least of the *conquistadores* and early settlers;[42] López de Gómara wrote approvingly in 1552 of the extent to which Spanish settlers had 'improved' Hispaniola and New Spain, while Gonzalo Fernández de Oviedo recounted with pride how 'we found no sugar mills when we arrived in these Indies, and all these we have built with our own hands and industry in so short a time.'[43] But it is uncertain whether Spaniards shared the English conception of America as a 'wilderness' waiting to be developed; and, if they did not, whether the difference derived from different attitudes to wealth in the two metropolitan societies, or from the fact that they had come to a different America.

For Spanish America, with its silver mines and its large sedentary Indian populations, *was* a different America, and this undoubtedly helps to explain the contrasting approaches to the occupation of Indian land. Where the English, if they were to justify the retention of their American settlements as valuable long-term investments (the short-term rewards being so disappointing), had no option but to develop with their own labour, or with that of imported African slaves, the resources of an apparently virgin continent, the prime concern of the Spaniards was to extract its rich mineral deposits and the labour and tribute of its indigenous peoples. This made the physical occupation of the land, once it had been formally conquered, a lesser priority for Spanish settlers and the Spanish crown. For Spanish crown and settlers alike the essential requirement was not so much the domination of the soil as

40   Cronon, pp. 77–8; Jack P. Greene, *Pursuits of Happiness* (Chapel Hill and London, 1988), pp. 197–8.
41   Quoted by Michael Zuckerman, 'Identity in British America: Unease in Eden', in *Colonial Identity in the Atlantic World, 1500–1800*, ed. Nicholas Canny and Anthony Pagden (Princeton, 1987), p. 133.
42   See France V. Scholes, 'The Spanish Conqueror as Businessman: a Chapter in the History of Fernando Cortés', *New Mexico Quarterly*, 28 (1958), pp. 1–29; Ward Barrett, *The Sugar Hacienda of the Marqueses del Valle* (Minneapolis, 1970).
43   Cited in J. H. Elliott, *The Old World and the New, 1492–1650* (Cambridge, 1970), p. 78.

54   John H. Elliott

the domination of its inhabitants. This requirement implied for the whole process of conquest different methods, and a different rhythm, from those that would characterize the later English conquest of North America. But at the same time the two societies would be faced by many of the same problems, and would adopt many of the same techniques for their solution — techniques that would also be used, with greater or lesser success, by Europeans attempting to seize territory in other parts of the non-European world.

EXECUTION

By 1800, Europeans had secured control over 35% of the total land area of the globe.[44] The development by Renaissance Europe of the gun-carrying sailing ship clearly played a crucial part in the establishment of European domination, especially in the initial stages of this process, when Europeans still enjoyed the advantage of surprise.[45] Sea-power not only facilitated the first establishment of Portuguese bases in Asia; it also allowed the Spaniards to secure a stranglehold over the Aztec capital of Tenochtitlán by dominating Lake Texcoco with their brigantines, and to destroy the highland empire of Atahualpa by bringing in their men and supplies over an ocean that the Incas regarded as an impassable barrier.[46] Similarly, it would be their command of the sea which would enable Europeans in the seventeenth and eighteenth centuries to maintain and extend their Asian bridgeheads, and dominate local trade through the use of terror and force.

On land, too, superior military technology gave Europeans important initial advantages, especially when combined with the use of the horse.[47] The use of cavalry had all the advantages of surprise in the Americas, where the horse was unknown; but it also enabled the Portuguese to make conquests in India, and to recapture Goa, benefiting from the local shortage of horses in regions which depended on Persia and

44   Geoffrey Parker, *The Military Revolution. Military Innovation and the Rise of the West, 1500–1800* (Cambridge, 1988), p. 119, citing D. R. Headrick, *The Tools of Empire: Technology and European Imperialism in the Nineteenth Century* (Oxford, 1981).

45   See Carlo M. Cipolla, *Guns and Sails in the Early Phase of European Expansion, 1400–1700* (London, 1965). For the careful weighing by Europeans of cost and operational factors in opting for wrought iron, bronze, or cast iron cannon, see especially John F. Guilmartin Jr., 'The cannon of the *Batavia* and the *Sacramento*: early modern cannon founding reconsidered', *The International Journal of Nautical Archaeology and Underwater Exploration*, 11 (1982), pp. 133–44.

46   C. Harvey Gardiner, *Naval Power in the Conquest of Mexico* (Austin, 1956); George Kubler, 'The Quechua in the Colonial World', in *Handbook of South American Indians*, ed. Julian H. Steward, vol. 2 (Washington, 1946), pp. 380–1.

47   See Parker, *The Military Revolution*, ch. 4, for a recent excellent survey of European military power and the non-European world; for European and indigenous arms in America, Alberto María Salas, *Las armas de la conquista* (Buenos Aires, 1950).

Arabia for their supply.[48] Yet European superiority in military, and horse, technology soon proved to be a diminishing asset in Asia, and even in the Americas. In Asia, itself already part of the gunpowder culture, sheer numbers were bound to tell after the first shock of the advent of the Portuguese. Portugal had a population of barely a million. In late sixteenth-century India, the Mughals had at least that number of men under arms, many of them equipped with muskets.[49] The Indians were quick to acquire European weaponry, and it was not until the middle of the eighteenth century, when a second military revolution gave Europeans a light, and relatively cheap, field artillery, that the latter were again able to seize the initiative, and move effectively into the interior of the sub-continent.[50] Further east, the Chinese, with their own indigenous firearms, and the Japanese, who both imported and copied European cannon in the sixteenth century, possessed military cultures and war machines which effectively made them formidable potential adversaries for Europeans, most of whom were in any event more interested in trade than in conquest in regions so remote from Europe.[51]

Although the technological gap between Europeans and non-Europeans was much wider in the Americas than in Asia, a grand total of less than seven hundred Spaniards, with a combined strength of eighteen cannons and eight-three horses, could hardly have toppled the Aztec and Inca empires, with their many millions of inhabitants, if they had not been able to draw on many other assets besides sheer technological superiority. The shock effect of horses and guns, although initially powerful, tended to wear off, and it was probably less difficult for Aztecs and Incas to adjust to such innovations than to a European style of warfare with objectives very different from those of the warfare to which they were accustomed. Where Europeans fought to conquer and kill, Aztecs fought to take captives, and the precise rituals which governed Aztec and Inca forms of combat placed them at a grave disadvantage in their first, critical, encounters with European warriors.[52]

The two great empires fell too rapidly for them to have time to adapt themselves to an unfamiliar style of warfare and unfamiliar technology, but it was a different story for the Indians on the fringes of Spain's American empire, and for those in North America. Decades of uneasy coexistence and of continued exposure to European influences, enabled some tribes at least to acquaint themselves closely with European

48   G. V. Scammell, 'Indigenous Assistance in the Establishment of Portuguese Power in the Indian Ocean', in *Indo-Portuguese History. Sources and Problems*, ed. John Correia-Afonso, S. J. (Bombay, 1981), pp. 166–7.
49   Parker, *The Military Revolution*, p. 129.
50   Philip D. Curtin, *Cross-cultural Trade in World History* (Cambridge, 1984), pp. 230–1.
51   For the European, and non-European, origin of Asian artillery, see C. R. Boxer, 'Asian Potentates and European Artillery in the 16th–18th centuries', in his *Portuguese Conquest and Commerce in Southern Asia, 1500–1750* (London, 1985), ch. 7.
52   For Aztec warfare see Inga Clendinnen, 'The Cost of Courage in Aztec Society', *Past and Present*, 107 (1985), pp. 44–89; for the Incas, Kubler, 'The Quechua', *Handbook of South American Indians*, II, p. 380.

56   John H. Elliott

military methods and acquire European weapons through trade, just as the peoples of
Asia acquired them. The Araucanian Indians of Chile, for instance, became formidable opponents of the Spaniards, incorporating the horse into their armies from the late
1560's, adapting the Spanish saddle to their own needs, and lengthening their pikes
to counter the attacks of Spaniards on horseback.[53] The Chichimec Indians on Spain's
northern frontier in Mexico showed a similar capacity for adaptation; the Great Plains
Indians acquired European war accoutrements and transformed themselves into a
horse culture; and northern tribes like the Pequots and the Iroquois assimilated
European firearms, and took to forms of guerrilla warfare which in turn forced
military acculturation upon their European enemies.[54]

In both North and South America, therefore, the European seizure of land was
slowed down, or stopped, by the resistance of scattered peoples who made use of the
time-lag before Europeans encroached seriously on their territory, to familiarize
themselves with European methods of warfare and devise appropriate responses. No
comparable time had been afforded to the great settled empires of the Aztecs and the
Incas; and here the very fact of their high degree of organization worked to their
disadvantage. As centralized empires they were peculiarly vulnerable to the strategy
employed successively by Cortés and Pizarro of seizing the emperor, and leaving the
imperial structure effectively headless. They were also made vulnerable by the
accumulated resentments of the peoples they had subjugated in the process of
extending their domination. Consequently, the conquest of Mexico and Peru was a
testimonial at least as much to Spanish political, as to Spanish military, skills. By
exploiting the internal divisions of the two empires, Cortés and Pizarro turned small-
scale European invasions into large-scale native uprisings which they orchestrated to
their own advantage, and conquered vast areas of territory in what were effectively
combined European and indigenous operations. The Portuguese in Asia made
comparable use of indigenous collaboration, although with less spectacular results.[55]
This kind of political machination was at its most effective where, as in Mexico and
Peru, Europeans were confronted by large and inflexible state structures. It proved
much more difficult to employ, and much less far-reaching in its results, when they
were faced by clusters of small states, or tribal groupings, as in Yucatan, with no
formal centre of domination commanding a reluctant loyalty.[56]

Biology, however, played a larger part than any conscious effort by European
intruders and invaders in undermining the resistance of the indigenous peoples of
America, and clearing the land for occupation. The impact of European-borne
diseases was devastating on peoples who had lived isolated from the plagues and

53   Alvaro Jara, *Guerre et Société au Chili. Essai de Sociologie Coloniale* (Paris, 1961), ch. 3.
54   Philip Wayne Powell, *Soldiers, Indians and Silver. The Northwest Advance of New Spain,
     1550–1600* (Berkeley, 1952); Edward H. Spicer, *Cycles of Conquest* (Tucson, 1962); Francis
     Jennings, *The Invasion of America* (Chapel Hill, 1975), pp. 165–70.
55   Scammell, 'Indigenous Assistance', in *Indo-Portuguese History*, ch. 11.
56   Ralph L. Roys, *The Indian Background of Colonial Yucatan* (Washington, 1943); Inga
     Clendinnen, *Ambivalent Conquests. Maya and Spaniard in Yucatan* (Cambridge, 1987).

ailments that had become endemic in the Eurasian landmass. Smallpox sapped the strength of the Aztec warriors defending Tenochtitlán against the forces of Cortés; and the Spanish conquest of Central and Southern America was accompanied, and followed, by demographic catastrophe. The English arrived in a North America to which European diseases had already preceded them, with the result that many of the areas into which they moved were already sparsely settled; and epidemics continued to reduce the numbers of North American Indians well into the eighteenth century. If, on the basis of an extrapolation from the figures for Central Mexico, the Indian population of the Americas as a whole can be regarded as having suffered a decline of the order of 90% in the century following its first contact with Europeans, the relative ease with Europeans were able to seize such vast areas of territory becomes far more comprehensible.[57]

The biological benefits enjoyed by Europeans in America, however, were replaced by a net biological loss in their dealings with Asia. Sharing the same pandemic diseases, the Asians were exposed to no mass biological effects from contact with Europeans who, for their part, were all too likely to succumb to the deleterious effects of climate and conditions in regions unfamiliar to them. A high rate of mortality was endemic to European enterprises in Africa and Asia, and the drain on human resources, especially for a country with a population as small as that of Portugal, must in time have come to operate as an inhibiting factor in the seizure of yet more territory. For the seizure and holding of territory carried costs that could at least be roughly appreciated, even when they did not necessarily lend themselves to precise calculation; and — as the anxious discussion by seventeenth century Spanish *arbitristas* of the impact of emigration to the Indies indicates[58] — there was liable to come a moment when the demographic costs to the metropolitan centre of overseas enterprise could not be entirely ignored in drawing up the balance sheet of empire.

Some such balance sheet, however rough and ready, was being drawn up from the very beginnings of European overseas enterprise. Expeditions of discovery and conquest required significant initial investment, either by the state, or private individuals, or both. The hope, and the intention, was that conquest and empire could soon be made to pay for themselves; and it was on the basis of this hope that the ruling houses of Portugal and Spain were prepared to raise loans and play some direct part in the financing of the early stages of overseas enterprise, before having any clear idea of what return could be expected for their investment. As soon as it became apparent that rich pickings were to be anticipated in Asia and America, local and international

57   The pioneer work of statistical analysis for Spanish America by Sherburne F. Cook and Woodrow Borah has been conveniently assembled in the three volumes of their *Essays in Population History* (Berkeley, Los Angeles, London, 1971–9). No work of comparable sophistication has been done for North America, for which see Francis Jennings, *The Invasion of America*, ch. 2. A recent overview of the impact of Europeans in the demography of the non-European world is to be found in Alfred W. Crosby, *Ecological Imperialism. The Biological Expansion of Europe, 900–1900* (Cambridge, 1986), ch. 9.

58   Eg. Pedro Fernández Navarrete, *Conservación de monarquías* (Madrid, 1626), *discurso* VIII.

merchants and financiers — Genoese, Florentines and Germans — moved in, and assumed the bulk of the financial responsibility. Then, as the first overseas settlements took root, it became possible, as in Spanish America, to mobilize an increasing porportion of resources locally for further expeditions of conquest. Here, investors in expeditions formed their own private partnerships or *compañías*, like that between Pizarro and Almagro preceding the conquest of Peru.[59]

Private investment, however, required relatively quick returns, and this requirement had a major impact on the character of European overseas enterprise, going far to determine both the character of colonization and the limits of territorial expansion.[60] Along the northern frontier of the sixteenth-century viceroyalty of New Spain, for example, it proved virtually impossible to mobilize adequate funds for war against the Chichimecs — a war in which further territorial expansion offered scant hope of reward. Such frontier areas, which required the establishment of defensive settlements and garrisons, imposed heavy financial burdens, which had to be set against the profits secured from the more lucrative regions of the viceroyalty.[61] This was to prove a common pattern in the overseas enterprises of Early Modern Europe whenever they involved the acquisition of territory. Yet the benefits of forcible acquisition were by no means necessarily short-term, as can be seen from Portuguese South Asia. Estimates prepared in the 1630's for the Estado da India indicate that the crown was then drawing at least 31% of its revenues from its land possessions, as against 47% from seaborne commercial activities. Moreover, in comparison with fluctuating customs dues, these land-derived revenues possessed a welcome stability.[62] Here, as elsewhere, however, the costs of defence were not only heavy but tended to rise, as local forces regrouped themselves and European rivals appeared on the scene.

Although Iberian adventurers and clerics might continue to propose ambitious expeditions of conquest in southeast Asia at the end of the sixteenth century,[63] an increasingly sombre awareness of the costs to the crown of empire helped to stifle such proposals at birth. Perhaps coercion was not after all the most cost-effective approach to the conduct of foreign trade. As George Cokayne put it after a visit to the

59   For the Portuguese, G. V. Scammell, *The World Encompassed* (Berkeley and Los Angeles, 1981), p. 264; for Spaniards in the Indies, Mario Góngora, *Studies in the Colonial History of Spanish America* (Cambridge, 1975), pp. 5–16; Hermann Kellenbenz, 'Die Finanzierung der spanischen Entdeckungen', *Vierteljahrschrift für Sozial- und Wirtschaftsgeschichte*, 69 (1982), pp. 153–181. The Pizarro-Almagro partnership, and the controversial role of Hernando de Luque, an entrepreneurially-minded priest, is discussed in James Lockhart, *The Men of Cajamarca* (Austin and London, 1972), pp. 70–3.

60   Cf. D. W. Meinig, *The Shaping of America* (New Haven and London, 1986), I, pp. 7 and 55.

61   Powell, *Soldiers, Indians and Silver*, esp. ch. 7.

62   See Anthony Disney, 'The Portuguese Empire in India, c. 1550–1650', in *Indo-Portuguese History*, ch. 10, pp. 150–1.

63   Boxer, 'Portuguese and Spanish Projects for the Conquest of Southeast Asia, 1580–1600', *Portuguese Conquest and Commerce*, ch. 3.

Moluccas: 'The trade that comes by compulsion is not profitable.'[64] It was easier, however, for purely commercial corporations to act on this maxim than governments subjected to a multiplicity of pressures from ecclesiastics and military men, bureaucrats and merchants, all lobbying for their particular projects and for state-protection and special privileges. By inserting themselves into existing trading relationships, and taking profitability, rather than 'victory or conquest',[65] as their yardstick, such corporations, with their restricted economic goals, were better placed to break free of the kinds of shackles that crippled the freedom of manoeuvre of territorially-conscious nation-states.

This at least would seem to be true in theory, and the activities of the Dutch and British East India Companies would suggest that, to some extent at least, it was also true in practice. But just as questions of profitability had a way of inserting themselves into the approach of the state to overseas enterprise, so too the chartered companies proved unable to rid themselves of the territorial preoccupations normally associated with states. This was particularly apparent in the experience of the Dutch, those late-comers to the practice of empire. In the Americas the West India Company was conceived from the beginning as an instrument for breaking the Iberian monopoly, and was soon involved in a long and ultimately abortive effort to conquer and colonize Brazil.[66] In Asia, the principal theatre of Dutch overseas interests, the VOC quickly discovered that, like the Portuguese, it needed entrepots, factories, and bases to protect its sea-lanes; this in turn involved securing voluntary or involuntary concessions from rulers; and in some instances, as in the Moluccas, open conquest, whether from the Portuguese or from weak local potentates. 'Trade', argued Coen in 1614, 'cannot be maintained without war, nor war without trade.'[67] The directors at home might attempt to rein him in, but neither then, nor later in the century, was the VOC immune to the temptations of conquest and colonization that afflicted other European peoples engaged in overseas enterprise.

It could, of course, be argued that the VOC from its early years was in some ways contaminated by its close association with the rulers of the Dutch Republic, and that the English East India Company, with its independence from 'existing political institutions',[68] provides a fairer test. But although many of its directors fought hard to save their company from incurring the kind of military protection costs that bore so heavily on the Portuguese and the Dutch, they, too, proved in the end to be fighting a losing battle. The experiences of the East India Company, indeed, provide a paradigm of the dilemmas involved in attempting to isolate commerce from conquest.[69]

64 Cited by Steensgaard, *The Asian Trade Revolution*, p. 123.
65 Steensgaard, *ibid.*, p. 137.
66 C. R. Boxer, *The Dutch in Brazil, 1624–1654* (Oxford, 1957).
67 Cited by Parker, *The Military Revolution*, p. 132.
68 Steensgaard, *The Asian Trade Revolution*, p. 120.
69 See particularly K. N. Chaudhuri, *The Trading World of Asia and the English East India Company, 1660–1760* (Cambridge, 1978), ch. 6, and I. Bruce Watson, 'Fortification and the "Idea" of Force in Early English East India Company Relations with India', *Past and Present*, 88 (1980), pp. 70–87.

60   John H. Elliott

The seventeenth-century directors of the company clearly hoped to ensure themselves a relatively trouble-free existence by concentrating trading activities in areas like the Carnatic and Bengal where European rivals offered no strong competition and the native Indian states themselves were weak.[70] But, like the Portuguese and the Dutch before them, they came to depend for their trade on the presence of fortified settlements defensible from the sea. These settlements, like those of the Portuguese and the Dutch, proved to be both assets and liabilities — assets in that, in the event of local disorders and attack, they offered protection to English nationals and the Indian merchants with whom they traded, and liabilities in that they were capable of absorbing and diverting into local defence costs a sometimes substantial portion of the profits arising from commercial operations. This in turn intensified the search for alternative sources of income, with the result that local revenue-raising became an increasingly important part of the company's activities.

However hard the company's directors in London might work to steer their agents in India clear of local involvements, changes in the sub-continent itself had come to make this a totally unrealistic policy by the mid-eighteenth century.[71] The establishment of French settlements in the area of the company's activities meant that it could not escape being embroiled in an increasingly global Anglo-French conflict; the northward drive of the Marathas sent shock-waves through the entire region, and inflicted grave damage on the rich and productive areas of western Bengal; and deteriorating political and economic conditions compelled the company's agents to intervene increasingly at the local level, whether to protect, or intimidate, local clients, and to salvage company interests. With a large army to be paid for, the company needed still larger resources, which could only be obtained by securing the cession of more territory. The 1765 treaty with the Mughal Emperor, which in effect gave the company control of the rich province of Bengal, was no more than the logical outcome of the process by which the East India Company had been progressively sucked into an Indian quagmire from which it must have seemed to the directors that there was no way of escape. By the 1780's the company was described as possessing a 'voracious desire' for lands and territory, and at the end of the 1790's the Governor-General, Richard Wellesley, was asserting Britain's right to India by conquest.[72]

This process seems characteristic of the entire European overseas enterprise in the Early Modern period: every forward step created a fresh disturbance which weakened the ground beneath the feet and made it harder to draw back. But the image, while telling some of the story, does not tell it all. These Europeans who, in the words of La Popelinière, were prepared to hazard 'their lives, their goods, their honour, and their consciences' to disturb the peace of the world, were no passive victims of a

---

70   Parker, *The Military Revolution*, p. 133.
71   See P. J. Marshall, *Bengal: The British Bridgehead (The New Cambridge History of India*, II, 2, Cambridge, 1987), ch. 3.
72   C. A. Bayly, *Indian Society and the Making of the British Empire (The New Cambridge History of India*, II, 1, Cambridge, 1988), pp. 79 and 81.

natural phenomenon. Nor were their failings simply those of execution. Rather, they were implicit in the very preconditions and preconceptions which sent them overseas. Consumed by the lust for profit; driven forward by a strong territorial imperative which made concepts of empire and sovereignty as natural to them in their dealings with non-Europeans as in their dealings with themselves; and arrogant, and increasingly self-confident, in their attitude to the non-Christian peoples of the world, they proved incapable of observing or preserving a distinction between the pursuit of trading relationships and the exercise of power. If, in consequence, they were sucked into a quagmire, they went into it with their eyes half open, and they made it for themselves.

7

Dispossessing the Barbarian: The Language of Spanish Thomism and the Debate over the Property Rights of the American Indians

Anthony Pagden

I

In 1537 the Spanish Dominican Francisco de Vitoria, Prime Professor of Theology at the University of Salamanca, delivered a lecture entitled *De indis* whose purpose was, he declared, to discover 'by what right the barbarians' – by which he meant the American Indians – 'had come under the rule of the Spaniards'.[1] For although, he professed, the conscience of the Spanish kings and their advisors was of itself sufficient guarantee that everything 'had been well-done', all men are compelled to consult the wisest and best-informed persons they can find before reaching a decision on any issue where matters of conscience are involved.

Vitoria's *relectio* belongs to a tradition of ritual legitimation which the Castilian crown had, since the later Middle Ages, regularly enacted when confronted by uncertain moral issues. The conclusions which the crown's advisors reached on these occasions were frequently ignored since, as Vitoria himself observed, kings were, of necessity, pragmatic beings compelled to 'think from hand to mouth'.[2] But the declarations issued by the theologians and jurists on crown policy formed an important part of the ideological armature of what, after the defeat of the *comunero* revolt in 1520, has some claims to being the first early-modern nation state. With the accession of Philip II, that state had, effectively, secured the consensus of its own political nation. Unlike France, and even England, it had, therefore, no further need to assert its own legitimacy against particular and faction interests, and its principal ideological concern

---

[1] Francisco de Vitoria, *De indis recenter inventis.* I have used the edition in Teofilo Urdanoz (ed.), *Obras de Francisco de Vitoria* (Madrid, 1960), pp. 643–4.

[2] Quoted in Anthony Pagden, *The Fall of Natural Man: The American Indian and the Origins of Comparative Ethnology* (Cambridge, 1982), p. 28.

became instead its self-appointed role as the guardian of universal Christendom. In order to safeguard this role, it was crucial that the crown was seen to act on all occasions in strict accordance with Christian ethico-political principles. The task of the theologians and jurists under Habsburg rule was to establish just what those principles were.

The legitimacy of the conquests had consequently been a subject of debate ever since the New World was discovered to be truly new and inhabited by non-Christian peoples living in what, to European eyes, were remarkably un-civil, 'barbarian' societies. Vitoria's *relectio* was, however, the most detailed and far-reaching discussion of the subject. It was also the first to claim that 'the affair of the Indies', as it had come to be called, was a question neither of the limits of papal jurisdiction, nor of Roman law, but of the law of nature, the *ius naturae*, and that the issue was consequently one not of juridic but of *natural* rights. What was at issue in the prolonged debates over the conquest of the Americas was not the Castilian crown's sovereignty in America (no one, not even Bartolomé de las Casas, the 'Apostle to the Indians' and the most radical defender of their interests, denied that) it was the nature of the rights and, in particular, rights of property, which that sovereignty entailed.

Vitoria and his pupils, and the pupils of his pupils down to the generation of the Jesuits Luís de Molina (1535–1600) and Francisco Suárez (1548–1617), have come to be called 'The School of Salamanca', although the Italian term 'seconda scholastica' is a better description. Their project was to create a moral philosophy based upon an Aristotelian and Thomist interpretation of the law of nature. Central to that project was an understanding of what we refer to loosely as 'property', but which, in the language of natural jurisprudence, was called *dominium* or more exactly in this case *dominium rerum*. By the terms of the social contract, men had renounced their primitive freedom in exchange for the security and the possibility of moral understanding which only civil society could provide; but they retained certain natural and hence inalienable rights of which *dominium* is the most fundamental. During the seventeenth century, the application of the term was successfully limited, by Grotius and then Pufendorf, to private property.[3] But for the scholastics, men could be said to have *dominium* over not only their private property,

---

[3] James Tully, *A Discourse on Property: John Locke and his Adversaries* (Cambridge, 1980), p. 69; and see Richard Tuck, *Natural Rights Theories: Their Origin and Development* (Cambridge, 1979), pp. 58–81. I am greatly indebted to this book for my discussion of *dominium*.

Dispossessing the barbarian 81

their goods (*bona*), but also over their actions, their liberty and even – with certain important qualifications – their own bodies. *Dominium* described the relationship which held together the three parts of the triad into which the Roman jurist Gaius had divided the natural world: persons, things and actions.[4]

Civil society was, by definition, a society based upon property, and property relations were what constituted the basis for all exchanges between men within society. It might, therefore, be argued that if, in objective fact, a society possessed no such relationships, and hence could not be described as a civil community, its individual members could make no claims to *dominium rerum* when confronted by invaders attempting to seize their lands. This, the jurist Palacios Rubios had claimed in 1513, provided one justification for the Spanish occupation of the Caribbean islands.[5] For the theologians, however, such arguments were deficient. All rights were natural whether they were exercised in social practice or not. The conquest of America could only be made legitimate by demonstrating that the native populations had forfeited these rights by their own actions. And this, as we shall see, had to be done without endangering the claim that all rights were the products of God's laws and not of God's grace.

The definition of the term *dominium* had itself been the subject of a prolonged debate for which, in the end, Grotius's reductive solution was the only satisfactory one. Most of the Spanish schoolmen, however, operated until important changes were introduced by Suárez and Molina in the seventeenth century, with the definition provided by Domingo de Soto in his *De iustitia et iure* of 1556. '*Dominium*', he said, 'is a faculty and a right (*facultas et ius*) which one has over anything to use it for his own benefit by any means which is permitted by law.' But since the Thomists upheld the distinction in Roman law between *dominium* and mere possession, he went on, '*dominium* is to be distinguished from possession, use or usufruct . . . for *dominium* is not simply the ability to use something and take its produce, but to alienate it, give it away, sell it or neglect it'.[6] As Richard Tuck has pointed out, the phrase 'by any means which is permitted by law' presented considerable difficulties because with

[4] Paolo Rossi, 'La proprietá nel sistema privatistico della seconda scolastica', in Paolo Grossi (ed.), *La seconda scolastica nella formazione del diritto privato* (Milan, 1972), pp. 117–222.

[5] Juan López de Palacios Rubios, 'Libellus de insulanis quas vulgus Indias apelat', in S. Zavala, *De las islas del Mar Océano* (Mexico, 1954), p. 27.

[6] *De iustitia et iure* (Salamanca, 1556), p. 280 and cf. F. J. Brufau Prats, 'El pensamiento político de Domingo de Soto', *Acta salamanticensis*, IV (1960), pp. 280–4.

that qualification it was hard to see what distinguished Soto's account of usufruct from the *dominium utile* which Accursius – and Aquinas – had granted to the user as distinct from the *dominium directum* possessed by the superior lord, but whose existence the Spanish Thomists vigorously denied.[7] The qualification had, however, important consequences for the arguments over the rights of the Amerindians because it was introduced by Soto precisely to deal with the problem of the rights of children before the age of reason; for children clearly do have *dominium* even if they cannot be allowed to exercise it – a condition in which, as we shall see, the Indians might be said to be.

II

Before 1539, the Castilian crown's principal claim to *dominium* in America had rested on the Bulls of Donation made by Alexander VI in 1493. These had granted to Ferdinand and Isabella sovereignty over all the lands inhabited by non-Christians they might discover in the Atlantic. Since, however, the power to make such donations rested on the papal assumption of temporal authority over both Christians and pagans – an assumption which only the Canonists were willing to endorse – the Bulls provided very shaky grounds indeed for conquest. Once they had been detached from their Caesaro–papal claims they only imposed upon the Castilian crown a duty, the duty to evangelise; but they could not confer upon it a corresponding right.[8] Vitoria, therefore, set the Bulls aside and turned his attention to those arguments for *dominium* which could be expressed in a language of natural rights.

It was clear, he said, from all that he had heard, that before the arrival of the Spaniards, the Indians had been 'in public, private and pacific possession of their things'.[9] There were, therefore, only four possible grounds for claiming that they did not, at the time of the conquest, also enjoy *dominium* over them: either because they were sinners, or because they were infidels, or because they were *insensati* (i.e., animals) or idiots (*amentes*). Only the first three of these had any

[7] *Natural Rights Theories*, pp. 48–9.
[8] *De indis*, pp. 682–5. Vitoria also considered, and rejected, the claims of the emperor to universal *dominium* (pp. 666–75) and the right by virtue of discovery (pp. 684–5). On this last claim he observed that it would only be valid if the Indians were not, prior to the discovery, 'private and public owners of their things' which, as he goes on to show, they were. The rejection of the universalist ambitions of both the papacy and the empire is repeated by all of Vitoria's followers. See, e.g. Soto, *De iustitia et iure*, p. 241.   [9] *De indis*, pp. 650–1.

direct bearing on the case of the Indians, since the mad are a special case whose rights can only be considered under the positive law, which clearly cannot apply to the Indians.

The first claim – that the Indians had forfeited their natural rights by reason of their sins – invoked an old heresy associated with Wycliff and Huss which had now been revived by 'the modern heretics', that 'no-one can have civil *dominium* if he is in a state of mortal sin'.[10] It was central to Vitoria's whole project to refute the claim of these 'modern heretics' that the authority of a prince depended not upon God's laws but upon God's grace, and the subsequent argument that if any prince fell from grace he might legitimately be deposed by his subjects or by another more godly ruler. The Thomists' attack on the arguments which the crown's apologists had hitherto used to legitimate the occupation of America and those used, as we shall see, by such men as Juan Ginés de Sepúlveda and a number of canon lawyers, came ultimately back to this. For, in the end, Vitoria and his successors were far less concerned with the particulars of the American case than they were with the opportunities it provided for a refutation of Lutheran and, later, Calvinist theories of sovereignty.

The accepted refutation of Wycliff's thesis provided by the Gersonian nominalists Pierre d'Ailly and Jean Almain depended – in Vitoria's somewhat schematised account of it – on the case of a sinner on the edge of starvation. If such a man does not have *dominium rerum* he cannot even possess the bread he needs to eat in order to stay alive. He is thus faced with an impossible moral choice: in order not to die voluntarily, which would be to commit one kind of mortal sin, he is compelled to commit another, theft. Since it is clearly impossible that God should have placed any of his creatures in such a position it follows that *dominium* must be independent of grace.[11]

This account of *dominium* implied, however, a theory of unlimited rights which, in effect, denied the Thomists' claim that *in extremis* all the necessities of life reverted to their common state, that every man may take what he truly *needs* from 'another man's plenty' without being guilty of theft.[12] It also obscured what, for Vitoria, was the

[10] *De indis*, pp. 651–2. [11] *De indis*, pp. 652–5.

[12] *Summa theologiae* Ia.IIae. q.66 a.7, Anthony Parel, 'Aquinas' theory of property', in A. Parel and T. Flanagan (eds.), *Theories of Property: Aristotle to the Present* (Calgary, 1879), pp. 89–111. For a discussion of this point, see Istvan Hont and Michael Ignatieff, 'Needs and justice in the wealth of nations: an introductory essay', in Istvan Hont and Michael Ignatieff (eds.), *Wealth and Virtue: The Shaping of Political Economy in the Scottish Enlightenment* (Cambridge, 1983), pp. 28–9.

main argument against Wycliff's thesis, namely that *dominium* derives from the fact that man is a rational being made in God's image, and that he cannot lose that characteristic of himself through sin. The Sun, he said, quoting Matthew 5.45, shines on both the just and the unjust. And if this is the case then *dominium* is inalienable since, by Vitoria's own account, no act, however irrational it might seem, can be anything other than a temporary aberration. There may, of course, be certain acts which are so deviant as to suggest that their agents are not, in fact, men at all. As Locke was to argue, slavery was an option only for a man who had violated the law of nature and thus shown himself to be not a man but a beast.[13] But, in Vitoria's view at least, the Indians were not guilty of such acts. If, as he explained, neither their supposed cannibalism nor the practice of human sacrifice could deprive them of *dominium* then neither could their paganism.

This left Vitoria with the last two claims. Truly irrational beings do not have *dominium* since this is a right (*ius*) and rights can only be held by those creatures who are capable of receiving injury. Since, for Vitoria, *ius* could only be defined objectively as 'that which is allowed under law', creatures who were incapable of receiving injury clearly could not be subject to laws and and could not thus be the object of rights.

The definition of *dominium* as natural to man by virtue of his rationality, which is what makes him an object of justice, raised for Vitoria what seemed to be a potential threat to any definition of *dominium* which made it a natural right independent of possession: namely the status of children. Children, claimed Vitoria, have *dominium*, 'which is nothing other than a right to use something according to its proper use'[14] because unlike, say, lions, they can be said to suffer injury; and because in law their goods are held independently from those of their tutors. But, as they cannot make contracts, they own these goods only as their inheritance.[15] The legal concept of inheritance can also, he implied, be transferred to a consideration of infantile psychology, for however irrational children may seem to be – and they are, he claimed in another lecture on the limits of human obligation, truly un-rational – [16] their reason is potential (just as their goods are potentially theirs) and since

[13] *The Two Treatises on Government*, ed. Peter Laslett (Cambridge, 1970), p. 292, and see Tully, *A Discourse on Property*, p. 114.
[14] *De indis*, p. 661, 'dominium nihil aliud est quam ius utendi re in usum suum'.
[15] *De indis*, pp. 663–4.
[16] 'De eo ad quod tenetur homo cum primum venit ad usum rationis', in *Obras de Francisco de Vitoria*, pp. 1307–8.

Dispossessing the barbarian 85

'nature never fails in what is necessary', that potential cannot ever fail to become actual. As we shall see, this observation offered a powerful analogy with the condition of the Indian.

Having thus rejected all these categories as possible grounds for denying the Indians *dominium* before the arrival of the Spaniards, Vitoria introduced what was to prove the most contentious claim of all. In 1510 the Scottish Dominican John Major had suggested that the Indians were the 'natural slaves' described by Aristotle in Books I and III of the *Politics*.[17] This had seemed to some to offer an objective proof that they had never had any property rights even in their pre-contact state for, both by the terms of Aristotle's psychology and in law, *servus* is the antithesis of *dominus*. Nor did the undeniable fact that the Indians had been legally 'free' in their own societies necessarily make them any the less slaves since, as Vitoria pointed out, a slave does require a master in order to be a slave.[18] The theory of natural slavery is also predicated upon the claim that such slaves are men who do not *possess* but have only a share in the faculty of deliberation and who, though they might be capable of understanding, are not capable of practical wisdom (*phronesis*). Since, therefore, such creatures lack free will, they cannot have any subjective right to *dominium* either.

But even if the American Indians appeared to be 'very little different from brute animals who are incapable of ruling themselves' they did, in fact, have 'a certain rational order in their affairs'. They lived in cities, had a recognised form of marriage, magistrates, rulers, laws, industry and commerce, 'all of which', as Vitoria observed, 'require the use of reason'.[19] This is a simplified version of Aristotle's requirements for civil life and it is clear that no people who fulfil them can be described as society-less and hence rights-less beings. At the very end of his lecture, however, Vitoria reconsidered this argument. Indian communities, he now claimed, possessed only the minimal requirements for social life. They had, for instance, no knowledge of the liberal arts, no proper agriculture, no true artisans. Theirs were societies in which no true *nobilitas* – in the Aristotelian and Thomist sense of the word – could exist and in which it would therefore be impossible to live a life of true *optium*.[20] But if the Indians do, in fact, live 'almost like beasts and wild animals' this is not because they belong by innate disposition to a state of semi-

[17] For a more detailed discussion of the theory of natural slavery, see Pagden, *The Fall of Natural Man*, pp. 27–56.   [18] *De indis*, p. 651.   [19] *De indis*, pp. 664–5.
[20] *De indis*, pp. 723–5. For the argument that the highest moral life is one of *otium*, or pacific contemplation, see pp. 127–8 below.

rationality, but because their 'poor and barbarous education' has rendered them incapable of fully rational behaviour. Since the cause of their cultural condition is to be found in the state of their education, then they may be, not natural slaves, but some kind of natural children and, like all children, heirs to a state of true reason. By the terms of Soto's definition of *dominium* they may be said to be in full possession of their rights without being able to exercise them. The Castilian crown might thus claim a right to hold the Indians, and their lands, in tutelage until they have reached the age of reason. The acceptance by any civil prince of such peoples 'into his care' might even, Vitoria concluded, be considered an act of charity.[21]

None of these arguments, of course, could provide the Castilian crown with *dominium* in America. In place of claims which made a direct appeal to either the natural or the civil law, Vitoria therefore substituted three based on the law of nations, the *ius gentium*. This was, by the definition given in the *Institutes* (1.2.1), 'that which is constituted by natural reason among men'. Just what this implied was a subject of much debate, but Vitoria took it on this occasion to be that which is 'of the natural law or derives from the natural law' and which, consequently, like the natural law, cannot be modified in any way by human agency.[22]

Under the *ius gentium*, the Spaniards possessed what he called the 'right of society and natural communication'.[23] Seas, shores and harbours are necessary for man's survival as a civil being and they have, therefore, by the common accord of all men, been exempted from the original division of property. It had always, Vitoria claimed, been an objective right in law that no man could be forbidden to land on any stretch of beach, no matter to whom it actually belonged, which is why Aeneas had rightly described the ancient kings of Latium as 'barbari' when they refused him anchorage. This right to travel, the *ius peregrinandi*, therefore, gave the Spaniards right of access to the Indies. There was also, under the heading of *communicatio*, an implied right to trade. As the Spaniards had come to America, or so Vitoria claimed, as ambassadors (*legati*) and traders, they had to be treated with respect and be permitted to trade with all those who wished to trade with them. And since this was a right under the law of nations, it could only (at least by the terms of Vitoria's present definition) be changed by the consensus of the

---

[21] *De indis*, p. 725.
[22] *De indis*, p. 706. The Spanish Thomists generally held the *ius gentium* to be a form of positive law, see e.g., Francisco de Vitoria, *Commentarios a la Secunda secundae de Santo Tomás*, ed. Vicente Beltrán de Heredia, III, pp. 8–9.   [23] *De indis*, pp. 705–6.

entire human community, not by the will of an individual ruler.[24] Vitoria also claimed that the *ius gentium* granted the Spaniards the right (the *ius predicandi*) to preach their religion without interference – although it did not compel anyone to accept it – and that it permitted them to wage a just war against any tyrant 'in defence of the innocent'.

In the first two of these cases – the *ius peregrinandi* and the *ius predicandi* – the Spaniards could enforce their rights if opposed because any attempt to deprive a man of his natural rights constitutes an injury. The vindication of injuries constitutes a just war, and ultimately it was only by means of such a war that the Spaniards could legitimate their presence in America.[25] By the terms of such a war the belligerent acquires the status of a judge with respect to his opponents and he may, therefore, appropriate their private property (their *bona* and usually only their moveable goods) as he sees fit.[26] Similarly, the victor acquires authority over the vanquished in order to defend himself against any future injuries, and prisoners taken in a just war may legitimately be enslaved. But in no other case may the enemy be deprived of his *dominium rerum*. In circumstances, however, where the offence is very great – and this might apply to the Indians – or where the enemy seems to be incapable of arriving at a peaceful solution, it is possible to depose ruling princes, to *tollere principem* or *mutare principatum*.[27] The Spaniards might then be able to send 'ministers' to protect their future interests and to depose troublesome local rulers should the need arise.

Vitoria's third title, the 'defence of the innocent', is even more limited in its application. The Spaniards may not, he insisted, make war on the Indians because of their supposed crimes against nature, since all nations are guilty of such crimes. If a prince has no right to invade the territory of another in order to punish cases of 'simple fornication' – since no nation on earth is free of that sin – no prince can punish another for cannibalism or sodomy.[28] For the Thomists, crimes against nature do not admit of degrees, since such crimes are offences against God not man, and only God can punish them. To suggest that any prince however godly, even the emperor himself, could act as *flagellum dei* was to fall, once again, into the Lutheran error of supposing that *dominium* is conferred by God's grace, not God's law.

---

[24] *De indis*, pp. 707–14. [25] *De indis*, pp. 715–21.
[26] Francisco de Vitoria, *Relectio de iure belli*, ed. L. Pereña *et al.* (Madrid, 1981), pp. 187–99. [27] *Relectio de iure belli*, p. 200. [28] *De indis*, pp. 698–9.

Vitoria had thus left the Castilian crown with a slender claim to *dominium iurisdictionis* in America but no property rights whatsoever. And, of course, the rights the crown might claim under the *ius gentium* would only be valid if the Indians had indeed 'injured' the Spaniards. If, however, as seemed to be the case, 'these barbarians have not given any reason for a just war, nor wish voluntarily to accept Christian princes, the expeditions must cease'. In the end, all that remained was the starkly objective claim that, since the Spaniards were already there, any attempt to abandon the colonies would only result in 'a great prejudice and detriment to the interests of [our] princes which would be intolerable'.[29]

III

Over the next three decades all of Vitoria's pupils re-described parts of these arguments in their own lectures on the subject of *dominium*. Perhaps the most important of these, partly because it is among the most radical, at least as far as its implications are concerned, partly because its author was later involved in the most widely publicised debate on the subject, was delivered by the Dominican theologian Melchor Cano in 1546. The Indians, Cano argued, may only be said not to possess *dominium* if they can be shown to be irrational beings. Since they clearly are not simpletons (*stulti*) the only possible argument is that they are 'slaves by nature'.[30] But this theory is, he claimed, incoherent, not only because – as Vitoria himself had argued elsewhere – no man who merely had a share in the faculty of reason could properly be described as a man,[31] but because slavery could, by definition, only be a category in law. Aristotle's mistake had been to confuse a legal classification with a psychological disposition. Since the accepted definition of slavery given in Roman law (Digest 1.1.4) was 'someone who has been deprived of his liberty contrary to nature', there could evidently be no such creature as a *natural* slave. This confusion had, furthermore, been made in the interest of the parochial claim that Athenians were the wisest of all living creatures. And even if we understand Aristotle only to be stating the general principle that the wise should always rule the foolish,

---

[29] *De indis*, p. 725.
[30] Melchor Cano, 'De dominio indorum', Biblioteca Vaticana MS Lat. 4648, fol. 30r.
[31] For a discussion of this argument, see Pagden, *The Fall of Natural Man*, pp. 57–97.

this, although it might indubitably be the case, cannot confer *dominium*, since *dominium* does not derive from wisdom any more than it does from grace. *Dominium iurisdictionis* derives from the will of the community and *dominium rerum*, of course, from the natural law.[32]

It may, of course, still be the case, as Vitoria had argued, that the Indians really are like children in need of education. But even if this were so, the Christians would not be entitled to 'take them into their care' if, in order to do so, they had to conquer them first, since any act whose purpose is to secure the utility of another is, as Vitoria had rightly suspected, a precept of charity, and no precept of charity can involve coercion. The position of the Castilian crown was thus, Cano concluded, analogous only to that of the beggar to whom alms may be due but who is not empowered to extract them.[33]

Cano also rejected Vitoria's other claims. The title 'society and natural communication' does not, he claimed, provide a right of entry to another's territory because even if the *ius gentium* is of the natural law, it can only be so in the third degree and is consequently, like any code which relies upon an interpretation of the natural law, subject to abrogation and alteration. Like Vitoria himself on other occasions, Cano could not really accept the *ius gentium* as anything other than a positive law. For it was, he pointed out, clearly absurd to suggest that there could exist a law of nations which might forbid a prince from controlling the movement of foreigners over his lands. Such a law would prevent the king of Spain from denying entry to the French, which would be contrary to actual practice and in violation of the positive law of Castile. Furthermore, even if it were the case that merchants and travellers might claim the right of free access under the law of nations, the Spaniards had clearly not presented themselves to the Indians as such. They had gone to America as conquerors. 'We would not', he concluded drily, 'be prepared to describe Alexander the Great as a "traveller" '.[34]

This left only the *ius predicandi* and the right to defend the innocent. These Cano was prepared to accept, but he made it clear that they did not have the power to confer property rights upon any secular prince. The Castilian crown's rights in the Indies were, by the terms of Cano's argument, severely limited to political sovereignty. It clearly did not possess rights of *dominium rerum* in America any more than it did in Naples or Aragon. The Indians were, as Las Casas was to insist time and again, free subjects of the Castilian crown, and their

---

[32] 'De dominio indorum', fols. 30r–31v.   [33] 'De dominio indorum', fol. 39r.
[34] 'De dominio indorum', fol. 39v.

property – including both their land and, more polemically, what lay beneath it –[35] remained their own.

IV

By the middle of the century, this modified version of Vitoria's argument was widely accepted by all the Thomists. They may not quite, as Dr Johnson supposed, have given it 'as their opinion that it was not lawful'[36] to deprive the Indians of their property, but they had come perilously close. And the changing tone of the legislation governing the crown's relationship with both the colonists and the Indians in the years after 1540 suggests that they voiced their views to some effect in the influential circles where they moved. In 1550, however, both Soto and Cano, together with Las Casas and a number of lesser figures, were confronted by a quite different set of arguments over the property rights of the American Indians. These were set out in a short dialogue, entitled *Democrates secundus*, by Juan Ginés de Sepúlveda, one of the Emperor's chaplains, and his official historian.[37] Sepúlveda stridently denied that the Indians had been capable of *dominium* before the arrival of the Europeans. John Major, says Democrates, Sepúlveda's mouthpiece in the dialogue, had rightly claimed that as these peoples had had no rulers, no laws, they might legitimately be appropriated by the first civil man to reach their shores. For Sepúlveda (as, in this case, for Major) and for most Roman lawyers and their humanist commentators, all property relations are the product of civil society. They constitute, that is, objective not subjective rights.[38]

To the Thomists, Sepúlveda seemed, by this claim, to have recast the whole issue in the language of humanist jurisprudence. Worse still, in order to make good his claim that not merely the Taino and the Arawak of the Caribbean, but also the Mexican and the Inca, were pre-social men, Sepúlveda was committed to a far starker read-

---

[35] Most of the Thomists rejected any claims that the Indians were not the rightful owners of the gold and silver mined on their lands. See, e.g. Soto, *De iustitia et iure*, p. 424, who argued that the Spaniards had no more right to mine for precious metals in America than the French had to come looking for buried treasure in Spain. And see Bartolomé de las Casas, *Tratado de las doce dudas*, in *Biblioteca de autores Españoles*, Cx, p. 523, who insisted that to deny this was 'to fall into the heresy of Huss'.

[36] Quoted in *Boswell's Life of Johnson*, ed. G. B. Hill (Oxford, 1934), I, p.45.

[37] For a discussion of this text and its reception by Cano, Soto and Bartolomé de Carranza, see Pagden, *The Fall of Natural Man*, pp. 109–18.

[38] *Democrates segundo, o de las justas causas de la guerra contra los indios*, ed. Angel Losada (Madrid, 1951), pp. 83–6.

ing of Aristotle's theory of natural slavery than any previous author had been. The Indians, he claimed, were evidently not civil beings since they consistently violated the law of nature. To the objection of the speaker in the dialogue (a mild-mannered German called Leopoldus who speaks throughout in the language of political Aristotelianism) that all men violate the law of nature and that in many societies such crimes are not even proscribed by civil law, Democrates replies that a man may perform certain unnatural acts *as an individual* and still retain his humanity. What he may not do is to set up 'laws and institutions' which are contrary to nature. Single individuals frequently, even in Christian societies, falter in their understanding of the law of nature. But if the consensus of the entire community, which is the only means of knowing the precepts of that law, is itself at fault, then it is clear that this cannot have been arrived at by a collectivity of rational beings. The 'crimes committed against human society' by such creatures therefore constituted, as the Canonists had always insisted, grounds for a just war in which the vanquished might be deprived of all their rights, including their liberty, their *dominium corporis suis*.[39]

Sepúlveda was extremely proud of what he believed to be his discovery of the weakness in the Thomists' rejection of the argument that 'crime against nature' constituted legitimate grounds for depriving a man of his natural rights. Leopoldus, however, objects that Mexican society, even if guilty of such crimes, has any number of other features characteristic of civil communities. Certainly, replies Democrates, for the Indians obviously possess some power of understanding; even natural slaves are men, not 'bears or monkeys'. But the communities they have created are not like those of 'truly civil beings'. For there are, he points out, many forms of natural association among animals which share some of the features of a true society but which are clearly not in any sense civil ones. A closer look at the Indian world would, he concludes, reveal that it was really not much better organised than a colony of bees or ants.[40]

Before the arrival of the Spaniards, the Indians had, Sepúlveda conceded, been lords in their own lands, they had enjoyed, that is, *imperium* under the terms of the law of nations which grants rights of occupancy to the first settler. But, he insisted, not only was *imperium* not *dominium*, any claim made under the *ius gentium* may be abrogated since it was, as the humanists had maintained, a positive, not a

[39] *Democrates segundo*, p. 97. [40] *Democrates segundo*, p. 36.

natural law. The Castilian crown's claims to *dominium* in America rest, however, on the dictate of the natural law which grants *dominium* to all those who are civil beings over all those who are not.[41]

It might, however, be argued that, under the new civil regime created by the Spaniards, the Indians could still retain their use rights over their lands and, more importantly, over their gold and silver. To this Democrates replies that God gave property to man for his use, but since use, unlike *dominium*, is limited, man may not *abuse* it. The Indians have clearly abused their property, cannibalism and human sacrifice being the most grisly violations of those limited use rights which men have over their own bodies. More importantly, they had only used their gold and silver for idolatrous ends. Like the Egyptians, then, they may be said to have forfeited whatever rights they had had over these metals because, in Augustine's words, 'they were sacriligeous and made ill-use of their gold'.[42] Furthermore, since no Indian society had had a monetary economy, no Indian could be said to have exercised any rights over any precious metal. These were, therefore, still a common part of Adam's patrimony, to which the Spaniards had a high moral claim by having traded metals which had been useless in the ancient Indian world for such useful things as iron, European agricultural techniques, horses, donkeys, goats, pigs, sheep, and so on.[43] For Sepúlveda, as for such eighteenth-century natural-law theorists as Wattell who, in the generation after Grotius and Pufendorf, rewrote the language of iusnaturalism in a more fully humanistic idiom, *dominium* could only exist if it were exercised. The cultivation of the land allotted by God to man is not, as Wattell claimed, merely useful: it is an obligation 'imposée à l'homme par la nature'.[44] Any people who failed to fulfil that obligation could have no claim against other more industrious nations who occupied and cultivated its lands. It followed, therefore, that the Christians might, in Democrates' words, take possession, 'by private and public law', of all Indian goods. The Indians' historical relationship to their property may now, he concluded, be likened to that of a man who has been deprived of his goods by the court but granted the *ius utendi* until sentence has been formally promulgated by a judge. The arrival of the Spaniards, directed to America by divine providence, constituted that promulgation.[45]

[41] *Democrates segundo*, pp. 79–83.
[42] *Democrates segundo*, pp. 87–90, citing *Contra Faustum*, Bk XXII, cap. 7.
[43] *Democrates segundo*, pp. 78–9.
[44] M. de Wattell, *Le Droit de gens ou principe de la loi naturelle* (Paris, 1820), I, p. 113.
[45] *Democrates segundo*, pp. 90–1.

Dispossessing the barbarian   93

Sepúlveda's argument, couched as it was in the language of a humanist jurisprudence which restricted all rights – and rights of property in particular – to the members of civil societies, met with fierce opposition from the Salamanca theologians. Their hostility to his work was, so Cano told Sepúlveda, based on the fact that his doctrines were unsound, that he was ignorant of what Vitoria had written on the subject and that he seemed to know more about history and philosophy than he did about theology.[46] In part, as Sepúlveda himself recognised, this was the reaction of a professional intellectual coterie to interference from an outsider. But Cano's increasingly acrimonious correspondence with Sepúlveda makes it clear that the Thomists were concerned by two other issues. In the first place, Sepúlveda's objective (and conceptually somewhat confused) use of *ius* had allowed him to translate concepts from the positive into the natural law. In the second, his reliance on the Canonists' defence of the thesis that no man who has committed crimes against nature may possess *dominium* seemed, once again, to open the way to an ultimately Lutheran definition of sovereignty.

The most sustained attempt to meet Sepúlveda's arguments on these issues came in a series of lectures given between 1560 and 1563 by Juan de la Peña, a pupil of Soto and a close friend of Las Casas.[47] Peña began, as Cano and others had before him, by dismissing the theory of natural slavery. It was, he claimed, not only inapplicable, as Cano had argued, it was also incoherent. For if it were possible for there to exist whole races of partially rational men capable of performing some, but not all, of the actions of civil beings, this would seriously threaten the doctrine of the perfectibility of man and the unity of the whole species, both of which have been guaranteed by divine revelation. If natural slaves do exist, they must be very rare beasts indeed, and they must *be* beasts. Peña was willing to concede the minor premise – that the wise should always rule the less wise – but the fact remains, he said – *factum tenet* – that in no actual society is this ever the case.[48]

If the Indians are rational men they have *dominium rerum*, since 'the foundation of *dominium* is that man is a rational creature',[49] and no act

---

[46] *Jo. Genesius doctor theologus Melchiori Cano doctori theo* in *Joannis Genesii Sepulvedae cordubensis opera* (Madrid, 1780), III, pp. 34–5, and see Pagden, *The Fall of Natural Man*, pp. 110–13.

[47] *De bello contra insulanos* and *De libertate indorum contra Sepulvedam*, parts of a commentary on the *Secunda secundae* of Aquinas and printed in *De bello contra insulanos*, ed. L. Pereña *et al.* (Madrid, 1982), pp. 136–393.

[48] *De bello contra insulanos*, pp. 245–9. Like Cano, Peña also accused Sepúlveda of being 'mediocriter in theologia exercitatus' (*Ibid.*, p. 213).

[49] *De bello contra insulanos*, pp. 146–7.

they might perform can, *of itself*, deprive them of that right. The manifest errors of their society before the arrival of the Spaniards, like the errors of all non-Christian societies, were, Peña insisted, merely probable. They were, that is, the kind of errors into which any individual might fall if he were deprived of proper guidance, the kind of guidance which, in the end, only a Christian civil society can provide. But a man who is in error is still in full possession of all his natural rights. Sepúlveda's claim that only civil men could enjoy *dominium* (the assumption which underwrites all Roman legal thinking on the subject) is merely the legislative norm of a tyranny, and may ultimately prove to be as parochial as Aristotle's assumption that all those who are not Athenians are natural slaves.[50]

Sepúlveda's claim that the Indians had also forfeited their use rights in the lands they occupied was similarly false. Use rights were, Peña pointed out, not *dominia* and thus came under not the natural but the civil law. From this it clearly followed that whatever misuse the Indians might have made of their property could only be punished by those who enjoyed civil jurisdiction over them. Since, however, they had had *dominium* before the arrival of the Spaniards and were guilty of no offence 'in respect of another republic', they could not be punished under a new regime – even supposing that regime to be a legitimate one, which, in this case, was by no means certain – for crimes committed under another. If they were in fact unworthy (*indigni*) of *dominia*, then it was up to *their* judges to deprive them of such rights and not the Spaniards, 'who have no authority over them'.[51] Far, therefore, from being, as Sepúlveda had suggested, under sentence of confiscation, the Indians were now in the position of persons from whom a judge has taken far more than the law allows and, like all such persons, they were entitled to restitution.[52] And, Peña concluded, if that was the case, then in order to press their claims for restitution, the Indians were perfectly within *their* rights to make war on the Spaniards.

Like Cano before him, Peña was willing to accept that the Spaniards could make just war on the Indians, and thereby deprive them of their rights, in defence of innocent parties. This, at least, would provide a legitimate reason among Christian princes. Henry VIII of England, whose *respublica* was, because of the offences he had caused its citizens, already in disarray, might legitimately be attacked

[50] *De bello contra insulanos*, pp. 247–9.
[51] *De bello contra insulanos*, p. 261.
[52] *De bello contra insulanos*, p. 239. Soto had come to much the same conclusion with regard to the Africans enslaved by the Portuguese, *De iustitia et iure*, p. 289.

Dispossessing the barbarian **95**

in order to prevent further collapse.[53] Similarly, it was legitimate for the Spaniards to prevent such tribes as the Caribs from eating each other by force. It was, however, by no means clear that the Mexicans – who did not eat their subjects – had sufficiently offended a large enough number of their people to warrant European interference. The Aztec kings had only been accused of one major violation of the rights of their citizens: human sacrifice. But from what Peña had heard (and this must have been a piece of information given him by Las Casas), this was, in fact, only a ritualised mode of execution.

In the end it was impossible for Peña, faced as he was by the need to refute Sepúlveda, to find sufficient grounds in any of Vitoria's original titles to deny the American Indians their natural property rights. The only title which could escape careful scrutiny in the light of an increasingly detailed body of ethnographic information was the *ius predicandi*, the right to preach. But, as Vitoria himself had recognised, this only gave the Spaniards the right to be heard.

The obvious conclusion, and it had been obvious now for some time, was that if the consequences of these arguments were going to be taken seriously, the Spaniards had to withdraw and return to the Indians all that they had taken from them. Although this was never considered as a real possibility because, as Vitoria had observed, it would be intolerable in practice, it was at one point widely believed in the colonies themselves that Charles V intended to 'abandon the Indies' to satisfy his conscience. The only possible argument which could preserve both Indian rights and the Spanish claim to, if not *dominium rerum*, at least *dominium iurisdictionis*, was the claim by Las Casas in 1554 that 'the only title which Your Majesty has is this: that all, or the greater part of, the Indians wish voluntarily to be your vassals and hold it an honour to be so'.[54] But this, of course, did not mean that the Indians had thereby voluntarily forfeited their natural rights, for it is obviously in no man's power to do that, nor that they were any the less due for restitution of their goods, and their

---

[53] In the interests of peace, which required the recovery of the well-ordered society, otherwise legitimate princes might be deprived of their goods (*bona*) and, if they continued to be unfit to rule, of their *dominium*. See, e.g., Francisco Suárez, *Disputatio XII: de bello*, in *Opus de triplici virtute theologica: fide spe et charitate* (Paris, 1621), p. 819.

[54] 'Sobre el título del dominio del rey de España sobre las personas y tierras de los indios', in *De regia potestate*, ed. L. Pereña *et al.* (Madrid, 1969), pp. 171 f. Vitoria himself had discussed this point in *De indis* (pp. 721–2). Just as the French had elected Pipin, so the Indians might 'elect' Charles V, since every *respublica* 'may constitute its own *dominium* with the consensus of the majority'. But he recognised that it would prove impossible in fact to discover what the consensus of the majority was.

liberties, even the liberty of self-government. For, by the terms of this formulation, the rights which the crown now had in the Indies were similar, not to those it had over the people of Castile, but to those it had in Milan. The Indian chieftains, like the Dukes of Milan, ruled over polities which were, in all respects, 'perfect republics', and their subjects were consequently free men with full *dominium* under their own laws. Philip II could no more parcel out the Amerindians to his Castilian subjects than he could give away the Milanese to the French.[55]

It followed from this, Las Casas wrote in 1555 to the Archbishop of Toledo, Bartolomé de Carranza, who had been fighting the Council of the Indies on his behalf, that the colonists must abandon the Indies, leaving only 'the universal principate of the King of Castile'. A limited number of soldiers should remain to protect the missionaries, and once restitution had been made, the crown might begin to trade for the precious metals it required.[56] Under this description, America resembled less the Duchy of Milan than a Portuguese factory in India, an analogy which Vitoria himself had drawn at the very end of *De indis*, pointing out that there was no evidence to suggest that the crown of Portugal had acquired any less through licit trade than the Castilian crown had through illicit occupation.[57]

V

With the death in 1566 of Las Casas, who had done so much to keep it alive, the debate over the rights of the Indians lost much of its immediate force. The rapid decline of the Indian population itself and the collapse of the missionary ambition, which Las Casas had shared, to create a New Jerusalem in the New World, greatly reduced the urgency of the whole issue. The Castilian crown's own concerns with political legitimacy were now focused on the Netherlands and Italy, where the issues – despite attempts by both Netherlanders and Neapolitans to turn Las Casas's arguments to

[54] *De regia potestate*, pp. 33–9, 83–5. This treatise, which was printed in Frankfurt in 1571, was the last Las Casas wrote. It relies heavily on the arguments of the work of the fourteenth-century jurist Lucas da Penna and consequently proposes a strongly contractualist account of government which contrasts markedly with the weaker versions proposed by the Thomists in which political authority is said, in, e.g. Suárez's formulation, to be held by the people only *in fieri* and not *in conservari*. (*Defensio fidei catholicae et apostolicae adversus anglicanae sectae errores* (Coimbra, 1613), p. 225.)

[56] 'Carta al maestro fray Bartolomé de Miranda sobre la perpetuidad de las ecomiendas', in *De regia potestate*, pp. 441–5.   [57] *De indis*, p. 275.

their own advantage – were quite unlike those which had applied in America. When in 1631 the jurist Juan de Solórzano y Pereira attempted to write what was, in effect, a history of the whole debate, the nature of the Vitorian project, the over-arching concern to refute the Lutheran account of *dominium*, had become invisible. In Solórzano's view, the entire debate had, from the moment Vitoria delivered his famous lecture, simply been couched in the wrong language. The Castilian crown's claims to *dominium* had derived, in the first instance, from Alexander VI's Bulls of Donation. But ever since Vitoria had cast doubt on these by denying the pope any degree of temporal power, the entire issue had been conducted in the vocabulary of natural rights. The point which had, therefore, escaped all the natural-law theorists was that even if the Bulls were invalid – and Solórzano seems inclined to accept that they were – neither Ferdinand nor Isabella were aware of this. As no less a person than Cardinal Bellarmine had pointed out, the Catholic Monarchs had believed in good faith that the pope had conferred full *dominium* upon the crown, and the crown had, therefore, behaved in good conscience of acting as it did. What Solórzano was now arguing, by recasting the whole debate in the language of Roman jurisprudence, was that if the crown had come into possession of the Indies by what it believed to be a legitimate right, then it could claim *dominium* by virtue of subsequent occupation. It was, as Solórzano pointed out, precisely this argument which had traditionally been used to legitimate the Roman conquests retrospectively. 'Even a tyranny', wrote Solórzano, and in this respect the Roman Empire was a tyranny, 'becomes in time a perfect and legitimate monarchy.'[58] Time, the Spaniards' historical presence, is then the sufficient condition of *dominium*, for it is the objective condition which confers legal rights; and, in the end, it is legal, not natural rights, which are under debate. A similar acceptance of an historical basis for rights was, as he pointed out, the only claim made by the other European maritime state to *dominium* over the seas closest to its shores. No one (except the wretched and heretical Grotius) denied the right of Alexander III to grant *dominium* over the Adriatic to Venice, or the right of the

[58] *Politica indiana sacada en lengua castellana de los dos tomos del derecho i govierno municipal de las Indias* (1648) in *Biblioteca de autores Españoles*, CCLII, p. 108. The argument which underpins this claim is set out by Vitoria himself in the prolegomenon to *De indis* (pp. 643–8). If someone, after due consultation with 'the most learned doctors', is convinced that an act is legitimate, then he cannot be held guilty of any offence, even if those doctors subsequently prove to be wrong. What Vitoria was not claiming, however, was that an illicit act performed in good faith could render the consequences of that act legitimate, particularly once it was recognised that the act itself had been illicit.

Genoese to the Ligurian Sea. Turn, he told his readers, to John Selden's *Mare clausum*, where you will find arguments which will do quite as well for Spanish claims to rights in the lands of America, as they do for the English king's claims to the North Sea and the North Atlantic.[59] Selden, of course, was writing in the terms of the language of 'modern' iusnaturalism (described here by Richard Tuck), a language in which objective conditions play a far larger role than they did for the Spanish Thomists. But the terms of that discourse were already beginning to look by the 1630s distincly unwieldy and outmoded. As Solórzano concluded, the whole issue to which Vitoria and his pupils had addressed themselves was now only of 'antiquarian interest' and was raised, when at all, only by 'certain heretics out of envy of our nation'.[60]

[59] *Politica indiana*, p. 114. On Selden's *Mare clausum*, see Richard Tuck, *Natural Rights Theories*, pp. 86–7.
[60] *Politica indiana*, pp. 112–13.

An earlier version of this essay was read as a paper at a conference on the Roman Law held at the Warburg Institute and at the Social and Political Theory Seminar at Cambridge. I am grateful to those present, and in particular to John Dunn, Quentin Skinner, Geoffrey Hawthorn and Istvan Hont, for their comments and suggestions.

8

The Ideology of English Colonization: From Ireland to America

Nicholas P. Canny

ALTHOUGH the lordship of Ireland had long been in English hands, effective control over the country had been lost during the late medieval period, with the result that independent and autonomous Irish jurisdictions covered much of the island until the end of the sixteenth century. Attempts to reassert English authority over Ireland produced under Elizabeth I a pattern of conquest, bolstered by attempts at colonization, which was contemporaneous with and parallel to the first effective contacts of Englishmen with North America, to plans for conquest and settlement there, and to the earliest encounters with its Indian inhabitants. The Elizabethan conquest of Ireland should therefore be viewed in the wider context of European expansion.

David B. Quinn has stressed the connection between English colonization in Ireland and the New World, and he has established the guidelines for a full investigation.[1] No historian, however, has dealt with the legal and ethical considerations raised by colonization in Ireland or with

* Mr. Canny lectures on history in the National University of Ireland at University College, Galway. He wishes to thank Professors Richard S. Dunn and Edward M. Peters of the University of Pennsylvania for their criticism of this work when in dissertation form; Professor David B. Quinn of the University of Liverpool for his encouragement, criticism, and valuable suggestions; Professor F. X. Martin and Dr. John Bossy for their helpful comments.

[1] See the following works by David Beers Quinn: *Raleigh and the British Empire* (London, 1947); *The Elizabethans and the Irish* (Ithaca, N. Y., 1966); "Ireland and Sixteenth-Century European Expansion," *Historical Studies,* I (1958), 20-32; "Sir Thomas Smith (1513-1577) and the Beginnings of English Colonial Theory," American Philosophical Society, *Proceedings,* LXXXIX (1945), 543-560; "The Munster Plantation: Problems and Opportunities," *Cork Historical and Archaeological Society Journal,* LXXI (1966), 19-41. See also Theodore K. Rabb, *Enterprise and Empire: Merchant and Gentry Investment in the Expansion of England, 1575-1630* (Cambridge, Mass., 1967); Howard Mumford Jones, *O Strange New World: American Culture, The Formative Years* (New York, 1964); Charles Verlinden, *Les Origines de la Civilisation Atlantique: De la Renaissance a l'Age des Lumières* (Paris, 1966), and *The Beginnings of Modern Colonization* (Ithaca, N. Y., 1970).

the means by which these were resolved to the satisfaction of the aggressors' consciences. It is the purpose of the present article to tackle this problem and to show how the justifications for colonization influenced or reflected English attitudes toward the Gaelic Irish and, by extension, toward the imported slave and the indigenous populations in North America. It will also be shown that those sixteenth-century Englishmen who pondered the Irish problem did so in secular terms, and that through their thinking on the social condition of the Irish they approached a concept of cultural evolution no less "advanced" than that of the Spaniard José de Acosta in his writing (1590) on the indigenous population of the New World.[2]

The question of how to treat the native Irish first confronted the Tudors during the years 1565-1576 in the context of establishing English colonies in the Gaelic areas of the country. There had been earlier attempts at plantation in sixteenth-century Ireland but always in terms of defending the Pale—the loyal area in the vicinity of Dublin—from Gaelic Irish marauders. The strategic consideration had never been absent, but an offensive dimension was added in 1565 when it became the avowed purpose of the government to bring all of Ireland under English control. Equally significant was the fact that all subsequent attempts at colonization in Ireland were privately sponsored, the adventurers being members of the gentry and younger sons of England's aristocracy rather than soldiers in the government's pay. All could justify their presence on the grounds of pursuing the public good, but there were some who had scruples about seeking private gain at the expense of the original inhabitants of the lands to be colonized, and each colonizer had to justify the attendant aggression for himself. The years 1565-1576 therefore produced an outpouring of justifications for colonization and conquest. These arguments were to be elaborated upon and drawn together in later years, notably in Edmund Spenser's *A View of the Present State of Ireland* (1596).[3]

[2] José de Acosta, *Historia Natural y Moral de las Indias,* ed. Edmundo O'Gorman, 2d ed. rev. (Mexico, 1962); J. H. Elliott, *The Old World and the New, 1492-1650* (Cambridge, 1970), 39-51; J. H. Rowe, "Ethnography and Ethnology in the Sixteenth Century," *Kroeber Anthropological Society Papers,* XXX (1964), 1-19; J. R. Hale, "Sixteenth-Century Explanations of War and Violence," *Past and Present,* No. 51 (May 1971), 3-26.

[3] Edmund Spenser, *A View of the Present State of Ireland* (1596), ed. W. L. Renwick (Oxford, 1970).

The leading personality behind the colonization scheme was Sir Henry Sidney who was appointed lord deputy of Ireland in 1565 and remained a controlling influence in Irish affairs until 1579. Sidney enjoyed the almost undivided support of the English government in his colonization ventures, particularly those of his brother-in-law, the earl of Leicester, and of Sir William Cecil and Sir Thomas Smith, all three of whom sponsored colonization in Ireland. The personnel of the various Irish expeditions reflected this sponsorship.[4]

The first attempt (1565-1566) was to colonize that part of Ulster lying east of the river Bann. The leader of this expedition was Sir Arthur Champernoun of Devon who was accompanied by a closely-knit group of West Country gentry, notably Sir Humphrey Gilbert, John Champernoun, and Philip Butshed. In 1567 some of these adventurers shifted their interest to the coastal areas of southwest Munster, this time under the direction of Sir Warham St. Leger of Kent, a close friend of Sidney. Others of the West Country gentry joined them; the leading spokesmen were Gilbert, Sir Peter Carew, Edmund Tremayne, and Richard Grenville. So far most of the colonizers had been lured to Ireland by Sidney or Leicester, and this exclusiveness persisted into the following year when Carew attempted by himself to carve out a colony in the barony of Idrone, in Leinster. After 1568 we notice a wider representation. There is evidence that Cecil was called upon to aid the flagging Munster expedition, and a second effort to colonize northeast Ulster was organized in 1572 by Smith.[5] In 1573 Walter Devereux, first earl of Essex, mobilized the greatest expedition to date in an attempt to establish title to those parts of northeast Ulster not claimed by Smith. The Essex expedition was almost a national effort in that it not only enjoyed the support of the queen and Privy Council, but also in its early stages attracted to its ranks the sons of many aristocratic families.[6] The persons most closely associated with this bloody and financially

[4] For details of those involved with colonization in Ireland see Nicholas P. Canny, "Glory and Gain: Sir Henry Sidney and the Government of Ireland, 1558-1578" (Ph.D. diss., University of Pennsylvania, 1971), esp. ch. 3. An expanded version of this work will be published by Irish University Press under the title *The Elizabethan Conquest of Ireland: A Pattern Established 1565-76.*

[5] Quinn, "Smith and Colonial Theory," Am. Phil. Soc., *Procs.,* LXXXIX (1945), 543-560, and Mary Dewar, *Sir Thomas Smith: A Tudor Intellectual in Office* (London, 1964).

[6] For a list of those involved in the Essex expedition see S.P. 63/41, fol. 64, Public Record Office.

disastrous campaign were Essex himself, Carew, Gilbert, Sir John Norris, and Edward Barkley. Financial and physical exhaustion forced the abandonment of this expedition in 1576, thus closing a chapter in the history of English colonization in Ireland.

It is apparent that the same names recurred in the successive colonization efforts. The majority of these were from the West Country, and many of them, like Gilbert and Grenville, afterwards became involved in colonization ventures in the New World and again in later plantation attempts in Ireland. Men from the West Country were prominent in all English expansionist ventures of the seventeenth century. Historians have noted this regional aggressiveness,[7] and the continued involvement of West Countrymen with colonization can be partly explained by the fact that so many of them were responsible for expounding a secular ideology to justify colonization in Ireland.

The sites for colonies selected by Sidney were northeast Ulster and southwest Munster. Both of these areas had long been considered by the government to be strategically dangerous, and proposals had earlier been made to remove the Scots settlement from northeast Ulster and to prohibit the arrival of Spanish ships in southwest Munster. Sidney intended to secure these objectives by laying claim to and colonizing extensive territories in both regions, thus disturbing the indigenous population as well as the foreign intruders. His decision was determined in part by the fact that those areas were inhabited by Gaelic Irish rather than by Old English. This distinction manifested itself again when the government restricted the claims of St. Leger in Munster to lands held by Gaelic lords.[8] The rationale behind this was Sidney's assertion that the Gaelic Irish were unreliable and could be subdued only by force, while the Old English could be brought to civility by persuasion. Sidney thus justified colonization on the grounds of strategic necessity and expediency, but this did not satisfactorily explain either how the crown could establish legal title to the lands in question or how the indigenous population might be removed from their lands

[7] Karl S. Bottigheimer, *English Money and Irish Land: The 'Adventurers' in the Cromwellian Settlement of Ireland* (Oxford, 1971), 65-66, 158-160; for West Countrymen in America, especially Virginia, see the many books on the subject by A. L. Rowse, and Rabb, *Enterprise and Empire*.

[8] Letter of the lords of the Privy Council, Mar. 1569, in David Beers Quinn, *The Voyages and Colonising Enterprises of Sir Humphrey Gilbert*, II (Hakluyt Society, *Publications*, 2d Ser., LXXXIII-LXXXIV [London, 1940]), 494-496. See *ibid.*, 493-494, for the petition to the Privy Council.

to make room for colonies of Englishmen. The answers to these questions, derived from experience in Ireland and ideologically articulated by the colonizers and their spokesmen, would prove readily applicable to other peoples in other places, not merely beyond the Irish Sea but beyond the Atlantic Ocean.

The first of these problems presented little difficulty to the English legal mind. England, after all, had established title to most of Ireland by right of conquest during the Norman offensive of the twelfth and thirteenth centuries. Although the native Irish had reoccupied much of this land in the fourteenth and fifteenth centuries, they had never established legal title to it and could therefore be considered trespassers on land that really belonged to the crown or to the descendants of the original conquerors. It was by right of conquest by his ancestors, for example, that Carew claimed title to lands in Ireland.[9] Again it was by right of inheritance from the long extinct line of the earls of Ulster that the queen claimed the lands of that province. Smith for example was granted title to lands in Ireland as "parcel of the county of Ulster in Ireland" to hold from the crown as heir to the earldom of Ulster by service of a knight's fee, and Essex likewise sought a patent for "the dominion of Clandeboy [etc.] . . . in the earldom of Ulster."[10] There was in fact only one attempt to colonize lands to which legal title had not been established, that of St. Leger in southwest Munster, and in that case it was hoped to have the Munster lords who resisted attainted as rebels. The accepted legality was, in the words of Spenser, that "all is the conqueror's as Tully to Brutus saith."[11]

Although the legal question involved in establishing title to land was easily answered to the satisfaction of the queen's, and England's, conscience, the treatment of the indigenous population was another matter. The Normans had driven off merely the ruling elite from the lands they conquered and had retained the majority of the inhabitants as tenants and cultivators. The Old English, the descendants of the

[9] John Vowell [Hooker], *The Life of Sir Peter Carew*, in J. S. Brewer and W. Bullen, eds., *Calendar of the Carew Manuscripts, preserved in the Archiepiscopal Library at Lambeth, 1515-1624* (London, 1867-1873).

[10] Smith's patent was granted on Nov. 16, 1571; see [N. J. Williams, ed.], *Calendar of the Patent Rolls, preserved in the Public Record Office* (London, 1966), V, patent no. 2167. The draft patent was granted to Essex in May 1573; see Brewer and Bullen, eds., *Calendar of Carew Manuscripts*, 441-442.

[11] Spenser, *Ireland*, ed. Renwick, 9.

580   WILLIAM AND MARY QUARTERLY

earlier conquerors, followed the same pattern. They clearly regarded the struggle in Ireland as a conflict between cultures, Gaelic and English, but while they considered the Gaelic system of government to be tyrannical, hence barbarous, they did not consider those living under Gaelic rule to be incapable of being civilized. On the contrary, they held that once the [Gaelic chieftains were overthrown and Gaelic law abolished, the native inhabitants, thus liberated from thralldom] would be accepted as subjects under English law. Even the statutes of Kilkenny (1366), which some historians have labeled apartheid legislation, allowed for a procedure by which Irishmen could be granted exactly the same legal status as English subjects. The fact that native Irish in the sixteenth century were being freely accepted as tenants to land within the Pale proves the persistence of these attitudes among the Old English.[12]

The queen seems to have accepted this view of the matter. She recognized that the Scots who inhabited lands in northeast Ulster were interlopers and not her subjects, and could therefore be forcibly removed with impunity. She directed, however, that the native Irish population there should be "well used," and on the subject of the Essex enterprise she stated specifically that "our meaning is not that the said Erle nor any of his company shall offend any person that is knowne to be our good subject."[13] Both Smith and Essex promised to observe this instruction, but Essex's assurance that he would not "imbrue" his "hands with more blood than the necessity of the cause requireth" was somewhat short of convincing.

Essex did follow the queen's instructions by concentrating his energies against the Scots settlement in Ulster. It was with the intention of breaking their power that he mobilized the nocturnal expedition to Rathlin Island in 1574, which succeeded in slaughtering the entire population of the island to the number of six hundred people.[14] The earl was

[12] For the statutes see Geoffrey Hand, "The Forgotten Statutes of Kilkenny: A Brief Survey," *Irish Jurist*, N.S., I (1966), 299-312, esp. 299; Terence de Vere White, *Ireland* (London, 1968); J. A. Watt, *The Church and the Two Nations in Medieval Ireland* (Cambridge, 1970), ix, 200-215. On the Irish tenants in the Pale see Nicholas P. Canny, "Hugh O'Neill, and the Changing Face of Gaelic Ulster," *Studia Hibernica*, X (1970), 25-27.

[13] Queen to William Fitzwilliam, July 17, 1573, Carte MSS. 56, no. 260, Bodleian Library, Oxford University.

[14] Essex to Privy Council, July 13, 1575, S.P. 63/52, no. 78, P.R.O., and Essex to the queen, July 1575, in Walter Bourchier Devereux, *Lives and Letters of the Devereux, Earls of Essex in the Reigns of Elizabeth, James I, and Charles I, 1540-1646*, I (London, 1853), 113-117.

frustrated by the queen's directive that he should not molest the Gaelic Irish inhabitants of Ulster, and when the local chieftain, Sir Brian McPhelim O'Neill, broke his compact with Essex he considered "all this to fall out to the best . . . so in the manner of their departure and breach of their faiths they have given me just cause to govern such as shall inhabit with us in the most severe manner, which I could not without evil opinions have offered if their revolt had not been manifest." One of the lieutenants of the expedition, Edward Barkley, was glad of the opportunity to extend stern rule over the Ulster Irish, who, he wrote, would be commanded by the queen or starve. Barkley gave a graphic description of how Essex's men had driven the Irish from the plains into the woods where they would freeze or famish with the onset of winter, and concluded with the smug observation: "how godly a dede it is to overthrowe so wicked a race the world may judge: for my part I thinke there canot be a greater sacryfice to God."[15]

The most extreme action of the enterprise took place at a Christmas feast in 1574, where O'Neill, his wife, and his kinsmen were seized by Essex, later to be executed in Dublin, and two hundred of O'Neill's followers were killed. This massacre went beyond the queen's original instructions, but it is significant that the attitude of the London government had hardened sufficiently to countenance the actions of Essex. The queen even commended his service in Ulster and was satisfied that her instructions had been complied with, "because we do perceive that, when occasion doth present, you do rather allure and bring in that rude and barbarous nation to civility and acknowledging of their duty to God and to us, by wisdom and discreet handling than by force and shedding of blood; and yet, when necessity requireth, you are ready also to oppose yourself and your forces to them whom reason and duty cannot bridle."[16] It appears, therefore, that the Essex experience had convinced the queen and her advisors that the Irish were an unreasonable people and that they, no less than the Scots intruders in Ulster, might be slaughtered by extralegal methods.

Similar extreme action was taken by Gilbert against those who

[15] See Devereux, *Lives of Devereux,* I, 30-31, for Essex to Burghley, July 20, 1573, and *ibid.,* 37-39, for Essex to Privy Council, Sept. 29, 1573. Barkley to Burghley, May 14, 1574, S.P. 63/46, no. 15, P.R.O.

[16] R. Bagwell, *Ireland under the Tudors, with a Succinct Account of the Early History* (London, 1885-1890), II, 288-289, and queen to Essex, July 13, 1574, in Devereux, *Lives of Devereux,* I, 73-74.

opposed the colonization effort in Munster. When the expected resistance occurred, Gilbert was, in October 1569, appointed military governor of Munster with almost unrestricted power of martial law.[17] Thereafter war in Munster became total war, and Gilbert extended his action
to "manne, woman and childe," so "the name of an Inglysh man was
made more terryble now to them than the syght of an hundryth was
before."[18] The pamphleteer, Thomas Churchyard, who accompanied
Gilbert to Munster, justified the slaughter of noncombatants on the
grounds of expediency. Their support, he claimed, was essential to
sustain the rebels "so that the killyng of theim by the sworde was the
waie to kill the menne of warre by famine." Even in granting mercy
to former rebels, Gilbert displayed the utmost cruelty and inhumanity.
All who submitted were compelled to demean themselves utterly before
him, to take an oath of loyalty to the queen, and to provide pledges
and recognizances as assurance of their future loyalty. The impact of
Gilbert's severity is brought home by Churchyard's graphic description
of his practice:

that the heddes of all those (of what sort soever thei were) which
were killed in the daie, should be cutte of from their bodies and brought
to the place where he incamped at night, and should there bee laied
on the ground by eche side of the waie ledyng into his owne tente
so that none could come into his tente for any cause but commonly
he muste passe through a lane of heddes which he used *ad terrorem,*
the dedde feelyng nothyng the more paines thereby: and yet did it
bring greate terrour to the people when thei sawe the heddes of their
dedde fathers, brothers, children, kinsfolke and freinds, lye on the
grounde before their faces, as thei came to speake with the said collonell.

Churchyard recognized that some would criticize this conduct, but he
justified it by asserting that the Irish had been first in committing
atrocities and more especially on the grounds of efficiency: "through
the terrour which the people conceived thereby it made short warres."[19]

   The significant factor is that both Essex and Churchyard, in ac-

[17] Sidney and Council to Privy Council, Oct. 26, 1569, S.P. 63/29, no. 70, P.R.O.
[18] Sidney to Cecil, Jan. 4, 1570, S.P. 63/30, no. 2, P.R.O.
[19] Thomas Churchyard, *A Generall rehearsall of warres and joyned to the same
some tragedies and epitaphes* (London, 1579), QI-RI.

knowledging the possibility of criticism of their actions, were admitting that what they were about was innovative. The Norman lords were not known to have committed such atrocities in Ireland, and there is no evidence that systematic execution of noncombatants by martial law was practiced in any of the Tudor rebellions in England. It is obvious that Gilbert and Essex believed that in dealing with the native Irish population they were absolved from all normal ethical restraints. The questions that we must pose are how, at the mid-sixteenth century, the Irish, a people with whom the English had always had some familiarity, came to be regarded as uncivilized, and what justifications were used for indiscriminate slaying and expropriation.

One important consideration is that this was probably the first time since the original Norman conquest that large numbers of Englishmen had come into direct confrontation with the Gaelic Irish in their native habitation.[20] Various lords justices had first been screened through the English Pale and thus had been prepared for the cultural shock of encountering the native Irish. Few English emissaries had actually penetrated deep into the Gaelic areas, and no lord deputy had ever made such comprehensive tours through the country as Sidney. Even more to the point is the fact that such colonizers as the younger Smith, Essex, and St. Leger went directly by ship to the proposed site of the colony and thus did not experience the gradual acclimation that an approach through the Pale would have effected.

Another important consideration is the peculiar nature of Catholicism in Gaelic Ireland. That the Irish were Christian was never doubted by the Normans or their successors, but it was always recognized that Christianity in Gaelic Ireland did not fully conform to Roman liturgical practice, and that many pre-Christian traditions and customs were only slightly veneered by Christianity. Criticism of unorthodox practices was frequent but deviance of this nature was not uncommon in medieval Europe, and two systems—an episcopal church on English lines in the Pale and environs, and an Irish-speaking, loosely structured church in the Gaelic areas—continued to tolerate each other's presence.[21]

[20] Witness the wonder caused by the appearance of Shane O'Neill at Queen Elizabeth's court as reported in William Camden, *Annales rerum Anglicarum et Hibernicarum, regnante Elizabeth ad annum salutis M.D. LXXIX* (London, 1615), 69-70.
[21] See John Bossy, "The Counter-Reformation and the People of Catholic Ireland," *Historical Studies,* VIII (1971), 155-169, and "The Counter-Reformation and the People of Catholic Europe," *Past and Present,* No. 47 (May 1970), 51-70.

This arrangement was accepted by the Old English but not by those adventurers who joined Sidney in Ireland. These were, for the most part, extreme Protestants; many of them, like Carew, had fled England in Queen Mary's reign and associated themselves with the exiled English divines on the continent.[22] They were hypercritical of Catholicism in the Pale, but religious observance in Gaelic Ireland was so remote from anything they had previously experienced that they branded the native Irish as pagan without question.

The groundwork for this view had been laid by the Old English who over the centuries had attributed to the Gaelic Irish certain vices which, they claimed, were fostered by Gaelic law. The most famous of such indictments was the "counter-remonstrance" of 1331, but the accusations were regularly repeated down through the years, even into the sixteenth century. A Palesman was clearly the author of the unpublished pamphlet, "On the Disorders of the Irishry" (1572), in which all the customary criticisms were leveled at the native Irish and Gaelic law was declared "contrary to God his lawe and also repugnant to the Queens Majesties lawes." Even more severe was the assertion that the "outwarde behavyor" of the Irish made it "seme" that "they neyther love nor dredd God nor yet hate the Devell, they are superstycyous and worshippers of images and open idolaters." The author was probably aware that much of what he said was rhetorical, and clearly his purpose was to impress upon the government the idea that the Old English were the only true representatives of civility in Ireland and therefore deserved support. Literature of this nature served, however, to prepare the minds of Englishmen for the worst, and many of these who came to Ireland saw what they had been conditioned to expect.[23]

What the English adventurers encountered in the remote areas of Ireland was taken as confirmation of the assertions of the Old English, leading many to despair of Christianity there. Tremayne found religion "totally lacking" in Munster and refused to declare the Irish "ether Papists nor Protestants but rather such as have nether feare nor love of God in their harts that restreyneth them from ill. Thei regarde no othe, thei blaspheme, they murder, commit whoredome, hold no wedlocke, ravish, steal and commit all abomination without scruple of conscience." The most startling features were the decay of the churches,

[22] Christina Hallowell Garrett, *The Marian Exiles: A Study in the Origins of Elizabethan Puritanism* (Cambridge, 1966 [orig. publ. 1938]).

[23] Watt, *Church and Medieval Ireland*, 183-197, and "On the Disorders of the Irishry," S.P. 63/1, nos. 72, 73, P.R.O.

which Tremayne found were "onlie like stables," and the ignorance of
the "priests and ministers of their owne race werse than shepherds."[24]
Sidney, a moderate Protestant, wrote an equally astonished report of
the state of religion in Munster in 1567:

Swerlie there was never people that lived in more miserie than they
doe, nor as it should seme of wourse myndes, for matrimonie emongs
them is no more regarded in effect than conjunction betwene unreasonable beastes, perjurie, robberie and murder counted alloweable, finallie
I cannot finde that they make anny conscience of synne and doubtless
I doubte whether they christen there children or no, for neither finde
I place where it should be don, nor any person able to enstruct them
in the rules of a Christian, or if they were taught I cannot see they
make any accompte of the woorlde to com.[25]

The clear implication is that Sidney considered himself to be dealing
with people who were essentially pagans. He, like Spenser, was arriving
at the conclusion that while the Irish professed to be Catholics they had
no real knowledge of religion: "They are all Papists by their profession
[wrote Spenser], but in the same so blindly and brutishly informed for
the most part as that you would rather think them atheists or infidels."[26]
   The English adventurers of the 1560s and 1570s thus had little difficulty in satisfying themselves that the Gaelic Irish were pagans, and
this became an accepted tenet of all Englishmen. Lord Deputy Mountjoy,
for example, was convinced that "the poore people of" Ulster "never had
the meanes to know God," and he described one of the Gaelic chieftains
of Ulster as "proud, valiant, miserable, tyrannous, unmeasurably covetous,
without any knowledge of God, or almost any civility."[27] That such
views could be offered without explanation in 1602 is a measure of the
success of the colonizers of the previous generation in propagating them.
   We must now ask why it was so important to the English adventurers to convince themselves that the Irish were pagan. The first
point to note is that the English recognized a distinction between
Christianity and civilization, and believed that a people could be civilized
without being made Christian but not christianized without first being

[24] Tremayne, Notes on Ireland, June 1571, S.P. 63/32, no. 66, P.R.O.
[25] Sidney to the queen, Apr. 20, 1567, S.P. 63/20, no. 66, P.R.O.
[26] Spenser, *Ireland,* ed. Renwick, 84.
[27] Fynes Moryson, *An Itinerary: Containing His Ten Yeeres Travell through
the Twelve Dominions of Germany, Bohmerland . . . Ireland* (1617) (Glasgow,
1907), II, 381; III, 208-209.

made civil. It was admitted that the Romans had been civilized despite being pagans, and sixteenth-century Englishmen were not ignorant of the existence of civilizations beyond the boundaries of Christian Europe. Supremacy was claimed for western civilization because it combined the benefits of Christianity with those of civility. To admit that the native Irish were Christian would, therefore, have been to acknowledge them as civilized also. By declaring the Irish to be pagan, however, the English were decreeing that they were culpable since their heathenism was owing not to a lack of opportunity but rather to the fact that their system of government was antithetical to Christianity. Once it was established that the Irish were pagans, the first logical step had been taken toward declaring them barbarians. The English were able to pursue their argument further when they witnessed the appearance of the native Irish, their habits, customs, and agricultural methods.

We must bear in mind that of the group of adventurers who flocked to Ireland many were widely travelled and some well read. There is evidence that a few of the West Countrymen had fought on the Continent, even against the Turks in Hungary, while others had visited the New World.[28] All were interested in travel and adventure, and through their exploits and reading of travel literature, such as the English translation of Johann Boemus (1555), they had familarized themselves with the habits of peoples who were considered barbarians by European standards.[29] It was natural that they should now strive to assimilate the Irish into their general conception of civilization. One early example of this was Sidney's comparing the Ulster chieftain Shane O'Neill with Huns, Vandals, Goths, and Turks.[30] Sidney was well versed in travel literature, and it is significant that the translator Thomas Hacket, in dedicating one of his works to Sidney, associated Sidney's task in Ireland with that of the Spaniards in the New World when he praised "such as have invented good lawes and statutes for the brideling of the barbarous and wicked, and for the maintayning and defending of the just."[31]

[28] For the careers of many of those mentioned see Churchyard, *General rehearsall.*

[29] Joannes Boemus, *The Fardel of facions, conteining the aunciente maners, customes, and Lawes of the peoples enhabiting the two partes of the earth, called Affrike and Asie,* trans. W. Waterman (London, 1555). See also Margaret T. Hodgen, *Early Anthropology in the Sixteenth and Seventeenth Centuries* (Philadelphia, 1964), esp. ch. 3.

[30] Sidney to Leicester, Mar. 1, 1566, S.P. 63/16, no. 35, P.R.O.

[31] André Thevet, *The new found worlde, or Antarticke,* trans. T. Hacket (London, 1568).

What is significant is that many of the colonizers came to Ireland with a preconception of what a barbaric society was like, and they found features in Gaelic life to fit this model. The ultimate hallmark of barbarism was the practice of cannibalism. While the Irish were seldom accused of cannibalism, Sidney referred to Shane O'Neill as "that canyball," and Sir John Davies, some fifty years later, asserted that those living under Gaelic rule "were little better than Cannibals who do hunt one another."[32] In addition, the English took the Irish practice of transhumance as proof that the Irish were nomads, hence barbarians. In the travel literature that was read by sixteenth-century Englishmen nomadic people were considered to be at the opposite pole of civilization from themselves. Boemus, for example, found the Scythians and their offshoot, the Tartarians, to be the most barbarous people in the world because they "neither possessed any grounds, nor had any seats or houses to dwell in, but wandered through wilderness and desert places driving their flockes and heardes of beasts before them."[33] This view became entrenched in the English mind and was repeated in the introduction of almost every sixteenth-century pamphlet dealing with travel and exploration. This explains why the practice of transhumance so readily caught the Englishman's attention in Ireland.

Smith, who sponsored a colony in Ireland even though he never visited the country himself, was particularly vehement against the "idle followyng of heards as the Tartarians, Arabians and Irishe men doo," thus categorizing the Irish with those whom he considered to be at the lowest level of civilization. Spenser went so far as to take the practice of transhumance as proof that the Gaelic Irish were descended from the Scythians. There was a custom in Ireland, said Spenser, "to keep their cattle and to live themselves the most part of the year in bollies [summer-quarters] pasturing upon the mountain and waste wild places, and removing still to fresh land as they have depastured the former; the which appeareth plain to be the manner of the Scythians as ye may read in Olaus Magnus et Johannes Boemus, and yet is used amongst all the Tartarians and the people about the Caspian sea which are naturally Scythians." Here was evidence to satisfy Spenser, and

[32] John Davies, *A Discovery of the True Causes why Ireland was never Entirely subdued, nor brought under obedience of the Crowne of England until the beginning of the happy reign of King James*, in Henry Morley, ed., *The Carisbrooke Library*, X (London, 1890), and Sidney to Leicester, Mar. 1, 1566, S.P. 63/16, no. 35, P.R.O.

[33] Joannes Boemus, *The Manners, Lawes, and Customes of all Nations . . .* (London, 1611), 106.

probably his readers, that the Irish were indeed barbarians. He was further convinced by Gaelic dress, hairstyle, and weapons, all of which he found to be "proper Scythian, for such the Scyths used commonly, as we may read in Olaus Magnus."[34] The Irish were also declared to be exceedingly licentious. Incest was said to be common among them, and Gaelic chieftains were accused of debauching the wives and daughters of their tenants.

The Irish appeared therefore not only as pagan but also as barbaric. Gilbert certainly treated them as if they were a lower order of humanity, and Carew considered one of his purposes in Ireland to be "the suppressing and reforming of the loose, barbarous and most wicked life of that savage nation." Barnaby Rich, a friend of Churchyard, argued against those who thought English conduct in Ireland "too seveare" by pointing out that the Irish preferred to "live like beastes, voide of lawe and all good order," and that they were "more uncivill, more uncleanly, more barbarous and more brutish in their customs and demeanures, then in any other part of the world that is known."[35]

So persuaded, Englishmen produced a moral and civil justification for their conquest of Ireland. Although most of the colonizers avowed that their long-term purpose was to convert the Irish to Christianity, they made no effort to accomplish this end, contending that conversion was impossible as long as the Irish persisted in their barbarous way of life. All were agreed that their immediate object should be the secular one of drawing the Irish to civility. Proclaiming this responsibility, Smith asserted that God "did make apte and prepare this nation . . . to inhabite and reforme so barbarous a nation as that is, and to bring them to the knowledge and lawe were both a goodly and commendable deede, and a sufficient work of our age," adding that it was England's civic duty to educate the Irish brutes "in vertuous labor and in justice, and to teach them our English lawes and civilitie and leave robbyng and stealing and killyng one of another." In Smith's view, the English were the new Romans come to civilize the Irish, as the old Romans had once civilized the ancient Britons: "This I write unto you as I do understand by histories of thyngs by past, how this contrey of England, ones as uncivill as Ireland now is, was by colonies

[34] J. Boemus, *A Letter Sent by J. B. . . .* (London, 1572), C. 1, and Spenser, *Ireland,* ed. Renwick, 49, 50, 54, 56.

[35] Vowell, *Peter Carew,* in Brewer and Bullen, eds., *Calendar of Carew Manuscripts,* civ; Barnaby Rich, *Allarme to England, foreshadowing what perils are procured, where the people live without regarde of Martiall lawe* (London, 1578), D. 2, and *A Short Survey of Ireland, truely discovering who it is that hath so armed the hearts of that people, with disobedience to their Princes* (London, 1609), 2.

of the Romaynes brought to understand the lawes and orders of thanncient orders whereof there hath no nacon more streightly and truly kept the mouldes even to this day then we, yea more than thitalians and Romaynes themselves."[36]

In accepting this idea, Smith was totally abandoning the notion of the Old English that the native Irish were enslaved by their lords and were crying out for liberation. The Irish, in his view, were indeed living under tyranny but were not yet ready for liberation since they were at an earlier stage of cultural development—the stage at which the English had been when the Romans had arrived. They needed to be made bondsmen to enlightened lords who would instruct them in the ways of civil society. In his major writing, *De Republica Anglorum*, Smith claimed superiority for England over all other nations, even the ancient Romans, on the grounds that bondsmen were by the sixteenth century virtually unknown in England.[37] He recommended that the Irish should be made subservient to the colonizing English so that through subjection they could come to appreciate civility and thus eventually achieve freedom as the former English bondsmen had done.

It is probable that the Roman parallel was used by Smith to justify his own actions in Ireland. This approach had already been taken by writers of the Italian Renaissance, such as Machiavelli, who contrasted medieval "barbarism" with old Roman "civilization" in order to justify the eradication of the last vestiges of that barbarism. This antimedievalism was easily transmitted by English Renaissance scholars, such as Smith, and further transformed when applied to the Irish who were considered even more "barbarian" than their medieval monkish counterparts. This helps explain why the Roman allusion appears so frequently in sixteenth-century writing on Ireland. Spenser repeated almost verbatim the sentiments of Smith when he remarked that "the English were at first as stout and warlike a people as ever were the Irish and yet you see are now brought to that civility that no nation in the world excelleth them in all goodly conversation."[38]

Almost fifty years later, Davies, urging completion of the conquest of Ireland, alluded to the Roman general Julius Agricola who had civilized "our ancestors the ancient Britons"—a "rude and dispersed"

---

[36] Boemus, *Letter sent to J. B.*, C. 6, and Smith to Fitzwilliam, Nov. 8, 1572, Carte MSS. 57, no. 236.

[37] Thomas Smith, *De Republica Anglorum: A Discourse on the Commonwealth of England* (1685), ed L. Ashton (Cambridge, 1906), 130-131.

[38] Spenser, *Ireland*, ed. Renwick, 11.

people, "and therefore prone upon every occasion to make war."[39] It was
only by retaining such a concept that cultivated men could allow themselves to bring other people to subjection, which was one purpose of
English colonization in Ireland. Thus Walter, earl of Essex, assured
the Privy Council that he "never mente to unpeople the cuntrie Clandy-
boy of their naturall inhabitauntes, but to have cherished them so farre
fourthe as they woulde live quiett and deutifull." It was his intention
to eliminate the military caste in Gaelic Ulster by having them "executed by martiall lawe whensoever they be founde ydell and weaponed."
Otherwise he wanted the natives retained as cultivators of the soil, "and
the more Irishe the more profitable so as the Englishe be hable to
master them."[40] Smith also envisaged the Irish husbandmen continuing
to occupy land in his colony and even being instructed in the English
methods of cultivation. This was to be done, however, under the strict
supervision of those who would undertake the task of colonizing. It
was no part of his plan that any native Irish should "purchase land,
beare office, be chosen of any jurie or admitted witnes in any reall or
personall action, nor be bounde apprentice to any science or arte that
may indomage the Queenes Majesties subjectes hereafter." They were
to be allowed to "beare no kind of weapon nor armoure," and the only
benefits he had to offer them were that their "plowinge and laboure"
would be "well rewarded with great provision," and that they would
be free from "coyne, lyverye or any other exaction."[41] What Smith and
Essex wanted to accomplish was to drive out the ruling elite and
retain the majority of the population as docile cultivators. Smith, and
later Spenser and Davies, pointed to Roman precedent to justify this
policy. They thought the example pertinent because England was now
the new Rome, the center of civilization.

We can see clearly that Smith had developed a sense of cultural
process which could be used as a rationale for reducing the Irish to
servitude and, if they resisted, for killing and dispossessing them. No
other colonist in Ireland articulated this view as clearly as he, but there

[39] Davies, *Discovery*, 272-273.
[40] Essex to Privy Council, undated, Add. MSS. 48015, fols. 305-314, British
Library (formerly British Museum).
[41] "Petition of Thomas Smythe and his Associates," c. 1570, in C. L. Kingsford,
ed., *Report on the Manuscripts of Lord de L'Isle and Dudley preserved at Penshurst
Place* (Historical Manuscripts Commission, *19th Report* [London, 1934]), II, 12-15,
and Smith to Fitzwilliam, May 18, 1572, in *Calendar State Papers Foreign, 1583,
and Addenda 1547-83*, 49-50.

is evidence that all had a sense of cultural superiority to the Irish. Essex professed his mission to be "grounded on Her Majesty's commiseration of the natural born subjects of this province, over whom the Scots did tyrannise," but when the same subjects refused to accept the substitution of a new form of slavery for the old, he had no scruples about slaughtering them.[42]

Sidney, too, seems to have had a vague sense of cultural process and at least approached a concept of cultural classification when he observed and compared the three segments of society that confronted him in Ireland—the Gaelic world, feudal Ireland, and the "civilized" society of the Pale. It was clear to the lord deputy that Irish feudal society was preferable to that of Gaelic Ireland, but he was equally conscious that feudal society in Ireland was more independent and authoritarian than its English counterpart and was still at a stage of development beyond which England had advanced. Even more emphatic on this point, Gilbert condemned the independence of the Irish feudal lords, warning against the danger to a prince whose "subjectes greatly followed for themselves, as may partlie appear by Nevell earll of Warruicke, by the prynce of Orrainge in the lowe countryes, and by the Faccions betwene the howsse of Bourbon and Gwysee in France."[43] It seemed to Gilbert that the Irish feudal lords were at a stage of development similar to that prevailing in France and the Netherlands but through which England had passed. Others saw this as an intermediary stage between total license, as in Gaelic Ireland, and final, if reluctant, acceptance of a centralized state, as in England. We get an example of this thinking in 1607 from Davies, the then attorney-general for Ireland, in his recommendation that Hugh O'Neill, earl of Tyrone, be deprived of control of his tenants and reduced "to the moderate condition of other lords in Ireland and in England at this day." Davies reminded his readers that "when England was full of tenants-at-will our barons were then like the mere Irish lords, and were able to raise armies against the crown; and as this man was O'Neal in Ulster, so the Earl of Warwick was O'Nevill in Yorkshire, and the Bishopric and Mortimer was the like in the Marches of Wales."[44]

The evidence is admittedly scattered and no individual writer stuck

[42] Essex to Burghley, Sept. 10, 1573, in Devereux, *Lives of Devereux*, I, 34-36.
[43] See Gilbert's discourse on Ireland, Feb. 1, 1574, Add. MSS. 48017, fols. 136-143.
[44] Davies to Salisbury, July 1, 1607, in C. W. Russell and J. P. Prendergast, eds., *Calendar of the State Papers for Ireland 1606-8* (London, 1873), 213.

consistently to one point of view, but we can state confidently that the old concept of the Irish as socially inferior to the English was being replaced with the idea that they were culturally inferior and far behind the English on the ladder of development. The colonizers were assisting in the development of a concept of historical process and cultural development, as the widening of the horizons of the articulate citizen of sixteenth-century England, both intellectually and geographically, slowly eroded the old idea of a static world.[45] It was only natural that the aggressive men who sought their fortunes in Ireland should try to fit Gaelic society into their expanding world view. But what provided Englishmen with a growing confidence and pride spelled disaster for Gaelic Ireland, which was now seen as a cultural throwback that must be painfully dragged to modernity. In the minds of these adventurers it no longer held true, as it had under the statutes of Kilkenny of 1366, that an Irishman could be accepted under English law. To do so, said Spenser, would be as absurd as to "transfer the laws of the Lacedemonians to the people of Athens." Laws, according to Spenser, "ought to be fashioned unto the manners and condition of the people to whom they are meant, and not to be imposed upon them according to the simple rule of right, for then . . . instead of good they may work ill, and pervert justice to extreme injustice." The central theme of Spenser's *Ireland* was that "the common law . . . with the state of Ireland peradventure it doth not so well agree, being a people altogether stubborn and untamed." The Gaelic law, which Spenser saw as fashioned to the manner and condition of the people, could not, however, be tolerated, since it was opposed to all civility. The only solution was to forbid the practice of Gaelic law and subject the Irish by force so that they could then by "moderation" be brought "from their delight of licentious barbarism unto the love of goodness and civility."[46]

It is only when we appreciate this reasoning that we can fully understand the attitudes and policies of Sidney and his adherents in Ireland. The lord deputy was critical of feudal society there, but argued that it was capable of being reformed and made to conform to the English model of civility. In the words of William Gerrard, one of Sidney's subordinates, the native Irish could be subdued only by arms, while the "degenerate" Old English could be improved by "the rodd

_____

[45] On the emergence of the concept of process in England see A. B. Ferguson, "Circumstances and the Sense of History in Tudor England: The Coming of the Historical Revolution," Medieval and Renaissance Studies, *Proceedings*, III (1967).

[46] Spenser, *Ireland*, ed. Renwick, 10-11.

of justice" for "in theim yet resteth this instincte of Englishe nature generally to feare justice."[47] Sidney was more moderate in holding that even those areas of Gaelic Ireland which were within easy reach of Dublin and had had some contact with civility were amenable to justice: extreme action was reserved for Gaelic Ulster and the Gaelic areas of southwest Munster.

The English Privy Council seems to have reasoned similarly, as is suggested by their confining of St. Leger's claims to the Gaelic areas of Munster. Fitzwilliam, who was generally a moderate, admitted that "nothing but feare and force can teach dutie and obedience" to this "rebellious people." The same view was held by Sir John Perrott, who prided himself on his stern rule while lord president in Munster and concluded that "there ys no waye better then to make those wylde people . . . to feare, so they be not kepte in servile feare." Essex, too, "put litell difference betweene the Irishe and the Scott saving that the Skott is the less ill of disposition, more inclinable to civility though more dangerous."[48] The Irish were thus categorized as the most barbarous of peoples, and Englishmen argued that it was their duty and responsibility to hold them down by force so that through subjection they could achieve liberty.

We should not attribute to the English complete originality in this. Many of the conclusions at which they were arriving about the Irish had already been reached by the Spaniards with respect to the Indians. J. H. Elliott has argued that the Spaniards had come to consider the indigenous population of the New World as culturally inferior to themselves and, like the Elizabethans in Ireland, were approaching a concept of cultural classification.[49] It can be established that many of the English associated with colonization were familiar with Spanish thinking, and it is quite probable that their attitudes and actions were influenced by Spanish precedents.

The most potent Spanish influence was undoubtedly communicated by Richard Eden's partial translation of Peter Martyr Anglerius's *De Orbe Novo*. Eden was well known to the group of West Country adventurers who came to Ireland in the 1560s, and Smith had been Eden's tutor at Cambridge, which is sufficient reason to assume his

[47] "Gerrard's Notes," Irish Manuscripts Commission, *Analecta Hibernica*, II (1931), 95-96.
[48] Fitzwilliam to queen, Sept. 15, 1572, S.P. 63/37, no. 59; Perrott to Smith, Jan. 28, 1573, S.P. 63/39, no. 16; Essex to Ashton, June 1, 1575, S.P. 63/52, no. 5, P.R.O.
[49] Elliott, *Old World and the New*, 39-51.

familiarity with the translation. Sidney was also acquainted with the work and may have had more direct acquaintance with Spanish colonial theory while in Spain, 1553-1556, in Queen Mary's service.[50] In any event it is difficult to imagine how any of the adventurers in Ireland could have been ignorant of Eden's work. It is more than likely that Champernoun, St. Leger, and the others saw themselves as *conquistadores* subduing the barbaric and pagan Irish, just as their Spanish counterparts were bringing the Indians to subjection.

Smith certainly recognized that his venture in Ireland was being compared by others with colonization in the New World. He voiced no objection, other than the fear that his exploit would be tainted by association with the none-too-successful Anglo-French venture of 1563, and that he and his son would be "accompted deceivers of men and enterprysers of Stowelies [Stukeley's] voiage of Terra Florida, or a lattarye as som evill tongues did terme it." Essex acknowledged a parallel with Spain and expected "that within two yeares, you shall make restraint for the Englishe to come hither [to Ireland] without license as at this date it is in Spaine for going to the Indyes."[51] Leicester, who also appears to have been influenced by Spanish thinking, admitted that his attitude toward the Irish was affected by the information he had of the treatment meted out to other "barbarous" peoples. He argued that since the Irish were "a wild, barbarous and treacherous people, I would deall as I have hard and redd of such lyke how they have byn used." In this he was, seemingly, suggesting that since the native Irish were barbarians there was no reason why the Spanish precedent should not be followed. Leicester's many statements make it clear that he favored a tough policy for Ireland; his sentiments came remarkably close to those of Eden who recommended that Englishmen emulate the example of the Spaniards in the New World.[52] If, however, Leicester was in fact influenced by the Spanish experience, he acknowledged the debt by implication rather than overtly. Less hesitantly and despite their hatred of the Spaniards, other Englishmen occasionally cited Spanish actions to justify their own extreme measures in Ireland. Davies, for

[50] Petrus Martyr Anglerius, *The Decades of the newe worlde or West India,* trans. Richard Eden (London, 1555); Elliott, *Old World and New,* 91; Quinn, "Ireland and Expansion," *Hist. Studies.,* I (1958), 26.

[51] Smith to Fitzwilliam, Carte MSS. 57, no. 227, and Essex to Privy Council, Add. MSS. 48015, fols. 305-314.

[52] Leicester to Fitzwilliam, Aug. 24, 1572, Carte MSS. 57, no. 227, and Anglerius, *Decades of the newe worlde,* trans. Eden, preface. For other extreme statements by Leicester see Carte MSS. 56, nos. 39, 97.

example, in defending the transplantation of natives during the course of the Ulster plantation, cited the precedent of "the Spaniards [who] lately removed all the Moors out of Granada into Barbary without providing them with any new seats there."[53] It is evident, therefore, that the English were aware of the severity of the Spaniards in dealing with those who did not measure up to their standards of civility, and it appears that this knowledge strengthened the English in their conviction that they were justified in their own harsh treatment of the native Irish.

The events of 1565-1576 in Ireland have a significance in the general history of colonization that transcends English and Irish history. The involvement in Irish colonization of men who afterwards ventured to the New World suggests that their years in Ireland were years of apprenticeship. Quinn has established that the use of a propaganda campaign to muster support for a colony and the application of the joint-stock principle to colonization were both novel techniques which were employed none too successfully in Ireland, but without which the English could hardly have pursued successful colonization in the New World.[54] An even more significant break with the past was the change in attitude toward the native Irish, and this too was to have consequences in the history of American colonization.

It has been noted how Sidney and his adherents fitted the native Irish into their mental world picture. Certain traits of the Gaelic way of life, notably the practice of transhumance, were accepted as evidence that the Irish were barbarians, and the English thus satisfied themselves that they were dealing with a culturally inferior people who had to be subdued by extralegal methods. Many of the English colonizers were at first unsure of themselves and looked to Roman practice for further justification for their actions. The Roman example seems to have been abandoned as unnecessary by the colonizers who ventured to North America, but not so the concept of cultural evolution that had been sharpened as a result of their Irish experience. Writers such as Thomas Hariot, who had Irish as well as American experience, frequently compared the habits of the Gaelic Irish with those of the Indians. Contemporary observers like Theodore De Bry claimed to see a resemblance between the ancient Britons and the Indians drawn by the artist John

[53] Davies to Salisbury, Nov. 8, 1610, in Sir John Davies, *Historical Tracts* (Dublin, 1787).
[54] See the works of Quinn, as cited in n. 1.

White, thus implying that they considered the Indians, like the Irish, to be at the same primitive level of development as the ancient Britons had been.[55] It appears therefore that the Irish experience confirmed and reinforced the English notion of barbarism and that those, such as Gilbert, Raleigh, and Frobisher, who had experience in both spheres had little difficulty in applying that notion to the indigenous population of the New World.[56]

We find the colonists in the New World using the same pretexts for the extermination of the Indians as their counterparts had used in the 1560s and 1570s for the slaughter of numbers of the Irish. The adventurers to Ireland claimed that their primary purpose was to reform the Irish and, in the words of Smith, "to reduce that countrey to civilitie and the maners of England." It is evident, however, that no determined effort was ever made to reform the Irish, but rather that at the least pretext—generally resistance to the English—they were dismissed as a "wicked and faythles peopoll" and put to the sword.[57] This formula was repeated in the treatment of the Indians in the New World. At first the English claimed their mission to be that of civilizing the native inhabitants, but they quickly despaired of achieving this purpose. When relations between the English and the Indians grew tense, emphasis was given to the barbaric traits of the native population. After the Indian insurrection of 1622 we find the colonizers exulting in the fact that they were now absolved from all restraints in dealing with the Indians.[58] We also find the same indictments being brought against the Indians, and later the blacks, in the New World that had been brought against the Irish. It was argued that the Indians were an unsettled people who did not make proper use of their land and thus could be justly deprived of it by the more enterprising English. Both Indians and blacks, like the Irish, were accused of being idle, lazy, dirty, and licentious, but

[55] Quinn, *Elizabethans,* 106-122, and Paul H. Hulton and David Beers Quinn, *The American Drawings of John White, 1577-1590, with Drawings of European and Oriental Subjects* (Chapel Hill, N. C., 1964).

[56] Quinn, *Raleigh and Empire,* and Jones, *Strange New World,* esp. ch. 5.

[57] Smith to Fitzwilliam, Nov. 8, 1572, S.P. 63/39, no. 30, and Barkley to Burghley, May 14, 1574, S. P. 63/46, no. 15, P.R.O.

[58] Gary B. Nash, "The Image of the Indian in the Southern Colonial Mind," *William and Mary Quarterly,* 3d Ser., XXIX (1972), 197-230, and Roy Harvey Pearce, *The Savages of America: A Study of the Indian and the Idea of Civilization,* rev. ed. (Baltimore, 1965), esp. 4-16.

few serious efforts were made to draw any of them from their supposed state of degeneracy.[59]

We have here a few of the lessons that the English gained from their Irish experience and later applied in the New World. Equally significant are the lessons that they failed to learn. The sixteenth-century colonizer was a proud disdainful person, but he was also insecure and needed to remind himself constantly of his own superiority by looking to the imputed inferiority of others. Those who came to Ireland had a preconceived idea of a barbaric society and they merely tailored the Irishman to fit this ideological strait jacket. There were, of course, many aspects of Gaelic life that did not so easily fit this model, but the English refused to make any adjustment, lest, perhaps, it disturb their own position at the top of the ladder of cultural development.

The most flagrant example of this blindness and obstinacy was the belief, retained in despite of all evidence, that "barbaric" societies were invariably divided into two neat categories—the barbarous tyrants or "cruell cannibales" and the meek laborers whom they held in utter bondage.[60] Tremayne's censures were reserved for the ruling caste in Ireland who, he claimed, had "mor authoritie than any lord over bondmen." Rich agreed with this and thought England's role in Ireland should be to defend the poor tenants from the "thraldome" to which they were being subjected by those "helhounds" of lords whose only ethic was to "defend me and spend me." Even Essex claimed this to be his mission in Ireland, and Smith idealized "the churle of Ireland as a very simple and toylesome man desiring nothing but that he may not bee eaten out with" Irish exactions.[61] It was of course some of these "simple and toylesome" men, whom the younger Smith had taken into his service, who murdered him, but not even this could disabuse the English. Spenser could still state emphatically that "there are two sortes of people in Ireland to be considered of . . . the one called the kerne,

[59] Nash, "Indian in the Southern Mind," *WMQ*, 3d Ser., XXIX (1972), 197-230; Pearce, *Savages of America*, 4-16; Winthrop D. Jordan, *White over Black: American Attitudes toward the Negro, 1550-1812* (Chapel Hill, N. C., 1968). See also P. E. H. Hair, "Protestants as Pirates, Slavers, and Proto-missionaries: Sierra Leone, 1568-1582," *Journal of Ecclesiastical History*, XXI (1970), 203-224, esp. 221-223.

[60] Anglerius, *Decades of the newe worlde*, trans. Eden, preface, 172.

[61] Tremayne, Notes on the Reformation of the Irish, June 1571, S.P. 63/32, no. 66, P.R.O.; Rich, *Allarme to England*, E. 1; Essex to Privy Council, Add. MSS. 48015, fols. 305-314; Boemus, *Letter*, B. 1.

the other the chorle. The kerne bredd up in idleness and naturally inclined to mischiefs and wickednesse, the chorle willing to labour and take pains if he might peaceably enjoy the fruites thereof.'[62]

Spenser might have been speaking of the Indians because, as Edmund S. Morgan has shown, the English in the New World used the same form of categorization and displayed the same reluctance to learn from experience. Morgan suggests that this blindness to reality can be explained by wishful thinking on the part of the English who expected to find a ready work force in America. There is certainly some truth to this as can be seen in Smith's desire, like that of the English in Virginia, to retain the supposedly docile natives as "fermors or copie-holders" in his colony. The retention of such a myth in the face of adversity must, however, be taken as indicating the colonist's insecurity: he needed to think of himself as setting out on a crusade, bringing the "gentle government" of the English to the oppressed. If he was to admit that the oppressed did not exist or were not anxious to avail themselves of English justice, then the colonist's *raison d'être* was called in question.[63]

The intent of this article has been to furnish an insight into the mind of the English colonist. At the outset the English were somewhat unsure of themselves and went to great lengths to establish the inferiority of others so as to provide a justification for acts of aggression. It can be seen also that the experience gained by the Elizabethans in Ireland opened their minds to an understanding of process and development, thus enabling them to arrive at a concept of cultural evolution. Other Europeans, notably the Renaissance theorists of Italy and France, had advanced the notion of social superiority, but it was only those who came into contact with "barbaric" peoples who drew practical conclusions from the idea in order to provide moral respectability for colonization.

[62] Spenser, *Ireland,* ed. Renwick, 179.
[63] Smith to Fitzwilliam, Nov. 8, 1572, Carte MSS. 57, no. 236, and Edmund S. Morgan, "The Labor Problem at Jamestown, 1607-18," *American Historical Review,* LXXVI (1971), 595-611.

9

Sovereignty-Association, 1500–1783

W.J. Eccles

AT THE CLOSE OF THE SIXTEENTH CENTURY all of present-day Canada was in the possession of the Indian and Inuit peoples. No Europeans resided anywhere in the land. Fishermen landed on the Atlantic coast and in the Gulf of St Lawrence to dry their cod, obtain wood, water, fresh meat, and to trade with the Indians for furs – but permanent settlements there were none.[1] Today the Indian peoples retain title to only a small fraction of their ancient lands. Sovereignty over the entire country is claimed by the federal and provincial governments of Canada; the rights of the indigenous peoples are either ignored or given short shrift. Some of these native peoples have, in recent years, resorted to the courts to assert their claims to their ancestral lands. It is, therefore, of some consequence that the history of how this situation came about should be investigated. It is also important that future legal judgments should not be based on ignorance or misconceptions of history, as has happened on occasion.[2]

The historical process of this centuries-long development in Canada has passed through three main stages: that of the French regime, that

1 Marcel Trudel, *The Beginnings of New France 1524–1663* (Toronto 1973), 82–4
2 *Supreme Court of Canada Reports*, vol. XIII, pp. 643–50, *St Catharine's Milling and Lumber Co.* v *The Queen*, 1887; *House of Lords, Judicial Committee of the Privy Council*, vol. XIV, Appeal Cases, 1888, pp. 46–61. In this all too frequently cited case Chief Justice Taschereau, of the Supreme Court of Canada, declared to the Judicial Committee that the King of France, in the 600 seigneuries extending from the Atlantic to Lake Superior, never recognized an Indian title to the land. There were, in fact, only 245 seigneuries in Canada during the French regime, the most westerly being La Petite Nation, some 20 miles west of the mouth of the Ottawa River, and it was not settled. See Marcel Trudel, *Atlas de la Nouvelle-France / An Atlas of New France* (Quebec 1968), 175–9; Richard Colebrook Harris, *The Seigneurial System in Early Canada* (Madison, WI 1968), endpaper. Moreover, the French kings most certainly did recognize Indian land title and sovereignty.

of the ensuing British colonial period and, post-1867, that of the Dominion of Canada. The relations of the French with the Indians were markedly different from those of the British prior to 1760, and those of both the British and the later Dominion of Canada different from the policies and attitudes of the United States authorities in this regard. Yet, after the cession of Canada to Great Britain in 1763, the end result for the Indians of Canada was roughly the same as for those caught within the confines of the burgeoning republic to the south.[3]

At the turn of the fifteenth century when the Americas were redis-covered by Europeans, rivalry, hostility, and warfare between the ma-jor European powers were the norm. The countries first making these discoveries, both in the Americas and the Orient, were determined to exclude all other nations from the benefits to be derived from the new-found lands. Although military force was the real determinant, various theories were promulgated on how title to these lands not occupied by Christian peoples could be acquired. Spain and Portugal claimed that prior discovery and conquest gave them title to pagan lands in Africa, Asia, and the Americas, to the exclusion of all others. Papal bulls granted by Alexander VI in 1493 were interpreted to repre-sent the division, between themselves, of the world beyond the confines of Europe. The dividing line was at first drawn from pole to pole, 100 leagues west of the Azores, then hastily amended at the behest of Jean II of Portugal by the Treaty of Tordesillas, to 370 leagues west of those islands. Portugal thereby retained Brazil but the whole of North Amer-ica fell under Spanish sovereignty.[4]

Although this was a much more civilized way to proceed than by force of arms, the other maritime powers could not accept being denied overseas ventures. Francis I of France, for one, rejected the notion out of hand. He asserted that title to pagan lands had to rest on three things: prior discovery, conquest, and occupation. Lands that might have been discovered first by the subjects of a Christian prince but were not subsequently occupied by them had, perforce, to be open to trade for all comers.[5] At that time the French were more interested in overseas commerce than in the establishment of colonies.

3 Robert M. Berkhofer, jr, *The White Man's Indian: Images of the American Indian from Columbus to the Present* (New York 1978), 127–45
4 Ch.-André Julien, *Les voyages de découverte et les premiers établissements (XVe–XVIe siècles)* (Paris 1948), 30–3; Pierre Renouvin, ed., *Histoire des relations internationales*, II (Paris 1953); Gaston Zeller, *Les temps modernes: 1 De Christophe Colomb à Cromwell* (Paris 1953), 35–9; Charles Gibson, *Spain in America* (New York 1966), 14–23; David B. Quinn, *North America from Earliest Discovery to First Settlements: The Norse Voyages to 1612* (New York 1977), 104–5, 110–12. For the text of the Treaty of Tordesillas see Frances Gardiner Davenport, *European Treaties Bearing on the History of the United States and Its Dependencies* (Washington 1934), I, 84–100.
5 Julien, *Les voyages de découverte*, 114–17

SOVEREIGNTY-ASSOCIATION, 1500–1783 477

The English, when they came to settle Virginia, quickly resorted to force of arms to seize land from the resident Indians. As Governor Wyat put it in 1623–4: 'Our first work is Expulsion of the Salvages ... for it is infinitely better to have no heathen among us, who at best were but as thornes in our sides, then to be at peace and league with them.'[6] Some 132 years later Hermon Husband of Orange County, North Carolina, reported to John Earl Granville, Viscount Carteret: 'Some here I find are so stupified as to secretly think & desire an occasion against those savages to have them destroyed in order to possess their lands with Negroes & have more room to employ their slaves upon.'[7]
In New England the Puritans occupied land left vacant when the great plague of 1616–17 killed a third or more of the Indians between Narraganset Bay and the Penobscot River. This the Puritans regarded as 'divine providence.'[8] When they began to expand inland the New Englanders were constrained to adopt the practice of the Dutch West India Company and to buy land from the Indians.[9] The ravages of disease had left the survivors with more land than they needed, and for the New Englanders acquisition of land title by purchase was cheaper than seizing it by force of arms. It required the drawing up of deeds to which Indian representatives affixed their symbols. The deeds were then registered and preserved for future reference.[10] No matter that too many of these deeds were fraudulent, the fact remained that a prior Indian title to the land was explicitly recognized.[11]
According to European custom, sovereignty carried with it four

6 Alden T. Vaughan, '"Expulsion of the Salvages": English Policy and the Virginia Massacre of 1622,' *The William and Mary Quarterly*, 3rd Series, xxxv (Jan. 1978), 58. See also K.G. Davies, *The North Atlantic World in the Seventeenth Century* (Minneapolis 1974), 285–6; William S. Simmons, 'Cultural Bias in the New England Puritans' Perception of Indians,' *The William and Mary Quarterly*, 3rd Series, xxxviii (Jan. 1981), 56–72.
7 A. Roger Ekirch, '"A New Government of Liberty": Hermon Husband's Vision of Backcountry North Carolina 1755,' *The William and Mary Quarterly*, 3rd Series, xxxiv (Oct. 1977), 642
8 Alden T. Vaughan, *New England Frontier: Puritans and Indians 1620–1675* (rev. ed., New York 1979), 104–20; Neal Salisbury, *Manitou and Providence: Indians, Europeans, and the Making of New England, 1500–1643* (New York 1982), 101–9, 190–215. See also Francis Jennings, *The Invasion of America: Indians, Colonialism and the Cant of Conquest* (Chapel Hill, NC 1975), a controversial work that gives pause for serious thought.
9 Allen W. Trelease, *Indian Affairs in Colonial New York: The Seventeenth Century* (Ithaca, NY 1960), 40–1; Berkhofer, *The White Man's Indian*, 130
10 Vaughan, *New England Frontier*, 107–9
11 On fraudulent land claims see Peter Wraxall, *An Abridgement of the Indian Affairs ... in the Colony of New York ... 1678 to 1751*, C.H. McIlwain, ed. (Cambridge, MA 1915), *passim*; Charles Thomson, *An Enquiry into the Causes of the Alienation f the Delaware and Shawanese Indians from the British Interest* (London 1759), *passim*. Other references on this topic could be added almost *ad infinitum*.

rights: that of the sovereign power to impose taxes on the people residing on the land over which sovereignty was claimed; to enact laws and enforce them; to demand military service from the adult males; and the right of eminent domain. It therefore follows that a European state could not be regarded as sovereign if it could not exercise those rights. Put another way, external sovereignty meant that the 'state was entirely free to regulate its relations with other states.' It also meant that a sovereign people 'did not yield habitual obedience to any other power.' If they were independent, that is, they were not subject to any legal superior power, then they were a sovereign people.[12] The Indian nations with whom the French had dealings could, and did, maintain that they satisfied all those requirements.

Some of the English colonies claimed, by virtue of their royal charters, that they held title to the land within lines of latitude westward to the Pacific Ocean.[13] Virginia, under the royal charter of 1609, with only a handful of settlers clinging desperately to a foothold in the malarial swamps on the St James River, laid claim to all the land enclosed by the line of latitude at approximately 35°, and a northwestern line from, roughly, the northern shore of Delaware Bay through Lake Ontario, Georgian Bay, and on across present-day Ontario, Manitoba, and the North West Territories.[14]

Claims were made by the interested European powers to vast areas in North America merely by virtue of a subject's having been the first to travel through them. Title was also claimed to lands by monarchs whose subjects had never seen, only heard of them. Thus France claimed the entire Ohio and Mississippi valleys by virtue of the voyages of Jolliet, Marquette, and La Salle. In fact, La Salle had not voyaged down the Ohio and he did not lay claim to having done so, yet France rested its claim to the region on his supposed voyage of discovery.[15] Needless to say, neither England nor Spain recognized these claims. Indeed, had they been deemed worthy of credence then Venice, in the fourteenth century, could have claimed title to all of China as a consequence of Marco Polo's journey to the court of the Great Khan. In the final analysis sovereignty rested on two things: occupation and military force sufficient to impose the will of the occupying power on the people in the territory to which title was claimed.

12 Dennis Lloyd, *The Idea of Law* (London 1965), 153–4, 157, 165
13 Francis N. Thorpe, ed., *The Federal and State Constitutions, Colonial Charters and Other Organic Laws of ... the United States of America* (Washington, DC 1909), VII
14 *Ibid.*, 3795
15 Fernand Grenier, ed., *Papiers Contrecœur et autres documents concernant le conflit anglo-français sur l'Ohio de 1745 à 1756* (Quebec 1952), 57, 217; Theodore Calvin Pease, *Anglo-French Boundary Disputes in the West, 1749–1763* (Springfield, IL 1936), xlii, lix–lx, 14, 73, 377; Jean Delanglez, *Some La Salle Journeys* (Chicago 1938), 3–39

SOVEREIGNTY-ASSOCIATION, 1500–1783 479

The French crown early adopted the practice of granting letters patent to certain of its subjects, giving them the right to seize land from the pagans by conquest or to obtain it by other means – this, it was piously stated, in order to bring them to a knowledge of God. It was hoped that the establishment of the King's authority in the new land would bring benefits to the commerce of his kingdom.[16] In this early period the French hoped to find sources of mineral wealth such as Spain had discovered in Mexico and Peru.[17] The disappointment occasioned by the discovery that Cartier's famous gold and diamonds were mere dross and worthless quartz did not end the search for minerals,[18] but by the end of the century a more tangible source of wealth had been found in the furs that the Indians were eager to exchange for European goods. This was enough to attract Europeans in large numbers to Acadia and the Gulf of St Lawrence. Companies were now formed and monopoly charters granted by the Crown in an attempt to exclude foreigners from this lucrative trade.[19]

From that point on the notion of seizing land from the aborigines by conquest had to be abandoned by the French. Good relations had to be maintained at all costs with the Indians who supplied the coveted furs. When permanent settlements were eventually established in the Bay of Fundy they were made on dyked tidewater land that was of no value to the Indians.[20] These settlements posed no threat to the indigenous peoples, who welcomed the French in their midst since they provided a year-round supply of trade goods at their posts. Moreover, in Acadia the French were so few in numbers that they represented no tangible or imaginable threat to the Micmacs, Malecites, and Abenakis.[21]

Similarly, in the St Lawrence valley the French established a trading

16 See H.P. Biggar, ed., *A Collection of Documents Relating to Jacques Cartier and the Sieur de Roberval* (Ottawa 1930), 128–31, 178–85, for Cartier's commission for his third voyage and Roberval's commission.

17 *Ibid.*, 42, grant of money to Cartier for his first voyage, 'pour descouvrir certain ysles et pays où l'on dit qu'il se doibt trouver grand quantité d'or et autres riches choses...' See also p. 77, letter from Lagarto to John the Third, King of Portugal, 22 Jan. 1539.

18 H.P. Biggar, ed., *The Works of Samuel de Champlain* (Toronto 1922), I, 180–5. On his 1603 voyage to Canada, Champlain was led to believe that rich veins of copper and silver had been found in a bay appropriately named Baie des Mines.

19 Robert Le Blant and René Baudry, eds, *Nouveaux documents sur Champlain et son époque (1560–1622)* (Ottawa 1967), I, 74, 407–14, 137–43; Trudel, *The Beginnings of New France*, passim

20 Andrew Hill Clark, *Acadia: The Geography of Early Nova Scotia to 1760* (Madison, WI 1968), 24–31, 67–9, 158–62

21 In 1714, after the cession of part of the area to Great Britain, the Acadian population was estimated to be less than 4,000. *Chronological List of Canadian Censuses*, Dominion Bureau of Statistics, Ottawa

post at Tadoussac with the sanction of the local Indians, nomadic hunters who transported their surplus trade goods to nations far in the interior in exchange for furs. As for occupying any part of that inhospitable region, the French cetainly had no such desire. The French Crown laid claim to the land but it was really a claim intended to exclude all but French subjects from the Indian trade, the Gulf fishery, and the seal and whale hunt.[22] The French then had no interest in the land itself, only with what it and its adjacent waters produced. They brought no womenfolk with them and made no attempt to cultivate the soil. When settlement was eventually undertaken its purpose was solely to make the fur trade and the fishing stations secure from foreign attack. These tiny French settlements were a means to an end, and the end required that the Indians and their way of life be preserved.

In 1608 the French established a trading post at Quebec under the local command of Samuel de Champlain. The region from Quebec to the island of Montreal had, when Jacques Cartier visited it in the 1530s and 1540s, been occupied by the St Lawrence Iroquois. It was they who had forced Cartier and Roberval to abandon their attempt to establish a colony near Quebec, or Stadacona as it then was.[23] When Champlain arrived on the scene those Indians had disappeared. Their warriors, archaeological evidence indicates, were killed in battle, their womenfolk and children absorbed by their triumphant Huron foes, likely after being decimated by some disease contracted from European traders.[24] The entire St Lawrence valley was unoccupied. There was, therefore, no need for the French to seize the land by conquest or to obtain title by purchase. The Hurons and Algonquins welcomed them since they provided a secure supply, close at hand, of European goods. Moreover, to consolidate this commercial alliance Champlain felt compelled to give them military aid in their war with the Iroquois Confederacy. In 1611 the Algonquins requested that Champlain establish a settlement at the Lachine rapids to shorten their journey and remove the need to run the Iroquois gauntlet along the St Lawrence from the mouth of the Ottawa to Quebec. It was not until 1634 that Champlain was able to establish a second post, not at Montreal as requested, but at Trois Rivières. He did so with the concurrence and at the behest of the Hurons and Algonquins, who wished to make use of the French as an auxiliary military force.[25]

In 1627 Cardinal Richelieu, who had had himself appointed Grand

22 Le Blant and Baudry, *Nouveaux documents*, 407–14
23 Trudel, *The Beginnings of New France*, 43–53
24 J.V. Wright, *Quebec Prehistory* (Toronto 1979), 64–75
25 Bruce G. Trigger, *The Children of Aataentsic: A History of the Huron People to 1660* (Montreal and London 1976), II, 270; Trudel, *The Beginnings of New France*, 185

SOVEREIGNTY-ASSOCIATION, 1500–1783 481

Master and Superintendant General of the Navigation and Commerce of France, organized the Company of One Hundred Associates, each associate providing 3,000 livres of working capital. All previous charters were thereby rendered null and void. The stated aims of the new company were, first and foremost, to convert the Indians to Christianity and cause them to adopt a civil mode of life; second, it was hoped that by establishing royal authority in the fledgling colony with its pathetic population of 107, the King's subjects could reap economic benefits. Provision was made for the establishment of 4,000 French Catholic settlers in the colony within fifteen years, this to prevent the King's enemies seizing the lands now claimed by France. This claim was nothing if not extensive – from the lands previously claimed in Florida, along the Atlantic seaboard to the Arctic circle, and inland from Newfoundland to the *mer douce*, Lake Huron, including all the land drained by the St Lawrence River and all waters flowing into it, and then as far beyond as His Majesty's subjects would find it possible to go. There was, however, no mention of lands being seized by right of conquest. The officials in France who drafted the charter could have had only the vaguest notion of what was being claimed. Their obvious purpose was to forestall claims by other powers.

French attitudes and policy for the Indians were clearly revealed in Article 17 of the charter, wherein it was stated that descendants of the French who would inhabit the colony, along with those Indians who became practising Christians, would be treated as French subjects. As such they would have the right to reside in France whenever they desired and there acquire, bequeath, succeed to property, and accept grants or legacies just as could the King's subjects in France, without the necessity to make any declaration of intent or obtain letters of naturalization. In short, Indians who were converted to Christianity were entitled to all the rights and privileges of French citizenship. The authors of the letters patent here manifested a lamentable ignorance of Indian predilections, but at least they had what they imagined to be the Indians' best interests at heart.[26]

Subsequently, when on 17 December 1640 title to a large part of the island of Montreal was ceded to the 'Messieurs de Saint-Sulpice,' the opening sentence of the patent stated: 'Notre plus grand désir étant d'établir une forte colonie en la Nouvelle-France, afin d'instruire les peuples sauvages de ces lieux en la connoissance de Dieu et les attirer à une vie civile...'[27] In 1644 the concession was ratified and again it was

26 *Edits, Ordonnances Royaux, Déclarations et Arrêts du Conseil d'Etat concernant le Canada* (Quebec 1854), 5–11, Acte pour l'établissement de la Compagnie des Cent Associés...

27 *Ibid.*, 20–3, Concession d'une grande partie de l'Isle de Montréal...

spelled out in great detail that the sole purpose of the settlement was to serve the Indians.[28]

In 1645 the Company ceded its monopoly on the fur trade to the colonists and once more it was stated that the King had no other purpose than 'l'avancement de la gloire de Dieu, et l'honneur de cette couronne en la conversion des peuples sauvages, pour les réduire à une vie civile sous l'autorité de Sa dite Majesté.'[29] It was then believed that the only effective way to Christianize the Indians was, by one means or another, to persuade them to abandon their nomadic, hunting life and to settle at Montreal as sedentary farmers merged with the French settlers. That this would have destroyed the fur trade was either not considered or was regarded as inconsequential. The fact that this policy enjoyed virtually no success whatsoever does not detract from its altruistic intent.[30] It was implicit that since the Crown wished, and expected, the Indians to occupy and exploit the land their title to it would have been recognized, as was that of the French settlers. When some of the Hurons who had survived the Iroquois holocaust of 1649 fled to Quebec they were granted land at Sillery under seigneurial tenure with the Jesuits acting for them, in exactly the same manner as seigneurial concessions were made by the Crown to French settlers.[31]

In theory the King was the true proprietor of all property, movable and immovable, in his kingdom. In his memoirs Louis xiv declared: 'les rois sont seigneurs absolus et ont naturellement la disposition pleine et libre de tous les biens, tant des séculiers que des ecclésiastiques, pour en user comme sages économes, c'est à dire selon les besoins de leur état.'[32] He maintained that his subjects were merely allowed the use of whatever property they might have acquired, during his pleasure. In New France Louis xiii had granted title to the land under seigneurial tenure in perpetuity to the Company of One Hundred Associates. The Associates merely had to make obeisance, swear fealty, and present the King with a gold crown of eight marks weight at each succession to the throne.[33]

28 *Ibid.*, 24–6, Ratification de la concession de l'Isle de Montréal...
29 *Ibid.*, 28–9, ...traité fait ... entre la dite Compagnie et le député des habitans de la Nouvelle-France
30 W.J. Eccles, *Canada under Louis XIV 1663–1701* (Toronto 1964), 97; Jean Delanglez, *Frontenac and the Jesuits* (Chicago 1939), 35–65
31 *Rapport de l'Archiviste de la Province de Québec pour 1943–1944* (hereafter RAPQ) 1–16, La Seigneurie de Sillery; Marcel Trudel, *Les débuts du régime seigneurial* (Montreal 1974), 52, 171
32 Jean Longnon, ed., *Mémoires de Louis XIV* (Paris 1927), 197; Marcel Marion, *Dictionnaire des institutions de la France aux XVIIᵉ et XVIIIᵉ siècles* (Paris 1968), 489–93; Roland Mousnier, *Les institutions de la France sous la monarchie absolue* (Paris 1974), I, 510–15
33 *Edits, Ordonnances Royaux, Déclarations et Arrêts...* 7–8 – Acte pour l'établissement de la Compagnie des Cent Associés

The 'in perpetuity' clause availed the Company nothing when Louis xiv, in 1663, decided to take the colony out of its hands on the grounds that it had failed to live up to the terms of its charter.[34] Title to all lands claimed by France in Canada, Acadia, Newfoundland, the West Indies, and Africa was now vested in the newly created Compagnie des Indes Occidentales. The Company's charter stipulated that all these lands in America, as far as they extended, by virtue of occupation by the French, or would extend in the future by right of conquest, were conceded to the company under seigneurial tenure, which meant that title ultimately rested with the Crown. This charter repeated in a modified form Article 17 of the charter of the defunct Company of One Hundred Associates. French subjects who emigrated to the colonies were guaranteed the same rights and privileges as were subjects residing in France. These rights were also extended to children born of marriages with Indians. It was the earnest desire of the minister responsible for the colonies, Jean-Baptiste Colbert, to have the French colonists and the Indians intermarry and form one race. This, he fondly believed, would serve two purposes: populate the colony without the need to ship a large number of emigrants from France at great expense, and bring the Indians to accept the French way of life by assimilation.[35]

Royal policy toward the Indians was succinctly stated by Louis xiv in a directive to the governor of New France, Daniel de Rémy de Courcelle:

Le Roy a deux objets principaux à l'esgard des Indiens naturels.

Le premier est de procurer leur conversion à la foy chrestienne et catholique le plustost qu'il sera possible, et pour y parvenir, outre les instructions qui leur seront donnez par les missionaires que Sa Majesté entrestient à cet effet, soubs la direction de Mgnr de Petrée, son intention est que les officiers, soldats et tous ses aultres subjets traitent les Indiens avec douceur, justice et équité, sans leur faire jamais aulcun tort ny violence; qu'on n'usurpe point les terres sur lesquelles ils sont habituez soubs pretexte qu'elles sont meilleures ou plus convenables aux François.

Le second objet de Sa Majesté est de rendre dans les suittes ces Indiens ses subjets travaillans utilement à l'accroissement du commerce qui s'establira peu à peu dans le Canada quand il sera bien cultivé; mais son intention est que tout cela s'exécute de bonne volonté et que ces Indiens s'y portent par leur propre intérest.[36]

34 Ibid., 31–2
35 Delanglez, *Frontenac and the Jesuits*, 35–65; H. Charbonneau and Y. Landry, 'La politique démographique en Nouvelle-France,' *Annales de démographie historique* (1979), 29–57
36 *Collection de manuscrits contenant lettres, mémoirs et autres documents historiques relatifs à l'histoire de la Nouvelle-France, recueillis aux archives de la province de Québec ou copiés à l'étranger* (Quebec 1873), I, 175, Le Roy à Courcelle

The clergy, who had originally espoused the policy of 'Frenchification,' became convinced that contacts between the Indians and lay Frenchmen had to be reduced to the minimum since, it seemed to them, each acquired the worst traits of the other.[37] They therefore sought to introduce what can be likened to latter-day South African 'apartheid,' but with a difference. In New France it was espoused by the clergy purely for the benefit and protection of the Indians. The French were eventually constrained to abandon their attempts to make the Indians into Europeans, and accept them as Indians.

Although Colbert strongly espoused the policy of assimilating the Indians and was very critical of the clergy for their rejection of it, at the same time he strongly opposed any territorial expansion of the settlements west of the island of Montreal.[38] He also ordered that the colonists were not to voyage to the Indian country to trade for furs. They had to remain in the settlements and let the Indians bring their furs to trade at Montreal or Trois Rivières. He wanted the central colony strengthened rather than allow its meagre manpower resources to be scattered about in the wilderness.[39]

In the colony, however, certain of Colbert's officials disagreed with this policy. The Intendant Jean Talon had quickly come to realize the great wealth to be garnered from the fur trade. He also warned of the potential threat to French interests posed by the English in New York, recently seized from the Dutch, and their presence in Hudson Bay. Within a few weeks of his arrival at Quebec he wrote to Colbert advising him that there was nothing to prevent the French expanding their claims on the continent as far south as Mexico. He proposed the establishment of garrisoned forts on both sides of Lake Ontario with a sailing barque to supply and maintain communications between them. By this means, he declared, the Iroquois would be cowed and French control of the fur trade assured.[40] Colbert would have none of it. He informed Talon that they had to concentrate their activities within an area that they could expect to hold securely, rather than grasp at too great an expanse and one day be forced to abandon part of it with a consequent loss of prestige.[41]

Undeterred, Talon sent what he called 'exploration parties' north to

37 Delanglez, *Frontenac and the Jesuits*, 35–47
38 W.J. Eccles, *Frontenac: The Courtier Governor* (Toronto 1959), 54–8
39 RAPQ 1930–1, p. 43, Colbert à Talon, Versailles, 5 jan. 1666; RAPQ 1926–7, p. 87, Lettre du Roi au Gouverneur Frontenac, Paris, 15 avr. 1676, AN C11A, vol. 4, f. 82, Ordonnance du Roy, St Germain-en-Laye, 12 mai 1678
40 AN C11A, vol. 3, f. 97, Au Roy. Mémoire sur le Canada. Talon. Qué, 10 nov. 1670. Addition au présent mémoire, Talon, 10 nov. 1670
41 AN, B, vol. 3, ff. 12–24, Colbert à Talon, [1671]; *ibid.*, vol. 7, f. 31, Le Roy à Frontenac, St Germain, 12 avr. 1676

Hudson Bay, down the Mississippi, and west into Lake Superior.[42] He stated that their purpose was to search for mineral deposits and also to claim for France the lands traversed. In reality they were little more than a means to circumvent Colbert's restrictive fur trade edict and garner large quantities of the choicer northern furs. One such party was sent out by Talon in October 1670 with orders to voyage as far west as possible to discover the copper deposits of Lake Superior, the route to the western ocean, and at the same time to lay claim to the Great Lakes for France. Led by Simon-François Daumont, sieur de Saint-Lusson, with Nicolas Perrot as interpreter and four Jesuits in attendance, an assembly was held near Sault Saint-Marie on 14 June 1671 with representatives of fourteen western tribes. According to Perrot's account, written several years after the event, and the edited version of the Jesuits, a post bearing the arms of France was erected, an official act of possession drawn up and read to the tribesmen, who were thereby considered to have placed themselves under the protection of, and in submission to, the King of France.[43]

It is extremely doubtful that the Indians had any understanding of what the ceremony purported. The notion that these strangers could somehow claim to have taken possession of their lands would have seemed utterly ridiculous to them; they might as well have laid claim to the air. As for their now being under the protection of a king thousands of miles away, that too would have appeared nonsensical since it was obviously the French who required the protection of the Indians in that part of the world. The episode is likely an early example of what might be termed the 'Janusian' – two-faced – attitude of the French toward the Indians at that time: tell Europeans – friends or foes – one thing, and the Indians something quite different, or nothing at all.[44]

42 John Bartlet Brebner, *The Explorers of North America, 1492–1806* (London 1933); RAPQ 1930–1, pp. 157–8, Mémoire de Talon au Roi sur le Canada, 2 nov. 1671

43 Ministère des Affaires Etrangères, Paris. Public Archives of Canada (hereafter PAC) transcripts, Série Amérique, vol. v, part 2, p. 13. Copie du Procès verbal de la prise de possession du Sr de Saint-Lusson, 16 May 1671; RP J Tailhan, SJ, ed., *Mémoire sur les mœurs, coustumes et relligion des sauvages de l'Amérique septentrionale par Nicolas Perrot* (Montreal 1973), 126–8, 292–4; Reuben Gold Thwaites, ed., *The Jesuit Relations and Allied Documents* (Cleveland 1899), LV, 105–15

44 A later example of this propensity occurred in 1742 when the chevalier de La Vérendrye, while on his epic trip across the western plains to the Bighorn Mountains, built a stone cairn near the future site of St Pierre, South Dakota, and beside it buried a lead plaque bearing the arms of France, brought from Quebec, to signify the taking of possession of the land. He noted in his journal, 'Je posai sur une éminence, près du fort, une plaque de plomb aux armes et inscriptions du Roy et des pierres en pyramide pour Monsieur le Général. Je dis aux Sauvages, qui n'avoient pas connaissance de la plaque de plomb que j'avois mise dans la terre, que je mettois ces pierres en mémoire de ce que nous étions venus sur leurs terres.'

A more likely version of the Saint-Lusson episode was related four generations later by a metis descendant of one of Saint-Lusson's companions. (The memories of illiterate peoples are far more reliable than those of the literate, who do not have to rely on their memory and hence rarely do.) This metis recalled that according to the collective memory of his mother's people Saint-Lusson had requested free passage to the Indians' country at all times to trade in their villages. 'He asked that the fires of the French and the Ojibway nations might be made one, and everlasting. He promised the protection of the great French nation against all their enemies ...'[45] There is no mention in this recollection of any awareness that they had ceded their lands to the French, and something as significant as that, had it actually transpired, would not easily have been forgotten. That the Indians were uneasy over the ceremony is indicated by the fact that immediately afterward they removed the copy of the act of possession that Saint-Lusson had attached to the post behind the coat of arms and threw it in the fire, fearing that it was intended to cast a deadly spell on them.[46]

Talon, seemingly in some trepidation as to Colbert's reception of his account of this expedition, assured the minister that it, and his other expeditions, had not cost the Crown a sou. He blandly stated that after taking possession of the Indians' lands Saint-Lusson had, in the King's name, granted them back to those who occupied them and in return had received several packs of beaver pelts.[47] Certainly on an occasion such as this there would have had to be an exchange of presents; Indian protocol insisted on it. It is difficult to escape the conclusion that this episode had been nothing more than a profitable trading venture to cement commercial ties with the northwest tribes. The asserted act of possession was, in reality, an empty gesture likely fabricated to assuage Colbert. The Indians remained in complete possession of their lands and in no way submissive to the French, who could travel through their territory only with their permission and establish trading posts only

Lawrence J. Burpee, ed., *Journals and Letters of Pierre Gaultier de Varennes de La Vérendrye and His Sons* (Toronto 1927), 427; Antoine Champagne, *Les La Vérendrye et le poste de l'ouest* (Quebec 1968), 293

45 William W. Warren, *History of the Ojibway Nation* (Saint Paul 1885; Minnesota Historical Society Collections 1974), 130–2

46 N. Perrot, *Mémoire sur les mœurs*, 295

47 Ministère des Affaires Etrangères, Paris, Série Amérique, v, 288–9, Au Roy. Mémoire sur le Canada, Talon. Qué., 2 nov. 1671. In a lengthy memoir on the fur trade written in 1695, de Lagny, the Intendant de Commerce, wrote: 'Ce fut à l'arrivée de M. Talon en Canada que sous pretexte des découvertes les voyages dans la profondeur des terres furent autorisés et qu'il permet ce commerce et pour son compte.' AN C11A, vol. 13, f. 400, Colonies fev. 1695. Commerce du Castor de Canada

SOVEREIGNTY-ASSOCIATION, 1500–1783 487

with their consent. The Indian nations were in the stronger position. The French dared do nothing that might offend them. They had to be provided with trade goods at favourable prices; trading practices that offended them had to be curbed swiftly.[48]

These proud nations refused to submit to French justice when, in their own country, they committed crimes against French subjects. All that the French authorities could do in cases where Canadians were murdered or pillaged by Indians was appeal to the chiefs of the offenders' nation and demand that those responsible be either punished or handed over to the French, but these appeals appear to have been consistently rejected.[49] In 1708 Governor General Vaudreuil and the Intendant, Jacques Raudot, wrote to the Council of Marine, following one such incident, that 'ces Sauvages luy representerent quils nétoient pas assez les maitres, les uns des autres, comme il est vray, pour pouvoir remettre un de leurs gens...'[50] François Clairambault d'Aigremont, naval commissary, after his tour of inspection in the west, reported: 'on ne parviendra jamais a establir la subordination parmy eux, Ils n'en connoissent aucune et ils n'obeissent pas mesme a leurs Chefs lesquels ne les parlent jamais en comande ny n'oseroient le faire, mais seulement en disant qu'il faudroit faire telle chose.'[51] The Indians had their own concept of justice and in their own country they meted it out as they saw fit.[52] When the presumptuous Jean-Louis, comte de

48 In 1748 the nations trading at La Baye complained to Governor General Galisso-nière that the leaseholder was charging too much for his goods. He immediately assured them that in future the post would not be leased to a monopolist but that the trade would be carried on by the issuing of *congés* to free traders. Galissonière did this out of fear that were he not to do so the Indians would go over to the English. AN C11A, vol. 93, f. 42, Jonquière et Bigot au Ministre, Qué., 9 8bre 1749. See also Grenier, *Papiers Contrecœur*, 265, Duquesne à Contrecœur, Qué., 21 oct. 1754. Governor General Duquesne here ordered Capitaine Contrecœur, commandant at Fort Duquesne, to have the price of trade goods fixed to put an end to the Indians' complaints that they were being cheated.

49 RAPQ 1946–7, p. 398. Vaudreuil au Ministre, Qué., 3 nov. 1710; *ibid.*, 427, Mémoire du Roi à MM de Vaudreuil et Raudot, Marly, 7 juillet 1711; AN C11A, vol. 102, f. 276, 1er 9bre 1757. Canada

50 RAPQ 1939–40, p. 446. Vaudreuil et Raudot au Ministre, Qué., 14 nov. 1708

51 AN C11A, vol. 29, f. 165v. Le Sr Daigremont, 14 nov. 1708

52 When 3 soldiers who had murdered a Seneca chief and robbed his cache of furs were convicted and executed before a large assembly of visiting Iroquois and western Indians the tribesmen were appalled, regarding it as barbaric that 3 should be put to death for the murder of 1. The Iroquois declared that they would have preferred to receive 10 belts of wampum as compensation rather than see the 3 soldiers die. In cases of murder the Indians always demanded *wergeld* in order to avoid a blood feud. See Etienne-Michel Faillon, *Histoire de la colonie française en Canada* (Ville-Marie 1865–6), III, 324–5. See also Joyce Marshall, ed. and trans., *Word from New France: The Selected Letters of Marie de l'Incarnation* (Toronto 1967),

Raymond, submitted a memoir on colonial affairs wherein he recommended that *haute, moyenne,* and *basse* justice be imposed on the Indians of the north, Governor General Duquesne declared that the man was clearly out of his mind to have made such a preposterous suggestion.[53]

Even in the case of crimes committed inside the colony by Indians, either by those residing there or those coming from afar, the French authorities had great difficulty in bringing those responsible to justice. The crimes were, invariably, acts of violence against a person, committed while the perpetrator was intoxicated. The Indians claimed, with cause, that they could not be held accountable for their actions under those circumstances since it was the alcohol, and not they, that had been responsible.[54] In 1676 the Sovereign Council had decreed that all Indians would be subject to the penalties required by French law for the crimes of theft, murder, rape, drunkenness, and other misdemeanours.[55] The Indians refused to comply; they declared that they were not subject to French law and could not be imprisoned against their will.[56]

During the period 1712–48 three Indians were convicted of murder and two of them were swiftly executed.[57] Significantly, although all three were mission Indians, resident in the colony at Sault Saint-Louis and Lac des Deux Montagnes, they were not tried in the Royal Court at Montreal but by military tribunal, for, as Governor General Vaudreuil and the Intendant Michel Bégon explained, to bring Indians into the courts risked 'de soulever contre nous les nations sauvages, et qu'ils ne prissent le party de celuy qu'on auroit puny.'[58]

The French authorities had to admit there was little they could do

---

240; and the case that unfolds in Archives Nationales du Québec à Montréal (hereafter ANQM), Pièces judiciares, 15 aoust–9 sept. 1722, wherein the Sault Saint-Louis Iroquois refused to allow one of their warriors to stand trial for the murder of a Canadian because he and his companions had been intoxicated at the time. The Governor General had to intervene and order the prisoner released, whereupon the Iroquois promised to make due retribution to the widow and child of the victim.

53 AN C11A, vol. 99, ff. 257–8, Duquesne au Ministre, Qué 7 8ᵇʳᵉ 1754
54 ANQM, Documents judiciares, 25 jan. 1719. Information contre Jacques Detaillis
55 *Arrêts et réglements du Conseil Supérieur de Québec et ordonnances et jugements des Intendants du Canada* (Quebec 1855), 70
56 RAPQ 1947–8, p. 241. Le Roi à Vaudreuil et Bégon, Versailles, 19 mars 1714
57 André Lachance, *La justice criminelle du Roi au Canada au XVIIIᵉ siècle* (Quebec 1978), 16–17
58 AN C11A, vol. 34, ff. 27–32, Vaudreuil et Bégon au Ministre, Québec, 15 nov. 1713. See also ANQ, Pièces judiciares, 15 aoust–9 sept. 1722. In this case a Canadian was killed and another wounded by 5 or 6 inebriated Iroquois in Montreal. One of them was apprehended and imprisoned for interrogation. At the insistence of the Sault Saint-Louis Iroquois council the Governor General was obliged to have the prisoner released after questioning to establish the facts of the case. Vaudreuil stated that he

SOVEREIGNTY-ASSOCIATION, 1500–1783 489

except to punish severely the Canadians who had provided the liquor to Indians when a crime ensued in consequence, as in the case of Jacques Detaillis in 1719. He was tried for selling liquor to a group of Sault Saint-Louis Iroquois who, while drunk, killed a Canadian child. They denied their culpability, blamed the incident, which they deeply regretted, on the liquor that they had drunk, and were not brought to trial.[59] The usual fine for anyone convicted of giving or selling liquor in excess to the Indians, in defiance of the Royal Ordonnance of 14 May 1679, was 50 livres; but in serious cases, where death had resulted from the offence, the fine could be 500 livres.[60] In some cases the penalties were more severe than that but still they proved to be no deterrent. In October 1735 Father Nau of the Sault Saint-Louis Mission reported that in the past two months one Frenchman had been sent to the galleys, two whipped in public by the hangman, and one put in the stocks to be reviled, yet the Indians of his mission were still obtaining supplies of liquor.[61] Clearly, the King's writ was ineffective at Sault Saint-Louis. To all intents it was an independent republic, in no wise subordinate to French authority.

Where territorial rights were concerned the French had conflicting claims only with the Five Nations Iroquois Confederacy. The Iroquois claimed that all the land south and west of the Ottawa River and around the shores of Lakes Erie and Huron belonged to them, they having conquered it from the Hurons, Petuns, and Neutrals in the mid-sixteenth century.[62] They were bitterly resentful when Governor General Louis de Buade de Frontenac established his trading post at Cataracoui in 1673. When, during the 1689–97 war between France and England, the French were constrained to abandon and destroy the fort the Iroquois swore that they would never allow them to reoccupy the site.[63] However, during that war their manpower losses were so

had to do so to calm the irate Indians, who would not permit the imprisonment of their people. The same thing had happened in a similar case previously and he had, on that occasion, declared that it was necessary 'd'agir a l'avenir avec beaucoup de précaution avec lesd Sauvages pour les menager.' A Canadian and his wife who, in the later case, had sold the liquor to the Iroquois were fined 500 livres, a year's wages for a skilled artisan.

59 ANQM, Documents judiciares, 25 jan. 1719. Information contre Jacques Detaillis
60 *Ibid.*, 13 mai 1700, procès de François Noir; *ibid.*, 14 mai 1700, procès de Jean Cuillerier; *ibid.*, 10 fev. 1719; *ibid.*, 25 juillet 1719; *ibid.*, 9 avr. 1721; *ibid.*, 27 juin–22 juillet 1721; *ibid.*, 13–31 juillet 1721
61 RAPQ 1926–7, pp. 282–3, RP Nau au RP Bonin, Sault Saint-Louis, 2 oct. 1735
62 Edmond B. O'Callaghan, Berthold Fernow, eds, *Documents Relative to the Colonial History of the State of New York* (Albany 1856–87), (hereafter NYCD), IV, 908–11, deed from the Five Nations to the King of their beaver hunting ground, 19 July 1701
63 *Ibid.*, 122, answer of the Five Nations to the Governor of Canada, Onondaga, 4 Feb. 1694/5

great that they were unable to enforce their mandamus and the French subsequently restored the fort.[64] Under pressure from their northern Algonquin foes they were also obliged to abandon all the villages that they had established on the north shore of Lake Ontario. Only a few families remained ensconced near Fort Frontenac.[65] Similarly the western Iroquois claimed sovereignty over the Ohio Valley by right of conquest. This vast area they maintained as their hunting territory and it was not until the 1720s that they allowed a few bands of Delawares and later, Shawnee, to settle there.[66] The British subsequently claimed that the region belonged to them since the Iroquois were their subjects, hence the Iroquois title ultimately rested in the British Crown,[67] a pretension that both the Iroquois and the French refused to countenance.[68]

For their part the French, on occasion, claimed that the Iroquois had been their subjects since the initial French discovery of their lands.[69] They also claimed title to the Mohawks' land by right of conquest. When Alexandre de Prouville de Tracy marched a few hundred French troops and Canadian militia into their abandoned villages he had an official act proclaimed taking possession of the land for Louis

64 *Ibid.*, 337–8, Comparative Population of Albany and of the Indians in 1689 and 1698; *Calendar of State Papers, Colonial Series, America and the West Indies* (hereafter CSPAWI) (London 1860–); 1699, 135, Earl of Bellomont to Council of Trade and Plantations, New York, 13 Apr. 1699; *ibid.*, 1700, p. 543, Council of Trade and Plantations to Mr Secretary Vernon, Whitehall, 4 Oct. 1700; *ibid.*, 615, Bellomont to Council of Trade and Plantations, New York, 24 Oct. 1700

65 AN C11A, vol. 29, f. 152, D'Aigremont au Ministre, Qué., 14 nov. 1708; Leroy V. Eid, 'The Ojibwa-Iroquois War: The War the Five Nations Did Not Win,' *Ethnohistory*, XXVI (Fall 1979), 297–324; Victor Konrad, 'An Iroquois Frontier: The North Shore of Lake Ontario during the Late Seventeenth Century,' *Journal of Historical Geography*, VII (1981), 129–44

66 Bruce G. Trigger, ed., *Handbook of North American Indians: Northeast* (Washington 1978), XV, 588–93; Delf Norona, ed., 'Joshua Fry's Report on the Back Settlements of Virginia,' (8 May 1751), *The Virginia Magazine of History and Biography*, LVI (Jan. 1948), 22–41; AN C11A, vol. 50, f. 43, Beauharnois et D'Aigremont au Ministre, Qué., 1 oct. 1728; AN F3, Moreau de Saint-Méry, vol. 12, f. 40, Mémoire du Roy aux Srs Beauharnois et Hocquart, Versailles, 22 avr. 1732

67 CSPAWI 1681–5, pp. 422–3, no. 1059, Apr. 1683. Draft of a memorial in answer to Monsieur de la Barre; *ibid.*, 1685–8, p. 645, no. 2091, Memorial for the French Ambassador; NYCD, IV, 908–11, deed from the Five Nations to the King of Their Beaver Hunting Ground, 19 July 1701

68 AN C11A, vol. 103, ff. 31–3. Acte Authentique des Six Nations Iroquoises sur leur Indépendance, 2 nov. 1748. See also AN C11A, vol. 39, f. 241. Conseil de Marine, juin 1718, Canada, for an example of the Iroquois' ability to work both sides of the street. The Five Nations having sent His Majesty a wampum belt to assure him of their fidelity, the Regent approved their being sent a gift in return – 2,000 pounds of gunpowder and 4,000 musket balls.

69 AN B, vol. 11, f. 104, Le Ministre à Mʳ. Barillon, Versailles, 10 mars 1685

SOVEREIGNTY-ASSOCIATION, 1500–1783 491

XIV. The fact that he had not conquered the Mohawks did not deter him. After burning their longhouses and corn fields the French marched back to Canada. The Mohawks then rebuilt their villages, reoccupied them, and all went on as before.[70] The French claim proved merely to be a futile gambit in their diplomatic skirmishes with the British.

Subsequently the French acquired a healthy respect for the martial prowess of the Iroquois. After the Five Nations, in the 1701 peace treaty, declared their intention to remain neutral in future Anglo-French hostilities the French were extremely careful not to do anything that might cause them to abandon that stance.[71] When, in 1719, the French learned that the New York authorities intended to establish a fort at Niagara to give them access to the northwest, and at the same time sever the French communication route through the Great Lakes to the far west and Louisiana, the Governor General of New France, Philippe de Rigaud de Vaudreuil, forestalled them by establishing a post there before the English of New York were able to move. Before proceeding, however, Vaudreuil was careful to obtain the sanction of the Senecas, who claimed the territory as theirs. He dispatched one of his officers, Chabert de Joncaire, who had been adopted into the Seneca nation, to request permission to build a house at Niagara. This the Senecas could not deny to one of their own, as Joncaire was.

Upon receiving the accord of the Seneca council Joncaire swiftly garnered a squad of soldiers from Fort Frontenac and built his 'house.'[72] A few years later it was replaced by a massive stone building but, significantly, it was not constructed in the form of a fort but rather as a large manor house in order not to upset the Senecas. Had the

70 CSPAWI 1699, no. 1109, p. 588. Copy of the Treaty Made with the Iroquois by M. de Tracy on 13 Dec. 1655; AN C11A, vol. 2, ff. 270–1, Prise de Possession des forts Dagnié, 17 oct. 1666

71 AN F3 Moreau de Saint-Méry, vol. 8, ff. 278–9, Assemblée faite par M. Le chevalier de Callières de tous les nations Iroquoises ... Mtl 7ᵉ aoust 1701; *Nouvelle-France: Documents historiques, Correspondance échangée entre les autorités françaises et les gouverneurs et intendants* (Quebec 1893), I, 44–5, Mémoire du Roy aux Srs Chevalier de Callières et de Champigny, Versailes le 31 mai 1701; RAPQ 1938–9, pp. 24–5, Vaudreuil au Ministre, Mtl., 3 avr. 1704; *ibid.*, 29, Le Roy à Vaudreuil et Beauharnois, Versailles, 14 juin 1704; *ibid.*, 160–1, Vaudreuil au Ministre, Qué., 4 nov. 1706; RAPQ 1939–40, p. 445, MM de Vaudreuil et Raudot au Ministre, Qué., 14 nov. 1708; RAPQ 1946–7, p. 453, Vaudreuil au Ministre, Qué., 8 nov. 1711

72 Yves F. Zoltvany, *Philippe de Rigaud de Vaudreuil: Governor of New France 1703–1725* (Toronto 1974), 168–70. Earlier, when Canadian officials proposed establishing a post at Toronto to stop the Mississaugas and Amicoués from trading their furs with the Iroquois, the King agreed only on condition that the Iroquois gave their prior consent. See RAPQ 1947–8, p. 300. Mémoire du Roi à Vaudreuil et Bégon, Paris, 15 juin 1716

Senecas refused their consent to Joncaire the French would not have dared to make the move. As it was when the New York authorities protested that the fort represented an invasion of British territory the Iroquois told them to remain quiet and live in peace with the French. They also stated that they had 'given the French liberty of free Passage thru Lake Ontario.'[73] At that time the Iroquois still were, in North American terms, a power to be reckoned with, one whom the French feared and respected far more than they did the English colonies.[74]

It was under the cover of the war with the Iroquois that began in 1684 with their attacks on the French in the Illinois territory, a war that lasted until 1699, that the French expanded their influence throughout the west. Although this was ostensibly to enlist the support of the western nations, in reality it was a concerted drive by rival fur trade factions to increase their trade. Posts were established around the northern shores of the Great Lakes, down Lake Michigan and into the Mississippi valley.[75] As the intendant Jean Bochart de Champigny put it: 'Il ny a point de nations a cinq ou Six Cent lieues d'Icy ou Il ny ayt les françois avec des Marchandises pour les traitter avec les Sauvages a mesure quils tuent leurs Castors.'[76] The predictable result was that the market for beaver in France became glutted. In desperation the Minister of Marine finally issued orders that all the western posts save Saint-Louis des Illinois were to be burned and abandoned. Saint-Louis was to be retained solely to prevent the Indian nations of the region forming an alliance with the English. No more *congés* were to be issued for voyages to the west. In future, the Indians were to bring their furs to trade at Montreal.[77] The Governor General and the Intendant were quick to point out that to abandon the western posts while the war with the English and the Iroquois raged would merely invite the enemy to fill the political vacuum, win over all the Indian allies of the French, and bring on the ultimate destruction of New France.[78] The Minister was thereupon constrained to relax his Draconian edict and the western posts were maintained.[79] Four years later an abrupt shift in European

73 Peter Wraxall, *An Abridgement of the New York Indian Records* C.H. McIlwain, ed., (Cambridge, MA 1915), 161
74 Vaudreuil, who knew better than most, wrote: 'Il est de notre interet Monseigneur de n'avoir aucune guerre avec cette nation tant qu'il nous sera possible et les cinq villages Iroquois sont plus a craindre que toutte la nouvelle angleterre.' RAPQ 1946–7, p. 453. Vaudreuil au Ministre, Qué., 8 nov. 1711. See also RAPQ 1939–40, p. 455, MM de Vaudreuil et Raudot au Ministre, Qué., 14 nov. 1708.
75 Eccles, *Frontenac*, 273–94
76 AN C11A, vol. 13, f. 198, Mémoire pour le Castor. Champigny. Que., 26 oct. 1694
77 Eccles, *Frontenac*, 285–8
78 *Ibid.*, 289–91
79 AN B, vol. 19, ff. 240–2, Mémoire du Roy pour les Srs comte de Frontenac et de Champigny, Versailles, 27 avr. 1697

SOVEREIGNTY-ASSOCIATION, 1500–1783 493

power politics confirmed the wisdom, or in the long run the folly, of that reluctant decision.

In 1701, on the eve of the War of the Spanish Succession, Louis XIV made a decision that was to have drastic consequences for everyone in North America, French, English, Spanish, and Indian. On 31 May 1701 he signed a memoir to Callières and Champigny, Governor General and Intendant respectively at Quebec, stating in part: 'Elle a pris la resolution de former un establissement au bas du Mississipy ... qui ... est devenue d'une necessité indispensable pour empecher le progrez que les Anglois de la Colonie [sic] et de la Nouvelle York ont commencé de faire dans les terres qui sont entre eux et ce fleuve.'[80] In addition a settlement was ordered established at Detroit to maintain control of the Great Lakes. Significantly, the lands here to be occupied were vacant. The founder of the new post, Antoine Laumet *dit* de Lamothe Cadillac, had to persuade Ottawa and Huron Indians to move there from Michilimackinac.[81] Here too there was no need for the French either to seize the territory by force or to offer monetary compensation to anyone. The French mission posts in the Illinois country were also ordered to be strengthened. They had been established with the agreement of the resident Indians, who saw no cause for concern at the presence among them of traders, hunters, and farmers. The way of life of these settlers differed little from that of the Illinois nation and intermarriage was common.[82]

During the ensuing war the Iroquois honoured their treaty obligation and remained neutral. On the earnest advice of Champigny, who had been recalled to France to serve as Intendant at Le Havre and also as the Minister's adviser on Canadian affairs,[83] a tacit understanding was reached with New York that neither would attack the other unless attacked first. This was agreed to by the French for fear that an attack on New York would cause the Iroquois to give the British their military support.[84]

Against New England it was a different story. The New England authorities claimed that they had title to all the land up to the St

80 AN B, vol. 22, ff. 231–2 / 245–6, Mémoire du Roy au Srs Chevalier de Callières ... et de Champigny, Versailles, 31 may 1701

81 Zoltvany, *Vaudreuil*, 38–41

82 Natalie Maree Belting, *Kaskaskia under the French Regime* (Urbana, IL, 1948); AN F3, Moreau de Saint-Méry, vol. 11, ff 180–1, Arrest de la Chambre du Conseil en Canada, 18 déc. 1728

83 PAC transcripts, AN B, vol. 22–4, p. 368, Ministre à M. de Champigny, Versailles, 4 juin 1701; *ibid.*, B, vol. 27–33, pp. 437–9, Ministre à M. de Champigny, Versailles, 2 juin 1706; Francis H. Hammang, *The Marquis de Vaudreuil: New France at the Beginning of the Eighteenth Century* (Brussels 1938), 21–2

84 *Ibid.*, 120–2, 176; AN C11A, vol. 21, f. 52, Vaudreuil au Ministre, Qué., 14 oct. 1703; RAPQ 1939–40, p. 423, Vaudreuil au Ministre, Qué., 28 juin 1708

Lawrence River and west along it to the border of New York.[85] To hold them well back from the St Lawrence Governor General Vaudreuil had to rely on the Abenakis. To make sure they remained at war with the English he launched a series of devastating raids by war parties composed of Canadians, Mission Iroquois, and Abenakis on New England towns along the coast and well inland. That on Deerfield, Massachusets, in February 1704 which resulted in the sacking of the village, the killing of 47 villagers, and 111 taken back to Canada as prisoners, was typical.[86]

The Treaty of Utrecht that ended the war in 1713 saw France make sweeping territorial concessions in North America to avoid having to make them elsewhere. Newfoundland, part of Acadia, and Hudson Bay were yielded to Great Britain. In addition, in Clause 15, which declared that all Indians were permitted to trade with both the English colonies and New France without molestation or hindrance, the Five Nations were described as being 'subject to the Dominion of Great Britain.'[87] This assertion was made without the knowledge of the Iroquois and when the French subsequently challenged them on the point they specifically denied that they were the subjects of any foreign power. In 1748 the Onondaga chief, Cachouintioni, declared that they had ceded their lands to no one, that the land was still theirs, given them by the Great Spirit. He declared that he spoke for all Five Nations in attendance. The Cayuga chief, Tomahae, repeated the same declaration and for proof that the Iroquois were not the subjects of the British King he pointed to their refusal to join the British in their current war with the French. The mere fact that they were in Canada discussing the issue indicated that they were an independent power. Tomahae also declared that he spoke for all the nations of the Confederacy and the forty-eight Iroquois delegates concurred.[88]

Despite the Iroquois rejection of British claims the French officials, in the years after 1713, had to make every effort to undo the harm caused by the concessions thoughtlessly made in the treaty. Cape Bre-

85 *Nouvelle-France: Documents Historiques*, I, 89, Instruction particulière pour M. de Vaudreuil, Versailles, 1 avr. 1755; Theodore Calvin Pease, ed., *Anglo-French Boundary Disputes in the West 1749–1763* (Springfield, IL 1936), xxxiii–xxxiv, 42–7 – Lord Halifax on French encroachments, 15 Aug. 1753; Trudel, *Atlas de la Nouvelle-France / An Atlas of New France*, 139

86 RAPQ 1922–3, pp. 95–6, Observations et réflexions servant de réponses aux propositions de Messieurs les commissaires au sujet des limites a régler pour la Baie d'Hudson [1720]; Max Savelle, 'The Forty-Ninth Degree of North Latitude as an International Boundary, 1719: The Origin of an Idea,' *Canadian Historical Review*, XXXVIII (Sept. 1957), 183–201

87 Frances Gardiner Davenport, *European Treaties Bearing on the History of the United States and Its Dependencies, 1698–1715* (Washington 1934), III, 193–214

88 RAPQ 1921–2, between 108–9, Acte authentique des six nations iroquoises sur leur indépendance (2 nov. 1748)

ton had been retained along with fishing rights on the northeast coast of Newfoundland. The major threat to French interests was in the northern and western interior of the continent. The British over-reached themselves when they insisted that the term 'ceded' Hudson Bay to His Britannic Majesty be replaced by 'restored,' this to make explicit their assertion that they had always had the prior claim. The French readily agreed, then riposted by asserting that, by definition, the British could have restored to them only the territory that they had previously occupied, namely their posts on the shores of the Bay.[89] The French rejected out of hand British claims to all the lands that drained into the Bay, later defined as north and west of a line from Cap Perdrix at $58\frac{1}{2}°$ Lat. on the Labrador coast down through Lake Mistassini to the 49th parallel and westward along it to the Pacific.

The Hudson's Bay Company was brazenly claiming most of present-day Canada despite the fact that, with the exception of Henry Kelsey's voyage to the Saskatchewan River in 1690, no Englishman had seen more than the coastal strip of the Bay.[90] As with the French the Indians were pleased to have the Bay posts there to provide competition for the French and did not see that they could ever constitute a threat to their interests. The Company made only two attempts to establish a post inland before the conquest of Canada – Henley House on the Albany River. The first post, built in 1743, was destroyed by the Indians twelve years later. When re-established in 1759 it was again destroyed in a matter of weeks.[91] Thus the Hudson's Bay Company could by no stretch of the imagination be deemed to have established British sovereignty over the lands it claimed. All it had, at best, was squatter's rights to its posts on the shores of the Bay.[92]

89 RAPQ 1922–3, pp. 95–6, Observations et réflexions servant de réponses aux proposi-tions de Messieurs les commissaires anglais au sujet des limites a régler pour la Baie d'Hudson
90 CSPAWI, 1719–20, no. 360, Memorial of Governors, Hudson's Bay Company, no. 443 (1719), 4 Nov., Whitehall
91 Charles A. Bishop, 'The Henley House Massacres,' *The Beaver* (Summer 1976), 36–41
92 Elaine Allan Mitchell, *Fort Timiskaming and the Fur Trade* (Toronto 1977), 209. Two Canadian governments later disputed the Hudson's Bay Company's claims to Rupert's Land. In 1856 the Honourable Philip Van Koughnet, president of the Executive Council of Canada, declared that 'no charter could give to a body of men control over half a continent' and that he would not rest 'until that Charter was abolished.' Eleven years later, at the first session of the federal parliament of the Dominion of Canada, the Honourable William McDougall, Minister of Public Works, on 4 Dec. 1867, declared in Parliament that the government was not pre-pared to heed the Hudson's Bay Company's demands for a large payment by Canada for the lands in question. The government proposed, he declared 'to claim this country as being part of New France, as having been ceded to the English government in 1760 [*sic*], and as having remained in that position from that time down to the present.' See Alexander Begg, *History of the North-West* (Toronto 1894), I, 330–42.

In Acadia after 1713 the Massachusetts authorities tried to lay claim to the lands of the Abenakis on the grounds that the King of France had ceded them to Great Britain by the Treaty of Utrecht. The Governor of Massachusetts also demanded that the Abenakis proclaim their new British monarch, take an oath of fidelity to him, and allow the English to settle among them on what was now regarded as British territory.[93] These claims the Abenakis vehemently rejected more than once. They declared that no king had ever taken possession of their lands, not by cession, conquest, or purchase. In the presence of French officials they declared that they had never been French subjects and that since no one could cede to another that which had never belonged to him, the French could not have ceded their lands to the English.[94]

Earlier during the war the French had rejected New England protests about the atrocities committed by the Abenakis during their raids on New England settlements, declaring that they could do nothing since the Abenakis were not French subjects.[95] Here was another example of the French 'Janusian' attitude. They still claimed title to the lands of the Abenakis but they did so merely to deny them to the English.[96] To the Abenakis they never would have dared make such a claim, for it would have alienated totally a vital ally who would have given them the same answer as they had given the English. The French had to support the Abenakis to keep the English from occupying territory within three days' march of the St Lawrence, which would have put the neck of New France in a noose. The Abenakis reminded the French that they had supported them in all their wars with the English, hence it was now their turn to come to the aid of their ally.[97] The French had good cause to fear that if they failed to provide the requested military support the Abenakis would be forced to make peace with the English on English terms and, as Governor General Vaudreuil pointed out, they would then assuredly turn their wrath on the French. It would, he stated, be all too easy for them to devastate the

93 AN C11A, vol. 35, f. 113, Bégon au Ministre, Qué., 25 7ᵇʳᵉ 1715; AN F3, Moreau de Saint-Méry, vol. 2, ff. 413–6, Parole de toute la Nation Abenaquise ... au gouverneur de Baston ... 28 juillet 1721
94 *Ibid.*, II, ff. 410–12, Parole des Abenakis au Roy, sur ce que les Anglois depuis la paix d'Utrecht s'emparent de leurs terres; NYCD, X, p. 253, Propositions of the Abenakis of St Francis to Captain Phineas Stevens, Delegate from the Governor of Boston... See also L.F.S. Upton, *Micmacs and Colonists: Indian-White Relations in the Maritimes 1713–1867* (Vancouver 1979), 37.
95 AN C11A, vol. 31, ff. 121–5 (Vaudreuil). Lettre à M. Nicholson du 14 jan. en réponse à la sienne du 11 oct. 1710
96 *Nouvelle-France: Documents Historiques*, I, 89, Instruction Particulière pour M. de Vaudreuil, Versailles, 1ᵉʳ avr. 1755
97 AN C11A, vol. 43, ff. 372–7, Mrs de Vaudreuil et Bégon au Ministre, Qué., 8 8ᵇʳᵉ 1721

SOVEREIGNTY-ASSOCIATION, 1500–1783 497

French settlements along the south shore of the St Lawrence, from Gaspé to above Quebec.[98] By no stretch of the imagination could either the French, or the English, at that time, have pretended to exercise sovereignty over the Abenakis and their land. Both powers wanted something from them; both feared that the other would acquire, if not the support of the Abenakis, then their acquiescence in the attainment of its aims.

A similar situation developed in the west, where the French were determined to prevent the English occupying the lands west of the Appalachian Mountains to the Mississippi. They had no intention of occupying the territory themselves, and even if they had they lacked the means to do it.[99] Nor did they covet the fur trade of that region. The better furs were to be had to the north, where the French garnered the lion's share in competition with the Hudson's Bay Company.[100] To prevent the English flooding over the mountains into the west the French had to enlist the aid of the Indian nations which, all too often, were their own worst enemies. The task for the French was to strive to keep those belligerent nations from constantly warring with one another and to weld them into an alliance, amenable to French direction, against the relentless encroachment of land-hungry speculators and settlers from the English colonies.[101]

From the French viewpoint, despite Clause 15 of the Treaty of Utrecht, the western nations had to be prevented by one means or another from having any dealings with the English colonials. To this end posts were established down the Mississippi Valley, on both sides of Lake Superior, at Lake of the Woods, on the Red and Assiniboine rivers, and far up the Saskatchewan. The latter posts, forming the Mer de l'Ouest district, and those at Lakes Nipigon, La Carpe, and Timiskaming, were intended to reduce the flow of Indians and furs to the

98 AN C11A, vol. 39, ff. 160–2, Vaudreuil au Conseil Marine, 31 oct. 1718
99 AN C11A, vol. 91, ff. 116–23, De La Galissonière au Ministre, Qué., 1 sept. 1748
100 W.J. Eccles, 'The Fur Trade and Eighteenth Century Imperialism,' *The William and Mary Quarterly*, 3rd Series, XL, July 1983, 341–62; W.J. Eccles, 'A Belated Review of Harold Adams Innis, *The Fur Trade in Canada*,' *Canadian Historical Review*, LX (Dec. 1979), 419–41
101 BN, Collection Clairambault, vol. 882, f. 137, La Mothe Cadillac [à M. de Lagny, Missilimackinac 1695]; AN C11A, vol. 24, ff. 3–5, Vaudreuil au Ministre, Qué., 28 avr. 1706; *ibid.*, vol. 39, f. 212, Vaudreuil au Conseil de Marine, 12 8bre 1717; *ibid.*, ff. 149–155, Vaudreuil au Conseil, Qué., 30 oct. 1718; *ibid.*, vol. 71, f. 35, Beauharnois au Ministre, Qué., 30 juin 1739; Archives du Séminaire de Québec (hereafter ASQ), Fonds Verreau, Carton 5, no. 33, Mémoire pour servir d'instruction au Sr le Gardeur de Saint-Pierre ... La Jonquière, Mtl, 27 may 1750; Archives Université de Montréal, Collection Baby (hereafter Baby) Céloron de Blainville à [M. de Lavalterie, commandant, Niagara?] Detroit, le 26 jan. 1752; AN F3, Moreau de Saint-Méry, vol. 14, ff. 36–7, Le Ministre à Duquesne, 16 juin 1752

Hudson's Bay Company posts.[102] Fort Rouillé, near the Toronto portage, was built specifically to stop the Mississaugas from going to the New York post at Oswego.[103] In every instance these posts were established with the sanction of the Indians. In 1736 the Cree and Assiniboine demanded that La Vérendrye establish a post at the foot of Lake Winnipeg, declaring that he had promised them the post to supply their needs.[104]

Dr Toby Morantz, in discussing the relationship between the northern Cree and the Hudson's Bay Company, remarked that the Cree did not regard themselves as dominated by Europeans. They exercised considerable influence over the trading policies of the Company.

Trade rituals, giving of presents, value of goods traded and their quality, respect of the factor toward the Indians, and the expansion of trade were all affected. The Indians had the upper hand for they could always take their furs to the opposition. It was a weapon they knew how to use well to their own advantage.[105]

The western posts of the French, all but the main bases Niagara, Detroit, Michilimackinac, and eventually, Grand Portage, consisted of little more than a three- to four-meter-high log palisade thirty-odd meters long on each side, enclosing four or five clay-chinked log cabins with bark roofs.[106] The 'presents' that the French were constrained to give the Indian nations every year were regarded by the latter as a form of rent for the use of the land where the posts stood and as a fee for the right to travel on the Indians' territory.[107] As early as 1650 Father Ragueneau, SJ, was made embarrassingly aware of this Indian customary law. While fleeing to Quebec from the Iroquois with a party of Hurons he refused to pay the customary Ottawa River toll to the Algonquins of Allumette Island, declaring that the French were now

102 Champagne, *Les La Vérendrye*, 99–104; ANQM, Congés et Ordonnances 1721–30, Charles, marquis de Beauharnois, 9 juillet 1729; Baby, G 1 / 3 Congé de La Barre au Sr D'Argenteuil, 1683; AN F3 Moreau de Saint-Méry, vol. 14, f. 14, Ordonnance de M. de la Jonquière, 27 fév. 1751

103 AN C11A, vol. 93, f. 43, Jonquière et Bigot au Ministre, Qué., 9 8bre 1749

104 Champagne, *Les La Vérendrye*, 191–2

105 Toby Morantz, 'The Fur Trade and the Cree of James Bay,' in Carol M. Judd and Arthur J. Ray, eds, *Old Trails and New Directions: Papers of the Third North American Fur Trade Conference* (Toronto 1980), 54

106 RAPQ 1926–7, p. 289, RP Aulneau au RP Bonin, Fort Saint-Charles, 30 avr. 1736; RAPQ, XLI, 1963, p. 263, Journal de Marin fils; Lawrence J. Burpee, ed., 'Journal of Anthony Hendry,' in *Transactions of the Royal Society of Canada*, (1907), 431–4; Champagne, *Les La Vérendrye*, 152–3

107 Wilbur R. Jacobs, *Dispossessing the American Indian* (New York 1972), 50–7; Wilbur R. Jacobs, *Wilderness Politics and Indian Gifts* (Lincoln, NB 1966); RAPQ, XLI, 1963, Journal de Marin fils, passim.

SOVEREIGNTY-ASSOCIATION, 1500–1783 499

the masters of the land and its people. The Algonquin chief, Le Borgne, promptly had the priest strung up in a tree by his armpits to teach him who was master there.[108]

In the 1680s, when Pierre-Charles le Sueur first travelled to the Sioux country, the Sioux described the territorial limits of their land and stated 'que ce n'estoit pas leur habitude de chasser sur les terres des autres, sans y estre invitez par ceux à qui elles appartenoient.'[109] In 1754 the Sioux complained bitterly to Capitaine Joseph Marin, commandant at La Baie des Puants (Green Bay), that the Saulteux were trying to steal their land. They drew a map and explained that from the mouth of the Wisconsin River to Lac Sangsue belonged to them, it having been granted them by the 'Master of Life.' Three years earlier, on making peace with the Saulteux at Marin's behest, they had allowed them to hunt at L'Aile du Corbeau, and the Saulteux subsequently claimed that the land was, in consequence, now theirs.[110] This pretence the Sioux vehemently denied. After the conquest of New France the British fur traders early learned that the Indians guarded access to their lands jealously. In a memoir on the Indian trade the Montreal merchants stated: 'the Indians are so tenacious of their property, and jealous of other nations that they will not suffer them in passing through their lands to hunt for their support.'[111]

Occasionally the Indians came to resent the presence of the French. Posts were destroyed or had to be abandoned hastily, as was the case with Fort la Reine on the Assiniboine in 1752.[112] During the Fox wars

108 Trigger, *The Children of Aataentsic* II, 785. The source of the account of this incident is Tailhan, ed., *Mémoire sur les mœurs, coustumes et relligion des sauvages de l'Amérique septentrionale*, 95. Perrot mistakenly names RP Allemand as the victim. See p. 245, n. 11. Other examples of toll charges being levied on the Ottawa in the first half of the seventeenth century are mentioned in Gabriel Sagard, *Le grand voyage au pays des Hurons*, George M. Wrong, ed. (Toronto 1939), 257. Sagard also mentioned that the Montagnais levied tolls on their rivers (257). The Huron and Nipissing permitted no one to cross their territory to trade in that early period. See R.G. Thwaites, ed., *The Jesuit Relations and Allied Documents* (Cleveland 1896–1901), VII, 215; VIII, 21, 83; IX, 275; X, 77; XV, 151; XXI, 171, 241. I am indebted to Conrad Heidenreich for the above references.

109 Pierre Margry, *Mémoires et documents pour servir à l'histoire des origines françaises des pays d'outre mer: Découvertes et établissements des Français dans l'ouest et dans le sud de l'Amérique septentrionale* (Paris 1876), VI, 78, Extrait du Mémoire de M. Le Chevalier Beaurien sur la Louisiane. Voyage de le Sueur chez les Sioux

110 RAPQ, XLI, 1963, pp. 280–1, Journal de Marin fils; *ibid.*, 295–8. A M. le Général. Lettre du 1er juin 1754

111 PAC transcripts, Shelburne MSS: MG 23, A4, vol. 12, pp. 138–9, Montreal fur merchants, memorial on the Indian trade, sent by Governor Carleton to the Board of Trade, 20 Sept. 1767. Included with Mar. 1766 dispatches

112 ASQ, fonds Verreau, Boite 5, no. 54. Mémoire ou Extrait du Journal Sommaire du voyage de Jacques Legardeur ... Sr de Saint-Pierre...

the Sioux posts had to be abandoned.[113] After being re-established at the request of the Sioux, they again had to be abandoned owing to the mounting hostility of the tribesmen. In fact, the French had lots of practice with that particular post. In 1700 Pierre-Charles le Sueur had established the first Sioux post at the junction of the Minnesota and Blue Earth rivers; three years later the garrison had to flee for their lives to Mobile.[114] The uprising of the Detroit Hurons and some Saulteux against the French in 1747 indicated all too clearly that their hold over the tribes was tenuous.[115]

Twice a year the fur and supply brigades voyaged to and from Montreal in convoy for security, with an officer of the colonial troops in command. One or two canoes was an invitation to pillage and, possibly, murder. Every voyageur was required by law to take a musket with him for self-defence and have it with him on his return on pain of three months in jail. The organization was that of a military expedition into enemy country and the casualties were not inconsiderable.[116] The French, despite their claims to sovereignty over all the land west of the Appalachians, Iroquoia, and Hudson Bay were, in fact, sovereign only inside their garrisoned forts, and beyond, only within the range of their muskets.

As early as 1704 a gathering of western tribesmen, when challenged by French officers at Lake Erie and asked where they were taking their furs, defiantly replied: 'Cette terre n'est pas a vous, elle est à Nous et nous la quitterons pour aller ou bon nous semblera.'[117] Three years later the Intendant, Jacques Raudot, admitted to the Minister of Marine: 'à légard des Sauvages, nous ne pouvons que les soliciter de ne point aller aux anglois et nous ne pouvons pas les en empecher.'[118] A

113 Ibid., Boite 11, no. 36–1 / 2. Relation des aventures de M. de Boucherville a son retour des Scioux
114 Jay Higginbotham, Old Mobile: Fort Louis de la Louisiane 1702–1711 (Mobile, AL 1977), 111
115 W.J. Eccles, The Canadian Frontier 1534–1760 (Albuquerque, NM 1969), 151–4
116 A.S. Morton, A History of the Canadian West to 1870–71 (London 1939), 252–3; Adolph B. Benson, ed., The America of 1750: Peter Kalm's Travels in North America (New York 1966), II, 561: AN C11A, vol. 35, Ramezay et Bégon au Ministre, Qué., 13 7bre 1715; ANQM, Pièces judiciares, 11 mars 1720; AN C11A, vol. 43, f. 324, Conseil. M. le Marqs de Vaudreuil, 6 8bre 1721; Champagne, Les la Vérendrye 157, n10; Huntingdon Library, Loudoun Collection, Vaudreuil à Beauharnois, Nouvelle Orléans, 9 nov. 1745; AN C11A, vol. 93, ff. 143–4, Galissonière au Ministre, le 26 juin 1759; ASQ, Fonds Verreau, Boite 5, no. 26, Congé. De La Jonquière à Le Gardeau de Saint-Pierre, Qué. 17 avr. 1750. Vu par Bigot; Grenier, Papiers Contrecœur, 193: ANQM, Greffe J. David, no. 173, 11 aoust 1720; ibid., no. 215, 16 sept. 1720; ASQ Fonds Verreau, Boite 8, no. 96, Ordonnance de Beauharnois, Mtl, le 8 juin 1743; Baby G 1 / 22 Ordonnance de Beauharnois, 31 may 1738
117 Quoted in E.E. Rich, The History of the Hudson's Bay Company 1670–1870 (London 1958), I, 482
118 AN C11A, vol. 26, ff. 221v–222r, Raudot au Ministre, Qué., 12 nov. 1707

half century later Governor General François-Pierre de Rigaud de Vaudreuil sought to have an Onondaga of his choosing appointed a chief and member of the Council at the Iroquois mission post, La Présentation. The Iroquois were outraged at this attempted interference in their affairs. They informed Vaudreuil that although it was true that they had taken an oath of fidelity to the French, they were governed by a council made up of twelve village chiefs, six war chiefs, and twelve council women. Their spokesman added that when they had been regenerated in the same baptismal water as had christened the Governor General they had not renounced their freedom or the rights they held from the Master of Life. If one wished to deprive them of those rights then they would regard themselves as no longer bound by their oath; their agreement was a reciprocal one. 'C'est a nous seuls a nous donner nos chefs,' their spokesman declared. He then demanded why Vaudreuil sought to impose on them the Onondaga who was not even a Christian: 'Mon pére explique nous cette parole. Elle nous a troublé l'esprit,' the spokesman bluntly requested. Vaudreuil was obliged to back down, with the face-saving statement that he thought it would be a good thing were his Onondaga nominee to be made a member of their Council.[119]

One area that France claimed for purely strategic reasons was Lake Champlain, but this had to be done without offending the Mohawks, who claimed that much of the area belonged to them. The lake and the Richelieu River flowing out of it to the St Lawrence had long been the main invasion route into Canada from New York. In 1708 the Minister of Marine instructed the Governor General and the Intendant that the English could not be allowed to establish themselves near the lake.[120] In 1730, when Governor General Beauharnois learned that the Lieutenant Governor of New York intended to place settlers on Wood Creek, which flowed into Lake Champlain from the south, he replied by having Fort Saint-Frédéric built at the narrows of the lake near its southern end.[121] Two years later the plans to replace the wooden fort with a masonry structure were approved and the Quebec officials were instructed to use force if necessary to prevent the English settling in the area.[122]

In 1739 the Mohawks obtained the erroneous information that the

119 RAPQ 1939–40, p. 260.' Journal de l'Expédition d'Amérique commencé en l'Année 1756, du 26 avr. 1757
120 RAPQ, 1939–40, 413. Mémoire du Roi à MM de Vaudreuil et Raudot, Versailles, 6 juin 1708
121 Francess G. Halpenny, ed., *Dictionary of Canadian Biography*, III (Toronto 1974), Beauharnois de La Boische, p. 45; AN F3, Moreau de Saint-Méry, vol. 12, f. 40, Mémoire du Roy aux Srs Beauharnois et Hocquart, Versailles, 22 avr. 1732
122 *Ibid.*, f. 140, Mémoire du Roy aux Srs Beauharnois et Hocquart, Versailles, 12 may 1732

French intended to occupy Wood Creek. They reported this to the Albany authorities and declared that all the land around the lake as far north as Ochjargo belonged to them.[123] This was a dubious claim; they hunted in the area but had no villages there. The Mohicans had once occupied the region and in 1730s the western Abenakis established a village at Missisquoi Bay.[124] Since before Champlain's day no tribe had been able to dominate the region.[125] The Mohawks sent a delegation to discuss the issue with the Governor General of New France. He informed them that the King of France claimed title to all the lands whose waters drained into the lake as far south as the portage to Lac Saint-Sacrement. He also stated that he would not allow the English to settle anywhere on those lands. Despite the fact that some sections on both sides of the lake had been conceded as seigneuries, but not settled, he declared that the French Crown's rights to the land from Crown Point to the head of the lake at the carrying place would be given as a deed of gift to the Mohawks and Abenakis to 'make use of it for a hunting Place for them and their Posterity...' He also assured them that no French would be allowed to settle there.[126]

In the west, at the conclusion of the War of the Austrian Succession, a war that changed nothing, settled nothing, and had to be refought, the French, English and Iroquois all claimed title to the entire Ohio Valley. The Iroquois claimed it by right of conquest;[127] the English of Virginia by virtue of their colonial charter and because they regarded the Iroquois as subjects of the British Crown;[128] and the French by virtue of La Salle's pretended prior discovery.[129] The French sought to deny the region to the English, not because they had any use for the land then or in the foreseeable future, but because the English coveted it and were they once to occupy the valley their potential military power would increase immeasureably and the water route from Canada to

123 Wraxall, *New York Indian Records*, 212–13, Albany, 7 June 1739; *ibid.*, 11 July 1732
124 Thomas Charland, OP, 'Un village d'Abenaquis sur la rivière Missisquoi' in *Revue d'Histoire de l'Amérique Française*, xv (Dec. 1961), 319–32
125 Biggar, *The Works of Samuel de Champlain*, II, 90–1. Champlain remarked of the lake in 1609: 'Ces lieux ne sont habitez d'aucuns sauuvages [*sic*], bien qu'ils soient plaisans, pour le subiect de leurs guerres, & se retirent des riuieres le plus qu'ils peuuent au profont des terres, afin de n'estre si tost surprins.'
126 Wraxall, *New York Indian Records*, 215, Albany, 26 Oct. 1739
127 *Nouvelle-France: Documents Historiques*, I, 89, Instruction Particulière pour M. de Vaudreuil, Versailles, 1ᵉʳ avr. 1755; Grenier, *Papiers Contrecœur*, 53–7, Conseil tenu par les Tsonnontouans venus de la Belle Rivière, du 2ᵉ 7ᵇʳᵉ 1753
128 Guy Frégault, *La guerre de la conquête* (Montreal and Paris 1955), 114
129 ASQ, Fonds Verreau, Boite 1, no. 11, Duquesne à Contrecœur, Mtl, 14 avr. 1753; Grenier, *Papiers Contrecœur*, 96, Duquesne à Contrecœur, Mtl, 30 jan. 1754; *ibid.*, 98–9, Duquesne à St Pierre, Mtl, 30 jan. 1754; *Nouvelle-France: Documents Historiques*, 89, Instruction Particulière pour M. de Vaudreuil, Versailles, 1ᵉʳ avr. 1755

SOVEREIGNTY-ASSOCIATION, 1500–1783 503

Louisiana then could be severed too easily.[130] Captain Pierre-Joseph de Céloron de Blainville was dispatched with 213 men in 1749 by Governor General Roland-Michel Barrin, comte de La Galissonière, to map the route from Lake Erie down the Ohio, to claim the region for France, and to drive out any English traders encountered there.[131]

In 1753 a French military expedition began clearing a route from Lake Erie to the forks of the Ohio. A party of Virginians that had begun to build a fort was driven off and Fort Duquesne was hastily constructed.[132] When the Iroquois protested they were bluntly told to accept the French presence, which was there for their protection against English encroachment, or be destroyed.[133] The French thus seized control of the region by force of arms, just as had the Iroquois three-quarters of a century earlier. During the ensuing hostilities that endured from 1754 to 1760 the Indian nations of the region, Shawnee, Delaware, Miami, Huron, Illinois, even many of the Six Nations Iroquois, initially fought with the French.[134] They did so because the French appeared to be the winning side, but also because they had been outraged over the years at the treatment they had received from American traders who had used rum to befuddle, cheat, and debauch them.[135] Worse still, they had been defrauded of vast tracts of land by Pennsylvania and New York.[136]

Once engaged in the war they fought as independent, sovereign powers, as allies of the French but in no way subservient to them; rather they regarded the French as their allies in a war being fought to protect

130 AN C11A, vol. 91, ff. 116–23, Galissonière au Ministre, Qué., 1 sept. 1748; Pierre Margry, *Mémoires et documents*, VI, 727–8, Jonquière au Ministre, Qué., 20 sept. 1749

131 George F.G. Stanley, *New France: The Last Phase 1744–1760* (Toronto 1968), 37–41; *Collections of the State Historical Society of Wisconsin*, XVIII, 57, Céloron de Blainville's Journal, 9 Nov. 1749

132 Lawrence Henry Gipson, *The British Empire before the American Revolution: Zones of International Friction. North America South of the Great Lakes Region 1748–1754* (New York 1939), IV, 302–10

133 Grenier, *Papiers Contrecœur*, 116, Paroles de Contrecœur aux Sauvages, 16 avr. 1754

134 War parties of Onondaga, Cayuga, and Seneca are specifically mentioned as having served with the Canadians in raids on Anglo-American settlements. See *Minutes of the Provincial Council of Pennsylvania*, VIII, 182, 185; Carl Van Doren and Julian P. Boyd, eds, *Indian Treaties Printed by Benjamin Franklin* (Philadelphia 1938), 220; AN C11A, vol. 101, f. 265, Conférence. 5 Nations. Mtl, 21 déc. 1756; RAPQ 1923–4, p. 250, Journal de l'expédition d'Amérique commencée en l'année 1756. 8 fev. 1757. Bougainville

135 Wraxall, *New York Indian Records, passim*; Charles Thomson, *An Enquiry into the Causes of the Alienation of the Delaware and Shawanese Indians from the British Interest*, 16–57

136 Thomson, *Enquiry*, 16–57

their interests. They depended on the French for supplies and usually, but by no means always, accepted French tactical direction of the campaigns. They fought when and how they saw fit, greatly to the consternation at times of the French high command.[137] The British generals, throughout the war, demanded that it be fought according to eighteenth-century European rules and held the French responsible for the atrocities committed by their Indian allies.[138] They could not conceive that since the war was being fought for the Indians' lands, and much of it on their land, then Indian concepts of warfare, not European, would obtain.

The independence of these sovereign nations was made startlingly clear in 1758 when the government of Pennsylvania offered to restore to the Shawnees and Delawares the lands that had been taken from them by fraudulent means, in return for their ending hostilities. The initial stages of the resultant Easton Treaty were negotiated by Frederick Post with the Indians encamped across the Ohio River from Fort Duquesne. The officers of the French garrison who attended the meeting were not allowed to intervene, or even to speak. They had to watch in angry, frustrated silence as their erstwhile allies agreed to a separate peace and to withdraw from the war. At the conclusion of the negotiations a chief naïvely remarked to Post, 'Now Brother, we love you, but can't help wondering why the *English* and the *French* don't make it up with one another, and tell one another not to fight on our land.'[139]

In September 1760 the hopelessly outnumbered French forces, following on the defeat at Quebec the preceding year, were forced to surrender to the armies of Major-General Jeffery Amherst. Governor General Vaudreuil drafted the terms of capitulation that he was pre-

137 Their attack on the surrendered garrison at Fort William Henry in 1757 is a case in point. See also the plaintive statement of Capitaine de Contrecœur after the crushing defeat of Major-General Edward Braddock's army near Fort Duquesne in 1755: 'Tous les sauvages du Détroit et de Michilimackinac sont partis le lendemain de l'action, sans que j'aye pu les arrester.' See AN F3, Moreau de Saint-Méry, vol. 14, f. 120. Extrait. Contrecœur à M. de Vaudreuil, Fort Duquesne, 14 juin 1755. In a similar vein see AN C11A, vol. 101, ff. 117–19v, Vaudreuil au Ministre, Mtl, 13 8bre 1756; AN F3, Moreau de Saint-Méry, vol. 15, ff. 75–9, Vaudreuil au Ministre, Mtl, 15 sept. 1757

138 The British, in contrast to the French, throughout the war were able to secure the services of only some 50 Stockbridge Indians, whose role is barely mentioned in the massive documentation of this war. The British thus were able to adopt a 'holier than thou' attitude toward the French. See Stanley McCrory Pargellis, *Lord Loudoun in North America* (New Haven 1933), 301; John Clarence Webster, ed., *Journal of William Amherst in America, 1758–1760* (Toronto 1931), 68; Henri-Raymond Casgrain, ed., *Collection des manuscrits du Maréchal de Lévis*, x, 14, Bernier à Lévis, Qué., 10 oct. 1759; *ibid.*, 18–19, Bernier à Lévis, 20 oct. 1759

139 Thomson, *An Enquiry into the Causes of the Alienation*, 138–46, 163–6

SOVEREIGNTY-ASSOCIATION, 1500–1783 505

pared to accept. Amherst agreed to most of them, rejected some, and qualified others. One clause that he accepted with an inconsequential amendment was Article 40, which stated:

The Savages or Indian allies of his most Christian Majesty, shall be maintained in the lands they inhabit; if they chuse to remain there: they shall not be molested on any pretence whatsoever, for having carried arms, and served his most Christian Majesty; they shall have, as well as the French, liberty of religion, and shall keep their missionaries. The actual Vicars General, and the Bishop, when the Episcopal see shall be filled, shall have leave to send them new Missionaries when they shall judge it necessary.

Amherst minuted the clause with the comment: 'Granted except the last article, which has already been refused'.[140]

The part of the article that Amherst did accept is highly significant. It was not revoked in the Treaty of Paris. In Article 4 of that treaty, by virtue of which France ceded to Great Britain 'Canada with all its dependencies,' no mention was made of the Indian nations.[141] Article 40 of the Capitulation of Montreal, not having been rescinded, therefore remained binding on Great Britain and also on whatever government subsequently acceded to the sovereignty then exercised by Britain such as, for example, the Dominion of Canada, or as surrogate any of its provincial governments. Article 40 tacitly acknowledged that the Indians retained title to their lands; therefore any attempt to dispossess them or to dispose of their lands without their prior consent would constitute 'molestation' and be in breach of the article in question.

In 1763 the British blandly assumed that the Treaty of Paris had confirmed their old claims to sovereignty over the territory west of the Allegheny Mountains to the Mississippi. They also assumed that the territories north and west of the St Lawrence and Great Lakes, as well as the lands between the St Lawrence and New England and New York, had been dependencies of Canada, hence they had acquired sovereignty over them. They based these claims on the presumption that France had held title to the lands in question, despite the fact that prior to 1763 they had rejected all such assertions. In fact, the French had never been able to exercise sovereignty in those territories. When, in 1715, the Abenakis had denied that they had ever been French subjects the Canadian officials had not disputed the assertion; they had thereby tacitly admitted the truth of the Abenakis' claim.[142]

140 Adam Shortt and Arthur G. Doughty, eds, *Documents Relating to the Constitutional History of Canada 1759–1791* (Ottawa 1918), I, 20, 33
141 *Ibid.*, 99–101, 115–17
142 AN F3, Moreau de Saint-Méry, vol. 2, ff. 413–16, Parole de toute la Nation Abenaquise et de toutes les autres nations sauvages ses alliés au gouverneur de Baston...

Similarly, in 1763 the British admitted that the Indians residing in the newly created Province of Quebec were not their subjects. In Article 60 of the Royal Instructions of Governor Murray, dated 7 December 1763, it was stated: 'And whereas Our Province of Quebec is in part inhabited and possessed by several Nations and Tribes of Indians, with whom it is both necessary and expedient to cultivate and maintain a strict Friendship and good Correspondence, so that they may be induced by Degrees, not only to be good neighbours to Our Subjects, but likewise themselves to become good Subjects to us.'[143]

Two things stand out in that policy statement: first, since it is hoped that eventually the Indian nations will be pleased to become the subjects of His Britannic Majesty, then clearly they were not, in 1763, considered to be his subjects; and since they were not considered to be the subjects of any other foreign power, then they were considered to have been independent, sovereign nations; second, this is confirmed by the phrase 'inhabited and *possessed*,' [emphasis added] for if they are considered to have 'possessed' the land, then it has to be acknowledged that, under the circumstances, they held title to it.

The lands lying between the north side of the lower St Lawrence River and the territory claimed by the Hudson's Bay Company were also deemed to have been ceded to Great Britain by France in 1763. Yet when, in 1766, a dispute arose over exploitation of the resources at the old King's Domain of the French regime, Governor James Murray informed the Lords of Trade:

The lands of the King's Domain were never ceded nor purchased by the French King, nor by his Britannic Majesty; but by compact with the savages inhabiting the said lands, the particular Posts or Spots of ground, whereon the Kings buildings are erected and now stand, were ceded to the French King, for the purpose of erecting storehouses & other conveniences for the Factors, Commis or servants employed to carry on the trade; and the savages residing within the limits of the Domain, & who resort to the said Posts of His Majesty at certain seasons of the year, were adopted as Domicile Indians under the sole and immediate protection of the King, & so remained till the reduction of the Province, & a Missionary was sent to reside constantly among them. The lands of the Domain therefore, are to all intents & purposes reserved, as hunting grounds to the savages, of which they are ever jealous, on the least appearance of an encroachment amongst themselves.[144]

143 Shortt and Doughty, *Documents Relating to the Constitutional History of Canada*, I, 199. Instructions to Governor Murray, St James's, 7 Dec. 1763

144 As cited in Brian Slattery, 'The Land Rights of Indigenous Canadian Peoples, as Affected by the Crown's Acquisition of Their Territories' (D.Phil. thesis, Oxford University 1979), 224. The Domaine du Roy, or Traitte de Tadoussac, encompassed the territory from a point opposite the eastern end of Ile-aux-Coudres, downstream to 2 leagues (5 miles) below Sept Iles, and inland stretching within an

SOVEREIGNTY-ASSOCIATION, 1500–1783 507

Exactly the same could have been said of the French posts in the northwest, although in both instances the Indians likely would have quarrelled with the notion that they had 'ceded' the 'spots of land' upon which the trading posts stood. In their view they had merely granted the French those spots of land during their pleasure and they expected compensation, 'presents', virtually rent, in return. In 1761 General Jeffery Amherst, with his customary ignorance and arrogance, ordered the granting of presents to cease. The Indians were, he stated, not to be bribed, but punished when they failed to submit. The Indians were outraged. The old understanding that they had had with the French had been unaccountably broken.[145]

They rejected totally all British claims to sovereignty over their lands. The attitude and intentions of the Anglo-Americans, despite anything the royal officials might declare, was all too clear.[146] The response of the Great Lakes Indians was the so-called 'uprising' of Pontiac. In fact it was not an uprising since, by definition, such an act has to be against duly constituted authority, and this the British had not then established. It was rather a pre-emptive strike by the Indians to defend their lands from invasion and occupation by the Anglo-Americans. British posts were attacked and several captured. American frontier settlements were once again ravaged by heavy casualties, and as in the preceding war, the American provincial assemblies sought to avoid voting money and supplies or raising troops for defence. Once again it was British regulars who had to do the fighting to defend those who were actually responsible for the hostilities.[147]

The reaction to the news of the Indian assults by the British commander-in-chief, Amherst, was uncomprehending, savage, and ruthless. He instructed his subordinate commanders that the Indians were to be treated 'as the vilest race of beings that ever infested the earth, and whose riddance from it must be deemed a meritorious act, for the good of Mankind. You will therefore take no prisoners, but put to death all that fall into your hands.' He also instructed his field commander, Colonel Henri Bouquet: 'Could it not be contrived to send the small pox among the disaffected tribes?' Bouquet replied that he would

---

east-west line from the western point at Ile-aux-Coudres to the height of land, and on the downstream side, from Cap-aux-Cormorans beyond Lake Mistassini to Hudson Bay. Included were the posts at Tadoussac, Chicoutimi, Lac Saint-Jean, Nekoubau, Mistassini, Papinachoix, Naskapie, Rivière Moisy, Sept Iles, and Malbaie. AN F3, Moreau de Saint-Méry, vol. 12, f. 147, Ordonnance de M. Hocquart qui fixe l'étendue du Domaine du Roi appelé la Traite de Tadoussac, 23 mai 1733

145 Howard H. Peckham, *Pontiac and the Indian Uprising* (Chicago 1961), 71–3; James Sullivan *et al.*, eds, *The Papers of Sir William Johnson* (Albany 1921–65), III, 245

146 Peckham, *Pontiac*, 282, 285

147 Jack M. Sosin, *Whitehall and the Wilderness* (Lincoln, NB, 1961), 66–76

make the attempt.[148] Whether or not he actually did is not known.[149] However, the commanding officer of Fort Pitt, Captain Simeon Ecuyer, like Bouquet a Swiss mercenary, replied to a Delaware demand that he surrender the fort with a present of two blankets and a handkerchief from the fort's smallpox ward. An epidemic raged through the villages of the Delawares, Shawnees, and Mingoes. Although there is a possibility that it began before Bouquet received his orders, the incident at Fort Pitt could only have extended and intensified the spread of that dread disease, to which the Indians had no resistance.[150]

Unable to support a long-drawn-out campaign without external logistic aid, such as they had previously received from the French, the Indians were forced to submit.[151] Now obliged to allow the British to reoccupy the old French posts, they still maintained that the French had neither conquered them nor purchased a foot of their land, hence the French could not have ceded to anyone what had never belonged to them.[152]

The British government, by the terms of the Royal Proclamation of October 1763, strove, for expediency's sake, to stop the usurpation of Indian lands by the American colonists. The Proclamation stated, unequivocally, that Indian lands could be ceded only to the Crown and not acquired by private purchase. Persons who had, by one means or another, acquired such lands were ordered to relinquish and depart from them forthwith.[153] Despite this order, land speculators were very active in London and the colonial capitals, striving by all means, licit and otherwise, to obtain title to some 2,400,000 acres in the Ohio Valley, ceded for a pittance by the Six Nations at Fort Stanwix in October 1768 – a cession that was later bitterly protested by the Senecas, Shawnees, and Delawares.[154] Companies such as the Mississippi Company, the Walpole Company, and the Illinois Company employed every device available to gain their ends, eventually challenging the Crown's right to prevent them dealing directly with the Indian nations.[155] Meanwhile, American squatters continued to flood in their tens of thousands onto the Indians' lands. Again the tribes began to

148 Peckham, *Pontiac*, 226–7
149 See Bernard Knollenberg, 'General Amherst and Germ Warfare,' *The Mississippi Valley Historical Review*, XLI (1954–5), 489–94.
150 Peckham, *Pontiac*, 170. The bacteria spores in the cloth would be released into the air and inhaled by whoever handled the material. I am indebted to Dr H. Velland of the Toronto General Hospital for information on this point.
151 Sosin, *Whitehall and the Wilderness*, 71–2
152 Peckham, *Pontiac*, 282, 285
153 Shortt and Doughty, *Documents*, Part I, 166–7, by the King. A Proclamation, 7 Oct. 1763; *ibid.*, 200, Instructions to Governor Murray, Article 60, 7 Dec. 1763
154 Sosin, *Whitehall and the Wilderness*, 186, 193
155 *Ibid.*, 227–32

SOVEREIGNTY-ASSOCIATION, 1500–1783 509

prepare for war.[156] South of the Great Lakes the royal proclamation proved to be an exercise in futility.

With the advent of the American Revolution the British policy of striving to defend the Indians' right to their lands, *pro tempore*, went by the board. Ironically, one cause of the Revolution was this attempt to thwart such avid land speculators as George Washington, his kinsmen the Lees, Benjamin Franklin, Samuel Wharton, Phineas Lyman, and others later prominent in the revolutionary cause.[157]

In 1783, despite outraged but belated protests from the French foreign minister, Charles Gravier, comte de Vergennes, the Americans negotiated, behind the backs of their French allies and in contravention of their treaty, a separate peace with Great Britain whereby they were granted not only their independence but also the dubious, to say the least, British claim to the vast area between the Appalachian Mountains and the Mississippi.[158] The Indian nations in that vast area were thereby abandoned to certain despoliation by the Americans.

In May 1783 Brigadier Allan Maclean at Niagara reported to General Haldimand that the Indians were very uneasy over 'certain pretended boundaries.' He stated that they considered themselves a free people subject to no power upon earth. Having served the King of England faithfully as allies, not as his subjects, during the war with the Americans they declared that he had no right whatsoever to grant their lands or their rights to the enemy. Maclean went on:

They added that many years ago their ancestors had granted permission to the French King to build trading houses, or small forts on the water communications between Canada and the western Indians in the heart of their country for the convenience of trade only, without granting one inch of land but what these forts stood upon, and that at the end of the last war they granted leave to Sir William Johnson to hold these forts for their ally the King of England, but that it was impossible from that circumstance to imagine that the King of England should pretend to grant to the Americans all the whole country of the Indians lying between the Lakes and the fixed boundaries as settled in 1768.

Maclean added, 'I do from my soul pity these people.'[159] The Indian nations were then driven off their lands by the Americans and brought close to annihilation. By 1840 the Indians east of the Mississippi, with

156 *Ibid.*, 106–23, 135–41, 154–7, 193, 205, 225
157 *Ibid.*, 138–9, 252
158 Marcel Trudel, *Louis XVI, le congrès américain et le Canada 1774–1789* (Quebec 1949), 130–1, 210–19
159 British Museum [now British Library] Additional Mss, 21,763m, ff. 118–19v. (calendared in PAC Report 1886, B 103, Haldimand Collection, I, 32–3, Brigadier General Allan Maclean, Niagara, to General Frederick Haldimand, Que., 18 May 1788)

the exception of a few small enclaves, 'had either been removed to the trans-Mississippi or had died in the process of moving.'[160]

To the north, on what remained of British North America, the royal proclamation of 1763 was honoured for the time being since there was no immediate rush of immigrants to seize the hunting lands of the northern Indians and metis. Then in the nineteenth century things changed. External forces made their lands economically desirable. The Indian and metis hunting societies, therefore, had to go, to make way for staid farmers, ranchers, the exploiters of timber and mineral resources who would play a 'proper' role in the eastern market economy. Force was not used until late in the nineteenth century, but eventually the result was the same in Canada as it was south of the border. Destruction of the plains Indians' main food supply and economic resource, the buffalo,[161] an appalling flood of alcohol,[162] epidemics that decimated the Indian population some seven times in less than 150 years,[163] and finally, sordid political and bureaucratic bungling and chicanery, brought them low.[164]

Such were the means whereby sovereignty and title to the lands of the Indians were eventually acquired by the Crown in Canada. They certainly were not acquired by virtue of France having ceded a non-existent title to the British Crown in 1763.

160 Clyde A. Milner, ii, 'Indulgent Friends and Important Allies: Political Process on the Cis-Mississippi Frontier and its Aftermath,' in Howard Lamar and Leonard Thompson eds, *The Frontier in History: North America and Southern Africa Compared* (New Haven and London 1981), 144

161 Between 1830 and 1888 the great herds were reduced from some 75,000,000 to a few hundred. See Frank Gilbert Roe, *The North American Buffalo* (2nd ed., Toronto 1970), 416–88.

162 E.E. Rich, *The Fur Trade and the Northwest to 1857* (Toronto 1967), 141, 164, 194

163 René Fumoleau, omi, *As Long as This Land Shall Last* (Toronto 1975), Appendix 1

164 *Ibid., passim*; D.N. Sprague, 'Government Lawlessness in the Administration of Manitoba Land Claims, 1870–1887,' *Manitoba Law Journal*, x, (1980), 415–41; D.N. Sprague, 'The Manitoba Land Question, 1870–1882,' *Journal of Canadian Studies / Revue d'études canadiennes*, xv (Autumn 1980), 74–84; Peter A. Cumming and Neil H. Mickenberg, eds, *Native Rights in Canada* (2nd ed., Toronto 1971)

10

Freitas Versus Grotius

C.H. Alexandrowicz

I

IN 1627, nearly nineteen years after the anonymous publication of his *Mare Liberum*, Hugo Grotius mentioned in one of his letters a work written by Franciscus Seraphin de Freitas in response to his treatise.[2] Freitas was a professor at the University of Valadolid, and the significant title of his work was *De Justo Imperio Lusitanorum Asiatico*. Grotius referred to it in the following words: 'Scriptum est satis diligens et vir dignus cui rescribatur.' But though he considered Freitas 'a man worthy of reply' and though he was urged to answer him he never did so. Instead he suggested in his letter that 'some one of our judges should be sought out and the duty delegated to him', a remark full of irony and perhaps bitterness, written after his trial and imprisonment by his own compatriots whose case he had so ably defended.[3]

Mare Liberum was not an academic treatise in the strict sense of the word but was one of the chapters of *De Jure Praedae* which Grotius produced, probably at the request of the Dutch East India Company and which was in the nature of a lawyer's plea relating to a particular case in which the Company was involved. This case arose out of the seizure of a Portuguese vessel in the Straits of Malacca by a Dutch Admiral in the employment of the Company. Its capture was questioned by some members of the Company who opposed the adjudication of the prize by the Dutch Admiralty Court.[4] In defending the case of the Company Grotius dealt in Chapter XII with the general aspects of the Portuguese–Dutch conflict in the Indian Ocean, and the freedom of the high seas as its central problem.

While Grotius pleaded the case of the Dutch East India Company Freitas was chosen to state a case for the King of Spain who was at that time also the sovereign of Portugal.[5] He fulfilled his task with scholarly care and precision, countering Grotius's reasoning chapter by chapter and pointing out numerous mistakes. Grotius himself admitted in another letter[6] that 'my work about the freedom of the sea was conceived in the best patriotic spirit but it was written "aetate juvenili"'. When it was

---

[2] Hugonis Grotii *Epistolae* (Amsterdami, 1687), Epistola No. 144, p. 796. Freitas's treatise was published in 1625.

[3] Grotius escaped in 1621 from Holland to France and later became Swedish Ambassador in Paris; see Knight, *The Life and Works of Hugo Grotius*.

[4] Knight, op. cit., p. 81.   [5] Amzalak, *Trois Precurseurs Portugais*, pp. 41–94.

[6] See *Recueil de Burman* as quoted by Guichon de Grandpont in his translation of Freitas's *De Justo Imperio Lusitanorum Asiatico* (Preface).

published he was only twenty-five years old. Indeed, in comparing *Mare Liberum* with *De Justo Imperio Lusitanorum Asiatico* the reader is struck by Freitas's perfect legal erudition and scholastic skill. But while Freitas was an expert in Roman and Canon law and had a profound grasp of the Commentators, Grotius appeared in spite of his young age as a legal reformer of great flexibility and foresight. This is perhaps the reason why Freitas's work, overshadowed by Grotius's spectacular success, has been so utterly forgotten. However, if the history of the classics of the law of nations of the seventeenth century is to be complete, Freitas deserves a proper place among all the other opponents of *Mare Liberum*, particularly Selden and Welwood with whose arguments Grotius dealt in due course.

In considering Freitas's work[1] it is important to remember that it refers to problems arising out of actual State practice in south Asia and the Indian Ocean in the sixteenth and seventeenth centuries. The same is true of *Mare Liberum* which in spite of the generality of its propositions concentrates on the Portuguese–Dutch conflict in the above region and the rôle played in it by the local rulers. Before engaging in a discussion of the legal aspect of this conflict its historical background deserves to be briefly recalled. Vasco da Gama's arrival on the west coast of India marked the opening of a new direct sea route from Europe to Asia, and had in effect a threefold significance—economic, political and religious. It undermined the trade monopoly established by Moorish (Arab) traders, and at the same time attacked the *hinterland* of Islam which drew vital resources from south Asia for carrying out its holy war against Christian Europe. The Moorish trading and navigating community in the East was intimately linked with Venice and with certain Asian ports, particularly the harbour of Calicut on the west coast of India, and it relied on the support of Turkey and Egypt, the latter being the area of transloading of goods shipped from India to European destinations. Spain and Portugal were at that period united under the Spanish Crown and enjoyed in all respects the support of Papal Rome not excluding the conferment on them of a legal title to overseas expansion. The three East India Companies (Dutch, English and French) only gradually came into the picture; the first to appear on the Asian scene in the seventeenth century were the Dutch who were out to break the back of the *Imperium Lusitanorum Asiaticum* irrespective of any ideological conflict. Though these companies were separate legal entities they were endowed by their sovereigns with authority to exercise rights of external sovereignty to the effect that their transactions with other independent powers created rights and duties in the law of nations.[2]

[1] *De Justo Imperio Lusitanorum Asiatico* (1625), and translation into French by Guichon de Grandpont (1882).
[2] See Dr. Kemal, 'The Evolution of British Sovereignty in India', *Indian Year Book of*

II

The first question with which the historian of the law of nations is confronted in assessing the situation in south Asia and in the Indian Ocean from the legal point of view is this: Did the struggle in this region start in a legal vacuum or was it determined by the existence of certain principles which were observed by all the participants in the local game of power politics in accordance with their various express or implied legal traditions? What was the status of the local rulers with whom the European powers exchanged envoys, concluded treaties and waged wars? In the absence of a precise local system of inter-State law, what was the actual contribution of regional State practice to the adaptation of legal notions concerning sovereignty, *bellum justum*, treaty making and maritime custom to new conditions? Grotius was intimately concerned with these questions and he gave in his *Mare Liberum* a tentative answer to each of them. These answers were no doubt based on a thorough study of the relevant factual material which he must have carried out in the archives of the 'United Company' in the Netherlands, and they were formulated in a manner reflecting the typical Grotian blend of the naturalist and positivist conceptions of law.

In Chapter II of *Mare Liberum*[1] Grotius refers to those parts of the East Indies in which the Dutch-Portuguese conflict developed most acutely, i.e. Ceylon, Java and the Moluccas (which is not an exhaustive enumeration), and says that these countries 'always have had their own Kings (*suos reges*), their own government (*suam republicam*), their own laws (*suas leges*) and their own legal systems (*sua jura*). The inhabitants allow the Portuguese to trade with them, just as they concede to other nations the same privilege. Therefore, inasmuch as the Portuguese pay tolls and obtain leave to trade from the Rulers there (jus mercandi a principibus exorant), they thereby give sufficient proof that they do not go there as sovereigns but as foreigners. Indeed they only reside there on sufferance (*precario*).' From this Grotius draws the conclusion that 'the Portuguese have no title at all to sovereignty' (*titulus dominii*). It is quite obvious that he considered the local Asian rulers as sovereigns capable of entering into diplomatic and treaty relations with European powers and in fact a survey of treaties concluded between them and the Portuguese in the sixteenth and seventeenth centuries supplies sufficient proof of actual State practice in this respect.[2] It should be remembered that the Portuguese, unlike the Dutch, English and French, had no real ambition of establishing themselves as a

---

International Affairs (1957); Hanataux and Martineau, *Histoire des Colonies Françaises*, vol. 5, p. 9; van der Burg and Groot, *The Dutch in Malabar; Selection from the Records of the Madras Government, Dutch Records* (1911).

[1] *The Freedom of the Sea* (transl. by Ralph van Daman Magoffin, ed. by J. B. Scott).

[2] Biker, *Collection of Treaties* (Colleccao de Tratados) (Lisboa, 1881).

land power in Asia. Their policy first aimed at controlling the sea routes and eliminating Moorish navigation from them, establishing coastal strong-holds and trading stations, and securing a monopoly of trade. Later they acquired certain territories under their own sovereignty such as, for instance, Goa and Malacca. Grotius was definitely aware of these exceptions as he added to the above-mentioned text in Chapter II the following words: 'Non enim de Malacca, non de Goa loquimur, coloniis Lusitanorum', but he crossed the words out from the original text which is only too charac-teristic of a writer engaged in writing a practical advocate's plea.[1] Grotius supports his opening remarks in Chapter II by the concluding text of Chapter IV in which he excludes the possibility of considering the terri-tories of the East India Rulers as *res nullius* and this opinion found its expression in the attitude of the Dutch to these rulers with whom out-standing questions were settled by a long series of treaties.[2]

Freitas hardly disagrees with Grotius as to problems of sovereignty and treaty making, but he adds in all sincerity that some of the possessions which the Portuguese acquired in the East Indies are based on a title of conquest. In this respect he argues in Chapter II that the Portuguese first acquired certain rights by treaties with local rulers, but that in case of breach of treaty on the part of the latter they had to go to war—and their war was *bellum justum*.[3]

Though Grotius accepted the sovereignty of local rulers and stressed the need of a legal title on the part of a European power for the acquisition of rights in their territories, he nevertheless argued in Chapter I that accord-ing to the primary (not secondary) law of nations (*jus gentium primarium*) every nation has the right of free access to, and of trade with, every other nation. Freitas rejects this artificial division between a primary and a secondary law of nations. He considers international law a monolithic system though some of its rules are according to the law of nature immut-able and some are subject to change. In case of conflict between the right of access to foreign nations and their sovereignty, the latter must prevail. If Asian rulers conceded to European powers access to their territories, such a concession was subject to change and could be withdrawn, otherwise there would be freedom of trade and navigation for the latter at the cost of sovereignty of the former. That Freitas's argument was legally justified follows from the attitude which the Dutch adopted in their conflict with the English over their rights in the East Indies (Indonesian Islands). The argument of the English in the London negotiations for the settlement of

[1] *De Jure Praedae Commentarius* (a collotype reproduction of the original manuscript, in the Classics of International Law, 1950), p. 97.
[2] Heeres, *Corpus Diplomaticum Neerlando-Indicum* (1907).
[3] As to their war against Islam Freitas describes it in a true Crusader's spirit as 'bellum justissi-mum'; see below.

the conflict (1613) was that after their arrival in the territories in question they established a good title to trade with local communities as all countries should by the law of nations have equally free access to the East Indies for trading purposes. The Dutch reply to this argument was that this universal freedom of the law of nations may be limited by special arrangements. The Dutch claimed priority on the basis of treaties with local rulers whom they considered as 'bound by their own consent'. To this the English rejoinder was that these treaties were unjust and contrary to the law of nature and that anyhow 'the Dutch would not be unaware of what had been written on this head by the "assertor maris liberi".'[1] Grotius, who might not have expected to be hoist by his own petard,[2] acknowledged the reliance of the English on the above argument but argued again that the Dutch relied on treaties concluded with local rulers and that the 'contract extinguished the liberty of the law of nations'. The effect of these negotiations on Grotius was that in his later writings the statements about the universal freedom of commerce (as limiting national sovereignty) were restated subject to careful qualifications.[3]

It may be noted, however, that while Freitas argued against the principle of free access to territories under foreign sovereignty for trading purposes, he adopted the same principle for another purpose by advocating free access of Europeans to Asian lands for the purpose of preaching the Christian faith. The consequences of adhering to this doctrine will be discussed below. It is essential to stress that its adoption is a corollary to the ideological conflict between Christianity and Islam which was transplanted by the Portuguese from the European scene to the Asian *hinterland* of Islam in south Asia.

However, in spite of these controversies over limitations of sovereignty, Grotius and Freitas seem to have shared the fundamental view that independent and politically organized societies in Asia were endowed with statehood and sovereignty in the law of nations, and this view was by no means an isolated one. As pointed out by Lindley,[4] the majority of the classic writers followed the opinion of St. Thomas Aquinas (as expressed in his *Summa Theologica*) that dominion was based on *jus humanum* and should not be obscured by the distinction between Christian and non-Christian religion and civilization which was based on *jus divinum* and was irrelevant to sovereignty as a temporal matter. Recognition of sovereignty of Asian or other extra-European States found its expression in the writings of Bodin,[5] Franciscus de Vitoria, Ayala, Gentili, Selden and Puffendorf,

---

[1] Clark, 'Grotius's East India Mission in England', *Transactions of the Grotius Society*, 20 (1935), p. 79.   [2] Knight, op. cit., p. 137.   [3] See Clark, loc. cit., p. 61.
[4] *The Acquisition and Government of Backward Territory in International Law* (1926), pp. 12 et seq.
[5] *Les Six livres de la république* (transl. by Richard Knowles, 1606); see L. I, C. VIII where

and it was later supported by eighteenth-century writers such as Vattel and G. F. de Martens. Vattel dismissing differences of religion as a relevant factor considered any independent State 'which govern itself by its own authority and laws' as sovereign and as a member of the natural society of nations 'subject to the law of nations'.[1] Martens, a writer with a positivist outlook, who relied to a great extent on treaties between European Powers as the basis of the law of nations, also referred to a long series of treaties between European and Asian Powers which obviously appeared as sovereign participants in extra-European treaty arrangements.[2] Thus, there was an overwhelming body of opinion among the classic writers to the effect that diplomatic and treaty relations between European and Asian Powers were based on a footing of equality and that (as stressed by Grotius and Freitas) the former could acquire rights from the latter by legitimate title only such as cession or conquest.

III

Assuming that a number of Asian communities were endowed with statehood and sovereignty and capable of entering into transactions with the Portuguese and other European powers which produced rights and duties in the law of nations, we have to exclude the possibility of acquisition of their territories by occupation or discovery. Grotius states in Chapter IV that 'the property and the sovereignty of the East Indies ought not to be considered as if they had been previously *res nullius* and as they belonged to the East Indians, they could not have been legally acquired by other persons . . .', and he adds that 'this is not denied even by the Spanish doctors'. Indeed, Freitas does not join issue on this point. Neither could the Portuguese according to Grotius have claimed 'to have discovered India which had been famous for so many centuries'. Originally Grotius had added the words: 'Alia enim India, alia Americana ratio est' (Chapter II) but he crossed them out from the text though the remark was, contrary to Vitoria's views, quite feasible.[3] Again it might have been inconvenient in a lawyer's plea. Freitas refers to two meanings of the word 'discovery': the geographical and the legal. He does not maintain that the Portuguese acquired a legal title by discovery but he stresses the fact that they opened the direct sea route to India by circumnavigating the Cape of Good Hope. As will be seen below he attaches legal significance to this fact and considers his Sovereign to have the right on the basis *prior tempore potior jure*.

Bodin refers to the sovereignty of the rulers of Turkey, Egypt and Persia and the Caliph (p. 147). Bodin considers 'the Kings of Calicut, of Malachie, of Cambar and of Canor' as vassals of the King of Portugal (p. 147).   [1] *Le Droit des Gens*, L. I, C. I, p. 4.
     [2] de Martens, *A Compendium of the Law of Nations* (1789, transl. by Cobbett, 1802); *Cours Diplomatique* (1801); *Recueil de traités* (1817).
     [3] 'De Jure Praedae' (Manuscript), op. cit., p. 98.

While Freitas has little to say on occupation and discovery, he engages in a lengthy controversy with Grotius over the title of Papal donation in favour of the Portuguese. In Chapter III of *Mare Liberum* Grotius had referred to 'the partition (of overseas possessions between Spain and Portugal) made by Pope Alexander VI used by the Portuguese as authority for jurisdiction in the East Indies' and had expressed the view that though it had been in the power of the Pope 'to settle the disputes between the Portuguese and the Spaniards' by *arbitration* if asked to do so, the conferment by him of any legal title in the East Indies had no effect in the law of nations. To this Freitas gives a lawyer's as well as a theologian's reply. He admits that the authority of the Pope is spiritual and only indirectly temporal. Thus if he intervenes in the secular sphere, it can only be for religious purposes. He can send missions to non-Christian communities and if they have to go by sea and to engage in trade to keep themselves going ('sub commercii colore') he can confer on them the right of navigation and trade to the exclusion of 'others'. As a theologian Freitas wrote on the assumption of the unity of the Church under the authority of the Pope and he therefore considered the Dutch as being outside this unity and as belonging to the category of 'others'. He also emphasizes in Chapter VIII that the King of Spain had as Count of Flanders acquired sovereignty over the Netherlands and that the Dutch Senate should act in deference to his legal authority. Whatever the objective value of these arguments (which Guichon de Grandpont, the translator of Freitas's work, rightly considers as untenable)[1] it is abundantly clear from the context of Freitas's treatise that the contemplated mission of the Portuguese had, apart from its religious aspect, the undermining of Islam's 'hinterland' in the Indian ocean as its ultimate purpose.[2] At the back of this political purpose loomed the anxiety of the inhabitants of the Iberian peninsula (who had experienced Islamic domination) to check Islam's progress in Asia.[3] It may be relevant to note that the Islamic power block acted on the doctrine of *Jihad* according to which the world was divided into *Dar-al-Islam* (Islamic

---

[1] Guichon de Grandpont, op. cit., p. 149; but see Knight, 'Seraphin de Freitas: Critic of *Mare Liberum*', *Transactions of the Grotius Society*, 11 (1926), p. 5.

[2] But it is important to emphasize that the greatest Islamic dynasty in south Asia, i.e. the Moguls, were, at the period of Vasco da Gama's mission and afterwards, ideologically outside the Islamic world in the proper sense of the word. Akbar, the Mogul Emperor of India, had applied a policy of tolerance and religious co-existence throughout his dominions. The position was different on the west coast of India which remained practically outside his Empire. The most powerful among its rulers was the Zamorin of Calicut and he, unlike other Hindu rulers on the west coast, was an intimate ally of the Arab trading community which with the support of Turkey and Egypt tended to dominate the sea routes in the Indian Ocean and the Arabian Sea. This explained *inter alia* the friendly relations and treaties of the Portuguese with other Hindu rulers on the west coast who welcomed the latter as their allies against the menacing pressure of Islam. See *The Book of Duarte Barbossa* (transl. from the Portuguese by Mansel Longworth Dames, 1918), vol. 2, p. 74.

[3] Panikkar, *Asia and Western Dominance* (1954), p. 13.

sphere) and *Dar-al-Harb* (the rest of the world). *Jihad* implied a state of continuous warfare between the two which could be interrupted by treaties of a temporary character only as if in the nature of a truce.[1] Freitas states that King Emmanuel of Portugal being in charge of the anti-Islamic crusade in Asia had invited other European sovereigns to participate in it, and moreover the promulgation in 1492 of the Bull 'Inter caetera' of Pope Alexander VI *urbi et orbi* constituted a sufficient notification of this policy to all concerned.[2] Freitas notes the complete lack of reaction on the part of other west European powers and this inaction meant in his view their acquiescence in the exclusive mission of the Portuguese in the East Indies.[3]

However, as to the implementation of this mission, Freitas realized that the legal position of the Pope in relation to non-Christians in the East Indies presented difficult problems. He agreed with Grotius that the Pope, as head of the Church, could not exercise jurisdiction over non-Christians. Already Vitoria had emphasized, in defiance of Spanish policy, that difference of religion did not justify political and military action.[4] Thus the Pope could not make grants to Christian powers at the expense of non-Christians though he could authorize 'missionary' activities in their territories. In trying to reconcile all controversial factors Freitas says in Chapter IX that three legal points occurred to him: first, non-Christians could not be compelled to accept the Christian faith; second, if they did not accept the Christian faith preached to them, they could not for this reason be deprived of their property rights and this also excluded *debellatio* ('non tamen ex eo eos debellare et bonis spoliare licet'); third, that the Pope could himself, or by the intermediary of Christian Princes, secure freedom of preaching the law of Christ in non-Christian countries.[5] The subjects of such countries who were prevented by their rulers from accepting the Christian faith, or from exercising it, in case of conversion, could be absolved from their allegiance to their rulers. The significant conclusion drawn by Freitas from the last point was that the Portuguese could go to

---

[1] *Jihad* meant, according to Islamic legal theory, *bellum justum*, but it is doubtful whether it reflected the ideology of the Koran. See Nawaz, 'The Doctrine of Jihad', *Indian Year Book of International Affairs* (1959).

[2] The line of demarcation between Spanish and Portuguese overseas interests had been later modified by the Treaty of Tordesillas in 1494, but it lost much of its significance during the period of temporary unification of Spain and Portugal under the Spanish Crown.

[3] There is also another reason for which Freitas supports the preference given to the Portuguese in the East Indies, i.e. their technical superiority. Since the reign of Henry the Navigator, Portuguese experience in oceanic navigation, including ship building, astronomy, geography, the use of instruments, &c., had reached a level incomparably superior to that of other maritime Powers. The spectacular achievements of Portuguese admirals since Vasco da Gama gave full expression to this technical superiority throughout the sixteenth century, and thus the Portuguese claim to monopoly in navigation and trade in the East Indies was, in Freitas's view, entirely justified by the Papal grant (Chapter VIII).

[4] de Vitoria, *De Indis* (ed. by E. Nys; Classics of International Law).

[5] Which excluded the ancient Christian community of St. Thomas on the west coast of India from Portuguese interference; Brown, *The Indian Christians of St. Thomas* (1956).

war with a non-Christian ruler who disregarded the freedom of preaching or preserving the Christian faith and thus a war for the purpose of securing such freedom was *bellum justum*,[1] a conclusion with which Grotius utterly disagreed though he accepted the principle of free access of Europeans to the East Indies for trading purposes. However, Freitas emphasized that in practice the Portuguese waged war only exceptionally against non-Moslem countries,[2] as for instance against the rulers of Calicut and Ceylon as to which Freitas remarks in Chapter XVII: 'Constantinus Brigantini filius Indiae Prorex potentissimum Janafatam in Taprobane Tyranum debellavit, coronaeque Lusitanae subegit anno 1560. . . .' But whatever the policy of the Portuguese in this respect, Freitas made it abundantly clear in Chapter IX that they would always avail themselves of the title of conquest against the Turks and Moors: 'Cum tamen contra Turcos et Mauros bellum ex nostra parte semper justissimum sit.'

It may be mentioned here that one of the legal consequences of this uncompromising attitude towards the Islamic world was the condemnation by Freitas (in Chapter XIII) of alliances between Christian and Islamic powers. Such alliances, if offensive, were illicit; if defensive they were tolerable but fraught with evil results. In support of this legal theory Freitas quotes one of the leading authorities on the subject, Octavianus Cacheranus, whose work under the title *Disp. an Principi Christiano fas sit, foedus inire cum infidelibus* (Taurini, 1569) was later mentioned by Ompteda[3] as an authoritative work on alliances of Christian Princes with infidels.[4]

Thus, while Grotius and Freitas broadly agree as to the application in the East Indies of legal principles relating to acquisition of territory, they disagree fundamentally as to the conception of *bellum justum* and conquest, particularly in relation to the Islamic world.

IV

Before discussing the Grotius–Freitas controversy over the freedom of the high seas with special reference to the position in the Indian ocean,

[1] This conclusion meant in fact the transplantation by Freitas of Vitoria's views to the Asian political scene.

[2] Their relations with the Hindu world were not dictated by any doctrinal conception, hence their alliances with the Vijayanagar Empire, the Ruler of Cochin, &c., against Muslim powers and their allies.

[3] *Litteratur des Völkerrechts* (Regensburg, 1785), p. 592. Ompteda refers also to Pott's work on the subject. Pott enumerates as infidels in the first instance Turks, Saracens and Tartars with whom offensive alliances are forbidden to Christian princes even if such alliances contemplated *bellum justum*. He criticizes particularly the treaty concluded between Francis I of France and Turkey against Emperor Charles V; Pott, *C. D. de Foederibus Fidelium cum Infidelibus* (Jenae, 1686).

[4] In Chapter XVIII Freitas refers to the alliances between the Dutch and infidels in the East Indies directed against the Portuguese and deplores the lack of solidarity of the Dutch in the common cause of Christendom.

the question may arise whether any legal régime existed in the above maritime region before the arrival of the Portuguese at the end of the fifteenth century. Grotius must have concerned himself with the question during the study of the relevant factual material, as he included at the end of Chapter VII of *Mare Liberum* the following passage: 'Praeterae accolae totius tractus Africani et Asiatici partem maris quisque sibi proximam piscando et navigando perpetuo usurparunt, nunquam a Lusitanis prohibiti.' In the light of this statement it seems that the various Asian communities had acquired vested rights of fishing and navigation in certain zones adjacent to their territories (as distinguished from the high seas) and thus Grotius draws from this and other arguments the general conclusion that the Portuguese 'are in possession of no right whereby they may interdict to any nation whatsoever the navigation of the ocean to the East Indies'.

As to sources of maritime law in South Asian countries, it may be noted that the oldest comprehensive treatise on inter-State relations in ancient India, Kautilya's Artashastra, which originates in all probability from the early period of the Buddhist Mauryan Empire (fourth century B.C.), makes numerous references to maritime regulations (L. II, C. XXVIII). It speaks about the existence of a superintendent of shipping and his jurisdiction over vessels navigating the ocean close to the shore (*Samudrasanyana*) and inland waters. One of his duties was the care of weather-beaten vessels which arrived at harbours. It is most characteristic of this treatise that it prescribes the application of measures against ships bound for an enemy country and the destruction of all pirate ships (*Himsrika*). It also appears from its text that sea routes along the shore were considered preferable to mid-ocean navigation in the Indian sea (L. VII, C. XII). The turning-point in shipping came with the discovery by the Romans (about A.D. 45) of the navigational use of monsoon winds blowing regularly across the Indian ocean which made mid-ocean sailing a practicable proposition.[1] After that a regular import of various luxury goods by sea route from the East to the Roman Empire became an important factor in the latter's economy. Moreover, oceanic trade between India and South-East Asia and the Far East experienced a spectacular development following the expansion of maritime activities of south Indian rulers. The sea route between India and China was in common use in the fifth century A.D. Commercial intercourse developed in the ninth century and up to the fifteenth century Chinese junks frequently arrived on the west coast of India.[2] The Indian Ocean became, therefore, much earlier than the Atlantic or the Pacific a maritime

---

[1] Rawlinson, *Intercourse between India and the Western World* (1926).

[2] Nilakanta Sastri, *A History of South India* (1955); Panikkar, op. cit., pp. 35–37. Reference may be made to *The Travels of Ibn Batuta* (transl. by S. Lee, 1829) who in the middle of the fourteenth century went on a mission to China and left an account of Chinese shipping regulations relating to the crews of vessels and cargo registers.

centre of far-distant shipping on a big international scale. This tended to lead to the spontaneous growth of a customary régime governing oceanic activities whose primary concern was the fight against maritime anarchy and the suppression of piracy. There were also examples of lcgislation which regulated controversial problems of maritime law, to mention only the edict of Maharaja Ganapati the purpose of which was to assure 'safety to foreign traders by sea whose vessels might be wrecked on the coast of his territories'.[1] Thus the Indian Ocean could hardly be considered *mare clausum* before the expansion of Moorish navigation and the advent of the European Powers.[2] The situation changed only later with the arrival of the Portuguese in the East Indies who tended throughout the sixteenth century to eliminate Moorish trade and to enforce a régime of far-reaching control of navigation which was *mutatis mutandis* similar to that imposed by the western Powers in various parts of European waters (England, Venice, Genoa, &c.). In the above circumstances it might not be impossible to assume that Grotius in the formulation of his new doctrine found himself to a great extent stimulated by the existence of an ancient maritime tradition in the Indian Ocean which for its vastness and extensive network of sea routes was bound to lend itself to a *mare liberum* outlook. Grotius's distinction between the high seas and territorial zones in which south Asian communities exercised rights of navigation and fishing certainly supports this supposition.

The formulation of this new outlook and its application to the Dutch–Portuguese conflict led Grotius to the denial of all possible titles claimed by the Portuguese in the Indian Ocean whether by occupation, by prescription or custom or by Papal donation. In support of his basic argument that the sea is *res communis* he refers *inter alia* to Roman law and quotes in Chapter V a reply made by Ulpian in which the latter stated that 'the sea could not be subjected to a servitude because it was by nature open to all persons'. To this argument Freitas replies that Ulpian excludes the imposition of a servitude on the sea only by private law and not by public law. The fact that a servitude cannot be imposed by an individual does not mean that it cannot be imposed by a sovereign. Thus though the sea may

[1] While formerly the whole cargo of such ships had been forfeited to the State, the ruler decreed that henceforth nothing but the normal custom duties would be levied on them (*Epigraphia Indica*, vol. xii, 1913–14, p. 188). The appropriation of wrecks and cargoes by rulers was a principle established by immemorial custom but it was gradually modified by legislation and treaty until it disappeared. As to piracy it might have been punishable according to the law or custom of a maritime State (see *Artashastra*) but State practice in the Indian Ocean seems to have evolved a certain identity of customs of oceanic tradition which lifted some principles to the inter-State level. Punishment of piracy as a crime against the safety of traffic and life in the open sea beyond the jurisdiction of any sovereign implied the existence of open oceanic highways.

[2] See Panikkar, op. cit., pp. 35–37. See also Ludovico di Varthemo who, in his *Itinerary from 1502 to 1508* (transl. by J. W. Jones, 1928), testifies to the freedom of navigation in the Indian Ocean.

FREITAS *VERSUS* GROTIUS

be *res communis jure gentium*, it can be charged with a servitude including a prohibition against foreign navigation if it is occupied by a sovereign. In Chapter XIV Freitas reiterates this idea and states that whenever the Roman people asserted their right over a portion of the high seas the latter ceased to be public by the law of nations and became public by the law of the sovereign. Though Grotius advocated a progressive doctrine which in due time proved more convincing than the views of his opponents he seemed to have underestimated the difficulty of transplanting conceptions of Roman law to the public law of nations.[1]

Nevertheless, it would be far from correct to consider Freitas an all-out antagonist of the freedom of the seas. In Chapter X he says: 'Maris ergo elementum commune omnibus est quia infinitum ita ut possideri non queat. . . .' In Chapter XI he discusses the use of the sea and the air and states: 'Haec enim naturaliter propter vastitatem, fluxumque vaguum, *integre* occupari non possunt omnibus hominibus communem decernit Celsus. . . .' The analogy between the high seas and the air space is characteristic. Freitas considers both *res communis* but subject to important limitations obviously dictated by the principle of effectiveness. First of all he emphasizes the existence of maritime zones to which the adjacent territorial State may extend its sovereignty. The question arises what are the limits of these zones. Freitas notes that lawyers found it impossible to agree on this matter—a state of affairs on which we cannot claim to have improved much even today.[2] As it is impossible to find a suitable formula in natural law, the jurisdiction of the territorial sovereign must according to Freitas extend into the high seas according to the possibilities of effective control —a proposition not alien to the tentative policies of some maritime powers today. In Chapter XIV Freitas refers to Grotius's remark about the rights of non-Christian States in Asia whose inhabitants had exercised from time immemorial rights of navigation and fishing in zones adjacent to their territories. He draws from this the logical conclusion that since Grotius admits national jurisdiction in certain portions of the sea, such rights are capable of being exercised not only by the Turks and Moors but also by

---

[1] Freitas encountered the same difficulties in his discussion of the Rhodian laws to which he refers in Chapter X. Their interpretation leads him to the conclusion that (1) the law of the sea must be considered as a system requiring the establishment of maritime jurisdiction; (2) the customary *lex maris* does not exclude the jurisdiction of the sovereign of the high seas but includes it; (3) it allows to assume the application of the *actio uti possidetis* to the high seas (a doubtful argument which is denied by Grotius); (4) even if private rights on the sea cannot exist, a sovereign may for their protection impose restrictions including tolls on foreign shipping in harbours as well as beyond them. This interpretation seems doubtful as the Rhodian laws tended to support the conception of the freedom of the sea in the East; see Champagne, *La Mer libre, la mer fermée ou exposition et analyse du traité de Grotius intitulé La Mer Libre et de la replique de Selden ayant pour titre La Mer Fermée*, &c. (Paris 1803); and see below.
[2] Johnson, 'The Geneva Conference on the Law of the Sea', *Year Book of World Affairs* (1959); Waldock, 'International Law and the New Maritime Claims', *International Relations*, vol. 1, April 1956.

174   FREITAS *VERSUS* GROTIUS

Christians. He does not limit national jurisdiction only to territorial zones but accepts its extension generally to the vast expanses of the high seas.

In this respect his views are revealing because he operates on the assumption of a possible quasi-occupation of the high seas by a particular sovereign. The rationale of this conception is explained in Chapter IV in the following way: the high seas cannot remain in a state of lawlessness and anarchy. To avoid a legal vacuum the régime of the high seas must be based on some law, whether national law or the law of nations. It must be kept in mind that in the absence of detailed rules supporting the doctrine of the freedom of the high seas as a practical proposition the sea was bound to be open to anarchy and this was evidenced in all periods of history by the concern of the navigating and trading communities with piracy. Asian history in the pre-Vasco da Gama period testifies to the friendly relations between maritime powers such as those between Buddhist India and China, or those developed during the period of the expansion of the maritime empire of Sri Vijaya. The problem of piracy was no doubt tackled in the inter-State practice of those Powers which seem to have treated the high seas as the common concern *generis humani*. To what extent these efforts were successful could only be ascertained by further historical research. As stated above, the Portuguese and other Europeans did not find themselves in the opening stages of their maritime career in the Indian Ocean in a *mare clausum*. But the monopolizing tendency of the Islamic trading community which carried valuable resources by sea to Egypt (already part of the Turkish Empire) and the opposition of the Portuguese to this potential monopoly which they considered a threat to Christian civilization became a highly disturbing factor in this region. In these circumstances the elements of maritime co-existence in the Indian ocean disintegrated into anarchy[1] and the Portuguese, not without selfish interest, arrogated to themselves the responsibility of converting the anarchy into conditions of security under their own jurisdiction. Freitas emphasizes in Chapter VIII that the Portuguese assumed the exploitation of the new direct sea route between Europe and Asia (which brought Asian merchandise at cheaper prices to the European consumer), and that to this end they diverted from the Arabian Gulf, which was constantly being invaded, the merchandise of India and undermined the uneconomic trade of Turkish merchants in Egypt. In Chapter XII he refers to Portuguese action against piracy in the Indian Ocean, and quotes Seleceus calling it 'ad auxilium purgandi orientis'. Thus the seventeenth century in the Indian Ocean witnessed a state of affairs to which the application of Grotius's doctrine was premature. Its realization proved possible at a later stage at which the

---

[1] See Lacour-Gayet, *La Marine Militaire de la France sous le Regne de Louis XIII et de Louis XIV*, pp. 13 et seq.; Hall, *History of South Asia* (1955), p. 453.

European Powers were able effectively to combat anarchy and to co-exist within a *mare liberum* régime. Prior to this period the situation in the Indian Ocean called for positive action, and this is exactly the reason why Freitas, far from abandoning entirely the *res communis* conception of the sea, tried to formulate certain principles of national maritime jurisdiction based on quasi-possession of the sea. He states in Chapter XI that in the absence of real occupation of the sea only its quasi-occupation is possible: 'Navigatione et piscatione quasi-occupatur', and he considers such quasi-occupation by the Portuguese as established without interference by the English or the French (Chapter XIV). The Dutch are according to him perfectly capable of establishing a similar right on other sea routes, but they cannot interfere lawfully with those leading to Portuguese trading stations and possessions. It will be seen that the right claimed by the Portuguese emerges as functional in character. In Chapter X Freitas makes it clear that the sea as *res communis* cannot be occupied for the sake of its occupation but rights in it can be acquired in relation to the purpose of their exercise, i.e. the preservation of the security on particular sea routes leading to specified territories. This functional character of quasi-occupation is also true of the maritime zones for, as Freitas states in the same chapter, it can take place only in relation to the land which envelops a particular portion of the sea. It seems that the sovereign asserting the above rights for himself acted in a way also as an agency of the law of nations for the common good of all concerned.

As to the legal title of the Portuguese to maritime jurisdiction, Freitas based it principally on prescription and custom. His main emphasis in Chapter XIV is on the fact that more than one hundred years had elapsed since Vasco da Gama's arrival in India in 1498 and that during this period the Portuguese, without any significant protest on the part of other Powers, asserted and exercised undisturbed control of navigation in the Indian Ocean. In this way they acquired a bona fide right of navigation by immemorial prescription or custom which, with the exception of the Moors, was generally accepted by the free consent of those against whom it was exercised. In this respect Freitas and Grotius differ fundamentally, for though both seem to view the Indian Ocean as practically an open sea before the arrival of the Europeans, Freitas considers it capable of quasi-possession ('mare navigationibus et piscationibus acquisitionis capax esse' —Ch. XIV), whereas Grotius finds any such acquisition of rights irreconcilable with the idea of the high seas conceived as *res communis*.[1]

---

[1] Under the impact of the opposition to his views Grotius modified to some extent his opinion about the freedom of the seas in his subsequent work *De Jure Belli ac Pacis* (see edition by William Whewell). Grotius says in L. II, C. II (13) that 'the Empire (imperium) of the sea claimed over a portion of it without any other property might easily proceed (from certain claims): Nor do I concede that the law of nations of which I have spoken would stand in the

V

Before concluding our considerations relating to maritime law it might be interesting to mention briefly the institution of the so-called *cartaz* which was instrumental in the exercise of the control of the seas by the Portuguese. The term 'connotes', according to Portuguese dictionaries, a safe conduct which the Portuguese authorities used to grant in Asia to the friends of Portugal to secure to them safe navigation.[1] The fact that the above term is found in the Arabic vocabulary indicates that the Arabs made early use of *cartazes* for the control of navigation.

Freitas, discussing *cartazes* in Chapter VIII, connects their introduction with the establishment in the East Indies of a Portuguese administration endowed with maritime jurisdiction. They were granted in the name of the King by the Viceroy or by a military or naval commander. Freitas explains the circumstances in which they became necessary and draws our attention to the need of distinguishing friends and allies from enemies on the high seas ('ut foederatos ab hostibus discernarent'). The influence of the Saracens on local rulers in the East Indies increased conditions of anarchy ('dolo ac fraudibus orientis reges in id excitantes') and the situation became even more acute when the Pasha of Egypt and the Emperor of Turkey sent their navies into Indian waters to attack Portuguese ships aᵣ d possessions ('cum Egypti Campson Turcorumque Imperator ad eandem nostrorum ab India exturbationem classes misissent aliquoties').[2] The *cartaz* appears therefore not only as the means of asserting Portuguese rights but also as an instrument for preserving order and security on international sea routes. Moreover, if we consider the region in question as subject to unlimited maritime warfare (*Jihad*) in which regular naval battles were fought in the sixteenth century, the *cartazes* bear certain similarities to navicerts[3] (see below). The authority issuing the *cartaz* applied a meticulous procedure of search to a foreign ship and ascertained whether its intended voyage was undertaken in good faith ('Fide prius illius qui navem conscendit diligenter explorata'). If the investigation proved satisfactory a safe conduct was issued which protected the ship from interference on her

way. It has often been asserted and conceded . . .' But Grotius emphasizes at the same time that 'He who holds the sea by occupation cannot prevent an unarmed and harmless navigation upon it' (12). Bynkershoek in his *De Dominio Maris Dissertatio* (ch. ix) refers to the fact that Grotius changed his views after the publication of *Mare Liberum* and expressed his doubts about the limits up to which occupation of the sea is possible (reference to *De Jure Belli ac Pacis*, L. II, C. III. 8).

[1] See, for instance, *Dicionario de Lingua Portugueza* (Lisboa, 1844).

[2] Suleiman the Magnificent of Turkey directed the Pasha of Egypt to support actively the Zamorin of Calicut and the Arab trading community. The Egyptian fleet which entered the Indian Ocean was defeated by the Portuguese in 1538 (see Panikkar, op. cit., pp. 51–53).

[3] Smith, *The Law and Custom of the Sea* (1959), p. 155; Colombos, *A Treatise on the Law of Prize*, p. 216; Higgins and Colombos, *The International Law of the Sea* (1951).

FREITAS *VERSUS* GROTIUS   177

voyage; if the ship sailed without it, she incurred the risk of being stopped and captured with all the consequences ensuing therefrom ('aliter enim a nostris navarchis capi, bonisque omnibus euerti et vita et saltem libertate privari possunt'). Freitas remarks in conclusion that the *cartaz* became part of Asian maritime law by immemorial custom and that the Dutch could not ignore it, the more so that even the author of *Mare Liberum* invokes the same law in relation to the Persians, Chinese, Arabs and others in the above region.[1]

A number of examples of *cartazes* were included by Judice Biker in his collection of treaties, and it may be of interest to give the content of at least one of them.[2] In a document issued on 9 August 1613 to Idalxa, King of Bijapur, a local Moslem ruler of an Indian State whose territories extended to the west coast, the Portuguese Viceroy in India states as follows:

'I, Dom Jeronimo D'Azevedo cause it to be known to all who may see it that in consideration of the ancient amity which El Rey Idalxa has with this State and in view of the treaty concluded with him, a licence and safe conduct are granted to him at the request of his ambassador, to enable six of his ships to sail to Mecca (Arabia), Ormuz (Persian Gulf) and other places. In particular I have the pleasure to issue a licence and safe conduct to his ship "Mamady" which carries four thousand khandis (of goods), her captain (Nacoda) being Melique Ambar aged thirty years, and which has for its defence twelve iron swivels (guns), twenty muskets and many moorish weapons so that she may start during the present monsoon from the port of Dabul where she is now, for Juda, and return without taking or bringing anything (anybody) prohibited that is to say Greeks, Turks, Abyssinians, cinnamon of Ceylon, pepper, ginger, iron, steel, lead, tin, timber, brass, saltpetre, sulphur, bamboo, and other things prohibited by the Government; neither will she be permitted to carry Portuguese (passengers) nor to bring horses without a licence, and she will be allowed to bring slaves, male and female of her own nationality only: And if there is any suspicion or information that some of these slaves are Christians or children of Christians, an enquiry will be instituted at the provincial council even if some of these children are not yet baptised; and before the ship departs from the port of Dabul she will be visited and searched by the agent of His Majesty who is at the spot and she will receive his certificate on the back of this document; and on these conditions her voyage both outward and homeward will be without any impediment on the part of the captains of the armadas of this State or on the part of other captains and persons, and all persons notified of the above will fulfill and observe these terms without any question; and this shall be sealed with the seal of the royal arms of the Crown of Portugal.'

Another *cartaz* quoted by Judice Biker was also granted to the King of Bijapur in the same year and is in identical terms. Portuguese *cartazes* granted at a later period, whether in favour of rulers or private merchants

---

[1] The text may be open to doubt, for Freitas says: 'Hinc fit Batavos sine hoc salvo conductu in Indiam navigare non posse, eo maximo quia incognitus [Grotius] idem ius implorat, quo Persae, Sinae, Saraceni et Ethnici in illis partibus utuntur. . . .' Guichon de Grandpont refers in his translation to the Persians, Chinese, &c., as subject to this law, but this may not give the precise meaning of *utuntur*.

[2] Biker, *Collecção de Tratados* (Lisboa, 1881), vol. iv, pp. 181 et seq.

differ little from the established pattern except that a clause was added to the effect that breach of the terms of the *cartaz* on the part of the grantee will render the *cartaz* invalid and that the ship will be seized and forfeited.[1]

The following conclusions may be drawn from the above: The *cartaz* could be viewed in a twofold way, first as an expression of Portuguese jurisdiction assumed in the Indian Ocean under their quasi-occupation, and second as a sort of navicert applied in conditions of continuous warfare against hostile Islamic powers. Navicerts, as is well known, were introduced during the two world wars and involved the submission of a neutral ship and its cargo by the shipper to investigation in advance. If the latter obtained a navicert from the relevant Allied authority at the point of departure the navicert, although it did not constitute a guarantee against being subjected to visit and search, provided the ship with a passport enabling it to pass easily through Allied maritime controls. Great Britain made navicerts compulsory during the Second World War to the extent that ships not protected by them were deemed to be liable to seizure and condemnation.[2] The *cartaz* covered not only contraband goods but also passengers which was obviously calculated to prevent unneutral service by excluding from the vessel persons liable to be of use to the enemy (Turks, Abyssinians, &c.). The distinction between conditional and unconditional contraband, well known to Grotius,[3] seems not to be reflected in the *cartaz* which enumerates indiscriminately items primarily of use in war as well as merchandise capable of peaceful use only.[4] But merchantmen were entitled to carry guns and weapons for their defence which indicates the existence of conditions of total war. Enemy destination is clearly stated in the *cartaz*, and the mention of Mecca seems to show that ships were also carrying Moslem pilgrims. The exclusion of Christian slaves is a corollary of the Portuguese policy of absolute protection given to their co-religionists. It also follows that the Portuguese exercised the right of search of all vessels on the high seas, a right already implied in the *Consolato del Mare*. But the submission of a ship at the port of departure to Portuguese investigation (which was compulsory) and the issue of the *cartaz* to a bona fide grantee exempted her from interference on the part of Portuguese and other captains and entitled her to their protection. Though some of the *cartazes* do not include a clause referring to sanctions, it is obvious that all ships not carrying a *cartaz* were liable to seizure and condemnation, as expressly confirmed by Freitas.

---

[1] Biker, op. cit.: *cartaz* granted to the King of Canares on 1 March 1714 (vol. iv, p. 183), to Govinda Das Nana on 15 July 1766 (vol. iv, p. 186), &c.

[2] See also British practice of issuing ships' warrants (Higgins and Colombos, op. cit.).

[3] *De Jure Belli ac Pacis*, L. III, C. I. 5.

[4] This may imply a policy prohibiting all trading with the enemy, a conception well known to English law at the period in question.

Thus the *cartaz* appears as an interesting forerunner of the navicert, and testifies to the early development of specific rules of international maritime law in the Indian Ocean. It would be difficult to ascertain to what extent the *cartaz* was a concomitant of maritime warfare on the one hand and the expression of Portuguese general maritime control on the other. The two functions seem intimately interwoven and the case of each *cartaz* must be judged on its own merits, but no doubt the Portuguese–Islamic conflict must have overshadowed maritime practice.

Cartaz arrangements were sometimes made between the Portuguese and Indian rulers by treaty[1] and similar arrangements were also concluded by other maritime powers in the Indian Ocean. State practice on the west coast of India in the seventeenth and eighteenth centuries also affords many interesting examples of maritime custom relating to the identification of ships on the high seas. Diplomatic correspondence between the Marathas and European Powers reveals that a vessel in the open sea was liable to capture if it carried neither a *cartaz* nor a passport nor flew the banner of its own State.[2] Frequent references to banners raise the problem whether there existed a proper law of the flag in the meaning of international law. There seems to be no evidence to this effect, but the flag, jointly with the type and name of the ship and the ship's documents, constituted the ways and means of identifying her nationality.[3] A vessel had the nationality of the ruler to which she belonged and if she was a private vessel her nationality was that of the ruler whose subject the owner was. Thus there existed what may be called in contemporary legal language a 'genuine link' between a ship and her home State.[4]

Wherever maritime custom was oppressive (as in the case of shipwreck) it was liable to be modified by treaty and this applied in course of time also to *cartazes*. It is interesting to note that in the Poonem treaty of 4 May 1779 concluded between the Portuguese and the Marathas, which is one of the relevant documents in the present Indo-Portuguese conflict before the International Court of Justice, it was stipulated in Article VIII that 'merchant vessels of both dominions proceeding to any port and encountering the fleets of both parties or any ship of war shall not be taken

---

[1] For instance, the treaty of 30 April 1559 concluded by the Portuguese and the ruler of Bakla. In Article V of this treaty the Portuguese Viceroy undertook to give to the ruler four *cartazes* authorizing Bakla ships to navigate freely in the Indian Ocean. Surendranath Sen, 'Historical Records at Goa', *Studies in Indian History* (1930). As to other examples of treaties see Sen, *Military System of Marathas* (1928).

[2] Sen, op. cit., pp. 178, 246, 250; see also *Dutch Records* (The Hague) (transl. by C. C. Remmerswaal in *Shivaji the Great*, by Bal Krishna, 1932).

[3] Edye, 'Description of the Various Classes of Vessels, &c.', *Journal of the Royal Asiatic Society*, 1 (1834); Edkins, 'Ancient Navigation in the Indian Ocean', ibid. 18 (1886); as to rules of navigation see Mohi't 1558 transl. by Hammer, *Journal of the Asiatic Society of Bengal*, 1 (1832).

[4] If a ship could not prove her national identity she ran the risk of being treated as piratical.

captive on the ground that they possess no safe conduct (*cartaz*) but shall be allowed to proceed freely'.[1] At that period conditions had radically changed in the Indian Ocean. The Portuguese–Islamic struggle had lost its significance and the prospects of co-existence of the several European East India Companies as well as the Asian Powers in the Indian Ocean warranted the establishment of a régime of freedom of the high seas. Martens gave expression to the impending general acceptance of the new doctrine at the end of the eighteenth century when he referred to the four great seas which compose the ocean and particularly to 'the Indian sea about which the great disputes have arisen' and said: 'The sole dominion (of the sea) may exist in the theory . . . the ocean then is free, indeed it ought to be so.'[2]

VI

Grotius and Freitas were not the only participants in the battle of wits around the freedom of the high seas and the problem of relations between European and Asian Powers. Gentili (1552–1608) concerned himself with these questions earlier and it is interesting to note that his views were in many respects similar to those of Freitas. Though he did not accept war 'on account of religion', he nevertheless stated that, with the Saracens (who were part of the Turkish Empire) 'we have an irreconcilable war'.[3] Consequently alliances of Christian States with infidels against other Christian States were according to him unlawful,[4] and Gentili draws our attention to the fact that treaties concluded with Islamic countries used to provide for cessation of hostilities only.[5] Thus similarly to Freitas but unlike Grotius, he envisages a state of affairs between Christian and Islamic Powers which reflected Jihad and the Christian counter-doctrine to a great extent formulated on the basis of Canon law.[6] In the field of maritime law also there are significant similarities between both writers. Gentili considers the sea *res communis*[7] but submits it to far reaching restrictions. He refers to State practice developed by European maritime Powers such as Venice and Genoa which claimed jurisdiction and sovereignty over the sea adjoining their territories up to 'a distance of one hundred miles and even farther'. As to England he says that 'immeasurable is the jurisdiction of

---

[1] *The Hindu*, 28 March 1956.

[2] Martens, *The Law of Nations* (transl. by W. Cobbett, London, 1829), p. 163.

[3] *Hispanicae Advocationis libri duo* (Classics of International Law), L. I, C. XX; *De Jure Belli* (Classics of International Law), L. I, C. XII.

[4] *De Jure Belli*, L. III, C. XIX. But commercial treaties with the Turks were not forbidden, see *Hisp. Advoc.*, L. I, C. XXV.

[5] *De Jure Belli*, L. I, C. IX. The state of undefined warfare had its repercussions in the law of contraband. Gentili discusses the case of an English ship loaded with powder and other merchandise which had been captured on its way to Constantinople by the Sardinians and Maltese. He does not consider 'other merchandise' as contraband goods.

[6] *Hisp. Advoc.*, L. I, C. XX.   [7] *De Jure Belli*, L. I, C. IV.

our King upon the sea'.[1] Though he denies the claims of these Powers to possession of the sea he nevertheless admits that it is possible for them to exercise jurisdiction and a protectorate over it.[2] Thus he comes near to Freitas's conception of quasi-possession of the sea without attempting a more precise definition.

Welwood, in his *Abridgment of all Sea Laws* published in 1613, also adopts a 100-mile limit of jurisdiction and though he advocates otherwise complete freedom of navigation he concedes to a national sovereign the right to impose restrictions on the freedom of fishing in the high seas. To this Grotius gave a critical reply in which he considered the 100-mile limit as arbitrary and anyhow untenable and rejected the dichotomy of navigation and fishing.[3] Ten years after the publication of Freitas's treatise appeared the most formidable reply to Grotius which came from the pen of Selden in 1635.[4]

Without going into further details which would be beyond the scope of this inquiry it must be stressed that Franciscus Seraphin de Freitas deserves his due place among the writers of the seventeenth century who contributed to the clarification of problems relating to the legal status of the sea[5] and to European–Asian inter-State relations. As the title of his work indicates his main purpose was, apart from replying to Grotius, to justify the 'Justum Imperium Lusitanorum Asiaticum' and to contrast it with another imperium 'justum' as implied in Islamic theory and practice. The fact that many of his views were ultimately overshadowed by Grotius's progressive ideas, does not detract from their significance for the development of certain principles of the law of nations such as those relating to

---

[1] *Hisp. Advoc.*, L. I, C. VIII.   [2] *De Jure Belli*, L. I, C. XIX.

[3] 'Hugonis Grotii Capitis quinti Maris liberi oppugnati a Gulielmo Welwood, etc.', in Muller, *Mare Clausum* (Amsterdam, 1872). Wright, *Some less known Works of Hugo Grotius* (Bibliotheca Visseriana, vol. 7, 1928). Welwood's *Abridgment* was followed up in 1615 by his *De Dominio Maris*.

[4] *Mare Clausum* (transl. by M. Nedham, London 1652; transl. by J. H. Gent, London 1663). Selden divides the British sea into four parts and though he considers the shores and ports of the neighbouring princes as bounds to the south and east, he maintains 'that in the open and vast ocean of the north and west, they [the bounds] are to be placed at the utmost extent of those most spacious seas which are possest by the English, Scots and Irish'. Among the nations claiming dominion of the sea Selden enumerates *inter alia* the Portuguese and the Turks. But his belief that the East had no conception of the freedom of the high seas seems open to doubt as pointed out by Champagne in his comparative study of Grotius and Selden *La Mer libre, la mer fermée* (Paris 1803), in which he discusses the Rhodian laws with special reference to the Byzantine Empire.

It is interesting to note Grotius's reaction to *Mare Clausum*; he stated in a letter to one of his disciples, Theodore Graswinckel: 'Sed ego libertatem maris dum propugno, meam amisi. Seldenus libertatem marie oppugnans suam recuperavit'; Hugonis Grotii *Epistolae* (1687), Epistola No. 697, p. 287.

[5] Pierre Margry draws our attention to the fact that France was one of the first countries to protest against the Spanish–Portuguese monopoly on the high seas and that she gave support to the conception of *mare liberum* before Grotius; *Les Navigations françaises du XIVᵉ au XVIᵉ siècle* (Paris, 1867). See also *Controversiae Illustres* (1599), by Vasquez, who opposed the claims of Spain, Genoa and Venice.

sovereignty, acquisition of territory, just war, maritime jurisdiction, contraband, unneutral service, navicerts and others. The application of these principles in Asian State practice in the sixteenth and seventeenth centuries is bound to disprove the view that the Europeans found themselves in Asia in a legal vacuum. Freitas formulates Portuguese rights in the Indian Ocean on the basis of territorial zones and quasi-possession, functional conceptions which in spite of offering a challenge to lawyers were defined with comparatively more caution than those of other opponents of *Mare Liberum*. All of them gave expression to an interim state of affairs prevailing in the seventeenth century which made it still premature to implement the principles of the freedom of the sea.

11
Millenarianism and Empire: Portuguese Asian Decline and the 'Crise de Conscience' of the Missionaries
G.D. Winius

Millenarian movements appeared in a number of European countries during the early modern era, but only in Portugal are any of them known to have manifested themselves in a colonial empire. In fact, one form, known as Sebastianism, persisted in Brazil longer than it did in the metropolis and even outlived the colony's independence in 1822. This article, however, does not concern itself with the belief that King Sebastião would return miraculously from the battlefield of El Ksar-el-Kebir to rule over his people and indeed all Europeans for a thousand years – a superstition already known well enough to Iberianists and to historians of witchcraft and the occult. Instead, it will deal with something much less familiar.

This is with the quite unrelated millenarian reaction of missionaries in Portuguese Asia to the inroads made by the Dutch in the seventeenth century, especially to the conquests of Malacca and Ceylon, which seemed to throw into reverse the pursuit of God's great design for the conversion of the peoples of the Orient. Only a handful of missionaries appear to have been involved, but I think their writings are especially revealing because they suggest all too clearly how devastating and incomprehensible were the hostile actions of the Dutch East India Company to a priesthood dedicated not to material ends, but to lofty, spiritual hopes. Their ideas should prove highly interesting to historians intrigued – like myself – with the twilight of empire and with the reactions which decline provokes among various groups in the colonizing society.

Most historians of European expansion who do not themselves specialize in Iberian studies tend to believe that the Spanish rather than the Portuguese were the ones most zealous in carrying out the missionary activities in the century following the papal donation and division of the non-Europe into hemispheres after Columbus' return from the Americas in 1493. What truth there is in this notion applies only to the first decennia after the discoveries, those when the Spanish were making their great territorial conquests. For at this time the Portuguese were indeed relatively sluggish in carrying the

Christian faith to Asia. But upon the arrival of the Jesuit, St. Francis Xavier, at Goa in 1542, all this changed dramatically. Before his departure from Lisbon, Xavier had made a deep impression on Portugal's King João III and convinced him of his sacred responsibility to support unstintingly a new propagation of the holy faith. Then, by the force of his own personality and with the support of pious colonial officials like the viceroy, D. João de Castro, he succeeded in launching a great wave of evangelization – sufficient to make Asia the place where most of the missionary action occurred in the second half of the sixteenth century and up until the disastrous arrival of the Dutch.

The anguish felt by the Portuguese in Asia over the plight of their declining Estado da India only intensified after the Dutch blockades of Goa began in 1636 and were followed by the invasion of Ceylon in 1638 and the fall of Malacca in 1641. Anyone familiar with this period of disaster (which bottomed out only in the 1660s) would be hard put to produce a single document or report from contemporaries which does not verge on hopelessness and despair.[1] God, observers believed, must surely be punishing a wicked Portugal for its sins.[2] But there most of the laity and clergy alike ceased to plumb the supernatural.

To some of the fathers engaged in missionary activity, however, a general conviction of sin was only the starting point for a much deeper and more distressing theological speculation than that, one which involved their very *raison d'être* and cast them into a dilemma whence it was no mean intellectual feat to emerge. One might term it 'the aftermath of *Inter caetera*'. For it involved the conflict the clergy and above all the missionaries had with their *Weltanschauung* when it dawned upon them that the great imperative supposedly launched by Pope Alexander VI in the three bulls of 1493 and undertaken with such zeal among the heathen was now about to be skewed by the actions of heretics.

This not only drove Iberian apologists like Frei Seraphim de Freitas to defend their Asian empire in terms of purely spiritual values, but also caused at least some of the missionaries in Goa to look for its salvation in the miraculous.

How I became aware of the topic only illustrates that moderns are likely to neglect historical evidence for which they are not attuned. In 1965, having just purchased the S.G. Perera translation of Fr. Fernão de Queyroz, S.J.'s *Conquista (Espiritual e Temporal) de Ceilão*, a book written in Goa in the 1680s but published only in 1916, I was offered the one other book written by Queyroz, which had been published in Lisbon in 1689, *A Vida do Veneravel Irmão Pedro de Basto*. I bought it if only because it was reasonably priced and contained one of the earliest Portuguese accounts of their rivalry with the V.O.C., or Dutch East India Company. But in all other respects it was such a puzzling tome that I relegated it to a forgotten corner of one of my bookshelves where it remained for nearly two decades. It was only a coincidence which brought it to mind again and helped me to fit it into the proper framework.

Then one summer years later, while back in Lisbon, I visited my old friend,

Alfonso Cassuto, the scholarly antiquarian bookseller who assembled large parts of the Bibliotheca Rosenthaliana, a collection of volumes and manuscripts now in the University of Amsterdam. It was a hot day, and we were to have lunch. Before leaving his display room for a restaurant, he asked me what I had on my afternoon agenda. I replied: 'Not much. I just wanted to look up a book at the Biblioteca Nacional which possibly has some bearing on something I am writing about the *Soldado Prático*. It is called the *Primor e Honra da Vida Soldadesca no Estado da Índia*, and I think it was published in 1630. If you happen to have it, by the way, maybe you can save me the long, hot trip out there.'

'Wait', he said, 'I may just have it.' He disappeared into a store room and was gone for some minutes. When he emerged, he looked disappointed and said: 'I must have sold it, but I came across this next to where it should have been.' He produced a volume of sermons preached in Goa by one Father Antonio Ardizone Spinola, and I recognized it as a book I had been shown in Rome twenty years before by the late Father Georg Schurhammer, S.J. Thereupon Cassuto presented it to me, saying that it was of little use to him because the binding had been so heavily damaged by worms, even though he believed all pages were intact.

As it turned out, my visit later in the day to the Biblioteca Nacional for the book I had really been seeking produced no more than a footnote. But the one my friend had given me, called (in its first edition) the *Cordel Triplicado de Amor a Christo Jesu Sacramentado*, by Ardizone Spinola and published in Lisbon in 1680, perfectly complemented the *Vida do Veneravel Irmão Pedro de Basto*. For the first time, in fact, I could see what that book really was all about. Before describing it, however, perhaps it would be wise to fill in a little background.

The Padroado and its Underpinnings

So far as most of the conquistadores and colonial officials were concerned, both in Asia and the Americas, the clergy were there mostly to say mass for them and assist in the holy sacraments. That the fathers quickly built up convents and launched missions must have seemed pious and useful, too, since Christianized natives, especially in Portuguese Asia, might give the secular arm far less trouble than those who professed the faith of some nearby enemy. At the same time, the fathers sometimes annoyed both officers and traders alike by their denunciations of greed and by their own manoeuvrings to obtain more than their fair share of the state's wealth for injection into the mission field.

To the padres themselves, of course, they were no mere servants of the secular authorities, but in fact one true reason for the whole state's existence overseas. It might be recalled that after Columbus' return from the New World in 1493, both Spain and Portugal sought papal mediation to protect their overseas discoveries. Papal mediation among monarchs was old enough in theory, but had seldom been practised, except in cases like this one where monarchs did not feel sanguine enough about something to fight over it.[3] (And one imagines that the post-Conciliar popes recognized themselves to be in a weak position vis-à-vis the New Monarchs and were eager to perform a task which could only increase their stature in the European community.) At any rate, the Borja pope's Aragonese friend, King Ferdinand, approached him with the mediation proposal and the Portuguese king, John II, whose nation had long enjoyed papal protection, was more or less bound to second the idea.

One imagines further that in the few weeks the papal legists had to draft the three mediatory bulls, they had to think very hard about a feasible basis on which their master could presume to allot areas of exclusive usufruct to each monarch with some expectation that the royal lawyers, both in Iberia and elsewhere, would accept it. I will spare here all the details, but essentially, what they decided seems to have rested upon Christ's spiritual dominion (and hence the pope's) over the heathen. If he did not actually rule them, then he could decide to whom to deputize as preachers to them on his behalf. He chose, of course, the two Iberian monarchs and in the second *Inter caetera* bull, of May, 1493, proposed a demarcation line to give each his own hemisphere as a parish. He further awarded each the unique right to exploit all lands to be discovered within his demarcated area, commanding the other Christian monarchs of Europe to keep out of them.[4]

From the above sketch, as telegraphic as it is, one can rightly suspect that other rulers would be less than acquiescent or happy about the arrangement. While Spain and Portugal signed an accord based upon it in 1494, the famous Treaty of Tordesillas, the battle to get other nations to recognize the papal decrees was a long and on the whole unsuccessful one. Already in 1496 King Henry VII of England sent out an explorer of his own, John Cabot, who may have reached Newfoundland. The only thing which probably made him desist from further exploration was Cabot's failure to return from a subsequent voyage. And of course King Francis I of France flouted the bulls and treaty openly, except on the occasions when defeats at the hands of Charles V temporarily restrained him.[5] In the end, it was more Spain's superior power than a willing recognition of the papal authority that kept the demarcated world mostly free of interlopers until the end of the sixteenth century, all due respects to Jacques Cartier, Jean Ribault, Nicolas Villegagnon and a few others, whose intentions were clear, but whose success was meagre.

Even though the papal mandate thus enjoyed a checkered success amongst the princes of Europe north of the Pyrenees, its implications were taken deadly seriously within the Iberian Peninsula, especially and initially in Spain. As early as 1512, members of the regular clergy were busy at court there, trying to convince King Ferdinand that if he did not oblige the colonists to treat the indigenes in a kind christian manner and support the fathers in their missionary needs, the papal rights accorded him might be voided.[6] Not only did Ferdinand listen, but all his successors as well. By and large, the kings decreed as the fathers bade them when it came to protecting what Lewis Hanke has called their 'title deeds'.

The Portuguese kings seem not to have had such delicate consciences as did the Spanish, at least they appear less preoccupied that lack of supportive behaviour toward mission work might lead to a loss of legal jurisdiction. As it was, Portuguese missionary activity really did not get rolling until around the time of St. Francis Xavier, or a little before, if only because the Portuguese conquered no extensive territories in Africa or Asia and because Moslems were nearly impossible to convert and Hindus far from easy. It was not until 1538 that Franciscans converted a large number of low caste *paravas* on the Fishery Coast of India near Cape Comorin and enjoyed the first mass success of the Portuguese *Padroado*, as the crown's jurisdiction over the missionary church was called. A few years later, Father Francis Xavier arrived in Lisbon, deeply impressed King D. John III and persuaded him to undertake a much more active missionary effort than he had hitherto contemplated. Not only did he lead the way so memorably, achieving sainthood on the basis of his intense missionary activities over the next decade (1542-1552), but the Jesuits became the shock troops of the *Padroado*, with the Franciscans and Augustinians, renewed in zeal, close behind. Despite setbacks, notably in Japan, and disappointments, as at Akbar, the Great Mogul's court, the missionaries made considerable progress, establishing Christian native colonies in the Moluccas, China, Japan, Malacca, Bengal, South India, Ceylon, Mozambique and Angola. It would seem that the Portuguese *Padroado* caught the spirit at just about the time in the mid-sixteenth century when, excepting some frontier areas like Paraguay, the Spanish counterpart *Patronato* was beginning to rest on its laurels. At any rate, the Asian *Padroado* was where the missionary action was occurring by the time the Dutch arrived.

The Heretics Attack

Although in the Atlantic Portuguese Brazil twice had had to expel French invaders during the sixteenth century, no Europeans save an occasional traveller by land violated the Asian *Padroado* until the Englishman James Lancaster sailed there in 1592. Three years later, a Dutchman, Cornelis de Houtman, arrived in the Moluccas. Then within a few years more, the Dutch were swarming in the area, and by 1605, Amboina was lost to them, followed in 1606 by Ternate and ten years later by Tidore. The fact that Xavier himself had converted Amboina could hardly have gone unnoticed by the missionaries. It meant that the spiritual conquests were now in peril.

That the Iberian church hardly viewed these reverses and others that followed as mere matters of losing colonial real estate is amply demonstrated by the reply of Frei Serafim de Freitas to Hugo Grotius' *Mare Liberum*, published anonymously in 1609. In it, as one will recall, Grotius argued the natural right of all nations to barter with one another, and asked: 'Can the vast, boundless sea be the appanage of any one country alone?'[7] This of course, might have been an effective rhetorical question, but it was a stupid thing to ask of a Portuguese. In 1625, one of them, Father Professor Doctor Serafim de

Freitas, a native of Lisbon and *catedrático* in canon law at the University of Valladolid, revealed the whole Grotian thesis to be devilish nonsense. His treatise, called *De Iusto Imperio Lusitanorum Asiatico*, does not leave the heretics a single toe to stand upon, not even an argument Grotius had drawn from the *Metamorphoses* of Ovid about the sun, the air and the water belonging to everyone. Virgil, wrote Freitas, could be cited against him; the poet said that Caesar Augustus ruled the very waves, and in truth, control over land masses did indeed impart sovereignty over seas which gave access to them. What was more, there was plenty of precedent in the ancient world and even in modern times for the levying of controls and tributes by virtue of maritime hegemony: witness the Venetians and their annual marriage to the sea. What was still more, one should not confuse the general utility to everyone of light, air or water with the commonality of ownership; if one gives another light from one's own flame, the owner's flame still remains his – so, if a prince concedes water rights to others, it does not mean he loses his rights to control the source.[8]

Having duelled with 'the anonymous one' on his own grounds, Freitas then returns to the legitimacy of the papal donation, the sacrifices of the Portuguese crown to achieve the road to India, and the heretical nature of the rebellious Hollanders, who in rejecting their prince committed a far greater misdeed than any the Portuguese may have committed in India. Finally, he closes his argument with Chapter XVIII, in which he justifies the entire exclusivity of the *Estado da Índia Oriental* on the basis of its missionary activity – verified by conversions and miracles from the Congo to Japan. Proof of this, he said, lies in the prophetic visions of the first Portuguese king on his coronation, in the five wounds of Christ corresponding to the five shields of the royal Portuguese coat of arms, and in the divine help the nation has continued to receive.[9]

Freitas' bold defense of the divinely sanctioned legitimacy and exclusivity enjoyed by the Estado da India must certainly be construed as the *Summa Theologica* of Portuguese Asia, and it stops only at the pearly gates of heaven. One will observe from it, that the *ad hoc* nature of the papal donation has now given way to an empire whose essential core is spiritual. When Freitas wrote, the Portuguese empire was already under military attack, and in the years ahead it actually became threatened with destruction. Now of course if something divinely ordained comes in peril, one can only conclude that God's will is being thwarted. But since He is omnipotent, He only permits the hindrance to exist to show His displeasure with, in this case, the sins of children of Portugal. Once they have repented, the divine plan would of course continue to unfold. Or so those concerned with the missions in Asia reasoned. It would almost seem that in their attempts to view all aspects of Portuguese Asia in the light of the papal donation – and a highly spiritualized interpretation of it at that – the fathers virtually put themselves in a plight where further reverses at the hands of the Protestant interlopers would either force them to abjure their faith – or else resort to highly original new explanations for what was happening and about to happen.

The Restauração

At what must have seemed the darkest moment of Portuguese Asia's history – and it certainly was up until then – news arrived in Goa of Portugal's revolt against Philippine Spain and the acclamation of John of Bragança as King John IV. I will not attempt to show in this article what role the prophetic and Sebastianist tradition played in this event – and it was not inconsiderable – but will only remark that it was easy for Portuguese to see the glorious restoration, or the Restauração, as the Portuguese called it, as a fresh start, a chance to reverse the tide. In my *Fatal History of Portuguese Ceylon*, I have indicated with what high hopes of retrieving their losses even the Portuguese ambassadors set out for The Hague. And how even the new king and his ministers expected that Portugal's regained independence would somehow induce the Dutch to return what the Portuguese considered as eternally and inflexibly their own.[10] So, I think, the fathers in Goa can be excused if they thought along the same lines. (Or, rather, it should perhaps be said that because the fathers thought and preached this way, the secular authorities reflected their thinking.) At any rate, it is now time to return to Fathers Ardizone Spinola and Queyroz.

Padre Antonio Ardizone Spinola was an Italian, as he tells us, a Genoese native of Naples. The new *Dicionário da Igreja em Portugal* further informs that he was born in 1609, studied philosophy and theology on his native soil and arrived at Goa via land passage, after a tiring journey. The date was October 25, 1640, just thirty-six days before the uprising and proclamation of independence back in Lisbon.[11] News of that event did not reach Goa until September 8 of the following year, right in the middle of Sunday mass in the cathedral church of Santa Catarina, where, as one might imagine, the solemnities dissolved into joyous confusion.[12] On the following Sunday, however, Father Spinola was ready to preach before Viceroy Aveiras and his council on the text from Deuteronomy 17: 'Thou shalt in any wise set him king over thee, whom the Lord thy God shall choose: one from among thy brethren shalt thou set king over thee: thou mayest not set a stranger over thee, which is not thy brother.'[13] This was the first of a dozen sermons, later collected into various tomes, but most notably into the *Cordel Triplicado de Amor a Christo Jesu Sacramentado*.

'Good news, good news!' he began appropriately enough by saying. Good news of a native king, chosen by God, good news, delayed so long, of the restoration of a monarchy eagerly prophesied and awaited. With the death of King Sebastian and the end of the native monarchy, he said, the Portuguese Empire 'nosedived (*hia de cabeça abaixo*) into pitiful losses, falling ever farther from that lustre and resplendency, those glories and greatnesses with which it shone in the days of its native kings.'[14] But now, just as the light was nearly extinguished, the wished-for event became reality and the one longed-for has taken up the sceptre and the crown of his empire.[15]

Although Padre Spinola openly professed his oneness with Portugal – he says in his dedicatory epistle to the Cordel that 'love made me a naturalized Portuguese since my passage to India' – he nevertheless was hardly blind to the faults of his adopted race. In his second series of sermons preached two years later in the same cathedral and devoted to the theme of Holy Communion, he says: 'Ah, it is not without cause that we have so many losses. Not without cause that we suffer the loss of our goods in India. Not without cause that the riches of our *conquistas* do not glisten before us . . . not without cause that God punishes you with ever renewed and ever unexpected punishments, losses and miseries.' The reason for this, he believes, is that white masters sin by not allowing their slaves and negroes to take holy communion.[16] Enlarging on this theme in another sermon he says: 'It is incomprehensible, this assumption that because they [the Portuguese] are white men they should disrespect with such regality the blacks of this *conquista*, freemen as well as slaves, that being blacks they are of no account to anybody – never considering that a black face does not prejudice the soul and that God far more values a good enslaved Christian than a great, very white senhor of bad life.' Why, he wonders, do the Portuguese not make friends with the Christian king of Monomatapa? He is a baptized Christian king, and his brother even a Dominican friar, residing in a convent of this city. It is, he says, because fidalgos are haughty to blacks – ironic, he says, because Saint Benedict the Black is so venerated in Portugal, and even in these *conquistas*. So why do the whites only talk to them condescendingly?'[17]

In his final group of four sermons, preached, incidentally, in Lisbon, before the king himself, Spinola makes it clear that John IV has work cut out for him: the Portuguese empire can only be renewed through his fusion of its purpose with the divine empire of Jesus Christ. As such, the king will become a new messiah, a light unto the gentiles, and the restorer, not only of Portugal's independence, but of faith, harmony, peace and unity to the world as well.[18] This was clearly a large order for so modest a man as King John to fill, incidentally, but the monarch at least liked the ideas enough to invite Dr. Spinola back to preach on four of his birthdays.

Spinola, though, however improbably his imagination might have soared into the empyrean, was but a link midway between the modest reality of a king created by acclamation at an unpromising moment and another churchman who likewise wrote about the predicament of *Asia Portuguesa*, Father Fernão de Queyroz, S.J.

The World of Pedro de Basto

Unlike the 'naturalized' Padre Ardizone Spinola, Fernão de Queyroz was a native Portuguese, born probably at Amarante in 1617, which makes him eight years younger.[19] He arrived in Goa in 1635, five years earlier, and it would be somewhat surprising if the two priests did not have a nodding acquaintance with one another, especially if Ardizone Spinola is known to have preached several sermons at the cathedral. At least they breathed the same air and were preoccupied with the same problem of explaining a contracting temporal empire, whose decline menaced the holy mission to which both friars were dedicated. In fact, the two men were very similar in their views, and I suspect it was little more than timing and circumstance that account for the differences between them. For one thing, Queyroz wrote some decades after Ardizone Spinola, when it was no longer possible to look forward to King John IV's restoration as an event which would set all things with the empire aright; Queyroz needed a new set of expectations in substitute. Then, secondly, Queyroz's insertion point was not the occasion of the Restauração itself, but a desire to write the biography of one Brother Pedro de Basto, a clairvoyant who enjoyed (or perhaps one should say 'suffered') visions which pertained chiefly to the island of Ceylon, where the Dutch had begun actions to expel the Portuguese. In the process of his writing and research, Queyroz of necessity had to consider the interpretation and accuracy of Basto's visions.

This dual task, of writing a biography and then verifying the visions of its subject, accounts for the apparently chimerical structure of the book: half of it (to p. 282) is full of Basto's inner life, while the remainder appears a straightforward politico-military chronicle of the struggle in Asia and particularly Ceylon between the Dutch and the Portuguese. By this expedient Queyroz simply wanted to demonstrate how the two dovetailed: he writes in his introduction that he did not 'set out to ramble on about political events of the whole Orient, but because so many of them were contained in revelations [. . .] and many others in the future, it would be impossible to form any concept of all God revealed to [Basto] unless one was aware of them'. It is worth noting, incidentally, that after finishing the work on Basto, Queyroz went on to 'ramble' for a thousand more folio pages of political events. This was his manuscript *A Conquista (Temporal e Espiritual) de Ceilão*, not published until this century, but invaluable to scholars. One must really consider it an extension of the *Vida do Veneravel Irmão Pedro de Basto* being scrutinized here.

Practically everything known of Basto's life comes via Queyroz, who not only made a thorough study of his hero, but possessed autobiographical material of him which has subsequently been lost. The brother was born in Portugal in 1570, shipped out to Goa as a soldier in the fleet of 1586, but then almost immediately began a novitiate with the Jesuit Order there. He was at the Collegio de São Paulo until 1589, then transferred to Cochin, where he remained until his death in 1645. He was a lay coadjutor, never consecrated as a priest, and he filled menial jobs in the cloister there, notably as keeper of the chapter's linen. But everybody knew and heeded his prophesies. Even as a boy of eight, he was said to have warned against King Sebastian's expedition to Africa,[20] while after his arrival in Cochin, he proved his worth to many people, like the two Portuguese whom he warned not to journey to Bengal on a certain ship. They took his advice and stayed home; the ship was wrecked. Once he even was said to have read the mind of Dom Felipe Mascarenhas, later a viceroy, and simply told him: 'Don't do what you're thinking about! Certainly not in the way you're thinking about it!'[21] But such prophesies of a personal variety were hardly Basto's main interest, though: he was most concerned with the supernatural forces in conflict to determine the fate of Portuguese Asia. In short, the struggle between God and Satan.

What the conflict was really about, and what gave Satan such power, Queyroz makes clear, was the corruption of the Portuguese. 'Portugal could have been today a flourishing kingdom if by every manner and means, we had not disposed it to ruin so great that we can neither repair it with right sentiments nor strong medication [. . .] today the income of the State is very limited and always distributed in such a manner that the king is always poor in India.'[22] It was no wonder, he felt, that the Devil had gained such ascendancy there.

Thus it was, too, that despite all his fervent prayers, Basto himself was literally haunted by satanic forces. Incubi grappled with him at the communion rail or tried to keep him from entering the choir by tugging at his clothing and shouting 'AY, HY!!'. Sometimes even cloistermates were frightened, as when a fellow Jesuit, Padre João de Silva, heard all sorts of 'commotions in the corridor and hauling of chains on its flooring, so much that he became deathly afraid, it seeming to him that they were entering into his cell when he felt the door shaking. Whereupon he called Basto, who said, "Father, have no fear – this happens to me every day at mealtime". Showing clearly', Queyroz said, 'that he knew clearly all this to be the work of demons, and how importunate they were in his persecution. At which the Padre de Silva could not hide his fear and remained astounded both at the way the malignant spirits worked and the divine spirit revealed.' Once, the devil himself, being especially angry with Basto, came accompanied by the same foul army, sought the brother out in his linen closet, grabbed him by the neck and would have choked him, had Basto not invoked the holy name of Jesus, whereupon all the devils suddenly disappeared, leaving him breathless.[23] Such a price the poor clairvoyant had to pay for being a window on God.

In the earlier days, Basto's visions ranged over a wide geographical area and even brought him news of what was occurring in the Straits of Malacca. In 1629, he had a vision of:

'[. . .] Fleets, being a cannon shot apart, about to start battle and our [sailors] shout "Santiago!" at the enemy. I saw coming from the side of the city of Malacca, with the wind at its stern and all in a great hurry with all its sails piled on, a handsome and powerful ship, its canvas, masts and spars resplendent, of rare materials, its hull of the finest, polished gold, which was topped off with a great poop, from which came many courtesans of glory, all armed from head to toe with the finest, glistening armour – who at their appearance stuck such great terror and dismay into the hearts of the enemy, and with the intrepid assaults they made upon it, in a short time it was defeated.'[24]

Such was Basto's splendid vision of Nuno Alvares Botelho's triumph over the King of Achin, fully borne out, as Queyroz affirms, by subsequent reports.

When after this glorious achievement, Admiral Botelho drowned a year later, Basto had another of him in 'a glory exceeding all his previous victories'.[25]

After the Dutch invasion of Ceylon in 1638, Basto's powers became focussed upon the seesaw battle for that island, and he foresaw events in a panoply of psychic images. He fervently besought God to save it, but the best he was able to obtain were mixed signals, doubtlessly an expression of the conflict between the heavenly will and the sins of Portugal which were thwarting it. One of the most ominous of these signs was a vision of Christ, with three lances in his hands, saying: 'All of these three I must break in Ceylon.'[26]

As mediator between himself and the Deity, Basto had frequent visions of none other than Saint Francis Xavier in person 'in the middle of the Host (no doubt while exposed on the altar), with his countenance toward the Gospel side, his hands together upon his breast, his eyes downcast, pleading with enormous fervour for the fortress (in this case, the strategic one of Galle) and Christianity'.[27] As matters worsened, Xavier's image was seen to pray even more fervently, so inclined to the ground that 'his back appeared to make a line parallel to it'. Simultaneously, he heard a voice saying: 'The danger is very great, the danger is very great.' Then, when Galle finally fell, on the same day Basto was overheard as saying to Padre Manuel de Leiva: 'Father, I saw a man as bloodied as an *ecce homo*; these are signs, but I don't know from where.' About a week later, the sad news arrived of Galle's loss.

Practically the only comfort the heavens could send through the venerable brother involved temporary stays of execution; when a Portuguese officer feared Dutch reinforcements were en route to Ceylon, Basto made a novena. Thereupon the Holy Spirit was seen as hovering above the island and God disclosed to him three factors greatly in its favour. Of these, incidentally, only one factor proved necessary: the fleet had been bound for another destination and passed Ceylon harmlessly by![28]

Brother Basto did not live to see the end of the conflict, but before his death, Queyroz affirms that God showed him both visions of the subsequent ruin of Ceylon and happy visions of its ultimate redemption. First, he experienced more visions of Xavier, prostrate on the ground, with a voice saying: 'Colombo was lost.' But other visions were more comforting: one week, while praying for Colombo, he saw 'a cross, elevated, covered with many precious diamonds and all sorts of other precious stones, and on both sides a multitude afoot, celebrating the feast, or victory of this same cross, with great joy'. And, finally, he experienced a super vision: 'I saw in the Host St. Francis Xavier, very resplendent, yet vested in red, and with him the Resurrected Christ, with a standard or flag in his hand, and an illustrious Portuguese man, of great authority, on a large and handsome throne [. . .] The generals of Ceylon were treated like kings, and held sway over all the natives of the island from a magnificent Portuguese encampment. And then I heard a voice which repeated thrice these words: "Long live the Church and the seat of Saint Peter!".'[29] Soon thereafter, on April 6, 1645, the venerable monk died. Colombo fell eleven years later.

Even though Pedro de Basto was dead, Queyroz had still more to communicate, not only about the subsequent perfect preservation and sweet aroma of the holy man's body after years in the grave, but about the future of Ceylon and the Portuguese empire. It is clear that he considers Basto a prime candidate for sanctification. He also warns: 'It is incumbent upon us to believe that [God] is punishing us like a father, and that he will remedy us as befits a Lord – for the examples of [restored] Portugal, Brazil, Angola, Maranhão and São Tomé facilitate this hope, even though all of India has had to suffer, being more guilty. The favour with which God embraces us in other parts of the world still excludes us from the singular grace which God has imparted to us in Europe, America and Africa.'[30]

In the end, though, he believed nothing could prevent a final, glorious outcome – the restoration of Ceylon, the conversion or destruction, like reeds in a raging fire, of the heretical Dutch, and finally, in the year 1702, according to calculation, the establishment of a thousand-year (fifth) monarchy under the Portuguese king.[31] One will note here that Queyroz is no longer drawing from his original material derived from the study of Pedro de Basto, but has switched into a prophetic, Portuguese metropolitan strain of thinking, whose roots, perhaps in the writings of one Padre Luz de Granada, I hope to untangle in the future. Suffice it here, however, that it was based on some doggerel verses of a shoemaker and on the prophetic Book of Daniel and involved a bit of manipulation of his first four Biblical empires to bring them forward in time and allow the last of these to fall on the Caliphate, making room for the final Portuguese world empire of John IV, who had already died in 1656. No matter – even the famous Padre António Vieira, S.J., believed John would be resuscitated for the purpose and successfully defended his viewpoint before the Inquisition in 1663-67.[32] So nobody can blame Padre Queyroz for borrowing the prophesies which morticed so well into his own.

One can only observe from a perspective of three hundred years since the time of Queyroz's writing that chroniclers have vastly preferred to report the foundations of empires over their dismal declines and that the few who did needed all the divine help they could get to console them. At the time of conquest only strong, right arms were needed and men like Barros, Castanheda and Corrêa quickly produced heroic chronicles of high quality to record the feats for posterity. Even writers who largely derived their facts from them, like Damião de Góis and Jerónimo Osório, could not resist participating in the fun. But the dark sadnesses of defeat are not pleasant to write about, and the arthritic old priest needed his self-deceptions in order to take up his pen.

The Impossible Dream

If one is to compare Fernão de Queyroz with Ardizone Spinola and both of them with the *Iusto Imperio Lusitanorum Asiatico* of Serafim de Freitas, it would seem that the Portuguese empire became, in the eyes of the missionaries, anyway, an increasingly spiritual entity. It moved in this direction most rapidly as a result of the incursion into it – and the challenge to Portuguese power – by the Protestant Dutch. If one remembers that the original papal grant had seemingly been based upon the only possible authority at the popes' disposal – that of imposing the pursuit of missionary activity in return for an exclusive right to occupy such vast areas – then the moment it came under attack by the heretics, the rather *ad hoc* and flimsy mediation which had never convinced even the Catholic powers became the all-important justification.

Meanwhile, the missionary clergy, once it had begun to enjoy measure of success with the gentiles of Asia, began to see itself as the instrument of God's supreme will for his creation, the very vessel of his love and grace. Seldom in modern history seem men to have felt so compelling a sense of purpose, as did the missionaries.

By 1640, the date of the Restauração, however, they were already in danger of disillusion, and one can perceive this event gave them fresh hope that the new king John IV might somehow return Portugal and the Asian empire to its golden era. Hence Ardizone Spinola's ecstatic sermons with their expectations of just this. Queyroz, though, speaks of clairvoyant saints, resuscitations and thousand-year empires. Certainly, he was no more of a madman than Spinola, with whom he shared the identical vision: it was only that he wrote thirty years later. King John was by then dead, and his reign had not halted the ruin of Portuguese Asia. So the Jesuit had to reaffirm his militant faith in still more apocalyptic terms, or else lose it altogether. To him there must have seemed no other way out.

Some cynic has defined a fanatic as one who redoubles his efforts when he has lost sight of his goal, and while I would not go so far as to label either of the authors as fanatics, I would rather emphasize their quandary: the vision of a Christian Orient with themselves in the central role was too compelling not to pursue, while the actual events were too threatening not to explain away. The only thing to do was to take refuge in fancy. And this was all too easy while living in an age which could still bring itself to believe in miracles.

Time has not been particularly kind to the protagonists. Basto, whom Queyroz hoped to elevate into sainthood through his scholarly study, has instead been all but forgotten; the *Catholic Encyclopaedia* does not mention him at all, while the *Grande Encyclopedia Luso-Brasileira* gives him only a few lines. Queyroz himself is known today almost entirely for his book on Ceylon, in short as a historian pure and simple. And Ardizone Spinola is remembered only as the founder of the Theatines in Goa and Portugal. In 1775, his *Cordel Triplicado* was condemned and put on the Index 'for containing intolerable, erroneous and scandalous propositions', doubtlessly those which practically equated King John IV with the holy one.[33]

In the end, most priests of the *Padroado* must have been willing to accept things as they came, even though the mighty dream had obviously turned into a nightsweat. The new opportunities may have been modest, but at least clerics were found who continued to present themselves for preaching and administration of the Sacraments. As the book by Robrecht J. Boudens shows, by the early eighteenth century, Portuguese fathers were back in Ceylon – on the sly.[34] It seems the Dutch East India Company, too parsimonious to staff its own churches adequately, had half-solicited their return, because they had noticed that Christian natives were always more loyal and easier to handle than Buddhist ones. Those returning priests most likely never thought of themselves as belonging to a front line of realists, but the fact is that in any society – or institution – there are the thinkers and the doers, the fantasts and the practical souls. In this case, one is tempted to speculate that it might be a good thing for society that some of us do not dream too much when there is work to be done.

Notes

1. For instance, see the *Documentos Remetidos da India*, Arquivo Nacional do Torre do Tombo, Livros 43-62; they form an almost unbroken litany of despair.
2   It is curious how few writers simply ascribed the Portuguese plight to the superior resources of their rival(s). One has the feeling that both the clergy and reformers like Francisco Rodrigues de Silveira were so eager to score their points against the conduct of governmental employees that they were only too glad to make it appear that the reverses were really due to the corruption and discrimination they attacked!
3   For information regarding the papal mediation, the best source I have found is Charles Martial de Witte, *Les bulles pontificales et l'expansion portugaise au XVe siècle* (Louvain 1958), which is also available as four articles, in *Revue d'Histoire Ecclésiastique* 48 (1953), 49 (1954), 51 (1956) and 53 (1958). There is a good short discussion in Hélio Vianna, *História do Brasil* (14th ed. (and all others); São Paulo 1980) 32-36. The text of the *Inter caetera* bulls, as well as of *Eximiae devotiònis*, can be found in Frances G. Davenport ed., *European Treaties Bearing on the History of the United States and Its Dependencies* (4 vols.; Washington D.C. 1914) I, 77-96.
4   Davenport ed., *European Treaties* I, 77-78. I am aware that the interpretations are legion, and that the Vatican may have simply assumed that it did indeed possess temporal power over kings.
5   See Paul E. Hoffman, 'Diplomacy and the Papal Donation, 1493-1584', *The Americas* 30, 2 (1973) 156-165.
6   See Lewis Hanke, *The Spanish Struggle for Justice in the Conquest of America* (Philadelphia 1949) 23-36 and chapter X.
7   Of the various translations of the *Mare Liberum*, I have employed the English translation of 1916 by J.B. Scott, published by the Carnegie Foundation.
8   Frei Serafim de Freitas, *Do Justo Império Asiático dos Portugueses* (De Iusto Imperio Lusitanorum Asiatico). tr. Miguel Pinto de Meneses, with an introduction by Marcello Caetano (2 vols.; Lisbon 1959-1961). These arguments are contained in chapter 10, in Vol. I, 247-261; in Vol. II (the original Latin), 120-130.
9   Ibidem, Chapters XII, 287-291 in I; 150-153 in II; 353-359 in I; 201-205; 371-382 in I; 217-225 in II. In making this 'synthesis', I have not attempted to present all the arguments of Freitas, but more to give the flavour of the debate.
10 G.D. Winius, *The Fatal History of Portuguese Ceylon; Transition to Dutch Rule* (Cambridge, Mass. 1971) chapter IV and V.
11 António Alberto Banha de Andrade ed., *Dicionário da Igreja em Portugal* (2 vols.; Lisbon 1982) I, 494-495.
12 Winius, *Fatal History*, 51.

13   Antonio Ardizone Spinola, *Portugal Restituido na Decima Sexta Geraçam de Seus Reys Naturals, prometido por Deos ao Sancto & Invicto Rey Dom Affonso Henriques & emparada do Ceo com prodigios e milagres* (Lisbon n.d., but before 1680) 3. An early edition, apparently in three volumes, of the *Cordel Triplicado de Amor a Christo Jesu Sacramentado* (Lisbon 1680). The earlier volume is curious in that it contains no licenses or imprimatur, nor even a printer and date.

14   Ibidem, 31.

15   Ibidem, 32.

16   *Cordel Triplicado*, 363.

17   Ibidem, 553.

18   Ibidem, 652-735. Spinola was invited to Lisbon by King John, after news had reached him of the Italian's strong support of his legitimacy. The sermons of the third and last book were preached in his presence.

19   Fernão de Queyroz, *Conquest of Ceylon.* tr. S.G. Perera, S.J. (3 vols.; Colombo 1930) I, 5*.

20   Fernão de Queyroz, *A Vida do Veneravel Irmão Pedro de Basto* (Lisbon 1689) 7.

21   Ibidem, 138.

22   Ibidem, 132-136.

23   Ibidem, 145-146.

24   Ibidem, 364.

25   Ibidem, 365.

26   Ibidem, 382.

27   Ibidem, 378.

28   Ibidem, 388.

29   Ibidem, 389.

30   Ibidem, 390.

31   Ibidem, 421 ff.

32   There are few monographs on Fifth Monarchist, prophetical nationalism in regard to Portugal, and most writing on it concerns António Vieira, S.J. Modern Portuguese historians pointedly avoid it. The best work on the subject is Raymond Cantel, *Prophétisme et messianisme dans l'oeuvre de António Vieira* (Paris 1960). See also Charles R. Boxer, *The Church Militant and Iberian Expansion* (Baltimore and London 1978) 116-118.

33   Andrade, *Dicionário da Igreja* I, 495. He does not seem to have been affected by the millenarist thinking which was so prevalent in Portugal, however, and which was doubtless so effective in preparing the ground for the Restauração. Perhaps the fact that he was an Italian who had reached India by land helps explain this. He was also shrewd enough to use his royal pulpit to get what he most wanted: permission to introduce a convent of his Theatine Order into Portugal at a time when the country could scarcely afford such luxuries and the crown was trying to keep church expenditure down. He boldly asked for this in a sermon to the king – and got it. See *Cordel Triplicado*, 733-734.

34   Robrecht Boudens, O.M.Z., *The Catholic Church in Ceylon under Dutch Rule* (Rome 1957) passim.

12

Power Versus Plenty as Objectives of Foreign Policy in the Seventeenth and Eighteenth Centuries

Jacob Viner

IN the seventeenth and eighteenth centuries economic thought and practice were predominantly carried on within the framework of that body of ideas which was later to be called "mercantilism." Although there has been almost no systematic investigation of the relationship in mercantilist thought between economic and political objectives or ends in the field of foreign policy, certain stereotypes have become so prevalent that few scholars have seriously questioned or examined their validity. One of these stereotypes is that mercantilism was a "system of power," that is, that "power" was for mercantilists the sole or overwhelmingly preponderant end of foreign policy, and that wealth, or "plenty," was valued solely or mainly as a necessary means to attaining or retaining or exercising power. It is the purpose of this paper to examine in the light of the available evidence the validity of this interpretation of mercantilist thought and practice. Tracing the history of ideas, however, always runs to many words, and limitations of space force me to confine myself, even with respect to bibliographical references, to samples of the various types of relevant evidence. That the samples are fair ones I can only attest by my readiness in most cases to expand them indefinitely.

The pioneer historians of mercantilism were nineteenth-century German scholars, predominantly Prussians sympathetic to its economic and political philosophy, and especially to its emphasis on state interests as opposed to the private interests of citizens. The interpretation of mercantilism by Schmoller as primarily a system of state-building is familiar, and com-

278 —————— THEORIES OF EMPIRE, 1450–1800 ——————

2   WORLD POLITICS

monly accepted by economic historians.[1] A similar stress on the political aspects of mercantilist commercial policy is common in the German writings. The proposition that the mercantilists sought a favorable balance of trade, wealth, and the indefinite accumulation of the precious metals solely as means to power seems first to have been launched by Baron von Heyking, who indeed claims priority for his interpretation.[2] Schmoller similarly interpreted the uncorrupted mercantilism of Prussia and of the non-maritime countries in general, but he maintained that the "imperialism" of the maritime powers was a debased mercantilism, characterized by an unscrupulous use of military power to promote ultimate commercial ends, and half-condemned it on that ground.[3]

This distinction between "pure" mercantilism, a "Staatsmerkantilismus," which can obtain its full development only in an absolute monarchy, and the mercantilism of countries where the commercial classes are influential and the state has to serve and to reconcile private economic interests, is also made much of by a later German writer, Georg Herzog zu Mecklenburg Graf von Carlow. For "pure" mercantilism, the ruling principle is not economic but the promotion of the power of the state.[4] In general, however, the historians have not distinguished between the mercantilism of the absolute and the constitutional

[1] I suspect, nevertheless, that it is highly questionable. The economic unification of the nation-state appears mostly to have occurred before the advent of mercantilism, as in England, or after its decay, as in France, Spain, Russia, Switzerland, Italy, the United States, or the British Dominions, if the national unification of tariffs or other significant criteria are applied. Even Colbert promoted regional as well as national self-sufficiency. As Moritz Bonn has commented (*Journal of Political Economy*, LIV [1946], 474), "A parochialist like Gustav Schmoller naturally deduced his impressions of mercantilism from the policies of primitive Prussia."

[2] *Zur Geschichte der Handelsbilanztheorie*, Berlin, 1880, Ch. 2, "Die Beziehungen der Theorie der Handelsbilanz zur Theorie des politischen Gleichgewichtes." The claim for priority is on p. 43. This chapter is a pioneer and valid demonstration of the existence of a close relationship between mercantilist balance-of-trade and balance-of-power theorizing and policy, but there is not a trace of valid demonstration in it that wealth considerations were made wholly subservient to power considerations.

[3] See his *Umrisse und Untersuchungen*, Leipzig, 1898, especially Ch. I, "Das Merkantilsystem in seiner historischen Bedeutung," pp. 42-60; see also "Die englische Handelspolitik des 17. und 18. Jahrhunderts," in *Jahrbuch für Gesetzgebung, Verwaltung, und Volkswirtschaft*, XX (1899), 1211-1241. F. Brie, *Imperialistische Strömungen in der Englischen Literatur*, 2nd ed., Halle, 1928, p. 68, characterizes English mercantilism of the eighteenth century, along Schmollerian lines, as "kaufmännisch gefärbte Imperialismus."

[4] *Richelieu als merkantilistischer Wirtschaftspolitiker und der Begriff des Staatsmerkantilismus*, Jena, 1929, pp. 198ff..

POWER vs. PLENTY UNDER MERCANTILISM   3

states, and where they have dealt at all with the questions of the ultimate aims of mercantilism they have almost invariably asserted that these were solely or preponderantly political, although only too often with ambiguity or even outright self-contradiction, and almost invariably without presentation of substantial evidence.

A case in point is William Cunningham, the English economic historian. His predominant interpretation of English mercantilism was that it sought power rather than or much more than plenty, and that it valued plenty solely or mainly as an instrument or support of power, although he easily slipped, in this as in other analytical issues, into ambiguity if not hopeless contradiction.[5] An English economic historian sympathetic to mercantilism, W. A. S. Hewins, regarded this interpretation as unfair to the mercantilists, and offered the following rendition of Cunningham's position to indicate its inacceptability:

> . . . one might almost imagine him [i.e., Cunningham] saying: "The mercantile system is concerned with man solely as a being who pursues national power, and who is capable of judging the comparative efficacy of means to that end. It makes entire abstraction of every other human passion or motive, except those which may be regarded as perpetually antagonizing principles to the pursuit of national power—viz., neglect of shipping and aversion to a fish diet. The mercantile system considers mankind as occupied solely in pursuing and acquiring national power."[6]

[5] Cf., for contradiction with the view that power was the predominant objective, *The Growth of English Industry and Commerce in Modern Times*, Vol. II, *In Modern Times, Part I*, Cambridge, 1903, p. 459: "From the Revolution till the revolt of the colonies, the regulation of commerce was considered, not so much with reference to other elements of national power, or even in its bearing on revenue, but chiefly with a view to the promotion of industry." Cf. also, *The Wisdom of the Wise*, Cambridge, 1906: "In the pre-scientific days the end which men of affairs kept in view, when debating economic affairs, was clearly understood; the political power of the realm was the object they put before them, . . ." (p.21) "We recognize [today] that the defense of the realm is essential to welfare, but we are no longer so much concerned about building up the power of the country, or so ready to engage in aggressive wars *for the sake of commercial advantages,* as Englishmen were in the eighteenth century." (p. 22) The italics are mine. The contradiction the italicized words seem to indicate may not be real, since Cunningham may have had in mind that the "commercial advantages" were sought for the sake of their contribution to British power, but such exposition, ambiguous, if not contradictory, is so common in the literature that it provides of itself a justification for an article such as the present one.

[6] In a review of Cunningham's *Growth of English Industry and Commerce* in *The Economic Journal*, II (1892), 696. Cunningham, in a reply to Hewins and other reviewers, *ibid.*, IV (1894), 508-16, permitted this interpretation of his position to pass without comment, although it must have been obvious to him that Hewins regarded it as a *reductio ad absurdum*.

All the German and English economic historians who found in mercantilism the complete subordination of economic to political considerations seem to have been themselves sympathetic to the subordination of the individual to the state and to the exaltation of vigorous nationalism characteristic of mercantilism, and to have been hostile to nineteenth century liberalism and its revolt against the residues of mercantilist legislation. Where this was combined, as in Schmoller and Cunningham, with a dislike of the rise of the bourgeois and his values to dominance over politics, to attribute to the mercantilists the conception of power as the sole or preponderant end of national policy was to praise rather than to blame them.

Eli Heckscher, the great Swedish economic historian and the outstanding authority on mercantilism today, follows the standard interpretation of the mercantilist objectives, but clearly to add to their shame rather than to praise them. Heckscher is an outstanding liberal, an individualist, a free-trader, and clearly anti-chauvinist. When to the section of his great work dealing with the foreign policy of the mercantilists he gives the heading "Mercantilism as a System of Power,"[7] and applies it to mercantilism in general and not only to the mercantilism of the absolute monarchies or of the non-maritime countries, he is reinforcing the indictment of it which he makes on other grounds, for to him "power" is clearly an ugly name for an ugly fact. More systematically, more learnedly, and more competently than anyone else, he supports his thesis that the mercantilists subordinated plenty to power. His argument calls therefore for detailed examination if this proposition is to be questioned.

Heckscher really presents an assortment of theses, ranging from the proposition (1) that for mercantilists—whether for most, or many, or only some, not being made very clear—power was the *sole* ultimate end of state policy with wealth merely one of the means to the attainment of power through the "eclectic" thesis (2) that power and plenty were parallel ends for the mercantilists but with much greater emphasis placed on power than was common before or later, to the concession (3) that mercantilists occasionally reversed the usual position and regarded power as a means for securing plenty and treated purely com-

[7] *Mercantilism,* translated by Mendel Shapiro, 2 vols., London, 1935, II, 13-52.

POWER vs. PLENTY UNDER MERCANTILISM   5

mercial considerations as more important than considerations of power. His central position, however, and to this he returns again and again, is that the mercantilists expounded a doctrine under which all considerations were subordinated to considerations of power as an end in itself, and that in doing so they were logically and in their distribution of emphasis unlike their predecessors and unlike the economists of the nineteenth century.

It is difficult to support this account of Heckscher's position by direct quotation from his text, since he presents it more by implication and inference from mercantilist statements than by clear-cut and explicit formulation in his own words. That mercantilists according to Heckscher tended to regard power as the *sole* end is to be inferred by the contrasts he draws between the position he attributes to Adam Smith—wrongly, I am sure— that "power was certainly only a means to the end . . . of opulence," and the "reverse" position of the mercantilists,[8] the "reverse," I take it, being the proposition that wealth was only a means to power. That there is something special and peculiar to mercantilism in conceiving power as an end in itself underlies all of Heckscher's exposition, but the following passages come nearest to being explicit. "The most vital aspect of the problem is whether power is conceived as an end in itself, or only as a means for gaining something else, such as the well-being of the nation in this world or its everlasting salvation in the next."[9] This leaves out of account, as an alternative, Heckscher's "eclectic" version, where both power and plenty are ends in themselves. On John Locke's emphasis on the significance for power of monetary policy, Heckscher comments, with the clear implication that the injection into economic analysis of considerations of power is not "rational," that it is "interesting as a proof of how important considerations of power in money policy appeared even to so advanced a rationalist as Locke."[10]

Heckscher later restated his position in response to criticisms, but it seems to me that he made no important concession and

8 *Ibid.*, II.
9 *Ibid.*, II, 16.
10 *Ibid.*, II, 47.

indeed ended up with a more extreme position than at times he had taken in his original exposition.

> The second of the aims of mercantilist policy . . . —that of power— has met with a great deal of criticism from reviewers of my book . . . I agree with my critics on that point to the extent of admitting that both "power" and "opulence" . . . have been, and must be, of importance to economic policy of every description. But I do not think there can be any doubt that these two aims changed places in the transition from mercantilism to *laissez-faire*. All countries in the nineteenth century made the creation of wealth their lode-star, with small regard to its effects upon the power of the State, while the opposite had been the case previously.[11]

The evidence which Heckscher presents that the mercantilists considered power as an end in itself and as an important end, and that they considered wealth to be a means of power need not be examined here, since there is no ground for disputing these propositions and, as far as I know, no one has ever disputed them. That the mercantilists overemphasized these propositions I would also not question. Nor will I enter here into extended discussion of the rationality of these concepts beyond stating a few points. In the seventeenth and eighteenth centuries, colonial and other overseas markets, the fisheries, the carrying trade, the slave trade, and open trade routes over the high seas, were all regarded, and rightly, as important sources of national wealth, but were available, or at least assuredly available, only to countries with the ability to acquire or retain them by means of the possession and readiness to use military strength.

In the seventeenth and eighteenth centuries also, "power" meant not only power to conquer and attack, and the prestige and influence which its possession gave, but also power to maintain national security against external attack. "Power as an end in itself" must, therefore, be interpreted to include considerations of national security against external aggression on the nation's territory and its political and religious freedom. Given the nature of human nature, recognition of power as an end in

[11] "Revisions in Economic History, V, Mercantilism," *The Economic History Review*, VII (1936), 48. The foreign policy implications of the nineteenth century economics, I believe, need investigation as much as do the aims of mercantilism. Until such investigation is systematically made, comparisons with mercantilism are liable to be misleading with respect to the true position of both bodies of doctrine.

itself was therefore then neither peculiar nor obviously irrational unless there is rational ground for holding that the promotion of economic welfare is the sole sensible objective of national policy to which every other consideration must be completely subordinated.

There remains, therefore, to be examined only whether Heckscher has demonstrated that mercantilists *ever* regarded power as the *sole* end of foreign policy, or ever held that considerations of plenty were *wholly* to be subordinated to considerations of power, or even whether they ever held that a choice has to be made in long-run national policy between power and plenty.

Despite his wide knowledge of the mercantilist literature, Heckscher fails to cite a single passage in which it is asserted that power is or should be the *sole* end of national policy, or that wealth matters *only* as it serves power. I doubt whether any such passage can be cited, or that anyone ever held such views. The nearest thing to such statements which Heckscher does cite are statements maintaining that wealth is a means of power and is important as such, unaccompanied by express acknowledgment that wealth is also important for its own sake. In almost every case he cites, it is possible to cite from the same writer passages which show that wealth was regarded as valuable also for its own sake. The passage of this type which Heckscher most emphasizes is a "passing remark" of Colbert in a letter: "Trade is the source of finance and finance is the vital nerve of war." Heckscher comments that Colbert here "indicates clearly the relationship between means and ends."[12] But argument from silence is notoriously precarious, and if it were to be pressed would work more against than for Heckscher's thesis, since there is a great mass of mercantilist literature in which there is no mention whatsoever, and no overt implication, of considerations of power. Colbert does not here indicate that the relationship was a one-way one. To make a significant point Heckscher would have to show that Colbert would not also have subscribed to the obverse proposition that strength is the vital nerve of trade and finance the source of trade.

Of all the mercantilists Colbert is the most vulnerable, since he carried all the major errors of economic analysis of which

[12] *Mercantilism*, II, 16.

8   WORLD POLITICS

they were guilty to their most absurd extremes both in verbal
exposition and in practical execution, and since, either as expressing his own sentiments or catering to those of his master,
Louis XIV, he developed more elaborately than any other author the serviceability to power of economic warfare, the possibilities of using military power to achieve immediate economic
ends, and the possibilities of substituting economic warfare for
military warfare to attain national ends. Even in his case, however, it is not possible to demonstrate that he ever rejected
or regarded as unimportant the desirability for its own sake of
a prosperous French people or the desirability of guiding French
foreign policy, military and economic, so as to augment this
prosperity. In many of his official papers he is obviously catering to Louis XIV's obsession with power and prestige, or perhaps to a conventional fashion of *pretending* that a great monarch would be so obsessed,[13] so that there is no reason to reject
as unrepresentative of his genuinely-held views, such passages
as the following:

> . . . comme toutes les alliances entre les grands rois ont toujours
> deux fins principales, l'une leur gloire particulière et quelquefois la
> jonction de leurs intérests, soit pour conserver, soit pour acquérir
> . . . et l'autre les avantages de leurs sujets, . . . Et quoyque dans l'ordre
> de le division, celuy de l'avantage de leurs sujets soit le dernier, il
> est néanmoins toujours le premier dans les esprits de bons princes . . .
>
> Les avantages de leurs sujets consistent à les maintenir en repos
> au dedans et à leur procurer par le moyen du commerce, soit plus de
> facilités de vivre aux nécessiteux, soit plus d'abondance aux riches.[14]

Certain peculiar features of mercantilist economic analysis-
features incidentally which modern apologists for mercantilist

[13] Cf. the following passage in his famous "Mémoire au Roi sur les Finances" of 1670:
"Il est certain, Sire, que Vostre Majesté . . . a dans son esprit et dans toute sa nature la
guerre par préférence à toute autre chose . . . Vostre Majesté pense plus dix fois à la guerre
qu'elle ne pense à ses finances." *Lettres Instructions et Mémoires de Colbert*, P. Clément,
ed., Paris, 1870, VII, 252. This long memoir is a plea to the king to look to his economic
policy, including economic warfare, as an essential instrument for attaining his ends.
Even in the case of Louis XIV, himself, it is easy to show from his writings that the
prosperity of his people, while no doubt inexcusably underemphasized, was a matter of some
concern to him for its own sake.

[14] "Dissertation sur la question quelle des deux alliances de France ou de Hollande peut
estre plus avantageuse à l'Angleterre," March, 1669. *Lettres*, VI, 261. A letter of Colbert
to Louis XIV in 1681 contains the following passage: "Ce qu'il y a de plus important, et
sur quoi il y a plus de réflexions à faire, c'est la misére très-grande des peuples." C.
Dareste de la Chavanne, *Histoire de l'Administration en France*, Paris, 1848, II, 258.

POWER vs. PLENTY UNDER MERCANTILISM   9

economics such as Lipson seem strangely to avoid discussing—
do seem to imply a disregard on the part of mercantilists for
economic welfare.[15] What was apparently a phase of scholastic
economics, that what is one man's gain is necessarily another
man's loss, was taken over by the mercantilists and applied to
countries as a whole. They incorporated this with their tendency
to identify wealth with money, and with their doctrine that, as
far as money was concerned, what mattered was not the absolute
quantity but the relative quantity as compared with other countries. Since the quantity of money in the world could be taken
as constant, the quantity of wealth in the world was also a
constant, and a country could gain only at the expense of
other countries. By sheer analogy with the logic of military
power, which is in truth a relative matter, and with the aid of
the assumption of a close relationship between "balance of
power" and "balance of trade," which, however, they failed in-
telligently to analyze, the mercantilists were easily led to the
conclusion that wealth, like power, also was only a relative
matter, a matter of proportions between countries, so that a
loss inflicted on a rival country was as good as an absolute
gain for one's own country. At least one mercantilist carried
this doctrine to its logical conclusion that plague, war, famine,
harvest failure, in a neighboring country was of economic advantage to your own country.[16] On such doctrine, Adam Smith's
trenchant comment is deserved, although he exaggerates its role
in mercantilist thought and practice:

> By such maxims as these, however, nations have been taught that
> their interest consisted in beggaring all their neighbours. Each nation
> has been made to look with an invidious eye upon the prosperity of
> all the nations with which it trades, and to consider their gain as its
> own loss. Commerce, which ought naturally to be, among nations, as
> among individuals, a bond of union and friendship, has become the
> most fertile source of discord and animosity. The capricious ambition
> of kings and ministers has not, during the present and the preceding
> century, been more fatal to the repose of Europe, than the impertinent
> jealousy of merchants and manufacturers. The violence and injustice
> of the rulers of mankind is an ancient evil, for which, I am afraid, the

[15] See Ephraim Lipson, *The Economic History of England*, Vols. II-III, "The Age of
Mercantilism," 3rd edition, London, 1943.
[16] Theodor Ludwig Lau, *Aufrichtiger Vorschlag*, 1719, as reported in Walther Focke,
Die Lehrmeinungen der Kameralisten über den Handel, Erlangen (dissertation), 1926, p. 59.

nature of human affairs can scarce admit of a remedy. But the mean rapacity, the monopolizing spirit of merchants and manufacturers, who neither are, nor ought to be, the rulers of mankind, though it cannot perhaps be corrected, may very easily be prevented from disturbing the tranquillity of any body but themselves.[17]

Heckscher cites mercantilist doctrine such as Adam Smith here criticizes as evidence that the mercantilists were not interested in economic welfare for its own sake, but subordinated it to considerations of power. Adam Smith's assumption that the exposition of such doctrine was confined to merchants rather than statesmen (or philosophers) is invalid. But in so far as it was expounded by merchants, it is scarcely conceivable that these were so different from merchants at other times that they were governed more by chauvinist patriotism than by rapacity. The significance of such doctrine is not that those who adhered to it placed power before plenty, but that they grossly misunderstood the true means to and nature of plenty. What they were lacking in was not economic motivation but economic understanding.

What then is the correct interpretation of mercantilist doctrine and practice with respect to the roles of power and plenty as ends of national policy? I believe that practically all mercantilists, whatever the period, country, or status of the particular individual, would have subscribed to all of the following propositions: (1) wealth is an absolutely essential means to power, whether for security or for aggression; (2) power is essential or valuable as a means to the acquisition or retention of wealth; (3) wealth and power are each proper ultimate ends of national policy; (4) there is long-run harmony between these ends, although in particular circumstances it may be necessary for a time to make economic sacrifices in the interest of military security and therefore also of long-run prosperity.

The omission of any one of these four propositions results in an incorrect interpretation of mercantilist thought, while additions of other propositions would probably involve internal dispute among mercantilists. It is to be noted that no proposition is included as to the relative weight which the mercantilists attached to power and to plenty, respectively. Given the general

[17] *Wealth of Nations*, Cannan, ed., I, 457-58.

POWER vs. PLENTY UNDER MERCANTILISM 11

acceptance of the existence of harmony and mutual support between the pursuit of power and the pursuit of plenty, there appears to have been little interest in what must have appeared to them to be an unreal issue. When apparent conflict between these ends did arise, however, differences in attitudes, as between persons and countries, did arise and something will be said on this matter later.

That plenty and power were universally regarded as each valuable for its own sake there is overwhelming evidence, in the contemporary writings of all kinds, and what follows is more or less a random sampling of the available evidence. In the text accompanying and interpreting the Frontispiece of Michael Drayton's poem, *Polyolbion*, 1622, there is the following passage:

> "Through a Triumphant Arch see Albion plac'd,
> In Happy site, in Neptune's arms embrac'd,
> In Power and Plenty, on her Cleevy Throne"

In Barbier d'Aucour's *Au Roy sur le Commerce, Ode*, 1665,[18] an early French equivalent of *Rule Britannia,* appear the following lines:

> "Vos vaisseaux fendant tous les airs,
> Et cinglant sur toutes les Mers,
> Y porteront vostre puissance;
> Et ce Commerce plein d'honneur,
> Fera naistre dans vostre France,
> Un flus et reflus de bon-heur."

Montchrétien opens his book with this passage: "Ceux qui sont appellez au gouvernement des Estats doyvent en avoir la gloire, l'augmentation et l'enrichissement pour leur principal but."[19] Another Frenchman, writing in 1650 says:

Deux choses sont principalement necessaires pour rendre un Estat florissant; c'est assavoir le Gouvernement, & le Commerce; & comme sans celuy-là il est impossible qu'il puisse longtemps subsister; de mesme sans celuy-cy on le voit manquer de mille sortes de choses im-

---

[18] The citation from D'Aucour in the text is made from a reprint extracted from J. Carnandet, *Le Trésor des Pièces Rares . . . de la Champagne*, Paris, 1863-1866. D'Aucour was a tutor of Colbert's son. F. C. Palm, *The Economic Policies of Richelieu*, Urbana, 1920, pp. 178-79, quotes from an earlier *Ode à . . . Richelieu*, in much the same vein by Jean de Chapelain (1595-1624), which similarly stresses power and plenty.

[19] *Traicté de l'œconomie politique* [1615], Th. Funck-Brentano ed., Paris, 1889, p. 11.

portantes à la vie, & il est impossible que les peuples acquierent de grandes richesses.[20]

John Graunt, in 1662, states that "the art of governing, and the true politiques, is how to preserve the subject in peace, and plenty."[21] An anonymous English writer, in 1677, declares that: "The four main interests of a nation are, religion, reputation, peace, and trade . . ."[22] William III, in his declaration of war against France in 1689, gives as one of the reasons that Louis XIV's "forbidding the importation of a great part of the product and manufactures of our Kingdom, and imposing exorbitant customs upon the rest, are sufficient evidence of his design to destroy the trade on which the wealth and safety of this nation so much depends."[23] In the preamble of 3 and 4 Anne, cap. 10, are the following words: "The Royal Navy, and the navigation of England, wherein, under God, the wealth, safety, and strength of this Kingdom is so much concerned, depends on the due supply of stores for the same."[24] An English pamphlet of 1716 on the relations with Russia, after describing the Czar as "a great and enterprizing spirit, and of a genius thoroughly politic" attributes to him and his people "an insatiable desire of opulency, and a boundless thirst for dominion."[25] William Wood, a noted mercantilist writer, refers to the English as "a people . . . who seek no other advantages than such only as may enlarge and secure that, whereby their strength, power, riches and reputation, equally encrease and are preserved . . ."[26] Bernard Mandeville discusses how "politicians can make a people potent, renown'd and flourishing."[27] An anonymous English writer states in 1771 that:

[20] Cited from Ch. Vialart dit St. Paul, *Histoire du Ministère d'Armand . . . Duc de Richelieu*, Paris, 1650, I, 332.

[21] *Natural and Political Observations made upon the Bills of Mortality* [London, 1662], Johns Hopkins University Reprint, Baltimore, 1939, p. 78.

[22] *The Present State of Christendom, and the Interest of England, with a Regard to France* [1677], in *The Harleian Miscellany*, London, 1808, I, 249.

[23] As cited in *Mercator, or Commerce Retrieved*, No. 1, London, May 26, 1713.

[24] Cited in G. S. Graham, *Sea Power and British North America 1783-1820*, Cambridge Mass., 1941, p. 143.

[25] *The Northern Crisis; or Impartial Reflections on the Policies of the Czar* [London, 1716], as reprinted in Karl Marx, *Secret Diplomatic History of the Eighteenth Century*, London, 1899, p. 32.

[26] *Survey of Trade*, 2nd ed., London, 1719, Dedication, pp. iv-v.

[27] *The Fable of the Bees* [6th ed., 1732], F. B. Kaye ed., Oxford, 1924, I, 185.

POWER vs. PLENTY UNDER MERCANTILISM   13

"Nature, reason and observation all plainly point out to us our true object of national policy, which is commerce; the inexhaustible source of wealth and power to a people."[28] In an undated memoir of Maurepas to Louis XVI, on the commerce of France, occur the following passages: "Le commerce est la source de la félicité, de la force et de la richesse d'un état ... La richesse et la puissance sont les vrais intérêts d'une nation, et il n'y a que le commerce qui puisse procurer l'une et l'autre."[29]

Such evidence as the foregoing that in the age of mercantilism wealth and power were both sought for their own sakes could easily be multiplied many fold. In English literature of the period of all kinds, from poetry to official documents, the phrases "power and plenty," "wealth and strength," "profit and power," "profit and security," "peace and plenty," or their equivalents, recur as a constant refrain. Nor is there any obvious reason, given the economic and political conditions and views of the seventeenth and eighteenth centuries, why power *and* plenty should not have been the joint objectives of the patriotic citizen of the time, even if he had freed himself from the mercantilist philosophy. Adam Smith, though not a mercantilist, was speaking for mercantilists as well as for himself when he said that "the great object of the political œconomy of every country, is to increase the riches and power of that country."[30]

In all the literature I have examined, I have found only one passage which is seriously embarrassing for my thesis, not because it subordinates in extreme fashion economic to political considerations, but for the reverse reason. The passage, in an anonymous and obscure pamphlet of 1754, whose authorship I have been unable to determine, is as follows:

> You want not, Gentlemen, to be informed by me, that commerce is the nearest and dearest concern of your country. It is what should be the great object of public attention in all national movements, and in every negotiation we enter into with foreign powers. Our neighbours on the continent may, perhaps, wisely scheme or quarrel for an aug-

[28] *Considerations on the Policy, Commerce and Circumstances of the Kingdom,* London, 1771, as quoted in the preface to G. S. Graham, *British Policy and Canada, 1774-1791,* London, 1930.

[29] *Mémoires du Comte de Maurepas,* Paris, 1792, III, 195.

[30] *Wealth of Nations,* Cannan ed., I, 351.

mentation of dominions; but *Great Britain, of herself, has nothing to fight for, nothing to support, nothing to augment but her commerce.* On our foreign trade, not only our wealth but our mercantile navigation must depend; on that navigation our naval strength, the glory and security of our country.[31]

It is much easier indeed to show that power was not the sole objective of national policy in mercantilist thought than to explain how historians ever came to assert that it was. The evidence they cite in support of this proposition is not only extremely scanty but is generally ambiguous if not wholly irrelevant to their thesis. It would be extremely difficult, I am sure, for them to cite even a single passage which unmistakably rejects wealth as a national objective worth pursuing for its own sake or unconditionally subordinates it to power as an ultimate end. It is only too probable that there has been operating here that intellectual "principle of parsimony" in the identification of causes which, whatever its serviceability in the natural sciences, has in the history of social thought worked only for ill.

Cunningham and Heckscher[32] make much of a passage of Francis Bacon's made famous by modern scholars in which he speaks of King Henry VII "bowing the ancient policy of this estate from consideration of plenty to consideration of power" when in the interest of the navy he ordered that wines from Gascony should be imported only in English bottoms. As a fifteenth century measure, this falls outside the period of present interest, but Bacon, no doubt, put much of his own ideas, perhaps more than of Henry VII's, in his *History of the Reign of King Henry the Seventh*. It is relevant, therefore, that Bacon speaks of Henry VII as conducting war for profit, and attributes to him even over-developed economic objectives. In 1493, Henry VII had declared an embargo on all trade with the Flemish provinces because the pretender, Perkin Warbeck, was being harboured there. The embargo after a time "began to

[31] *Mercator's Letters on Portugal and its Commerce*, London, 1754, p. 5. The italics are not in the original text.
[32] Heckscher refers to this as "a very characteristic passage" (*Mercantilism*, II, 16), but I find it difficult to cite a duplicate, whether from Bacon's writings or in the period generally. See also Heckscher, "Revisions in Economic History, V, Mercantilism," *Economic History Review*, VII (1936), 48: "I think Cunningham was right in stressing the famous saying of Bacon about Henry VII: 'bowing the ancient policy of this Estate from consideration of plenty to consideration of power.'"

POWER vs. PLENTY UNDER MERCANTILISM   15

pinch the merchants of both nations very sore, which moved them by all means they could devise to affect and dispose their sovereigns respectively to open the intercourse again." Henry VII, no longer apprehensive about Warbeck, was receptive. "But that that moved him most was, that being a King that loved wealth and treasure, he could not endure to have trade sick, nor any obstruction to continue in the gate-vein, which disperseth that blood," and by the *intercursus magnus* of 1495-96 with the Archduke of Austria he negotiated the end of the trade war.[33]

Not so frequently stated is that power and plenty are properly joint objectives of national policy, but undoubtedly a pervasive element in the thought of the period, is the proposition that they are also harmonious ends, each reinforcing and promoting the other. The idea is expressed in the maxim attributed to Hobbes: "Wealth is power and power is wealth."[34] There follow some passages in which the idea is spelled out somewhat more fully: "Foreign trade produces riches, riches power, power preserves our trade and religion."[35] "It is evident that this kingdom is wonderfully fitted by the bounty of God almighty, for a great progression in wealth and power; and that the only means to arrive at both, or either of them, is to improve and advance trade . . ."[36] "For as the honesty of all governments is, so shall be their riches; and as their honour, honesty, and riches are, so will be their strength; and as their honour, honesty, riches, and strength are, so will be their trade. These are five sisters that go hand in hand, and must not be parted."[37] "Your fleet, and your trade, have so near a relation, and such mutual influence upon each other, they cannot well be separated; your trade is the mother and nurse of your seamen; your seamen are the life of

[33] See *The Works of Francis Bacon*, James Spedding, ed., London, 1858, VI, 95-96; 172-73. Cf. also *Considerations touching a War with Spain* [1624], in *The Works of Francis Bacon*, Philadelphia, 1852, II, 214, where he says that: "whereas wars are generally causes of poverty or consumption . . . this war with Spain, if it be made by sea, is like to be a lucrative and restorative war. So that, if we go roundly on at the first, the war in continuance will find itself." On the other hand, in his *Essays or Counsels* [2nd ed., 1625], *Works*, London, 1858, VI, 450-51, he makes what appears to be a clear-cut statement that the prestige of power ("grandeur") is more important than plenty.

[34] J. E. Barker, *Rise and Decline of the Netherlands*, London, 1906, p. 194.

[35] Josiah Child, *A Treatise concerning the East India Trade*, London, 1681, p. 29.

[36] *Ibid.*, *A New Discourse of Trade*, 4th ed. (ca. 1690), Preface, p. xliii.

[37] Andrew Yarranton, *England's Improvement by Sea and Land*, London, 1677, p. 6.

your fleet, and your fleet is the security and protection of your trade, and both together are the wealth, strength, security and glory of Britain."[38]

"By trade and commerce we grow a rich and powerful nation, and by their decay we are growing poor and impotent. As trade and commerce enrich, so they fortify, our country."

"The wealth of the nation he [the 'Patriot King'] will most justly esteem to be his wealth, the power his power, the security and the honor, his security and honor; and by the very means by which he promotes the two first, he will wisely preserve the two last."[39]

"De la marine dépendent les colonies, des colonies le commerce, du commerce la faculté pour l'État d'entretenir de nombreuses armées, d'augmenter la population et de fournir aux entreprises les plus glorieuses et les plus utiles."[40]

George L. Beer has commented, with particular reference to the statement from Lord Haversham quoted above, that "The men of the day argued in a circle of sea power, commerce and colonies. Sea power enabled England to expand and to protect her foreign trade, while this increased commerce, in turn, augmented her naval strength."[41] Circular reasoning this may have been, but it was not, logically at least, a "vicious circle," since under the circumstances of the time it was perfectly reasonable to maintain that wealth and power mutually supported each

---

[38] Lord Haversham in the House of Lords, November 6, 1707, *Parliamentary History of England*, VI, 598. Cf. also James Whiston, *A Discourse of the Decay of Trade*, London, 1693, p. 3:

"For, since the introduction of the new artillery of powder guns, &c., and the discovery of the wealth of the Indies, &c. war is become rather an expense of money than men, and success attends those that can most and longest spend money: whence it is that prince's armies in Europe are become more proportionable to their purses than to the number of their people; so that it uncontrollably follows that a foreign trade managed to the best advantage, will make our nation so strong and rich, that we may command the trade of the world, the riches of it, and consequently the world itself. . . . Neither will the pursuing these proposals, augment the nation's wealth and power only, but that wealth and power will also preserve our trade and religion, they mutually working for the preservation of each other . . . "

[39] Lord Bolingbroke, "The Idea of a Patriot King," in *Letters on the Spirit of Patriotism*, London, 1752, pp. 204, 211.

[40] Petit, a colleague of the French Foreign Minister, Choiseul, in 1762, as cited by E. Daubigny, *Choiseul et la France d'Outre-Mer après le Traité de Paris*, Paris, 1892, p. 176.

[41] *The Old Colonial System, 1600-1754*, New York, 1912, I, 16.

POWER vs. PLENTY UNDER MERCANTILISM   17

other, that they were, or could be made, each a means to the augmentation of the other. [42]

In contending that for the mercantilists power and plenty were regarded as coexisting ends of national policy which were fundamentally harmonious, I do not mean that they were unaware that in specific instances economic sacrifices might have to be made in order to assume national security or victory in an aggressive war. But as a rule, if not invariably, when making this point they showed their belief that such economic sacrifices in the short run would bring economic as well as political gains in the long run. The selfishness from a patriotic point of view of taxpayers resisting wartime impositions for armament or for war was always a problem for statesmen in the age of mercantilism, and sometimes the parsimony of monarchs was also a problem. It was also necessary at times for statesmen to resist the pressure from merchants to pursue petty commercial ends which promised immediate economic gain but at the possible cost of long-run military security and therefore also of long-run national prosperity. The mercantilist, no doubt, would not have denied that if necessity should arise for choosing, all other things would have to give way to considerations of the national safety; but his practice might not rise to the level of his principles, and his doctrine would not lead him to recognize that such choice was likely to face him frequently. It is not without significance that it was an anti-mercantilist economist, Adam Smith, and not the mercantilists, who laid down the maxim that "defence is more important than opulence." A typical mercantilist might well have replied that ordinarily defence is necessary to opulence and opulence to effective defence, even if momentarily the two ends might appear to be in conflict.

[42] Edmond Silberner, *La Guerre dans la Pensée Économique du XVI° au XVIII° Siècle*, Paris, 1939, concentrates on the search for attitudes toward war, idealizing or pacific, rather than on the motivations of foreign policy, but it presents a rich collection of extracts from the contemporary literature which in so far as it is pertinent to the present issue is, I believe, wholly confirmatory of my thesis. Cf. also, by the same author, *The Problem of War in Nineteenth Century Economic Thought*, Princeton, 1946, p. 286: "In the protectionist view, there is a reciprocal action between the economic and war: industrialization facilitates the conduct of war, and military victories increase the possibilities of industrialization and of economic prosperity. This point of view recalls that of the mercantilists: wealth increases power, and power augments wealth." The thesis presented in the text above is also supported not only by the title but by the contents, if I understand his Italian aright, of Jacopo Mazzei's article, "Potenza Mezzo di Ricchezza e Ricchezza Mezzo di Potenza nel Pensiero dei Mercantilisti," *Rivista Internazionale di Scienze Sociali*, XLI (1933), 3-18.

Queen Elizabeth was notoriously parsimonious and one of her diplomatic agents, Buckhurst, in reasoning with her in 1587 when the safety of England against the menace from Spain appeared to call for rearmament, anticipated Adam Smith's maxim:

> And alwaies when kinges and kingdoms do stand in dout of daunger, their safetie is a thing so far above all price of treasure, as there shold be no sparing to bring them even into certainty of assurans.

He accordingly advised Elizabeth to

> unlock all your cofers and convert your treasure for the advauncing of worthy men and for the arming of ships and men of war, that may defend you, sith princes' treasures serve only to that end and lie they never so fast nor so full in their chests, can no waies so defend them.[43]

Statesmen frequently found it necessary to warn against endangering political ends by unwise pursuit of temporary or petty commercial gains in response to pressure from business interests. This was especially true in connection with the relations between England and France during the Seven Years' War, which to many contemporaries seemed to be conducted with too much attention to economic considerations of minor importance. Just before the outbreak of the conflict, when it was still being debated whether the issue between the two countries should be settled by economic or military means, Lord Granville was reported as "absolutely against meddling with trade—he called it, vexing your neighbours for a little muck."[44] And in the face of the struggle itself, Mirepoix, the French Ambassador to England, is said to have commented "that it was a great pity to cut off so many heads for the sake of a few hats."[45] In the course of controversy over the Newfoundland fisheries after the ending of hostilities, in 1763, Choiseul appealed to Halifax: "mais pour l'amour de Dieu, ne laissons pas des querrelles de pêcheurs dégénérer en querelles de nations."[46]

[43] "Correspondentie van Robert Dudley Graaf van Leycester," Part II, *Werken uitgiven door het Historisch Genootschap*, Utrecht, 3rd Series, No. 57 (1931), pp. 239, 240.

[44] *The Diary of the Late George Bubb Dodington*, new ed., London, 1784, pp. 344-45.

[45] [William Knox], *Helps to a Right Decision*, London, 1787, p. 35; cf. also a slightly different version in *Letters Military and Political from the Italian of Count A. Algorotti*, Dublin, 1784, p. 129. The hats were involved, of course, because beaver skins were the main prize of the American fur trade, and the hair from these skins was the basic raw material for the men's hats of the time.

[46] Cited in *Mélanges d'histoire offerts à M. Charles Bémont*, Paris, 1913, p. 655.

POWER vs. PLENTY UNDER MERCANTILISM   19

To some extent this point of view may have been a reflection of a certain disdain for trade in general which was beginning to affect the aristocratic class who conducted the foreign relations of the time. It would be a mistake, however, to explain it in terms of basic disregard for economic considerations, rather than as belief that the pursuit of temporary and minor economic benefits should not be permitted to dominate foreign policy. Such is the position of John Mitchell, who makes clear elsewhere that "power and prosperity" are the proper ends of policy:

> It is well known, that our colonies in America are rather more under the tuition and influence of the merchants in Britain, than the government perhaps, and that all public measures relating to them are very much influenced by the opinions of our merchants about them. But the only things that they seem to attend to are the profits of trade . . . This, it is true, is necessary to be considered likewise, but it is not the only thing to be attended to. The great thing to be considered by all states is power and dominion, as well as trade. Without that to support and protect our trade, it must soon be at an end.[47]

While mercantilist doctrine, moreover, put great stress on the importance of national economic interests, it put equally great stress on the possibility of lack of harmony between the special economic interests of the individual merchants or particular business groups or economic classes, on the one hand, and the economic interest of the commonwealth as a whole, on the other. Refusal to give weight to *particular* economic interests, therefore, must never be identified with disregard for the national economic interest as they conceived it, in interpreting the thought of the mercantilists. In human affairs, moreover, there is always room for divergence between dogma and practice, be-

---

[47] *The Contest in America between Great Britain and France,* London, 1757, Introduction, p. xvii. Cf. also *A Letter to a certain Foreign Minister, in which the grounds of the present war are truly stated,* London, 1745, p. 6: "That we receive great benefits from trade, that trade is a national concern, and that we ought to resent any attempt made to lessen or to injure it, are truths well known and out of dispute, yet sure the British people are not to be treated like a company of merchants, or rather pedlars, who, if they are permitted to sell their goods, are to think themselves well off, whatever treatment they may receive in any other respect. No, surely, the British nation has other great concerns besides their trade, and as she will never sacrifice it, so she will never endure any insult in respect to them, without resenting it as becomes a people jealous of their honour, and punctual in the performance of their engagements."

The occasion for this outburst was a Prussian "rescript" insisting that Britain should not intervene in quarrels between German states, since they had nothing to do with British commerce.

tween principles and the actual behavior of those who profess them. It is doctrine, and not practice, which is the main concern here. The task of ascertaining how much or how little they corresponded in the age of mercantilism, and what were the forces which caused them to deviate, is the difficult duty of the historian, in whose hands I gladly leave it.

It was the common belief in France, however, that commercial objectives and particular commercial interests played a much greater role in the formulation and administration of British than of French foreign policy, and some Englishmen would have agreed. There was universal agreement, also, that in "Holland" (*i.e.*, the "United Provinces"), where the merchants to a large extent shared directly in government, major political considerations, including the very safety of the country or its success in wars in which it was actually participating, had repeatedly to give way to the cupidity of the merchants and their reluctance to contribute adequately to military finance. Whether in the main the influence of the commercial classes, where they had strength, worked more for peace or for war seems to be an open question, but there appears little ground for doubt that with the merchants, whether they pressed for war or for peace, the major consideration was economic gain, either their private gain, or that of their country, or both.

The material available which touches on these strands of thought is boundless, and there can here be cited only a few passages which give the flavor of contemporary discussion. We will begin with material relating to the influence of the merchant and of commercial considerations on British policy.

Sir Francis Bacon, in reporting a discussion in Parliament, in the fifth year of James I's reign, of the petition of the merchants with regard to their grievances against Spain, makes one of the speakers say that: "although he granted that the wealth and welfare of the merchant was not without a sympathy with the general stock and state ["estate?"] of a nation, especially an island; yet, nevertheless, it was a thing too familiar with the merchant, to make the case of his particular profit, the public case of the kingdom." The troubles of the merchants were partly their own fault: they so mismanaged their affairs abroad that

POWER vs. PLENTY UNDER MERCANTILISM   21

"except lieger ambassadors, which are the eyes of kings in foreign parts, should leave their sentinel and become merchants' factors, and solicitors, their causes can hardly prosper." Wars were not to be fought on such minor issues. Another speaker was more sympathetic to the merchants, who were "the convoy of our supplies, the vents of our abundance, Neptune's almsmen, and fortune's adventurers." Nevertheless, the question of war should be dealt with by the King and not by Parliament, presumably because the merchants wielded too much influence there. Members of Parliament were local representatives with local interests; if they took a broader view it was accidental.[48]

Allies or potential allies of England sometimes were troubled by England's supposed obsession with commercial objectives as making her an unreliable ally where other interests were involved. In September, 1704, a minister of the Duke of Savoy issued a memorial which the English representative at that Court reported as holding that England and Holland, "the maritime powers, (an injurious term, I think, which goes into fashion,) were so attentive to their interests of trade and commerce, that, perhaps, they would . . . abandon the common interests of Europe" in the defeat of France in the war then under way.[49] When Pitt declared to Catherine the Great of Russia that no Russian conquest could give offense to England, she was skeptical, and replied: "The acquisition of a foot of territory on the Black Sea will at once excite the jealousy of the English, whose whole attention is given to petty interests and who are first and always traders."[50]

Montesquieu and Quesnay both thought that in England, unlike France and other countries, the interests of commerce predominated over other interests:

> D'autres nations font céder des intérêts de commerce à des intérêts politiques; celle ci [i.e. England] a toujours fait céder ses intérêts politiques aux intérêts de son commerce.[51]
> en Angleterre . . . où les lois du commerce maritime ne se prêtent point aux lois de la politique; où les intérêts de la glèbe et de l'État

---

[48] *The Works of Sir Francis Bacon*, Philadelphia, 1852, II, 193-99.

[49] *The Diplomatic Correspondence of the Right Hon. Richard Hill*, London, 1845, I, 479; see also II, 751.

[50] Cited by Edward Crankshaw, *Russia and Britain*, New York, no date (ca. 1943), pp. 45-46.

[51] Montesquieu, *De l'Esprit des Lois*, Book XX, Ch. 7.

sont subordonnés aux intérêts des négociants; où le commerce des productions de l'agriculture, la propriété du territoire et l'État meme ne
sont regardés que comme des accessoires de la métropole, et la métropole comme formée de négociants.[52]

The history of British policy and practice with respect to
enemy and trade with the enemy during war provides abundant
and occasionally startling evidence that considerations of
plenty did not always automatically give way to considerations
of power. There is much in British history, as in the history of
Holland, of France, and of Spain, to support the statement of
Carl Brinkmann that: "The history of war trade and trade
war is a rich mine of interest to the economic and social historian just for the peculiar ways in which the autonomy of
business connexions and traditions is seen cutting across even
the sternest decrees and tendencies of political *ultima ratio*."[53]

That in Holland commercial interests predominated was
taken for granted in both France and England when foreign
policy was formulated. Thurloe commented, in 1656, that all
proposals "of alliances of common and mutual defence, wherein
provision was to be made for the good of the Protestant religion"
failed "in respect the United Provinces always found it necessary for them to mingle therewith the consideration of trade . . .
The Hollanders had rather His Highness [Oliver Cromwell] be
alone in it than that they should lose a tun of sack or a frail of

[52] *Oeuvres Économiques et Philosophiques de F. Quesnay*, Auguste Oncken, ed., Paris,
1888, p. 429. Quesnay is referring here specially to Britain's policy with respect to the trade
of the colonies. Adam Smith's comment on the monopolistic aspects of this policy was
more acid: "To found a great empire for the sole purpose of raising up a people of cus-
tomers, may at first sight appear a project fit only for a nation of shopkeepers. It is,
however, a project altogether unfit for a nation of shopkeepers; but extremely fit for a
nation whose government is influenced by shopkeepers." *Wealth of Nations*, Cannan, ed.,
II, 114.

[53] *English Historical Review*, CLIII (1924), 287. There is not space here to elaborate
on this theme, but reference to one striking instance will serve to bring out the nature of
the evidence available. In the 1740's, during the War of the Austrian Succession, English
marine insurance companies insured French vessels against capture at sea by the British
navy, and Parliament, after protracted debate, refused to make the practice illegal. Cf.:
Parliamentary History (Cobbett, ed.), XII, 7-26 (for 1741); [Corbyn Morris], *Essay towards
Illustrating the Science of Insurance, particularly whether it be Nationally Advantageous to
Insure Ships of our Enemies*, London, 1747; Admiral H. W. Richmond, *The Navy in the
War of 1739-48*, Cambridge, England, 1920, III, 248-250; C. Ernest Fayle, "The Deflection
of Strategy by Commerce in the Eighteenth Century," and *ibid.*, "Economic Pressure in the
War of 1739-48," *Journal of the Royal United Service Institution*, LXVIII (1923), 281-
294, 434-446; Charles Wright and C. Ernest Fayle, *A History of Lloyds*, London, 1928, pp.
80 ff.

POWER vs. PLENTY UNDER MERCANTILISM   23

raisins."[54] A French naval officer, writing to Colbert with reference to the failure of the Dutch to provide the fleet which they had promised for the Levant, said that he was not at all surprised: "les Hollandais n'agissent en cette occasion que par leur propre intérêt; et comme ils ont peu ou point de bâtiments en Levant, et qu'en leur pays ils ne regardent qu'au compte des marchands, ils n'ont garde d'envoyer et de faire la dépense d'une escadre de ce côté-là."[55]

In the summary given in Cobbett's *Parliamentary History* of the principal arguments made in Parliament in favor of moderating the peace settlement to be made with France to end the Seven Years' War, a contrast was made as to the policy proper for England and that for a country like Holland. The economic value of the British conquests of French colonies in America was great. Nevertheless it was to be remembered:

> ... that the value of our conquests thereby ought not to be estimated by the present produce, but by their probable increase. Neither ought the value of any country to be solely tried on its commercial advantages; that extent of territory and a number of subjects, are matters of as much consideration to a state attentive to the sources of real grandeur, as the mere advantages of traffic; that such ideas are rather suitable to a limited and petty commonwealth, like Holland, than to a great, powerful, and warlike nation. That on these principles, having made very large demands in North America, it was necessary to relax in other parts.[56]

There was general agreement that in France economic considerations played a lesser role in foreign policy than in England and Holland. In part, this was to be explained by the lesser importance even economically of foreign trade to France

[54] Cited by F. M. Powicke, "The Economic Motive in Politics," *Economic History Review* XVI (1946), 91.

[55] A. Jal, *Abraham Du Quesne et la Marine de son Temps*, Paris, 1883, I, 470.

[56] *Parliamentary History of England*, XV (1813), 1271-1272 (for December 9, 1762). For similar views as to the propriety of a country like Holland confining her foreign policy to commercial matters and to defense, without attempting to participate otherwise in *Haute Politique*, see the instructions prepared in 1771 by the French foreign office for the French Ambassador to Holland, *Recueil des Instructions Données aux Ambassadeurs et Ministres de France*, XXIII, Paris, 1924, 308.

For the comments of the Anglophile Prince of Orange in the course of his attempts to keep Holland neutral during the War of the American Revolution, which proved unsuccessful because of both pressure from France and the financial ambitions of the commercial classes in Holland, see *Archives ou Correspondance Inédite de la Maison d'Orange-Nassau*, 5th Series, F. J. L. Kramer, ed., Leyde, 1910, I, 607 ff., 618, 635 ff., 677 ff., *et passim*.

and by the lesser role of French merchants in French politics. George Lyttelton, an English observer at the Soissons Congress of 1729, where the question of the maintenance of the alliance with England was at issue, reported to his father:

> Affairs are now almost at a crisis, and there is great reason to expect they will take a happy turn. Mr. Walpole has a surprizing influence over the cardinal [Cardinal Fleury, in charge of French foreign policy]; so that, whether peace or war ensue, we may depend upon our ally. In truth, it is the interest of the French court to be faithful to their engagements, though it may not entirely be the nation's. Emulation of trade might incline the people to wish the bond that ties them to us were broke; but the mercantile interest has at no time been much considered by this court. . . . The supposition, that present advantage is the basis and end of state engagements, and that they are only to be measured by that rule, is the foundation of all our suspicions against the firmness of our French ally. But the maxim is not just. Much is given to future hopes, much obtained by future fears; and security is, upon many occasions, sought preferably to gain.[57]

Frenchmen in the period occasionally professed readiness to yield to Britain predominance in maritime trade if Britain would give France a free hand on the Continent,[58] but it would be a mistake to conclude that this reflected a readiness to concentrate on political objectives alone. Even on the Continent there were economic prizes to be won, though less glittering ones than those naval power could win overseas.

Historians, moreover, may have been too ready to find sharp differences in kind between the role of economic considerations in the making of foreign policy in England and France, respectively, in the age of mercantilism. The differences, though probably substantial, seem in the matters here relevant to have

[57] *The Works of George Lord Lyttelton*, G. E. Ayscough, ed., 3rd ed., London, 1776, III, 243-44.

[58] An instance in point is in a despatch by Louis XIV to his ambassador in London, in 1668: "Si les Anglais voulaient se contenter d'etre les plus grand marchands de l'Europe, et me laisser pour mon partage ce que je pourrais conquérir dans une juste guerre, rien ne serait si aisé que de nous accommoder ensemble." Cited by C.-G. Picavet, *La Diplomatie Française au Temps de Louis XIV*, Paris, 1930, p. 171.

About a century later, in 1772, George III of England, alarmed by the coalition of Austria, Prussia, and Russia to partition Poland, expressed sympathy for the idea of an alliance between Britain and France despite their traditional enmity: "Commerce the foundation of a marine can never flourish in an absolute monarchy; therefore that branch of grandeur ought to be left to England whilst the great army kept by France gives her a natural pre-eminence on the Continent." (Sir John Fortescue, ed., *The Correspondence of King George the Third*, London, 1927, II, 428-429.)

POWER vs. PLENTY UNDER MERCANTILISM   25

been differences in degree rather than in kind. In particular, the extent of the influence which commercial interests in France could in one way or another exercise on policy has been seriously underestimated by many historians, and both in theory and in practice absolutist government was not as absolute in power nor as non-commercial in motivation as the school textbooks have taught us. French records have been misleading in this regard because the older generation of historians were not interested in economic issues and tended to leave out of their compilations of documents matter of a markedly economic character, and French historians seem for some time to have been moving toward a reconsideration of the role of economic factors in the formulation of foreign policy under the Ancien Régime.[59]

There may have been monarchs who recognized no moral obligation to serve their people's interests, and there were no doubt ministers of state who had no loyalties except to their careers and perhaps to their royal masters. Frederick the Great is said to have declared, with brutal frankness, that "Je regarde les hommes comme une horde de cerfs dans le parc d'un grand seigneur et qui n'ont d'autre fonction que de peupler et de remplir l'enclos," and there is little in the King's voluminous writings which makes this incredible.[60] Some monarchs were, to modern taste, childish in the weight they gave to the routine symbols of prestige and protocol.[61] The personal idiosyncrasies

[59] For representative contemporary evidence in support of these points, see: *Mémoires de Louis XIV*, Jean Longnon, ed., Paris, 1927, p. 73; a proclamation of Louis XIV reprinted in P. M. Bondois, "Colbert et l'industrie de la dentelle," *Mémoires et Documents pour Servir à l'Histoire du Commerce et de l'Industrie en France*, VI (1921), 263; Vauban, "Description Géographique de l'Élection de Vézeley" [1696], in A. de Boislisle, *Mémoires des Intendants sur l'État des Généralités*, Paris, 1881, I, 738-49; G. Lacour-Goyet, *L'Éducation Politique de Louis XIV*, 2nd ed., Paris, 1923, pp. 341 ff. For reconsiderations of the traditional views by modern historians, see A. Jal, *Abraham du Quesne et la Marine de son Temps*, Paris, 1883, II, 352-53; P. Muret (a book review), *Revue d'Histoire Moderne*, IV (1902-3), 39-43; J. Hitier, "La Doctrine de l'Absolutisme," *Annales de l'Université de Grenoble*, XV (1903), 106-113, 121-31; Charles Normand, *La Bourgeoisie Française au XVIIᵉ Siècle, 1604-1661*, Paris, 1908, pp. 195, 279-287; Henri Hauser, La *Pensée et l'Action Économique du Cardinal de Richelieu*, Paris, 1944, pp. 185 ff.; Philip Dun, "The Right of Taxation in the Political Theory of the French Religious Wars," *Journal of Modern History*, XVII (1945), 289-303.

[60] Frederick the Great did recognize, however, at least in principle and in his better moments, that the economic well-being of his people should be one of the major objectives of a monarch. See his "Essai sur les Formes de Gouvernement et sur les Devoirs des Souverains," of which he had printed a few copies only in 1777, *Oeuvres*, IX (1848), 195-210.

[61] To a letter from Louis XIII in 1629 proposing closer commercial relations, Czar Michel Federowitz of Russia replied favorably, but complained about the manner in which he had

of rulers and, above all, dynastic ambitions, exerted their influence on the course of events. Occasionally religious differences made the course of diplomacy run a little less smoothly by injecting an ideological factor into the range of matters out of which disputes could arise or by which they could be sharpened. But it seems clear that predominantly diplomacy was centered on and governed by considerations of power and plenty throughout the period and for all of Europe, and that religious considerations were more often invoked for propaganda purposes than genuinely operative in fashioning foreign policy. Even the cardinals, who in some degree monopolized the diplomatic profession on the Continent, granted that religious considerations must not be permitted to get in the way of vital national interests, and even genuine missionary enterprises could get seriously entangled with the pursuit of commercial privileges. When Louis XIII in 1626 sent an emissary to Persia with the primary purpose of promoting the Catholic religion, he instructed him at the same time to seek special privileges for French trade as compensation for the diplomatic difficulties with the English and the Dutch which would result from a French attempt to catholicize Persia. "Sa Majesté pensait qu'on ne pouvait éviter cet inconvénient qu'en se rendant maître du commerce du pays, lequel, outre le gain des âmes, qui est celui que sa Majesté recherchait, offrirait encore à son royaume de notables avantages."[62]

been addressed: "Mais nous ne savons à quoi attribuer que notre nom, nos titres et nos qualités aient été oubliés à la lettre que vous nous avez écrit. Tous les potentats de la terre . . . écrivant à notre grande puissance, mettre notre nom sur les lettres et n'oublient ancun des titres et des qualités que nous possédons. Nous ne pouvons approuver votre coutume de vouloir être notre ami, et de nous dénier et ôter les titres que le Dieu tout-puissant nous a donnés et que nous possédons si justement. Que sí, à l'avenir, vous désirez vivre en bonne amitié et parfaite correspondance avec notre grande puissance, en sorte que nos royales personnes et nos empires joint ensemble donnent de la terreur à tout l'univers, il faudra que vous commandiez qu'aux lettres que vous nous récrirez à l'avenir toute la dignité de nostre grande puissance, notre nom, nos titres et nos qualités soient écrits comme elles sont en cette lettre que nous vous envoyons de notre part. Nous vous ferons le semblable en écrivant tous vos titres et toutes vos qualités dans les lettres que nous vous manderons, etant le propre des amis d'augmenter plutôt réciproquement leurs titres et qualités que de les diminuer ou retrancher." *Recueil des Instructions*, VIII (1890), 29.

[62] G. deR. de Flassan, *Histoire Générale et Raisonnée de la Diplomatie Française*, 2nd ed., Paris, 1811, II, 396.

In 1713 Charles XII of Sweden wrote to Queen Anne demanding that England, in conformity with her treaty obligations, give him assistance in regaining his territories in the Germanic Empire. "It was not possible," he said, "that Anne could allow her mind to be

POWER vs. PLENTY UNDER MERCANTILISM   27

The role of the religious factor in Cromwell's foreign policy has been much debated. The literature of historical debate on this question is voluminous, but it is not apparent to the layman that any progress toward a definitive decision has been made, unless it is that Cromwell was a complex personality on whom economic, religious, and power considerations all had their influence, but in varying degrees and combinations at different times. George L. Beer quotes Firth as saying about Cromwell that: "Looked at from one point of view, he seemed as practical as a commercial traveller; from another, a Puritan Don Quixote," and gives as his own verdict that "It was 'the commercial traveller' who acted, and the 'Puritan Don Quixote' who dreamt and spoke."[63] Other historians have given other interpretations.[64]

I have unfortunately not been able to find an orthodox neo-Marxian study dealing with these issues for this period. If there were one such, and if it followed the standard pattern, it would argue that "in the last analysis" the end of foreign policy had

influenced by the sordid interests of trade; the protectress of the Protestant religion could not fail to support the Protestant power of the north," as against Russia. But Russia at the time was seeking admittance into the Grand Alliance against Louis XIV, and England, alarmed at the ambitions of both monarchs, made no choice. See Mrs. D'Arcy Collyer, "Notes on the Diplomatic Correspondence between England and Russia in the First Half of the Eighteenth Century," *Transactions of the Royal Historical Society*, New Series, XIV (1900), 146 ff.

[63] Cromwell's Policy in its Economic Aspects," *Political Science Quarterly*, XVII (1902), 46-47.

[64] Cf. John Morley, *Oliver Cromwell*, New York, 1901, p. 434; Guernsey Jones, *The Diplomatic Relations between Cromwell and Charles X. Gustavus of Sweden*, Lincoln, Neb., 1897, pp. 34-35; Frank Strong, "The Causes of Cromwell's West Indian Expedition," *American Historical Review*, IV (1899), 245; M. P. Ashley, *Financial and Commercial Policy under the Cromwellian Republic*, Oxford, 1934; [Slingsby Bethel], *The World's Mistake in Oliver Cromwell* [1668], in *The Harleian Miscellany*, London, 1810, VII, 356-57.

I have not been able to find any systematic or comprehensive study of the role of the religious factor in power politics. The following references are a fair sample of the material bearing on this which I have come across: Leon Geley, *Fancan et la Politique de Richelieu de 1617 à 1627*, Paris, 1884, pp. 264-290; "Discours sur ce qui peut sembler estre plus expedient, & à moyenner au sujet des guerres entre l'Empereur & le Palatin," [1621], in *Recueil de Quelques Discours Politiques*, no place given, 1632, pp. 314 ff; C. C. Eckhardt, *The Papacy and World Affairs as Reflected in the Secularization of Politics*, Chicago, 1937, p. 89; S. Rojdestvensky and Inna Lubimenko, *Contribution à l'Histoire des Relations Commerciales Franco-Russes au XVIII° Siècle*, Paris, 1929, p. 4; *Mémoires de Noailles*, Paris, 1777, I 126; Cheruel, "Le Baron Charles D'Avangour Ambassadeur de France en Suède" (1654-1657, *Revue d'Histoire Diplomatique*, III (1889), 529; [Jean Rousset de Missy], *The History of Cardinal Alberoni*, London, 1719, p. 105; W. E. Lingelbach, "The Doctrine and Practice of Intervention in Europe," *Annals of the American Academy*, XVI (1900), 17, note; "Les Principes Généraux de la Guerre," *Oeuvres de Frédéric le Grand*, XXVIII (Berlin, 1856), 50; C.-G. Picavet, *La Diplomatic Française au Temps de Louis XIV*, Paris, 1930, pp. 8, 160-166; Georges Pagès, *La Monarchie d'Ancien Régime en France*, Paris, 1928, pp. 67 ff.

been not power, and not power and plenty, but plenty alone, and plenty for the privileged classes only, and it would charge that members of these classes would always be there in every major diplomatic episode, pulling the strings of foreign policy-making for their own special benefit. Writing a few years ago in criticism of this theory as applied to more recent times, I ventured the following comment: "While I suspect that Marx himself would not have hesitated to resort to the 'scandal' theory of imperialism and war when convenient for propaganda purposes, I am sure that he would basically have despised it for its vulgar or unscientific character."[65] I was "righter" than I deserved to be.

Karl Marx studied the British diplomacy of this period, even making use of the unpublished records in the British Foreign Office, and discussed the role played by commercial objectives in British foreign policy. The ruling oligarchy needed political allies at home, and found them in some section or other of the *haute bourgeoisie*.

> As to their *foreign policy*, they wanted to give it the appearance at least of being altogether regulated by the mercantile interest, an appearance the more easily to be produced, as the exclusive interest of one or the other small fraction of that class would, of course, be always identified with this or that Ministerial measure. The interested fraction then raised the commerce and navigation cry, which the nation stupidly re-echoed.

Eighteenth century practice thus "developed on the Cabinet, at least, the *onus* of inventing *mercantile pretexts*, however futile, for their measures of foreign policy." Writing in the 1850's, Marx found that procedure had changed. Palmerston did not bother to find commercial pretexts for his foreign policy measures.

> In our own epoch, British ministers have thrown this burden on foreign nations, leaving to the French, the Germans, etc., the irksome task of discovering the *secret* and *hidden* mercantile springs of their actions. Lord Palmerston, for instance, takes a step apparently the most damaging to the material interests of Great Britain. Up starts a State philosopher, on the other side of the Atlantic, or of the Channel, or in the heart of Germany, who puts his head to the rack to dig out

[65] "International Relations between State-Controlled National Economies," *American Economic Review Supplement*, XXXIV (1944), 324.

POWER vs. PLENTY UNDER MERCANTILISM   29

the mysteries of the mercantile Machiavelism of "perfide Albion," of which Palmerston is supposed the unscrupulous and unflinching executor.[66]

Marx, in rejecting the economic explanation of British friendship for Russia, fell back upon an explanation of both a sentimental pro-Russianism in high circles in Britain and an unjustified fear of Russian power. It is a paradox that the father of Marxism should have sponsored a doctrine which now sounds so non-Marxian. I cannot believe, however, that the appeals to economic considerations which played so prominent a part in eighteenth-century British discussions of Anglo-Russian relations were all pretext, and I can find little evidence which makes it credible that friendly sentiment towards foreigners played a significant role in the foreign policy of England in the eighteenth century. Leaving sentiment aside, England's foreign policy towards Russia in the eighteenth century, like English and European foreign policy in general, was governed by joint and harmonized considerations of power and economics. That the economics at least was generally misguided, and that it served to poison international relations, is another matter which, though not relevant *here*, is highly relevant now.

[66] Karl Marx, *Secret Diplomatic History of the Eighteenth Century*, Eleanor Marx Aveling, ed., London, 1899, pp. 55-56. The italics are in the original.

13

New Wine in Old Skins? American Definitions of Empire and the Emergence of a New Concept

Norbert Kilian

When the thirteen British colonies in North America issued their Declaration of Independence, they not only rejected George III as their lawful sovereign, but also renounced all further ties with the British Empire.[1] The one seems to be a logical consequence of the other, even by eighteenth-century standards. The term "empire", as Richard Koebner convincingly demonstrated,[2] then retained still much of the Latin *imperium,* implying that somewhere in the body politic there had to be a sovereign, be it king, parliament or both, who was to rule the empire and to whom every part of that empire owed allegiance and submission, the colonies of course not excepted. Considering, however, John Adams' dictum of 1775, that "an Empire is a despotism",[3] it seems odd that Americans after 1776 did not discard the term from their political terminology as unfit and obsolete to describe conditions in the emerging republic in the same way that they dropped monarchy, king, nobility, etc. On the contrary, they began to talk about a rising American empire as soon as independence seemed inevitable. Their empire, however, was not styled after the British Empire, it was rather created in opposition to the political entity they were rejecting – as such, this concept as applied to America became part of the revolutionary ideology. With this they blended the vision of the constant westward move of empires, a movement which was to come to an end in America, where the final and most glorious empire of all would arise.

This paper proposes to study this change in the use of the term "empire" in America more closely. This will be done in four steps: First, the British use of the word will be considered; secondly, the changing American interpretation of the term between 1765 and 1776 will be analyzed, and then I shall attempt to discuss the different uses of the phrase "American empire" before and, in conclusion, after Independence. My findings will be based primarily on American public opinion as expressed in pamphlets and other printed works of the Revolutionary period.

I.

It was not until the end of the French and Indian War that the term "British Empire" was raised "on both sides of the Atlantic, to the level of a concept signifying a political cause, which implied a constitutional system."[4] At the very time, it should be noted, when the first wave of protest and resistance swept through the American colonies in 1765, Englishmen and Americans alike began to discuss the character of their relationship in terms of the "British Empire" meaning thereby the mother country and the colonies taken collectively. Both, however, had a different objective in mind. The *Americans* made use of the term to denote the common interest and strong ties that continued to exist between Great Britain and the colonies in spite of the latters' resistance to British measures after 1763. *English* statesmen and writers, however, used the term to stress the leading role which out of necessity the mother country and Parliament, in particular, had to play to make the various parts of the extensive British Empire act in concert to further the common interest. Accordingly only the center of the Empire was in a position to judge what benefited the whole and what did not. The mother country alone had the perspective and the institutions to act in the interest of her whole Empire, she alone could decide where particular interests had to be encouraged or restricted, depending on whether they worked to the advantage or disadvantage of the whole. This position was shared by the majority of Englishmen up to the beginning of hostilities in America. Thomas Whately stated it very clearly at the beginning of the controversy in 1765: "The British Empire in *Europe* and in *America* is still the same Power: Its subjects in both are still the same people; and all equally participate in the adversity or prosperity of the whole. ... It is an indisputable consequence of their being thus one nation, that they must be governed by the same supreme authority."[5] This quasi-official statement of the British point of view by Grenville's secretary entered the statute book one year later, when, in the Declaratory Act of 1766, it was proclaimed for the first time in British history that the colonies in America were subordinate to "the *Imperial* Crown and *Parliament* of Great Britain".[6] The theory of parliamentary sovereignty was thus given its legal sanction.

Such claims the *colonials* were not ready to accept. They seriously doubted that Parliament had always had the good of the whole Empire in mind when it legislated for the colonies. This suspicion increased considerably when the British government launched its new fiscal policy with the passage of the Revenue Act of 1764. Americans were forced to realize that a good many Englishmen within and without Parliament still favored the old mercantilist doctrine that whatever was good for England was also good for the Empire, or, as some people preferred to put it: What other reasons could there be for founding colonies than to make them subservient to the demands of the mother country?

II.

In 1764 this doctrine which took the subordination of the colonies to the needs of the mother country for granted was no longer acceptable to the colonies as their opposition to the Sugar Act showed. Prompted by a post-war depression they began to demand equality and recognition of their own interests. This they did in the established framework of mercantilism. The colonies were neither ready to develop completely new economic models nor did they confront the mother country with their own brand of mercantilism. Instead they recurred to those recent and more advanced mercantilist doctrines, which viewed different parts of the Empire as economic units with complementary functions. When the colonies sent their raw and staple products to the mother country, they thereby paid for the manufactured goods which they received in return. The northern colonies even went so far as to claim that it did not matter at all from where they procured the money to pay for British manufactures. They therefore demanded unhampered access to foreign markets, particularly the foreign West Indies and southern Europe. In their pamphlets the colonists cited exclusively those passages from mercantilist writers like Josiah Child, Malachy Postlethwayt, Josiah Tucker, William Wood – as well as Cato and Montesquieu where appropriate –, where this "natural relationship"[7] between colonies and mother country was discussed. They neglected, of course, all other aspects of mercantilist thinking in which, by definition, the subordination of the colonies to the mother country was taken for granted.

The colonies wanted recognition of their particular economic needs, and it was this they had in mind whenever they referred to the British Empire.[8] "To represent them as an 'expensive appendage of the British Empire...' is certainly one of the greatest errors; ... Every advantage accruing to the colonies by their connection with the mother-country is *amply – dearly –* paid for ... by the restrictions of their commerce", wrote John Dickinson in 1765.[9] He consequently defined the Navigation Acts as "intended to preserve an intercourse between the mother-country and her colonies, and thus to cultivate a *mutual affection;* to promote the interests of *both* by an exchange of *their* most

137

valuable productions for *her* manufactures, thereby to increase the shipping of both, and thus render them capable of affording aid to each other."[10]

What the colonies claimed was membership in the Empire on an equal footing with the mother country, not a second-class membership. They did not want dramatic changes which would have endangered their remarkable growth. They expected recognition of their growing importance, and the British Empire was the frame of reference in which they voiced their demands. "Let it be demonstrated that the subjects of the British Empire in Europe and America are the same, that the hardships of the latter will ever recoil upon the former. In theory it is supposed that each is equally important to the other, that all partake of the adversity and depression of any. The theory is just and time will certainly establish it . . ."[11] Daniel Dulany, who stated this in 1765, was already advancing to more broadly conceived political demands.

The call for equality in the economic field, which was triggered off by the news of the Sugar Act, was but a foretaste of what the British government would be confronted with when it passed the Stamp Act and the Townshend Acts and thus brought to a test the question of the legal status of the colonies and of parliamentary sovereignty. Both these measures led the colonials to demand political equality within the Empire. In this debate the term "empire" was used as a rhetorical device which was to indicate that in spite of the new political theories proposed by the colonists they still considered themselves as part of the larger community, i. e. the British Empire.[12]

This is not the place to discuss in detail the development of the arguments used by the Americans, beginning with the denial of Parliament's right to lay internal duties to the final point where all legislation without the explicit consent of the colonies was considered illegal. It should be noted, however, that while Americans asserted their rights against parliamentary "encroachments", they were very vague about a positive description of what Parliament did have the right to do. From their point of view this was not even necessary. It was the firm belief of many Americans that they only opposed a novel, unheard-of exercise of power by the British Parliament. When Americans talked about the British Empire, they meant the *status quo* of legal, commercial, and other ties that existed between mother country and colonies. A passage from John Dickinson's *Farmer's Letters* which in 1768–69 motivated opposition as no other publication had done thus far, may illustrate the point: "He, who considers these provinces as states distinct from the *British empire,* has very slender notions of *justice,* or of their *interests.* We are but parts

138

of a *whole;* and therefore there must exist a power somewhere, to preside, and preserve the connection in due order. This power is lodged in the Parliament; and we are as much dependent on *Great-Britain,* as a perfectly free people can be on another."[13]

The British Empire among other things still meant protection from outside interference, loyalty to the king, acceptance of parliamentary legislation (with the exception of specific measures which the colonies opposed), and regulation of trade. Clinging to this concept of the British Empire in the 1760s and early 1770s, they were not just trying to minimize the serious difficulties that were to separate them from the mother country only a few years later. They had a far more practical reason for their attitude: As long as they were members of the British Empire they were also entitled to the rights of Englishmen as a birthright inherited from their ancestors. In the beginning of the controversy these rights which could be claimed in a British court were an argument much more convincing to loyal-minded subjects of George III than doctrines of natural law derived from philosophical principles.[14]

The appeal to the rights of Englishmen had helped the colonies to ward off unwanted taxes. They were of little use, however, when Parliament, in reaction to the Tea Party, passed the "Intolerable Acts" and used troops to enforce them. The interference with the internal constitution of Massachusetts the colonies countered by declaring that Parliament had no such power and that they were "entitled to a free and exclusive power of legislation in their several provincial legislatures."[15] The equality they had until then claimed for all the subjects of the Empire was now extended to include the equality of their assemblies with Parliament. Parliament was no longer to have that "superintending power" it was formerly conceded. This "commonwealth theory of the empire" began to gain ground in the colonies after 1774.[16]

Loyalist writers, wherever they could still publish, launched a vigorous campaign against this new theory and also against the Continental Congress for endorsing it. The constitution of the British Empire became a major issue in this campaign. A very characteristic and for our purpose very instructive debate took place in 1774–75 in Massachusetts between Daniel Leonard and John Adams, who in an exchange of letters in the public newspapers justified their respective stands in the controversy as "Massachusettensis" and "Novanglus". Leonard as *Massachusettensis* referred to the British Empire to make sure that his readers never lost sight of the fact that the colonies had always been – and still continued to be – only part of a whole and should not be considered as "distinct a state from Great-Britain as Hanover".[17] Therefore, and this is the essence of the argument which he repeated several times, if "we are a part of the British empire, we must be subject to the supreme power of the state, which is vested in the estates of Parliament, notwithstanding each of the colonies have legislative and executive powers of their own ... which are subordinate to ... the checks, controul and regulation of the supreme authority." He added the sarcastic remark that "this doctrine is not new, but the denial of it is." The doctrine of legislative equality in the assemblies was an absurdity which to Leonard hardly required refutation, for, as he pointed out: "Two supreme or independent authorities cannot exist in the same state. It would be what is called *imperium in imperio*, the height of political absurdity." Statements of this kind were to be repeated over and over again by authors who, in their pamphlets, denied the notion of a federal government.[18]

If it had not been for the "republican party"[19] in the province, everybody in Massachusetts might have admitted the benefits which the colonies had derived from their being part of the Empire, for the "effects of our connection, and subordination... to Britain" Leonard considered obvious: "Our merchants are opulent ... Population is so rapid as to double the number of inhabitants in the short period of twenty-five years: Cities are springing up in the wilderness: Schools, colleges, and even universities are interspersed through the continent... These are infallible marks not only of opulence but of freedom." To Leonard it was the Empire alone which ensured stability and freedom to the colonies. This the provincial assemblies, were they to act on their own, could not guarantee: "They are but faint sketches of the estates of Parliament," they "have no principle of stability within themselves... and... [would] become wholly monarchical or wholly republican, were it not for the checks, controuls, regulations and supports of the supreme authority of the empire."[20]

Never doubting that Britain and her colonies were but parts of a whole, he could meet his republican opponents (e. g. John Adams), who advanced the theory "that government in the dernier resort is in the people", on their own ground: "for admitting" – he writes in his last letter – "that the collective body of the people, that are subject to the British empire, have an inherent right to change their form of government, or race of Kings, it does not follow, that the inhabitants of a single province or of a number of provinces, or any given part under a majority of the whole empire, have such a right. By admitting that the less may rule or sequester themselves from the greater, we unhinge all government."[21]

I have quoted Massachusettensis so extensively to exemplify how effectively the concept of the British Empire could be employed in the political debates and what meaning it had acquired for many people as tension heightened. The patriots were made to look like troublemakers who kept demanding more and more till all lawful government would succumb to anarchy. For selfish reasons they were defying the freest yet strongest government in the world which, in Leonard's words, had "the power to make us subject to the supreme authority of the Empire."[22] Massachusettensis seemed to demand no more than John Dickinson, the "Pennsylvania Farmer," who five years before had contended for the same with the unanimous support of the whole continent. Leonard's proposition – which the Stamp Act Congress of 1765 had already dismissed as impracticable – that the colonies should be represented in Parliament, suggested a willingness to bring about reconciliation and more peaceful times, a quality the demands of the patriots obviously lacked.

In his response *Novanglus* John Adams strove to show that his opponent's interpretation of the British Empire had no foundation in law and that "empire" was, in fact, an inappropriate word to describe the relationship of Britain to her American colonies. Consequently he attempted to avoid the term, although he was not always successful in doing so. In his third letter Novanglus frankly stated that "the terms [!] 'British empire' are not the language of the common law, but the language of newspapers and political pamphlets," and similarly: "This language, 'the imperial crown of Great Britain', is not the style of the common law, but of court sycophants". To him "empire" implied "dominion", something which the colonies never conceded to Parliament. According to Adams it had always been held, "that America is not parcel of the realm, state, kingdom, government, empire or land of England, or Great Britain in any sense which can make it subject universally to the supreme legislature of that island."[23] As Parliament had no right to legislate for the colonies, except where the colonies made a voluntary concession as they had done in the regulation of their trade,[24] the only link that connected the different parts of the Empire was the king. In a very learned though rather dubious legal argument he even stated that the colonies owed their allegiance only to the person of the king and not to the crown, as the latter was held by act of Parliament.[25] He thus created, as Massachusettensis mockingly pointed out, "a King of Massachusetts, King of Rhode Island, King of Connecticut, etc. etc.", who depended on the consent of the respective assemblies. This Adams readily admitted.[26]

It is obvious that Adams tried to get away from the implications which the traditional idea of an empire, centered in Britain, would have on colonial thinking, if allowed to continue unchallenged. Not only did he try to destroy the myth of the British Empire as hitherto maintained, but he even proceeded to give the word a new meaning that would reconcile it with the rising tide of republican thought in the colonies. In so doing, he gave the term such a bend as to make it a ready tool for the rhetoric of the emerging republic.

In his seventh Novanglus letter Adams stated that "we are not a part of the British empire; because the British government is not an empire". According to him only three empires existed at the time in Europe: the German, or Holy Roman, the Russian, and the Ottoman Empire, all of which he considered as despotisms, because it was the will of the prince alone that prevailed. The British government, however, was "a limited monarchy. If Aristotle, Livy and Harrington, knew what a republic was, the British constitution is much more like a republic than an empire. They define a republic to be *a government of laws, and not of men*". As "empire", in another sense of the word, to Adams also meant government,[27] i. e. rule or dominion in general, he could write ten months later in 1776: "... there is no good government but what is republican. That the only valuable part of the British constitution is so; because the very definition of a republic is 'an empire of laws, and not of men'."[28] The term "empire", which only recently had been rejected for its dangerously despotic connotations and for smacking too much of absolute monarchy, was thus reclaimed for the republican ideology. Surprising indeed is the apparent ease as well as the rapidity with which the transition to republican principles was thus accomplished.

There are other examples of this easy transition of ideas and loyalties within the imperial context. Perez Morton of Massachusetts in April 1776 simply declared every part of the Empire outside of America so rotten that the colonies could reap only advantages from a timely separation: "Now is the happy season, to seize again those Rights ... which have been repeatedly and violently attacked by the *King, Lords and Commons of Britain*. Ought we not then to disclaim forever the forfeited Affinity; and by a timely Amputation of the rotten Limb of the Empire, prevent the Mortification of the whole?"[29] His empire would preserve equal rights and leave no room for the mother country and her pretensions. William Smith, the provost of the College of Philadelphia, had similar notions. He saw "one part of a great Empire" opposing the other with a completely different set of values, thus judging actions as virtuous and patriotic, which the other condemned as treasonable – the implication being, of course, that Americans acted the more virtuous parts and thus came to represent the better part of the Empire.[30]

142

By 1776 two sets of ideas could be associated with the word "empire". On the one hand, there were those of loyalist leanings, who, when talking about the British Empire, had protection, security, lawful government, parliamentary supremacy, and loyalty to the king in mind. On the other hand there were the patriots, who demanded equality of rights, liberty from outside interference, popular sovereignty and, before long, an independent American empire.

The reason why Americans very easily accepted this latter view was not only to be found in the political developments which favored the patriots. It was also due to the fact that it was quite familiar for Americans to talk about an empire in America even before Independence.

III.

When Americans mentioned the Empire before 1776 they sometimes were more specific and meant only that part of the British Empire which lay in North America. In the short time of 150 years this *"British empire in America"* or "empire on this side of the Atlantic"[31] had grown immensely in wealth and population and had expanded over a considerable part of the continent. It had, as one writer said in 1766, acquired "the resources of Empire". Its future development was the object of constant speculation. Extrapolating past developments people calculated that the population in America would double every twenty-five years. On both sides of the Atlantic it seemed an established fact "that this vast Country will, in Time, become the greatest Empire that the world has ever seen."[32] It was openly discussed how many years it would take America's population to exceed that of the mother country and how that would affect mutual relations. Some only saw an increase in trade, others warned the mother country of further taxation measures, because this might disaffect the future larger part of the Empire from the smaller part.[33] As early as 1755, young John Adams talked about the "transfer [of] the great seat of empire into America".[34] Massachusettensis – among others – elaborated on this prospect twenty years later: "After many more centuries", he wrote, when "the colonies may be so far increased as to have the balance of wealth, numbers and powers in their favour, the good of the empire [shall] make it necessary to fix the seat of government here; and some future GEORGE ... may cross the Atlantic, and rule Great Britain by an American parliament". By 1775, however, John Adams had already lost faith in the reigning George and ridiculed the idea as the surest means of driving the colonies into independence.[35]

143

Although it was occasionally pointed out that a future "American empire" might try to be independent from Great Britain, this idea was dreaded and anticipated with horror.[36] "America ... will become a mighty empire" only "after many revolutions and great distresses," an anonymous writer said in 1768.[37] It seems therefore reasonable to assume that as long as Americans did not discuss independence, which they did not until 1775, the empire in America they were talking about was generally considered to be a part of the more extensive British Empire. Repeatedly the colonials were at pains to point out this fact. Jonathan Mayhew envisioned "a mighty empire" in America, but added in parentheses "I do not mean an independent one". Joseph Reed said in a prize essay written at the College of Philadelphia in 1766 that "the difficulties of an Union for the purposes of empire, are almost insuperable" for the colonies. John Dickinson in his *Essay On The Constitutional Power Of Great Britain over the Colonies in America* still reiterated these thoughts in 1774.[38]

Yet, no one harbored any doubts about "The Rising Glory of America" which was the title of a poem by Philip Freneau and Hugh Henry Brackenridge published in 1772. These verses asked the question "what empires yet must rise" before "Britain's sons shall spread, Dominion to the north and south and west Far from th'Atlantic to the Pacific shores?"[39]

The territorial expansion of the colonies over the whole continent was repeatedly discussed in colonial literature, particularly after the French lost Canada in the French and Indian War.[40] The two young poets were not expounding any strikingly new ideas (that would have been expecting too much from a Princeton commencement exercises address of 1771 anyway). All they were expressing by joining the idea of territorial expansion and empire was that the British Empire in America would eventually extend over the whole continent. Undoubtedly, there was a certain sense of destiny in pronouncements of this kind. "Providence will erect a mighty empire in America" wrote Samuel Adams to Arthur Lee in 1774 with almost religious conviction,[41] explaining that the mother country eventually would depend on America for its existence. Sam Adams's belief may very well have been rooted in the old myth that since antiquity all great empires had been moving from east to west like the sun. Bishop Berkeley had applied this myth to the settlements in America in his poem "On the Prospect of Planting Arts and Learning in America" with its often quoted last stanza:

> Westward the course of empire takes its way;
> The first four Acts already past,

144

A fifth shall close the Drama with the Day;
Time's noblest offspring is the last.[42]

The point should however be made here that Berkeley was not concerned with "empire" as a political concept or with territorial expansion. He was profoundly pessimistic about the future of Britain, where complacency and private interest worked against a badly needed spiritual regeneration. The aim he propounded in the poem was to accomplish this regeneration in a new society on unspoiled ground.[43]

No prospect could have been more pleasing to the colonial mind; it was eagerly adopted and propagated. Nathaniel Ames wrote in his almanac for 1758: "Arts and Sciences will change the Face of Nature in their Tour from Hence over the Appalachian Mountains to the Western Ocean." By 1764 empire and progress in the sciences were again combined: "we may anticipate America as the destined seat of science, where she may found an empire uncontrouled; ... here a new empire arises, and tho' in its infancy, yet the human mind is in full exertion of all its faculties, the basis of science large and expanded, and the art of printing preserving all its investigations." Four years later the concept seemed firmly established, so that the *American Whig* could address his audience: "Courage then Americans! Liberty, religion and sciences are on the wing to these shores. The finger of God points out a mighty empire to your sons. ...." It should be noted that by then liberty as well as religion had caught up with the sciences on their journey to the new world, which Independence did not stop.[44]

IV.

Independence did not basically change the pattern of thought which had developed around the British Empire in America. It opened, however, new perspectives. Americans were quick to point out, in 1776, that they were now a new and "Independent empire" which became the new focus for the already familiar thoughts. "Religion, Learning, and Liberty" continued to flourish there and were the assets of a "new people rising to empire and renown".[45]

As a result of their being "a distinct empire",[46] a new sense of finality entered the writings of the former colonists. After commenting on the "progress of Liberty, of Science and of Empire ... from east to west since the beginning of time", Timothy Dwight said: "It may as justly be observed that the glory of empire has been progressive, the last constantly outshining those which were before it". The conclusion to be drawn from this was "evident": The "Empire of North America will be the last on earth" as well as "the most glorious". Americans were assured that this empire would be the scene of the millenium.[47]

Joel Barlow, the poet, came to a similar conclusion by noting that when the course of empire reaches the "western shore" – meaning the Pacific ocean – "earth-born empires rise and fall no more". To expansionists, echoing earlier statements, these were intriguing thoughts. If the extensive American empire was to be the last and most glorious in the world, it would eventually extend over the whole continent. No one was more explicit than Timothy Dwight, who exclaimed in 1776 in an unparalleled outburst: ". . . the moment our interest demands it, these extensive regions will be our own; . . . the present race of inhabitants [i. e. the Spanish settlers, not the Indians] will either be exterminated, or revive to the native human dignity, by the generous and beneficent influence of just laws, and national freedom". This was in marked contrast to the peaceful empire and the golden age which Freneau envisioned in 1778.[48]

There was yet another line of thought which Americans ardently pursued after Independence. "Exalted to the rank of empire" themselves, they began to reflect on the rise and fall of empires, particularly on what they considered the "downfall of the British empire".[49] This was set in contrast to the rise of the infant American empire. William H. Drayton said in an address to the grand jury of Charlestown, S. C., about the "rise of the American empire": "And thus has suddenly arisen in the world, a new empire, styled the United States of America. An empire that as soon as started into existence, attracts the attention of the rest of the universe, and bids fair by the blessing of God, to be the most glorious of any upon record. – America hails Europe, Asia, and Africa! – She proffers peace and plenty!"

"God Almighty" had already chosen his own people. According to Drayton he "made choice of the present generation to erect the American empire". Loyalists and those who still harbored doubts about the wisdom of declaring Independence were admonished not "to repine that, in our day, America is dissolved from the British state", for this would be impiously ignoring the will of divine providence.

Britain's fate was attributed to more secular causes. Although advancing "that the duration of empire is limited by the Almighty decree", Drayton saw the rise and fall of empires as natural events. Britain "experienced the invariable fate of empire", because she succumbed to riches and luxuries;[50] others attributed her fall from the glory of empire to pride and ambition.[51] Drayton as well as all other Revolutionary writers failed to consider "the invariable fate of empires" with regard to the

146

American empire. The optimism of the Revolutionary generation apparently ruled out thoughts of this nature – a fact which illustrates more than any other how closely all statements about the rising American empire must be set in the context of Revolutionary rhetoric.

I have already mentioned how John Adams, by reviving Harrington's dictum, made "empire" and "republic" compatible terms. Thereafter the republican character of the American empire was no longer open to discussion. Republicanism, in fact, had become the "link of empire". America was designated the "seat of freedom and the nurse of empire".[52] The Boston Massacre Oration of 1781 celebrated the American republics as the "abodes of empire and liberty". American statesmen were hailed for "the task of forming and defending a free and extensive empire".[53]

Americans were, at the same time, made aware of their unique and incomparable station in the international community as a free people. "To measure the freedom, the Rights and Privileges of the American Empire by those enjoyed by other Nations would be folly."[54] The American empire represented man's advances in "every species of knowledge, natural and moral". Washington struck a similar note in 1783, when he maintained in the *Circular to the States:* "The Foundation of our Empire was not laid in the gloomy age of Ignorance and Superstition, but at an Epocha when the rights of mankind were better understood and more clearly defined, than at any former period."[55]

Washington wrote at a time, when American independence had been secured at Yorktown and the peace treaty of 1783 was ready to be signed. By then, Noah Webster and the Society of the Cincinnati had already become concerned about the "future dignity of the American Empire". Washington himself was widely acclaimed for the "formation and establishment of an empire". The republic, by then risen "into a powerful and polished empire", as one author stated, had begun creating its own heroes – other requisites of empire were to follow in due time.[56]

The quotations presented in this paper seem to suggest that Americans of the Revolutionary period used the term "empire" almost as a household word. This, however, would certainly be a wrong impression. Although there were occasional discussions of the character of the British Empire before 1776,[57] no similar detailed analysis of the nature of the rising American empire was published from 1776 to 1783; references to the term are scattered throughout the bulk of the political writings and public addresses. This apparently haphazard use accounts for the different connotations that have been presented here. Two things stand out: If we take the word of the colonials as our starting point there was no independent American empire before 1775–76. After Independence the term began to appear with a wide range of meanings. These encompassed territorial expansion, republican ideals, the idea of God's chosen people, progress in the arts and sciences, and an equal rank of the United States in the international community of nations. By reducing these rather imprecise ideas to just one aspect, for example to that of territorial expansion, later historians invite the charge of not only reducing a complex set of ideas to a crude belief, but indulge in the questionable practice of transferring backwards concepts which are of much later origin.[58] Modern historians should indeed be cautious about using eighteenth-century quotations when presenting, in their analyses, a more recent concept of "empire".

Notes

[1] When used as a proper name I have capitalized "empire", e. g. as in "British Empire".

[2] Richard Koebner, *Empire* (Cambridge, 1961), 87; in the period under discussion the word was still frequently used in this sense, e. g. [Carter Braxton,] *An Address To The Convention of the Colony ...* (Philadelphia, 1776), 12 (Evans No. 14669), "gaining the empire of the sea."

[3] Charles Francis Adams, ed., *The Works of John Adams* (Boston, 1850–56), IV, 107 (Novanglus Letters).

[4] Koebner, *Empire* (cf. n. 2), 145.

[5] [Thomas Whately,] *The Regulations Lately Made ...* (London, 1765), 39–40.

[6] Koebner, *Empire* (cf. n. 2), 157; italics mine.

[7] [John Dickinson,] *The Late Regulations ...*, in Bernard Bailyn, ed., *Pamphlets of the American Revolution*, I (Cambridge, Mass., 1965), 668–691, is a good illustration of the point. In his footnotes Dickinson quotes extensively from those authors that were usually selected to support the colonists' point of view.

[8] Why the colonies introduced the concept "British Empire" at this point is explained by Koebner, *Empire* (cf. n. 2), 86. There he says that before 1750 its main connotation was "trade, shipping and the navy." Quite early the term "empire" had already been used to describe a "nation extended over vast tracts of land, and number of people," as Koebner, *Empire,* 59, and Gerald Stourzh, *Alexander Hamilton and the Idea of Republican Government* (Stanford, Cal., 1970), 190, both indicate by quoting Sir William Temple. See also James Truslow Adams, "On the Term 'British Empire'," *AHR*, XXVII (1922), 485–489. In the discussion of this paper, Gerald Stourzh also pointed out that in the 18th century an empire was commonly considered a composite entity, where territories with varying degrees of sovereignty and with different jurisdictions coexisted under one head. Such a vast, composite empire was the Holy Roman Empire. Stephen Hopkins, *The Rights of Colonies Examined* (Providence, R. I., 1765), 19–20, in Bailyn, ed., *Pamphlets* (cf. n. 7), I, 519, concluded from the analogy of the British Empire with the Holy Roman Empire that Parliament had no right to tax the colonies: "In an imperial state, which consists of many separate

148

governments each of which hath peculiar privileges and of which kind it is evident the empire of Great Britain is, no single part, though greater than another part, is by that superiority entitled to make laws for or to tax such lesser part; ... This may be fully verified by the empire of Germany, which consists of many states, some powerful and others weak, yet the powerful never make laws to govern or to tax the little and weak ones, ..." I have not been able to locate additional references to the Holy Roman Empire which bring out this analogy. It would be interesting to know, whether the "Thirteen States in Congress Assembled" still considered themselves a composite empire.

⁹ [Dickinson,] *Late Regulations*, 29, in Bailyn, ed., *Pamphlets* (cf. n. 7), I, 686.

¹⁰ *Ib.*, 38 (691); italics Dickinson's.

¹¹ [Daniel Dulany,] *Considerations on the Propriety of imposing Taxes ...* ([Annapolis,] 1765), 46, in Bailyn, ed., *Pamphlets* (cf. n. 7), I, 649–650.

¹² "British dominions", "British nation" were used in the same sense.

¹³ Paul Leicester Ford, ed., *The Writings of John Dickinson*, I (Historical Society of Pennsylvania, *Memoirs*, XIV [Philadelphia, 1895]), 312 (beginning of Letter II).

¹⁴ *JCC*, I, 68. This is the so-called "Declaration of Rights and Grievances" and still makes the point. See also Daniel Shute, *A Sermon Preached Before His Excellency Francis Bernard ...* (Boston, 1748 [i. e. 1768]), 59, "The happiness of THIS PEOPLE in the enjoyment of their natural rights and privileges under providence is provided for by their being a part of the *British* empire, by which they are intitled *[sic]* to the privileges of that happy constitution."

¹⁵ *JCC*, I, 68.

¹⁶ See Randolph G. Adams, *Political Ideas of the American Revolution*, 3d ed. (New York, 1958), 68–85.

¹⁷ [Daniel Leonard,] *Massachusettensis* (Boston, 1775), 6 (Evans No. 14157). See also p. 11: "We had always considered ourselves, as a part of the British empire, and the parliament, as the supreme legislature of the whole." The recent edition of the Massachusettensis-Letters by Bernard Mason, ed., *The American Colonial Crisis* (New York, 1972), which also reprints the bulk of John Adams' Novanglus-Letters, is of little use as it does not reprint both series of letters in full.

¹⁸ [Leonard,] *Massachusettensis* (cf. n. 17), 42, 41.

¹⁹ *Ib.*, 93; see also 23.

²⁰ *Ib.*, 103; 43–44.

²¹ *Ib.*, 114–115.

²² *Ib.*, 6.

²³ Adams, ed., *Works of John Adams* (cf. n. 3), IV, 37–38, 163.

²⁴ *Ib.*, 130; see also 158.

²⁵ *Ib.*, 114; see also 142.

²⁶ [Leonard,] *Massachusettensis* (cf. n. 17), 43. Adams, ed., *Works of John Adams* (cf. n. 3), IV, 114–115.

²⁷ *Ib.*, 106–107.

²⁸ *Ib.*, 194 (*Thoughts on Government*). The quotation is apparently derived from Harrington's *Oceana* as Yehoshua Arieli, *Individualism and Nationalism in American Ideology* (Cambridge, Mass., 1964), 55, points out. References to this statement by Harrington are not uncommon in the colonies, see, for instance, *Four Dissertations, On The Reciprocal Advantages Of A Perpetual Union Between Great-Britain And Her American Colonies* (Philadelphia, 1766),

149

3 (Dissertation I); [John Dickinson and Arthur Lee,] *The Farmer's and Monitor's Letters* (Williamsburg, Va., 1769), 94 (Evans No. 11239).

29 Perez Morton, *An Oration; Delivered At the King's Chapel In Boston, April 8, 1776* ... (Boston, 1776), 13 (Evans No. 14892).

30 William Smith, *An Oration In Memory Of General Montgomery* ... (Philadelphia, 1776), 13 (Evans No. 15084). See also Thomas Paine's statement in William M. Van der Weyde, ed., *The Life and Works of Thomas Paine*, II (New Rochelle, N. Y., 1925), 26 *(A Dialogue Between the Ghost of General Montgomery ... and an American Delegate)*.

31 Edmund S. Morgan, ed., *The Stamp Act Crisis: Prologue to Revolution* (Chapel Hill, N. C., 1959), 77 (from the *Providence Gazette*, May 11, 1765); *A Letter To The North American* ... (Barbados, 1766), 11.

32 [Nicholas Ray,] *The Importance of the Colonies of North America* ... (New York, 1766 [orig. publ. London, 1766]), 5; see also the quotation from Sir William Draper in Richard W. Van Alstyne, *Empire and Independence* (New York, 1965), 42. The first known mention of this rate of increase is found in Benjamin Franklin's *Observations Concerning the Increase of Mankind* as pointed out in J. Potter, "The Growth of Population in America, 1700–1860," in D. V. Glass and D. E. C. Eversley, eds., *Population in History* (London, 1965), 632.

33 The great future of the colonies is referred to in William Wood, *New England's Prospect* ... (Boston, 1764), iv (Evans No. 9884); Maurice Moore, *The Justice And Policy Of Taxing The American Colonies* (Wilmington, N. C., 1765), 15 (Evans No. 10076); [James Otis,] *A Vindication Of The British Colonies* ... (Boston, 1765), 15 (Evans No. 10117); *Letter To The North-American (cf. n. 31)*, 27; [Stephen Johnson,] *Some Important Observations* ... (Newport, R. I., 1766), 33 (Evans No. 10346), which contains the warning to the mother country.

34 Adams, ed., *Works of John Adams* (cf. n. 3), I, 23.

35 [Leonard,] *Massachusettensis* (cf. n. 17), 45; Adams, ed., *Works of John Adams* (cf. n. 3), IV, 121.

36 The phrase is taken from Malachy Postlethwayt, *The Universal Dictionary of Trade and Commerce*, I (London, 1774), xxiv. Englishmen frequently voiced their fears that America wished "to be an Empire by itself", see the quotations in Van Alstyne, *Empire and Independence* (cf. n. 32), 74, 55.

37 *The Power And Grandeur Of Great Britain, Founded On The Liberty Of The Colonies* ... (New York, 1768), 22.

38 Jonathan Mayhew, *Two Discourses Delivered Oct. 25, 1759* ... (Boston, 1759), as quoted in Bailyn, ed., *Pamphlets* (cf. n. 7), 84–85; *Four Dissertations* (cf. n. 28), 101 [J. Reed]; [John Dickinson,] *An Essay On The Constitutional Power of Great Britain* ... (Philadelphia, 1774), 56–62, particularly the extensive footnote.

39 Fred L. Pattlee, ed., *The Poems of Philip Freneau*, I (New York, 1963), 73.

40 Franklin's very advanced views on the expansion of the colonies are discussed in Gerald Stourzh, *Benjamin Franklin and American Foreign Policy*, 2d ed. (Chicago, 1969), 54–82.

41 H. A. Cushing, ed., *The Writings of Samuel Adams*, III (New York, 1907), 102; the letter is dated April 4, 1774.

42 A. C. Fraser, ed., *The Works of George Berkeley*, IV (Oxford, 1901), 365–66. Werner Goez, *Translatio Imperii. Ein Beitrag zur Geschichte des Ge-*

schichtsdenkens und der politischen Theorien im Mittelalter und in der frühen Neuzeit (Tübingen, 1958), gives an account of the origins of the idea.

43 Koebner, *Empire* (cf. n. 2), 96; Hans Kohn, *American Nationalism* (New York, 1957), 10–11. The main idea of the poem, as expressed in its title, has very often been disregarded. For a recent example see Loren Baritz, *City on a Hill* (New York, 1964), 94.

44 Ames is quoted in Jack P. Greene, ed., *Settlements to Society: 1584–1763*, in David Donald, gen. ed., *A Documentary History of American Life*, I (New York, 1966), 380; William Wood, *New-England's Prospect* (cf. n. 33), xvii, the quotation is from the introduction which was written by James Otis, Jr., or Nathaniel Rogers; *American Whig* as quoted in Koebner, *Empire* (cf. n. 2), 172.

45 The Secret Committee to Silas Deane, October 1, 1776, as quoted in Van Alstyne, *Empire and Independence* (cf. n. 32), 79; Samuel Sherwood, *The Church's Flight Into The Wilderness* ... (New York, 1776), 17 (Evans No. 15082).

46 Van der Weyde, ed., *Works of Thomas Paine* (cf. n. 30), II, 260.

47 [Timothy Dwight,] *A Valedictory Address To The Young Gentlemen, Who Commenced Bachelors of Arts, At Yale College, July 25th. 1776* (New Haven, Conn., [1776]), 13, on p. 14 the millennarian aspect is further discussed. For a recent view of millennarian thinking in early Puritan New England see J. F. Maclear, "New-England and the Fifth Monarchy: The Quest for the Millennium in Early American Puritanism," *WMQ*, 3d Ser., XXXII (1975), 223–260.

48 Joel Barlow, *The Prospect of Peace* ... (New York, 1778), 11 (Evans No. 15729); [Dwight,] *Valedictory Address* (cf. n. 47), 10; Pattlee, ed., *Poems of Philip Freneau* (cf. n. 39), I, 281.

49 *A Dialogue, Between The Devil and George III* ... (Boston, 1782), 22 (Evans No. 17520).

50 William H. Drayton, *A Charge, On the Rise of the American Empire* ... (Charleston, S. C., 1776), in Hezekiah Niles, ed., *Principles And Acts Of The Revolution In America*, repr. ed. (New York, 1971 [orig. publ. Baltimore, 1822]), 81–82. It is interesting to note that the American empire apparently did not imply the idea of a strong, centralized government. Judge Drayton is a good example. Although he celebrated the rising American empire in 1776 he opposed the adoption of the Articles of Confederation 16 months later as giving too much power to the central government, *ib.*, 98–114.

51 See James Murray, *An Impartial History of the War in America* (Boston, 1781 [orig. publ. Newcastle, 1778]), 49 (Evans No. 17241).

52 Niles, ed., *Principles And Acts* (cf. n. 50), 49; Josiah Meigs, *An Oration Pronounced Before a public Assembly in New Haven* ... (New Haven, Conn., 1782), 4 (Evans No. 17604).

53 Niles, ed., *Principles And Acts* (cf. n. 50), 52, 26.

54 Quoted from Willi Paul Adams, *Republikanische Verfassung und bürgerliche Freiheit* (Darmstadt, 1973), 141.

55 [Dwight,] *Valedictory Address* (cf. n. 47), 12; John C. Fitzpatrick, ed., *The Writings of George Washington*, XXVI (Washington, D. C., 1938), 485; in the Newburgh Address Washington refers also to "our rising Empire", *ib.*, 227.

56 Noah Webster, *A Grammatical Institute, Of The English Language* ... *Part I* ... (Hartford, Conn., [1783]), 15 (Evans No. 18297); *Observations On A Late Pamphlet, Entitled* [sic], '*Considerations upon the Society or Order of the Cincinnati*', ... (Philadelphia, 1783), 7 (Evans No. 18073); Meigs, *Oration*

(cf. n. 52), 11; [Charles Henry Wharton,] *A Political Epistle To His Excellency George Washington, Esq.* . . .(Providence, R. I., 1781), 24; Meigs, *Oration*, 4. Aspects of the empire in America after 1783 are presented in Stourzh, *Hamilton* (cf. n. 8), 189–201, and Julian P. Boyd, "Thomas Jefferson's 'Empire of Liberty'," *Virginia Quarterly Review*, XXIV (1948), 538–554.

[57] A good example is [John Joachim Zubly,] *An Humble Enquiry Into The Nature of the Dependency of the American Colonies* . . . ([Charleston, S. C.,] 1769).

[58] Inviting criticism of this kind is, e. g., Walter LaFeber, "Foreign Policies of a New Nation: Franklin, Madison, and the 'Dream of a New Land to Fulfill with People in Self-Control', 1750–1804" in William Appleman Williams, ed., *From Colony to Empire* (New York, 1972), 9–37. Studies about the international aspects of the American Revolution tend to conceive the idea of the American empire too narrowly, see Arthur Burr Darling, *Our Rising Empire, 1763–1803* (New Haven, Conn., 1940). Richard W. Van Alstyne, *The Rising American Empire* (Oxford, 1960), is another example: He concentrates almost exclusively on the territorial aspects of the American empire; his *Empire and Independence* (cf. n. 32), is, however, more broadly conceived.

152

14

Spain and the Breakdown of the Imperial Ethos: The Problem of Equality

Timothy E. Anna

S PAIN'S dominion in the New World was supported more by ideas than by force of arms. Though based initially on the right of conquest—an a priori right that few Spaniards, even in the late colonial period, disputed—other concepts arose during three centuries to legitimize further Spain's rule of so many vast lands. This nexus of ideas was complex and can barely be touched upon here. What interests us is the process of the collapse of the imperial ethos. Though ultimately encrusted with centuries of complex ramifications, the concepts of empire were always simple, for they had to be understood by ordinary subjects. The essential simplicity, and, nonetheless, the strength, of these ideas are impressive, as is the way in which Spain, in a period of extreme stress, debunked and disproved them.

The three fundamental concepts of empire in the late colonial era, particularly as they appear in documents that demonstrate Spain's resistance to independence in America, are: (1) the father king; (2) the ties that bind; and (3) the equality of citizens and of territorial units within the empire. The last concept, which emerged very late in the era and as a direct consequence of the crisis of 1808, is the focus of this article.

The overarching idea was of the empire as a family united under the father king, the *rey padre*, as he was frequently called in loyalist propaganda. Originating during the Hapsburg era, the idea was based on the legal view that the American territories were the patrimonial property of the king. The "modern" Bourbons had resisted this traditional role, but those living in the colonies "clung to the Hapsburg image of the patriarchal state and resisted the Bourbons' political philosophy."[1] The king was señor, or lord, to whom, according to Spanish political philosophy, the nation at some time in the remote past had transferred au-

---

1. Richard Graham, *Independence in Latin America*, (New York, 1972), pp. 6–7.

thority.[2] He was limited in his exercise of absolute authority by the precepts of Thomism, which required him to rule justly and in the best interest of the people. Also limiting the king's absolutism was the practice of colonial or peninsular officials of refusing to obey or implement laws or decrees of the crown perceived as being inappropriate to local conditions. This principle of *obedezco pero no cumplo* can be seen frequently at work in the colonial era.

Though the emphasis was on centralism during the era of Bourbon reforms, the essentially Hapsburg concept of father king, of patrimonial rather than "modern" absolutism, remained paramount.[3] So central was the patrimonial authority of father king that one writer has asserted that the overthrow of the royal father figure was "the central and 'traumatic' event in all Spanish American history. It represented the acting out of Oedipal desires to slay the father, creating a collective guilt which Spanish America has never overcome. Much of the rebelliousness in modern Spanish American history represents a search for a paternal replacement for the Kings of Spain."[4]

More enduring perhaps than the concept of the patrimonial king and state was the concept of the "ties that bind," the cultural unity "of these and those Spaniards"—the belief that Spain was a transoceanic state composed of many states, united by the event of the conquest and of Spain's having brought civilization to the New World. Many explicitly stated the idea during the independence era, but rarely as cogently as when the Junta Central of Spain wrote the Cabildo of Bogotá in 1809:

> There exists a union between the two hemispheres, between the Spaniards of Europe and of America, a union that can never be destroyed either by intrigue or force of tyrants because it is grounded upon the most solid bases that tie men together: a common origin, the same language, laws, customs, religion, honor to

2. Richard M. Morse, "The Heritage of Latin America" in Howard J. Wiarda, ed., *Politics and Social Change in Latin America: The Distinct Tradition*, (Amherst, 1974), pp. 25–69; Frank Jay Moreno, "The Spanish Colonial System: A Functional Approach," *Western Political Quarterly*, 20 (June 1967), 308–320; John L. Phelan, "Authority and Flexibility in the Spanish Imperial Bureaucracy," *Administrative Science Quarterly* (Ithaca), 1 (June 1960), 47–65; Magali Sarfatti, *Spanish Bureaucratic-Patrimonialism in America* (Berkeley, 1966).

3. Brian R. Hamnett, "Mexico's Royalist Coalition: The Response to Revolution 1808–1821," *Journal of Latin American Studies*, 12 (May 1980), 55–86; Hamnett, *Politics and Trade in Southern Mexico, 1740–1821* (Cambridge, 1971), pp. 72–94; Jacques A. Barbier, "Tradition and Reform in Bourbon Chile: Ambrosio O'Higgins and Public Finances," *The Americas*, 34 (Jan. 1978), 381–399; Barbier, *Reform and Politics in Bourbon Chile, 1755–1796* (Ottawa, 1980).

4. Marvin Goldwert, "The Search for the Lost Father-Figure in Spanish American History: A Freudian View," *The Americas*, 34 (Apr. 1978), 532–536.

principles and sentiments, and relations and interests. These are the ties that unite us.[5]

As different a source as Simón Bolívar's "Letter from Jamaica" made essentially the same observation: that Spain's authority over America was founded on these "ties that bind." In Bolívar's words, these were "the habit of obedience; a community of interest, of understanding, of religion; mutual goodwill; a tender regard for the birthplace and good name of our forefathers."[6] Much of the royalist propaganda in response to the American uprisings centered on the cultural unity of the empire and its church, the role of Spain as the civilizer of America, and the ingratitude of those who would rebel.[7]

There were many potential and actual weaknesses in the concept of the cultural unity of the empire, not the least of which were the implied, but obvious, disregard for the Indian contribution to colonial culture and the creoles' lack of parity with Spaniards in church and state bureaucracies. The weaknesses of the concept, however, did not induce Spain to abandon it as an official point of view. The American dominions were not considered equal to the provinces and kingdoms of peninsular Spain, yet semantically, at least, every effort was made to obscure that fact. Formally the American territories were not colonies; they were kingdoms, vicekingdoms, or dominions. Only at the height of Bourbon mercantilist reform did the term "colony" creep into use, and even then it was used chiefly in internal state papers and not as proclaimed official terminology. When the wars of independence erupted in America, the word "pacification" was officially decreed for use instead of "reconquest" so as not to offend American sensibilities.

The crisis lasting from March to May 1808 seriously wounded the Old Regime in Spain, and, subsequently, the liberal bourgeoisie made a rapid rise to power. The accession of the liberals, whose position was supported by an emerging economic middle class deeply dependent on the preservation of Spain's monopoly of American trade and symbolized by the principal merchants of Cádiz, brought the dialectical problem of equality to the fore.

Desperate to secure the support of America in the struggle under way in Spain, the liberals spoke out in favor of America's nominal equality.

5. Junta Central to Cabildo of Bogotá, Seville, Jan. 14, 1809, Archivo Histórico Nacional, Madrid (hereinafter AHN), Estado 60.

6. "Letter from Jamaica" in Vicente Lecuna, comp.; Harold A. Bierck, Jr., ed.; Lewis Bertrand, trans., *Selected Writings of Bolívar*, 2 vols. (New York, 1951), I, 103–122.

7. Hugh M. Hamill, Jr., *The Hidalgo Revolt* (Gainesville, 1966), pp. 163–164; Hamill, "Early Psychological Warfare in the Hidalgo Revolt," *HAHR*, 41 (May 1961), 206–235.

In the last days before joining the Junta Central, the separate Junta of Seville instructed its delegates to sponsor the liberal position that the overseas provinces be permitted to "have the government of their own provinces in the same manner enjoyed by the Juntas of Spain," that these American juntas be permitted to propose candidates to be selected by the Junta Central as their viceroys, and that matters of trade and navigation be decided by the juntas in the American ports and in the Spanish ports engaged in American trade. The Junta of Seville's argument was for regional autonomy, which, it insisted, "is inviolably sacred, since it comes from the people."[8] The Junta Central overrode Seville's attempt to speak for America and consolidated itself by September 1808 as the single government of a free Spain, but in the process, it absorbed and accommodated the liberal thinking of Seville. By January 1809, the Junta Central, still desperate to affirm American support, invited the New World colonies to send delegates to join the Junta Central and announced that Spain, that is, free Spain, no longer considered the overseas dominions colonies, but "an essential and integral part of the Spanish monarchy." Four months later, the Junta announced its intention to call into session the Cortes and to include representation from America. When, in the following January, the Junta Central collapsed in the face of its own failures and the French successes in Andalusia and Seville, the Regency Council (which replaced the Junta) announced to America the convocation of the Cortes, and added: "From this moment, Spanish Americans, you see yourselves raised to the dignity of free men; . . . your destinies no longer depend on ministers, viceroys, or governors: they are in your hands."[9]

The Cortes began its sessions in September 1810, and under pressure from American deputies, proclaimed on October 15 that Spain recognized the "indisputable concept that the Spanish dominions of both hemispheres form a single monarchy, a single nation, and a single family," and that "natives derived from the said European and overseas dominions are equal in rights to those of this peninsula."[10] Thus did Spain take its first steps toward declaring the overseas territories equal parts of the monarchy and of recognizing the equality of Americans with peninsulars.

Before proceeding, a critical proviso needs to be made. The termi-

8. Instrucción de la Junta Suprema de Sevilla a sus diputados a la Junta Central, Seville, Aug. 24, 1808, AHN, Estado 82.

9. Regency decree, León, Feb. 14, 1810, Archivo General de Indias, Seville (hereinafter AGI), Ultramar 795.

10. "Bando declarando a los Indios con iguales derechos que a los Españoles" in Juan E. Hernández y Dávalos, ed., Colección de documentos para la historia de la guerra de independencia de México de 1808 a 1821, 6 vols. (Mexico City, 1877–82), II, 379.

nology of the October 15 decree purposely excluded Blacks and their descendants of full or mixed blood—those "derived from Africa"—from equality. This prohibition was incorporated into the Constitution of 1812, a hallmark of Spanish liberalism, which declared that all Indians, mestizos, castes, and whites were "Spaniards," but limited the rights of citizenship to "Spaniards who on both sides trace their ancestry to the Spanish dominions of both hemispheres." This peculiar and subtle distinction generally reflected the American creoles' own social and cultural prejudices, for while they were prepared to insist on the equality of American whites, and even Indians, with Spaniards, they could not bring themselves to recognize the equality of the colored castes.[11]

For larger purposes, however, the point is that in 1810 Spain added the principle of equality to the other leading concepts upon which the imperial ethos was based; in so doing, it stumbled into a hopeless dialectical trap. The issue of equality became the cutting edge that would demonstrate to moderate Americans the inherent ideological contradiction of empire, for neither the Constitution and the Cortes, nor after 1814 the restored absolutist regime of Ferdinand VII, would prove able to deal satisfactorily with the issue. Once officially declared, imperial equality could not be withdrawn without doing irreparable damage to political relations between America and Spain. At no point, not even after 1814, was the official principle nullified; neither, however, was it ever implemented, for to have done so would have deprived Spain of important benefits of empire. These benefits were primarily psychological. Spain's definition of itself and of its greatness was deeply involved with its role as founder of a New World empire.

The view of American substitute and proprietary deputies who took their seats in the Cortes of Cádiz, however, differed sharply from that of peninsular deputies on the matter of equality. Until 1812, most of the American deputies were substitutes, chosen from among the native sons of each territory who were then resident in Spain. In general, they were more influenced by the ideology of liberalism than the proprietary deputies, who traveled to Cádiz from their home territories, and who emphasized the need for domestic reforms in government, administration, and economics. Many substitutes retained their seats in the Cortes in order to fill their region's complement of numbers.[12] Still, there was an

11. James F. King, "The Colored Castes and the American Representation in the Cortes of Cádiz," *HAHR*, 33 (Feb. 1953), 33–64.

12. Charles R. Berry, "The Election of the Mexican Deputies to the Spanish Cortes, 1810–1822" in Nettie Lee Benson, ed., *Mexico and the Spanish Cortes, 1810–1822* (Austin, 1966), pp. 10–42; Jorge I. Domínguez, *Insurrection or Loyalty: The Breakdown of the Spanish American Empire* (Cambridge, Mass., 1980), pp. 184–185.

essential continuity and cohesion of demands among all the American deputies up to 1814.

It should be noted that those overseas territories already well ad-vanced along the road to independence or involved in civil warfare, such as the Río de la Plata and Venezuela, did not send proprietary deputies and were represented throughout the extraordinary and ordinary Cortes (until 1814) by their substitutes. What happened in the Cortes cannot be said to have had either a positive or a negative impact upon those ter-ritories represented only by substitutes.

The members of the American caucus, at any rate, threw themselves into the struggle to make operational the concept of equality. They con-centrated their efforts in two areas: the implementation of political equal-ity, by which they meant full parity in appointment to positions in church and state bureaucracies; and equal apportionment of representation in the Cortes. Less energetically, at first, they pursued equality in trade and commerce.

The struggle to secure equal representation in the Cortes was led by the young liberals José Mejía Lequerica of New Granada and Vicente Morales Duárez of Peru. Since the peninsular population was 10.5 mil-lion, while the overseas population was between 15 and 16 million, con-trol of the Cortes rested on the outcome of this matter. The day after the Cortes opened, the Americans made known their expectation of parity in representation. This demand, if accepted, would have doubled the representatives from America since the existing provisions allowed one deputy for each 100,000 inhabitants, while peninsulars had one deputy for each 50,000. The Americans demanded that they receive one deputy for each 50,000, and that the apportionment be based on a count of all free subjects, regardless of caste identity. The peninsular deputies strong-ly rejected that demand. At issue was the fact that while there were far more Americans than peninsulars, there were far fewer American whites.[13]

The Question of Citizenship

In December 1810, the American deputies produced eleven propo-sitions that came to constitute their basic program in the Cortes. The demands included equality of representation between Spain and the In-dies for "natives derived from both hemispheres, Spaniards as well as Indians," which effectively constituted the Americans' giving in to the

13. Mario Rodríguez, *The Cádiz Experiment in Central America, 1808–1826* (Berke-ley, 1978), p. 54.

inevitable exclusion of Blacks from apportionment. James F. King believes that some Americans adopted the formula merely as a minimum demand, intending to return to the question of caste representation at a future date. The matter was thus carried over to later debates surrounding the writing of the Constitution.

In the draft constitution presented to the Cortes for discussion in August 1811, Article 1 defined the Spanish nation as "the union of all Spaniards of both hemispheres"; Article 5 defined Spaniards as "free men born and domiciled in the domains of the Spains," naturalized foreigners, and freedmen at the moment of their emancipation. Thus, all American Indians, mestizos, and castes were proclaimed "Spaniards." Being a "Spaniard," however, was not the same as being a citizen. Article 18 proclaimed that citizens—upon whose number apportionment would be based—were "Spaniards who on both sides trace their ancestry to the Spanish dominions of both hemispheres." In short, the compromise of the October 15 decree in reference to equality was retained as written in the Constitution, over the strong objections of American deputies. Article 22 dealt with persons of African origin as a separate element in the population, proclaiming for them the creation of "a door of virtue and merit" by which the Cortes would grant citizenship—to persons who had given "meritorious services" to the nation and who were of good conduct, legitimately born, married, and exercising some "useful" profession. Article 29 declared that the basis for apportioning representation in Spain and the Indies was "the population composed of those native-born who from both lines are derived from the Spanish domains." These principles having been accepted, there was no danger in Article 28, which declared that "the base for national representation is the same in both hemispheres," or in Article 31, which provided that there would be one deputy for every 70,000 enumerated inhabitants in both Spain and America.[14]

The refusal of the Cortes to accept equal representation (by means of limiting citizenship rights) provided fuel for the anti-Spanish elements among the creoles, encouraged and justified the revolts breaking out in America, and permanently skewed the outcome of future Cortes debates on all questions affecting American appointments, trade, and pacification. As Peruvian deputy Ramón Feliú observed: "America is no longer . . . a child who, put to bed with promises, will forget them when he awak-

---

14. King, "The Colored Castes," 33–64; David T. Garza, "Mexican Constitutional Expression in the Cortes of Cádiz" in Benson, ed., *Mexico and the Spanish Cortes*, pp. 43–58; the most readily available copy of the Constitution is in Hernández y Dávalos, ed., *Colección de documentos*, IV, 50–118.

ens."[15] Even at its best, Spanish liberalism did not extend to the point of risking Spain's domination of its colonial territories, and this resulted in the fundamental failure of the vision of the Cortes as it affected American questions. Agustín Argüelles, leader of the peninsular liberals, admitted that he saw as "an insuperable obstacle" a citizenry "that exceeds that of the mother country."[16] In the course of the debate over representation, the Americans were repeatedly outraged by what they considered the myopic vision of peninsulars living both in Spain and America. José Baquíjano, a Peruvian who sat on the Council of State, said that "the leader of the liberals [Argüelles] reproduced the most contemptible sophisms to argue that the Indians were slaves by nature." He continued: "One ecclesiastical deputy said, 'If they [the Indians] are equal in rights, it will be necessary to suppress the tributes, and that is not convenient'; another asked if Americans were white and professed the Catholic religion; and ultimately one deputy, who had extracted his wealth from South America, concluded 'that it has never been known to what genus of animal the Indians belonged.'"[17]

During the continuing efforts to limit the number of citizens, there appeared a memorial from the Consulado of Mexico City. Read in the Cortes on September 16, 1811, the memorial condemned all Americans of the three racial categories as unfit for equal representation in the Cortes. Concluding that Mexico was Spanish by right of conquest, the memorial advocated that the country be represented in the Cortes by designated Spaniards only, and expressed the thought that the only appropriate parallel between the Indian and the Spaniard was that between a "flock of gibbon monkeys" and an advanced urban society.[18] After the reading, the entire American deputation attempted to withdraw from the floor, but was blocked by orders of the president.

From Parity to Economic Equality

Once the question of equality of representation was resolved in a manner prejudicial to the Americans, all other questions in which the interests of Spain differed from those of America followed suit. The two

15. For the role of the five Peruvian substitute deputies in the equal apportionment debate, see Timothy E. Anna, *The Fall of the Royal Government in Peru* (Lincoln, 1979), pp. 46–47.

16. King, "The Colored Castes," 33–64.

17. Memoria of José Baquíjano, Madrid, Aug. 31, 1814, AGI, Estado 87.

18. "Informe del Real Tribunal del Consulado de México," May 27, 1811, Hernández y Dávalos, ed., *Colección de documentos*, II, 450–466.

most important expressions of American demands were those presented by the overseas deputies on December 16, 1810, and August 1, 1811. The December 16 presentation comprised eleven fundamental reforms. They were: (1) equal proportionate representation in the Cortes; (2) freedom to plant and manufacture all previously restricted commodities; (3) freedom of trade with allied and neutral powers; (4) free trade with the Asiatic possessions; (5) free trade with any other part of Asia; (6) suppression of all state and private monopolies; (7) free mining of mercury in America; (8) equal rights of Americans, whether white or Indian, to any political, military, or ecclesiastical appointment; (9) distribution of half of the positions in each American kingdom to natives of that kingdom; (10) creation of advisory committees in America for the selection of local residents to be given those public offices; and (11) restoration of the Jesuit order in America.[19]

These demands represented a shift in focus. The American demand for implementation of equality began to center around the question of free trade, of economic equality. Each of the demands held implications for the entire empire, yet each was also local, since terms of implementation would differ according to the conditions prevailing in each locality.

All the demands were eventually debated in the Cortes in one form or another, but only three were acted upon favorably, and these were modified or otherwise rendered meaningless. Item 1, as we have seen, was approved on the basis of an incomplete count of inhabitants, and it did not apply to the Cortes that was actually sitting. Item 2 was granted, but it had little impact in a war-torn America. Item 7, the request for free mining of mercury in America, the Cortes partially accepted, granting on January 26, 1811, the privilege of free trade in mercury—that is, the right of anyone who had the capital to import as much mercury as he could from peninsular sources. (This was chimerical since the mines at Almadén were occupied by the French. In 1811 and 1812 there were no mercury shipments to Peru; in 1813 and 1814 large shipments were sent after allied military forces captured reserves held by the French; after 1814, it seems that no further shipments reached Peru.)[20] Of the other demands, one (Item 11) was rejected outright in a Cortes vote; three (Items 3, 4, and 5) were delayed pending the collection of further opinion; three (Items 8, 9, and 10) were reserved for later action and then never acted upon; and one (Item 6) was postponed.

19. W. Woodrow Anderson, "Reform as a Means to Quell Revolution" in Benson, ed., *Mexico and the Spanish Cortes,* pp. 185–207; John Preston Moore, *The Cabildo in Peru under the Bourbons* (Durham, 1966), pp. 208–209.
20. J. R. Fisher, *Silver Mines and Silver Miners in Colonial Peru, 1776–1824* (Liverpool, 1977), p. 84.

Having run up against the immovable obstacle of state and private peninsular interests, some of the American delegates attempted a flanking action, to acquire expanded liberty of commerce for their countries. On August 1, 1811, thirty-three of them presented a report in a closed session of the Cortes, advocating a political reform first suggested by Mexican deputy José Beye de Cisneros. The scheme was that a system of provincial juntas would be established in America and that they would be authorized to open free trade with foreign powers should the metropolis itself fall to French conquest. If this happened, the American countries would then rescue Spain with their own great resources. Mexico, for example, would make massive loans to Spain by mortgaging its mines to the British. This concept was deemed revolutionary and allowed to die on the table without being presented to the full house.[21]

In addition to the general demands of the American delegation, many of the individual deputies, both substitute and proprietary, had received specific instructions from their home provinces, normally drafted by the city councils of their capitals. Their demands can be pieced together by reviewing recommendations for pacification of America submitted by at least thirty-two former deputies after the king's restoration.[22] The request that appeared most often in instructions from the cabildos was for the creation in the local jurisdictions of various new agencies or offices of royal government, such as new audiencias, new viceroyalties, or royal mints. The next most frequent demand involved matters relating to the Indians, mostly either to continue the suppression of the tribute or to reinstate it. Next in line was the demand to lower various taxes, customs duties, and interest rates. Then came requests for the improvement or opening of ports and navigational systems. Ten deputies asked for local agricultural improvements, mining reforms, and a variety of changes in the civil and clerical bureaucracies. Seven deputies wanted the abolition of some royal office, usually of the most local nature. The next most frequent requests were for the establishment of universities or seminaries, city councils, mining tribunals, or professional agencies, or the granting of special distinctions, arms, or titles to home towns and provinces. Nine deputies demanded universities for their home districts; eight asked for new dioceses or archdioceses. Many deputies wanted major public works—roads, bridges, military highways, and fortifications. These in-

21. "Informe que hizo el Dr. D. José Beye de Cisneros a las Cortes," 1811, Archivo del Ex-Ayuntamiento, México, Elecciones de diputados a Cortes, vol. 870, no. 9; Baquíjano memorial, AGI, Estado 87.

22. Nota de los diputados de las Américas a quienes se les ha comunicado la circular de 17 de junio de 1814, AGI, Indiferente general 1354. The replies are scattered throughout Indiferente general 1354 and 1355.

dividual "wish lists" make it clear that the creoles were prepared to settle for parity of treatment rather than a thorough ideological transformation of the empire; it should be remembered, however, that these lists represented the wishes of those creoles who were prepared to try parliamentary methods for the solution of grievances.

By mid-1811, the Cortes had received a clear statement from the Americans of the political solution to the rebellions then raging in their homelands. All of them advocated equality of career opportunity, free foreign trade, and abolition of internal hindrances to production, while most of them supported provincial autonomy. That was the American political solution; that was what imperial equality meant to them. It expressed the aspirations of a still loyalist creole elite continuously engaged in a contest for influence against the peninsular elites who administered America, but who could not bring themselves to support the homegrown radicalism of lower-class revolt. The creole elite represented a middle position between absolutism and separatism.[23]

By switching the focus of their efforts from parity to the free-trade question, the Americans sealed their fate; by refusing economic equality, Spain did the same to itself. Politically, Spain could not give in to the American demands for economic equality. To have done so would have threatened the existence of the empire and the overseas territories from which Spain, according to the Conde de Toreno, derived 55.5 percent of total government revenues in 1810, and 35 percent in 1811. The Cádiz merchants controlled the Cortes, and their survival was basic to that of Spain. José Baquíjano declared that the Consulado of Cádiz was "the absolute dictator of the resolutions of the Regency and the Cortes."[24] The most clear-sighted members of the Cádiz regime understood that there was no room to maneuver, but even they deluded themselves into imagining that such apparent reforms as the decree of individual equality, or else the Constitution itself, would answer the Americans' demands. The Conde de Toreno, a major leader of the peninsular liberals, recognized, however, that even the Constitution, with its long-term object of increasing centralization in America, was a European enactment suitable mainly to European conditions. He wrote:

> It might appear at first glance a great delirium to have adopted for the remote countries of Ultramar the same rules and Constitution as for the peninsula; but from the moment that the Junta Central declared the inhabitants of both hemispheres equal in

23. Hamnett, "Mexico's Royalist Coalition," 55–86.
24. Baquíjano memorial, AGI, Estado 87.

rights, and from the moment the American deputies were seated in the Cortes, [the Cortes] either could not approve reforms for Europe, or it was necessary to extend them to those countries. There were already too many indications and proofs of disunion for the Cortes to add fuel to the fire; and where compulsory means do not exist to check hidden or open rebellions, it becomes necessary to charm the spirits in such a way that while independence may not be impeded in the future, the instant of a total and hostile break is at least postponed.[25]

This startling confession indeed makes clear that Spain had maneuvered itself into a hopeless political trap. Either the overseas territories were colonies or they were not; Spain, however, had decided to have it both ways, to "charm the spirits" by telling the Americans they were equal while treating them as before.

In a powerful memorial submitted in 1814, José Baquíjano condemned Spain and the Cortes for failing to implement the vast promises of the Constitution. According to Baquíjano, the fault lay not so much in misgovernment, though there was plenty of that, but in unfulfilled promises. The two chief insults of the Cortes, he said, were its refusal to grant equal representation and its refusal to establish free commerce. He declared that "this antipolitical conduct has been the true origin of the desperation of the American peoples; the Cortes never wanted to listen to their complaints, or hear their proposals."[26]

Perceptive observers echoed Baquíjano's thinking, among them José García de León y Pizarro, who served briefly in 1812 as minister of state and returned to that position in 1816–18. He believed that "America should follow the fortune that nature has destined for all those distant possessions separated geographically from their centers; it should emancipate itself." The moment of separation and the damage it inflicted on Spain, however, were the fault of "inexperience, slovenliness, and blindness" on the part of the rulers of Spain. The Junta Central and the Cortes, he argued, had excited and legitimized American rebellion by proclaiming equality one moment and infringing upon it the next.[27] It was not merely that Spain had broken faith with colonial elites; it had raised new hopes that it had no will to satisfy.

The failure to implement economic equality played a role in the dis-

25. Conde de Toreno, *Historia del levantamiento, guerra y revolución de España,* Biblioteca de Autores Españoles, no 64 (Madrid, 1953), p. 393.
26. Baquíjano memorial, AGI, Estado 87.
27. José García de León y Pizarro, *Memorias,* ed., prol., and notes by Alvaro Alonso-Castrillo, 2 vols. (Madrid, 1953), I, 148–150.

cussion of possible British mediation in the American rebellions, discussions that began in May 1811 and continued in a desultory fashion long after the Cortes was dissolved. The British proposed that in return for their involvement, they be permitted free trade with the American territories for at least as long as the mediation effort lasted. Disagreement over the bases of mediation prevailed and always resulted in the negotiations coming to naught.[28] The English were quite cogent in their arguments, pointing out that unless the Americans were permitted commercial advantages equal to those of Spaniards, their separation from the metropolis was inevitable. They argued that the pacification of America was as simple a matter as removing the restrictions on colonial commerce. Americans, they said, simply could not be treated as colonials once Spain had declared their equality.

In 1812 the British government proposed as possible bases of mediation that America be granted free foreign trade, equality of appointment to state offices, and the "concession of interim or provincial governments under the viceroys or governors to the cabildos or ayuntamientos."[29] This would have led to genuine equality and the creation of a federative government in the empire. These propositions were submitted to the Cortes for discussion and on July 16, 1812, rejected by a vote of more than two to one. (The American deputies strongly endorsed the proposals, while the European deputies just as strongly opposed them.)[30] By the end of the year, Spanish Minister of State Pedro Gómez Labrador informed the British that the publication of the Constitution had completely altered Spain's relation with America: for the first time, a European nation, he said, had given its colonies complete equality; therefore, no more special favors could be considered. The question of mediation emerged again in 1815 and appeared periodically until 1820, but no final agreement was ever reached.

The Restoration Response to Equality

The restoration of Ferdinand VII to the throne in early 1814 and his May coup, in which he overthrew the Cortes and Constitution and re-

28. See Michael P. Costeloe, "Spain and the Latin American Wars of Independence: The Free Trade Controversy, 1810–20," *HAHR*, 61 (May 1981), 209–234; John Rydjord, "British Mediation between Spain and her Colonies: 1811–1813," *HAHR*, 21 (Feb. 1941), 29–50; Wecenslao Ramírez de Villa-Urrutia, *Relaciones entre España e Inglaterra durante la guerra de la independencia*, 3 vols. (Madrid, 1912), II, 366–411; William W. Kaufmann, *British Policy and the Independence of Latin America, 1804–1828* (New Haven, 1951), pp. 64–75; Extracto histórico y razonado de la negociación seguida entre el Gobierno Inglés y la España acerca de la mediación, AGI, Indiferente general 1571.

29. Toreno, *Historia*, p. 439.

30. Rydjord, "British Mediation," 29–50.

established absolutism, did not, strangely enough, eliminate the concept of equality of the overseas territories. Although a succession of royal decrees throughout the latter half of 1814 ordered the abolition of all constitutional and elected bodies and the restoration of the Old Regime, at no point was there a decree annulling the grant of equality. In November, the king provided for the restoration of all government offices in America to the persons who held them before the Cortes.[31] Minister of the Indies Miguel de Lardizábal called upon American Cortes deputies still in Spain to submit recommendations on means to pacify America. In response, many of them urged implementation of the concept of equality. Their requests were not, however, acted upon and the reforms they demanded remained unattended during the restoration. Indeed, in the first year of the restoration the basic policy of the king toward America was to do nothing. In this he accepted the advice of Ramón de Posada, a member of the Council of Indies, who suggested: "At the moment all reforms and general means are inopportune. Reforms might be useful, and at times necessary, but despite that they do not fail to be odious." Posada continued: "This is not the time either to annul or to confirm the inopportune grants and declarations of the Cortes in favor of the Americans." In a second letter he urged the following policy: "No new taxes, no alleviation of taxes, no grants and declarations, no revocation of those opportunely or inopportunely conceded; keep totally silent about everything."[32] Although it revoked the constitutional system in all its aspects, the absolute regime made no other changes, whether negative or positive. How could the king deny the principle of October 15, 1810, that his dominions "form[ed] a single monarchy, a single nation, and a single family"? Not even the king could tell Americans that they were reduced again to colonial inferiority.

During the restoration, the concept of father king received a massive impetus in official mythology and came to predominate in Spain's appeals for America to return to loyalty. The Conde de Puñorrostro insisted that Ferdinand's restoration would end the American rebellions, for "those vassals, through the nature of their climate and their temperament, are docile, submissive, and gentle, and, above all, lovers to the point of idolatry of the name and person of their sovereign."[33] Minister of Indies Lardizábal asked for reports from Americans about the insurrections and informed them that "His Majesty, once he knows the truth, will place himself in the midst of his European and American children and will

31. Council of Indies consulta, Madrid, Sept. 5, 1814, AGI, Indiferente general 803.
32. Ramón de Posada to Lardizábal, Toledo, Aug. 6, Aug. 10, 1814, AGI, Estado 87.
33. Puñorrostro to San Carlos, Madrid, May 22, 1814, AGI, Estado 87.

bring to an end that discord that never would have happened among brothers except for the absence and captivity of the father."[34] Absolutist periodical *El Procurador* insisted that "the name of Ferdinand is a magic or mysterious name for all good people."[35]

This "love of king" thesis among Spanish policy-makers failed to restore loyalty on the part of the Americans. The restoration was dominated by hardliners and militarists, those closest to Ferdinand and most influential in his councils, whose view that force was "the only thing that [could] suffice in the state to which things had arrived" prevailed.[36] It is not surprising that in September 1814 the decision was made to dispatch the expedition of Pablo Morillo to New Granada and Venezuela, or in early 1815 to gather a second large expedition for use against Buenos Aires.

The voices of moderation at court coalesced around Minister of State José García de León y Pizarro. At all times, however, the camarilla was able to prevent the adoption of moderate reforms, and in September 1818, with Pizarro's dismissal, it succeeded in winning control over the regime.[37] The absolutists who surrounded the king and possessed his confidence, urged total opposition to equality of trade. Even Martín Garay, the moderate minister of finance, told the king that adoption of commercial equality between Spain and America would result in a "political monstrosity never before seen in either ancient or modern overseas establishments." He meant that an empire of equal parts would be no empire. "The Indies," he continued, "by their situation, state, needs, and relations, have perforce to carry out the role of colonies, . . . and it is not humanly possible to identify or equalize the colonies with their metropolis, because they and it have different and even contrary objectives, obligations, and functions."[38] A member of the Council of State declared: "I would look upon the decree of free commerce as the same as the emancipation of America and the sentence of our degradation."[39]

The debate over equal trade that occurred among the highest policy advisers to the king isolated for the first time and discussed, in however

34. Melchor Fernández Almagro, *La emancipación de América y su reflejo en la conciencia española*, 2d ed. (Madrid, 1957), p. 76.

35. Jaime Delgado, *La independencia de América en la prensa española* (Madrid, 1949), p. 214.

36. Memoria on pacification of Juan Antonio Yandiola, Madrid, Jan. 29, 1815, AGI, Estado 87.

37. Russell H. Bartley, *Imperial Russia and the Struggle for Latin American Independence, 1808–1828* (Austin, 1978), pp. 122–127.

38. Apuntes del Sr. Garay sobre el papel de Casa Flores para pacificación de América, Jan. 1817, AGI, Estado 87.

39. Voto particular, unnamed councillor of state, Madrid, July 1817, AGI, Estado 88.

inadequate a way, the fundamental issue of the relationship between America's colonial status and Spain's sense of national greatness. The Junta of Pacification pointed out that "the project [of free trade] is bound up historically with . . . our own [national] preoccupations," and that Spain was the dependent part. "In effect, much thought is required to combine their [Americans'] liberties with the metropolis's dependency. To concede them the same privileges as Spain . . . it would be necessary to be very sure of their loyalty."[40] Pizarro bluntly had reminded the king that American pacification was the premier topic, beside which all other questions paled into insignificance, and upon the solution to which the glory of the king's reign and of generations to come depended. He was convinced that Spain could win great advantages by accommodating itself to American independence and building a new and greater trade relationship, as Britain had with the United States. In the Council of State, Minister of War Francisco Eguía took a decidedly different stance. He branded both free trade and amnesty for liberals and *afrancesados* treason, and he blocked any discussion of the several proposals for dividing the empire into a confederation of states. In the absolutists' view, such projects were fatal to the king's majesty.

The king's camarilla, in September 1818, finally engineered the removal from court and the exile of Pizarro and his colleagues, thus bringing to an end any hope for acceptance of the concept of equality for America. The new minister of state, the Marqués de Casa Irujo, advised abandonment of all Pizarro's policies, including the effort to seek European mediation in return for free trade. Foreign trade was always the vehicle of revolution, he said, and the king agreed.[41] Shortly thereafter, the United States and European powers were informed that all foreigners were barred from further contacts with Spanish America and that armed foreigners caught while in the service of the rebels in America would be subject to the same penalties as Spanish nationals.[42] The only policy left, according to Casa Irujo, was to hasten the outfitting of the great expedition being gathered at Cádiz for dispatch to Buenos Aires, the expedition that in January 1820 revolted and brought down the absolutist regime.

The Constitutional Triennium

During the constitutional triennium (1820–23), a succession of four increasingly radical governments did nothing to advance the cause of

40. Junta of Pacification consulta, Madrid, Feb. 8, 1817, AGI, Estado 86-A.
41. Casa Irujo to King, Madrid, Sept. 21, 1818, AGI, Estado 89.
42. Royal order, Madrid, Nov. 23, 1818, AGI, Estado 89; Eguía to Secretary of State, Madrid, Feb. 12, 1819, AGI, Estado 103.

American equality, now again officially enshrined in law. Distracted by the effort to make the revolution at home and by the outright hostility and conspiracies of the king to destroy the constitutional regime, the liberals made no important advances except to recognize the need for a negotiated political settlement. In the first weeks of the new regime, the Provisional Junta that ruled before the meeting of the Cortes ordered ceasefires in America and dispatched commissioners to negotiate with the rebels for acceptance of the Constitution. The Junta declared that restoration of the Constitution "equalized in every way the rights of Spanish Americans with peninsulars." As a result, "the Junta is firmly convinced that the pacification of America is now more the work of politics than of force, and that only the Constitution can reestablish the fraternal bonds of union with the mother country."[43] Yet, the same gap between promise and performance that had paralyzed the first constitutional government in 1812 continued to exist during the triennium.[44]

In much of America it was too late by 1820 to adopt political reforms that would save Spain's control. Pablo Morillo, writing from Venezuela, advised: "It is nonsense, in my view, to believe that this part of America wants to reunite with Spain and adopt the Constitution. . . . The American dissidents . . . have not been fighting to improve the system of government and it is an error to believe that they will ever be agreeable to uniting with the metropolis. They do not want to be Spaniards."[45] American deputies to the Cortes once again urged in passionate voices the redress of American grievances, but they met with even stronger resistance than that of 1812. In November 1821, the Council of State urged abolition of trade exclusion, arguing that "free commerce is so much in the natural order of things that only by tyrannical violence can it be withdrawn." In January 1822, the ministry, in its major pronouncement on the American crisis, urged the Cortes to grant free trade for six years.[46] The Cortes, however, rejected these and other similar proposals, and ended instead by dispatching a second set of commissioners to "hear" the complaints of America. At that point, American deputies still remaining in the Cortes left Madrid, and one after another of the American

43. Cardinal Bourbon to Secretary of Ultramar, Madrid, Apr. 19, 1820, AGI, Indiferente general 1568.
44. Free trade in Peru was firmly resisted, even though the Peruvian viceroy demonstrated that his kingdom was about to be lost for lack of trade with Spanish vessels and began on his own authority to permit foreign trade at Callao. He was reprimanded.
45. Morillo to Secretary of Ultramar, Cuartel General de Valencia, July 26, 1820, AGI, Indiferente general 1568.
46. Council of State consulta, Madrid, Nov. 7, 1821, AGI, Indiferente general 1569; Informe del Gobierno a las Cortes sobre medidas de pacificación de Ultramar, Madrid, Jan. 17, 1822, AGI, Indiferente general 1571.

countries became independent. After the United States recognized the independence of Buenos Aires, Mexico, and Colombia in March 1822, Spanish Minister of State Martínez de la Rosa dispatched a manifesto to the courts of Europe, declaring that Spain had decided to abandon its exclusive monopoly and that all the actions of the liberal regime since 1820 tended toward an attitude favorable to foreign trade and settlement in America.[47] Yet, the Cortes had made no such specific decisions and no such laws were enacted. By the last months of 1822, Spain was once again in the grip of domestic crisis as the liberal regime fell apart amid the rivalry of *moderados* and *exaltados* and as the king conspired with France for the overthrow of the constitutional system. In January 1823, a French army of 100,000 "Sons of Saint Louis" invaded Spain and restored the absolute regime.

Conclusion

All three of the basic concepts of empire were broken down by the actions of Spain during the independence era. Most damaging to the concept of the "ties that bind" was the decision to dispatch military forces from Spain to suppress the rebellions. José Baquíjano denounced the Cortes for punishing the overseas vassals instead of addressing their grievances. In 1812 Baquíjano had warned that "to make war on vassals is not a triumph or an advantage."[48] Bolívar, in the "Letter from Jamaica," wrote that the war in Venezuela had destroyed the ties that bind, converting Spain from the benign mother into a raging serpent bent on destruction. The Mexican delegation to the Cortes in Spain informed the government as late as August 1821 that the chief cause of the rebellion in Mexico was "the despotism and constant arbitrariness of the government."[49] America had outgrown its dependence. The ties that bind had become chains of oppression.

The concept of father king, meantime, had undergone a remarkable transformation. In 1808, the symbol of Ferdinand as *el deseado* was the strongest single thread holding together Spain's resistance to Napoleon and, after 1810, the resistance of American loyalists to domestic insurrection. His restoration in 1814 was overwhelmingly popular and there was a near total absence of resistance or reaction to the coup by which he overthrew the Constitution. Yet, by the time Pizarro came to office as minister of state in 1816, the prestige of the king had begun to decline.

47. Manifesto to Spanish ambassadors, Madrid, 1822, AHN, Estado 3024.
48. Baquíjano memorial, AGI, Estado 87.
49. Cortes Delegates of New Spain to Ultramar, Madrid, Aug. 8, 1821, AGI, Indiferente general 1569.

There were good reasons for the king's loss of standing. The Conde de Toreno traced the process by which the camarilla gathered around the king on his return to Spain and pointed to "the unwise advice of those who imprisoned his will or gave it a deplorable bias."[50] Pizarro blamed all the errors of the royal policy on the camarilla, referring to the members of the clique as "vermin." Year after year, the king rejected the advice of moderates at home, while he utterly ignored the pleas of the predominant element among loyalist creoles in America. The revolution of 1820 finally disproved the ideology of throne and altar, as the king abjectly requested his American subjects to forgive his error in having overthrown the Constitution in 1814, urging them to remember that "errors in judgment are not crimes."[51] Then the king spent the rest of the triennium conspiring against his own governments and declaring to the world that he was their prisoner.

It was the declaration of equality and then the failure to implement the concept that most weakened Spain's hold over the hearts of its New World subjects. It pointed up the inherent ideological contradiction of empire. To paraphrase what Baquíjano said in 1814, the Americans quite rightly demanded: "if we are equal, then treat us that way." The Americans were forced to recognize that equality was a sham. At the end of 1821 and beginning of 1822, the liberal constitutional government, while still debating a possible American policy, recommended free trade and absolute job equality as essential to the restoration of order in America. The colonists' grievance over job and economic equality was "converted into a pretext that for some made independence not only plausible but necessary."[52] Even the most loyal or inert Americans had only one conclusion to draw. The principle of equality, proclaimed in 1809–10 as the keynote of Spain's attempt to preserve the empire, had become merely the leading example of Spain's duplicity. Under both the constitutional and the absolutist regimes, in the name of both liberals and conservatives, the metropolis toyed with the aspirations of those still loyal Americans who were prepared to give it one more chance, throwing away the legacy of American goodwill through the proclamation of impossible and unachievable promises.

50. Toreno, *Historia,* p. 519.

51. Proclama del Rey a los habitantes de Ultramar, Madrid, Apr. 1820, AGI, Indiferente general 1568.

52. Voto particular de los Consejeros Aycinena, Luyando, Flores y Príncipe de Anglona, Madrid, Nov. 7, 1821, AGI, Indiferente general 1570.

15

Aboriginal Property and Western Theory: Recovering a Middle Ground

James Tully

I. INTRODUCTION

During the last forty years, the Aboriginal peoples of the Americas, of the British Commonwealth, and of other countries colonized by Europeans over the last five hundred years have demanded that their forms of property and government be recognized in international law and in the constitutional law of their countries. This broad movement of 250 million Aboriginal people has involved court cases, parliamentary politics, constitutional amendments, the United Nations, the International Court of Justice, the development of an international law of Aboriginal peoples, and countless nonviolent and violent actions in defense of Aboriginal systems of property and cultures. The Aboriginal peoples of New Zealand, Canada, and the United States have been at the forefront of the movement, and it is in these countries that the greatest legal recognition has been achieved.[1]

I have come to the conclusion that many of the representative Western theories of property do not provide an impartial conceptual framework in which these demands for justice with respect to property can be adjudicated. Even the recent attempts to stretch some Western liberal theories to accommodate a plurality of systems of property do not give fair recognition to Aboriginal property.[2] However, it does not follow that there is no impartial conceptual framework available. I will argue that the constitutional common law of the British Commonwealth, Canada, and the United States does provide a form of recognition and negotiation of Aboriginal and European-American systems of property that meets the criteria of justice shared by both Aboriginal peoples and non-Aboriginal North Americans.[3] This form of conceptualization of property developed

* I would like to thank Ellen Frankel Paul and the other contributors to this volume for their exceptionally helpful comments.

[1] See Julian Burger, *First Peoples: A Future for the Indigenous World* (New York: Anchor Books, 1990), for an overview; see *ibid.*, p. 15 for the figure of 250 million, not including Africa. See also Augie Fleras and Jean Leonard Elliott, *The Nations Within: Aboriginal-State Relations in Canada, the United States, and New Zealand* (Toronto: Oxford University Press, 1992).

[2] See, for example, Will Kymlicka, *Liberalism, Community, and Culture* (Oxford: Clarendon Press, 1991).

[3] Although I believe my argument could be extended to other countries, this essay is restricted to Canada and the United States.

154   JAMES TULLY

in practice during the early modern period and was given authoritative expression in the documents accompanying the Royal Proclamation of October 7, 1763, and in the Supreme Court decisions of Chief Justice John Marshall in the early nineteenth century. In the Royal Proclamation and the decisions of John Marshall, the ways in which Aboriginal and Western property in North America had been conceptualized in major European and European-American political theories were replaced by a fairer common-law alternative.

During the same period, the Aboriginal peoples, or "First Nations" as they are called in Canada, developed a form of mutual recognition and negotiation of French and British property in North America which is commensurable with the common-law tradition. The cross-cultural "middle ground" composed of early modern Aboriginal and common-law conceptions of the constitutional relations between their two systems of property, and their authoritative traditions of interpretation, is now being rediscovered and reconstructed by a young generation of Aboriginal and non-Aboriginal legal scholars, and is being employed to justify the property rights of the Aboriginal peoples of North America.[4] I do not mean to suggest that this Aboriginal and common-law system (as I will call it)[5] for the establishment and adjudication of property relations has been faithfully followed in practice by governments and courts since 1763. Quite the contrary. It has been criticized, denied, ignored, and violated many times.[6] Nonetheless, it provides a normative framework for property rights that meets both Aboriginal and non-Aboriginal criteria of justice.

The reason why many Western theories of property do not provide an impartial framework is that they share a set of assumptions which misrecognize the political organizations and property systems of the Aborig-

[4] See Joseph William Singer, "Sovereignty and Property," *Northwestern University Law Review*, vol. 86, no. 1 (1991), pp. 1–56; Charles Wilkinson, "Native Sovereignty in the United States: Developments during the Modern Era," in *Aboriginal Self-Determination*, ed. Frank Cassidy (Halifax: Institute for Research on Public Policy, 1991), pp. 219–32; Brian Slattery, "Understanding Aboriginal Rights," *Canadian Bar Review*, vol. 66, no. 1 (1987), pp. 727–83; and Brian Slattery, "Aboriginal Sovereignty and Imperial Claims," in Cassidy, ed., *Aboriginal Self-Determination*, pp. 197–219.

[5] "Aboriginal and common-law system" refers to both the Aboriginal and common-law modes of argument, authoritative traditions, and concepts, *and* the institutions of property and practices of cross-cultural negotiation these modes of argument are associated with. The *locus classicus* for this approach is Ludwig Wittgenstein, *Philosophical Investigations* [1953], trans. G. E. M. Anscombe (Oxford: Basil Blackwell, 1988), sections 240–42. See James Tully, "Wittgenstein and Political Philosophy: Understanding Practices of Critical Reflection," *Political Theory*, vol. 17, no. 2 (May 1989), pp. 172–204; and compare Philip Bobbitt, *Constitutional Interpretation* (Oxford: Basil Blackwell, 1991), pp. 141–77, and Dennis Patterson, "Conscience and the Constitution," *Columbia Law Review*, vol. 93, no. 1 (January 1993), pp. 270–307.

[6] For judicial and government deviation from the Aboriginal and common-law system, see Milnar Ball, "Constitution, Court, Indian Tribes," *American Bar Foundation Research Journal* (now *Law and Social Inquiry*), vol. 1 (1987), pp. 1–139; Robert N. Clinton, "The Proclamation of 1763: Colonial Prelude to Two Centuries of Federal-State Conflict over the Management of Indian Affairs," *Boston University Law Review*, vol. 69 (1989), pp. 329–85; and the works cited in note 4 above.

inal peoples. From the seventeenth century to the present, Western theories of property conventionally begin from one of the following three premises that purport to represent the initial conditions for thinking about property: (1) equal individuals in a state of nature, behind a veil of ignorance, or in a quasi-ideal-speech situation, prior to the establishment of a legal system of property, and aiming to establish one society; (2) individuals within a set of shared and authoritative traditions and institutions derived from European history; or (3) a community bound together by a set of shared and authoritative traditions and institutions. The suggestion of this essay is that a theory of property which begins from any of these three conventional and well-known premises of liberal, critical, and communitarian theory cannot be justly applied to reflect on property in Canada and the United States, because the premises misrecognize and occlude the initial conditions of property in North America. The initial conditions are that when Europeans arrived and began to establish systems of property, the Aboriginal peoples were already there, organized into First Nations with their own systems of property and authoritative traditions, many of which are over ten thousand years old. As Chief Justice Marshall classically stated in *Worcester v. the State of Georgia* (1832):

> America, separated from Europe by a wide ocean, was inhabited by a distinct people, divided into separate nations, independent of each other and the rest of the world, having institutions of their own, and governing themselves by their own laws. It is difficult to comprehend the proposition, that the inhabitants of either quarter of the globe could have rightful original claims of dominion over the habitants of the other, or over the lands they occupied; or that the discovery of either by the other should give the discoverer rights in the country discovered, which annulled the pre-existing rights of its ancient possessors.[7]

This would be of interest only to historians of political theory if the Aboriginal peoples had been subsequently and justly conquered or assimilated, and their original systems of property and government superseded; for then one, perhaps any one, of the three conventional premises would represent their (changed) status accurately. But this has not occurred. Neither the Aboriginal people themselves nor international law acknowledge the conquest, assimilation, or supersession of the First Nations.[8]

---

[7] *Worcester v. the State of Georgia*, 6 Peter 515 (U.S.S.C. 1832), p. 542, reprinted in John Marshall, *The Writings of Chief Justice Marshall on the Federal Constitution* (Littleton, CO: Fred B. Rothman & Co., 1987), pp. 426–27.

[8] For international law, see Maureen Davies, "Aspects of Aboriginal Rights in International Law," in *Aboriginal Peoples and the Law*, ed. Bradford Morse (Ottawa: University of Carleton Press, 1991), pp. 16–47, esp. pp. 37–40. Although there is agreement that the

156   JAMES TULLY

Consequently, the initial conditions for theorizing and reflecting on property rights in America are of a (European) people who arrive on a continent of roughly five hundred established Aboriginal nations and systems of property and who do not wish to become citizens of the existing Aboriginal nations, but wish to establish their own nations and systems of property in accordance with their European institutions and traditions. The question of justice with respect to property is thus a question of political and cultural pluralism: How can non-Aboriginal systems of property be justly established under such conditions? This is the fundamental problem of property in North America properly stated—a problem for which, I will argue, there is a solution: the Aboriginal and common-law system. To imagine or presuppose that the conditions are a state of nature, a veil of ignorance, or an ideal-speech situation of pre-political and undifferentiated individuals, in which no system of property exists, or a set of authoritative European traditions and institutions, or an already existing community, is to beg the problem—it is to dispossess the Aboriginal peoples of their property rights, forms of government, and authoritative traditions without so much as an argument. The imposition of any one of these three premises constitutes the injustice.

The historical reason why the Western theories of property constructed on these three premises misrepresent the initial condition of property in North America is *not* that the theorists were uninterested in European settlement in America or unaware of the Aboriginal peoples of America and their systems of property. Just the opposite. One of the leading problems of political theory from Hugo Grotius and Thomas Hobbes to Adam Smith and Immanuel Kant was to justify the establishment of European systems of property in North America in the face of the presence of "Indian Nations." Almost all the classic theorists advanced a solution to this problem of justifying what was seen as the one of the most important and pivotal events of modern history. They constructed and used these three premises to justify European settlement on the one hand, and to justify the dispossession of the Aboriginal peoples of their property on the other. Substantial sections of the early modern theories are given over to trying to show that the three premises do fairly represent the initial conditions in North America—sections which are standardly overlooked today because the three premises are taken for granted. Hence, to understand how they misrecognize the initial conditions, and why Chief Justice Marshall repudiated them, it is necessary to survey the errors in the arguments and assumptions the classical theorists used to establish the premises.

Aboriginal peoples are not conquered, there is less agreement on what their status is. The United Nations' forthcoming declaration on the rights of indigenous peoples may clarify this. See *Discrimination against Indigenous Peoples: First Revised Text of the Draft Universal Declaration on the Rights of Indigenous Peoples*, U.N. Doc. E/CN.4/Sub.2/1989/33 (1989).

Accordingly, the remainder of this essay consists of three sections. Section II is a critical survey of the shared assumptions of representative theories of property used to justify the establishment of European property in North America. Section III is a recovery and reconstruction of the overlapping common-law and Aboriginal conceptions of their two systems of property and of the reasons for believing this normative framework meets both Western and Aboriginal criteria of justice. It provides a system for establishing and adjudicating property relations, by consent, in a genuinely bicultural and bilegal situation. Section IV seeks to show what effect this argument should have on property *theory* in North America today. Western theories of property are not invalid just because their premises misrecognize, in a biased manner, the initial conditions of property relations in North America. Rather, once their bias has been corrected, they have a legitimate role to play in the critical reflection on property in North America today, but only within the broader framework of the Aboriginal and common-law system.

One further introductory point is necessary to situate this essay in its appropriate context. There are two opposed views in the literature on Aboriginal property in North America. Some argue that the property systems of Canada and the United States are unjust, because they rest on the theft of Aboriginal property and the usurpation of Aboriginal governments.[9] The only remedy would be to overthrow the present systems of property. Others argue that the Canadian and U.S. systems are just, in virtue of the legal positivist principle of effective occupation and use over the last three centuries.[10] No remedy would be required. This essay can be said to present a third view somewhere between these two.[11] I agree with the proponents of the first view that many grave injustices have been and continue to be committed, and that the principle of effective occupation and use applies in the first instance to the Aboriginal peoples, rather than to the land claims of the Canadian and U.S. governments. It does not follow, however, that justice demands the overthrow of the present systems of property in the two countries. For the Aboriginal and common-law system is a normative framework that is just by both Aboriginal and non-Aboriginal standards. It has been consented to and

[9] See, for example, Ward Churchill, *The Struggle for the Land: Indigenous Resistance to Genocide, Ecocide, and Expropriation in Contemporary North America* (Toronto: Between the Lines, 1991); and John Howard Clinebell and Jim Thomson, "Sovereignty and Self-Determination: The Rights of Native Americans under International Law," *Buffalo Law Review*, vol. 27, no. 1 (1987), pp. 669–714.

[10] See, for example, L. C. Green, "Claims to Territory in Colonial America," in *The Law of Nations and the New World*, ed. L. C. Green and Olive P. Dickason (Edmonton: University of Alberta Press, 1989), pp. 1–131.

[11] For two different middle positions, see Russell Barsh and James Youngblood Henderson, *The Road: Indian Tribes and Political Liberty* (Berkeley: University of California Press, 1980); and Brian Slattery, "First Nations and the Constitution: A Matter of Trust," *Canadian Bar Review*, vol. 71, no. 1 (1992).

is immanent to some extent in the practice of the present systems of property, specifically in the treaty system. It thereby provides the already shared framework for the negotiated redress of claims to property in North America. (It is sufficient to note in passing that the claims of injustice advanced by the first view appeal to standards that are part of the Aboriginal and common-law system.) To say this is not to endorse the status quo, as the proponents of the second view conclude, but to reform it in accordance with its best standards.

II. WESTERN THEORIES OF PROPERTY

In this section, I seek to show how Western theories tend to misrepresent the initial conditions of appropriation in America; I do this by critically analyzing assumptions of some exemplary and influential theories. This critical survey provides the clarification necessary to appreciate the superiority of the Aboriginal and common-law system, which I reconstruct in the next section, and to see the appropriate place for Western property theory, suitably corrected, within the conceptual framework established by the Aboriginal and common-law system in the final section.[12] I start with John Locke because he gathered together many of the arguments of the early seventeenth century and because his theory set the terms for many of the later theories that were used to justify the establishment of European property in America. Also, it was Locke's theory that Chief Justice Marshall repudiated, in *Johnson and Graham's Lessee v. M'Intosh* (1823), before he put forward his alternative.[13]

A. Locke's theory

In the *Second Treatise* of the *Two Treatises of Government* (1690), Locke set out four sets of arguments, contrasts, and assumptions that were widely accepted and taken for granted by later theorists, providing the unexamined conventions of many Western theories of property. The four sets of arguments conjoin to misrecognize two conditions of Aboriginal peoples at the time of European arrival and settlement: their systems of property and their political organizations. I do not mean to suggest that all four sets of arguments have found their way into theories of property that start from any of the three premises set out in the introduction. The Lock-

---

[12] The argument of Sections II and III is constructed on the basis of detailed historical scholarship in two previous essays: James Tully, "Rediscovering America: The *Two Treatises* and Aboriginal Rights," in Tully, *An Approach to Political Philosophy: Locke in Contexts* (Cambridge: Cambridge University Press, 1993), pp. 137–78, and "Placing the *Two Treatises*," in *Political Discourse in Early Modern Britain*, ed. Nicholas Phillipson and Quentin Skinner (Cambridge: Cambridge University Press, 1993), pp. 253–82.

[13] *Johnson and Graham's Lessee v. M'Intosh*, 8 Wheaton 543 (U.S.S.C. 1823), pp. 567–71, reprinted in Marshall, *Writings of Chief Justice Marshall*, pp. 257–61.

ean arguments are most closely associated with theories constructed on the first premise. I do, however, wish to suggest that assumptions of some of the four sets of arguments have found their way into theories of property which start from the other two premises, and these assumptions function there to misrecognize Aboriginal property and political organization.

The first set involves the belief that Aboriginal peoples are in a pre-political "state of nature." The state of nature represents the "pattern" of a "first age" in a process of historical development all societies go through: "[I]n the beginning all the World was *America*." European societies represent the most advanced or "civilized" age in this process.[14] In the first age there is no established system of property or government and economic activity consists of subsistence hunting and gathering. In contrast, the European civilized age is characterized by established legal systems of property, political societies, and commercial or market-oriented agriculture and industry.[15] This first set of contrasts makes up the background assumption of the "stages view" of historical development which tends to be taken for granted in political (and economic) theory to this day.[16]

Second, the Aboriginal peoples of America, possessing neither government nor property in their hunting and gathering territories, have property rights only in the products of their labor: the fruit and nuts they gather, the fish they catch, the deer they hunt, and the corn they pick.[17] Unlike citizens in political societies, anyone in a state of nature is free to appropriate land without the consent of others, as long as the land is uncultivated and "there is enough, and as good left in common for others."[18] Illustrating his theory throughout with examples drawn from America, Locke draws the immensely influential conclusion that Europeans are free to settle and acquire property rights to vacant land in America by agricultural cultivation without the consent of the Aboriginal people:

> [L]et him [a European] plant in some in-land, vacant places of *America*, we shall find that the *Possessions* he could make himself upon the *measures* we have given, would not be very large, nor, even to this day, prejudice the rest of Mankind, or give them reason to complain, or think themselves injured by this Man's Incroachment. . . .[19]

[14] John Locke, *Two Treatises of Government*, ed. Peter Laslett (Cambridge: Cambridge University Press, 1970), *Second Treatise* (II), sections 14, 30, 49, 108, 109; the quote in the text is from section 49.

[15] *Ibid.*, II, 30, 38, 45, 50, 87, 107, 108.

[16] See Ronald Meek, *Social Science and the Ignoble Savage* (Cambridge: Cambridge University Press, 1976); and Tully, "Placing the *Two Treatises*," pp. 262–66.

[17] Locke, *Two Treatises*, II, 28, 30, 34, 36, 37, 41–43, 48–49.

[18] *Ibid.*, II, 27.

[19] *Ibid.*, II, 36.

It might appear from the phrase "vacant places" that Locke means that Europeans may cultivate and settle without consent only in those parts of North America that are not the hunting and gathering territories of the Aboriginal peoples. But the text will not bear this interpretation. Locke stipulates that he means by "vacant" land any land that is "uncultivated" or "unimproved" by labor: that is, land that is used for hunting and gathering is vacant.[20] The reason why the American Indians have no property in their hunting and gathering territories is that the title to property in land is "labor," and labor is defined in terms of European agriculture and industry: cultivating, subduing, tilling, and improving.[21] Consequently, the hunters and gatherers have no rights in the land and thus no reason to complain. Moreover, if the Aboriginal peoples attempt to subject the Europeans to their laws and customs or to defend the territories that they have mistakenly believed to be their property for thousands of years, then it is they who violate natural law and may be punished or "destroyed" like "savage beasts" by the European settlers.[22]

At the beginning of chapter 5 of the *Second Treatise*, Locke explains that the justification of appropriation without consent is the problem he sets out to solve, and he repeats twice that he has solved it.[23] The reason why the argument was so contentious is that it bypasses one of the basic principles of Western law, the principle of consent, or *quod omnes tangit ab omnibus tractari et approbari debet* ("what touches all must be agreed to by all"). This principle constrained most earlier theorists of European settlement to insist on deeds or treaties as a sign of consent and a condition of legitimate property acquisition. This second set of arguments came to be called the "agricultural" or "cultivation" justification for settlement, and it was widely used in the eighteenth and nineteenth centuries until Chief Justice Marshall repudiated it.

Whereas the second set of arguments justifies appropriation by alleging that the Aboriginal peoples have no rights in the land, the third set of arguments justifies appropriation by claiming that the Aboriginal peoples are better off as a result of the establishment of the commercial system of private property in land. Locke claims that a system of European commerce based on the motive to acquire more than one needs, satisfied by surplus production for profit on the market, is economically superior to the American Indian system of hunting and gathering based on fixed needs and subsistence production. It is superior in three crucial respects: it uses the land more productively; it produces a greater quantity of conveniences; and it produces far greater opportunities to work and labor by expanding the division of labor.[24] The standard of comparison of the two

[20] *Ibid.*, II, 42, 45.
[21] *Ibid.*, II, 32.
[22] *Ibid.*, I, 130–31; II, 10, 11, 16.
[23] *Ibid.*, II, 25, 39, 51.
[24] *Ibid.*, II, 37, 40–43, 48–49.

systems is which produces the "greater quantity of conveniencies" (an early formulation of the gross domestic product), including not only finished products but also the opportunities to labor.[25] Commercial agriculture, Locke suggests, uses one-tenth the amount of land that hunting and gathering does to produce the same quantity of conveniences. Then he revises the ratio to one one-hundredth the amount of land. In the following sections commercial societies are said to create one hundred, and then one thousand, times as many "conveniencies of life" as hunting and gathering from the same amount of land, and Locke famously concludes that a day-laborer in England is one hundred times better off than an Indian King with his huge yet unimproved territory in America.[26]

The Aboriginal peoples are better off as a result of conversion to the commercial system, for they too share in its greater abundance of commodities and jobs. As we have seen, Locke sets out the problem of original appropriation without consent with the proviso that any legitimate appropriation must leave enough and as good in common for others. Although agricultural appropriation does not leave enough and as good *land*, it unquestionably leaves more than enough and as good of the objects of comparison: namely, opportunities to labor and products of labor. Appropriation by means of cultivation and industry is non-zero-sum in this (much celebrated) sense.[27] It is difficult to overestimate the influence of this argument in justifications of original acquisition and in normative comparisons of competing property systems. Even theorists who believe that Aboriginal peoples have rights in their territories, contrary to Locke, often argue that they are nevertheless more than *compensated* for their loss of land by the material bountifulness and greater productivity of the commercial system. Locke's standard of comparison of "greater conveniences" in its many reformulations is taken for granted as an impartial standard, whereas it measures all systems in terms of the goods of the commercial system without weighing these against the goods of, for example, a steady-state, hunting and gathering system.[28]

The fourth set of arguments establishes a broad and influential picture of the historical development of systems of property and government. It explains why Aboriginal peoples have no recognizable systems of property and government and why Europeans do. A fixed and recognizable system of property in land is defined as an institutionalized legal system of property, and a political society is defined as an institutionalized sys-

---

[25] *Ibid.*, II, 34, 37.

[26] *Ibid.*, II, 40, 41, 42.

[27] *Ibid.*, II, 37, 43. For this interpretation of Locke's solution to the "enough and as good" or "sufficiency" proviso, see Stephen Buckle, *Natural Law and the Theory of Property* (Oxford: Clarendon Press, 1990), pp. 150–53; Barbara Arneil, *All the World Was America: John Locke and English Colonization* (London: University of London Ph.D., 1993); and Gopal Sreenivasan, *The Limits of Lockean Rights in Property* (Oxford: Oxford University Press, 1994).

[28] For a critical survey of the recent literature and a defense of this argument, see Tully, "Property, Self-Government, and Consent" (forthcoming).

tem of law, with legislature and executive.[29] By defining systems of property and government in terms of the institutions of early modern European state-formation, it is easy for Locke to show that Aboriginal societies lack both. He concedes that American Indians govern themselves by means of popular councils and chiefs, and that they are usually called nations and kingdoms by Europeans. However, in chapter 8 of the *Second Treatise*, a chapter on the history of state and property formation, he points out that the authority of the chief rests on the unanimous, non-delegated and ongoing consent of the council of the people, not on delegated and institutionalized majority rule through a legislature, and the right to declare war remains vested in the people, not delegated to the executive.[30] Hence, Aboriginal societies are not recognized as "political societies" or states by these defining criteria, but are considered to be in the state of nature. It follows that Europeans can deal with the Aboriginal peoples not on a nation-to-nation basis but as individuals under natural law.[31]

Aboriginal peoples lack the institutions of government and property according to Locke because they have no need of them at their level of economic development. They have "few Trespasses, and few Offenders," "few controversies" over property, and therefore "no need of many laws to decide them."[32] They can thus decide controversies on an *ad hoc* basis as in the state of nature. In turn, the explanation for this underdevelopment, which explains their whole system, is that they have limited and fixed desires for property, and thus produce for the sake of subsistence rather than for surplus. That is, they lack the desire to enlarge their possessions which comes into effect with the introduction of money and markets and leads to disputes over property, and so to the need for institutionalized political and property systems to settle the disputes.[33] Europeans, in contrast, live in commercial societies. Once money and trade develop, they spur the growth of population and the applied arts. An elastic desire for more than one needs comes into effect, uprooting forever the pre-monetary economy of limited desires and needs. People seek to enlarge their possessions in order to sell the surplus on the market for a profit.[34] As a result of the dynamic productivity of market-oriented labor, land becomes scarce, property disputes increase, and people set up political societies with institutionalized legal and political systems to regulate and protect property.[35]

[29] Locke, *Two Treatises*, II, 30, 38, 87.

[30] *Ibid.*, II, 107–8, and the quotation in the editorial footnote to II, 107.

[31] *Ibid.*, II, 9, 108.

[32] *Ibid.*, II, 107.

[33] *Ibid.*, II, 108.

[34] *Ibid.*, II, 37, 48–49.

[35] *Ibid.*, II, 50. See Tully, "Rediscovering America," pp. 164–66, for a defense of this interpretation.

B. Aboriginal governments

Let me draw a rough sketch of Aboriginal forms of government and property that Europeans encountered in eastern North America, in order to show how Locke's four sets of arguments misrecognize them. After observing and studying the Indian nations of the northeast in the early seventeenth century, Roger Williams famously concluded, in opposition to Locke's later view, that "the wildest Indians in America agree on some forms of Government . . . [and] their civill and earthly governments be as lawfull and true as any Governments in the World."[36] The typical form of Aboriginal government was a nation governed by a council or longhouse of chiefs (*sachems*) drawn from the clans. Each nation had a clearly demarcated and defended territory, a decision-making body, a consensus-based decision-making procedure, and a system of customary laws and kinship relations. The nations, in turn, often associated in international relations of confederation of various kinds and engaged in the international activities of trade, diplomacy, war, and peace. There were no standing armies, bureaucracies, police forces, prisons, or written laws. They did not have the definitive institutions of European states, yet they governed themselves and their complex systems of property.[37] Aboriginal societies were not only called "nations" by Europeans, and often treated as such, as we shall see; they were seen by many Europeans besides Chief Justice Marshall to meet the four criteria of nationhood or statehood in international law: a permanent population, a form of government, the recognized occupation of a territory over time, and the ability to enter into relations with other governments.[38]

Locke was knowledgeable about American Indian societies from his interest in the colony of Carolina, his seat on the Board of Trade, which

[36] Roger Williams, "The Bloody Tenant . . . ," in *The Complete Writings of Roger Williams* (New York: Russell & Russell, 1963), vol. 3, p. 250. See Ruth Barnes Moynihan, "The Patent and the Indians: The Problem of Jurisdiction in Seventeenth-Century New England," *American Indian Culture and Research*, vol. 2, no. 1 (1977), pp. 8–18.

[37] See Francis Jennings, *The Ambiguous Iroquois Empire: The Covenant Chain Confederation of Indian Tribes with English Colonies from Its Beginnings to the Lancaster Treaty of 1744* (New York: W. W. Norton and Co., 1984); and Daniel Richter and James Merrell, eds., *Beyond the Covenant Chain: The Iroquois and Their Neighbours in Indian North America* (Syracuse: Syracuse University Press, 1987).

[38] For these four criteria for statehood and sovereignty in international law, see Davies, "Aspects of Aboriginal Rights" (*supra* note 8), pp. 24–28. For the argument that Aboriginal nations meet the criteria, see Grand Council of the Crees (of Quebec), *Status and Rights of the James Bay Crees in the Context of Quebec's Secession from Canada*, submission to United Nations Commission on Human Rights, 48th session (January 27–March 6, 1992). For the widespread recognition of their nationhood in the early modern period, see Richter and Merrell, *Beyond the Covenant Chain*; Richard White, *The Middle Ground: Indians, Empires, and Republics in the Great Lakes Region, 1650–1815* (Cambridge: Cambridge University Press, 1991), pp. 305–17; and Six Nations, *The Redman's Appeal for Justice: The Position of the Six Nations That They Constitute an Independent State* (Brantford, Ontario: The Six Nations, 1924). For doubts, see generally S. James Anaya, "The Capacity of International Law to Advance Ethnic or Nationality Rights Claims," *Iowa Law Review*, vol. 75 (1990), pp. 837–82; and L. C. Green, "Claims to Territory in Colonial America" (*supra* note 10).

administered the colonial system, and his collection of anthropological literature on travel and exploration in the Americas.[39] In his interpretation of Aboriginal government, he highlights three features of their organization to the neglect of the customary system of government that underlies them. He interprets the war-chief from a European perspective, as a kind of proto-European sovereign, and stipulates that because he does not possess the right to declare war and peace he does not, by definition, possess the degree of sovereignty necessary to statehood. But the war-chief was not, and is not today, a proto-sovereign. He was a temporary military commander subordinate to political authority. Second, the chiefs and the council often appointed *ad hoc* arbitrators of justice. These *ad hoc* procedures may be a source of Locke's concept of individual and non-delegated self-government in the state of nature, but he overlooks the appointment procedure and the unwritten yet orally transmitted culture of customary law and sanctions that governs it. Third, Locke emphasizes the lack of crime, property disputes, and litigation in Aboriginal societies, and he explains these by reference to their limited desires and material possessions. Yet he disregards the national, clan, and family systems of sanctions that help prevent and resolve disputes.

With respect to Aboriginal property, the territory as a whole belongs to the nation (or, more accurately, the nation belongs to the territory) and jurisdiction over it is held in trust by the chiefs. The identity of a nation as a distinct people is inseparable from their relation to and use of the land, animals, ecosystems, and spirits that co-inhabit their territory. Clans and families have a bundle of rights and responsibilities, usually matrilineal, of use and usufruct over the land and waterways for various purposes. That is, property rights and duties inhere in the clans and families and apply to forms of activity and to the geographical territories or ecosystems in which the activities take place, not to the products of the activities, as in Locke's account. The activities include hunting, trapping, gathering berries, seasonal agriculture, clam-bed cultivation, fishing, and so on. The distribution and trade of the products is governed by custom and kinship traditions. These systems of property are transmitted from generation to generation, not by myths of a state of nature or veil of ignorance but by the stories families and clans are responsible for learning and telling at public feasts. When the coastal nations made property agreements with the settlers, as Roger Williams explained, they were granting them rights and responsibilities of co-use of the land, not alienable rights to the land itself.[40] Finally, families and individual members own their goods, yet there is a relatively casual attitude toward possessions and an overriding custom of sharing and gift-giving (typical of subsistence econ-

---

[39] See Tully, "Rediscovering America" (*supra* note 12), pp. 140–41.

[40] John Cotton, "John Cotton's Reply to Roger Williams," in *The Complete Writings of Roger Williams*, vol. 2, pp. 46–47. See Moynihan, "The Patent and the Indians."

omies). From an Aboriginal perspective, the European settlers were appropriating land that was not in the state of nature, but in their nations, and was not unowned, but was under their ownership and jurisdiction.[41]

In his depiction of Aboriginal property, Locke highlights one specific, European form of property-generating activity, industrious labor, and in this light, so to speak, fails to recognize the Aboriginal system of national territories, the bundle of property rights and responsibilities in activities and their locales, and the customs governing distribution. Of course, if he had recognized these forms of property, settlement in America without consent would have been unjust by his own criteria, for the land would have been owned, rather than unowned and common as the original-appropriation argument requires.

C. Later Western theorists

The four sets of argument presented by Locke were widely used throughout the eighteenth and nineteenth centuries to simultaneously dispossess Aboriginal peoples of their nationhood and property, and justify European settlement and expansion in America. In 1725, for example, John Bulkley of Connecticut published "An Inquiry into the Right of the Aboriginal Natives to the Land in America" in order to refute the claim advanced by the Mohegan nation that they constituted a sovereign nation with jurisdiction over their territory in Connecticut.[42] His argument was based entirely on the passages of Locke's *Two Treatises* that I have summarized above. In *The Law of Nations or the Principles of Natural Law* (1758), one of the most widely cited legal texts in America, Emeric de Vattel echoed Locke in using the agricultural argument to justify French and British settlement:

> The cultivation of the soil . . . is . . . an obligation imposed upon man by nature. Every Nation is therefore bound by the law of nature to cultivate that land which has fallen to its share. There are others who, in order to avoid labour, seek to live upon their flocks and the fruits of the chase. Now that the human race has multiplied so greatly, it could not subsist if every people wished to live after that fashion. Those who still pursue this idle mode of life occupy more land than they would have need of under a system of honest labour, and they may not complain if other more industrious nations, too

---

[41] This synopsis of Aboriginal property systems is based on numerous anthropological studies. Two of the best are Anthony F. Wallace, "Political Organization and Land Tenure among Northeastern Indians, 1600–1830," *Southwestern Journal of Anthropology*, vol. 13 (1957), pp. 301–21; and William A. Starna, "Aboriginal Title and Traditional Iroquois Land Use," in *Iroquois Land Claims*, ed. Christopher Vecsey and William A. Starna (Syracuse: Syracuse University Press, 1988), pp. 31–49.

[42] John Bulkley, "An Inquiry into the Right of the Aboriginal Natives to the Land in America," in Roger Wolcott, *Poetical Meditations* (New London, 1726), pp. i–lvi.

> confined at home, should come and occupy part of their lands. . . .
> [W]hen the Nations of Europe . . . come upon lands which the sav-
> ages have no special need of and are making no present and contin-
> uous use of, they may lawfully take possession of them and establish
> colonies in them.[43]

Ronald Meek and other scholars have traced how Locke's four sets of
arguments became conventional features of the four-stages theories of
property in the Scottish and French Enlightenments, even when the theorists disagreed with Locke in other respects.[44] Once the broad picture
that Locke's arguments set in place was accepted to different degrees, the
inevitability of European settlement and dispossession was assured.
When theorists of what John Pocock calls the "competing traditions" of
rights, virtues, and commerce debated the nature of modernity in terms
of the relative merits of Locke's rights-bearing and industrious agricultur-
ist, James Harrington's virtuous republican, and Adam Smith's polished
and civilized commercialist, they gave the implantation of European civilization in America the impression of historical inevitability; for all three
conceptions of modernity were defined in contrast to, and in supersession of, the Aboriginal peoples they displaced in practice—the property-
less and economically wasteful hunter-gatherers, the vicious savages, and
the rude and primitive Indians, respectively.[45]

Features of Locke's four sets of arguments did not come to be accepted
only in the background conventions of the great liberal and republican
theories of property. Similar modes of argument are woven into the
theory of Immanuel Kant, who is often seen as founding an independent
tradition of liberal political theory. In "Idea for a Universal History with
a Cosmopolitan Intent" (1784) and "Perpetual Peace" (1795), Kant argues
that humanity can achieve full moral progress and freedom only after
commerce and republican constitutions are spread around the world.[46]
Although there are important differences between Kant's concept of a
republican constitution and Locke's concept of a political society, they
both share the characteristically European features that are said to mark

[43] Emeric de Vattel, *Le droit des gens, ou principes de la loi naturelle* [1758]; reprinted as
The Law of Nations or the Principles of Natural Law, trans. Charles G. Fenwick (Washington:
Carnegie Institute, 1902), pp. 207–10.

[44] See note 16 above.

[45] I defend this claim in "Placing the *Two Treatises*" (*supra* note 12), pp. 279–80. For the
authors cited, see John Pocock, *Virtue, Commerce, and History* (Cambridge: Cambridge Uni-
versity Press, 1985); James Harrington, *The Political Writings of James Harrington*, ed. J. G. A.
Pocock (Cambridge: Cambridge University Press, 1977); and Adam Smith, *Lectures on
Jurisprudence*, ed. Ronald Meek, D. D. Raphael, and L. G. Stein (Indianapolis: Liberty
Press, 1982).

[46] Immanuel Kant, "Idea for a Universal History with a Cosmopolitan Intent" and "Perpetual Peace: A Philosophical Sketch," in *Perpetual Peace and Other Essays*, trans. Ted Humphrey (Indianapolis: Hackett Publishing Company, 1983), pp. 29–40 and pp. 107–44; see
esp. pp. 33, 111, 114.

them as different from and superior to Aboriginal forms of government: institutionalized legal and constitutional rule of law and representative government.[47] Once these civilizing institutions are established, progress toward moral freedom occurs by means of the mechanism of "unsocial sociability": that is, markets and constitutional government constrain self-interested individuals ("a people comprised of devils") to cooperate with others in order to satisfy their desires for more than they need for bare subsistence.[48]

In contrast, the systems of property and government of Aboriginal peoples are misrecognized and dismissed, and European institutions are set in their place and justified as the baseline for moral and political theory and practice. The uncivilized hunting and gathering peoples of America, Kant argues, lack secure property because they have not made the transition to the life of agriculture. They have, in their pre-political state of nature, what he calls the "lawless freedom of hunting, fishing, and herding," which, of "all forms of life, . . . is without doubt most contrary to a civilized constitution."[49] Agriculture, commerce, and republican constitutions are spread to non-Europeans by means of war, and then commerce.[50] Although Kant condemns the excesses of the European wars of imperial expansion, especially outright conquest,[51] and prefers expansion by means of trade, economic sanctions, and diplomacy, he commends the overall effect of spreading the economic and political institutions of moral progress, going so far as to say that it is "our duty to work towards bringing about this goal."[52] The justification European nations possess, again quite similar to Locke, is the third definitive article for perpetual peace that Kant proposes for international law.[53] This is "the right of hospitality," which gives Europeans the right to engage in commerce with native inhabitants, and to defend their traders if the native inhabitants deny the right. "In this way," Kant concludes, "distant parts of the world can establish with one another peaceful relations that will eventually become matters of public law, and the human race can gradually be brought closer and closer to a cosmopolitan constitution."[54]

In contemporary political theory the premises and modes of argument laid down by theorists such as Locke and Kant continue to be taken for

[47] *Ibid.*, pp. 112–15.

[48] *Ibid.*, pp. 31–32, 124. For the philosophical background to the concept of "unsocial sociability," see Istvan Hont, "The Language of Sociability and Commerce: Samuel Pufendorf and the Theoretical Foundations of the 'Four Stages Theory'," in *The Languages of Political Theory in Early-Modern Europe*, ed. Anthony Pagden (Cambridge: Cambridge University Press, 1987), pp. 253–76.

[49] Kant, "Perpetual Peace," pp. 111, 122 and note.

[50] *Ibid.*, p. 123.

[51] *Ibid.*, p. 119.

[52] *Ibid.*, p. 125.

[53] *Ibid.*, pp. 118–19.

[54] *Ibid.*, p. 118.

granted as the initial conditions for theorizing about property in North America. Whereas Locke and Kant at least presented arguments to justify the elimination of Aboriginal claims to aboriginal property and government, contemporary theorists tend to take the conclusion of their arguments for granted as the original starting point of a theory, without even raising the question of Aboriginal property. Original-acquisition theories overlook Aboriginal acquisition. This is obvious, of course, in theories which start from what I call the first premise, some variation of a Lockean state of nature and individual self-ownership, such as Robert Nozick's theory in *Anarchy, State, and Utopia*.[55] But it is no less true in theories which start from a more Kantian premise, such as John Rawls's *A Theory of Justice*, as Vernon Van Dyke has pointed out.[56]

In the last decade Rawls has suggested that his theory can be seen in a slightly different way, as a theory written within the framework of an authoritative moral and political tradition and history (what I have called the second premise). The tradition which sets the horizons of the theory consists entirely of a set of institutions and forms of thought that derive from post-Reformation Europe (toleration, rule of law, representative government, markets, and individual rights), and the role of the philosopher is to articulate "the basic intuitive ideas that are embedded in the political institutions of a constitutional democratic regime and the public traditions of their interpretation."[57] This move thus effectively posits Kant's threshold institutions, and their traditions of interpretation, as the authoritative framework for theorizing about property, thereby effacing the pre-existence of independent Aboriginal government, property, and traditions, and assimilating Aboriginal peoples into this European-derived framework. Theorists working within this framework who notice Aboriginal property claims, such as Will Kymlicka, take up these claims *within* the Kant-Rawls framework, failing to recognize that the Aboriginal claim is to a system of property and tradition that is independent of, and prior to, the one Rawls posits.[58] Nor do recent communitarian theories of property and justice fare any better. They generally agree with Rawls that political theory must take a set of entirely European traditions and institutions as the authoritative framework, disagreeing with Rawls only over

[55] Robert Nozick, *Anarchy, State, and Utopia* (New York: Basic Books, 1974). See David Lyons, "The New Indian Claims and Original Rights to Land," in *Reading Nozick: Essays on Anarchy, State, and Utopia*, ed. Jeffrey Paul (Totowa, NJ: Rowman and Littlefield, 1981), pp. 355–79.

[56] John Rawls, *A Theory of Justice* (Cambridge, MA: Harvard University Press, 1971); see Vernon Van Dyke, "Justice as Fairness—For Groups," *American Political Science Review*, vol. 69 (1975), pp. 607–14.

[57] John Rawls, "Justice as Fairness: Political not Metaphysical," *Philosophy and Public Affairs*, vol. 14 (1985), p. 225. This premise is incorporated in John Rawls, *Political Liberalism* (New York: Columbia University Press, 1993).

[58] See Kymlicka, *Liberalism, Community, and Culture*; and Allen Buchanan, *Secession: The Morality of Political Divorce from Fort Sumter to Lithuania and Quebec* (Boulder: Westview Press, 1991).

which European traditions are authoritative and over their interpretation, as for example in the work of Alasdair MacIntyre and Michael Walzer.[59] Aboriginal claims are either ignored or, at best, misrecognized as claims for some sort of minority status within the European-derived normative framework of an overarching national community, to the same effect. Many theorists of "difference," finally, continue to work within some of the four sets of assumptions associated with the three main Western premises, for they misrecognize Aboriginal property claims as demands for the recognition of difference within, again, some overarching framework of non-Aboriginal institutions and modes of argument, not as an independent system of property and authoritative traditions.[60]

III. The Common-Law System

Let us now turn to the Europeans and colonists who did recognize, to some extent, the property and government of the Aboriginal peoples. Most of the colonists were aware that the Aboriginal peoples possessed political organizations and forms of property. A second form of property acquisition, in competition with the Lockean agriculturalist argument for appropriation without consent, arose on this basis. Colonists (even some who paid lip service to the agriculturalist argument) often negotiated a treaty or deed of cession, on the presumption that the Aboriginal people had some sort of prior claim and that consent was thus required. One of the most bitter struggles over property in New England in the mid-seventeenth century was between Roger Williams and his Plymouth followers, who negotiated treaties with the local First Nations for the use of their land, and Governor Winthrop and his Boston followers, who claimed, in a proto-Lockean way, that settlement and cultivation were sufficient to establish property.[61]

The classic statement of the "treaty" theory of property acquisition was written by Samuel Wharton in his famous text *Plain Facts: Being an Examination into the Rights of the Indian Nations of America to Their Respective Territories* (1781) to justify the acquisition of, and speculation in, the rich lands of the Ohio Valley in the latter half of the eighteenth century. Wharton dismisses the argument that the land of the Aboriginal peoples can be appropriated without consent. He argues that the Enlightenment ideals of rights and equality must be applied to the Aboriginal peoples. Consequently, they have "an absolute exclusive right to the countries

[59] Alasdair MacIntyre, *Whose Justice? Which Rationality?* (Notre Dame: University of Notre Dame Press, 1988); Michael Walzer, *Spheres of Justice: A Defense of Pluralism and Equality* (New York: Basic Books, 1983).

[60] For example, see the otherwise impressive work by Iris Marion Young, *Justice and the Politics of Difference* (Princeton: Princeton University Press, 1990).

[61] Francis Jennings, *The Invasion of America: Indians, Colonialism, and the Cant of Conquest* (New York: W. W. Norton and Co., 1975), pp. 128–46.

they possess" in virtue of their occupation and use of them and of their (ironically) Lockean right to the means of preservation.[62] It follows from this absolute and therefore alienable property right, according to Wharton, that the Aboriginal peoples may sell parcels of their land to individual colonists or, as in his own case, to land speculation companies. The land then falls under colonial law.[63]

A third, widely employed claim to property was a land grant from a colonial assembly. The assumption was that a colonial assembly had sovereignty over its territory and thus possessed the right to allocate property to its citizens. This justification was often based on the compact theory of colonial independence, derived from the *Two Treatises* — as, for example, in the writings of James Otis and Thomas Jefferson.[64] The question it raises is how the colonial assembly acquired independence from the Crown and sovereignty over the lands of the Aboriginal peoples. The answer to the question about sovereignty was: either through a Lockean settlement and cultivation argument, an argument that the land had been ceded to the assembly by treaties, or an argument that it had been acquired through conquest.

The British Crown dismissed all three of these theories of property acquisition and slowly developed a common-law way of conceptualizing the status and relations of the different systems of property of the Aboriginal peoples and the European newcomers that was fair to both. The Crown formalized this in the Royal Proclamation of 1763 by recognizing the Aboriginal First Nations as a mirror image of itself: as equal in status to European nations and to be dealt with on a nation-to-nation basis.[65] It followed from this form of recognition that the Crown (or other European crowns) was the only agent with the authority to negotiate with the Aboriginal peoples, considered as nations, and to secure non-Aboriginal title to property in North America. If an individual were to negotiate property acquisition from a First Nation by agreement (although this was discouraged by the Crown), then he would hold it under the Aboriginal law of that nation. The motivation for formalizing this form of recogni-

[62] Samuel Wharton, *Plain Facts: Being an Examination into the Rights of the Indian Nations of America to Their Respective Territories, and a Vindication of the Grant of the Six United Nations* (Philadelphia, 1781), p. 7.

[63] For the context, see Robert A. Williams, *The American Indians in Western Legal Thought: The Discourse of Conquest* (Oxford: Oxford University Press, 1990), pp. 257–300.

[64] James Otis, *Rights of the British Colonies Asserted and Proved* (Boston, 1764); Thomas Jefferson, *A Summary View of the Rights of British America* [1775], ed. T. P. Abernethy (New York: Columbia University Press, 1943). See Tully, "Placing the *Two Treatises*" (*supra* note 12), pp. 266–75.

[65] For this way of articulating the form of mutual recognition expressed in the Royal Proclamation, see John Pocock, "A Discourse of Sovereignty: Observations on the Work in Progress," in *Political Discourse in Early Modern Britain*, pp. 417–21. The Royal Proclamation is reprinted in *Documents of the Canadian Constitution, 1759–1915*, ed. W. P. M. Kennedy (Toronto: Oxford University Press, 1918), pp. 18–21.

tion in the Royal Proclamation is obvious.[66] The Aboriginal nations of the Ohio Valley and the Old Northwest (up to the Great Lakes) resisted the invasion of their territories and property rights by settlers and land speculators, bearing agriculturalist arguments and dubious deeds, and this defensive war threatened to disrupt British-Native trade and military relations. The recognition of the Aboriginal peoples as nations concentrated the control of all property relations in the Crown's Privy Council and gave it the authority to remove the interloping settlers from the Ohio Valley. This move was a major cause of the War of Independence, because it blocked the expansion of the colonies, especially Virginia and New York, and land speculators into the Aboriginal nations of the Ohio Valley. Consequently, one of the great ironies of American legal history is that Chief Justice Marshall, a Virginian, decided that the way to solve the post-revolutionary conflict over title to land in the west, and to strengthen the Union, was to transfer the old, hated doctrine of Crown recognition of Aboriginal sovereignty to the new federal government.[67]

The common-law recognition of two different but juridically equal systems of property in America, enunciated in 1763, is based on the practice of the Privy Council and the North American agents of Indian Affairs over the previous century. As early as 1665, a Royal Commission repudiated the "agriculturalist" argument that land in North America was "vacant waste" and concluded that it belonged to the Aboriginal people: "[N]o doubt the country is [the Indians'] till they give it or sell it, though it be not improoued [sic]." In the 1690s, the colony of Connecticut claimed jurisdiction over Mohegan lands on a combination of Lockean and treaty grounds (as argued by John Bulkley; see Section II above). The Mohegan nation claimed sovereignty under the law of nations and appealed to the Privy Council that it would negotiate only with the Crown. This was one of the most famous cases in colonial history, lasting over eighty years and employing some of New York's brightest lawyers on the Mohegan side. The Privy Council found in favor of the sovereignty of the Mohegan nation in 1705 and, when Connecticut appealed, again in 1743.[68]

---

[66] For the context, see Brian Slattery, *The Land Rights of Indigenous Canadian People as Affected by the Crown's Acquisition of Their Territory* (Saskatoon: University of Saskatchewan Press, 1979); and Jack Stagg, *Anglo-American Relations in North America to 1763 and an Analysis of the Royal Proclamation of 7 October 1763* (Ottawa: Department of Indian and Northern Affairs, 1981).

[67] Dorothy V. Jones, *License for Empire: Colonialism by Treaty in Early America* (Chicago: University of Chicago Press, 1982).

[68] The quotation is from N. B. Shurtleff, ed., *Records of the Governor and Company of the Massachusetts Bay in New England* (Boston: W. White, 1853–54), p. 213, cited in Clinton, "The Proclamation of 1763" (*supra* note 6), p. 334. The Mohegan case is in J. H. Smith, *Appeals to the Privy Council from the American Plantations* (New York: Oxford University Press, 1950), pp. 417–22. See Clinton, "The Proclamation of 1763," pp. 335–36; and Bruce Clark, *Native Liberty, Crown Sovereignty: The Existing Aboriginal Right of Self-Government in Canada* (Toronto: McGill-Queens University Press, 1990).

The Royal Proclamation and Chief Justice Marshall's interpretation of it provide the classic enunciation of the Aboriginal and common-law system. We are now in a position to appreciate its superior recognition of the initial conditions of property in America. First, as Chief Justice Marshall later explained, when the Crown discovered and occupied territory in America, it gained a right to continue to occupy this territory, on the internationally recognized title of use and occupation, but only with respect to the exclusion of all other *European* nations. The title of long use and occupation did not, however, confer on the Crown any right with respect to the Aboriginal peoples, since, from their perspective, they held the superior title of long use and occupation. Discovery and occupation confers sovereignty only if the land is "vacant" (*terra nullius*), and, contrary to Locke, this was not the case in North America.[69]

Therefore, the second and crucial step in establishing the Crown in America was to establish a juridical relationship with the Aboriginal peoples. This could be done by conquest or consent. Although Chief Justice Marshall entertained the fiction of conquest in an earlier case (*Johnson and Graham's Lessee v. M'Intosh* [1823]), he repudiated it in the later and authoritative *Worcester v. the State of Georgia* (1832). Conquest was never the doctrine of the Crown.[70] It should be noted that even if the wars against the Aboriginal peoples were considered wars of conquest, the systems of property and government of the Aboriginal peoples would have continued intact by the international convention of "conquest and continuity." When one civilized nation conquers another, the property and government of the conquered nation continue, under the *imperium* of the conqueror, unless and until the conqueror expressly discontinues them. If the conqueror recognizes them, then the option of discontinuity is extinguished. Chief Justice Marshall refers to this convention; the Crown applied it to Canada in the Quebec Act (1774), after the "conquest" of 1760, and to Grenada in *Campbell v. Hall* (1774), and Locke himself applies this liberal convention to the Norman Conquest of Anglo-Saxon England.[71]

Hence, the principle governing relations between the Crown and Aboriginal nations is the oldest principle of Western law: the principle of consent (*quod omnes tangit*, or "what touches all must be agreed to by all"), which Locke sought to get around by his theory that appropriation could

---

[69] *Johnson and Graham's Lessee v. M'Intosh*, pp. 573–74, in Marshall, *Writings of Chief Justice Marshall* (supra note 7), pp. 263–64; and *Worcester v. the State of Georgia*, pp. 543–47, in ibid., pp. 427–33. Compare Brian Slattery, *Ancestral Lands, Alien Laws: Judicial Perspectives on Aboriginal Title* (Saskatoon: University of Saskatchewan Press, 1983), p. 26, and see quotation accompanying note 7 above.

[70] *Johnson*, pp. 588–89, in Marshall, *Writings of Chief Justice Marshall*, pp. 274–75; and *Worcester*, pp. 544–45, in ibid., pp. 428–29.

[71] *Johnson*, p. 589, in *ibid.*, p. 275; *Worcester*, p. 547, in *ibid.*, p. 431; *Campbell v. Hall*, 1 Cowp. 204 (1774); *The Quebec Act*, 14 George III, c.88 (1774); Locke, *Two Treatises*, II, 182–85, 192–96.

proceed without consent because it did not affect the rights of the Aboriginal peoples. The Royal Proclamation sets out three conditions for consensual negotiations between the Crown and Aboriginal nations in which their coordinate "sovereignty" is recognized and continued through the negotiations of treaty relations between them: (1) the negotiations are between the Crown and the chiefs of an Aboriginal nation, thereby recognizing nation-to-nation status; (2) the negotiations must take place in a public place, recognizing and employing both Aboriginal and Crown forms of negotiation and reaching agreements; and (3) the negotiations cannot be initiated by pressure from the Crown. Although the subject of the negotiations can involve anything of concern to the parties, they typically concern land cessions to the Crown, or agreements on the co-use and management of resources, in exchange for protection and other benefits to the Aboriginal peoples. The land in America not ceded to the Crown in this manner is "reserved" to the Aboriginal peoples and remains under their governments and property systems.[72]

The three conditions of the Royal Proclamation provide the normative framework for over five hundred treaties that the Aboriginal peoples have negotiated with the Crown and, after 1867, the federal government of Canada. The Proclamation is constitutionalized in section 25 of the Canadian Charter of Rights and Freedoms, and all treaties are constitutionally protected.[73] The treaties have given rise to a network of trust-like relations of interdependent property and government between the First Nations and the federal government in Canada which constitutes a system of "treaty federalism": that is, the Aboriginal peoples and the federal government are recognized as forming a federation of nations bound together by treaties. In the U.S., Chief Justice Marshall's interpretation, rather than the Royal Proclamation itself, provides the normative framework. The crucial feature is that the Aboriginal nations' juristic status as nations and their systems of government and property remain intact through the negotiated relations of treaty federalism, even when, as is quite common, they conditionally entrust some powers of self-government and rights of property to the federal government over the lands reserved to themselves or placed under joint resource and environmental management.[74]

This normative framework has been violated, either by ignoring or denying it, on more occasions in the past than it has been honored in Canada and the U.S. However, in the last twenty years the courts of both

---

[72] "The Royal Proclamation," in Kennedy, ed., *Documents* (*supra* note 65), pp. 20–21. Compare Clinton, "The Proclamation of 1763," pp. 354–60; and Darlene Johnston, *The Taking of Indian Lands in Canada: Consent or Coercion?* (Saskatoon: University of Saskatchewan Native Law Centre, 1989).

[73] See Bruce Wildsmith, *Aboriginal Peoples and Section 25 of the Canadian Charter of Rights and Freedoms* (Saskatoon: University of Saskatchewan Native Law Centre, 1988).

[74] Compare the similar arguments of Barsh and Henderson, *The Road*, for the U.S., and Slattery, "First Nations and the Constitution," for Canada (*supra* note 11).

174   JAMES TULLY

countries, and constitutional amendments in Canada, have tended to
some uneven extent to approximate several features of it.[75] My argument
is not that this framework *determines* the legal and constitutional practice
of the two countries; nor is my argument that the Royal Proclamation and
Chief Justice Marshall give perfect expression to it. The framework can be
theoretically reconstructed and defended independently of either formulation, since its norms of recognition of equality, political and cultural continuity, and consent are shared by Western and Aboriginal traditions,
even though, as we have seen, they have not been adhered to in Western theory with respect to Aboriginal peoples. It is, however, part of my
argument that the Royal Proclamation and the interpretation of Chief Justice Marshall constitute two (partial) expressions of this framework, and
that at least some of the relations between Aboriginal peoples and the
governments of Canada and the U.S. over the last two hundred years are
based on the norms of the framework as formulated in the Royal Proclamation and by Chief Justice Marshall. If this is true, then the Aboriginal
and common-law system, with its institutions and traditions of interpretation, has priority with respect to the institutions and traditions which
the proponents of the three premises, especially the second, appeal to as
authoritative. Of course, many of the institutions and traditions these
proponents appeal to are included in the Aboriginal and common-law
system, albeit in a modified form (as we shall see in Section IV). This
practice-based part of the argument is thus important (but not indispensable), because it challenges the presumption of all three premises that
Aboriginal forms of property and traditions do not form any of the *actually* recognized authoritative institutions and traditions of property in
America—that is, that the argument I am advancing is not grounded in
the legal and constitutional traditions of North America. Therefore, I want
to defend my reading of the Royal Proclamation and Chief Justice Marshall's interpretation of it against the claim that neither one comes near
to recognizing the coexistence and equality of Aboriginal forms of property and government.

Lawyers, judges, and commentators often read the Royal Proclamation
and the Marshall cases to the effect that they assert sovereignty over the
Aboriginal peoples and their land and subject them to the Crown or the
federal government.[76] This interpretation is surprising, because the Crown
made no attempt to govern the Aboriginal peoples at the time, and the
documents surrounding the Proclamation and treaties repeatedly, though

---

[75] See notes 4, 6, and 11 above for recent court cases and constitutional developments.
For a comprehensive analysis of a recent Canadian lower court denial of the normative
framework (based on the four sets of Eurocentric assumptions summarized in Section II)
which has been successfully appealed, see Frank Cassidy, ed., *Aboriginal Title in British
Columbia: Delgamuukw v. The Queen* (Montreal: Institute for Research on Public Policy, 1992).

[76] See, for example, L. C. Green, "Claims to Territory in Colonial America," pp. 99–105,
110–11, 116–23; see also the examples in note 6 above.

ABORIGINAL PROPERTY AND WESTERN THEORY   175

not without exception, acknowledge the sovereignty and independence of the Aboriginal nations.[77] Here is the relevant passage:

> It is just and reasonable and essential to our Interest, and the Security of our Colonies, that the several Nations or Tribes of Indians with whom We are connected, and who live under our Protection, should not be molested or disturbed in the Possession of such parts of Our Dominions and Territories as, not having been ceded to or purchased by Us, are reserved to them, as their Hunting grounds.[78]

In *Worcester v. the State of Georgia* (1832), Chief Justice Marshall provides an answer to the attempt to read this passage as the assertion of Crown sovereignty over the Aboriginal peoples. *Worcester* also provides a step-by-step clarification and correction of Marshall's earlier views in *Johnson and Graham's Lessee v. M'Intosh* (1823), thereby providing a response to later commentators who take this earlier decision as authoritative.[79] First, the phrase "Our Dominions and Territories" does not imply sovereignty with respect to the Aboriginal peoples, but, as we saw above, a claim to exclude other European powers, to treaty with the Aboriginal nations for land cessions, and to assert sovereignty over the ceded land.

Second, the Proclamation does not discontinue the sovereignty of the Aboriginal nations to "live under" the protection of the Crown. Chief Justice Marshall lays this down in no uncertain terms, ironically invoking Emeric de Vattel's concept of "guardianship" to represent the continuity of Aboriginal sovereignty in relation to the federal government:

> [T]he settled doctrine of the law of nations is, that a weaker power does not surrender its independence, its right to self-government, by associating with a stronger, and taking its protection. A weak state, in order to provide for its safety, may place itself under the protection of one more powerful, without stripping itself of the right of self-government, and ceasing to be a state. Examples of this kind are not wanting in Europe. "Tributary and feudatory states," says Vattel, "do not thereby cease to be sovereign and independent states, so long as sovereign and independent authority are left in the administration of the state."[80]

---

[77] See Johnston, *The Taking of Indian Lands in Canada* (*supra* note 72); and *Worcester*, p. 547, in Marshall, *Writings of Chief Justice Marshall*, p. 431.

[78] "The Royal Proclamation," in Kennedy, ed., *Documents*, p. 20.

[79] There is considerable evidence that Marshall was dissatisfied with his judgment in *Johnson* and welcomed the opportunity to correct it. See Joseph C. Burke, "The Cherokee Cases: A Study in Law, Politics, and Morality," *Stanford Law Review*, vol. 21 (1968), pp. 500–31.

[80] *Worcester*, p. 560 in Marshall, *Writings of Chief Justice Marshall*, p. 446.

It was only in the late nineteenth century, when government policy in the United States and Canada came under the spell of doctrines of racial superiority, that "under the protection" was misinterpreted as a "guardian-child" relation and the independence and consent of the Aboriginal nations was systematically violated.[81]

Chief Justice Marshall goes on to show that the status of the First Nations as "sovereign nations" and "states" was never discontinued, but in fact was recognized and affirmed by the many treaties with the Crown and later with Congress. These treaties are not mere contracts but are like "international" treaties between crowned heads of state in Europe. The "several Indian nations" are "distinct political communities, having territorial boundaries, within which their authority is exclusive," and their "right to all the lands within those boundaries . . . is not only acknowledged, but guaranteed [sic] by the United States." Furthermore, the phrase "hunting grounds" does not in any sense restrict the Aboriginal peoples to that activity.[82]

Chief Justice Marshall concludes that the Aboriginal nations are to be conceived as, and to continue as, "domestic dependent nations." That is, they are independent, self-governing nations with internal sovereignty. Their protection by the United States government "diminishes" their sovereignty only in the following respects. They cannot engage in military alliances with foreign governments; their trade is regulated by Congress; and Congress may build roads through their nations and use their waterways for navigation. Any other relations of federalism must be worked out by fair treaty negotiations.[83]

Although this "diminished" sovereignty is acceptable to almost all the First Nations of the United States (with the exception of the Haudenosaunee confederacy, which claims undiminished sovereignty), the Canadian Royal Commission on Aboriginal Peoples has rejected this definition of "domestic dependent nations" as a diminution of their legitimate status. In advancing this reply, the First Nations of Canada do not signal a desire to form independent sovereign states, but rather to ensure that their equality and coexistence with the Canadian government is recognized and affirmed through all the negotiated relations of dependency.[84]

IV. THE ABORIGINAL SYSTEM

As we have seen, the Royal Proclamation form of recognition of Aboriginal and non-Aboriginal relations was formulated in the context of decades

[81] J. R. Miller, *Skyscrapers Hide the Heavens: A History of Indian-White Relations in Canada* (Toronto: University of Toronto Press, 1989), pp. 83–210.

[82] *Worcester*, pp. 544, 548, 551, 553–54, 559–61, in Marshall, *Writings of Chief Justice Marshall*, pp. 428, 433, 436, 438–39, 445–47.

[83] *Worcester*, p. 555, in *ibid.*, p. 440; and *The Cherokee Nation v. the State of Georgia*, 5 Peter (1829), pp. 14–20, in *ibid.*, pp. 412–18.

[84] Royal Commission on Aboriginal Peoples, *The Right of Aboriginal Self-Government and the Constitution: A Commentary* (Ottawa, February 13, 1992), p. 15.

of negotiations with the First Nations of northeastern North America. It is not surprising, therefore, that it is fairly close to, and overlaps with, the form of recognition that the Aboriginal peoples themselves developed to establish and negotiate property relations with the non-Aboriginal new-comers. Let us now turn to the Aboriginal side of the Aboriginal and common-law system. When the Europeans arrived, the Aboriginal peoples of the northeast were organized into nations and federations, and they had a system of international customary law developed over centuries of use. This is codified in an exemplary way in the oldest living constitution in North America, *Kaianereko:wa* or the Great Law of Peace of the Haudenosaunee (Six Nations or Iroquois) confederacy, established in the mid-fifteenth century.[85] The First Nations sought to understand and negotiate with the Dutch, French, and British in light of their centuries' old practices of federal and international negotiations, just as the Europeans conceptualized negotiations within their traditions as we have seen, developing from 1645 to 1815 a complex multinational system that spanned half the continent.[86] At the heart of their practice of international relations is a normative framework called the Two Row Wampum Treaty, or *Kahswentha*, of the Haudenosaunee, which has been adopted by many First Nations across North America. This representation of negotiated relations is symbolized in the belts made of wampum beads exchanged at treaty negotiations from the first French-Iroquois treaty in 1645 to the negotiations at Oka Quebec in the summer of 1990. A background of white wampum beads symbolizes the purity of the agreement; two rows of purple beads symbolize the Aboriginal and non-Aboriginal nations involved; and the three beads separating the two rows symbolize peace, friendship, and respect. The two central and parallel rows of purple beads

> symbolize two paths or two vessels, travelling down the same rivers together. One, a birch bark canoe, will be for the Indian people, their laws, their customs and their ways. The other, a ship, will be for the white people and their laws, their customs and their ways. We shall each travel the river together, side by side, but in our own boat. Neither of us will try to steer the other's vessel.[87]

First, the Aboriginal peoples and the European Americans, the two vessels, are reciprocally recognized as equal and coexisting nations, each

---

[85] A. C. Parker, ed., *The Constitution of the Five Nations, or The Iroquois Book of the Great Law* (Albany: State University of New York, 1916; Iroqrafts Reprints, 1984).

[86] For the history of early treaty relations, see Francis Jennings et al., eds., *The History and Culture of Iroquois Diplomacy* (Syracuse: Syracuse University Press, 1985); and White, *The Middle Ground* (*supra* note 38).

[87] The quotation is from the Haudenosaunee confederacy's presentation to the Canadian House of Commons Committee on Indian Self-Government (1983), reprinted with commentary in Michael Mitchell, "An Unbroken Assertion of Sovereignty," in *Drumbeat: Anger and Renewal in Indian Country*, ed. Boyce Richardson (Toronto: Summerhill Press—The Assembly of First Nations, 1989), pp. 109–10.

with its own customs and laws of government and property, just as in the Royal Proclamation. This is the principle (of recognition) of *Kahswentha* or equality. The second feature is that, as the two peoples become bound together by relations of trust by means of treaties, the Aboriginal traditions, governments, and property systems continue through their negotiated relations of interdependency and guardianship over time. It is symbolized by the parallel rows of beads, the vessels carrying on "side by side," and by neither people trying to steer the other. This feature, similar to the international principle of continuity expressed in the Royal Proclamation and in Chief Justice Marshall's judgment in *Worcester*, is one of the oldest conventions of Aboriginal international relations. The Great Law of Peace, for example, states that, "whenever a foreign nation is either conquered or has by its own will accepted the Great Peace [i.e., joined the Haudenosaunee confederacy], their own system of internal government may continue."[88]

The third feature of the Aboriginal normative framework is the treaty negotiations themselves. The Aboriginal negotiators negotiate in accordance with their complex traditions of consensus government and diplomacy. The negotiations can involve the delegation (but never the alienation) of some of their powers of self-government, cession of land, agreements on the co-use of land and co-management of resources, establishment of reserves, redress of injustices in past treaties, and so on. The form of political association with Canada and the U.S. is thus properly called "treaty federalism," since the Aboriginal nations have the ability to voluntarily delegate some powers to the Canadian and U.S. governments for specific purposes, thereby placing themselves in a guardian relationship, while retaining their status as independent nations. This Aboriginal form of federalism is also commensurable with the liberal traditions of federalism and continuity that underlie the Royal Proclamation. As long as the first two features are firmly established, as the initial and continuing conditions for negotiations over property, the negotiations cannot extinguish the status of Aboriginal societies as nations with independent systems of property and traditions of thought, any more than the negotiations can extinguish the equal status of the U.S. and Canada. As a result, the Aboriginal peoples cannot be brought under the sovereignty of non-Aboriginal laws, institutions, and traditions of interpretation without their consent. Rather, they bring themselves by their consent, expressed in their own ways, into the federation constituted by the Aboriginal and common-law system of laws, institutions, and traditions of interpretation.[89]

---

[88] Parker, ed., *The Constitution of the Five Nations*, section 84, p. 53.

[89] For Aboriginal accounts of treaty negotiations, see Richardson, ed., *Drumbeat: Anger and Renewal*. For liberal traditions of federalism commensurable with the Royal Proclamation and Two Row, see James Tully, "Diversity's Gambit Declined," in *Canada's Constitutional Predicament*, ed. Curtis Cook (Montreal: McGill-Queens University Press, 1994).

The Two Row Wampum Treaty has provided the Aboriginal people with a way of conceptualizing the foundation and negotiation of Aboriginal and Western systems of property in America for over three hundred years. Although Two Row is grounded in Aboriginal world-views and serves to protect Aboriginal systems of property, the features of it that serve to establish a framework for recognizing, establishing, and negotiating relations of property overlap with the three similar features of the common-law framework, based on Western traditions and designed to protect Western systems of property in America.

V. CONCLUSION

In conclusion, there exists in Aboriginal and common-law traditions and practices a cross-cultural form of recognition of and negotiation between two different systems of property in North America. This Aboriginal and common-law system is the normative basis of the constitutional history of Aboriginal-U.S. and Aboriginal-Canadian property relations. It is also a very flexible bicultural and bilegal system, capable of providing the framework for overlapping systems of property as diverse as the James Bay and Northern Quebec Agreement of 1975–81, the Sechelt Self-Government Agreement of 1987 in British Columbia, the new Inuit province of Nunavut of 1992 in Northern Canada, and the negotiated redress of hundreds of treaty and reserve violations, from the Haudenosaunee claims in New York to the Sioux claims in the Black Hills of South Dakota.[90] In addition, the negotiations, court cases, appeals, renegotiations, and armed resistances over the centuries in accordance with and in violation of the system have given rise to hundreds of intersubjective conventions (such as Marshall's concept of guardianship and Canada's concept of a fiduciary trust between the Crown and First Nations) which provide the common grounds for each successive property negotiation.

It is therefore the suggestion of this essay that a theory of property applicable to North America will be just only if it begins from the Aboriginal and common-law conceptual framework as its premise, for this is the just representation of the initial conditions of property at the foundation of Canada and the United States. Unfortunately, as we have seen, many current theorists of property either ignore the foundations of property in North America, by uncritically assuming that European-American institutions and traditions are exclusively authoritative and applying one or more of the three premises mentioned in the introduction, or they mistake Aboriginal property for a problem of recognizing some kind of cultural or

[90] For these examples, see Ken Coates, ed., *Aboriginal Land Claims in Canada: A Regional Perspective* (Toronto: Copp Clark Pitman Ltd., 1992); Vecsey and Starna, eds., *Iroquois Land Claims* (*supra* note 41); and Edward Lazarus, *Black Hills, White Justice: The Sioux Nation versus the United States, 1775 to the Present* (New York: Harper Collins, 1991).

180   JAMES TULLY

minority difference within the sovereignty of a liberal or communitarian framework. In either case the sovereignty of non-Aboriginal institutions and traditions of thought is taken for granted and the Aboriginal peoples are subjected to it without their consent, thereby unwittingly perpetuating a form of conceptual imperialism in legal and political philosophy. The legitimacy of these modes of argument and institutions of property rests on the prior recognition of the coordinate legitimacy of the Aboriginal traditions and institutions of property and the network of treaty relations between the two peoples.

Hence, the modes of argument of Western theories of property should be used in North America only *within* the Aboriginal and common-law framework. They are authoritative for an issue of property in North America that is concerned exclusively with the legitimate non-Aboriginal systems of property. Reciprocally, Aboriginal traditions are authoritative for any issue of property concerned exclusively with the Aboriginal systems of property. (Of course any interlocutor is free to introduce arguments from the other traditions as best he can.) For any issue of property on the now large middle ground where the Aboriginal and non-Aboriginal systems of property overlap in a multiplicity of ways, Aboriginal and non-Aboriginal modes of argument are always on equal footing. In this unique cross-cultural speech-situation, the negotiators are bound together by three shared norms (and by all previous, justified agreements) of the system: that the equality of their respective traditions and institutions is recognized and continued, that the negotiations and argumentation respect the forms of negotiation of both cultures, and that the treaty relations of property they reach by negotiation will be based on consent, not on force or deceit. The Aboriginal and common-law system comprising these three shared norms is the philosophical foundation and, to the extent that the existing property systems are just, practical foundation of property in North America.

Index